Christian Philosophy

PETER LANG
New York • Washington, D.C./Baltimore
Bern • Frankfurt am Main • Berlin • Vienna • Paris

Leo Sweeney, S.J.

Christian Philosophy

Greek, Medieval,
Contemporary Reflections

PETER LANG
New York • Washington, D.C./Baltimore
Bern • Frankfurt am Main • Berlin • Vienna • Paris

Library of Congress Cataloging-in-Publication Data

Sweeney, Leo.
Christian philosophy: Greek, medieval,
contemporary reflections/ Leo Sweeney.
p. cm.
Includes bibliographical references and index.
1. Philosophy and religion. 2. Christianity—Philosophy. I. Title.
BR100.S94   190—dc21   97-8544
ISBN 0-8204-1179-5

Die Deutsche Bibliothek-CIP-Einheitsaufnahme

Sweeney, Leo:
Christian philosophy: Greek, medieval, contemporary reflections/
Leo Sweeney. –New York; Washington, D.C./Baltimore; Bern;
Frankfurt am Main; Berlin; Vienna; Paris: Lang.
ISBN 0-8204-1179-5 Gb.

The paper in this book meets the guidelines for permanence and durability
of the Committee on Production Guidelines for Book Longevity
of the Council of Library Resources.

Printed in the United States of America.

Contents

Part II
Neoplatonism and Early Latin Authors

Part III
Medieval Scholastics

Part IV
Existence and Existentialism

Part V
Further Contemporaries and Aquinas

Preface

In 1990 Joseph Owens published *Towards a Christian Philosophy*, a book whose long introduction (pp. 1–62) discusses what Christian philosophy is, followed by thirteen chapters which reprint previously published papers on that topic.[1] My own volume, *Christian Philosophy: Greek, Medieval, Contemporary Reflections*, is similar to Owens' in that its initial portion (chapters 1–3) takes up what Christian philosophy is, followed by twenty-one chapters consisting of papers previously published (but now largely revised or updated) which are in turn followed by a chapter on Whitehead (presented here for the first time) and by a chapter which charts Aquinas' reaction to philosophers from Descartes to Jacques Derrida.

Owens' volume is helpful, first of all, by tracing the history of Christian philosophy in modern times, where two dates stand out: 1879, when Leo XIII published his encyclical, *Aeterni Patris*, and 1928, when Émile Bréhier lectured at Brussels. In the encyclical the pope aimed at "the 'restoration' of Christian philosophy in Catholic schools,"[2] a restoration which consisted in promoting

---

[1] Joseph Owens, *Towards a Christian Philosophy* [hereafter: Owens] (Washington, D.C.: The Catholic University of America Press, 1990).

[2] Owens, p. 63. Also see *ibid.*, pp. 4, 27–29, 52–53. For the text of the encyclical see Victor B. Brezik, *One Hundred Years of Thomism: "Aeterni Patris" and Afterwards* [hereafter: Brezik] (Houston, Tex.: Center for Thomistic Studies, 1981), pp. 172–97. Attention is also given to the encyclical by G. McCool in his books *Catholic Theology in the Nineteenth Century* (New York: The Seabury Press, 1977), ch. 10, and *From Unity to Pluralism: The Internal Evolution of Thomism* (New York: Fordham University Press, 1992). The second book would be more helpful if its author did not try to show, as a personal agendum, that traditional Thomism is dead but is reborn in the neo-Kantian theologies of K. Rahner and B. Lonergan. For a refusal of McCool's endeavor, see my paper, "Must Thomism Become Kantian to Survive? A Negative Response," in John F. X. Knasas (ed.), *Thomistic Papers VI* (Houston: Center for Thomistic Studies, 1994), all of whose chapters are relevant.

the use of philosophy to serve the Christian faith. This required a choice of philosophical problems on the ground of their relation to revealed doctrines. It required also that the faith give incentive and guidance to genuinely philosophical procedures in the solution of those problems.[3]

In his 1928 lectures (published in 1931)[4] Bréhier claimed that the two notions of "Christian" and "philosophy" contradict one another, since the first refers only "to a story known solely by revelation," the second concerns what is known by reason as to what "is in things and in the universe."[5] That is, the two elements of "Christian" and "philosophy"

> in Christian philosophy, taken as a notion, were contradictorily opposed to each other. Philosophy is based upon what is intrinsically evident, Christianity on what is authoritatively revealed without intrinsic evidence. The one, therefore, annuls the other. Instead of specifying philosophy, the characterization of "Christian" would destroy the generic philosophical nature. Consequently, the notion of "Christian" cannot be a specifying differentia of philosophy. The nature expressed by the one term would set aside the nature expressed by the other.[6]

Bréhier's claim was soon answered by E. Gilson[7] and by J. Maritain. For Gilson Christian philosophy is explained "in terms of its selection of topics," whereas Maritain's explanation is through a "distinction of the nature and state of a philosophy."[8] But basically

---

[3] Owens, p. 73.

[4] Émile Bréhier, "Y a-t-il une philosophie chrétienne?" *Revue de métaphysique et de morale* 38 (1931), 133–62.

[5] Owens, p. 6, quoting É. Bréhier, "La notion de philosophie chrétienne," *Bulletin de la Société française de Philosophie,* 31 (1931), 50. See also Maurice Nédoncelle, *Is There a Christian Philosophy?* trans. I. Trethowan (New York: Hawthorn Books, 1960), p. 55: "Either we know something or else we believe it: when knowledge supervenes, belief has no longer a place."

[6] Owens, pp. 6–7.

[7] In fact, Bréhier's lectures appear in the same issue and journal (see n. 4 above) as does Gilson's "La notion de philosophie chrétienne," to which Bréhier's article is a reply. See Owens, p. 6.

[8] Owens, p. 31. On Maritain's difference from Gilson, see *ibid.*, p. 11, n. 18, last prgr.; *ibid.*, pp. 83–86.

their two explanations amount to the same: Christian philosophy does exist as a respectable body of knowledge.[9] Authors subsequent to them fall into two groups—those who (with Bréhier) deny and those who affirm (with Gilson and Maritain) that philosophy can be and is Christian.[10]

The debate which Bréhier's attack on the existence of Christian philosophy set off

flared up brilliantly in the years immediately following the publication of his provocative article. The debate has continued ever since to excite intermittent attention and interest, though in restricted circles. [But] at least the endurance of the attention given it testifies that as a topic of discussion and of pursuit "Christian philosophy" is a label that seems here to stay. No common consensus on its nature has so far emerged.[11]

Owens' Position

What is Owens' own contribution to that debate or, more simply, does he agree with Bréhier or with Gilson/Maritain? With the latter, but he expresses his views in a complex manner in answering three questions, which themselves "arise spontaneously" from Sections I and II of his Introduction, which he summarizes before asking the questions.

The first of the preceding introductory sections brought out how Christianity and a developed philosophy are both accidental and external to each other. They are accidental in the sense that the concept of neither of them necessarily involves the concept of the other. They are external insofar as each may exist outside the other, for in historical reality they have ex-

---

[9] For fuller discussion of Gilson's and Maritain's positions, see my ch. 2 below: "Can Philosophy Be Christian?"

[10] In the first group are Ferdinand Van Steenberghen (see Owens, notes 21 and 32), C. Sierp (notes 17 and 32), Claude Tresmontant and Peter Redpath (n. 45). In the second group are Anton Pegis (Owens, p. 45) and Ralph McInerny (pp. 12–13).

[11] Owens, p. 8.

isted factually apart from each other. Then the second introductory section examined how Christian philosophy is a general philosophy and therefore receives its specification from
the subjective dispositions of the persons who are doing the
philosophizing.[12]

But what are the three questions themselves which issue from
those two sections and which "call for answers before the already
existing body of Christian philosophy may be probed for assurance
that it is genuinely philosophy and offers guarantee of a viable
future toward which one's efforts may still be devoted" (*ibid.*)?
Here is his list.

> First, how does something accidental and external bring about
> the essential differentiation that is intrinsic to a philosophical
> discipline? Further, does specification through subjective dis-
> position involve a radically pluralistic understanding of phi-
> losophy, to the extent that each side is rendered impervious to
> the probative force of the other's arguments? Third, how can a
> way of philosophizing that developed historically within sa-
> cred theology successfully cut the umbilical cord and carry on
> an independent life of its own? (*ibid.*)

His answer to the first inquiry runs from pp. 24–35, his answer to
the second from pp. 35–41 and to the third from pp. 41–47. Those
answers prompt still a fourth question:

> Even though Christian philosophy may claim to be erected
> only upon naturally accessible principles, does it not acknowl-
> edge subjection of its results to some kind of control by Chris-
> tian authority? It may verbally claim to be answerable solely
> to the court of human reason. But do not the preceding con-
> siderations seem to make it, like sacred theology, ultimately
> subject, in regard to its truth, to a magisterium based on re-
> vealed premises?[13]

His affirmative answer to that fourth question (*ibid.*, pp. 48–50) is
immediately followed by Section VI (pp. 50–59), in which he explains the relevance to Christian philosophy of his subsequent

---

[12] *Ibid.*, p. 23.
[13] *Ibid.*, p. 48.

thirteen chapters, which were previously published elsewhere as independent papers.

In the light of those five sections, then, what does Owens hold on Christian philosophy? Despite its complexity, his position can be outlined in the following statements.

(1) Philosophy of religion, metaphysics, cosmology, medical ethics, epistemology, philosophy of law and the like are "special" branches of philosophy in that each deals with a particularized area, with its own object or subject matter. Christian philosophy is not "special" in that sense.

(2) Rather, it is a "general" philosophy, as is Greek philosophy or medieval philosophy or Marxism or materialism or Kantianism or phenomenology or radical existentialism and the like. Each such philosophy deals with a broad area of philosophical reflection, and so too does Christian philosophy.[14]

(3) But Christian philosophy has several subdivisions, such as Catholic philosophy, Lutheran philosophy, Calvinistic philosophy— these are different inasmuch as they issue, to some extent, from different beliefs, which therefore are different approaches to achieving awareness of different starting points for the philosophies themselves.

(4) Let us concentrate upon the Catholic subdivision of Christian philosophy, which itself comprises such "special" philosophies as metaphysics, cosmology, epistemology, ethics, philosophy of God, philosophy of the human person, etc. (see #1 above). (a) All such "special" philosophies are each essentially philosophical because their starting points are evidences in material things that provide naturally known premises, which human reason uses to arrive at naturally known conclusions. (b) Each such "special" philosophy becomes aware of its starting points as natural evidence because the Catholic religion draws the philosopher's attention to such evidence due to its revealed truths on the Trinity and Incarnation (which invites the philosopher to reflect on nature and person), the Eucharist (invitation to reflection on substance and accidents), the human person with God as supernatural end attained through free cooperation with grace (reflection on the natural *vs.* the supernatural), sin as offense against God, etc. (c) Yet those revealed truths remain external to the philosophical processes themselves, even

---

[14] That wider area for Christian philosophy is, for Owens (p. 16) "its object or . . . the subject matter with which it deals," which is "all things human and divine." Also see pp. 17, 21–22.

though those truths genuinely help, in an external and accidental fashion, to specify the intrinsic results of such processes and to differentiate them from philosophical processes without such help or with help from different outside forces (as in the case of linguistic analysis, phenomenology, Marxism and liberation philosophy, and so on)[15] or with help because of different creeds (as in the case of Lutheran Christian philosophy or Calvinistic Christian philosophy, etc. [see #3 above]).

(5) But Christian philosophy in Catholic circles also is itself a psychological activity of the human person who is such a philosopher and is thus an accident inhering in a substance—the human person—(a) who is perfected by other such psychological accidents, one of which is his/her assent to Christ's revealed truths, which are presented to them by the magisterium and which are developed, "understood" and safeguarded by them if they are Christian theologians (see Owens, p. 30). (b) Such human persons also exist in definite historical settings and thus are conditioned also by cultural and political environments (both national and international).

(6) Although one may (in fact, must) abstract from such psychological and historical situations if one is to understand him/her as exemplifying in general what a Christian philosopher is, one should not separate them through precision by completely removing them from those concrete and actual situations.

(7) Such is the understanding of Christian philosophy which Étienne Gilson, Jacques Maritain, Anton Pegis and others contrast with that proposed by Émile Bréhier, (a) for whom (following Descartes) philosophy is a substance or essence, which is known in a clear and distinct idea and through precision from anything other than itself as that which starts from naturally known and evident premises and proceeds through careful reasoning to conclusions thus naturally known also and which thereby totally excludes Christian theology. The latter, as a development of divinely revealed truths, is itself a substance or essence known also in a clear and

---

[15] See Owens, p. 21: "An approach from language occasions linguistic analysis, and an approach from vivid existentials marks off the starting points for phenomenology, and an approach from economic crises results in development of Marxism or of liberation philosophy." Also *ibid.*, n. 29: "Specification by reason of the selection of starting points on the basis of various interests distinguishes one general philosophy from another without infringing upon the philosophy's general scope. Each in this way is a special philosophical discipline even though the range of its object is general."

distinct idea in precision from anything other than itself. (b) Hence, "philosophy" and "Christian" contradict one another and can never be assimilated into "Christian philosophy" as an acceptable and valid science. (c) Thus, Bréhier, as well as those agreeing with him (see note 10 above), is in irreconcilable opposition with those agreeing with Gilson and Maritain.

Evaluation

If those seven statements sketch Owens' position adequately, what evaluation may one make of it?

As already indicated, the initial portion of Owens' book is a helpful account of the modern history of Christian philosophy.[16] Moreover, his own interpretation of Christian philosophy is informative. But it is complicated—a complication which may be due largely to what Christian philosophy itself is but also to the approach Owens takes.

(a) McInerny on Maritain

In the initial part of his historical account, he to some extent relies on Ralph McInerny,[17] who himself is reflecting on Maritain's distinction between the nature of Christian philosophy and the state in which it is being exercised. McInerny orders the points he makes in this fashion.

(a) Maritain's distinction between nature and state is equivalent to substantive and modal levels or, again, to the activity of philosophizing as formally characterized and as "undertaken by so-and-so in such-and-such circumstances."[18] (b) Such equivalence or characterization is easily understood *re* philosophizing when appraised as morally good or bad—it is morally good if true (achievement of truth corresponds to nature [Maritain] or to substantive level or formal characterization [McInerny] of philosophizing). It is morally bad if done by someone who thereby neglects his/her duty. Such an appraisal deals with the state (Maritain) or with the

---

[16] See prgrs. corresponding to notes 2–11 above.

[17] Ralph McInerny, "Reflections on Christian Philosophy" [hereafter: McInerny] in Brezik, pp. 63–73. Also see *idem, The Question of Christian Ethics* (Washington, D.C.: The Catholic University of America Press, 1993).

[18] McInerny, p. 65.

modality or circumstantial characterization (McInerny) of philoso-phizing.[19]

(c) Again, Maritain's distinction between the nature and the state of philosophizing may be compared to a distinction between the intrinsic content of philosophizing (then it is judged as true or false) and its being carried on by "this concrete person here and now" (then it is judged morally as good or bad).[20] From this comparison one sees the difference between intrinsic and moral appraisals of philosophizing.

(d) But since philosophizing can be wrongly motivated, one might be led to conclude that unless philosophizing is carried on with morally right motives and "appropriate moral orientation," it is worthless. Thus Plato: moral virtue gives "that necessary affinity with the really real which enables knowledge to take place." Consequently, the moral dimension of philosophizing is lifted "from the mere modal status to a substantive feature of philosophizing"—or from state to nature (Maritain) or (see #b above) from circumstantial to formal characterization (McInerny) of philoso-phizing.[21]

(e) Moreover, not just Christian but all philosophers come "to the philosophical task with convictions and certainties"—namely, "implicit and explicit certainties about the world and ourselves," with the implication that "we *bring* truths to our philosophizing."[22]
(f) Hence, one should ask "what is *peculiar* about what the Christian brings to the activity of philosophizing and how it differs from what others, e.g., secular humanists, bring to that task." The answer: "the Roman Catholic philosopher . . . takes with the utmost seriousness documents emanating from Rome and having to do with his activity, documents like the encyclical *Aeterni Patris*," which among other things puts "before the Catholic intellectual, particularly the philosopher and theologian, Saint Thomas Aquinas as a model" to help a Catholic "attain the objectives of philosophy and theology."[23]

(g) What, then, is to be "the starting point of our philosophizing? With what author should we begin? . . . Why does he begin where he does?" The answer: he begins with someone he trusts. And here

---

[19] *Ibid.*, pp. 65–66.
[20] *Ibid.*, p. 66.
[21] *Ibid.*, p. 67.
[22] *Ibid.*, pp. 67 and 68.
[23] *Ibid.*, pp. 68–69.

the Catholic "is in a far better position" than others because of "the authority and trustworthiness of his advisor"—namely, Aquinas and those he especially has illumined (Gilson and Maritain).[24]

(h) Thus the existential attitude of the Catholic intellectual should be one not of apology but of gratitude "for the guidance he receives from the Church," for the gift of faith, for "the counsel and advice of those in whose keeping the deposit of faith is entrusted." Accepting such advice does not lead to "uniformity and homogeneity of thinking. . . . A single moral ideal for human persons," if pursued seriously, will lead not to "somber sameness" but to "a far greater differentiation among us."[25]

(i) Maritain (as McInerny notes in closing this portion of his paper) has not only "provided a modal religious context within which philosophical thinking takes place"[26] but also suggests "that the object of religious faith, believed truths, exercise an intrinsic influence on philosophical content, on philosophical truth"—without however intending that the origin of a philosophical truth (e.g., creation) "in a revealed truth . . . means that its acceptance is always and everywhere dependent upon religious belief."[27]

(j) After five paragraphs of commentary upon the then recently founded Society of Christian Philosophers (pp. 71–73), McInerny returns in a concluding paragraph to what a Christian philosopher is. Maritain's book, *Prayer and Intelligence*, reminds us (McInerny states) "that just as the ethical provides a wider context in which the activity of theoretical thinking can be appraised, so too does religion." What does that "wider context" of ethics and of religion provide? "The common supernatural goal of human persons"—namely, "contemplation, the fulfillment of the spiritual life." And

---

[24] *Ibid.*, p. 69.

[25] *Ibid.*, p. 70. Presumably that "single moral ideal" is identical with "the common supernatural goal of human persons" and of philosophers: "contemplation, the fulfillment of the spiritual life" (see McInerny, p. 73; #j below).

[26] "The modal context" which McInerny here ascribes to Maritain corresponds to the latter's state *vs.* nature of philosophy and to which McInerny himself earlier has called the "circumstantial characterization" (see #b above) or its "concrete exercise" (see #c) or its "moral appraisal and orientation" (see #d). And (here we have an important key to understanding McInerny) this moral dimension of philosophizing lifts it from a mere modal status to a substantive feature or from circumstantial to formal characterization or (in Maritain's language) from a state to the nature of philosophy. See #d above and n. 21.

[27] McInerny, pp. 70–71.

contemplation "is no less the goal of the philosophers." The result? Their thinking should not be dissociated from their spiritual (and ethical) life, the goal of which is contemplation of and thus union with God so that each becomes a "saintly philosopher," whose thought should be influenced by the spiritual and ethical or moral dimension of his life,[28] with the implied conclusion (in light of the points McInerny made previously—see #a–#i above) that such spiritual and moral influence is no longer merely modal and extrinsic but also substantive and intrinsic to his philosophizing.[29]

So far (#a–#j) I have traced the movement of thought in McInerny's reflection on Maritain so as better to understand Owens. But before turning to Owens, let me evaluate McInerny's attempt to complement Maritain. It is ingenious and interesting. But it also is not totally clear and, in fact, raises questions.

These do not arise from the parallel McInerny sets up between Maritain's nature and state with his own substantive and modal levels or formal and individual circumstances (#a). In this initial consideration Christian philosophy is taken intellectually—that is, as a general sort of philosophical knowledge. But in #b to #d McInerny inserts "morally good" and "morally evil" into the previous parallels (#a), with the result that if philosophy is true, it is morally good but if philosophizing is evilly motivated,[30] philosophy itself is morally bad (#b). But since philosophy as a science involves content (#c) and since content is intrinsic to it and since philosophy however can be done with evil intent, the contrast has become that between an intrinsic and a moral appraisal of it (#c). But since philosophy if wrongly motivated is (with Plato) in itself and in its content worthless,[31] the moral appraisal of philosophy

---

[28] *Ibid.*, pp. 72–73.

[29] Nowhere does McInerny explicitly link modal and extrinsic with accidental (as Owens does). The sole use of the word (p. 65) occurs in the phrase *per accidens*: "It is not necessary to think of philosophy as some inert nature having properties of its own which is then carried around by various sweating Atlases whose itinerary is the basis for a number of *per accidens* remarks about their burden." See Owens, p. 23: "[Christianity and philosophy] are accidental in the sense that the concept of neither of them necessarily involves the concept of the other."

[30] Such evil motives might be neglect of duty (see McInerny, pp. 65–66) or vanity, will to power, etc.—see *ibid.*, p. 67, quoted in n. 31 below.

[31] *Ibid.*, p. 67: "Once we remind ourselves that the truth can be sought out of motives of vanity or the will to power or to *épater la bourgeoisie*, we can see how one might want so to describe the philosophical ideal as to insist that the

has been raised from a mere modal status of philosophy to a substantive feature (or with Maritain) from state to nature, or with McInerny from circumstantial to formal characterization (#d).

McInerny next (#e–#g) returns to philosophy precisely as an intellectual discipline, to the truths which it contains and which for a Catholic Christian philosopher are worked out under the guidance of the magisterium and its faith-deposit and of Thomas Aquinas. But this elaboration is not conducted in such a manner as to be sacred theology (#i).

However in #h McInerny again mentions morality when speaking of the "single moral ideal," which as our "supernatural goal" is "contemplation, the fulfillment of the spiritual life" and thus of our ethical or moral life (#j).

McInerny's insertion of morality into intellectuality raises questions. For instance, why would the *moral* condition of the philosopher necessarily change *the content of his philosophy itself,* which would or at least could be worked out independently of that ethical condition? Socrates and Plato of the early dialogues would legitimately answer: because knowledge *is* virtue.[32] But moral conduct involves more than knowing what is right and wrong—it also involves freedom of choice, from which the morality of human actions also issues. And freely choosing what is known to be morally good produces the virtues of courage, temperance and justice. Experiencing such production of virtues in ourselves or in others can lead to our formulating a valid science of ethics, the content of which however can remain distinct from the personal moral condition of the ethicist himself.

But suppose we grant that no one living immorally can elaborate a morally good science of ethics (because its subject-matter is precisely human conduct) and thus his/her personal moral life intrinsically, formally, substantively affects its contents. The case would apparently be quite different in other philosophic knowledges. Consider the speculative science of metaphysics (which concerns all

---

right deed be done for the right reason and to suggest that without the appropriate moral orientation the whole thing is worthless. Plato held that it is moral virtue which gives us that necessary affinity with the really real which enables knowledge to take place."

[32] See Plato, *Protagoras*, 349E–360E. Also see J. Owens, *A History of Ancient Western Philosophy* (New York: Appleton-Century-Crofts, Inc., 1959), pp. 171–73 on "Knowledge is virtue" in Socrates, pp. 201–2 in Plato; W. K. C. Guthrie, *A History of Greek Philosophy* (Cambridge University Press, 1969 and 1975), III, 450–59, and IV, 227–31.

actual existents qua existent). Its content need not reflect directly the moral or immoral life of the metaphysician. Consider this four-fold scenario. (1) If the content of a metaphysics is true and is worked out and taught for right motives, such a philosopher is (I would say) morally good. (2) If the content of such a science is true but is worked out and taught from wrong motives, the philosopher is morally evil, but that moral condition of the philosopher would not change the content and truth of his philosophy itself. (3) If the content of such a science is untrue but is elaborated and presented from good motives, the philosopher is morally good subjectively but is a poor metaphysician. (4) If the content of such a science not only is false but is worked out and taught with bad motives, the philosopher is morally bad and is (again) a poor metaphysician.

The inference this scenario suggests is that anyone's moral life need not directly and intrinsically influence his/her philosophical sciences (except possibly the ethics they might propose). Consequently, the contents of metaphysics and other non-ethical knowledges of a Christian philosopher remain essentially independent of the personal moral lives of metaphysicians and other such philosophers. That independence would be replaced by dependence only if with Socrates and Plato one agrees all knowledge (even metaphysics) *is* virtue. Accepting the Socratic-Platonic identification of knowledge and virtue is too high a price to pay that morality might (as McInerny would seem to wish) be identified as an intrinsic and not merely an extrinsic determinant of Christian philosophy, as its substantive and not solely modal feature, as its formal and not merely circumstantial situation.

(b) Owens on McInerny

The longest of his six references to McInerny Owens initiates (p. 12) by locating the aim of McInerny's supplement to Maritain in the emphasis the former gave to the "appropriate moral orientation" of the Christian philosopher, issuing from Christianity's proclamation of the "common supernatural goal of human persons."[33] Christianity thus can "exercise the intrinsic influence necessary for the specification of philosophy."[34] In the moral orientation arising from that goal and the intrinsic influence it exercises on specifying philosophy, Owens finds McInerny making a "considered attempt

---

[33] Words in double quotation marks here are from McInerny, pp. 67 and 73. See my section "McInerny on Maritain" above, prgrs. #b, #d and #j.

[34] Owens, p. 12.

to explain how something accidental to the internal constitution of a philosophy can occasion intrinsic differentiation in its essence,"[35] because that "appropriate moral orientation . . . lifts the moral from mere modal status to a substantive feature of philosophizing,"[36] from what is accidental in philosophizing to what is its very essence. This "jump from external association to substantive differentiation is obviously the crucial consideration in the problem at issue," but it is so not just for Christian but for all philosophers, each of whom initially depends on external guidance to set philosophy afoot.[37]

Whether or not one decides morality is actually this external factor causing Christian philosophy to be specifically differentiated from other philosophies is (for Owens) questionable, but at least McInerny's observation is important: "for all philosophies determining of the starting points has been radically influenced by external environment." No Christian philosopher need be apologetic about Christian philosophy depending upon his "existential situation" (McInerny, p. 70)—every philosopher is similarly dependent (Owens, p. 12).

What needs more careful consideration (Owens adds) is "how a goal *common* to all can serve in specifying a particular type of philosophy." But at least this is true: McInerny's "distinctive contribution to the debate [on whether Christian philosophy is a viable notion] is the framework for a role to be played by moral orientation in the problem of Christian philosophy" (p. 13). And the challenge that remains is "to show how something extrinsic and accidental can cause the intrinsic specification" of Christian philosophy. Owens takes up that challenge in his subsequent paragraphs, which have been outlined earlier (see "Owens' Position" above), as well as those on pp. 14–15 of his *Towards a Christian Philosophy*, to be analyzed in my immediately subsequent section.

---

[35] On the meaning Owens gives to "accidental" (a word he uses often), see p. 23: "[Christianity and philosophy] are accidental in the sense that the concept of neither of them necessarily involves the concept of the other" (see note 29 above). On "accident" in contrast with "substance," see Owens, p. 30: "As an activity, it [philosophy] is inherent as an accident in the substance of the one from whom it proceeds." Presumably, "accidental" has also this meaning throughout Owens' discussions?

[36] McInerny, p. 67.

[37] Owens, p. 12. For restatement of Owens' position see pp. 307–26.

Reaction and Supplement

On his pp. 14–15 Owens moves the problem of how something "extrinsic and accidental" can intrinsically specify Christian philosophy from the level of morality/intellectuality to that of its causes. Any product has (he observes) internal causes. Thus a summer cottage consists of wood, glass and other materials, put together as an A-frame or in some other shape. But a product also results from final, exemplary and efficient causes. Thus,

> the specific characteristics that differentiate a summer cottage and any other type of house are caused respectively by the purpose of summer relaxation, the blueprint of the architect, and the work of the carpenter or mason. It would be idle to contend that the intrinsic differentiation is not brought about by those external causes, each functioning in its own way.

Owens then turns to philosophy as a product.

> When philosophy is looked upon in its exercise as an activity produced by a person, the external factors of purpose, model, and agent may work together harmoniously to bring about a specifically distinct type of philosophical procedure. The fact that they are external and accidental gives no ground for incompatibility. The extrinsic and accidental teaching or guidance can in its own way determine the intrinsically distinct type of philosophy in which a person molds his thought. Christian considerations can in this way bring about an intrinsic differentiation in a philosophy.[38]

(a) Content-Determining-Cause

Let us concentrate upon what determines the content of knowledge as possibly a sort of exemplary cause. What is known causes directly and intrinsically the very content of the knowledge, and thus the known is not accidental and extrinsic to the knowledge but (in nonconstructural knowledge) is intrinsic and essential to it.[39] In fact, as Aristotle and Aquinas both affirm, the known and

---

[38] *Ibid.*, p. 15.

[39] On nonconstructural knowledge see my *Authentic Metaphysics in an Age of Unreality*, 2d ed. [hereafter: *Authentic Metaphysics*] (New York/Bern: Peter Lang Publishing, Inc., 1993), p. 146, n. 10.

the knower share in and are united by a single actuation. This actuation is an entitative, precognitive formal determination of the knower's faculties but which is nonetheless common to both knower and known because the latter has caused it first efficiently by physically affecting the sense organs (through the media of light and sound waves, etc.) and, thereby, also "exemplarily" as content-determining-cause of it in the cognitive powers (the external and internal senses and the recipient intellect, the latter with the help of the agent intellect) of the knower, who, as so actuated, efficiently causes his/her awarenesses of what (say) a tiger is, his judgments that tigers are not elephants, and inferences for further judgments that tigers are best kept in their native forests rather than in zoos.[40]

Suppose, though, that what is causing the content of knowledge is not tigers in their local habitat or in zoos but (say) the Nazi Germans entering and occupying Paris in 1940. Then the content-determining-cause of Simone de Beauvoir's knowledge was not just human beings *tout courte* but human-beings-who-are-Nazis-bent-on-conquering-France-and-Europe.[41] The resultant knowledge issued into the philosophical position of radical existentialism, which is not a "pure" philosophy unaffected by what is exterior. In fact, what might be exterior in a noncognitional situation is not so in a cognitional situation because it functions as content-determining-cause of cognition and thus is intrinsic to cognition: as noted above, the known and the knower share in and are united by a single entitative, precognitive actuation. Thus the radical existentialism of Simone de Beauvoir or of Jean-Paul Sartre is genuinely philosophical (because it is due to reflection and reasoning) and yet it is

---

[40] See my ch. 21 below, "Preller and Aquinas: Second Thoughts on Epistemology," especially the section "Aristotle's Theory of Knowledge," as well as prgrs. corresponding to notes 4–10. On nonconstructural knowledge, see *ibid.*, n. 21.

Content-determining-cause can be viewed as a sort of exemplary cause if this is taken as an "external formal cause": *formal* because the known produces actuation "a" as an entitative determinant of the faculty, *external* because, although that actuation belongs to both knower and known, it is solely *in* the knower but also is an actuation *of* the known. Obviously, such exemplary causality is analogous. On efficient and final causes, see my *Authentic Metaphysics*, pp. 236–311; on exemplary cause see *ibid.*, pp. 312–17.

[41] See S. de Beauvoir, *The Ethics of Ambiguity*, trans. B. Frechtman (New York: The Citadel Press, 1968), pp. 74–75.

intrinsically and essentially permeated by events in the 1940s and later and thus is radically existentialist and atheistic.[42]

The situation of Christian philosophers is not unlike theirs. Take a Christian philosopher who is an authentic existentialist. He or she has experienced this world of actual existents—tigers, Concord grape vines, the earth with its atmosphere, human persons of many talents and nationalities in various circumstances of pain and joy. From such experiences they have realized that what gives such existents worth and value (that is, what makes them real) is not directly the fact that such existents are tigers or grape vines or humans, but rather each does exist and yet exists contingently: each exists in such a way that it does so not *of and in itself* because what it is (= its essence or nature) makes it be *what* it is but not *be*. And yet it *is*, and thus it must be caused *to be* by an Existent whose very essence must be existence and who thus as agent properly causes it to exist and thus who has created it, since creation is to cause something to actually exist which in no way before or even now exists *in and of itself.*

In all those steps in the authentically existentialist metaphysics just sketched, one proceeds philosophically—i.e., from our experience of naturally known starting points (existing tigers, vines, coal, human persons) by inductive inferences to naturally known conclusions. It is, in other words, genuinely *philosophical.* But it is also a *Christian* philosophy because its initial awareness of "creation" came from divine revelation in the sacred Scriptures, elaborated by theologians such as Thomas Aquinas. But theologians' function in my philosophizing is to point to natural evidence present in ourselves and other actual existents, serving as content-determining-causes of our philosophical knowledge but heretofore overlooked. "Creation" and "existence" (not merely as fact but evidence of an intrinsic component) are not intelligible content superimposed by Aquinas "upon the data already gained from material existents

---

[42] *Ibid.*, Section 3: "The Antinomies of Action," pp. 96–115; Jean-Paul Sartre, *Existentialism*, trans. B. Frechtman (New York: Philosophical Library, 1947); *idem, Existentialism and Humanism*, trans. P. Mairet (Brooklyn, N.Y.: Haskell House Publishers, 1948). See James Collins, *The Existentialists: A Critical Study* (Chicago: Henry Regnery Co., 1952); Frederick Copleston, *Contemporary Philosophy* (Westminster, Md.: The Newman Press, 1963), chs. 10 and 11. On existentialism see the following chapters below: ch. 20: "The Mystery of Existence," ch. 22: "Existentialism: Authentic and Unauthentic," ch. 24: "The Christian Existentialism of Jacques Maritain."

through direct perception."[43] Such intelligibilities were already present in those existents, functioning as content-determining-causes, which however could not disclose their full content until sacred Scripture and theology had pointed out the fuller actuation actual existents could give. Hence, authentically existential metaphysics is a *Christian* philosophy because Christianity played an illuminative role in its development, but it is a Christian *philosophy* because its starting points are the evidences from actual existents themselves as its content-determining-causes, and its procedure is natural reflection upon and inductive inference from such evidence.[44]

Let me reflect again on the relational situations a human person can find him/herself in and their relevance to those persons as content-determining-causes of knowledge. As indicated in the invasion of Paris by the Nazis in the mid-forties, as well as that of Kuwait by the Iraqis and the resultant "Desert Storm" warfare in the late eighties and early nineties or the 1994 surprise attack on the American figure-skater Nancy Kerrigan or the dire influence of TV and other communication media upon violent youth or (a happier example) the repair of the Hubble telescope by astronauts and their safe return, human persons are constituted also by the situations they find themselves in—where they are, with whom, when, in what circumstances (stressful or relaxing). Such situations are the skeins of relationships in which human persons exist and which intrinsically help make them be who they are. Thus they function as content-determining-causes not in precision from but concretely in their actual relational situations. They are, then, rich in intelligibilities by their openness to joys and sorrows and to other influences, by their very vulnerability. And even though in working out an authentically existentialist philosophy of the human persons who are determining its content I produce a philosophical science which is abstract in that it is not of this or that individual person, still it is of human persons as "individual"—i.e., what it means to be *an* individual human person. Thus that philosophical science must be open to constant enrichment in content insofar as the philosopher is constantly experiencing more and more of what

---

[43] See my ch. 2 below, p. 35.

[44] On inductive inference see my *Authentic Metaphysics*, pp. 325–33, especially pp. 328–33. For a listing of texts (early, middle, late) in which Thomas speaks of existence/essence see my ch. 19 below.

actual persons are conveying by determining further the content of his or her knowledge through entitative actuations. And if that authentic existentialist is a Christian philosopher, he/she finds himself in a situation in which he hears the word of God, assents to it through faith, understands it through theology and, also, independently works out a philosophy but under the influence of divinely revealed truth indicating perceivable evidence in actual existents which might be overlooked.

If my previous paragraphs are accurate, human persons and other actual existents in all their ample relationships are content-determining-causes of knowledge and thus are intrinsic to it. One result is that there seemingly is less need to speak of morality *vs.* intellectuality, of modal *vs.* substantive levels, of individual *vs.* formal characterizations, even of state *vs.* nature. As content-determining-cause of cognition the known is on a par with the knower through the single actuation they have in common.

(b) Can There Be "Pure" Philosophy?

Another result of knowledge having actual existents as its content-determining-causes (which thereby produce entitative and precognitive actuations) is that no philosophical science—whether general or special (see paragraphs corresponding to notes 14–15 above)—would be "purely" philosophical because, even though proceeding from natural evidence through reflection and reasoning to naturally accepted conclusions, each philosopher would have gained that evidence by being actuated in an entitative, precognitive formal manner by actual existents in their concrete relational situations constituting what/who they are.[45] Thus French men and women in and after the 1940s produced radical existentialism,[46] which is distinctively what it is because of life in France in that era. Marxism arose, as Owens notes, "from economic crises" in the nineteenth century, which in the twentieth century also helped produce liberation philosophy.[47] Lenin and his contemporaries for-

---

[45] In ch. 21 below, I label such entitative actuations as "actuations *a*" to distinguish them from "actuations *b*," which are the awarenesses, judgments and inferences efficiently produced by the knower when entitatively and precognitively actuated (#a) by the known as content-determining-cause. See ch. 21, section "Aristotle's Theory of Knowledge," as well as prgrs. linked with notes 4–10. On relations see *Authentic Metaphysics*, ch. 7.

[46] See prgrs. corresponding to notes 41–42 above. On atheism within an American context, see references to Paul Kurtz, ch. 26, n. 37.

[47] Owens, p. 21, quoted in n. 15 above.

mulated communism as (in part, at least) a reaction to Czarist repression of the Russian serfs and thus to the then economic and historical milieu.

Certainly philosophers in countries such as the Czech Republic, now freed from communism, will produce distinctive philosophies inasmuch as they are free not only politically but also from the internal structure forcefully imposed by the Communists. As Václav Havel explained in a speech on April 22, 1993,

> communism was far from being simply the dictatorship of one group of people over another. It was a genuinely totalitarian system, that is, it permeated every aspect of life and deformed everything it touched, including all the natural ways people had evolved of living together. It profoundly affected all forms of human behavior. For years, a specific structure of values and models of behavior was deliberately created in the consciousness of society. It was a perverted structure, one that went against all the natural tendencies of life, but society nevertheless internalized it, or rather was forced to internalize it.

He speaks next of the post-Communist era.

> When Communist power and its ideology collapsed, this structure collapsed along with it. But people couldn't simply absorb and internalize a new structure immediately, one that would correspond to the elementary principles of civic society and democracy. The human mind and human habits cannot be transformed overnight; to build a new system of living values and to identify with them takes time.[48]

---

[48] Václav Havel, "The Post-Communist Nightmare," *New York Review of Books*, May 27, 1993, p. 8.

That the moral, political and personal devastation which Saddam Hussein and the Baath regime have inflicted upon Iraq far exceeds that which Communist power and its ideology inflicted (as described by Havel) upon Czechoslovak society, see Edward Mortimer's review of Kanan Makiya's book, *Cruelty and Silence: War, Tyranny, Uprising and the Arab World*, in *The New York Review of Books*, May 27, 1993, pp. 3–7. One can with assurance infer that the philosophy which will eventually issue from Iraq will be thoroughly influenced in content by what its intelligentsia have experienced, serving, however far in the future, as its content-determining-causes.

However unsettling this current period is, certainly with time Czech philosophers will undoubtedly set forth not a "pure" philosophy devoid of influence from the preceding decades but a markedly Czech philosophy made distinctive by the experiences which those philosophers went through and are going through now and in which are found the actual content-determining-causes of that philosophy.

More examples are available but those given make clear that a philosophy can be "pure" only with difficulty.[49] It would have to cut itself off through precision from the concrete relational contexts within which the philosopher lives and which are the content-determining-causes of his knowledge. It would be no more than logically correct reasoning from a starting point arrived at through precision from our actual *Lebenswelt*, the latter word taken not in Husserl's neo-Kantian sense[50] but as our world of actual noumena[51] directly serving as determinants of all our nonconstructural knowledges, authentic existentialism included.

Another avenue for seeing how difficult it is for philosophy to be "pure" is reflecting on Etienne Gilson's description of how a Christian philosopher submits to the influence of his/her Christian religion. Such submission shows itself in three ways, the first of which is that "the Christian philosopher . . . effects a choice between problems" (e.g., those concerning the nature and immortality of the human soul, freedom of the will, God's existence and nature, etc.). Second, such a philosopher rethinks any reasoning process which has culminated in a conclusion (e.g., the human soul perishes with the body, there is no God) opposed to divine revelation. Finally, a Christian philosopher grasps philosophical truths more easily and

---

[49] What comes closest to "pure philosophy" may be symbolic logic or linguistic analysis, which centers on meanings and language divorced from and not arising from actual reality. See H. A. Nielsen, "Linguistic Analysis," *New Catholic Encyclopedia*, VIII, 771–75; Morris Weitz, "Analysis, Philosophical," *Encyclopedia of Philosophy*, I, 97–105; William P. Alston, "Language, Philosophy of," *ibid.*, IV, 386–90.

[50] See Herbert Spiegelberg, *The Phenomenological Movement*, 3d ed. (The Hague: Martinus Nijhoff Publishers, 1982), pp. 144–47.

[51] See Thomas P. Rausch, "Thomas Merton: Twenty-five Years After," *America*, Jan. 1, 1994, p. 7, where after an introductory sentence he quotes Merton's *Contemplation in a World of Action* (1971): "The world is not a reality outside of ourselves: 'It is a complex of responsibilities and options made out of the loves, the hates, the fears, the joys, the hopes, the greed, the cruelty, the kindness, the faith, the trust, the suspicion of all.' "

deeply from studying the theologians who by using philosophy in trying to understand divine revelation see more deeply into philosophy itself, and this they do precisely as theologians.[52]

Gilson's words seem especially applicable today when our culture is permeated with abstract but potent factors often spelled with capital letters: Evolution, Computer Technology, Racism, Right to Life, Right to Self-Determination, Privacy, Consumerism, Greed, Science, Political Correctness. These factors are often taken for granted as true, valuable, significant without question or without giving an account or proof of them (either because we personally cannot do so or we think they do not need proof). Yet they influence (however quietly, latently, subtly) our explicitly and strictly philosophical activities.[53] Think, for instance, how Right to Life has affected Operation Rescue in its policies and practices, how Right to Self-Determination and Privacy have affected abortion-advocacy and radical feminism, how Science has influenced logical positivists and some linguistic analysts by giving them the "empirically verifiable" as a criterion of what they take to be true.

In these and other instances which could be given, Gilson's three ways of submitting to forces outside strictly philosophical areas seem relevant. Such capitalized words intimate to those working inside those areas what problems are worth attending to; they suggest the necessity of retracing one's steps upon arriving at destinations hostile to them; they furnish a touchstone of "truth" by stressing aspects of current society which otherwise might go unconsidered.

If those contemporary nonphilosophical factors are operative in contemporary thinkers, then a philosophy which is Christian is not unique but is merely one among many philosophies arising not only from philosophical but also from nonphilosophical sources. If so, there is no "pure" philosophy today any more than there was in nineteenth-century Germany or sixteenth-century France or thirteenth-century Europe or in fifth- or fourth-century Greece B.C.[54]

---

[52] See ch. 2 below, pp. 29–30.

[53] On the frequency and influence of capitalized words, see Saul Bellow, *Humboldt's Gift* (New York: Avon Books, 1976), p. 6, which I quote below, ch. 2, pp. 36–37. There I call such capitalized factors "the mythical 'gods' of our current culture" and thus the philosophies they influence I term "religio-speculations" or "religio-philosophies."

[54] Plato's *Phaedo* is a clear example of an absence of "pure" philosophy in Greece. In that dialogue his starting point is divine revelation from Orphic or other mystery religions that souls exist before and after their bodies (69C–E);

(c) Monism and Christian Philosophy

The attention given to Bréhier's debate on Christian philosophy with Gilson and Maritain, as well as its continuance up to and including Joseph Owens' *Towards a Christian Philosophy*, might suggest all Christian thinkers desire that Christianity and philosophy remain distinct while simultaneously working in tandem with revealed truths influencing philosophy in such a way however as to be (in Gilson's words) "an indispensible auxiliary to reason" but not to "descend as a constitutive element . . . into its texture . . . but [only] into the work of its construction."[55] Such a relationship between Christianity and philosophy is certainly found in Aquinas, where real distinctions are crucial, as the stress he puts on the real otherness between each human person and all other existents (including and especially God)[56] but also on the real otherness in him between his existence and essence, his soul and body, his faculties and the soul (from which they emanate), between the faculties themselves and their operations and the virtues thus acquired. Genuine otherness also obtains between the sciences he gains—for instance, geometry, computer science, economics,[57] as well as theology and philosophy. Although the latter is genuinely distinct from his theological knowledge, nonetheless it can (as we have seen) be influenced by divinely revealed truths in his choice of topics studied, in its correction (when necessary) of conclusions and in its deeper grasp of philosophical truths from reading theologians. And such influence renders his/her philosophy Christian, without however Christianity's becoming an intrinsic constitutive factor in that philosophy.[58]

---

his procedure is to understand and establish that the human soul is thus deathless by four arguments (*logoi*), which run from 70C–107B. Plato, accordingly, is working out not "pure" philosophy but religio-philosophy.

[55] For the quotation from Gilson see my ch. 2 below, p. 29.

[56] See *S.T.*, I, 8, 1 resp., where in one sentence Thomas intimates that God is transcendent and yet also is immanent to every creature but in such a way as to exclude monism: "Deus est in omnibus rebus, non quidem sicut pars essentiae vel sicut accidens, sed sicut agens adest ei in quod agit." For Aquinas' position on real distinctions, see my *Authentic Metaphysics*, chs. 4–6 and 10.

[57] On the distinction Thomas finds in sciences because of their distinct formal objects, see L. Sweeney, S.J., "The Distinction of Operative Habits in the Philosophy of Saint Thomas Aquinas" (Master's thesis, St. Louis University, 1945), ch. 3.

[58] See prgr. corresponding to n. 52 above. Also see ch. 12 below: "Scholasticism," especially section "Scholasticism's Golden Age," which discloses the academic milieu of Aquinas, Albert and Bonaventure.

But Bonaventure does not (in my interpretation—see chapter 3 below: "Augustine and Bonaventure on Christian Philosophy") hesitate to insert Christianity into the very content of metaphysics on one of its levels. This insertion is due to the fact that Bonaventure's intellectual position is monistic: everything (God and creatures, faith and reason, theology and philosophy) consists of light, and the otherness between each member in the three couplets is not totally and fully real because each differs from the other solely according to the degree of light proper to it. Hence, that insertion of divine truths into metaphysics is not, for the Franciscan author, a scandal but is the only means by which he can safeguard moral philosophy from the errors which afflict pagan Platonic philosophy. Hence, even though theology is other than philosophy, Bonaventure's "transcendent" metaphysics in its third stage must be completed by belief in divine revelation concerning Adam's sin and its serious effects on human agents, resurrection of the body, Christ as God-man and mediator, grace as necessary to gain eternal life, and so on.[59]

His transcendent metaphysics on its third level is, then, neither straight theology nor straight philosophy but may be called "Christian philosophy" in a sense as different from Thomas Aquinas' as the former's monistic reality of light differs from the latter's pluralistic reality of actual existence in really and fully distinct existents.

Monism and its effects on Christian philosophy in Bonaventure's position alert one to search for possible similar effects in other authors. In Gabriel Marcel one has not far to look. In *Creative Fidelity* he finishes his reflection on whether God exists by stating there is no "precise boundary between metaphysics and mysticism. . . . It is time that the metaphysician understands, if he wants once and for all to get out of the epistemological rut, that adoration can and ought to be a *terra firma* for reflection, a ground where he can find support."[60]

Bonaventure and Marcel are, accordingly, two cases in which monism blurred the distinction between faith and reason, between religious and metaphysical thought. Cannot one take monism (or its opposite, as in Aquinas) as a litmus test to detect what an

---

[59] See my ch. 3 below, especially "Conclusions."

[60] *Creative Fidelity*, pp. 145–46, quoted in ch. 23 below: "Gabriel Marcel's Position on God," section "Several Intellectual Stages," final prgr. On Marcel's possible monism of "Being," see *ibid.*, "Marcel's *Weltanschauung*," prgrs. corresponding to notes 9–18; *ibid.*, "Further Questions," prgrs. corresponding to notes 31–35.

author's attitude is on the relationship between philosophy and theology? If so, chapters 14–16 below on Albert the Great are significant since reality for him is also light.[61] So too the investigation of topics in Plotinus (chapters 4–6 and 16–18) is relevant since his monism apparently has repercussions on his philosophy, which is an henology (not an ontology, because reality is unity and not being) in metaphysics. It is also an ethics by pointing out how an individual soul may attain happiness and fulfillment, a religious theory by instilling a reverent dedication to God, and a mysticism by counseling ultimate identification with Him—and all this often expressed in one and the same treatise in the *Enneads*.[62]

Even though Augustine's reading Plotinus played a significant role in the process of his conversion,[63] he was not a monist.[64] But the influence of Plotinus upon him appears so strong (at least to some) that it is still a viable question as to whether Augustine was authentically a Christian or a Neoplatonist.[65] Moreover, for him "Christianity" and "true philosophy" are practically synonymous terms—in fact, he once defined Christianity as "the one true philosophy . . . the true and holy philosophy" learned from St. Paul.[66]

----

[61] See my ch. 15 below: "*Esse Primum Creatum* in Albert the Great's *Liber de Causis et Processu Universitatis*," especially "Conclusions." On Albert's immediate predecessor at the University of Paris see ch. 13 below: "Human Knowledge According to Guerric of St. Quentin," which shows Guerric's epistemology to combine an independent Aristotelianism on intellect with a plurality of forms.

On Thomas' distancing himself from Neoplatonism (especially as expressed in the *Liber de Causis*), see my ch. 19 below, "'Idealis' in the Terminology of Thomas Aquinas." Such distance also exists between him and Albert precisely on what *esse* means—a distance which illumines that the *esse* which Fran O'Rourke (following C. Fabro) characterizes as "intensive" and "synthetic" is *not* Aquinas' but *Albert's*. See O'Rourke, *Pseudo-Dionysius and the Metaphysics of Aquinas* (Leiden: E. J. Brill, 1992); M. Ewbank's review in *The Review of Metaphysics* 47 (1993), 375–77.

[62] See ch. 4 below, pp. 79 and 82.

[63] See *Confessions*, VII, 9, 13 and 10, 16.

[64] See *ibid.*, VII, 11, 17 and X, 6, 9.

[65] See my chs. 7 and 8 below. Also see James J. O'Donnell, *Augustine: "Confessions"* (Oxford: Clarendon Press, 1992), I, pp. xxiii–xxxii; Carol Harrison, *Beauty and Revelation in the Thought of Saint Augustine* (Oxford: Clarendon Press, 1992), pp. 8–12.

[66] *Contra Julianum*, IV, 4, 72 (*PL* 44, 774), quoted in ch. 3 below, n. 8. Also see ch. 2, p. 24.

If we use monism one last time in deciphering the relationship between philosophy and religious thought in an author, let us turn to Alfred North Whitehead in the twentieth century with this question: is his cosmology a monism because of the central position he gives there to creativity as the basic stuff which God and actual entities have in common and which is itself modeled on an electromagnetic field of force?[67] If the answer is affirmative, reflection on creativity may help us understand better how Whitehead conceives God and the cosmos, as well as religion, science and philosophy.

The final chapter, "Can Aquinas Help Our Contemporary World?" concentrates on those aspects of Thomas' thought which are most in contrast with modern and contemporary thinkers from Descartes to Derrida—actual existents are themselves the content-determining-causes of one's knowledge and thus one knows noumena; in each of them existence is an intrinsic actuating cause, which however reveals also that each is contingent and thus leads to God who *is* existence; the human soul is *by nature* not only the substantial form of matter but also is spiritual and, consequently, is immortal; hence, the human person is to be guided by natural law, which is itself a participation in the divine law in the same way that each human existent is a participant of divine existence. Although other aspects could be listed, enough has been said to illustrate the value of Aquinas' Christian philosophy in counteracting erroneous modern and current philosophical views and in helping us deliver our world from its moral and political disasters.

The preceding prefatory remarks will, I hope, help illumine the contents of this book as issuing from my reflecting on what philosophy (whether "pure" or religio-speculation) and, especially, Christian philosophy signify;[68] how especially the latter is prepared for by Greek authors[69] and is present in and practiced by medieval authors;[70] and how Gabriel Marcel and Alfred North

---

[67] See ch. 25 below: "Whitehead's Cosmology: A Monism of Creativity?" and John J. Furlong, "Recent Developments in Metaphysics," in my *Authentic Metaphysics*, ch. 11, pp. 355–59.

[68] Chs, 1–3 above.

[69] Plato, Aristotle and Plotinus, as studied in chs. 4–6, 11 and 18.

[70] See chs, 7–10 on Augustine, ch. 13 on Guerric of St. Quentin, chs. 14-16 on Albert, ch. 17 on Thomas' reading of the *Liber de Causis*, chs. 10–23, 24 and 26 on Aquinas.

Whitehead set forth, each in his own way, theories which clarify how science and philosophy, religion and theology are linked.[71]

Ten years ago someone initiated the "Preface" of his book by saying:

> This book brings together previously published articles bearing on issues which have defined my scholarly efforts for some years. Such a collection cannot, of course, have the cohesion of a planned book, but there is a not too fanciful sense in which these studies can be thought of as chapters of a book I was half-consciously composing.[72]

That paragraph fits my book on *Christian Philosophy: Greek, Medieval, Contemporary Reflections* sufficiently to allow me to end its "Preface" with it.

The only thing remaining—and it is a pleasant task—is to express gratitude to those who have helped in preparing this book: Charles Ermatinger, Vatican Film Library of St. Louis University, whose paleographic skill (together with Marvin Kessler's) made ch. 13 possible; Christopher Myers of Peter Lang Publishing, Inc. whose assistance was always at hand; Suzanne Mazurek, Erin Milnes, Jack Jasper, Juliana and Harry Dukov for editorial and computer expertise; Clement Kuehn for expertly keyboarding the Greek script; David Meconi, S.J., and John DeJak for judicious proofreading; Carol Szablewski for drawing up the indices and for securing copyright permissions; Loyola University Chicago, its Jesuit Community and its department of philosophy for providing the environment and opportunity to do research; my brother and sister, Paul and Bernice, as well as my sister Elizabeth and her husband, Monroe Koblitz, for helping finance the preparation of the manuscript.

Let me dedicate this volume to all my teachers and in a special way to four who were outstanding: Francis A. Preuss, S.J. (1889–1968), Augustine Klaas (1902–1966), Henri J. Renard, S.J. (1894–1981) of St. Louis University, and Etienne Gilson (1884–1978) of the Pontifical Institute of Mediaeval Studies and the University of Toronto.

---

[71] See chs. 23 and 25.

[72] Ralph McInenrny, *Being and Predication: Thomistic Interpretations* (Washington: The Catholic University of America Press, 1986), p. vii.

Acknowledgments

The author and publisher wish to thank the following for permission to reprint copyrighted material:

American Catholic Philosophical Association for "Existence/Essence in Thomas Aquinas' Early Writings", *Proceedings* of the American Catholic Philosophical Association 37 (1963), pp. 97-131.

Associated University Presses for Joseph Bracken, *Society and Spirit* (Cranbury, NJ: Associated University Presses, 1991), pp. 72-73, 140.

Augustinian Historical Institute, "Was St. Augustine a Christian or Neoplatonist? Old Question, New Approach" in J. C. Schnaubelt (ed.), *Collectanea Augustiniana* (Villanova: Augustinian Historical Institute, 1988); *idem*, "Augustine on Christ as God and Man: Exegesis of *Confessions*, VII, ch. 19" in Frederick Van Fleteren (ed.), *Collectanea Augustiniana*, (Villanova, PA: Augustinian Historical Institute, 1995).

Beacon Press for excerpts from Hans Jonas, *The Gnostic Religion* (Boston: Beacon Press, 1991).

A & C Black for excerpts from Gabriel Marcel, *Being and Having*, transl. Katherine Farrer (Huntingdon, Cambridge: A & C Black Publishers, 1965).

Bolchaza-Carducci Publishers, "Boethius on the 'Individual': Platonist or Aristotelian?" in R. Sutton (ed.), *Daidalikon: Studies in Memory of Raymond V. Schoder, S.J.*

The Catholic University of America Press for excerpts from Joseph Owens, *Towards A Christian Philosophy* (Washington, D.C.: The Catholic University Press, 1990).

Center for Thomistic Studies for "Can St. Thomas Speak to the Modern World?" in *One Hundred Years of Thomism*, Victor Brezik (ed.), (Houston: University of St. Thomas, 1981), pp. 119-41.

Franciscan Institute for "Augustine and Bonaventure on Christian Philosophy" in *Essays Honoring Allan Wolter*, edited by Girard J. Etzkorn and published by The Franciscan Institute, St. Bonaventure University, (Summer, 1985), pp. 271-308.

Editions Gallimard for excerpts from Gabriel Marcel, *Du refus à l'invocation; Creative Fidelity*, transl. R. Rosthal (Paris: Editions Gallimard, 1940; New York: Farrar, Straus & Giroux, Inc., 1964).

Good Will Publishers, Inc. for "Philosophy" in John P. Bradley (ed.), *Encyclopedic Dictionary of Christian Doctrine*, Vol. 9 of *The Catholic Layman's Library* (Gastonia, NC: Good Will Publishers, Inc., 1970), pp. 872-88.

HarperCollins Publishers for excerpts from Jacques Maritain, *Approaches to God.* (HarperCollins Publishers, Inc., 1954).

Harvard University Press for Rodolphe Gasché, *The Tain of the Mirror: Derrida and the Philosophy of Reflection* (Cambridge, MA: Harvard University Press, 1986), pp. 238-42.

Henry Holt and Company, Inc. for excerpts from Jacques Maritain, *Peasant of the Garonne* (Henry Holt and Co., 1968).

MacMillan Educational Co. for "Scholasticism" in *Collier's Encyclopedia* (1962), Vol. 20, pp. 487-89.

Modern Schoolman for "Preller and Aquinas: Second Thoughts on Epistemology" in *The Modern Schoolman*, Vol. 48, (1971), pp. 267-73; "The Mystery of Existence", *ibid.*, Vol. 44 (November, 1966), pp. 57-63.

New Scholasticism for "Existentialism: Authentic and Unauthentic" in *New Scholasticism*, 40 (January, 1966), pp. 36-61; "Gabriel Marcel's Position on God", *ibid.*, 44 (1970), pp. 101-24.

Oxford University Press for excerpts from Terence Irwin, *Aristotle's First Principles* (New York: Oxford University Press, 1990).

Pontifical Institute of Mediaeval Studies for "Are Plotinus and Albertus Magnus Neoplatonists?" in Lloyd Gerson (ed.) *Graceful Reason: Essays in Ancient and Medieval Philosophy Presented to Joseph Owens* (Toronto: Pontifical Institute of Mediaeval Studies, 1983), pp. 177–202.

Recherches Augustiniennes for excerpts from William Mallard, "The Incarnation in Augustine's Conversion, " *Recherches Augustiniennes*, 15 (1980), 80–98.

Regnery Publishing, Inc. for excerpts from Gabriel Marcel, *Metaphysical Journal*, transl. B. Wall (Washington: Regnery Publishing, Inc. 1952).

Regnery Publishing, Inc. for excerpts from Gabriel Marcel, *Mystery of Being*, transl. R. Hague (Washington: Regnery Publishing, Inc., 1960).

Salem Press, Inc. for "Plotinus' Conception of Neoplatonism" in E. G. Weltin (ed.), *Great Events of World History* II (1973), pp. 823–29.

Simon & Schuster for excerpts from Alfred North Whitehead, *Process and Reality* Corrected Edition, ed. David R. Griffin and Donald W. Sherburne (New York: Simon & Schuster, 1978).

Speculum for "*Idealis* in the Terminology of Thomas Aquinas", *Speculum*, 33 (October, 1958), pp. 497–507.

State University of New York for "Mani's Twin and Plotinus: Questions of Self" in *Neo-Platonism and Gnosticism*, Richard T. Wallis (ed.), (Albany: State University of New York Press, 1992), pp. 381–424.

Theology Digest for "Can Philosophy be Christian?" in *Theology Digest*, 34 (Winter, 1987), pp. 327–36.

The Thomist for "*Esse Primum Creatum* in Albert The Great's *Liber de Causis et Processu Universitatis*" in *The Thomist*, 44 (1980), pp. 599–646.

University of Montreal for "Human Knowledge According to Guerric of St. Quentin, O.P.", *Arts Libéraux et philosophie au moyen age*, (Montréal: Institut d'Etudes Médiévales; J. Vrin, 1969), pp. 1129–41.

University of Notre Dame Press for L. Sweeney, "Augustine's *De Doctrina Christiana*" from D. Arnold and P. Bright (eds.), *De Doctrina Christiana: A Classic of Western Culture*" (University of Notre Dame Press, 1995).

University of Oklahoma Press for "*Esse* in Albert The Great's Texts on Creation in *Summa de Creaturis* and *Scriptum in Libros Sententiarium*", *Southwestern Journal of Philosophy*, 10 (1980), pp. 65–95. Reprinted as chapter in F. J. Kovach (ed.), *Albert the Great: Commemorative Essays* (University of Oklahoma Press, 1980), pp. 65–95.

University of Ottawa Press for "The Christian Existentialism of Jacques Maritain" in Jean-Louis Allard (ed.), *Jacques Maritain: A Philosopher in the World*, (Ottawa: University of Ottawa Press, 1986), pp. 31–41.

University Press of America for Joseph Bracken, "The Issue of Panentheism in the Dialogue with the Non-Believers" in *Studies in Religion* 21 (1992), pp. 216–217.

University Press of America for Joseph Bracken, *The Triune Symbol: Persons, Process and Community*, (Lanham, MD: University Press of America, 1985), p. 7.

Walter de Gruyter and Co. for "Metaphysics and God: Plotinus and Aquinas" in *Miscellanea Mediaevalia*, Vol. 2: *Die Metaphysik im Mittelalter: ihr Ursprung und ihre Bedeutung* (Berlin: Walter de Gruyter and Co., 1963), pp. 232–39.

Washington Post Writers Group for George F. Will, syndicated column, *Chicago Sun-Times*, March 13, 1979.

I

Christian Philosophy:
Fact or Fiction?

1

Philosophy: An Overview

Before concentrating upon philosophy as "Christian, " it is useful to reflect briefly upon what "philosophy" in contrast to "science" and to "religion" has meant—a reflection augmented by subsequent chapters.

Philosophy etymologically comes from a Greek word (*philosophia*) signifying "love of wisdom." But that literal meaning is of little help in understanding contemporary usages of the word. Popularly, it occurs in such expressions as "his philosophy of life" or "the philosophy behind the merger." In technical contexts one hears of a "philosophy of art," "philosophy of nature," of science, of religion, of man, of history, of God, of being, of morality, of mathematics.

Again, philosophy currently is itself described in various ways. To some it is the science of sciences, but to others it is no science at all: it is a pursuit or mental attitude rather than a body of knowledge with sharply defined contents. Some call it a speculative cosmology, others a theory of language, or a theory of critical discussion, or a rational reconstruction, or a collection and evaluation of conclusions from various empiriological sciences (those based on the quantitative and the measurable), or a survey and critique of presuppositions taken throughout the history of scientific ideas, and so on.

What, then, is philosophy? The conclusion to be drawn from the current scene is that "philosophy" is used frequently in different contexts and is itself understood in many different ways. Accordingly, questions arise as to its meaning, nature, validity, function. It is a single term used in several diverse fashions, but does "philosophy" have a single although analogous meaning or is it merely equivocal? Is it genuinely a science, or is it mere speculation and opinion? If some sort of science, does it have distinct branches, divided according to their objects of study like the natural sciences? Is it distinct from religion and theology? Does it conflict with them? Are they in conflict with it?

Answers to these and other inquiries can be achieved if we view philosophy in relationship to science and, then, to religion or theology (these two are not synonyms: religion is man's acknowledgment of belief in God through prayer and cult, whereas theology is an intellectual elaboration and defense of the divinely revealed contents of this belief).

Philosophy and Science: Plato to Kant

The history of how philosophy is related to science may be viewed as falling into two main periods: (1) from Plato (427–347 B.C.) and Aristotle (384–322 B.C.) up to Kant (1724–1804); (2) from Kant to the present day. In the first period, philosophy was a science, because the latter word then signified certain and universal knowledge arrived at by demonstration, and such knowledge a philosopher was thought to attain.

Terms Used Interchangeably

In fact, the two words came to be used interchangeably. Let me explain. In comparing "philosophy" and "science," one does not begin with the terms themselves but rather with the actual states of mind they express. During this period a person was viewed as using his intellectual powers so as to arrive at certain and relatively universal conclusions by demonstration from principles. The resultant mental state in which such a thinker actually found himself was described as either "philosophy" or "science," without any difference of meaning.

True enough, the principles and conclusions helping to constitute that state pertained now to being as being, now to being as material and mobile, now to discrete and continuous quantity, and so on. In light of those different formal objects, those knowledges could be called metaphysics, physics and mathematics. But these were all merely subdivisions of "philosophy" or "science."

In this connection a comment by Mortimer Adler and William Gorman in *The Great Ideas: A Syntopicon of Great Books of the Western World* is worth noting:

> This use of the words "science" and "philosophy" persists well into modern times. Hobbes, for example, presents his classification of the types of knowledge under the heading "science, that is, Knowledge of Consequences, which is also called philosophy." Bacon proposes to divide sciences into theology and philosophy. Descartes uses the words "science" and "philosophy" interchangeably. . . . Even as near the end of the eighteenth century as Hume, the word "philosophy" continues to be the general name for the particular sciences. It covers the experimental study of natural phenomena as well as what are for Hume the nonexperimental sciences of mathematics and psychology. . . . [Also] the authors of the books which are today regarded as among the foundations of modern science—Galileo, Newton, Huygens and, in the eighteenth century, Lavoisier and Fourier—refer to themselves as philosophers and to the science in which they are engaged, e.g., mathematics, mechanics, physics, chemistry, as parts or aspects of natural philosophy.[1]

Comments

Before moving on to the second historical period, let us add a couple of comments. The heart of the notion which "science" expresses in the first period is that of necessary, relatively universal conclusions achieved by demonstration from previously known premises. These last can be obtained in various ways—e.g., by reflection upon innate ideas (Plato, Descartes), by induction from sense-data (Aristotle, Aquinas), even by divine revelation regarding religious mysteries (thus sacred theology could be a science for Aquinas).

But the manner of obtaining the principles from which demonstration proceeds is not relevant to science as such, which points instead to the demonstrative movement from them to necessary conclusions. Moreover, even the mode of carrying on the demonstration could vary without detriment to the scientific status of the

---

[1] Vol. 2 (Chicago: Encyclopedia Britannica, 1955), pp. 345–46; also see M. J. Adler, *The Condition of Philosophy: Its Checkered Past, Its Present Disorder, and Its Future Promise* (New York: Atheneum, 1965).

resultant knowledge. For example, Plato used the dialectical movements of division and collection; Aristotle relies on various sorts of syllogistic reasoning.

Second, some Greeks before Plato are exceptions to this identification of philosophy with science. The reason is not only the absence in them of such universal and demonstratively certain knowledge. It is also the fact that "philosophy" then had not yet acquired that meaning. For example, for Herodotus (484?–425? B.C.) the verb *philosophein* meant nothing more than the desire to find out and, thus, *philosophia* connotes the love of exercising one's curiosity and intelligence.

Again, Pythagoras (*ca.* 582–*ca.* 507 B.C.), who supposedly was the first to describe himself as a philosopher, claimed that philosophers were those who spurned both fame and profit so as to seek after truth by contemplation, thereby resembling those who attend festal games just to be spectators without seeking fame or gain.[2]

Still another exception to the identification is St. Justin (*ca.* A.D. 100–*ca.* 165). Minucius Felix (flourished second century A.D.) and other early Christians identify philosophy with Christianity itself.[3]

Philosophy and Science: Kant and After

The second historical period stretches from Kant to the present day. In it philosophy and science are sharply distinguished. The result is that philosophy is no longer considered a science, which now points to knowledges involving laboratory experimentation, whether they be its direct outcome (e.g., physics, chemistry, and other empiriological cognitions) or its necessary adjunct (e.g., mathematics, which is itself a purely formal discipline but which helps formulate the results of experiments).

The aim of science thus interpreted is to bring all phenomena of nature under the smallest number of generalizations, which have the utmost simplicity in mathematical statements.[4] Obviously, such a meaning and aim are applicable to few if any philosophical endeavors. Hence, philosophy is no longer classifiable as a science.

---

[2] See John Passmore, "Philosophy," *Encyclopedia of Philosophy*, VI, 216.

[3] See E. Gilson, *The History of Christian Philosophy in the Middle Ages* (New York: Random House, 1955), pp. 11–14, 44–51.

[4] See Adler and Gorman, *op. cit.*, pp. 363–66 and 686–89.

The one who initiated this new state is Kant, who distinguished between "empirical" and "rational" methods. Although he applied "science" to both sorts of investigation, still he restricted "philosophy" to the latter—to the pure, *a priori*, rational science. Moreover, he excluded mathematics from philosophy too.[5]

Auguste Comte (1798–1857) went further than Kant by refusing to refer to philosophy as a science at all. He explicitly affirmed that only the positive disciplines—the study of natural, mental, and social phenomena by empirical methods—are aptly called "sciences," whereas philosophy is merely empty speculation and religion is superstition.

Sigmund Freud (1856–1939) actually set science against philosophy and religion. The scientific *Weltanschauung* (general view of the world), he maintained,

> asserts that there is no other source of knowledge of the universe but the intellectual manipulation of carefully verified observations . . . and that no knowledge can be obtained from revelation, intuition, or inspiration. . . . It is inadmissible to declare that science is one field of human intellectual activity, and that religion and philosophy are others, at least as valuable. . . . The bare fact is that truth cannot be tolerant and cannot admit compromise or limitations, that scientific research looks on the whole field of human activity as its own, and must adopt an uncompromisingly critical attitude towards any other power that seeks to usurp any part of its province.[6]

Some Conclusions

The importance for our topic of Kant and those he influenced is evident. If one takes their attitude on "science," then philosophy occupies at best an inferior place among human endeavors. It cannot be a science, for it is not a knowledge issuing from or expressive of technical experiments (perhaps symbolic logic might come closest to being a science because of its kinship with certain forms of modern mathematics).

Philosophy deprived of scientific status. Thus deprived of scientific status, philosophy (when taken as transcendent) assumes diverse shapes and takes on various functions. It is thought but not

---

[5] *Ibid.*, p. 346.

[6] S. Freud, *New Introductory Lectures on Psycho-Analysis*, quoted by Adler and Gorman, *op. cit.*, p. 683.

knowledge (Kant). That is to say, it is thought empty of content because without data from intuition. It is meditation upon the inevitable but groundless Ideas of Soul, World and God, with which Kant's *Critique of Pure Reason* terminates.

For others, it is a spirit or method of approaching experience rather than a body of conclusions about experience (E. S. Brightman). It is critical and correlating reflection upon the findings of various empiriological knowledges. It is an historical survey of what absolute presuppositions various people have actually made in doing various pieces of scientific thinking (R. G. Collingwood). It is a quest in areas not yet explored scientifically. It is a technique for testing whether or not statements are meaningful (A. J. Ayer and other linguistic analysts).

In short, philosophy's bailiwick is anyplace where genuine sciences have not yet investigated or cannot investigate or prefer not to investigate, without, however, philosophical investigation's having any hope of becoming a science.

Philosophy can be a science. But if (as seems reasonable) one breaks the bond between "science" and experimentation, if one refuses to restrict science to knowledge based on the measurable and the quantitative, then philosophy can be a science. This is not to return to the previous position (see above, "Plato to Kant") if this be interpreted as affirming that philosophy *is* science, that the two are interchangeable. No, philosophical disciplines are sciences but not all science is philosophical. Science is more general and extensive. Let me explain.

The following definition appears to be sufficiently accurate and broad to do justice to various cognitions found on the contemporary scene: science is knowledge of conclusions which are to some extent universal and necessary and which are acquired by intellectual processes centering upon some sort of meaningful data. The processes are multiple: deduction (as in mathematics, logic), intellective induction (as in metaphysics, theory of morality, philosophical psychology), rational induction utilizing constructs (as in physics, chemistry, and other empiriological cognitions), and so on.

The source of significant and fertile data can also be multiple: direct perception (for metaphysics, intellectual psychology, ethics), previous spontaneous knowledge of quantified objects (for mathematics), experimentation (for empiriological sciences), even divine revelation (for sacred theology).

What makes all those cognitions sciences is, rightly understood, not solely the sort of processes engaged in or the origin of data but especially the fact that they consist of somehow necessary and universal conclusions and that science is no longer confined to knowledge involving laboratory experimentation.

In this view, then, empiriological and mathematical knowledges are genuine sciences. But so also are the philosophical disciplines of metaphysics, cosmology, intellectual psychology, theory of morality and the rest. Each of these is distinct from the others by reason of its own formal object and its own brand of abstraction, yet each is a science by reason of its being a relatively general and necessary knowledge issuing from intellection upon significant evidence.[7]

In what sense is philosophy a science? Is "philosophy," then, an analogous or an equivocal term? If one views it as a science, then it is analogous, since it has a single meaning ("a relatively general and necessary knowledge issuing from intellection upon significant evidence"), which is verified somewhat differently when applied now to being, now to the human person, art, morality, mathematics and the rest. If one does not view it as a science but as a pursuit or an approach or an historical survey and so on, then it is equivocal since in each instance it seems to have a rather totally different meaning.

Philosophy and Religion

The history of the relations between philosophy and religion can be charted in nine stages, which we shall now discuss within the necessarily restricted limits of this chapter.

Before the Birth of Greek Philosophy

The *first* of these nine stages occurred prior to the birth of Greek philosophy and was one of religion—i.e., man's awareness that gods existed and his acknowledgment through prayer and worship that they had dominion over him. It was religion unadulterated by and without challenge from philosophy. This is the age represented by the *Theogony* of Hesiod (flourished eighth century B.C.), by ear-

---

[7] See Leo Sweeney, S.J., *Authentic Metaphysics in an Age of Unreality*, 2d ed. (New York/Bern: Peter Lang Publishing, Inc., 1993), chs. 1 and 10.

lier Hittite and Phoenician mythologies, even by the inspired books
of the Jewish scriptures.

Thales to Plotinus

The *second* stage extended from Thales (*ca.* 636–*ca.* 546 B.C.)
through Plato and Aristotle to Plotinus (*ca.* A.D. 205–70) and other
pagan Neoplatonists. During this stage, philosophy became victorious over the gods of traditional religions. This triumph had two
characteristics. It was not accompanied by open hostility to the
gods (an exception is Lucretius, the Roman Epicurean poet in the
first century B.C., who spoke of philosophy as the remedy for the
deepest of human ills by "freeing the mind from the close bondage
of religion"). Second, philosophical systems themselves usually
culminated in theism. As proof, one need only mention such instances of philosophical divinities as Anaximander's the Infinite,
Plato's Demiurge or Craftsperson as described in the *Timaeus* (29D–
30C, 34A–B, 41A–D), Aristotle's First Mover, Plotinus' One.

Beginning of Christianity to the Thirteenth Century

The *third* stage began abruptly in Palestine with the life, teachings, and church of Jesus Christ. Here we come again upon stark,
unadulterated religion and divine revelation. There then arose an
intellectual climate which lasted until the thirteenth century and
which was marked by primacy given to faith and religion, together,
however, with a sane respect for reason and Greek philosophy
(although each of these two characteristics has exceptions, soon to
be noted).

An indication of the dominant role faith played during this period is the fact that early Christians took Greek and Latin words
(e.g., *prosopon, hypostasis, persona, substantia, relatio*) and rejected or
modified their then current meaning so as to express the deposit of
faith.

Or consider Augustine (354–430). He kept faith supreme, but he
also found room for reason. "We are induced to learn," he explained, "both by authority and by reason. In matters of authority, I
intend never to go away from that of Christ. But I impatiently
desire not only to believe but also to understand, and this latter I
am confident I shall find with the help of Platonism" (*Against the
Academicians,* III, 20, 43; see my chapters 3 and 7–10 below). His
entire intellectual career was equivalent to "faith seeking understanding" (*fides quaerens intellectum*) and set a precedent for Anselm,
Peter Lombard, Bonaventure and others.

But, as has already been mentioned, there were exceptions. Most of the early Trinitarian and Christological heresies (e.g., Subordinationism, Arianism, Tritheism, Docetism, Nestorianism, Monophysitism) had as authors Christians who were so deeply imbued with Greek philosophy (especially Neoplatonism) that they bent the Christian mysteries to fit Greek hierarchies of reality and categories of thought. On the other side, though, there also were harsh critics of reason and philosophy, e.g., Tertullian (against Gnosticism), Peter Damian, St. Bernard of Clairvaux (against the dialectics of Abelard and Gilbert of la Porrée).

Introduction of Aristotle's Writings

The *fourth* stage was occasioned by the introduction in the West, during the first half of the thirteenth century, of all of Aristotle's writing, translated into Latin from Arabic and Greek. Prior to this the Christian West had only Aristotle's logic; now it was inundated by his metaphysics, philosophy of nature, psychology and ethics, accompanied by commentaries or original treatises of Algazel, Avicebron, Avicenna and Averroës.[8] The Aristotelian worldview, especially as interpreted by Averroës, was quite different from and even openly opposed to the Christian. His universe was eternal, not temporal. God was a First Mover, not a creator. He was a final, but not an efficient, cause. He was multiple (either forty-nine or fifty-five), not unique. The human soul was mortal, not immortal. Man's highest cognitive faculty was imagination (the *intellectus passivus*), and all human beings shared a single *intellectus agens*, which was the intelligence of the lowest heavenly sphere. Human beings were determined, not free. Human ethics was man-centered, not God-centered.

Siger of Brabant. This inundation triggered at least three reactions. The Faculty of Arts at the University of Paris, under the leadership of Siger of Brabant (flourished 1260–77), permitted itself to be swept along by Averroës' Aristotle. The result was that the autonomy and even, at times, the primacy of reason and philosophy were strongly affirmed. But what if the Catholic Church put forth propositions on a topic which directly contradicted those set down by philosophy? Both sets of propositions would be true (the "double truth" theory). At least, this must be said: philosophy should not

---

[8] See James A. Weisheipl, "Albert's Disclaimers in the Aristotelian Paraphrases," in Joseph C. Schnaubelt *et al.* (eds.), *Proceedings of PMR Conference* 5 (1980), 5–8.

yield. It must hold its ground because it is autonomous, reason is invincible, and Aristotle is infallible.

Bonaventure. Another extreme reaction was experienced by St. Bonaventure (1221–74) and others, who claimed Augustine as guide. In bluntly rejecting Averroës' eternal and deterministic universe, as well as his theory of human knowledge, freedom and immortality, they reaffirmed strongly the supremacy of faith and revealed religion. In fact, philosophy practiced apart from Christ is harmful and error-prone. True philosophy begins and ends with God. It is "a journey of the mind to God," it is "faith seeking understanding" (see ch. 3 below).

Thomas Aquinas. Still a third reaction was initiated by Thomas Aquinas (1225–74). He tried to separate Aristotle's own thought from Averroës' by seeking out Latin translations made directly from Greek manuscripts, as well as commentaries written by Greeks rather than Arabians. Simultaneously he reemphasized the primacy of faith.

But he also distinguished philosophy from sacred theology: each is certain and universal intellection (hence, both are sciences), but the former proceeds from directly perceived evidence, the latter from divinely revealed truths. Even though distinct, philosophy is nonetheless subordinate to theology as handmaid to queen. Philosophy helps a theologian perform his proper functions, not only of defending the deposit of faith against heretical interpretations but also of explaining, developing and, rightly interpreted, understanding it.

Harmony between philosophy and theology. Aquinas' conception of the rapport between theology and philosophy was such that it enabled philosophy to be subordinate and yet simultaneously to gain from that subordination. As just noted, one task of theologians is to explain, develop and understand divine revelation. In accomplishing that development and understanding, theologians rely upon (among other items) what previous thinkers, including philosophers, have written.

That reliance results not only in their deeper awareness of individual theological dogmas but also in the development of various philosophical notions. For instance, because theologians worked out what "person" and "nature" meant with reference to the Trinity and to Christ, we can derive from their writings a philosophy of person and of nature which is more profound than anything found in philosophers who were not also trained as theologians. Again, because they investigated what "being" signifies when predicated of God and of creatures, we find implied in their treatises various metaphysics of being which utilize but far surpass previous philosophical tracts.

Hence, within the theological writings of Aquinas and those he influenced, one finds tremendous advances in metaphysics, natural theology, psychology, epistemology and the other philosophical disciplines. The outcome is that, paradoxically enough, philosophy at its best in the thirteenth century was found not in the Faculty of Arts but in that of Theology, even though Aquinas and his followers gave primacy to faith and considered philosophy its handmaid and servant.[9]

The Condemnation of 1277

The beginning of the *fifth* stage can be dated precisely: March 7, 1277, when Etienne Tempier, bishop of Paris, condemned two hundred and nineteen propositions. Some of them were Aquinas', expressing his position on the human soul as the substantial form of the body, on matter as the principle of individuation.

But the condemnation seems especially aimed at Siger and Averroës' other disciples in the Faculty of Arts at Paris, who were downgrading Christian religion and theology (with such propositions as: the Christian religion hinders education; there are falsehoods and errors in the Christian religion as in all the others; one does not know more for knowing theology; what the theologians say rests upon myths) and simultaneously upgrading philosophy (with such statements as: true wisdom is the wisdom of the philosophers, not of the theologians; there is no state superior to the practice of philosophy).

Effects of the condemnation. The effects of the condemnation were manifold. As viewed by those living in the decades immediately subsequent to 1277, Aristotle had been condemned (granted it was Aristotle as interpreted by Averroës but, nonetheless, it was Aristotle). But reason and philosophy had become equated with Aristotle. Therefore, Aristotle's condemnation was at the same time the condemnation of reason and philosophy.

Accordingly, the vigorous emphasis placed in 1277 on the supremacy of faith and Christian theology was at the expense of reason itself and of philosophical wisdom. In fact, the very nature

---

[9] L. Sweeney, "Scholasticism," in *Collier's Encyclopedia,* 20 (New York, 1967), 487–89, reprinted below as ch. 12; also see chs. 19–20 and 22 below.

of theological reflection was affected. Instead of the mutually help-ful and confident collaboration between philosophy and theology recommended by Aquinas, theologians viewed philosophy with suspicion and disdain. To give one instance: Duns Scotus and Wil-liam Ockham withdrew from metaphysical demonstration theo-logical conclusions (e.g., immortality of the soul) previously held to be rationally demonstrable, and posited them as knowable only in the light of revelation. After the fourteenth century, theology tended to be scriptural, positive and affective rather than intellectual in nature. No longer was "faith seeking understanding."[10]

Still another relevant effect was the birth pangs of modern sci-ence. Aristotle, as noted above, had been condemned; but natural sciences as conceived by Aristotle were qualitative and deductive (granted that he used observation to acquire principles, but deduc-tive demonstration and application of principles to less general areas then took over); therefore, Aristotle's views on natural science had been rendered suspect and new approaches could be attempted. These would be quantitative, permeated with experimentation, eventually postulating an infinite universe, and so on.

Man at the Hub of Reality

In the *sixth* stage, man was noticeably put at the hub of reality in two separate fashions. For the Renaissance humanists this move-ment coincided with their return to classical literature, which was pagan rather than Christian, the product of human ingenuity rather than of divine revelation. The outcome: the human person rather than God, reason rather than faith, philosophical wisdom (Platonic, Stoic, Epicurean, Neoplatonic) rather than religion occupied the place of honor.

On the other hand, René Descartes (1596–1650) also set the hu-man person in center stage, but without denial of or, possibly, even antagonism to faith and religion. Nonetheless, philosophy for him was totally separate from religion and theology; reason was com-pletely autonomous. Let everyone, he advised, shut out all influ-ences, whether external or internal and including even faith and revelation, so as to bring himself back to the core of his own self, which he then finds to be an indubitable starting point for the affirmation of all else: *cogito, ergo sum* (I think, therefore I exist). The philosophy Descartes then worked out was intended to be without

---

[10] See E. Gilson, *op. cit.*, pp. 385–410.

subordination to theology and without illumination from it: a philosophy completely autonomous and independent.[11]

Immanuel Kant

The *seventh* stage was occupied by Immanuel Kant (1724–1804), with whom reason continued to be autonomous. In fact, its autonomy was increased: when correctly understood, things themselves are dependent upon reason. Because space and time, together with cause, substance, necessity, and the other categories, are part of the very equipment of the human mind, pure reason imposes them upon sense data gained through intuition so as to structure and thus constitute "things" as phenomena.

Although man needs sense data in order to transform mere thought into knowledge (in this sense Kant is an empiricist), still his knowledge terminates with the sense-impressions on the periphery of his mind and not with things-in-themselves, not with noumena (here, the influence of Hume). Man is cut off from existents and the actual world they form (the influence of Descartes). But this is no hardship. It allows the human knower to assume an active and dominant role in knowledge, which in its entirety is constructural. "Things" are the phenomena constituted by the human knower. Obviously, reason is in a position of ascendancy. God plays only a second-rate role as a mere adjunct to man: He is either an empty Idea (in line with the *Critique of Pure Reason*) or a postulate so that morality can be viable (*Critique of Practical Reason*).[12]

Comment. The primacy reason enjoys is not communicable to philosophy. By contrasting empirical and rational sciences, by restricting knowledge to the empirical kind, by describing philosophy as a purely rational science, Kant reduced transcendent philosophy to the state of empty thought, incapable of knowing God and other noumena. Anyone who might assent to divinely revealed truths about God would find Kantian philosophy useless for defending, explaining, developing or understanding them. A "faith seeking understanding" would find little solace in reason or philosophy as conceived by Kant.

---

[11] See J. Collins, *A History of Modern European Philosophy* [hereafter: *HMP*] (Milwaukee: Bruce Publishing Co., 1954), ch. 4.

[12] See J. Collins, *HMP*, chs. 11–12; *idem, God in Modern Philosophy* [hereafter: *GMP*] (Chicago: Henry Regnery Co., 1959), ch. 6.

Hegel

Faith finds even less solace in the worldview of Georg Wilhelm Friedrich Hegel (1770–1831), with whom the *eighth* stage began. Why so? Because according to Hegel, religions, including Christianity, are only transient moments in the development of the Absolute Spirit as it moves to culmination, which it achieves as philosophy. But Philosophy (spelled now with a capital *P*) is no longer the personal achievement of now this, now that individual thinker. It is the Absolute Spirit itself at the apex of completion.

The path which led Hegel to this monistic view is rather easily traced. Kant, in his two *Critiques,* had given autonomy to pure reason and to practical reason in each person. But how explain the fact that the knowledge which your mind, functioning as pure reason, brings about is identical with that which mine effects (as our ability to communicate with one another and with others indicates)? Or how explain that it is identically one and the same moral law which resounds in your practical reason and in mine and in that of all other human beings?

The explanation, Hegel concluded, can only be that there is solely one Reason, one *Geist,* one Spirit, which is absolute, evolutionary, all-inclusive and of which each one of us is a transitory manifestation. Here, then, is an autonomy of Reason and Philosophy with a vengeance. The Christian Trinity as a reality independent of the Absolute Spirit, revelation as good news about an autonomous Christ, faith as an independent and free assent to Him—all are impossible and meaningless.[13]

The Contemporary Scene

The *ninth* and final stage in the history of the relations between philosophy and religion is the contemporary intellectual scene, at the start of which stand two quite disparate figures: Søren Kierkegaard (1813–55) and Edmund Husserl (1859–1938).

Kierkegaard reacted against Hegel's system of thought (especially its devaluation of the individual, its conversion of philosophy into the Absolute Spirit itself, its degradation of Christian mysteries); he also reacted against institutionalized religions, the growth of empirical sciences, and technology. His reaction took the form of a reassertion of the infinite significance of each individual and of a proclamation of the primacy of faith, the object of which now is a person: the reality of Christ Himself. Its object is not a doctrine,

---

[13] J. Collins, *HMP,* ch. 14; *idem, GMP,* ch. 7.

because then the relationship between faith and object would be intellectual. Nor does faith ground a doctrine: no science of theology is possible. Even philosophy as a systematic science would be futile and harmful.[14]

On the other hand, Husserl (see *The Idea of Phenomenology* and *Ideas Concerning a Pure Phenomenology and Phenomenological Philosophy*) wished to reinstate philosophy as a science but within a Cartesian and Kantian realm. Philosophy is a clear, certain and universal knowledge of essences, which are phenomena within the mind achieved by as complete a withdrawal as possible from the actual universe. This reinstatement took place without attention paid to faith or sacred theology.[15]

Existentialists. Many of those currently called "existentialists" or "philosophers of subjectivity" combine Kierkegaard with Husserl, although in varying ways and to different extents. They rather commonly follow Husserl in their attempt to isolate and describe factors within the human situation as carefully and fully as possible, viewing them as phenomena and equating reality with meaning. In accounting for meaning, though, they differ. Jean-Paul Sartre located it in man's free choices, the only norm for which is man himself and the values he creates. In this Sartre was somewhat akin to Kierkegaard, although he weakened this kinship by completely excluding faith from his universe.

Gabriel Marcel welcomed faith, which he found even at the start of one's philosophical approach to God, the Absolute Thou. Reality and meaning are rooted in human freedom, which is, however, the means by which we freely enter into mutual relationships with others and with God.

Martin Heidegger seems distant in his thinking from both Kierkegaard and Husserl but close to Hegel, whose Absolute Spirit can be viewed as the model for Heidegger's *Das Sein*. He gave faith or sacred theology no place in his theory, which culminates not in metaphysics (*re* beings) but in "Fundamental Ontology" (*re* Being).[16]

---

[14] See J. Collins, *GMP*, pp. 340–48; F. Copleston, *Contemporary Philosophy* [hereafter: *CP*] (Westminster, Md.: The Newman Press, 1963), pp. 105–109, 127–32, 148–56 and 221–23.

[15] See H. Spiegelberg, *The Phenomenological Movement: A Historical Introduction*, 3d ed. [hereafter: *PM*] (The Hague: Martinus Nijhoff, 1982), ch. 3, especially pp. 104–23.

[16] See ch. 22 below, especially prgrs. corresponding to notes 7–13; on Sartre see H. Spiegelberg, *PM*, ch. 10. On Marcel see ch. 23 below. On "God" in Jacques Derrida see my ch. 26 below, prgrs. corresponding to notes 85-87.

Linguistic analysis. The school of linguistic analysis (A. J. Ayer, etc.) owes no direct debt to Hegel, Kierkegaard or Husserl. Isolating themselves from influences of faith and theology, its adherents give prominence to empiriological sciences. The possibility of empirical verification is for many of them decisive as to whether or not philosophical and theological statements are meaningful. Philosophy is not a science but merely a technique of testing the significance of such statements.[17]

Whitehead. Alfred North Whitehead (1861–1947) also was appreciative of modern sciences, as well as of mathematics. But his appreciation helped rather than hindered his elaborating a philosophy, in which one even finds "God"—finite and functional but, nonetheless, a "God." Belief in a supernatural and transcendent deity would, however, be absurd.[18]

Maritain and Gilson. Finally, let us mention Jacques Maritain and Etienne Gilson as representatives of those who call themselves "Christian philosophers." Occasioned initially by Emile Bréhier's denial in 1927 of "Christian philosophy" as fact or possibility (see Preface above, pp. xi–xiii) and influenced by Henri Bergson and Thomas Aquinas (among others), they used history and speculation to establish the reality and nature of a philosophy which is Christian and yet is still philosophy.

It is philosophy because it reflects upon evidences furnished to intellection by perception and direct observation (thus, it is distinct from sacred theology, a science whose starting point is divinely revealed truths). It is Christian because it is subordinate to and influenced by theology. It is subordinate because theology uses it to defend, explain and develop the deposit of faith. It is influenced because theologians enrich and deepen the philosophical reflection they engage in while working out their theology.[19]

Having contrasted philosophy with science and religion, let us now consider philosophy as Christian in greater detail.

---

[17] F. Copleston, *CP*, ch. 1: "Contemporary British Philosophy."

[18] J. Collins, *HMP*, pp. 315–24. See ch. 25 below.

[19] J. Maritain, *An Essay on Christian Philosophy* (New York: Philosophical Library, 1955); E. Gilson, *The Spirit of Mediaeval Philosophy*, trans. A. H. C. Downes (New York: Charles Scribner's Sons, 1940). See ch. 2 below, "Can Philosophy Be Christian?" prgrs. corresponding to notes 13–30.

Also see J. Owens, *Towards a Christian Philosophy* [hereafter: *Christian Philosophy*] (Washington, D.C.: The Catholic University of America, 1990), "Introduction," pp. 1–59 and *passim*.

2

Can Philosophy Be Christian?
Its Relationship to Faith, Theology
and Religion?

The title of this chapter consists of two questions: Can philosophy be Christian? and What is the relationship of philosophy to faith, theology and religion? There are at least two ways of introducing the chapter. If one stresses "religion" in the title, then the paper touches on a practical, concrete and currently very controversial topic in view of rather recent decisions in various U.S. courts. For example, in 1986 Judge Brevard Hand ruled that secular humanism (hereafter: SH) is a religion and, hence, the forty-four textbooks for history, social science and home economics classes in use in public schools in Alabama were no longer to be used. But in August 1987, the Eleventh Federal Appeals Court ruled that Hand had not proved the forty-four books did indeed promote SH and hence the judge was overruled, although the court made no decision on whether or not SH is a religion (*Chicago Tribune*, August 26, 1987).

Or another instance: Louisiana state senator William Keith had a law passed requiring teachers in Louisiana schools to present the theories of both evolution and creation. But in June 1987, the Supreme Court by a decision of 7 to 2 declared that creationism cannot be taught in public schools because it is a religious viewpoint (*Newsweek*, June 29, 1987).

Simultaneously with the court decisions, syndicated columnists were taking sides. In the *Chicago Sun-Times* for February 18, 1986, James Kilpatrick asserted that SH is a religion; in fact, the Supreme Court itself had similarly declared in the Torcaso case of 1961 that "among religions in this country which do not teach what would generally be considered a belief in the existence of God are Buddhism, Taoism, Ethical Culture, Secular Humanism and others." Kilpatrick then comments: "As a matter of law Secular Humanism is as clearly a religion as Christianity or Judaism." In the *Chicago Sun-Times* for October 13, 1986, Charles Krauthammer concluded (with a University of Virginia sociologist) that "Secular Humanism is the functional equivalent of a religion," but, he added, so too are feminism, socialism and vegetarianism, all of which, however, should be ignored by the federal courts.

In the *Chicago Tribune* for March 11, 1987, Clarence Page declared that SH is not a religion but the very absence of religion. And *if* it were a religion, then should not secular humanists seek exemption from taxes on their property and from the military draft? Should they not demand legal holidays "to honor the founding fathers of rationalism, individualism, secularism, existentialism, pragmatism or . . . Epicureanism?"

Whatever one may personally think about the fairness of the decision in such court cases and the accuracy of the opinions of the syndicated columnists, this much is clear: such decisions and opinions recommend—indeed, demand—that one reflect upon the nature of religion, science and philosophy. How does religion differ from science and from philosophy? Perhaps this chapter (and chapter 1 above) will at least indirectly aid in that reflection.

Another way to introduce this chapter is less controversial. In September 1977 several American philosophers began forming a "Society of Christian Philosophy." To quote from their initial letter:

> As we conceive it, the society would be made up of philosophers who share a commitment to the Christian faith, and who wish to join in exploring the philosophical ramifications of that commitment. "Christian faith" is here construed in a broadly ecumenical fashion (but not so broadly as to include commitments that fail to embody the substance of the classical creeds). "Ramifications" is intended to include both philosophical problems about the Christian faith, its interpretation, its meaningfulness and rationality, and also implication of a Christian commitment for philosophizing in a variety of areas and on a variety of topics (Letter of September 1977).

In that quotation one should note that a description is given of "Christian faith" (namely, a commitment to the substance of classical creeds) but no attempt is made to determine in what "philosophy" itself consists, despite speaking of "philosophers," "philosophical ramifications," "philosophical problems" and "philosophizing."

That absence of determination on the part of the Society is extended even to "Christian" two years later (April 1979) in the Constitution its executive committee submitted to its members for approval. After stating that "the purpose of the organization shall be to promote fellowship between Christian philosophers, and to provide occasions for intellectual interchange between Christian philosophers on issues that arise from their joint commitment" and that "membership in the Society shall be open to all Christian philosophers," its authors added: "It is solely up to the applicant for membership to determine whether he/she is a philosopher and whether he/she is a Christian."

But if the Society is unwilling or, even, unable to decide on the nature of philosophy and of the Christian faith separately, how can it cope with them together? What would a Christian philosopher be? How does he or she differ from a theologian? from someone who believes in and/or practices a religion?

Such is the more direct topic of this chapter—namely, the speculative problem which "Christian philosophy" entails. It can be stated very simply as Can *philosophy* be *Christian*? If so, how? No one claims there is a "Christian mathematics" or "Christian physics"; why "Christian philosophy" then? Our interest in the notion itself of "Christian philosophy" will lead us to reflect on "philosophy" and, because linked with "Christian," on "faith" and "theology" and "religion," on "pure" (or "presuppositionless") philosophy *vs.* "religio-speculation." And our main goal is neither to evaluate whether "Christian philosophy" is good or bad nor to promote it but *to understand it* in itself and in its implications. The means to be used are a survey of what "Christian philosophy" has meant in the history of ideas and, second, the formulation of a series of concluding questions.

Now let us turn to the first stage in that history of ideas: St. Augustine of Hippo, whom Thomas Merton praises in this fashion: "The light of God shines to me more serenely through the wide open windows of Augustine than through any other theologian. Augustine is the calmest and clearest light."[1]

---

[1] *The Sign of Jonas* (New York: Harcourt, Brace and Co., 1953), p. 255.

The History of Ideas

St. Augustine

Prior to the mid-thirteenth century when Aquinas distinguished theology and philosophy, faith and reason, "Christian philosophy" was not a problem—at least in all those academic circles in which the thought of St. Augustine of Hippo (354–430) was operative. As R. A. Markus observes:

> From his conversion to "philosophy" at the age of eighteen to his conversion to Christianity some fifteen years later, and for the remainder of his life, Augustine conceived of "philosophy" in a sense which would be odd to twentieth-century usage, but was generally shared by his contemporaries. He included under this heading everything that was of ultimate concern to man, everything relevant to the question: how is a man to attain his ultimate fulfillment, that is "blessedness" (*beatitudo*)?[2]

Accordingly,

> "Christianity" and "true philosophy" are practically synonymous terms; and, indeed, Augustine later once defined Christianity simply as the one true philosophy. He often defines "philosophy" following the etymology, as the love of wisdom; and wisdom has to do with the truth about the nature and the attainment of the supreme good, that in which man finds his complete and ultimate fulfillment.[3]

And although Augustine on occasion speaks "of 'philosophy' in a narrower, technical sense akin to that of modern usage,"[4] nonetheless "the distinction between the two disciplines [philosophy/theology] did not exist in Augustine's world, and their realms are merged in his 'Christian philosophy.'"[5]

Thomas Aquinas

But around 1252 and thereafter Thomas Aquinas (d. 1274) distinguished philosophy from theology and from faith, a distinction which can be expressed in this simplified fashion:

---

[2] In *Cambridge History of Later Greek and Early Medieval Philosophy*, ed. A. H. Armstrong (Cambridge University Press, 1967), p. 344.

[3] *Ibid.*, pp. 344–45.

[4] *Ibid.*, p. 345.

[5] *Ibid.*, p. 353.

(1) *Faith* is a human person's assent to God revealing himself: it is my saying yes to the divine invitation within to believe that God exists, that He is triune, etc.

(2) *Theology* is the same human person's endeavor to reflect upon, "understand" and develop what one believes. It is the science one intellectually elaborates. It is a series of "syllogisms," where the major premise of each initial syllogism is a dogma of faith; the minor premise can be another dogma of faith but can also come from reason—even from that of a pagan philosopher such as Aristotle; the conclusion is that which logically follows from the two premises through the power of the middle term and which the human knower accepts as true.

We can illustrate this from *Summa Theologiae* I, 8, 1, where Aquinas asks, *Utrum Deus sit in omnibus rebus* ["Whether God is in all things"], and where the initial portion of his affirmative answer is an inferential process or sort of "syllogism," which can be reconstructed in this way for our purposes. Its major premise is given in the *sed contra* and is a quotation from the Old Testament:

Isaiah 26:12: "O God, You do whatever we do"—You it is who act whenever we engage in activity; You are the agent when we are agents.

Its minor premise is taken from the *respondeo* and is the intellectual awareness, based upon Aristotle, that

every agent must be joined to that upon which he is immediately acting and must affect it by his power, as Aristotle proves in *Physics* VII, ch. 2, 243a3 sqq.: "The mover and what is moved must be present simultaneously."

The mediation of the middle term, "agent," then results in the conclusion that God must be present to and in us while engaged in activity—in fact (as subsequent lines reveal) in us and in anything which *exists* because God properly causes existence in whatever exists and, hence, God exists in all existents.

One should note the psychological movement which theology entails: from a starting point which is divine revelation through syllogistic reasoning to a conclusion which explicates that revelation. The divine revelation, assented to by faith, illumines, controls and determines the entire human intellectual process.

(3) Next, what is *philosophy* to Aquinas? Although it is similar to theology in that each is a science, they differ in their starting points. As we have noted, a theologian moves from divine revelation,

accepted by faith, to further insights into what one believes. But a philosopher starts with actual individual existents in all their richness and variety (other human persons and oneself, as well as nonhuman beings), which one knows through sense perception and spontaneous intellection and which thereby give evidence that they are and what they are. From this evidence the philosopher realizes that to be real is actually to exist and thereafter infers (for example) that each existent entails not only an essence (itself composed of prime matter, substantial form and accidents), but also an act of existence by which it is real; that none of them exists by its very nature or essence and thus each exists in such a way that *of itself* it need not be; that accordingly there exists an Existent whose very nature is to be, who properly causes all else to exist and (as seen previously) who is present in all existents as creator and conserver.

This exposition of Aquinas' metaphysics has been rapid, but it is sufficient, perhaps, for us to understand what he intends by philosophy: the intellectual awareness (gradual, experiential, open-ended) which arises when a human person starts from and concentrates on this physical universe within which he or she exists, and realizes through reflection that reality is actuality and then elaborates the consequences of that realization.

It is also sufficient to help us analyze more deeply why a *philosophy* which is *Christian* is paradoxical or, even, problematic: the starting point of each seems opposed. Philosophy starts with individual material existents, whence comes the evidence through our sense perception and spontaneous intellection that they are and what they are, which in turn and through technical reflection and inference issues into a science of reality as reality. Christian belief centers on God Himself revealing, whence Christian theology begins and, under divine illumination and through technical reflection and inference, culminates in a science of God as God. Therefore, the problem: What can that which begins with God's disclosure of Himself have in common with the knowledge which begins with the perceptible data which physical things furnish of themselves? How can that science which starts with God contribute significantly to that which (if it reaches God at all) ends with God? Would not the one exclude the other?

René Descartes

A word of warning seems necessary. No one should think only Thomists find trouble with the conception of "Christian philosophy." Any philosopher who has read Descartes should experience a similar uneasiness. True enough, this French philosopher expressed respect for theology, as evidenced by the following facts: First, he dedicated the *Meditation on the First Philosophy* to "the very sage and illustrious Dean and Doctors of the Sacred Faculty of Theology of Paris." Second, while constructing a new philosophy "by eradicating from my mind all the wrong opinions which I had up to this time accepted," he formed for himself a code of morals by which he might live, the first of which is this:

> To obey the laws and customs of my country, adhering constantly to the religion in which by God's grace I had been instructed since my childhood.[6]

But once Descartes had accomplished that eradication and actually initiated the construction just mentioned, he described the two sorts of

> mental operations by which we are able, wholly without fear of illusion, to arrive at the knowledge of things. Now I admit only two, viz., intuition and deduction.
>
> By *intuition* I understand . . . the conception which an unclouded and attentive mind gives us so readily and distinctly that we are wholly freed from doubt about that which we understand. Or, what comes to the same thing, *intuition* is the undoubting conception of an unclouded and attentive mind, and springs from the light of reason alone; it is more certain than deduction itself in that it is simpler, though deduction . . . cannot by us be erroneously conducted.[7]

And what is deduction? It is "all necessary inference from other facts that are known with certainty." Why is this operation needed?

> Because many things are known with certainty, though not by themselves evident, but only deduced from true and known principles by the continuous and uninterrupted action of a mind that has a clear vision of each step in the process.[8]

---

[6] *Discourse on the Method of Rightly Conducting the Reason and Seeking for Truth in the Sciences* in *Descartes Selections*, ed. Ralph M. Eaton (New York: Charles Scribner's Sons, 1955), pp. 20 and 21.

[7] *Rules for the Direction of the Mind* in *Descartes Selections, op. cit.*, p. 46.

[8] *Ibid.*, p. 47.

Descartes concludes by contrasting intuition and deduction with faith.

> These two methods are the most certain routes to knowledge, and the mind should admit no others. All the rest should be rejected as suspect of error and dangerous. But this does not prevent us from believing matters that have been divinely revealed as being more certain than our surest knowledge, since belief in these things, as all faith in obscure matters, is an action not of our intelligence, but of our will.[9]

Intelligence *versus* will, intuition and deduction *versus* faith and theology—these contrasts reveal the distinction (separation, even) of philosophical knowledge from Christianity effected by Descartes, whose aim "was to elaborate a purely human wisdom in accord with the teachings of faith but apart from all theological schools and all influence of revelation."[10]

Etienne Gilson

We asked earlier how the science of theology which starts with God can contribute significantly to philosophy terminating with God. Let us now note how two contemporary philosophers, Etienne Gilson and Jacques Maritain, answered that question during the controversy on Christian philosophy which erupted in the second and third decades of this century.

Etienne Gilson (1884–1978) met the opposition led by (among others) Emile Bréhier,[11] in his Gifford lectures given in 1931–32.[12] Gilson's initial description of the content of Christian philosophy is "that body of rational truths discovered, explored or simply safeguarded, thanks to the help that reason receives from revelation."[13]

---

[9] *Ibid.*, p. 48.

[10] J. Collins, *God in Modern Philosophy* (Chicago: Henry Regnery Co., 1959), pp. 58–59.

[11] See Emile Bréhier, *Histoire de la philosophie*, vol. 1: *l'Antiquité et le moyen âge* (Paris: Alcan, 1927); "Y a-t-il une Philosophie Chrétienne?" *Revue de Métaphysique et de Morale* (April–June 1931). Also see J. Owens, *Christian Philosophy*, "Introduction," pp. 1–59, who parallels Bréhier's position with Descartes' in contrast with Aristotle's on pp. 32–34, 41; also see "Epilogue," pp. 307–26; for publishing data see my ch. 1, n. 19.

[12] These were published in English as *The Spirit of Mediaeval Philosophy*, trans. A. H. C. Downes (New York: Charles Scribner's Sons, 1940), especially chapters 1 and 2.

[13] *The Spirit of Mediaeval Philosophy*, p. 35.

Two pages later he says,

> If it is to deserve that name [Christian philosophy] the super-
> natural must descend as a constitutive element not, of course,
> into its texture which would be a contradiction, but into the
> work of its construction. Thus I call Christian, *every philosophy*
> *which, although keeping the two orders formally distinct, neverthe-*
> *less considers the Christian revelation as an indispensable auxiliary*
> *to reason.* . . . It is but one of the species of the genus philosophy
> and includes in its extension all those philosophical systems
> which were in fact what they were only because a Christian
> religion existed and because they were ready to submit to its
> influence.[14]

And how does that submission show itself? "In the first place [and,
perhaps, most obviously] the Christian philosopher . . . effects a
choice between philosophical problems." He attends to those most
worthy of attention because closest to the conduct of his religious
life—e.g., the nature and immortality of the human soul; whether
and how the will is free; God's existence and nature; the meaning
of "person," "self," "nature."

Second, faith cautions a philosopher to rethink any reasoning
process which may have culminated in a conclusion (e.g., the human soul perishes with the body; there is no God) opposed to
divine revelation.

Third, a theologian in Aquinas' (and Gilson's) conception, while
using philosophy in trying to "understand" divine revelation, may
thereby and *precisely as a theologian* see more deeply into philosophy
itself, which thereby becomes enriched, more fully developed precisely as philosophy but which is expressed within a *Summa*
Theologiae. This means that we philosophers, by reading his theological treatise, can learn philosophy better and more deeply. As an
instance let us see again how Gilson might interpret Aquinas' theological answer to the question, *Utrum Deus sit in omnibus rebus*. For
our purposes, Aquinas' answer can be formulated in this line of
argumentation:

O God, You are the agent when we are agents (*Isaiah*);
But every agent must be present to and in that upon which he
is immediately acting (Aristotle);

---

[14] *Ibid.*, p. 37.

Therefore, You are present in us when we are agents;

But we are agents only insofar as we exist;

But we exist only if You cause us to exist—in fact, existence is what You properly cause in us since Your essence is existence;

But existence is that which permeates us most thoroughly and deeply because existence is the actuation of all other perfections in a being (*Esse autem est illud quod est magis intimum cuilibet et quod profundius omnibus inest, cum sit formale respectu omnium quae in re sunt*).

Therefore, You are present in us most thoroughly and deeply as the agent or cause of our existing (*S.T.*, I, 8, 1 resp.).

According to Gilson, such a line of theological reflection has enriched philosophy in these areas: *re* an agent and, more generally, efficient cause and its proper effect; his presence within an effect and thus *re* divine immanence and transcendence; existence as the heart of reality and as the key to creation (i.e., to make something *exist* which did not actually exist on any level before). Those areas show the influence of theological reflection and thus constitute a philosophy which is Christian because their content is what it is due to that influence.

Jacques Maritain

The second proponent of Christian philosophy is Jacques Maritain (1882–1973). Maritain's reply to our inquiry of how divine revelation (faith, theology) contributes meaningfully to philosophy can be drawn from his *Essay on Christian Philosophy*[15] and *Science and Wisdom*.[16] Maritain distinguishes "between the *nature* of philosophy, or what it is in itself, and the *state* in which it exists in real fact, historically, in the human subject, and which pertains to its concrete conditions of existence and exercise."[17] In its nature philosophy is specified by the "object to which it makes our intelligence adapted and co-natured; . . . toward which it tends by virtue of itself (by no means the subject in which it resides)."[18] Viewed precisely in its nature, then,

---

[15] *An Essay on Christian Philosophy*, trans. Edward H. Flannery (New York: Philosophical Library, 1955).

[16] *Science and Wisdom*, trans. Bernard Wall (New York: Charles Scribner's Sons, 1940).

[17] *Essay on Christian Philosophy*, pp. 11–12.

[18] *Ibid.*, p. 13.

philosophy is wholly rational: no reasoning issuing from faith finds its way into its inner fabric; it derives intrinsically from reason and rational criticism alone; and its soundness as a philosophy is based entirely on experimental or intellectual evidence and on logical proof. From these considerations it follows that since the specification of philosophy hinges entirely on its formal object, and since this object is wholly of the rational order, philosophy considered in itself—whether in a pagan or Christian mind—depends on the same strictly natural or rational intrinsic criteria.[19]

Maritain continues, however, by saying that one must also consider philosophy as an actual *state* of mind.

As soon as it no longer is a question of philosophy considered in itself but of the manner in which men philosophize, and of the diverse philosophies which the concrete course of history has brought into existence, the consideration of the *essence* of philosophy no longer suffices; that of its *state* must be undertaken.
From this viewpoint of the state, or the conditions of exercise, it is manifest that before philosophy can attain its full, normal development in the mind it will exact of the individual many emendations and purifications, a disciplining not only of the reason but of the heart as well. To philosophize man must put his whole soul into play in much the same manner that to run he must use his heart and lungs.[20]

Stated another way: "Taken concretely, in the sense of being a *habitus* . . . existing in the human soul, philosophy is in a certain *state* [and] is either pre-Christian or Christian or a-Christian, which has a decisive influence on the way in which it exists or develops."[21]
In its actual state within a Christian thinker philosophy receives subjective and objective assistance.

[The Christian thinker] also believes that if reason is to attain without admixture of error the highest truths that are natu-

---

[19] *Ibid.,* p. 15.
[20] *Ibid.,* p. 17.
[21] *Science and Wisdom,* p. 79.

rally within its ken it requires assistance, either from within in the form of inner strengthening or from without in the form of an offering of objective data.[22]

That subjective reinforcement comes from the

> superior wisdoms, theological wisdom and infused wisdom, which rectify and purify in the soul the philosophical *habitus* with which they maintain a continuity not of essence but of movement and illumination, fortifying them in their proper order, and lifting them to higher levels.[23]

Such reinforcement is exemplified in the ability faith gives a "philosopher, who knows of the existence of God by purely natural means, to adhere rationally to this truth with a sturdier grasp." It is also exemplified in the clarification and spiritualization the contemplative *habitus* contributes to the philosophical *habitus*;[24] in the self-detachment and relief from ponderousness theology grants to a philosophy accepting its infraposition; in the freedom from futilities and opacities grace bestows on speculative intellects by its healing of nature.[25]

But in addition to such subjective corroborations philosophy also receives from faith and revelation objective data

> which deal primarily with revealed truths of the natural order. The highest of these have been regularly missed or misstated by the great pagan philosophers. Moreover, these objective data are also concerned with the repercussions of truths of the supernatural order on philosophical reflexion.[26]

Instances of such data are creation, the human soul as object of salvation, God as subsistent love,[27] substance and accident, nature and person, essence and existence,[28] God as subsistent Being, and sin as an offense against God.[29] Accordingly,

---

[22] *An Essay on Christian Philosophy*, p. 18.

[23] *Science and Wisdom*, p. 80.

[24] *An Essay on Christian Philosophy*, p. 26.

[25] *Ibid.*, pp. 27–28.

[26] *Science and Wisdom*, p. 80.

[27] *Ibid.*, pp. 90–91.

[28] *Ibid.*, p. 102.

[29] *An Essay on Christian Philosophy*, pp. 13–19, especially p. 19.

Christian philosophy is philosophy itself insofar as it is situated in those utterly distinctive conditions of existence and exercise into which Christianity has ushered the thinking subject, and as a result of which philosophy *perceives* certain objects and *validly demonstrates* certain propositions, which in any other circumstances would to a greater or lesser extent elude it.[30]

Concluding Questions

So far we have listed some of the stages in a history of philosophy that can be profitably taken into account if one is to understand the problems which the notion of Christian philosophy entails. In what follows I shall set down, albeit tentatively and often through questions, my own position.

(1) If we look at the history of philosophical ideas (as both Gilson and Maritain counsel), it appears certain Christianity did enrich that history. Take, as one example, the doctrine of creation. This kind of making involves the following: (a) the producer himself must undergo no change in the act of producing, neither losing nor acquiring any perfection, and the implication is that he is both all-perfect and entirely free; (b) what is produced must be really distinct from the producer and, finally, (c) must be wholly produced. That something could be freely made to exist now which had not actually existed before was unknown until it was disclosed in the Jewish, Christian and Islamic scriptures. But that notion itself is also philosophical, because data for each of its components are provided by the actual existents of this universe, and thus the notion is accessible to an attentive mind. Here, then, do we not have one contribution of divine revelation to the mainstream of Western philosophical thought? Do we not also have clearly indicated that we can assent to creation not only through faith but also through knowledge? If so, the result is that, although creationism is not an empiriological "science," it is a "science" in the sense of true and certain knowledge issuing from reflection upon the actually existing world, as well as upon all its human and nonhuman inhabitants (see chapter 1 above), because it *is* in such a way that *of itself* it need not have been and even now need not *be*.

---

[30] *Ibid.*, p. 30.

(2) "Existence" is another notion given by divine revelation to philosophy. Here the word refers not simply to the fact that things exist (Plato, Aristotle, Descartes and any other extra-mentalist certainly knew and accepted that fact) but to the fact that existence intrinsically perfects things and thus is an *evidence* of an intrinsic component (the act of existing or of be-ing) within each of them by which each is real. Thus to be real is actually to exist, an equation which eventually terminates in one's inferring that God *is* subsistent existence and is efficiently the proper cause of existence in all else.[31]

All those statements are philosophical inasmuch as we and other existents furnish the data upon which they are based. Yet, actually, he who first formulated those propositions was not a philosopher. It was the medieval theologian already referred to, Thomas Aquinas, who most likely became aware that reality *is* existence when reflecting theologically upon some such Scripture text as *Exodus* 3:14 (which Thomas quotes as early as *In I Sent.*, 8, 1, 1, sol., and as late as *Summa Theologiae*, I, 2, 3, *sed contra*, where it is the key to his famous "Five Ways"): "God replied to Moses: 'I am who am.' . . . This is what you shall tell the Israelites: 'He who is sent me to you.'" Although Aquinas never disclosed when and on what occasion he first became aware that actual existence is equivalent to reality, still it may have occurred while making some such reflections as this under the influence of the *Exodus* text:

(1) God is Being (*Exodus*);
(2) But God is supremely real;
(3) Therefore, Being is supremely real;
(4) But Being is existence;
(5) Therefore, existence is supremely real, whether in God or in creatures.

The fourth premise requires that Aquinas will have gone outside the Scriptures, which nowhere explicate the equation "Being is existence." Hence, he will have called upon his experience of himself and other existents (human and nonhuman) within this actual world as to the fact that he and they all exist. But now he realizes that *because they exist*, they *are real*—a realization which actually comes from the prior premises of the syllogism but the basis for which is actually also *in the existents themselves*. If so, one may conclude that, although a theologian originated the notion of existence

---

[31] See L. Sweeney, S.J., *Authentic Metaphysics in an Age of Unreality*, 2d ed. (New York/Bern: Peter Lang Publishing, Inc., 1993), chs. 4–5.

as the actualizing and perfective component within creatures, that doctrine does not belong of its very nature only to theology. It is not a strict mystery, transcending the grasp of human reason. That is to say, the illumination Thomas experienced while reflecting upon *Exodus* 3:14 did not superimpose any intelligible content upon the data already gained from material existents through direct experience. Rather, its function was to enable him to see what *actually was already contained within that data* but heretofore overlooked by previous thinkers (and by himself, for that matter).

If the preceding interpretation is accurate, has not divine revelation influenced philosophy *precisely as philosophy,* which through that influence exemplifies a "Christian philosophy?"

(3) The influence of what is nonphilosophical upon philosophy seems to have been so great in the case of Christian philosophy that I am tempted to think there never has been a "pure" philosophy (neither Plato's nor Aristotle's nor Descartes' nor Ayer's), nor is there today a "pure" philosophy, i.e., a philosophical position which arises *entirely* as the direct expression of what its formal object conveys to an alert and receptive intellect. This absence of a "pure" philosophical position stems from the side of the knower, who is the efficient cause of his assents not only to truths gained through philosophical reflection and other natural knowledges, but also to truths acquired through faith and theological argumentation and who simultaneously is on the receiving end of all sorts of outside forces.

The absence also arises from the side of the formal object of philosophy: the actual universe in which we, who are the efficient causes of philosophy and, more generally, of all our knowledges, are and live and think is not only composed of human beings and giraffes and geraniums and petroleum but also permeated with such abstract but potent factors as Evolution, Democracy, Science, Humanism, Computer Technology, Energy, Communications Media, Atheism, Black Race, Jewish Race, Right to Life, Right to Self-Determination, Psychotherapy, Consumerism, Greed. All these we of the twentieth century find ourselves spelling with a capital letter. They constitute the mythical "gods" of our current culture and we take and believe them to be valuable, significant, real without much question or reflection or proof. Yet these potent and "divine" abstractions also influence our philosophical positions of a moral and political sort by intimating which problems are worth attending to, by suggesting the necessity of retracing our intellectual steps when we have arrived at destinations hostile to them, by furnishing a criterion of truth (e.g., Science gave the "empirically verifiable" to positivist philosophers and some linguistic analysts), by illuminating aspects of reality which hitherto escaped notice. Are not those influences the very ones ascribed above to divine revelation as constituting Christian philosophy? If similar contemporary non-philosophical "divine" factors are operative on contemporary philosophers, then a philosophy which is Christian is not unique but is merely one among many philosophies arising not only from philosophical but also from nonphilosophical sources. If so, there is no "pure" philosophy today any more than there was in nineteenth-century Germany or sixteenth-century France or thirteenth-century Europe or in fifth- and fourth-century Greece B.C. Every actual philosophy is "religio-philosophical."

If so, let me put to others the questions I have been putting to myself: what nonphilosophical influences are exerting themselves upon each of us? What current "gods" do we worship, albeit unknowingly? What abstract nouns do we capitalize? Are we like Saul Bellow's Humboldt?

> Humboldt, that grand erratic handsome person with his wide blond face, that charming fluent worried man to whom I was so attached, passionately lived out the theme of Success. Naturally he died a Failure. What else can result from the capitalization of such nouns? Myself, I've always held the number of sacred words down. In my opinion Humboldt had too long a list of them—Poetry, Beauty, Love, Waste Land, Alienation, Politics, History, the Unconscious. And, of course, Manic and Depressive, always capitalized. According to him, America's great Manic Depressive was Lincoln. And Churchill with what he called his Black Dog moods was a classic case of Manic Depression. "Like me, Charlie," said Humboldt. "But think— if Energy is Delight and if Exuberance is Beauty, the Manic Depressive knows more about Delight and Beauty than anyone else. Who else has so much Energy and Exuberance? Maybe it's the strategy of the Psyche to increase Depression. Didn't Freud say that Happiness was nothing but the remission of Pain? So the more Pain the intenser the Happiness. But there is a prior origin to this, and the Psyche makes Pain on purpose. Anyway, Mankind is stunned by the Exuberance and Beauty of certain individuals. When a Manic Depressive escapes from his Furies he's irresistible. He captures History. I think that aggravation is a secret technique of the Uncon-

scious. As for great men and kings being History's slaves, I think Tolstoi was off the track. Don't kid yourself, kings are the most sublime sick. Manic Depressive heroes pull Mankind into their cycles and carry everybody away."[32]

Perhaps we do not spell instinctively as many abstract nouns as did Humboldt with capital letters. But if we capitalize any, it might be interesting and instructive to determine what they are so as to determine what nonphilosophical factors may be coloring our philosophical efforts in producing our own "religio-philosophy."

At the beginning of this chapter the question was asked, Can philosophy be Christian? Obviously, the answer now is, Of course it can! In fact, the philosophizing of all Christians must be Christian if and to the extent that their faith in Christianity is genuinely operative. Indeed, all philosophy will and must be "religious," provided we interpret "religious" broadly but accurately as pertaining to anything which we take to be valuable, true, significant, real (and, thus, spell with a capital letter) without question or reflection or giving an account or proof (either because we personally do not or cannot do so or the item itself transcends proof) and yet which influences (however quietly, latently, subtly) our explicitly and strictly philosophical activities.

---

[32] *Humboldt's Gift* (New York: Avon Books, 1976), p. 6.

3

Augustine and Bonaventure on Christian Philosophy

One problem concerning "Christian philosophy" in contemporary times consists of the seeming opposition between the adjective and the noun (see chapter 2 above). Let us begin with the noun: philosophy involves human reasoning on empirical data and achieves knowledge of God, if at all, only at the end of the reasoning processes. Christianity begins with God, to Whom it assents through faith in divine revelation. Reasoning on empirical data thus appears opposed to assenting to and dealing with divinely revealed data: they move in different directions. How can they be combined to form a single intellectual enterprise called "Christian philosophy?" Moreover, no one claims there is a "Christian mathematics" or "Christian physics"—why, then, "Christian philosophy"?

This chapter again tackles those problems by studying Saints Augustine and Bonaventure, two important Christian authors separated by eight centuries and yet set within a single tradition. Our study will perhaps help us to understand the problem more deeply and eventually to cope with it more intelligently and accurately.

St. Augustine

Let us start with St. Augustine (354–430), who "dominates the Middle Ages, representing and summing up patristic thought for that period."[1] His position on philosophy and related topics is rather complex. Although philosophy is, wherever found, a love of wisdom,[2] philosophers show themselves to be of two sorts: they are either pagan or Christian.[3] The former deal with this world, and St. Paul himself (*Colossians* 2:8) commands "that we avoid and esteem them for nought"; but Christian philosophers deal with "another world utterly remote from these eyes of ours," which Christ Himself designates as His Kingdom (*De Ordine*, I, 11, 32; *PL* 32, 993). Again: pagan philosophers "do not carry philosophy into religious observance or philosophize in a religious spirit," whereas Christian philosophers hold fast the Christian religion, which is "the prophetic history of the dispensation of divine providence in time— what God has done for the salvation of the human race, renewing and restoring it unto eternal life. When once this is believed, a way of life agreeable to the divine commandments will purge the mind and make it fit to perceive spiritual things which are neither past nor future but abide ever the same, liable to no change" (*De Vera Religione*, VII, 12 and 13; *PL* 34, 128).[4]

Again: the philosophers of Athens constantly wrangled among themselves (e.g., Epicurus *vs.* Stoics and *vs.* Anaxagoras, Aristippus *vs.* Antisthenes) about the world (Is there only one? Did it begin? Will it go on forever? Is it ruled by divine intelligence or by chance?), the soul (Is it immortal? permanently so?), the *summum bonum* (Is it body? mind? external goods?),[5] whereas the philosophers in the

---

[1] Maurice Nédoncelle, *Is There a Christian Philosophy?* trans. Illtyd Trethowan (New York: Hawthorn Books, 1960), p. 40. For a survey of the controversy on Christian philosophy in contemporary times, see *ibid.*, pp. 85–117; J. Owens, *Christian Philosophy*, [publishing data given above, ch. 1, n. 19], "Introduction," pp. 1–59; for Owens' numerous comments on Nédoncelle, see Index.

[2] For this definition see *De Ordine*, I, 11, 32 (*PL* 32, 993); *De Trinitate*, XIV, 1, 2 (*PL* 42, 1037); *Contra Julianum*, IV, 14, 72 (*PL* 44, 774). Another trait all philosophers have in common is their desire of a happy life, which they pursue "studendo, quaerendo, disputando, vivendo" (*Sermo* 150, 3; *PL* 38, 809).

[3] "Pagan philosophers" translates "gentium philosophi"—see *De Trin.*, XIII, 19, 24 (*PL* 42, 1034); *Contra Julianum*, IV, 14, 72 (*PL* 44, 774).

[4] Among the "spiritualia percipienda" are God as one and triune, all creatures as having being, form and order from the creative Trinity (*ibid.*).

[5] For other lists of pagan philosophers see *De Civitate Dei*, XIII, 8–10 (*PL* 41, 233 sqq.), where Augustine speaks of multiple philosophical sects and dissensions which issue from varying views on the good; *Sermo* 150, 4 (*PL* 38, 810): the Stoics and Epicureans were among the multiple philosophical sects St. Paul encountered at Athens.

City of God are "the true-speaking authors of Holy Scripture," who serve for its inhabitants as "their lovers of wisdom, their sages, their theologians, their prophets, their teachers." Granted that some pagan philosophers did glimpse some truths (e.g., "God's creation of the world, His providential governance of it, the excellence of virtue, of patriotism, of loyalty, of good works and all other things pertaining to morality") and tried to put them across by carefully worked out disquisitions; still they were ignorant of the final goal of such moral excellences.[6] On the other hand, such truths were conveyed to anyone living in the divine City not by tortuous argumentations but by prophets speaking God's own words ("propheticis, hoc est divinis vocibus, quamvis per homines, in illa civitate populo commendata sunt, non argumentationum concertationibus inculcata"; *De Civitate Dei*, XVIII, 41, 2 and 3; *PL* 41, 601).

Other texts might be cited which make the same contrast,[7] but enough has been said to indicate the point Augustine is making: to

---

[6] Among the pagan philosophers who achieved some partial insights into truth Augustine gives pride of place to Plato. See *De Civitate Dei*, VIII, 8–10 (*PL* 41, 233–35): for Plato to philosophize was to love and rejoice in the incorporeal God. In contrast to "materialistic philosophers, who give no thought to the creator of the world," Platonists, whether Ionian or Italian, agree with Christians "concerning one God, the Creator of the universe, who is not only incorporeal, transcending all corporeal beings, but also incorruptible, surpassing every kind of soul—our source, our light, our goal." Consequently, Christians prefer them to all other philosophers, while simultaneously rejecting their doctrines when wrong.

In *De Doctrina Christiana*, II, 40, 60 (*PL* 34, 63) Augustine recommends that Christians appropriate whatever truths Platonic philosophers have chanced upon and use them in the service of the Christian faith, while simultaneously discarding falsities and superstitions. In this they are following the lead of the Israelites fleeing from Egypt, who appropriated for themselves the gold and silver vessels and ornaments of the Egyptians and this they did "not on their own authority but by the command of God."

[7] See *De Trin.*, IV, chs. 15 and 16 (*PL* 42, 501): some philosophers there are who lightly touch the light of unchangeable truth, who grasp the exalted and unchangeable substance ("praecelsam incommutabilemque substantiam") through the things which have been made (*Rom.* 1:20), and who have beheld their sublime and eternal exemplars ("Illis summis aeternisque rationibus") but who cannot look into the exemplars themselves so as to understand temporal things in their variety and successions and yet who think themselves capable of purifying themselves by their own strength "so as to see God and to inhere in God, and yet whose very pride defiles them above all others." How different are the many Christians who humbly live by faith alone and

be authentic philosophy must be in line and, in fact, be identical with divine revelation or, more precisely, with Christianity.[8] Moreover, the same reason pagans use to work out their theories Christians use to develop and understand faith. Let us believe (Augustine advises in *De Trinitate*) that "the Father, Son and Holy Spirit are one God, the creator and ruler of all creation, that the Father is not the Son, nor is the Holy Spirit the Father or the Son but that there is a trinity of interrelated persons and the unity of an equal substance." But with our reason "let us also seek to understand this, imploring the help of Him whom we wish to understand; and in the measure that He shall grant, desiring to explain what we understand" ("Hoc autem quaeramus intelligere. . . . et quantum tribuit quod intelligimus explicare"). This understanding we initiate by seeing "whether that most excellent love [of which 1 *John* 4:16 speaks] is proper to the Holy Spirit, and if it is not so, whether the Father or the Son or the Holy Trinity itself is love, since we cannot contradict the most certain faith and the most weighty authority of Scripture which says: 'God is love' " (*De Trin.*, IX, 1, 1; *PL* 42, 962).

Comment. John's text calls us not only to believe that God is love but also to use our intellect to understand that equation: what is divine love? Is love properly attributed to all three persons of the Trinity or to the Holy Spirit alone? What are the factors that human love entails?[9] The knowledge resulting from that reflection will be

---

submit to the cross of Christ, wherein lies their salvation. Also see *ibid.*, XIII, 19, 24 (*PL* 42, 1034): pagan philosophers "were able to perceive that the invisible things of God are understood by those things that are made and yet they held back the truth in wickedness . . . because they philosophized without the mediator, that is, without the Man Christ." But for Christians Christ is our science and our wisdom. "He Himself plants the faith concerning temporal things within us; He Himself manifests the truth concerning eternal things. Through Him we travel to Him; through science we proceed to wisdom."

[8] See R. A. Markus in A. H. Armstrong (ed.), *Cambridge History of Later Greek and Early Medieval Philosophy* (Cambridge University Press, 1967), p. 344: " 'Christianity' and 'true philosophy' are practically synonymous terms; and, indeed, Augustine later once defined Christianity as the one true philosophy." For that definition see *Contra Julianum*, IV, 14, 72 (*PL* 44, 774: "Do not let the philosophy of Gentiles be more honest than our Christian philosophy, which is the one true philosophy . . . the true and holy philosophy [wherein we have learned from St. Paul, *Galatians* 5:17] that the flesh lusts against the spirit and the spirit against the flesh."

[9] See *ibid.*, ch. 2, where Augustine begins his attempt to answer those questions by reflecting on what human love involves: lover, beloved and love itself.

what subsequent ages will call "theology." But for Augustine it is "philosophy" in its authentic sense. Accordingly, if we put to him the question raised in this chapter of whether philosophy can be Christian, his answer will obviously be affirmative: philosophy can be Christian because it *is* Christian. Philosophy is the love of wisdom; but genuine wisdom consists in knowing and loving God here and hereafter as He is in Himself—i.e., as one and triune, as the Word incarnate, as creator and providential, as ruler and judge; but we know and love God as He is in Himself precisely as Christians—i.e., through our belief in and understanding of the Holy Scriptures under the aegis of the Church; therefore, philosophy by its very nature is Christian: it is "fides Christiana quaerens intellectum." There is, then, no conflict between reason and authority, between understanding and faith: the first word in each couplet complements the second.[10]

St. Bonaventure

Augustine's position is attractive and inspiring, but it is not without problems. If philosophy is identified with Christianity,[11] what of the sincere attempts of non-Christian believers to understand their faiths (Judaic, Eastern, Islamic)? More seriously, must one subordinate reason to authority, understanding and specula-

---

[10] On those couplets see F. E. Van Fleteren, "Authority and Reason, Faith and Understanding in the Thought of St. Augustine," *Augustinian Studies* 4 (1973), 33–72. For relevant studies on Augustine prior to 1960, see T. J. Van Bavel, *Répertoire Bibliographique de S. Augustin: 1950–1960* (The Hague: Martinus Nijhoff, 1963), pp. 403–13. For helpful studies since 1960 see the following: A. H. Armstrong, *Saint Augustine and Christian Platonism* (Villanova University Press, 1966); J. F. Anderson, *St. Augustine and Being: A Metaphysical Essay* (The Hague: Martinus Nijhoff, 1965); V. J. Bourke, *Augustine's View of Reality* (Villanova University Press, 1964); John F. Callahan, *Augustine and the Greek Philosophers* (Villanova University Press, 1967); Frederick Crossan, "Religion and Faith in St. Augustine's *Confessions*" in C. F. Delaney (ed.), *Rationality and Religious Belief* (University of Notre Dame Press, 1979), pp. 152–68; G. R. Lewis, "Faith and Reason in the Thought of St. Augustine" (Ph.D. diss., Syracuse University, 1959); D. J. Novak, "The Heart in the Philosophy of St. Augustine" (Ph.D. diss., Boston College, 1978); R. J. O'Connell, S.J., *St. Augustine's Early Theory of Man, A.D. 386–391* (Cambridge: Harvard University Press, 1968), ch. 9: "Faith and Understanding"; Eugene TeSelle, *Augustine the Theologian* (London: Burns and Oates, 1970), pp. 73–89 and *passim*.

[11] See R. A. Markus, *op. cit.*, p. 344, quoted in n. 8 above.

tion to faith, philosophy to theology, in such a way and to such a degree that reason, understanding and philosophy are without autonomy? Has philosophy no distinctive and independent area and methodology of its own? Perhaps St. Bonaventure (ca. 1217–1274) will help provide answers.

But attaining those answers has problems of its own, one of which is the abundance of secondary literature on Bonaventure which constitutes a "terrain . . . [that] resembles a jungle, or more pointedly, an embattled no-man's land."[12] Such scholars as Maurice De Wulf, Pierre Mandonnet, Etienne Gilson, Fernand Van Steenberghen, Patrice Robert, Joseph Ratzinger and Hendrikus van der Laan (to name a few) have entered the fray, as chronicled helpfully and at length by John F. Quinn in *The Historical Constitution of St. Bonaventure's Philosophy* (Toronto: Pontifical Institute of Mediaeval Studies, 1973), pp. 17–99.[13] There he isolates the questions debated: Is Bonaventure's philosophy (as distinguished from his theology) to be described more properly as Augustinian or as Aristotelian? To what extent may his philosophy be described as anti-Aristotelian? Is one justified in attempting to extract Bonaventure's philosophy from the theological context in which it is presented? To what extent may his philosophy be described as "Christian"?[14]

Quinn's own replies to those questions are interesting and, unfortunately, complex. By distinguishing between "universal" and "integral" wholes one realizes that "truths concerning the Creator and the creature" are integral parts of theology, but "taken separately, any one of those truths stands on its own ground" and can be treated also by a philosopher; yet when "taken as part of the whole, any one truth is a composite element of theology in which it is united and ordered to other truths" and thus forms the universal whole which is theology.[15] Philosophy and theology are, then, two distinct sciences inasmuch as the *lumen* and *habitus* of faith are distinct from the *lumen* and *habitus* of reason. Yet viewed with

---

[12] Ewert H. Cousins, "Response to Zachary Hayes," in David Tracy (ed.), *Celebrating the Medieval Heritage: A Colloquy on the Thought of Aquinas and Bonaventure*—Supplement of *Journal of Religion* 58 (1978), 97.

[13] Quinn gives his reaction to the positions of those scholars at the end of his book (pp. 841–96). He also furnishes bibliographies for each of them—see pp. 904–11. According to John P. Doyle, *Modern Schoolman* 54 (1976), 88, Quinn "seems most opposed to Gilson's views that Bonaventure's is a Christian philosophy which is essentially anti-Aristotelian."

[14] For this list of questions see John Wippel, *Thomist* 44 (1980), 143–44.

[15] Quinn, *ibid.*, p. 673.

respect to theology as a universal whole, philosophy is inseparable from Christian faith, even though it is separable when viewed with respect to theology as an integral whole. From this latter perspective a Christian theologian may be a philosopher when he utilizes "reasons to make intelligible the object of belief" but his philosophy is intrinsically and formally philosophical and not Christian.[16]

Manifestly, if one is to evaluate Quinn's and the others' interpretations[17] and, more important, to decide on one's own what Bonaventure's position is, one must turn to Bonaventure's own texts.

Bonaventure's Views of Pagan Philosophers

Philosophy was, for Bonaventure, initiated by the Greeks, who used human reason in an attempt to understand reality and thereby developed nine sciences, which are classified under three general headings and all of which are in turn called "philosophy," as this diagram shows.[18]

---

[16] *Ibid.*, pp. 815–16.

[17] Quinn's book has not stopped the onslaught of relevant literature. Besides the book edited by Tracy, referred to in n. 12 above, see Jacques Bougerol, "L'aspect spirituel de la spéculation bonaventurienne," *Antonianum* 52 (1977), 695–701; Ewert H. Cousins, *Coincidence of Opposites. The Theology of St. Bonaventure* (Chicago: Franciscan Herald Press, 1978); Bonaventure Hinwood, "Division of Human Knowledge in the Writings of St. Bonaventure," *Franciscan Studies* 38 (1978), 220–59; G. Iammarone, "Il projetto teologico di S. Bonaventura. Suvi presupposti antropologici e problematica della sua attualità," *Miscellanea Franciscana* 75 (1975), 637–705; T. Manferdini, "La ragione teologica in S. Bonaventura," *ibid.*, pp. 535–52; Thomas R. Mathias, "Bonaventurian Ways to God through Reason," *Franciscan Studies* 36 (1976), 192–232 and 37 (1977), 153–206; Letterio Mauro, *Bonaventura de Bagnoregio. Della Filosofia alla Contemplatio* (Genova: Accademia Ligure di Scienze e Lettere, 1976); David E. Ost, "Bonaventure: The Aesthetic Synthesis," *Franciscan Studies* 36 (1976), 233–47; P. Vignaux, "Le Christocentrisme de saint Bonaventure et le problème d'une philosophie de la religion," *Laurentianum* 19 (1978), 391–412; the multiple articles in Commissio Internationalis Bonaventuriana (eds.), *S. Bonaventura: 1274–1974* (Grottaferrata: Collegio S. Bonaventurae, 1973–74), Vol. II (*Studia de Vita, Mente et Operibus S. Bonaventurae*), Vol. III (*Philosophica*), Vol. IV (*Theologica*) and Vol. V (*Bibliographia Bonaventuriana: 1850–1973*, ed. J. G. Bougerol).

[18] See *Collationes in Hexaemeron*, IV, 1–5; V, 22; also see Leon Amoros *et alii* (eds.), *Obras de San Buenaventura* (Madrid: Biblioteca de Autores Cristianos, 1947), III, 158. In the diagram the first triad of sciences is called "essential" rather than "natural" because it embraces not only philosophy of nature or physics but also mathematics and metaphysics.

I shall base this chapter solely upon the *Collationes in Hexaemeron*, to which I shall refer (as above) by roman numerals (to indicate the *Collatio*) and arabic

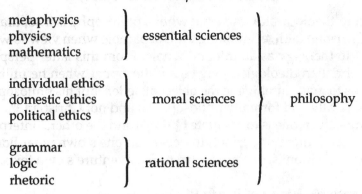

Obviously, the nine philosophical sciences culminate in metaphysics and the realization, on the part of at least the most worthy among ancient Greek philosophers, "that there exists a beginning and an end and an exemplary reason" (VI, 1: "Ad hoc venerunt philosophi et nobiles eorum et antiqui quod sunt principium et finis et ratio exemplaris").[19] This awareness of the First Being as exemplary cause sets metaphysicians apart from physicists (philosophers of nature), who also study the origin of things, and from moral philosophers, who also "lead all things back to the one Supreme Good as the final end." But only he who goes from the consideration of the principles of created and particular substance to universal and uncreated substance and to the very notion of being and then realizes that the First Being is the exemplary cause

numerals (indicating the section within the *Collatio*). The title itself will be abbreviated as *Hex.*, although this abbreviation is almost always omitted as unnecessary. The Latin text is found in vol. 5 of *S. Bonaventurae Opera Omnia* edita studio et cura PP. Collegii a S. Bonaventura (Quaracchi, 1891). It is reprinted in *Obras de San Buenaventura*, vol. 3, which is referred to in the previous paragraph and which also provides a translation. Besides that Spanish translation, I have consulted the English translation of José de Vinck, *The Works of Bonaventure* (Paterson, N.J.: St. Anthony Guild Press, 1970), vol. 5, which, however, needs modification rather often.

I have concentrated upon the *Hex.*, even though a *reportatio*, because of its ample relevant information and because these twenty-three university sermons are "a monument of outstanding historical and doctrinal value" and represent Bonaventure's final interpretation of philosophy and theology, delivered as they were between 9 April and 28 May 1273. See J. G. Bougerol, *Introduction to Works of Bonaventure*, trans. José de Vinck (Paterson, N.J.: St. Anthony Guild Press, 1964), pp. 125–26 and 130–33. Also see *S. Bonaventurae Opera Omnia*, vol. 5, pp. xxxvi–xxxix.

[19] These "nobiles et antiqui philosophi" would be Plato and his followers, among whom Plotinus looms large in Bonaventure's eyes—see n. 43 below.

of all creatures transcends the other philosophical sciences and thus is a true metaphysician (I, 13: "Metaphysicus autem . . . [assurgit] ex consideratione principiorum substantiae creatae et particularis ad universalem et increatam et ad illud esse ut habet rationem principii, medii et finis ultimi. . . . Sed considerat illud esse in ratione omnia exemplantis, cum nullo communicat et verus est metaphysicus").[20]

But not all pagan philosophers were as worthy and true in their metaphysics as were Plato and his followers: Aristotle and those influenced by him erred in three areas and were thereupon afflicted with a threefold blindness. Aristotle's errors were his denial of *rationes aeternae*, which might serve as divine exemplars for creatures; the elimination of providence from God, Who knows nothing but Himself; and the consequent refusal to view Him as governing the universe.[21] Those three errors blinded the Aristotelians as to the duration of the world (it is eternal), the status of the agent intellect (there is only one, existing independently of human knowers) and the afterlife (there is no heaven or hell).[22]

Aristotelians differ, then, from Platonists, but both are, in Bonaventure's eyes, pagan philosophers: they philosophize without the illumination which comes from the Christian faith.[23]

---

[20] At the end of the first Latin sentence quoted, Bonaventure adds: "non tamen in ratione Patris et Filii et Spiritus Sancti." Knowledge of the Trinity, then, is beyond the grasp of even an authentic metaphysician.

[21] *Hex.*, VI, 2–3. There and elsewhere in *Hex.*, Bonaventure attends to then current errors in Averroës' interpretation of the philosophy of Aristotle, which "had conquered the faculty of arts [at Paris]. Both dialectics and physics, the major subjects studied in this faculty, had become occasions for discussing problems in metaphysics and for penetrating beyond philosophy into the field of theology. The infrastructure of the philosophical studies of the 'artists' being trained with Averroistic interpretations" issued into the doctrinal current called "Latin Averroism," which produced "veritable disasters in theology." Hence, Bonaventure intended *Hex.* as a major attack upon the masters of Arts and of Theology who favored the doctrinal innovations (J. G. Bougerol, *Introduction to Works of Bonaventure*, p. 131).

[22] *Hex.*, VI, 4.

[23] Bonaventure has several ways of making that point—II, 21: pagan philosophers search for wisdom out of idle curiosity over creatures; III, 4: they deny that the multiple can proceed from one and the same Being, the temporal from the eternal, the possible from the actual, and so on, because the door to truth on those matters is understanding the Uncreated Word and that door is closed to them; IV, 1: many pagan philosophers, boasting of their knowledge, have become like Lucifer or grope in the densest darkness like the Egyptians

But what is the condition of Christians who philosophize within the context of that faith? Are they philosophers or theologians or what? Let us make the question more concrete. Franciscan and other students at the time of Bonaventure studied in their religious houses or in the faculty of Arts the nine philosophical sciences initiated by the ancient Greeks, while simultaneously professing and practicing their Catholic faith—would their study be purely philosophical or would it be Christian? Moreover, Bonaventure himself used his reason and called upon insights from Greek and other philosophical authorities in developing and understanding the faith—would that speculation be Christian philosophy or theology or what?

In trying to reply let us turn to Bonaventure's *Collationes in Hexaemeron*—sermons (see note 18 above) on the initial chapter of *Genesis*, where he separates the vision into reality which nature bestows upon our understanding ("Visio prima, quae est intelligentiae per naturam inditae") from the vision we attain when our understanding is lifted up by faith ("Secundo visio, scilicet intelligentiae per fidem elevatae"). In the first section (*Collationes* IV–VII)[24] one finds Bonaventure commenting not only upon pagan philosophers but also on his own conception of philosophy. The second section (*Collationes* VIII–XII) amounts to a discussion of theology as the "speculatio fidei."[25]

(also see VI, 5); VII, 3: such philosophers live in darkness because they are without the light of faith, which, however, Christians have; VII, 9: pagan philosophers philosophized without the Mediator, that is, without Christ.

[24] This section is preceded by three *Collationes* which are not only an introduction to the entire series but also a preview of them (see especially III, 24–31).

[25] After this section Bonaventure takes up the understanding achieved by meditation upon Sacred Scripture (*Collatio* XIII, 1: "Haec est tertia visio intelligentiae per Scripturam eruditae") not as to the content it furnishes theological speculation but as to the various spiritual interpretations (e.g., literal, anagogical, allegorical, tropological) it gives rise to (*Collatio* XIII), its sacramental figures (*Collationes* XIV–XV, 9) and the many theories (expressed through symbols of seeds and fruits) it provides a basis for (XV, 10–XIX). Next, he considers the understanding one gains through contemplation (*Collationes* XX–XXII). The series of academic sermons was to have terminated with remarks on prophecy, mystical rapture and the vision of glory (see III, 28–30), but Bonaventure's becoming a cardinal on 23 May 1273 put an end to the series. See J. G. Bougerol, *Introduction to Works of Bonaventure*, p. 133.

Collatio IV, 1–14

In the first section of that treatise, then, how does Bonaventure conceive philosophy? It is not easy to decide, because *Collationes* IV–VII are complex in content and literary expression. In them Bonaventure compresses an explanation of the nine philosophical sciences in terms of the threefold and ninefold illuminations that constitute them, a list (with refutation) of the multiple errors of pagan philosophers mentioned above, a consideration of light or truth with reference to its source, recipient and object (each of these is in turn threefold), and so on. And in expressing all this, he often cites the Old and New Testaments, as well as various Platonists, Aristotle, Cicero, Augustine and the Greek Fathers of the Church, and he profusely uses numerous symbols (e.g., in *Collatio* VII, 15–22, the cardinal virtues are likened to the four rivers of paradise, the four ornaments of the tabernacle, the four sides of the holy city, as well as to seven stars and women and loaves, etc.).

Accordingly, the complexity of *Collationes* IV–VII deters one from easily deciphering what "philosophy" and related topics mean technically. How can one overcome the deterrence? For our purposes we shall concentrate upon the data Bonaventure furnishes on essential (*vs.* moral and rational) philosophical sciences and, especially, on metaphysics and, even more precisely, on metaphysics with reference to God.

In the soul's desire to embrace the whole world ("Vult autem anima totum mundum describi in se") it acquires the essential philosophies of metaphysics, mathematics and physics, all three of which deal somehow with essences, but metaphysics has to do directly with the hidden differences within them ("ad quidditatum differentias occultas considerandas"; IV, 6). These are sixfold: substance and accident, universal and particular, potency and act, one and many, simple and composite, cause and caused (IV, 7). Four of them, when one reflects upon the errors they have encountered, disclose some facet of God. The relation of creature to Creator is not accidental but essential (IV, 8). There are three sorts of universals: "unum ad multa et unum in multis et unum praeter multa," the first of which entails the potency of matter, the second is the nature which individuals have in common, the third resides in the soul; but all three are in the eternal Art and Exemplar, and it is there they have reality ("in arte aeterna sunt; per illam enim artem et rationem consistit in re"; IV, 9). Only God is pure act and, hence, an angel is a composite of act and potency (IV, 12). Something cannot be made out of nothing and yet exist from all eternity, since something coming forth from nothingness begins to be ("quando [res] fit de nihilo, incipit esse"). Hence, the world is not eternal and God created matter and let no one think His power depends upon matter as a foundation ("absit quod potentia Dei fulciatur fundamento materiae"; IV, 13).

Bonaventure will next consider the other two essential sciences (mathematics and philosophy of nature), the rational sciences (grammar, logic, rhetoric; IV, 15–25) and the moral sciences (V, 10–21). But before beginning that consideration and immediately after his discussion of the six hidden differences a metaphysician attends to, he briefly alludes to faith: "These, then, are the foundations of faith, which examines everything" ("Haec igitur sunt fundamenta fidei quae omnia examinat"; IV, 13).[26]

Comments. Bonaventure here offers little direct information on how a metaphysician achieves knowledge of essences and their hidden differences, but his contrasting them with the essences a mathematician studies helps somewhat. Mathematical essences (e.g., numbers in themselves or in sounds, continuous quantity in general measurable proportions or as visible surfaces, etc.; IV, 15)[27] "are very clear because they offer themselves to our senses and we willingly deal with them because they fall under the imagination, which is strong within us but reason is obscured" ("istae sunt valde manifestae quia offerunt se sensui; et libenter homo negotiatur circa ista, quia cadunt in imaginatione, et imaginatio est fortis in nobis et ratio obscuratur"; IV, 14). From the clarity of mathematical essences and the ease with which a human knower deals with them by his imagination, may one not infer at least that he knows metaphysical essences less clearly and with greater difficulty?

Later Bonaventure gives more information on metaphysical knowledge. The cognitive powers a knower first uses are his external senses and his imagination, the objects of which are (respectively) "sensibilia per se (et propria et communia) et per accidens" and

---

[26] J. de Vinck's translation of the final clause is inaccurate: ". . . faith which every man should examine" (*The Works of Bonaventure*, V, 66). The Spanish translation is correct: ". . . de la fe, que examina todas las cosas" (*Obras de San Buenaventura*, III, 265).

[27] Corresponding to these essences are six mathematical sciences: arithmetic, music, geometry, perspective, astrology and astronomy (on the essences these last two consider, see IV, 15). We might add that physics (= philosophy of nature) studies "naturarum permixtas proprietates, scilicet partim occultas et partim manifestas" (see IV, 17, with several references to Aristotle's treatises). Thus it is intermediate between metaphysics and mathematics.

phantasms.[28] From these objects his reason abstracts universal *rationes* or essences from place, time and definite dimensions (V, 24) and, as a metaphysician, he begins to consider their hidden differences, which are the subject of his science (see IV, 6–7). Yet this consideration, as well as any intellectual operation which attains truth, is possible only because Christ's translucent *rationes* are illumining the universal but darkened and obscure *rationes* in our minds (XII, 5): "Ideo necesse est ut [Christus] habeat clarissimas species apud se.
. . . Suis speciebus clarissimis refulget super species intellectus nostri tenebrosas; et sic illustrantur species illae obtenebratae, admixtae obscuritati phantasmatum, ut intellectus intelligat").[29]

In view of those passages metaphysics, as well as any human knowledge, arises from two sources: Christ and the human agent. The former's eternal *rationes* are needed to transform our universal *rationes* from darkness and obscurity into light and clarity (XII, 5). But the human knower must first furnish the dim and opaque *rationes* to be illumined. This his reason does by abstracting them from the empirical data his senses provide (V, 24). Metaphysics results when the human knower studies the hidden differences within the essences (IV, 6–7) thus achieved by abstraction and by ensuing technical reflection which is divinely illumined (a divine illumination, nonetheless, which is needed for any true knowledge and which thus allows metaphysics to remain strictly philosophical—see note 29—and to serve as the basis of faith; IV, 13).

Collationes V, 22–33

The investigation of the eight philosophical sciences other than metaphysics which Bonaventure undertakes next (IV, 15 sqq., and

---

[28] Such is my interpretation of Bonaventure's words in V, 24: "objecta sensuum particularium et sensus communis . . . phantasmata sensibilium." On "sensibilia per se et per accidens" as objects of the external senses in Aristotle, see Henry B. Veatch, *Aristotle: A Contemporary Appreciation* (Bloomington: Indiana University Press, 1974), pp. 76–78.

[29] The divine illumination of which Bonaventure here speaks is a factor in any sort of intellectual knowledge, as XII, 5, discloses in sentences immediately prior and subsequent to those just quoted: "Christus est doctor interius, nec scitur aliqua veritas nisi per eum . . . interius illustrando. . . . Si enim scire est cognoscere rem aliter impossibile se habere, necessarium est ut ille solus scire faciat qui veritatem novit et habet in se veritatem."

Moreover, XII, 5, lies within the philosophical section of *Collatio* XII, not the theological section (XII, 7 sqq.)—see n. 71 below. Faith, as well as theology, requires a special divine illumination over and above that referred to in XII, 5.

V, 1–21) culminates in his commenting upon the wisdom pagan philosophers promised to their followers. After having worked out those nine justly renowned branches of philosophy,[30] they sought to reach and communicate the wisdom whither truth was leading them and which is the happiness which arises when an intellect attains its goal ("Postmodum voluerunt ad sapientiam pervenire et veritas trahebat eos; et promiserunt dare sapientiam, hoc est beatitudinem, hoc est intellectum adeptum"; V, 22).[31] But how did they come to separate themselves from the darkness of error and open themselves up to the light of truth? In the same way as any one of us does: our soul reflects upon itself, upon spiritual intelligences and upon the eternal exemplars ("Sed hoc ita fit ut anima convertat se primo super se, secundo super intelligentias spirituales, tertio super rationes aeternas"; V, 23).[32] When a soul reflects upon itself, it mentally sees itself first and other things subsequently ("primo videt se et postmodum alia") and this by attending to its three cognitive powers and their operations. The first of these are its sense faculties, by which the soul considers the objects of the external and internal senses and the phantasms of sensible things. The second is its twofold intellectual power, by which it abstracts universal *rationes* from place, time and definite dimensions and, thereafter, is raised so as to know itself and other spiritual substances into which it enters and where it shares aeviternity with them ("elevatur ad substantias separatas . . . et tunc ingerit se intelligentiis et tunc intrat aeviternum ipsarum"). Finally, by its divine powers of contemplation the soul directs its understanding so as to behold divine sights and directs its unifying power of love so as to savor divine joys—this last ability is secret and pagan philosophers knew little or nothing of it ("Similiter, operatio vel potentia divina duplex est: una quae se convertit ad contuenda divina spectacula; alia,

---

[30] Philosophers were able to elaborate those philosophical sciences because, Bonaventure adds from *Romans* 1:19, God revealed them: "Deus enim illis revelavit."

[31] "Intellectus adeptus" came originally from Avicenna, *De Anima*, V, 6, according to the editors of Bonaventure's *Opera Omnia*, V, 357, n. 7. On Avicenna's theory of intellect see E. Gilson, *History of Christian Philosophy in the Middle Ages* (New York: Random House, 1955), pp. 199–200 and 204–5; Soheil M. Afnan, *Avicenna. His Life and Works* (London: George Allen and Unwin, 1958), pp. 139–41. Also see n. 73 below.

[32] My paralleling what pagan philosophers did to escape from error with what we Christians do rests on the shift in verbs from past tenses in V, 22–24 ("voluerunt . . . trahebat . . . promiserunt . . . venerunt . . . converterunt") to present tense ("fit . . . convertat . . . oportet . . . videt," etc.).

quae se convertit ad degustanda divina solatia. Primum fit per intelligentiam, secundum per vim unitivam sive amativam, quae secreta est et de qua parum vel nihil noverunt"; V, 24).

Through these three powers and operations, then, the soul sees itself as a most beautiful and splendid mirror reflecting dazzling images ("sit spectaculum quoddam pulcherrimum et tersum, in quo videt quidquid est fulgoris et pulcritudinis"; V, 25). Second, it contemplates angels illuminating and uplifting it and thereby becomes interior to them and enters their world ("anima ingerit se angelis et intrat saeculum ipsorum"; V, 26–27.[33] Finally, the soul intellectually moves itself from effect to causes and passes over into the eternal exemplars by considering the conditions of being ("ipse intellectus considerans conditiones entis secundum relationes causae ad causatum, transfert se ab effectu ad causas et transit ad rationes aeternas") in the light of such a relationship between effect and cause as their difference: from the very fact that a cause differs from what it causes we realize with complete certitude that the First Cause is a Being which is first, simple, pure, stable, absolute and perfect (V, 28).

The soul is intellectually brought to this illuminating realization by reasoning, experience and understanding ("intelligentia autem fertur in hanc lucem tripliciter: ratiocinando, experiendo, intelligendo—rationaliter, experimentaliter, intelligentialiter"). Its reasoning rests on the opposition between effect and cause: e.g., if there is a produced being, i.e., a being which is "ab alio, secundum aliud et propter aliud"—there is a First Being—i.e., a being which is "a se, secundum se et propter se"; (V, 29).[34] Second, the soul's intellect is illumined through its experiencing within itself the awareness that a deficiency in something is knowable only if the perfection lacking is known—thus, the state of being a product points to there being a First Cause, the state of compositeness indicates that Cause's simplicity, and so on (V, 30). Finally, the soul's intelligence understands from what it has learned by reasoning and experience that there is a First Being and "being" properly belongs to Him

---

[33] Angels lift up the soul in three ways: by their lesser powers, which regulate the movement of heavenly bodies and influence earthly events (V, 26); by their higher powers, which convey light and prepare human intellects to receive illuminations; by their supreme power to turn to God so as to receive eternal light (V, 27).

[34] Also see I, 12; X, 14. This "ratiocinatio per oppositum" (as V, 32, describes it) applies not only to the divine being as first but also as simple, pure, stable, absolute and perfect—the characteristics listed in V, 28.

alone, that all else receives being from Him, that He is supremely simple and, thus, supremely perfect, that He cannot be thought of as not existing (V, 31).

And when the soul becomes more at home with that triple reflection, it can rest there ("quando anima videt hoc familiarius, . . . ibi potest quiescere") by becoming increasingly aware that the First Being entails also substance, power and operation, each of which is primal, most simple, pure, stable, absolute and perfect;[35] that He is unity, truth and goodness; that He is constancy, beauty and goodness; that He involves memory, intelligence and will; that He is life, wisdom and joy. With that awareness the soul understands that the First Being is good in His very essence and confers happiness upon all and, hence, is supremely desirable and must be supremely desired. In Him the soul finds peace and quiet (V, 32).

Accordingly, by reflecting upon itself, upon angels and upon the eternal exemplars (see above, V, 23), the soul rises to divine contemplation and declares that its intellect has reached the goal which was promised by the philosophers and to which truth leads ("consurgit ad divinum contuitum [et] dicit se habere intellectum adeptum, quem promiserunt philosophi; et ad hoc veritas trahit") with the necessary help of the virtues preached and practiced by philosophers such as Socrates (V, 33).

Comments. In the *Collationes* so far analyzed Bonaventure has provided a good deal of relevant information. Standing at the apex of the nine philosophical sciences is what might be called "general" metaphysics, which consists in a consideration of essence in its six basic and hidden differences: substance/accident, universal/particular, act/potency, one/many, simple/composite, cause/effect (IV, 7). This general metaphysics, in which one's awareness of God is as yet relatively undeveloped, becomes (literally) beatifying wisdom (V, 22) when the soul transcends the abstract and universal *rationes* of material things and knows itself and the angelic substances which illumine and elevate it into their realm (V, 24 and 26–27) and when, finally, it contemplates divine sights and lovingly savors divine joys (V, 24), into which reflection upon the difference between effect and cause initiates it.[36] Thereby it realizes that the

---

[35] This list of adjectives comes from V, 28, and Bonaventure applies them to the nouns in the subsequent clauses (e.g., divine unity, truth and goodness also are each primal, most simple, and so on; so too are constancy, etc.).

[36] When the metaphysician thus transcends the essences of material things so as to know himself, angels and God, his metaphysics is "transcendent,"

First Cause encompasses the divine exemplars and is primal, simple, pure, stable, absolute and perfect Being (V, 28). This realization has been acquired by reasoning based on the opposition between effect and cause (V, 29), by the experiential awareness that deficiency in creatures indicates fullness of perfection in their cause (V, 30) and by understanding that such a cause *is* Being, supreme simplicity and, thus, supreme perfection, from whom all else receives being (V, 31). Still further contemplation reveals to the soul such divine attributes of the First Cause and Being as substance, power and operation; unity, truth, constancy, beauty; intellection and will; life, wisdom and joy.[37] The First Being is, in a word, good in His very essence and, hence, is supremely desirable and is the source of happiness for all (V, 32).

In Bonaventure's mind all the preceding information on metaphysics and wisdom is the common property of pagan philosophers (Platonists would fully possess it, Aristotelians less so because of their three errors and triple blindness)[38] and of Christian students and faculty at the University of Paris and elsewhere. This is true, provided one attends to two qualifications. Pagan philosophers knew little or nothing of the divine joys a Christian tastes when his power of unifying love has lifted him up to God (V, 24). Second, that a soul knows angelic substances, enters into them, shares their aeviternal duration (*ibid.*) need not mean that Bonaventure intends such knowledge and cohabitation to arise from faith and supernatural grace. Plato's conceiving of the heavenly bodies as ensouled (e.g., see *Phaedrus, Timaeus, Philebus, Laws*) and, especially, Aristotle's positing a separate intelligence for each heavenly sphere (e.g., see *Metaphysics*, Lambda, chs. 7–8) would enable a Christian to posit separate intelligences and simply rename them "angels" without ceasing to consider himself a philosopher.[39] By keeping those qualifications in mind one may and can read Bonaventure as intending that his exposition of philosophy up to this point fits both pagans and Christians and is indeed philosophy.[40]

---

which will later show itself to consist of three stages (see paragraph below corresponding to note 51, as well as notes 55 and 56).

[37] All these divine attributes also are each primal, most simple, and so on— see n. 35 above.

[38] See VI, 2–4, discussed in the paragraph above corresponding to nn. 21–22.

[39] The point here is not whether Bonaventure is right and his proofs and inferences valid but that he apparently considers his position here on angels, as well as on soul and God, to be philosophical.

[40] See n. 32 above.

Will subsequent *Collationes* support that evaluation?

Collationes VI and VII

In the next two *Collationes* Bonaventure continues to discuss the vision which nature bestows upon our understanding (VI, 1: "visio intelligentiae per naturam inditae") by considering the four cardinal virtues (temperance, prudence, fortitude and justice) that are necessary if we are to achieve through contemplation the wisdom in which metaphysics culminates and happiness consists. Plato and his school arrived at this wisdom by positing "rationes exemplares" in the first cause (VI, 1), but Aristotle and those he influenced excluded exemplarity from that cause when he rejected Plato's theory of Ideas (VI, 2).[41] This exclusion was unfortunate because it extinguished the great light which had produced their previous sciences (VI, 5: "licet enim magna lux videretur in eis ex praecedentibus scientiis, tamen omnis extinguitur per errores praedictos").[42] That eternal light is also the exemplar of all things created and is attained when our minds are lifted up, as were those of the Platonists ("illa lux aeterna est exemplar omnium . . . et mens elevata, ut mens aliorum nobilium philosophorum antiquorum, ad hoc pervenit"). In that light there first comes to our soul the exemplars of the cardinal virtues ("in illa vero primo occurrunt animae exemplaria virtutum"; VI, 6), which flow thence into our cognitive, affective and efficient powers, as Plotinus and other worthy philosophers established.[43]

---

[41] On Aristotle's threefold errors and blindness see VI, 3–4, and paragraph above corresponding to notes 21–22. In VII, 1–2, Bonaventure returns to the Aristotelian errors.

[42] Here Bonaventure also notes that Aristotle led others into error because "he had been so great in other matters and had expressed truth so well."

[43] Mentioned by name in VI, 6, Plotinus is given special prominence in VI, 25–32, which are quotations from Macrobius reproducing *Enneads* I, 2, on virtue (VI, 25: "Macrobius narrans sententiam Plotini"). On Macrobius (*fl.* ca. 400) as the pagan Latin Neoplatonist who was influenced by Numenius, Plotinus and Porphyry, and who is the author of a commentary of Cicero's *Somnium Scipionis* and is very influential on medievals, see R. T. Wallis, *Neoplatonism* (New York: Charles Scribner's Sons, 1972), pp. 35, 36, 96 and 167.

Besides Plotinus, Bonaventure also names Philo (VI, 7), Augustine (VI, 12), Cicero (VI, 15) and Origen (VI, 25). Even Aristotle is quoted on virtue as the mean between two extremes (VI, 12).

Mention is made again of Plotinus and Cicero in VII, 3, as enlightened and eminent philosophers.

These thinkers indeed seem enlightened and capable of enjoying happiness, but they lived in darkness because they did not have the light of faith, as we do (VII, 3: "et ita isti videbantur illuminati et per se posse habere felicitatem. Sed adhuc isti in tenebris fuerunt quia non habuerunt lumen fidei: nos autem habemus lumen fidei").[44] Yes, such renowned, enlightened but faith-less philosophers posited the existence of the cardinal virtues ("illi autem praecipui philosophi posuerunt, sic etiam illuminati, tamen sine fide . . . virtutes cardinales"), which are called "political" inasmuch as they teach proper conduct with others, "purgative" inasmuch as they prepare us for contemplation by ourselves and "reformative" insofar as they enable a cleansed soul to rest in the Exemplar (VII, 4).

Comments. Here Bonaventure links the cardinal virtues needed to achieve wisdom and happiness with the divine Exemplar: our prudence, justice, temperance and fortitude flow from that eternal light and affect our powers of knowing, loving and acting (VI, 6). But Platonists gave a prominent place in their philosophy to exemplarity because of their theory of subsistent Forms and, thereby, also to the cardinal virtues. On the other hand, Aristotelians excluded the Platonic Forms from their philosophy and thus would consistently reject (by force of Bonaventure's argument) the four virtues likewise.[45] Yet his reaction to the Platonists takes an unexpected turn. Granted that they were in some sense aware of the cardinal virtues and their role in one's social, personal and transcendent life.[46] Yet their enlightenment and ability to achieve happiness on their own are only apparent, because they lack the light of faith and are thereby still in darkness (VII, 3: "Et ita isti *videbantur* illuminati et per se posse habere felicitatem. Sed adhuc isti in tenebris fuerunt, quia non habuerunt lumen fidei"). And the Franciscan devotes the rest of *Collatio* VII to laying out the reasons why darkness overtook such noble philosophers, who will be seen to possess only partial

---

[44] The final sentence of VII, 3, is from 1 *Peter* 2:9: we who have the faith "are a chosen race . . . [because] of Him who has called [us] out of darkness into his marvelous light."

[45] Bonaventure's interpretation has to contend with the fact that Aristotle's own ethical theory had a rather full doctrine of virtues—see H. B. Veatch, *Aristotle: A Contemporary Appreciation*, pp. 94–127, especially pp. 108–12.

[46] See for example VI, 6: "Illa lux aeterna est exemplar omnium et . . . mens aliorum nobilium philosophorum antiquorum ad hoc [pervenerunt]. In illa [luce] ergo primo occurrunt animae exemplaria virtutum"; VII, 3: "Alii philosophi illuminati posuerunt ideas; . . . posuerunt virtutes exemplares, a quibus fluunt virtutes cardinales"; also see VII, 4.

knowledge of the virtues and totally to lack the ability to practice them because of their ignorance and unacceptance of Christ.

Why (Bonaventure begins) are pagan philosophers still in darkness? Because the cardinal *virtutes* must first direct one's soul to its proper end, rectify its affections and heal its deficiencies before they can be certified as authentic. But the virtues of those philosophers are not capable of causing those three operations (VII, 5: "Sed adhuc in tenebris sunt quia necesse est ut hae virtutes prius habeant tres operations, scilicet animam ordinare in finem, secundo rectificare affectus animae, tertio quod sanentur morbidi. Has autem operationes non habuerunt in ipsis"). That the virtues of a pagan philosopher do not direct him to his proper and ultimate goal (and thus are not genuine) is proved in the light of Augustine, *De Civitate Dei*, XIX, 25, for whom no virtue is genuine which does not direct one's intention to God as his source in order that he may repose in an assured eternity and in perfect peace. Assured eternity ("certa aeternitas") demands that it cannot be lost; perfect peace, that the soul be reunited to the body after death. But pagan philosophers were unaware of an assured eternity by reason of their doctrine of the transmigration of souls (*ibid.*). They were ignorant of perfect peace because of their not knowing that the world would end and that bodies would rise from their dust—such ignorance is not surprising because they were investigating solely by the power of reason, which cannot conceive of the resurrection of bodies and other related facts.[47] Hence, they were ignorant of faith, without which virtues are of no value (VII, 6: "Nec mirum quia, cum essent investigatores secundum potentiam rationis, ratio nostra non potest ad hoc pervenire ut corpora resurgant. . . . Ignoraverunt ergo fidem, sine qua virtutes non valent").

A second reason pagan philosophers were in darkness is that their cardinal virtues did not rectify their emotions ("affectus") of fear, sorrow, joy and trust. This rectification requires that God's grace enable our free wills to trust in things unseen and thereby to merit eternal life. But pagans were unaware or disdainful of divine grace and of supernatural merit and, hence, their practice of virtue did not make their fear be holy, sorrow be just, joy be true, or trust be assured and thus their emotions were distorted (VII, 7).

---

[47] "Other related facts" refers to Bonaventure's position that contrary elements can endure forever in heaven without interaction—see J. de Vinck, *The Works of Bonaventure*, V, 112, with note; L. Amoros, *Obras*, III, 324, note 10 (with references to Aristotle and Augustine).

Moreover, our emotions must be healed, a process that demands that we understand the nature of the disease affecting them, and know its cause, a competent physician and an effective medicine. In all four areas the knowledge of pagan philosophers was deficient. They did not fully appreciate the fact that weakness, ignorance, malice and concupiscence, which a soul contracts when united to the body, permeate and radically affect not just our imagination but our very powers to understand, love and act (VII, 8). Nor did they realize that the cause of such diseases was the sin of Adam, known however not through reason but only through faith in the prophets. Such knowledge eluded them because of their disbelief: as Augustine, *De Trin.*, XIII, 19, 24, says, the foremost Gentile philosophers became aware of God through the things He made, but they philosophized without the Mediator, who is the Man Christ and whom they did not accept from the prophets or the Apostles, and thus wickedness held them back from admitting the truth (VII, 9; on Augustine see note 7 above). They did not know the doctor who could heal them—Christ, the God-man, who alone could atone for their sinfulness; Christ, the divine Word, who was incarnate and crucified and who later sent the Spirit into our hearts (VII, 10). The grace of this Spirit is the medicine which is needed for us to regain health but which unfortunately escapes the grasp of philosophy ("hanc gratiam philosophia non potest attingere"; VII, 11). Accordingly, philosophers should not glory in a science unable to know the disease afflicting them, its cause, and the doctor or remedy required.

Indeed, they were like ostriches, equipped with wings but incapable of flying.[48] So too the philosophers had the cardinal virtues, which, however, were unable to direct, cleanse or rectify their emotions because of their lack of faith. Thus, they came falsely to propose that a soul could attain beatitude in endlessly recurring cycles of transmigration, that it could achieve sufficient merit to earn eternal happiness through its own powers of free will, that its internal powers of knowing, loving and acting remain intact despite the diseases it contracts through its union with the body.[49] And so they fell into a threefold darkness ("Unde primo posuerunt falsam beatitudinis circulationem; secundo, falsam praesentium

---

[48] The comparison of pagan philosophers with ostriches is based on Pliny—see L. Amoros, *ibid.*, p. 326, n. 18.

[49] The diseases are listed in VII, 8: "infirmitas, ignorantia, malitia, concupiscentia."

meritorum sufficientiam; tertio, internarum virium perpetuam incolumitatem. In has tres tenebras inciderunt"; VII, 12).

Such darkness is dispelled only by faith, which indicates not only the nature and cause of the illness afflicting our human nature but also the physician and remedy it needs by locating the roots of our merits in the very God to be satisfied ("Fides . . . sanat animam, ponendo meritorum radices in Deo cui placeat"; VII, 13). Thus by the merits of Christ a soul proceeds through faith into sure hope and is thereby healed, straightened and rightly ordered. But pagan philosophers knew nothing of those meritorious roots in Christ and thus they were in darkness. Christians, though, "are light in the Lord" (*Ephesians* 5:8): faith accompanied by hope and especially by charity, heals the soul, cleanses and illumines it, makes it like God (*ibid.*). In fact, charity is the root of all the emotions ("radix omnium affectionum") and, once it is healed by divine love, they too are healed. Charity is also the end and form of all virtues (VII, 14)— those of a Christian are formed and clothed with charity, those of philosophers are not (VII, 15).[50]

Comments. Between the beginning of *Collatio* IV and the end of *Collatio* V Bonaventure sketched a twofold metaphysics, which for sake of convenience we can refer to as "general" and "transcendent" (see note 36 above). The first starts from sense data furnished by external and internal senses and from reason abstracting universal *rationes* or essences from the time, place and definite dimensions such data involve (V, 24); it proceeds by considering (under divine illumination) the hidden differences in those essences (substance/accident, universal/particular, potency/act, one/many, simple/complex and cause/effect—see IV, 7 sqq.); it terminates by reflecting on the errors such differences have occasioned (IV, 8–13).

"Transcendent" metaphysics centers on God, especially as the First Being and Primal Cause, who is the exemplar of all creatures, and as the supreme Good, who confers happiness upon all human and angelic existents seeking Him as their final goal (V, 22). Such a metaphysics deploys in two stages, in the first of which a soul, through reasoning on the opposition between effect and cause (V, 29), through experiencing the contrast between presence and absence of a perfection (V, 30) and through understanding (V, 31) comes to know itself in relationship to other spiritual substances and to the divine exemplars (V, 23–27). Thereupon the soul realizes

---

[50] The rest of *Collatio* VII is given over to symbolizing the cardinal virtues as four rivers of paradise, four sides of the city, four ornaments of the tabernacle.

that the First Cause is a Being which is primal, simple, pure, stable, absolute and perfect (V, 28). That realization next opens up—this is the second stage of "transcendent" metaphysics—into a fuller awareness of God as First Being—namely, that He is substance, power and operation; unity, truth, constancy, beauty; intellection and will; life, wisdom and joy.[51] He is, in brief, good in His very essence, bestows happiness upon all and, hence, is supremely desirable and desired, and in Him the soul rests (V, 32).

But how do pagan philosophers of ancient times stand with respect to metaphysics as Bonaventure understands it? Aristotelian metaphysics would obviously be "general" but not "transcendent" because of Aristotle's refusal to accept Plato's theory of Forms: God is not an exemplary cause of the universe.[52] Platonic philosophy would correspond to both "general" and "transcendent" metaphysics in Bonaventure's sense because of the place Plato gives to Forms and exemplarity in reality. This correspondence is what one expects from the Franciscan's praise of Platonists as philosophers who have escaped from the darkness which enveloped other pagans and emerged into the light of truth through their philosophy of exemplarism.[53]

But what takes one by surprise is Bonaventure's rather sudden and strong criticism of the Platonists' views on the cardinal virtues. Granted that the most worthy among the ancient philosophers "have come to this point: there exists a beginning and end and *ratio exemplaris*" (VI, 1). Granted, too, that they were aware that the "eternal light, which is the exemplar of all things," also contains the exemplars of the virtues (VI, 6), which thence flow into our cognitive, affective and efficient powers (VII, 4).[54] But their enlightenment was illusory and they were incapable of attaining true happiness: unlike us they actually lived in darkness because they did not have the light of Faith (VII, 3). This lack meant that their virtues were not genuine (VII, 5: "vera virtus non est quae non dirigit intentionem ad Deum fontem") and were powerless (VII, 6: "Ignoraverunt ergo fidem, sine qua virtutes non valent"). Why so? For three reasons: such virtues could not direct a soul to its final goal of finding eternal happiness (owing to their theory of the

---

[51] All these attributes are characterized as primal, simple, etc. (V, 28)—see notes 35 and 37 above.

[52] See paragraphs above corresponding to notes 41–42.

[53] See especially VI, 6.

[54] On Plotinus as foremost among such Greek philosophers, see n. 43 above.

transmigration of souls, which eliminates *certa aeternitas* and *perfecta pax;* VII, 5–6). Second, their virtues did not rectify their distorted emotions ("affectiones sunt obliquae") because such philosophers presumptuously attempted to achieve salvation solely by their own merits and free choices (VII, 7). Third, the cardinal virtues they practiced did not heal them because their lack of Faith concealed from them the nature of the diseases they had contracted when their souls entered matter (VII, 8), their cause (Adam's sin; VII, 9), Christ as doctor through His incarnation and crucifixion (VII, 10), and the grace of the Holy Spirit as remedy (VII, 11).

And this inauthenticity or inadequacy of their virtues did not have results merely in the practical order (e.g., in deficient ascetical practices) but in the speculative order as well. It issued into three errors, which can be formulated as follows: a soul achieves beatitude in endlessly recurring cycles of existence; a soul merits beatitude solely through its own free choices; a soul's powers of knowing, loving and acting are themselves safe from contamination from diseases contracted upon its union with a body (VII, 12; see note 49 above). Accordingly, the "transcendent" metaphysics of the Platonists, which those false conceptions help constitute, is in part erroneous and is the darkness within which they dwell and which only faith in Christ can dissipate (VII, 13).

In contrast to such philosophers are the Franciscan seminarians and other Christians studying philosophy at medieval universities or religious houses—they "are in the true light and are unlike those who . . . take the false for the true, an idol for God" (VII, 13: "modo [sunt] in vera luce; non sic illi...qui accipiunt falsa pro veris, idolum pro Deo"). How would this philosophy fit into Bonaventure's scheme of "general" and "transcendent" metaphysics?

Its initial position on sensible existents, whether approached from a Platonic or an Aristotelian point of view, would obviously be a "general" metaphysics. But in order to be "transcendent" their position on God would (for reasons too manifest to need repeating) have to be Platonic. But because of their faith they are in a position to work out a metaphysics which is without the falsities marring that of pagan Platonists. For as Christians they believe that a soul achieves eternal happiness and perfect peace by contemplating God, its source and end; that an individual soul is reunited with its body on the last day and, hence, that the world is not eternal (VII, 5); that divine grace is necessary for us freely to gain eternal life (VII, 7 and 11); that Adam's sin has grave effects on human agents and their moral life (VII, 8); that Christ, the God-man, is our mediator, redeemer and physician (VII, 9–10).

Their Christian faith results, then, not only in their having authentic virtues which are truly salvific by ordering, rectifying and healing their emotional and psychological lives but also in their developing a "transcendent" metaphysics which is totally true. They are aware, yes, that God exists as primal being and exemplary cause; that He is substance, power, operation, unity, truth, constancy, beauty, intellection, will, life, wisdom and joy (and each of these in the highest degree of primacy, simplicity, purity, immutability, necessity and perfection; see note 51). But they also realize (in contrast to their pagan counterparts)[55] that beatitude is a soul's eternal and peaceful possession of God through contemplation in heaven; that beatitude is merited through a soul's free cooperation with divine grace; that a soul contracts diseases upon its entrance into a body which radically affect its cognitive, affective and efficient powers, whose remote origin is Adam's sin and which are eradicated only through its faith in Christ's redemptive life and death and through the charity that forms and clothes its cardinal virtues. If those speculative truths are joined with the truths dealing with God, one has a considerable body of transcendent metaphysical knowledge.[56]

But is that knowledge philosophy? Certainly, the methodology a Christian uses during the first two stages of such transcendent metaphysics is (in Bonaventure's eyes) philosophical. Having started from sense data, having abstracted universal essences therefrom and having investigated their hidden differences (IV, 7–13; V, 24), he uses reasoning, experience and intellection (V, 29–31) to become aware of God as First Cause and Being and of all His additional attributes (V, 28 and 32). All such mental operations would be recognized as philosophical. But what of the (so to speak) "third" stage of transcendent metaphysics? There faith steps in to prevent a Christian from making the three mistakes pagan Platonic philosophers made regarding our human situation here and hereafter, and thus it completes metaphysics. Are the three speculative truths a Christian there formulates under the influence of his faith philosophical? If so, do they constitute what one may call "Christian"

---

[55] This realization is the third stage of what I call Bonaventure's "transcendent" metaphysics.

[56] If such metaphysical science were without such truths derived from faith (as is the case with the Platonists), it would not be simply incomplete, but wrong. Hence, in its third transcendent stage, metaphysics depends on faith to a considerable extent. See E. Gilson, *The Philosophy of St. Bonaventure* (London: Sheed and Ward, 1938), pp. 92–105, especially 99–102.

philosophy—that position on the nature of reality which is attained by human reason drawing upon data from the sensible universe but which is specially illumined in some areas by faith? Or does that illumination transform at least the third stage of transcendent metaphysics into theology?

Perhaps subsequent *Collationes* will help us decide.

Collatio X

Bonaventure starts to set forth his conception of theology ("speculatio fidei") in *Collatio* X.[57] Having considered the vision into reality achieved when our understanding is elevated by faith ("visio scilicet intelligentiae per fidem sublevatae") by discussing the scope of faith in *Collatio* VIII[58] and the certainty our assent through faith gives in *Collatio* IX,[59] he continues by speaking of "speciositas fidei" (X, 1)—this is the splendor, clarity, beauty which faith achieves when we explicate its contents through reason and which thereby transcend the clarity, refulgence and beauty of the stars themselves in the heavens and even of the twelve gates and pearls of the heavenly Jerusalem (X, 1 and 2: "Nunc de speciositate [fidei] dicendum est. . . . Pullulationes speculationum orientium ex fide sunt transcendentes claritatem siderum. . . . Hae autem orientes ex fide speculationes comparantur claritati margaritarum quia sunt fulgidae, vivificae, iucundae ad modum margaritae").[60]

Such explication centers on twelve truths of faith, which Bonaventure approaches in a complex manner. He lists them in a single

---

[57] He seems not to use the term "theologia" itself but "speculatio fidei" means for him what other authors call theology. Speculation on faith in *Collationes* X–XII is in contrast with *Collationes* IV–VII on philosophy and with XIII–XIX on Sacred Scripture itself (see n. 25 above).

[58] When commenting upon *Genesis* 1:8 ("vocavit Deus firmamentum caelum") and after noting that "caelum" is "sublime, stabile et spectabile" (VIII, 1), Bonaventure transfers those three adjectives to faith. Speaking of faith as "lofty" (*sublime*) is equivalent to speaking of its scope: it deals with the Trinity and the Incarnation (VIII, 7) and is articulated in the "Apostles' Creed" (VIII, 19).

[59] Speaking of faith as "stable," the second of the three adjectives mentioned in VIII, 1 (see previous note), is to discuss its certainty, which rests upon the sources of revelation: the uncreated Word, the incarnate Word and the inspired word of Scripture (IX, 1).

[60] Using stars and the gates and pearls of celestial Jerusalem as symbols of the truths of faith comes from *Genesis* 15:5 ("Suscipe caelum et numera stellas") and *Apocalypse* 21:10 ("Et vidi Jerusalem descendentem de caelo . . . et portae [factae sunt] ex singulis margaritis"; X, 1).

paragraph,[61] and he deals with the first three of them at some length but only after he has commented briefly upon the last nine (X, 4–9). To simplify matters let us list all twelve but incorporate within that list the gist of his brief comments on the last nine[62] and delay attending to his longer commentaries on the first three.[63]

Here, then, are the twelve truths we assent to by faith:[64]

1. God is;
2. He is triune and yet one;
3. He is the exemplar of all things;
4. He created the universe in time;
5. He forms human souls by illumining their intellects;
6. He gives the Holy Spirit by bestowing grace upon them;
7. God the Son became incarnate so as to make reparation for human beings and angels;
8. He was crucified for us;
9. He is medicine for our souls;
10. He is life-giving food for the Church militant and triumphant because He is merciful;
11. He avenges wrongdoing because He is just and truthful;
12. He is our eternal reward.

---

[61] See X, 3: "Duodecim speculationes sunt quas habemus ex fide: credere Deum primum, Deum trinum et unum, et exemplar rerum, ut creantem mundum, ut formantem animam, dantem spiritum. Deum carni unitum, Deum crucifixum, medelam mentium, vitale pabulum, ultorem scelerum, praemium aeternum."

[62] This brief "speculatio" constitutes his theological reflection upon the last nine articles. Much more speculative attention is given them in other treatises.

[63] He comments on the first article in *Collatio* X, on the second in XI, on the third in XII. We shall restrict our exegesis to *Collatio* X—that is, to his theological reflection upon the revealed truth that God is (see n. 66 below on this formulation instead of God is first): such is sufficient for our purpose of understanding the contrast between philosophy and theology. On God as exemplar (*Collatio* XII) see n. 71 below.

On the content of *Collationes* XIII–XXII, see n. 25 above; on *Collationes* III, see n. 24 above.

[64] Bonaventure further complicates these truths by specifying the first three as each "veritas praeexistens," the second three as each "veritas efficiens," the third three as each "veritas reficiens," the fourth three as each "veritas perficiens" (X, 5–9). I shall disregard this fourfold specification as an unnecessary complication.

Those twelve *credibilia* are also the *intelligibilia* for which the human intellect seeks *rationes*[65] and which thereby are allowed to shine forth in beauty and clarity. That search, when successful, constitutes what the Franciscan calls "speculatio fidei," or theology.

Let us observe his speculation on the first such *credibile*: God exists. He formulates three "proofs," the last of which has three divisions and one set of subdivisions.

Why, then, do we know that God exists and is first?[66] Because the first name of God is "being" (*esse*), which is the most manifest and most perfect of all names and is most properly God's own—otherwise, God would not have said to Moses (*Exodus* 3:14): "I am who am." Therefore, nothing is more obvious than that God exists, because whatever is said of Him is reduced to being (X, 10: "Primum speculabile est Deum esse. Primum nomen Dei est esse, quod est manifestissimum et perfectissimum, ideo primum; unde nihil manifestius quia quidquid de Deo dicitur reducitur ad esse; hoc est proprie proprium nomen Dei. Deus non dixisset Moysi sive latori Legis: 'Ego sum qui sum,' nisi esset primus").

Second, it is most clear that God exists and is first because any true proposition, whether affirmative or negative, indicates He exists [because He is truth].[67] Even if one were to say, "God does not exist," one can still infer that He is [because He is truth and the supposition is that it is true] that He is not (X, 11): "Deum esse primum manifestissimum est quia ex omni propositione, tam affirmativa quam negativa, sequitur Deum esse, etiam si dicas: 'Deus non est' sequitur: 'Si Deus non est, Deus est'").[68]

---

[65] Not all *credibilia* are "intelligibilia per rationem, ut Abraham genuit Isaac, sive facta particularia."

[66] For Bonaventure to affirm that God exists (X, 10; X, 15) is equivalent to affirming that He is first (X, 3, quoted above, n. 61; X, 11; X, 18). Why so? Because "esse divinum primum est quod venit in mente" (X, 6)—a reason which is reducible to the Latin Avicenna, as this argument suggests: being is what first falls into the human intellect (Avicenna); but God is Being (*Exodus* 3:14); therefore, God is what we first know; therefore, we know that God is and that He is first. On Avicenna, see E. Gilson, *History of Christian Philosophy*, p. 206; S. M. Afnan, *Avicenna*, pp. 115–16. Also see n. 73 below.

[67] At the end of the paragraph Bonaventure gives an example of a negative proposition that is true: "Si Socrates non currit, verum est Socratem non currere."

[68] Some help in understanding this elliptic argument can be found in *Quaestiones Disputatae de Mysterio Trinitatis*, q. 1, a. 1 ad 5; Thomas Aquinas, *De Veritate*, q. 10, a. 12 ad 3.

Third, creatures are a mirror reflecting the truth that God exists because of their order, origin and completion. With respect to order some creatures are posterior, others are prior—a situation which points to there being a First—namely, God (X, 12: "Manifestum . . . est si est posterius, est prius; ergo et primum"); again, some creatures are lower in perfection, others higher—a relationship that indicates their dependence in nature upon that which is highest: God (X, 13: "Secundo est ordo inferioris ad superius et superioris ad summum, quae habent essentialem ordinem et dependentiam secundum ordinem naturae"); some creatures are temporal, others aeviternal and, hence, there must be a being who is eternal, uncreated, self-sufficient and self-subsistent: God (X, 14: "Si est aliquid propter aliud creatum ergo et illud aliud est aliquid propter aliud, scilicet increatum et illud erit propter se; ut si est res temporalis propter animam, et anima propter Deum; necessario ergo Deus per se et propter se est").

With respect to origin creatures testify that God exists: because their being is characterized by creation, participation, composition and multiplicity, there is a Being which is uncreated, is essentially, with absolute simplicity and uniquely (X, 15: "Si est ens creatum est ens increatum; et si est ens per participationem est ens per essentiam; et si est ens per compositionem, est ens per simplicitatem; si est ens per multiformitatem, est ens per uniformitatem vel identitatem"; also see X, 16).

Finally, with respect to completion creatures witness to the fact that God is: because their being is potential, mutable, qualified, dependent and generic, there is a Being which is fully actual, immutable, without qualification and independent. And He is a Being which exceeds and transcends every genus; He is unrestricted power, being and operation (X, 17: "Si est esse potentiale, est esse actuale; si est esse mutabile, est esse immutabile; si est esse secundum quid, est esse simpliciter; si est esse dependens, est esse absolutum; si est esse in genere, est esse extra genus. . . . Ens enim in genere habet differentias coarctantes, et tale non habet posse, esse et agere universaliter. Unde Deus est ens extra genus et supra genus").

Consequently (Bonaventure concludes), viewing the order, origin and fulfillment of creatures leads us to that first Being, which they all mirror. Why so? Because "being" is written upon them all and those relationships (order, origin, completion) are the attributes of "being upon which one can base most certain inferences concerning God. Hence, although the author of the *Liber de Causis* said, 'Being is what is created first' [Proposition 4], I say: the First

Being is what is known first" (X, 18: "Hae igitur speculationes ordinis, originis et completionis ducunt ad illud esse primum quod repraesentant omnes creaturae. Hoc enim nomen scriptum est in omnibus rebus; et sunt hae conditiones entis super quas fundantur certissimae illationes. Unde dixit ille: 'Prima rerum creatarum est esse,' sed ego dico: prima rerum intellectualium est esse primum").[69]

Comments. In *Collatio* X Bonaventure has disclosed what "theology," or "speculation on the content of Christian faith" (*speculatio fidei*), means in these stages. First, he formulated the twelve propositions to which a Christian assents through faith (X, 3). Then he characterized those *credibilia* as *intelligibilia*, whereby he invites the believer to elaborate *rationes* to establish, develop and understand them and thereby to decorate them with beauty, clarity and splendor (*speciositas*).

Several of the *rationes* Bonaventure himself offers concentrate upon "being."[70] God exists and is first because "being" is His most perfect, manifest and proper name, as *Exodus* 3:14 discloses (X, 10). Everything other than God is being through creation, participation, composition and multiformity and, thus, testifies that the divine being is an uncreated essence of absolute simplicity and self-identity (X, 15–16). All beings other than God are marked by potentiality, change, qualification and dependence and, accordingly, they indicate that God's being is pure act, permanence, absoluteness and independence and, therefore, transcends every genus of being and is unrestricted in power, being and activity (X, 17). Since, then,

---

[69] The *Liber de Causis*, from which Bonaventure quotes Proposition 4, is an anonymous treatise which was also called *Liber de expositione bonitatis purae* and which was translated into Latin from Arabic by Gerard of Cremona (d. 1187). On its authorship see Richard C. Taylor, "St. Thomas and the *Liber de Causis* on the Hylomorphic Composition of Separate Substances," *Mediaeval Studies* 41 (1979), 506, n. 3 (with references to other secondary literature); *idem,* "The *Liber de Causis:* A Study of Medieval Neoplatonism" (Ph.D. diss., University of Toronto, 1981), pp. 54–70 (the anonymous author was probably a Muslim or Christian philosophical thinker living in the Middle East between A.D. 833 and 922); Denis J. Brand, *The Book of Causes* (Niagara, N.Y.: Niagara University Press, 1981), pp. 1–7. On its contents see L. Sweeney, S.J., *Divine Infinity in Greek and Medieval Thought* (New York/Bern: Peter Lang Publishing, Inc., 1992), chs. 13–14.

[70] Arguments which do not center on "being" as such are the second (X, 11: any true proposition indicates that God is) and the first portion of the third, based on the ordering of creatures (X, 12–14).

"being" is inscribed on all creatures in what and how they are, they reveal God as Being. In fact, they allow us to realize not only that what God first creates is being but also that what we first know is the First Being, or God (X, 18).[71]

Conclusions

Obviously, "theology" for Bonaventure is "fides Christiana quaerens intellectum": a believer seeks to understand, develop, establish the content of his faith. As observed in *Collatio X*, Bonaventure's starting point is an article of faith (e.g., "God exists") and Scripture (*Exodus* 3:14: "I am who am. . . . He who is"), which govern and illumine the psychological process coming next—namely, reasoning. This latter enables him to establish, understand, probe that article and its scriptural basis by developing *rationes* issuing from reflection upon "being" as the name most suitable for God and yet also applicable to creatures in their relationships to Him (X, 10 and 15–17), as well as upon the truth of propositions (X, 11), and so forth.

---

[71] The insights Bonaventure has provided in *Collatio X* are enough to illumine *Collatio XII* as a minuscule model of how philosophy and theology differ. The latter *Collatio* is dedicated to the third article of faith—namely, that God is the exemplar of all things (XII, 2). But before reflecting theologically upon it, Bonaventure turns to four truths which faith presupposes: God is He who creates all things, governs our actions, teaches our intellects and judges our merits (*ibid.*: "Supponendum enim est per fidem quod Deus est conditor rerum, gubernator actuum, doctor intellectuum, judex meritorum"). He next establishes each of those truths through reasoning and, thus, through philosophical reflections (see XII, 3–6; we used XII, 5, in the paragraph above corresponding to n. 29). Then his tactics change: he lists (XII, 7–8) texts from Scripture which to his mind establish that God is exemplary cause of all: *John* 1:3; *Jeremiah* 31:33; *Hebrews* 8:10; *Wisdom* 7:29; *Apocalypse* 20:12; *Psalm* 138:16. Subsequent to that listing comes the speculation which transforms them from *credibilia* to the *intelligibilia* of theology (XII, 9–13). At the end of that theological process he summarizes it and the earlier philosophical processes thus: "Ad hos splendores exemplares ratio ducit et fides" (XII, 14).

This statement is immediately followed, we might add, by paragraphs (XII, 14–17) which are a meditation on various spiritual interpretations and symbols of Scripture and which thus appear to anticipate briefly *Collationes XIII* sqq. (see n. 25 above).

But however one interprets these final paragraphs, those preceding them rather clearly show themselves to have arisen from distinct cognitive operations, the first set of which (XII, 3–6) is philosophical, the second is theological (XII, 7–13).

Obviously, too, theology differs in its starting point from meta-physics as "general." This latter starts (as we have noted) from sense data furnished by external and internal senses and from reason abstracting universal essences from the time, place and definite dimensions such data involve (V, 24) and proceeds by considering the hidden differences in those essences (IV, 7).

Granted, then, the diversity between theology and "general" metaphysics, but what of theology and "transcendent" metaphys-ics? In its first two stages the latter is genuinely different from theology inasmuch as in the first of those stages the soul begins by reasoning on the opposition between effect and cause (V, 29) and by experiencing the contrast between presence and absence of a perfection (V, 30) and thus comes to know itself in relationship to other spiritual substances and to the divine exemplars (V, 23–27); thereupon it realizes that the First Cause is a Being that is primal, simple, pure, stable, absolute and perfect (V, 28). The second stage of "transcendent" metaphysics consists simply of a fuller aware-ness of the divine Being thus reached by reasoning, experience and understanding: He is substance, power and operation; unity, truth, constancy, beauty; intellection and will; life, wisdom and joy—He is, in brief, good in His very essence, bestows happiness upon all and, hence, is supremely desirable and desired (V, 32).

But what of the third stage of "transcendent" metaphysics—is it distinct from theology? This question has no easy answer. Here is the situation. This third stage has to do with us as moral agents and with our ability to attain permanent happiness. On these topics a Platonic pagan philosopher was at a great disadvantage because he used reason alone, which injected three errors into his metaphysics at this stage: a soul (so he thought) achieves beatitude in endlessly recurring cycles of existence; it merits beatitude solely through its own free choices; its powers of knowing, loving and acting are themselves safe from contamination from diseases contracted upon its union with a body (VII, 12).

But Christians in this area of transcendent metaphysics are res-cued from those mistakes because they believe that a soul achieves eternal happiness and perfect peace by contemplating God, its source and end; that an individual soul is reunited with its body on the last day and, hence, that the world is not eternal (VII, 5); that divine grace is necessary for us freely to gain eternal life (VII, 7 and 11); that Adam's sin has serious effects on human agents and their moral life (VII, 8); that Christ, the God-man, is our mediator, re-deemer and physician (VII, 9–10). With such realizations a Christian has (in Bonaventure's eyes) completed the last stage of a metaphysics which is totally true.

But is it any longer philosophy, the starting point of which is empirical data and the instrument used is human reason? Has it not transcended the philosophical enterprise by the very fact that his faith prevents a Christian from making the threefold mistake a pagan Platonist makes concerning our human condition both here and hereafter? What reply can be made?

First of all, this third stage of transcendent metaphysics follows upon (and is likely influenced by) two earlier stages, as well as upon a general metaphysics: this last begins with data from the external and internal senses and with reason abstracting universal essences therefrom; transcendent metaphysics in its first stages starts with reasoning on the opposition between effects and causes and with experiencing the contrast between the presence and absence of perfections so as to know itself, angelic substances and divine exemplars and, finally, God as First Cause and Being. May not the fact that the third transcendent stage "follows upon" two earlier stages and a general metaphysics which Bonaventure considers to be philosophical be construed as indicating that at least to some extent it too is somehow philosophical? Especially is this somewhat plausible because the earlier transcendent stages result in (among other things) a soul's knowing *itself*, and the third stage has to do with human souls as moral agents. Surely they provide some empirical data which are valid and necessary for a theory of morality and salvation but which also must be corrected and supplemented by divinely revealed data.

Yet this correction and enrichment does not convert the third stage of transcendent metaphysics into theology as such, because the latter begins with articles of faith concerned with God, and it attempts to develop, establish and understand them. On the other hand, a metaphysician in the third stage of his science tries to understand human persons in their moral lives. He does so in an enterprise which initially was philosophical but for which reasoning and empirical data turn out to be insufficient (or even misleading) and must, to be true and adequate, be completed by belief in divine revelation on Adam's sin, resurrection of the body, Christ, grace, and so forth.

In the light of the previous paragraphs, then, transcendent metaphysics in its third stage is neither straight philosophy nor theology as such. But because it inherits a philosophical dimension from its earlier stages and yet depends to some degree on divinely revealed data, may one not legitimately call it "Christian philosophy"? The term is not used here as Etienne Gilson and Jacques Maritain apply it to Aquinas: for them faith cannot and should not enter into the content itself of philosophy.[72] Here, though, faith in divine revelation concerning human nature and destiny affects the very data itself upon which transcendent metaphysics builds—it enriches, rectifies and verifies what such a metaphysician holds regarding the human person and his attaining his ultimate end. In this sense, then, transcendent metaphysics in its third stage would be "Christian philosophy": it is that position on the nature of human beings which is attained by reason drawing upon empirical data that issue from such beings but that are supplemented, illumined and corrected in some areas by faith.

One reason Bonaventure (as I read him) allows faith to enter into the content of the third stage of transcendent metaphysics, which nonetheless continues to be philosophical, is that fully real or complete distinctions are rare in his *Weltanschauung*, wherein reality is light. God is supreme light; all creatures—angels, human souls, animals, plants, minerals—participate in the divine light in varying degrees and, thus, are also lights, arranged on descending levels of perfection. Human psychological processes—assent to divine revelation through faith, theological speculation through reasoning on that revelation, the nine philosophical sciences, which range from rhetoric at the bottom to metaphysics at the top (see paragraph above corresponding to note 18)—are all lights, too, as sharings in the divine light. But there is no separation or full distinction be-

---

[72] See E. Gilson, *The Spirit of Mediaeval Philosophy* (New York: Charles Scribner's Sons, 1940), pp. 35 and 37: "The content of Christian philosophy is that body of rational truths discovered, explored or simply safeguarded, thanks to the help that reason receives from revelation." Yet the supernatural must not descend as a constitutive element "into its texture, which would be a contradiction." J. Maritain, *An Essay on Christian Philosophy* (New York: Philosophical Library, 1955), p. 15: When viewed precisely in its nature rather than in the state in which it exists historically, "philosophy is wholly rational: no reasoning issuing from faith finds its way into its inner fabric; it derives intrinsically from reason and rational criticism alone; and its soundness as a philosophy is based entirely on experimental or intellectual evidence and on logical proof. From these considerations it follows that since the specification of philosophy hinges entirely on its formal object, and since this object is wholly of the rational order, philosophy considered in itself—whether in a pagan or Christian mind—depends on the same strictly natural or rational intrinsic criteria." See ch. 2 above.

tween (for instance) sunlight and the light of a candle set outdoors on a clear August day: although they differ, they fuse together and cannot be separated. So, too, with respect to God and creatures or the various kinds of mental processes: there is no separation, no full distinction, no rigid demarcation between light at its source (God) and in the rays of light going forth, which are individual creatures or various sciences. What is higher (God or faith or theology) differs but is not separate from what is lower (creatures or reason or philosophy) and vice versa. Hence, faith and reason, philosophy and theology differ, but reason is not separated from faith or philosophy from theology. In at least one case faith and metaphysics in its third stage combine, coalesce, cooperate to form a philosophy which is Christian.[73]

---

[73] On light as central to Bonaventure's thought see E. Gilson, *The Philosophy of St. Bonaventure*, ch. 9: "Inanimate Bodies. Light"; ch. 12: "Illumination of the Intellect"; ch. 13: "Moral Illumination." Also see John Quinn, *The Historical Constitution of St. Bonaventure's Philosophy*, pp. 241–61, 499–506 and *passim* (see "Index," p. 943); on Neoplatonism in Bonaventure see E. Cousins, *Coincidence of Opposites*, pp. 22–27 and *passim* (see "Index," p. 315).

On "theological metaphysics" (which perhaps corresponds somewhat to what I call "Christian philosophy") see Zachary Hayes, "Christology and Metaphysics in the Thought of Bonaventure" in D. Tracy (ed.), *Celebrating the Medieval Heritage*, pp. 82–96; E. Cousins, *Coincidence of Opposites*, pp. 10–15.

Like Bonaventure, Albert the Great also centers his position concerning God and creatures on light and is Neoplatonist in some areas—see ch. 15 below: "*Esse primum creatum* in Albert the Great's *Liber de Causis et Processu Universitatis*"; ch. 16 below: "Are Plotinus and Albertus Magnus Neoplatonists?" especially prgrs. corresponding to notes 52–77.

For additional information on Avicenna, on whom Bonaventure depends (see notes 31 and 63 above) for his conception of intellect and being, see Parviz Morewedge, *The "Metaphysica" of Avicenna: A Critical Translation-Commentary and Analysis* (New York: Columbia University Press, 1973, pp. 249–84 on intellect; pp. 15–16, 30–32, 300–302 in being (*hasti*).

II

Neoplatonism and Early Latin Authors

4

Plotinus' Conception of Neoplatonism

It seemed helpful to begin Part One on Christian Philosophy with a general overview of "philosophy." Accordingly, we start Part Two with a general consideration of Neoplatonism before examining particular topics and authors other than Plotinus in subsequent chapters.

Neoplatonism is a Greek philosophic doctrine (a) whose initial source is Plato (d. 347 B.C.), together with contributions from Aristotle (d. 321 B.C.) and the Stoics; (b) yet whose direct founder was Plotinus (A.D. 205–270); (c) which was prolonged by Porphyry (d. A.D. 301), Jamblichus (d. *ca.* A.D. 330), etc.; and (d) which in its pagan formulation terminated in Proclus (410–485). (e) Yet it also provided the answer to many speculative problems for such Christians as St. Augustine (354–430), Pseudo-Dionysius the Areopagite (perhaps late fifth century A.D.), John Scotus Erigena (ca. 810–878), Albert the Great (1206–1280), Meister Eckhart (1260–1327) and Nicholaus of Cusa (1401–1464), as well as for such Semitic writers as Avicenna (980–1037) and Avicebron (1021–1070). (f) It continued its influence upon such Italian Renaissance authors as George Gemistus Pleton (d. 1464), Marsilius Ficinus (1433–1499), John Pico della Mirandola (1463–1494), etc. (g) It is even matched by parallel doctrines in such modern philosophers as Jakob Böhme (1575–1624), Spinoza (1632–1677), and Hegel (1770–1831).

What, then, is this doctrine which had such a long and influential history? Let us trace its general outlines, and these primarily in Plotinus, because Neoplatonism is commonly identified with him and, moreover, his pagan successors did not radically change his basic insights into metaphysics.

The basic problem of Plotinus (205–270) was the nature of reality. What makes a thing real? What gives it value or significance? What makes it perfect? His answer is that reality is unity: to be real is to be one. Any item is real because of its unity, and a change into multiplicity is a fall into unreality. Moreover, since unity is reality, it follows that what is totally simple is the Prime Reality. Plotinus proposed a descending trinity of existents: the One, the Supreme Intelligence, and the Soul. The One is the absolutely first and highest Existent. Every other existent is less real because no other existent is sheer unity: each of them combines unity with multiplicity in varying degrees. The supreme Intelligence, together with the subordinate intelligences it contains, combines maximal unity with minimal multiplicity. In the Soul, as well as in souls subordinate to it, unity still predominates but plurality has grown stronger. But in the material universe plurality predominates because individual sensible things involve physical matter, which is sheer multiplicity and hence unreality. Consequently, existents fall into a pyramid of reality according to their degree of unity. At the apex is the One, at the base is the material world. In between, in ascending order, are souls and intelligences. "Being" for Plotinus begins only with the second level, that is, with intelligences, since "being" is equivalent to "one-many." Because the object of knowledge is being, the One, as transcending Being, also transcends knowledge. The One is incomprehensible to finite minds and even to Itself.

The identification of reality with unity has another relevant consequence. Because of its unity something is not only real but also perfect and powerful. As such, it automatically overflows and thereby produces other existents, which depend upon and tend back to their cause in love. Hence, something by reason of its unity is also a cause of others and, thereby, is good, for such is what "good" signifies when predicated of an item: a reality and unity insofar as it is both the source of subsequents and the term of their love and tendency. The result is that what is totally simple is also the supreme Good: as the ultimate source of absolutely all else and the universal goal of all appetition, the One is also the Good. Accordingly, the hierarchy stretching from the One to the material realm depicts degrees not only of reality but also of goodness, of capability and of causality.

In that hierarchy intelligences, souls and material things are other than the One because they entail multiplicity as well as unity. But they are not totally distinct from their primal Source; if they were, the oneness they do possess would vanish and, thereupon, their reality too. Hence, Plotinus' position is basically a monism, since all existents are radically of the nature of the One, and a pantheism, since the One is God. The supreme Intelligence and its contents are actually nothing more than the One-God as found on a lower level of multiplicity and dispersion, of less perfection and decreased power. The Soul, as well as the subordinate souls it contains, is little more than the Intelligence and its contents deployed on a still lower level where plurality, dispersion and incapacity are even greater. Individual material things are merely transient reflections of souls on the lowest level of all—namely, matter, which is multiplicity, unreality, sterility, impotence.

Obviously, Plotinus' monism has repercussions upon his view of human existents. A human soul becomes individual, unique and speciously autonomous by descending from the upper strata to the sensible universe and so "it comes to evil and so to nonbeing." Thus something other than true reality "has added itself to you, O soul, and you become less by the addition, for the addition did not come from real being . . . but from that which is not. You have become a particular person by the addition of nonbeing" (*Enneads*, VI, 5, [23], 12, 16 sqq.). In order to find the One-God and to become truly real again, the soul must put off that accretion of individuality and uniqueness. Or, to change the metaphor, it must "travel the opposite way, and so it comes not to be something else but to itself," to its true self. "Hence, when it is in itself alone and not in nonbeing, it is in the One, for everyone becomes oneself not as entity but beyond entity" by union with the Supremely Real, a union which is "a being out of oneself, a simplifying, a self-surrender, a pressing towards contact, a rest, a sustained thought directed to perfect conformity . . . deliverance from the things of this world, escape in solitude to the Solitary" (VI, 9, [9], 11, 35 sqq.). Plotinus' Neoplatonism thus refuses value to the unique, distinguishing characteristics of an individual human person. An individual, precisely in his individuality and actual existence, is unreal, valueless and unimportant.

Neoplatonism is nevertheless an attractive philosophy at other points. As an intelligible and comprehensive account of reality, it is a genuine system of metaphysics that is not an ontology but a henology, not a knowledge of being but of unity. It provides a system of ethics by pointing out the course of conduct by which the individual soul may attain happiness and fulfillment. It is religious in that it instills a reverent dedication to God, and it culminates in mysticism by counseling ultimate identification with him. Thus it is small wonder that Neoplatonism since its inception has exerted a profound, frequent and varied influence on the history of thought.

Christian writers were likewise not unaffected by this philosophy, although Neoplatonists were generally hostile to Christianity because of the doctrine of the Incarnation. Origen speaks of the generation of the Logos from the Father in the same manner as Plotinus describes the generation of the *Nous* from the One. Cyril of Alexandria sees a similarity of function between the Neoplatonist Soul and the Christian idea of the Holy Spirit. Much has also been written about the extent of Neoplatonism's influence on Augustine of Hippo (see ch. 7 below). Through him and Dionysius the pseudo-Areopagite, Neoplatonism profoundly influenced medieval mystics.

Before concluding, let us make two comments concerning Plotinus' view of God's causality and of divine infinity: He is not a creator, and He is infinite not as being but as transcending being. These arise in opposition to John M. Rist, *Plotinus: The Road to Reality* (Cambridge University Press, 1967), who apparently misinterprets what "creation" means and erroneously considers Plotinus' God to be "infinite being."

Rist speaks of many different existents as "creating." "The One," he affirms, "is the creator of all" (p. 27; see also pp. 26, 136, 163, 178). *Nous* creates Soul, which in turn creates matter (p. 90; see also p. 102). The World Soul "does not enter the world of sense and change, but produces and creates the world from above" (p. 113; see also pp. 114, 116, 120). The *logos*, as the outflow of the higher Soul and of *Nous*, is concerned with the creation and administration of the visible world (p. 96; see pp. 97, 102). Nature, which is a phase of the *logos*, actually creates the material world (p. 98). There is a kind of self-centeredness involved in the creative power of a particular soul: it is too weak to concentrate itself upon returning to its source and, thus, creates the world of matter (pp. 122–23; see also pp. 120, 134–35, 129, 165).

One interpretation of Rist's frequent use of the term is that he intends to use the word "create" merely as an equivalent of "produce." In the light of the Old and New Testaments, however, the term is (at least, should be) restricted to a special kind of productivity and, hence, has a technical meaning. When thus understood, creation is the sort of efficient causality in which the producer himself undergoes "no change in the act of producing, neither losing nor acquiring any perfection, and the implication is that he is both all-perfect and entirely free. Next, what is produced must be really distinct from the producer and, finally, must be wholly produced."[1] If such is an accurate understanding of creation, then *Nous*, Soul, *logos*, nature and individual soul are not creators for obvious reasons. Indeed, it is very questionable that the One himself is a creator, since his causality appears not to be efficient and, even if it were, it is not free. Moreover, it is disputable that his products are really and adequately distinct from him.[2] Accordingly, the One, as well as *Nous* and other existents in the Plotinian hierarchy, does not create if the verb is taken technically. At least Rist has not definitely established that it does.

But what of Plotinus' conception of infinity and God? When discussing what the Greek author meant when he "said that the One is 'beyond Being,'" Rist decides that "the *prima facie* meaning of the phrase 'beyond Being' should be 'infinite Being'" (p. 25). Later on in his discussion, Rist says that when Plotinus holds that the One is other than finite Beings, "what he is saying is that the One is a different kind of *being* from finite being, that is, that he is infinite *being*" (p. 35, italics added; also see pp. 30, 32, 33, 36). Rist's conclusion is, I submit, without textual warrant and is a rather grievous misunderstanding of Plotinus. The One does exist, and so do the *Nous* and its subsequents; but existence is not synonymous with being, which instead means unity-in-multiplicity. The One is sheer simplicity, whereas *Nous* and all else are mixtures (in varying degrees) of unity and multiplicity; hence, *Nous* and its subsequents are beings but the One transcends being and, thus, is nonbeing. To predicate "being" (unity-multiplicity) intrinsically of the One is to destroy his unique status. But is not the One infinite? Yes, for this reason: finitude is tightly linked with being; because the One transcends being, he also rises above finitude, limit, determination (they all amount to the same in Plotinus) and, thus, is infinite, unlimited, indeterminate. In fact, Plotinus may imply that the One is infinite in his very reality. But does not the last phrase indicate that he is infinite in being? No, because reality in Plotinus' view is not identical with being but with unity and goodness. Hence, if the One would be for Plotinus infinite in his very reality, it is precisely and necessarily because as absolute oneness he is nonbeing as

---

[1] See L. Sweeney, S.J., "Doctrine of Creation in the *Liber de Causis*," *Divine Infinity in Greek and Medieval Thought* (New York/Bern: Peter Lang Publishing, Inc., 1992), ch. 13, pp. 293–94.

[2] See L. Sweeney, S.J., *ibid.*, ch. 11: "Basic Principles in Plotinus' Philosophy," pp. 245–49.

beyond being and, thereby, beyond the determination and limit which he would encounter were he form and being.[3]

Conclusions

Plotinus did not, then, elaborate a metaphysics of being but of unity. His is not an "ontology" but an "henology." Accordingly, if the principle of contradiction is primally effective where being has primacy, it has been supplanted in the Plotinian universe by other more basic principles. These are at least the following: "Whatever is real, is one"; "Whatever is one, also is good"; and "Whatever is prior is of greater reality than that which is subsequent."

From the last of these seemingly issues Plotinus' doctrine of divine infinity, which is expressed in terms of what is prior to what is subsequent. In a threefold manner it illumines God's *rapport* with His products: He is without the determination proper to their way of being, His power is their endless source, His absolute supremacy sets Him above their comprehension.

Such, then, is the God who emerges from Plotinus' metaphysics. He is the One because supremely real. He is the Good because source and goal of all else. He is the First because pure unity, total power and complete autonomy. In union with Him each soul finds not only Him but also its own true self:

> When a soul goes down, it comes to evil and so to nonbeing but not to absolute nonbeing; and when it travels the opposite way, it comes not to something else but to itself; and so when it is not in anything else it is in nothing but itself. But when it is in itself alone and not in being, it is in That, for one becomes oneself not as entity but beyond entity by that intercourse (γίνεται γὰρ καὶ αὐτός τις οὐκ οὐσία ἀλλ' ἐπέκεινα οὐσίας ταύτῃ προσομιλεῖ). So if one sees that one's self has become this, one has it as a likeness of the Divine, and if one goes on from it, as image to original, one reaches the end of one's journey. And when a man falls from the vision, he wakes again the virtue in himself and considers himself in all his order and beauty, and is lightened and rises through virtue to Intelligence and through wisdom to the Divine. This is the life of gods and divine and blessed men—deliverance from the things of this world, a life which takes no delight in the things of this world, escape in solitude to the Solitary.[4]

---

[3] See L. Sweeney, S.J., *ibid.*, ch. 10: "Another Interpretation of Plotinus' *Enneads*, VI, 7, 32"; for my critique of Rist's book, see *Classical Journal* 64 [1969], 180–83.

[4] *Enneads*, VI, 9, 11, 35 sq.

5

The "Individual" in Plato, Plotinus and Aristotle

In his book *Modern Philosophers and Education*, Ralph Harper states that

both students and teachers are individuals. . . . The teacher should recognize the student . . . as an individual. . . . To see another man as an individual is to treat him as if he personally mattered, as if he was irreplaceable, as if he was different from all others. This requires a sensitivity to differences, a humor, and even a certain tenderness that one does not extend to a person insofar as one is thinking of him as of a type.[1]

---

[1] *Modern Philosophers and Education* (Chicago: National Society for Study of Education, 1955), p. 250. For "individual" in contemporary educational, social and political theory, which gives "priority in value or worth to the individual over all else," see R. W. Hall, *Plato and the Individual* (The Hague: Martinus Nijhoff, 1963), pp. 11–17, where he gives helpful references to writings of Ralph Barton Perry, F. A. Hayek, F. Knight, J. M. Clark, W. E. Hocking, C. L. Becker, Ernest Baker, H. Kelsen, R. H. Tawney, H. A. Myers and others.

For more directly and technically philosophical reflection on "individual," see these two articles of Jorge J. E. Gracia: "Boethius and the Problem of Individuation in the *Commentaries on the 'Isagoge,'*" *Atti del Congresso Internazionale di Studi Boeziani* (Roma: Herder, 1981), pp. 169–70, where he lists the six basic issues involved in the problem of individuation as the intention of individuality, the extension of individuality, the ontological status of individuality in the individual and its relation to the nature, the cause or principle of individuation, the discernibility of individuals, and the function of proper names and indexical terms; "Individuals as Instances," *Review of Metaphysics*

From those statements we realize that an individual is someone who personally matters, who is different from all others, who is irreplaceable. The last word should be taken seriously: an individual is someone who is so important, whose contribution to others so unique, whose influence so widespread that no one else can take his or her place: they are, literally, "irreplaceable." Names of several prominent people easily come to mind: Einstein in physics, Hegel in philosophy, George Balanchine in ballet, Johann Sebastian Bach in classical music, Abraham Lincoln in government, Martin Luther King, Jr., in civil rights, Mother Teresa of Calcutta in charitable works, Pope John Paul II in religion, Placido Domingo on the current opera scene, and so on.[2]

---

37 (1983), 37–59, where he dismisses five features traditionally assigned as constituents of individuality (distinction, division, identity, impredicability, indivisibility) as failing to serve as its necessary and sufficient conditions, which (he concludes) are best satisfied by conceiving individuality as incommunicability (to use the language of Boethius, Aquinas and other medievals) or noninstantiability (a contemporary word): "What is meant by saying that individuals are incommunicable [is the same as saying that it is impossible] that they be instantiated. Socrates, for example, cannot become instantiated in the way 'man' can. It is, then, non-instantiability that provides us with a precise understanding of individuality, since it is both a necessary and sufficient condition of it. Individuals cannot be instantiated as universals can. They are instances of instantiables and, therefore, non-instantiable themselves" (p. 57). Also see Gracia's book *Introduction to the Problem of Individuation in Early Middle Ages* (Washington, D.C.: Catholic University of America Press, 1984), pp. 17–63.

Also see Karl R. Popper, "Symposium: The Principle of Individuation," *Proceedings of Aristotelian Society for the Systematic Study of Philosophy*, supplementary vol. 27 (1953), 97–120; P. F. Strawson, *Individuals: An Essay in Descriptive Metaphysics* (London: Methuen, 1965), pp. 23 sqq., 227 sqq. One also may profitably consult the chapters in Michael J. Loux (ed.), *Universals and Particulars: Readings in Ontology* (Garden City, N.Y.: Doubleday, 1970), especially Loux's own two chapters, "The Problem of Universals" (pp. 3–15) and "Particulars and Their Individuation" (pp. 189–203), as well as David Higgins, "The Individuation of Things and Places" (pp. 307–335); also the chapters in Milton K. Munitz (ed.), *Identity and Individuation* (New York University Press, 1971), especially Munitz's "Introduction" (pp. iii–viii) and H. Hiz, "On the Abstractness of Individual" (pp. 251–61); B. J. Martine, *Individuals and Individuality* (Albany, N.Y.: SUNY Press, 1984). For secondary literature on Aristotle's position on "individual," see below, Appendix D.

[2] Such people are outstanding (and thus unique) in some sort of excellence, but one may easily list others outstanding in evil—Hitler, Stalin, Mao Tse-Tung, Fidel Castro, Idi Amin, Ayatollah Khomeini, Muammar Qaddafi, Jim Jones of Guyana, Saddam Hussein.

But individuality is not to be restricted to prominent people. It may and should, if taken seriously, be applied to every human existent because each one of us differs from all others (parents, spouses, children, students, neighbors, friends), each one of us is unique and, therefore, each is *irreplaceable*: absolutely no one is identical with me, no one else is me, no one is numerically the same. The twofold result is that no one can fill my shoes or replace me and, second, that because I am unique and I am, I have a right to be. This last result can perhaps be best gathered from a description a young lady gave of her experience when confronted with the fact that she had been an illegitimate child.

I remember walking that day under the elevated tracks in a slum area, feeling the thought, "I am an illegitimate child." I recall the sweat pouring forth in my anguish in trying to accept that fact. Then I understood what it must feel like to accept, "I am a Negro in the midst of privileged whites," or "I am blind in the midst of people who see." Later on that night I woke up and it came to me this way, "I accept the fact that I am an illegitimate child." But "I am not a child anymore." So it is, "I am illegitimate." That is not so either: "I was born illegiti- mate." Then what is left? What is left is this, "*I Am.*" This *act* of contact and acceptance with "I am," once gotten hold of, gave me (what I think was for me the first time) the experience "Since I Am, I have the right to be."[3]

From such a description one realizes that viewing an individual as he or she who is literally "irreplaceable" issues into our contem- porary awareness of the legitimate claim everyone has to civil and personal rights in all fields, of freedom as our precious and inalien- able property.[4]

The question then arises, Whence came this appealing notion of individuality? What is its source within the history of ideas? Cer- tainly one major origin is Christianity, as even its enemies recog-

---

[3] See Rollo May, *Existence, A New Dimension in Psychiatry and Psychology* (New York: Basic Books, 1958), p. 43. The girl continues her account by turn- ing the tables on Descartes: "[My experience of being] is my saying to Descartes, 'I am; therefore I think, I feel, I do.'"

[4] Such awareness of rights and freedoms must, of course, be balanced by awareness of the responsibilities they also entail. Lack of such concern for the rights of others would produce a "Me-Generation" with tendencies to ma- nipulate, bully or, even, enslave others.

nize. According to Karl Marx, "Political democracy is Christian in the sense that man, not merely one man but every man, is there considered a sovereign being, a supreme being. . . . Creations of fantasy, dreams, the postulates of Christianity, the sovereignty of man— . . . all these become, in democracy, the tangible and present reality, secular maxims."[5] Or Adolf Hitler: "To the Christian doctrine of the infinite significance of the individual human soul . . . I oppose with icy clarity the saving doctrine of the nothingness and insignificance of the human being."[6]

To confirm the accuracy of Marx's and Hitler's identification of Christianity as the origin of the realization that each human individual is significant and has primacy, one need (for our present purposes) only turn to two sources, the first of which is Søren Kierkegaard, the Danish nineteenth-century religious and philosophical author. In 1850 he wrote this entry in his diary: "In the eyes of God, the infinite spirit, all the millions that have lived and now live do not make a crowd: He only sees each individual." Two years earlier (1848): "Each human being has infinite reality."[7] Of course Kierkegaard was merely echoing the letter and spirit of the Judeo-Christian Scriptures. Take as an example *Psalm* 139:1 sqq.:

O Lord, you have probed me and you know me;
    you know when I sit and when I stand;
    you understand my thoughts from afar.
My journeys and my rest you scrutinize;
    with all my ways you are familiar.
Even before a word is on my tongue,
    behold, O Lord, you know the whole of it.
Behind me and before, you hem me in
    and rest your hand upon me.

[And why do you know me so well, O Lord?]

Truly you have formed my inmost being;
    you knit me in my mother's womb. . . .

---

[5] "On the Jewish Question," in R. C. Tucker (ed.), *Marx-Engels Reader*, 2d ed. (New York: W. W. Norton, 1978), p. 39. German text: *Karl Marx-Friedrich Engels Werke*, Band 1 (Berlin: Dietz Verlag, 1970), pp. 360–61.

[6] Quoted by Hermann Rauschning, *The Voice of Destruction* (New York: G. P. Putnam's Sons, 1940), p. 25.

[7] See G. M. Anderson (trans.) and P. P. Rohde (ed.), *The Diary of Søren Kierkegaard* (New York: Philosophical Library, 1960), pp. 106 and 103.

My soul also you knew full well;
  nor was my frame unknown to you
  when I was made in secret,
  when I was fashioned in the depths of the earth.
Your eyes have seen my actions;
  in your book they are all written;
  my days were limited before one of them existed.

Or *Psalm* 147:1, 3 and 4:

Praise the Lord, for he is good;
  sing praise to our God, for he is gracious. . . .
He heals the brokenhearted
  and binds up their wounds.
He tells the number of the stars;
  he calls each by name.[8]

The same message is given in Paul, Mark, Matthew, Luke and John, who speak of each individual lily or sparrow or human person as of value in and of itself. God the Son became incarnate in history as an individual human existent that He might save individual men and women. God freely causes all individual creatures each to exist and, as the efficient and creative cause, is thereby present to them but also is really distinct from them individually (hence, His simultaneous immanence and transcendence). Certainly, then, Judaism and Christianity are at least one (and perhaps the most important) root of our contemporary conception of what constitutes the individuality of each human being and our dedication to safeguarding it as his or her most precious commodity.[9] But does

---

[8] *Isaiah* 43:1 sqq. expresses similar sentiments *re* Jacob and Israel as nations: "Thus says the Lord, who created you, O Jacob, and formed you, O Israel: fear not, for I have redeemed you; I have called you by name: you are mine. When you pass through the water, I will be with you. . . . I will say to the north and to the south: . . . 'Bring back my sons from afar and my daughters from the ends of the earth: everyone who is named as mine, whom I created for my glory, whom I formed and made.'"

A typical example from St. Paul *re* Christ's concern for each human individual, is *Galatians* 2:20: "Christ is living in me. I still live my human life, but it is a life of faith in the Son of God, who loved me and gave himself for me."

[9] Besides the Judaic and Christian Scriptures another ultimate source of contemporary individualism is the stress put on "person" and "supposit" *vs.* "essence" and "nature" in early ecumenical councils and creeds of the Church. For documentation see L. Sweeney, S.J., *Authentic Metaphysics in an Age of Un-*

it arise from any other sources? What of the ancient Greek philosophers, who commonly are taken as ancestors of Western civilization and patterns of thought?[10]

Such is the precise topic of this chapter: Plato, Plotinus and Aristotle on the "individual."

Plato

On first reflection one would be inclined to answer affirmatively the question of whether Plato (428–347 B.C.) is a source of our Western conception of individuality. Yes, Plato has contributed to the primacy and value currently given to individual human existence—did he not conclude that the human soul, even when in a body, transcends the body? that it is thereby shown to be spiritual and immortal? that its proper activity is intellection? that it is capable of contemplating the highest realities (the Forms or Essences) and, in fact, exists with them prior to entering the body? Accordingly, a human soul is valuable as an apt companion of the

---

reality, 2d ed. [hereafter: *AM*] (New York/Bern: Peter Lang Publishing, Inc., 1993), pp. 181–87. Also see M. F. X. Millar, S.J., "The History and Development of the Democratic Theory of Government in Christian Tradition," in *The State and the Church* (New York: Macmillan Publishing Co., Inc., 1924), pp. 99–114; Caroline Walker Bynum, "Did the Twelfth Century Discover the Individual?" in *Journal of Ecclesiastical History* 31 (1980), 1–17 (with references to studies by W. K. Ferguson, W. Ullmann, P. Dronke, R. Hanning, R. W. Southern, John Senton, Peter Brown, Lynn White, Andre Wilmart, C. M. Radding); Colin Morris, *The Discovery of the Individual 1050–1200* (Toronto University Press, 1987).

[10] See R. S. Brumbaugh, *Philosophers of Greece* (New York: Thomas Y. Crowell Co., 1964), p. 2: "We are still seeing the world in an ancient Greek way and . . . there is a gain in seeing clearly that [their ideas] are now so built into our thinking that we are unaware of them"; F. Copleston, *A History of Philosophy*, vol. 1 (London: Burns Oates and Washbourne, 1951), p. 10: "As Hegel says, 'the name of Greece strikes home to the hearts of men of education in Europe.' No one would attempt to deny that the Greeks left an imperishable legacy of literature and art to our European world, and the same is true in regard to philosophic speculation"; Joseph Owens, *A History of Ancient Western Philosophy* (New York: Appleton-Century-Crofts, 1959), p. ix: In watching through the writings of the Greek philosophers "the themes of Western philosophy as they were progressively given their definite form, in reliving the problems and solutions as they actually arose, the student has as it were an experimental and laboratory introduction to European thought."

Forms, it is powerful, it transcends matter.[11] On the strength of
such elevated positions he was warmly applauded and his doctrine often adopted from his death in 347 B.C. to the mid-thirties of
our own century.[12]

Political and Social Doctrines

But what happened then? The rise of dictators (Hitler, Mussolini,
Stalin), the suppression of freedoms and the active persecution of
Jews and other minorities deemed undesirable in their totalitarian
regimes caused some scholars to reassess Plato's dialogues, especially those in which he developed his political and social positions.
They began to ask whether Plato's philosopher-king in the *Republic*
was not equivalent to a twentieth-century dictator, whether his
seemingly rigid threefold classification of citizens as guardians
(from whom philosopher-kings would alone be chosen), military
personnel and artisans (slaves were excluded even from this third
and lowest class) did not anticipate the regimentation marking
contemporary totalitarian states, how his "communism" (e.g., everything, including wives and children, is to be held in common)
differs from the Soviet and other socialist versions.[13] Manifestly, if

---

[11] For Plato's exalted conception of a human soul as by nature transcending
matter and consorting with Forms through contemplation before entering this
physical world, see for instance *Phaedo*, 65D–E, 74A–77A, 78D–79D; *Phaedrus*,
246A–248A; *Symposium*, 210E sqq.

[12] For a history of the almost universally favorable reaction to Plato up to
the 1930s, see Frantisek Novotny's valuable book *The Posthumous Life of Plato*
(The Hague: Martinus Nijhoff, 1977); E. M. Manasse, "Plato and French Revolution," *International Studies in Philosophy* 9 (1977), 93–110.

[13] For Plato's political theory see *Republic*, Books II–V, VII–IX; for helpful
commentaries see N. R. Murphy, *The Interpretation of Plato's "Republic"* (Oxford
University Press, 1951); R. C. Cross and A. D. Woozley, *Plato's "Republic": A
Philosophical Commentary* (London: Macmillan, 1970); R. K. Sprague, *Plato's
Philosopher-King* (Columbia, S.C.: University of South Carolina Press, 1976),
ch. 6; Nicholas P. White, *A Companion to Plato's "Republic"* (Indianapolis:
Hackett, 1979); Julia Annas, *An Introduction to Plato's "Republic"* (Oxford: Clar-
endon Press, 1981), esp. ch. 10, pp. 170–89; (select bibliography, pp. 188–89);
Jacqueline Bordes, *Politeia dan la pensée grecque jusqu'à Aristote* (Paris: "Belles
Lettres," 1982); David Grene, *Man in His Pride: Study in Political Philosophy of
Thucydides and Plato* (University of Chicago Press, 1950); D. Hellwig, *Adikia in
Platons Poiteia. Interpretation zu den Büchern VII und IX* (Amsterdam: Gruner,
1980); T. Irwin, *Plato's Moral Theory. The Early Middle Dialogues* (Oxford:
Clarendon Press, 1977); John Rist, *Human Value: Study in Ancient Philosophical
Ethics* (Leiden: Brill, 1982), ch. 7: "Society and the State," pp. 84–98.

this reassessment of Plato's dialogues should prove accurate, Plato can hardly be the father of our twentieth-century respect for individual persons but rather of the exact opposite attitude.

What scholars initiated this important reevaluation? In 1934 Warner Fite, a professor of moral philosophy at Princeton University, published *The Platonic Legend* (New York: Charles Scribner's Sons, 1934), devoted to destroying "'the legend of Plato . . . [as] the consummate artist, the shrewd interpreter of human nature, the stern and lofty moralist, and even of Plato the good Christian.'"[14] This destruction rests upon several denials, of which the following instances are enlightening. The *Republic* does not (in Fite's opinion) set forth "the ideal of maximal happiness and self-development for all the citizens" but only for "a small privileged leisure class, say, 10 percent of the population, guided by the arrogant and esoteric wisdom of a still smaller minority within this, 1 percent, at the cost of the exertion and sacrifice of the despised and cynically befooled 90 percent of the citizens. The goal of all this striving is not the humane fullness of a richly cultural existence, which his native Athens could have taught him to love; it is the largely Spartan ideal of a closely regimented state, a stratified caste society, its members carefully bred to type, their quality ruthlessly maintained by infanticide; it is organized largely for the practice of the military virtues, if not for conquest." Second, in the *Republic* and elsewhere Plato does not at all anticipate "the Christian, Kantian, democratic sense of the value and dignity of the individual. He fails to discern the very nature of personality, as we conceive it, and the conditions for the development of genuine moral freedom. Even his philosopher-kings are impersonal beings; the mass of the citizens are creatures guided only by habit and fear of consequences."[15]

Five years after Fite's book appeared, R. H. S. Crossman of Oxford University published *Plato Today* (New York: Oxford University Press, 1939), where the Greek philosopher is shown in the *Re-*

---

[14] In my analysis of Fite, as well as subsequently of Crossman and Popper, I am drawing upon R. B. Levinson, *In Defense of Plato* (Cambridge: Harvard University Press, 1953). This book gives accurate and clear surveys of their positions, as one can determine from studying their own books. Sentences from Levinson quoted within double quotation marks are from his book (as is the case with the quotation referred to by n. 14); sentences within single quotation marks are from Fite's volume (p. 271) but as quoted by Levinson (p. 10).

[15] Levinson, *In Defense of Plato*, pp. 10–11.

public to be "wrong, both for his times and for ours, at several points of his political program." He built an institutional structure of the ideal city intended to be immediately imposed upon actual communities of ordinary mortals; in reorganizing these communities he would assign some inhabitants hereditary power, others permanent subordination and this in line solely with aristocratic class prejudice; he would have sanctioned the use of repellent weapons of political power against dissidents.[16] And underlying Plato's failure to benefit in any way the Greek world of his time and the uselessness of his message in general are three cardinal errors: his despair of the potentialities of the common man; his mistaken belief that a just government can be established by revolution; and his conviction that final truth can be discovered and, once discovered, that freedom of thought ought to be suppressed. Because of Crossman's own faith in the power of reason and "the infinite possibility of self-development of every man," he counseled challenging and, if need be, altering any governmental form and breaking down every orthodoxy. And in this endeavor today "'it is Socrates, not Plato, whom we need.'"[17]

Socrates, too, is championed by Karl A. Popper, *The Open Society and Its Enemies* (London: George Rutledge, 1945 and 1957; Princeton University Press, 1950), where the initial words of the title refer to the Athenian democracy of the latter part of the fifth century—the "open society" which was marked by egalitarian individualism and humanitarianism and promoted by Pericles, Herodotus, Protagoras and other sophists and, especially, Socrates, "perhaps the greatest individualist of all times."[18] In contrast was the society cherished by the "oligarchic Spartophiles, who, by their disloyalty, sabotage, and on occasion outright treason, encompassed the ruin of their native city, the defeat of Athens by Sparta in 404 B.C., which only a revived democracy was able partially to make good." Where did Plato stand in relationship to that democracy? He reacted against it.

Scion of an aristocratic family with strong oligarchic affiliations, he was early indoctrinated with the love of Sparta, the worst features of which, un-Athenian infanticide and harsh-

---

[16] *Ibid.*, pp. 13–14.

[17] *Ibid.*, p. 16, where Levinson is quoting Crossman (p. 308 in the first edition but p. 187 in the second edition of 1959 and reprinted in 1971).

[18] *Ibid.*, p. 17.

ness to slaves and underlings, awakened in him no repug-
nance. The noble achievements of his native Athens he mocked
and denied. Though brought for a time by the powerful moral
magnetism of Socrates under the sway of humanitarian, individualist sentiments, he was unable to keep the faith. Frus-
trated by the turn of political affairs, he found no outlet in the
world of action for those consuming ambitions which remained
with him to the end. The dark struggle in Plato's soul between
the Socratic faith and his growing treason to its principles
accounts for the "spell of Plato," lending hitherto unexplained
fascination to his writings. For the record of Plato's thought, as
Popper reads it, is a story of continuous degradation, in which
the noble Socratic gospel, as Plato has sympathetically reported it in the *Apology*, the *Crito* and others of the earlier dialogues, is gradually and treasonably perverted, against the
inner protest of Plato's better self, into the poisonous crypto-
totalitarianism of the *Republic* with its scorn for all that the real
Socrates had held dear and its dishonest attribution to him of a
dogmatic authoritarianism which blasphemed the memory of
the modest and cautious doubter; finally it is transformed into
the "theory of inquisition" elaborated in the *Laws*, a polity in
which Socrates would, with Plato's full approval, have met the
death penalty for presuming to exercise the freedom of rational inquiry.[19]

Obviously, Popper stresses what he believes to be "the uncom-
promising totalitarian character of Plato's thought."[20] This emphasis called forth strong and numerous reactions, as one can judge by
the fact that Harold Cherniss lists twenty articles, reviews or books.[21]
Prominent among the latter is a volume which has already furnished us accurate surveys of Fite, Crossman and Popper himself:
Ronald B. Levinson, *In Defense of Plato* (Cambridge: Harvard University Press, 1953). Hoping to "meet the new charges [those of
Popper *et al.*] on their own grounds, accept of the indictment [of
Plato] what in conscience they [the friends of Plato] must, repel
what in honor they can," Levinson devotes eight long chapters to
those charges, the last of which asks an especially noteworthy

---

[19] *Ibid.*, p. 18.
[20] *Ibid.*, p. 16.
[21] "Plato (1950–57)," *Lustrum* 4 (1959), 18–21.

question: "Was Plato a Totalitarian?" In replying he collects the ten qualities Popper and others consider to constitute totalitarianism:

1. "historicism" or the doctrine that historical events are determined by inexorable laws;
2. Spartanism, the exaltation and imitation of Spartan institutions and ideals;
3. "holism" or the belief that the interest of the group is the criterion of morality and that it entirely supersedes the welfare of the individual;
4. the doctrine of racial superiority;
5. advocacy of the direction of the state by a specially trained and disciplined ruling class;
6. the "closing" of the society or the attempt to stabilize the state and to give security and peace to its members by predetermining all their choices and beliefs;
7. readiness to employ violence to achieve radical reforms;
8. inhumanity;
9. the recommendation of "autarky" [= commercial self-sufficiency or independence] to keep out the liberalizing effect of trade;
10. militarism, exercised against neighboring states, employed to unify the people and to prevent the entry of liberal beliefs from outside sources.[22]

Interestingly enough, Levinson eliminates five of those qualities (nos. 1, 4, 7, 9 and 10) from Platonic doctrine. "Plato was no historicist of any kind, no racialist—he felt indeed greater piety for those of kindred blood, but of racial scorn he was entirely free. He was scrupulous in disavowing violence, was in no modern sense an advocate of autarky, and was far rather a peace-lover than a militarist."[23] But somewhat surprising in a book the title of which is *In Defense of Plato* is the fact that its author concedes that the other five qualities do fit Plato to some extent at least: Plato did propose to "close" his society "insofar as this denotes regimentation of the ordinary citizens. . . . Plato's state, by depriving most of its citizens of independent moral action and freedom of belief, would in fact harm and diminish them as human beings"; also, he "would put an elite in control of his *Republic*, . . . he is entirely too harsh in the

[22] *In Defense of Plato*, p. 504.
[23] *Ibid.*, p. 572.

punishments imposed upon offending slaves in the *Laws*, and . . . he admires Sparta, approving in particular its endeavor to attain at least a part of virtue."[24]

Those concessions indicate that Plato's political and social theories do not give primacy to every individual person precisely qua individual in our contemporary sense and hence cannot be its direct source. As Frantisek Novotný, *The Posthumous Life of Plato* (The Hague: Nijhoff, 1977) observes, defenses such as Levinson's "showed that Popper did not take sufficient account of the historical and philosophical conditions of the constitution proposed by Plato. However, they were not able to refute Popper's main assertion that Plato's system is totalitarian."[25]

Is Novotný's assessment of Plato too harsh? It certainly is in the light of Robert William Hall's book *Plato and the Individual* (The Hague: Nijhoff, 1963).[26] There Hall contends that the three traits which constitute contemporary individualism—namely, the supremacy of each individual, freedom and equality—are present in Plato's theory of the individual (p. 3)—a contention which obviously opposes Novotny's evaluation, as well as Popper's, Crossman's and Fite's.[27] How does Hall establish his view? By tracing

---

[24] *Ibid.*, p. 571. But see next paragraph, where Levinson adds qualifications that those five qualities do not fully fit Plato. "We have shown that Plato sponsored and encouraged freedom of inquiry for the philosopher kings of the *Republic*, and for their nearest equivalents in the city of the *Laws*, and that he contemplated change in the direction of improvement in both communities; that he never limited the criterion of morality to state interest or upheld the amoral state, and that he intended the benefit of every citizen; that he despised the oppression practiced by the Spartans, the narrowness of their ideal, and the brutalizing effect of their education; that his elite was to be unified by no haughty scorn of its human cattle, his philosopher kings to be no breeder-shamans; that most of his particular inhumanities were shared with him by other enlightened Greeks of his day, while his own humanity vastly exceeded theirs in depth and in ideality of aim."

[25] Novotny, p. 543. For more general criticism see J. Agassi, *The Philosopher's Apprentice: In Karl Popper's Workshop* (Amsterdam: Rodopi, 1993)

[26] Other relevant publications by Hall are "Justice and the Individual in the *Republic*," *Phronesis* 4 (1959), 149–58; "Plato's Theory of Justice in the *Republic*," *Buckwell Review* 15 (1967), 59–69; "Plato's Just Man: Thoughts on Strauss' Plato," *New Scholasticism* 42 (1968), 202–25; "The Just and Happy Man of the *Republic*: Fact or Fancy?" *Journal of History of Philosophy* 9 (1971), 147–58; "Egalitarianism and Justice in the *Republic*," *Apeiron* 6 (1972), 7–19; "Plato's Political Analogy. Fallacy or Analogy?" *Journal of History of Philosophy* 12 (1974), 419–35.

[27] Hall lists Popper but not Fite or Crossman in his bibliography. In his book itself he refers only once to Popper and this in a footnote on p. 21 con-

Plato's ethical thought as it developed from its initial Socratic stage, expressed in dialogues up to the *Phaedo*, to its later and typically Platonic stage, expressed in the *Republic* and subsequent dialogues (e.g., *Phaedrus, Timaeus, Laws*).[28] Between the earlier and later dialogues there is a contrast between aristocratic and "demotic" ethics:

(1) only philosophers can achieve genuine morality and happiness, with others capable only of a "second best" sort *versus* a morality which is open to everyone inasmuch as all individuals can attain the excellences (*aretai*) proper to their stations and, thereby, gain happiness and a state of well-being (p. 149);

(2) the utilitarianism of Socrates (wherein morally good deeds are valuable because of their consequences solely) *versus* Plato's own nonutilitarian conception (wherein good deeds and the excellences they produce are valuable in themselves as inward conditions of the soul);

(3) the relatively undeveloped conception of soul in the *Phaedo versus* the more mature view in later dialogues of soul as a differentiated unity—its rational part entails the twofold faculty of reasoning properly so called (by which it attains intellection) and of opinion, plus the pleasures, desires and other affections proper to it (pp. 152, 153, 161–62).[29]

This interpretation of soul as a differentiated unity is especially significant because it furnishes the proper conditions under which "all men can achieve excellence of soul without knowledge of the forms."

The duty imposed on the philosophers in the *Republic* to rule the *polis* is so that its citizens may acquire justice, contrasts sharply with the self-imposed isolation of the philosopher in the *Phaedo*. This perhaps suggests Plato's intent to extend the scope of the application of justice as far as possible. The *Republic* retains that aspect of *aretê* which frees the body from all unnecessary pleasures and desires, and which places the remaining desires under the control of reason. It does reject the

---

cerning the latter's belief that a significant movement of abolishing slavery existed in Athens during Plato's time—a belief Hall does not accept.

[28] On the *Phaedo* as transitional between the two stages see *Plato and the Individual*, pp. 135–38.

[29] Soul as a differentiated unity is not identical with soul as tripartite (intellectual, spirited, appetitive), since each of these parts can be such a unity—see *ibid.*, pp. 144, 148–50.

knowledge of the forms as a *sine qua non* of *aretê* (which in the
Republic is justice).

Plato's theory of the individual emerges clearly here: any
man by nature potentially can acquire justice. By living within
the ideal *polis* of the *Republic* he himself can acquire his own
perfection or *aretê*. The philosopher ruler may help the individual by providing the proper environment and education,
but the actual acquisition of justice is the individual's own task
and responsibility (p. 162).

In brief: although the philosophers as craftsmen may help individuals to acquire the excellence proper to their states of life, still
"only the individual citizen himself can bring about and preserve
the just condition of the soul. . . . In the *Republic* every man by nature can acquire justice, and under the proper conditions of society
can in fact acquire it without knowledge of the forms, and such
justice constitutes the true worth of every individual" (p. 164). The
result is that Plato has necessarily extended "his analysis of the two
fundamental concepts of ethics, the right and the good, to all individuals." Although "he never did single out these two concepts as
the fundamental principles of ethics, as would have to be the case
today, nonetheless they clearly appear in his thought." Thus he is
"one of the first significant ethical thinkers" and deserves to be
ranked with Hume and Kant, who also "agree on the universal . . .
extension of these concepts" of right and good, of justice and happiness to all individual moral agents (p. 2).

Is Hall's eloquent exegesis of Plato accurate? There is no easy
answer. If moral goodness consists in the state of well-being which
is proportionate to an individual's function within the state and
which issues not from outside imposition but from his own free
choices, then philosophers and other members of the guardian
class of citizens, military people and artisans can each have
excellences uniquely their own and thus be valuable in their very
moral individuality. But that is a big "if." As reviewers have pointed
out, the function of an individual within a state is determined by
the class (guardian, military, artisan) within which he fits,[30] and the

---

[30] J. Brunschvig, *Revue de Metaphysique et de Morale* 72 (1967), 382. For other
informative reviews see John P. Anton, *Journal of History of Philosophy* 3 (1968),
260–61; Arthur W. H. Adkins, *Classical Review* 16 (1966), 28–31; Helmut Kuhn,
Gnomon 39 (1967), 6–13. Nowhere in his book does Hall face the ten qualities
which Levinson lists as characteristics of totalitarianism and some of which

good of the state takes precedence over his individual welfare.[31] Moreover, Plato did not elaborate a doctrine of freedom of choice— at least not nearly as explicitly or thoroughly as Hall's position on Platonic individualism needs.[32] Finally, even Hall admits that, un-

---

he finds within Plato's political theory (see prgr. corresponding to n. 22 above).

In the year after Hall's book appeared, another book with the same title was published: H. O. Rankin, *Plato and the Individual* (London: Methuen, 1966). It was not well received by reviewers (and justifiably so)—see W. K. C. Guthrie, *Philosophy* 40 (1965), 362–63; T. Gould, *Classical World* 59 (1965), 84; A. Ralls, *Philosophical Quarterly* 16 (1966), 271–72. Yet it does make the point that "there is no really comprehensive or completely satisfactory answer to Popper's criticism. Plato and the Greeks in general were historicists in their outlook on the world and in their view of man" (*Plato and the Individual*, p. 131). But even though "Popper protested that the whole tissue of Plato's social thinking was totalitarian," one must remember "that by modern standards, all ancient city-states had rather a totalitarian flavour. We should thus be careful about calling them totalitarian within the context of their own times" (*ibid.*, p. 137 and n. 3).

For other comments on Crossman and Popper see G. J. De Vries, *Antisthenes Redivivus: Popper's Attack on Plato* (Amsterdam: North-Holland Publishing Co., 1952); T. L. Thorson (ed.), *Plato: Totalitarian or Democrat?* (Englewood Cliffs, N.J.: Prentice Hall, 1963); W. K. C. Guthrie, *Twentieth-Century Approaches to Plato* (University of Cincinnati Press, 1963), pp. 14–17; Renford Bambrough (ed.), *Plato, Popper and Politics* (Cambridge University Press, 1967); idem, "Plato's Modern Friends and Enemies," *Philosophy* 37 (1962), 97–113; Richard Robinson, "Dr. Popper's Defence of Democracy," in *Essays in Greek Philosophy* (Oxford: Clarendon Press, 1969), pp. 74–99; J. B. Skemp, *Plato's Philosophy of History* (Washington: University Press of America, 1981), pp. 199–209; Richard Kraut, *Socrates and the States* (Princeton University Press, 1984).

[31] Even philosophers would be forced to return to the cave that they may care for and govern those incapable of philosophical contemplation of the Good—see *Republic*, 519C–520D. See T. C. Brickhouse, "The Paradox of the Philosopher's Role," *Apeiron* 15 (1981), 1–9.

[32] For Ludwig Koenen the thought in Homer, Hesiod and Aeschylus that "is a cornerstone of the intellectual tradition which led to the development of Western technology, civilization and culture" is that "man is the master of his fate." The Greeks generally "sought to explain the human condition as situated between the poles of fate and self-determination" ("Augustine and Manichaeism in Light of the Cologne Mani Codex," *Illinois Classical Studies* 3 [1978], 154 and 155). Also see A. Jannone, "Sur les notions *ekousion* et *akousion* dans la morale platonicienne," *Diotima* 2 (1974), 57–71.

There are some indications, however brief and implicit, that Plato gave a degree of self-determination to human existents—for instance see *Timaeus*, 41E sqq., where the Craftsman is disclosing the laws of Destiny to the newly

like Hume and Kant, Plato did not single out the right and good as fundamental concepts of ethics (see p. 2). Hence, if he is a significant ethical thinker, his significance does not consist in them but in notions proper to his own era and thought: excellences valued for the stability and prosperity they produced (hence, utilitarian in nature)[33] within a *polis* where every citizen found an assigned place and role and became just, temperate and courageous by participating in the Forms of Justice, Temperance and Courage and, ultimately, the Form of the Good but only through the philosopher-king.[34] He alone participated in such forms immediately since he alone knew the Forms firsthand. Only he contemplated them directly and thereafter communicated to the citizens below the wisdom so gained, which made him wise and virtuous primarily and them secondarily and derivatively. They could, indeed, be morally

---

produced but as yet unincarnate souls. If they should master the passions (sensations, desires, pleasure and pain, fear, anger) encountered when implanted in bodies, they would live in righteousness; but if they were mastered by them, in unrighteousness (42B). Moreover, the sorts of lives they would lead while in bodies (e.g., as men, women, various sorts of beasts) would depend upon themselves; they would escape such transmigration only if and when each of them, "letting the revolution of the Same and uniform within himself draw into its train all that turmoil of fire and water and air and earth that had later grown about it, should control its irrational turbulence by reason and return once more to the form of his first and best condition" 42B–D). These disclosures the Craftsman made that "he might be guiltless of the future wickedness of anyone of them." He then let the astral souls "mould mortal bodies" and fashion the spirited and appetitive parts of the soul so that they might "govern and guide the mortal existent to the best of their powers, save insofar as it should be a cause of evil to itself" (*kakôn . . . heautô aition;* 42D–E).

Rather obviously, Plato's considering a person to be the cause of evil and of good to himself, to be capable of mastering his passions and of controlling irrational turbulence, of determining the level on which he would lead his life intimates some awareness of human existents as somehow free. But such intimations need much more explicit and prolonged development before they can support Hall's interpretation of Plato as a proponent of individualism. According to Hall "freedom in Platonic thought is primarily moral freedom," which "consists in the self-determination of the immortal part of the soul, *to logistikon*. It signifies that the soul is determined not by the appetites and spirit but by reason." Only secondarily and with limitations would a citizen in Plato's ideal state enjoy economic freedom, political freedom and freedom of action and thought—see *Plato and the Individual,* pp. 216–18.

[33] See A. W. H. Adkins, *Classical Review,* p. 29.

[34] On Plato's doctrine of the Good, see Appendix A below.

good as members of such a political structure but not independently, not on their own, not precisely as individuals.

Accordingly, when Plato's political and social theories are reinserted into the metaphysics which produced them and in which subsistent Forms are primary realities and individual existents (human souls included) are real only to the extent they transiently participate in these Forms, one realizes that Plato's ethic does not anticipate current individualism so much as contemporary socialism. Let us reflect, then, upon his metaphysical doctrine so as to perhaps understand better his attitude on the individual as such.[35]

Metaphysics

In our interpretation metaphysics is the knowledge of the real as real;[36] but to be real for Plato is to be immutable; therefore, Platonic metaphysics concerns that which is immutable. But two sorts of existents are immutable:

primarily and in and of themselves subsistent Forms or Essences are immutable,

derivatively individual sensible existents share in immutability insofar as efficient causes make-them-be-images of Forms, which also cause them as models and goals.[37]

---

[35] According to Levinson this metaphysical doctrine is what is supremely important. "Plato, for all his concern with the political conditions of human life, was still, on our view, primarily a philosopher, and his *Republic* is not so much the plan of a city as it is a dramatically disguised essay on the True, the Good, and the Beautiful, in which is set forth its author's central convictions regarding the meaning of the world and man, the highest springs of value, and the way leading toward the vision of the eternal Good. And this is, for us aftercomers, the devotees of philosophy, the aspect of the *Republic* that far outshines all others, and which we should never permit to be made secondary to the particularities of political reform." On Plato's political theory see n. 13 above.

[36] "Real" means "that which has value, worth, perfection." Most philosophers would agree with that answer but disagreement begins in deciding what factor ultimately causes objective value, worth and perfection. For Plato that cause is immutability. See L. Sweeney, *AM*, pp. 29 sqq.

[37] For the contrast between Forms and sensible things in terms of the former's immutability and the latter's mutability see *Phaedo*, 74A–B and 78D; *Symposium*, 210E–211B; *Timaeus*, 27D-28A and 51E–52A; *Philebus*, 58A. In the first two dialogues mentioned, immutability resides in the fact that a Form is simple (*monoeides*—see *Phaedo*, 78D5; *Symposium*, 211B1); in the last two dialogues Forms are composite because they participate in other Forms (see *Timaeus*, 30C–D; *Philebus*, 23C–D, as answering the second of three questions

Several aspects of that participational situation deserve comment. The participated perfection never becomes an intrinsic and stable constituent of the participant.[38] Second, the participated perfection (e.g., beauty) is that which each participant has in common with the Form and, what is especially relevant, *with other participants*—in fact, such common perfections and the common names we use to designate them lead to our awareness (through recollection) that the Form itself exists and of what it is.[39] Third, that which

---

Plato asks earlier in 15B: how can Forms be one-many? His reply: they are *ousiai* which are combinations each of *peras* and *to apeiron;* see also *Sophist,* 251E–252D) and yet they are immutable.

In *Phaedo,* 100B–E, participation of things in a Form is designated simply as its presence in and association with them. In *Parmenides,* 131A–D, participation is further explained as the process by which things are-made-to-be-images of Forms—a process which is later disclosed to consist in the exemplary and telic causality of the Forms themselves and in the efficient causality of the Craftsman (*Timaeus,* 28A–29A and 29D–C; *Philebus,* 26E–27C and 28C–30D). See L. Sweeney, S.J., *Infinity in Plato's "Philebus": A Bibliographical and Philosophical Study* (forthcoming), chapters 4–6; R. Patterson, *Image and Reality in Plato's Metaphysics* (Indianapolis: Hackett, 1985).

[38] The participated perfection is the second of three factors in the participational situation of which Plato speaks in *Phaedo,* 102B, and *Parmenides,* 130B:

the form of (say) Beauty itself, which is a single Essence subsisting apart from the physical world but which is the radical cause (as model and goal) of why these petunias are beautiful;

the beauties present in the flowering plants, which are the multiple participated perfections in the petunias and through which the Form itself is present to them;

the plants themselves, which are the participants.

To them Plato adds a fourth factor—the Craftsman as efficient cause—when he realized that he must explain further how those multiple participated perfections come about (for references to *Timaeus,* see n. 37 above). Reflection upon the nature of participants induced him to add a fifth factor, which in the *Timaeus* (47E–49A, 50A–51B and 52D–53C) he called receptacle or space and in the *Philebus* (23C, 24A–25A) the indefinite or unlimited (*to apeiron*). On the three-factor theory of participation see L. Sweeney, S.J., *Divine Infinity in Greek and Medieval Thought* (New York/Bern: Peter Lang Publishing, Inc., 1992), chs. 3 and 4. But see K. M. Sayre, *Plato's Late Ontology: A Riddle Resolved* (Princeton University Press, 1983), pp. 238–53.

[39] On recollection as a human soul's recalling (on the occasion of sense-experience) the awareness it achieved by contemplating (and thereby participating in) the Forms before entering the physical world, see *Meno,* 81A sqq.; *Phaedrus,* 246D–252C. Also see Jacob Klein, *A Commentary on Plato's "Meno"* (Chapel Hill: University of North Carolina Press, 1965), pp. 108–72; J. C. B.

distinguishes one participant from other participants (and, of course, from the Form itself), that which is uniquely its own, that which makes it other than them is its "individuality." And what does that consist in? It is aligned with unreality because the reality of this individual participant is whatever participated perfection it has in common with other participants transiently and (so to speak) on loan. It is linked with negation: beauty (for example) in participant #a is not the beauty in participants #b and #c. It is other than their beauties. But that otherness is not something positive but simply the observable fact that somehow and for some inexplicable reason beauty in #a is not beauty in #b or in #c.

Already one can begin to see how individuality in moral agents is unreal and negative. Why so? Philosophers (let us restrict ourselves to this sort of human soul, since what is true of them is also true *a fortiori* of soldiers and tradesmen) are just, temperate, courageous and morally good only by participating in the Form of the Good and, thereby, in the Forms of Justice, Temperance and Courage. What such philosophically gifted participants have in common (however impermanently and on loan) is the participated perfection of goodness, justice, temperance and courage, which make them authentically be moral agents. What distinguishes one such participant from others, what makes him be other than them, what is unique to him would constitute his individuality as a moral agent. And what does that consist in? It could not be anything real since the justice, temperance, courage and goodness he has in common with other moral agents are the participated perfections, which alone are real. Again, it must not be anything positive but simply the negative fact that somehow the morality precisely of Socrates *is not* precisely that of Plato. And what "is not" expresses is actually and really nothing.[40]

Gosling, *Plato* (London: Routledge and Kegan Paul, 1973), pp. 125–27 and 160–66; Nicholas P. White, *Plato on Knowledge and Reality* (Indianapolis: Hackett, 1976), pp. 47–61.

[40] Apparently what corresponds in the realm of Forms to this negation is the Form of Otherness and Nonbeing in *Sophist*, 255C–E and 256D–258C, a Form which accounts for the fact that the Form of Rest is *other than* and, thus, *is not* the Form of Motion by their participation in Otherness and Nonbeing. More relevantly: the Form of Otherness and Nonbeing accounts for the fact that the Form of Justice is other than and is not the Form of Courage by their participation in Otherness and Nonbeing. So too Plato's justice is other than Socrates' by their participating in the Form of Otherness or Nonbeing. But their being other than one another constitutes their individuality. Hence, the Form of

Accordingly, the outcome of Plato's metaphysics is that individuality *as such* is not a perfection: in and of itself it is merely negation, unreality, nonbeing. An individual existent *qua* individual is unreal, worthless, insignificant. Consistently, then, Plato's position cannot have been an ancestor of our current dedication to the "infinite reality" (Kierkegaard) of each individual. Even if he had never written the *Republic* with its subordination of all ranks of citizens to philosopher-kings, themselves subordinate to the Form of the Good, his metaphysics would locate whatever reality individual human souls have in the perfections they share and not in their individuality.

The impact metaphysics has upon someone's interpretation of individuality is clear from a Greek philosopher separated from Plato by five centuries but greatly influenced by him: Plotinus (A.D. 205–270).

Plotinus

Here, as with Plato, metaphysics is the knowledge of the real as real; but to be real for Plotinus is to be one and, hence, Plotinian metaphysics deals with oneness.[41] But unity is found in two sorts of existents:

  primarily and fully in Plotinus' highest hypostasis—the One-Good, who is God and Who is sheer and subsistent unity;

Otherness and Nonbeing in the *Sophist* can be called the Form of Individuality, by participating in which individual existents are individual, even though their individuality as such is negation, unreality, absence. Consistently, Plato will no longer equate individuality with negation, unreality and absence in *Philebus*, 23C sqq., where an individual physical existent is no longer form or image or reflection solely (see *Timaeus*, 50B6, where *to sôma* is only the *eikôn* itself) but is a composite of *peras* and *to apeiron*, the latter serving as participant, the former as the formal determinant which directly affects the *apeiron*, which in turn receives, limits and thereby individuates the *peras*. Obviously in the *Philebus* Plato is closely approaching Aristotle's doctrine of individuation—see "Aristotle" section below.

[41] In Plotinus metaphysics is the knowledge of the real as real and not (as Aristotle expresses it) of being as being, since reality is not being but unity. Were Aristotle's formula taken literally, metaphysics would be restricted to reflection on Intellect, Soul and the physical world, since the One transcends being. Actually, though, such a restriction is unnecessary when the object of metaphysics is taken to be the real as real and the real is oneness and not being.

derivatively in all other existents—the Intellect (and the intellects it contains) and the Soul (and its contents: the World Soul, astral souls, human souls, subhuman souls). The Intellect and intellects come about by the One overflowing and by that overflow (which is intelligible matter and power) turning back to contemplate its source; the Soul and souls come about when the Intellect in turn overflows and the resultant overflow looks back at the Intellect and the One and fashions itself. In all those existents other than the One reality is unity and nothing else: each is real to the extent that it *is the One on a lower level.*[42]

Let us now concentrate on human souls, concerning whose individuality Plotinus speaks almost explicitly.[43] One such passage is

---

[42] On reality as identified with unity, which is primarily found in God as the One-Good, who is the source of all other existents, see *Enneads*, VI, 9 (9) 9, 1–8; III, 8 (30), 10, 14–31; V, 2 (11), 1, 10–21. For translation and commentary on those texts see ch. 16 below, "Are Plotinus and Albertus Magnus Neoplatonists?" prgrs. corresponding to notes 14–21; on monism as the essence of Plotinus' metaphysics see *ibid.*, prgrs. corresponding to notes 36–43.

[43] Explicit language has occurred in V, 7 (18), 1, where Plotinus asks, "Is there an Idea of each individual?" His answer there and in IV, 3 (27), chs. 5 and 12, is affirmative. But in other passages he seems to reply negatively: V, 9 (5), 12 and VI, 5 (23), 8. Those opposing texts have called forth a considerable amount of important secondary literature—e.g., John Rist, "Forms of Individuals in Plotinus," *Classical Quarterly* 13 (1963), 223–31; *idem*, "Ideas of Individuals in Plotinus: A Reply to Dr. Blumenthal," *Revue Internationale de Philosophie* 24 (1970), 298–303; H. J. Blumenthal, "Did Plotinus Believe in Ideas of Individuals?" *Phronesis* 11 (1966), 61–80, which the author reprinted in his *Plotinus' Psychology* (The Hague: Martinus Nijhoff, 1971) as ch. 9; Plato S. Mamo, "Forms of Individuals in the *Enneads*," *Phronesis* 14 (1969), 77–96; J. Igal, "Observaciones al Texto de Plotino," *Emerita* 41 (1973), 92–98. Carefully taking into account those publications in the light of the above-cited passages in the *Enneads*, A. H. Armstrong, "Form, Individual and Person in Plotinus," *Dionysius* 1 (1977), 49–68, comes to this conclusion: "Individual Forms are to be assumed wherever a real formal difference can be detected, as it can be clearly in the case of the true, higher selves of individual men (and of course of higher spiritual beings, gods and *daemones*); they should not be assumed where such differences cannot be observed, and it seems to have been Plotinus' normal thought that they should not be supposed to exist in the case of human bodies or anything lower than animal bodies in the scale of formal distinctiveness and complexity. His principles would, however, leave him free to suppose their existence at lower levels whenever and wherever he thought it necessary to do so" (*ibid.*, p. 56).

According to Armstrong, then, Plotinus assumes that with reference to humans and some higher existents there are individual Forms. But this as-

Enneads, VI, 4 (22), 14, where he is tracing the relationship between a human soul and Soul. [1] The latter contains all [individual] souls and intellects, and yet in spite of its distinguishable, multiple and, in fact, infinite contents it is one, since all such existents are there in an unseparated fashion and all-together, springing from but always remaining in self-identical unity (ch. 14, lines 1–15).[44]

> [2] But *we*—who are *we*? Are *we* that All-Soul or, rather, are we that which drew near to it and came to be in time? [3] Before this sort of birth came about we were There as men different from those we now are—some of us as gods, pure souls, intellects united with all reality, since we were parts of the intelligible world, not separated or cut off, but belonging to the whole—indeed we are not cut off even now. [4] But now there has come to that higher man another man who wishes to be and who finds us, for we were not outside the All. [5] He wound himself round us and fastened himself to that man that each one of us was There (as if there was one voice and one word, and someone else came up from elsewhere and his ear heard and received the sound and became an actual hearing, keeping present to it that which made it actual. [6] Thus we became a couple and [we were no longer] the one [= higher man] we were before. Sometimes we even become the other [= lower man] which had fastened itself to us, when the first man is not active and is in another sense absent (lines 16-31).

Ἡμεῖς δέ — τίνες δὲ ἡμεῖς; Ἆρα ἐκεῖνο ἢ τὸ πελάζον καὶ τὸ γινόμενον ἐν χρόνῳ; Ἢ καὶ πρὸ τοῦ ταύτην τὴν γένεσιν γενέσθαι

---

sumption does not affect our subsequent conclusion (see paragraph corresponding to n. 45 below) that individuality for Plotinus is negation, unreality, nonbeing. The Form of an individual soul would disclose that soul as it is: soul and individual. As soul its reality is its oneness with souls-Soul-Nous-One; as individual it is other than and distinct (at least, distinguishable) from souls, Soul, Nous, and One—an otherness, distinction and, hence, individuality which is not positive but negative, not an addition but a subtraction, not being but nonbeing (see VI, 5 (23), 16 sqq., analyzed below). The content of its Form would, then, re-present not only its reality but also its unreality, which is its individuality.

Porphyry uses these expressions for "individual": *atomon, to kath hekaston* and *to kata meros*—see Jorge J. E. Gracia, "Boethius and the Problem of Individuation," p. 171. For Aristotle's terms, see below, Appendix D.

[44] The Greek for the crucial lines 3–5: Καὶ γὰρ ἕν ἐστι καὶ ἄπειρον αὖ καὶ πάντα ὁμοῦ καὶ ἕκαστον ἔχει διακεκριμένον καὶ αὖ οὐ διακριθὲν χωρίς.

ἦμεν ἐκεῖ ἄνθρωποι ἄλλοι ὄντες καί τινες καὶ θεοί, ψυχαὶ καθαραὶ καὶ νοῦς συνημμένος τῇ ἁπάσῃ οὐσίᾳ, μέρη ὄντες τοῦ νοητοῦ οὐκ ἀφωρισμένα οὐδ' ἀποτετμημένα, ἀλλ' ὄντες τοῦ ὅλου· οὐδὲ γὰρ οὐδὲ νῦν ἀποτετμήμεθα. 'Αλλὰ γὰρ νῦν ἐκείνῳ τῷ ἀνθρώπῳ προσελήλυθεν ἄνθρωπος ἄλλος εἶναι θέλων· καὶ εὑρὼν ἡμᾶς — ἦμεν γὰρ τοῦ παντὸς οὐκ ἔξω — περιέθηκεν ἑαυτὸν ἡμῖν καὶ προσέθηκεν ἑαυτὸν ἐκείνῳ τῷ ἀνθρώπῳ τῷ ὃς ἦν ἕκαστος ἡμῶν τότε· οἷον εἰ φωνῆς οὔσης μιᾶς καὶ λόγου ἑνὸς ἄλλος ἄλλοθεν παραθεὶς τὸ οὖς ἀκούσειε καὶ δέξαιτο, καὶ γένοιτο κατ' ἐνέργειαν ἀκοή τις ἔχουσα τὸ ἐνεργοῦν εἰς αὐτὴν παρόν· καὶ γεγενήμεθα τὸ συνάμφω καὶ οὐ θάτερον, ὃ πρότερον ἦμεν, καὶ θάτερόν ποτε, ὃ ὕστερον προσεθέμεθα ἀργήσαντος τοῦ προτέρου ἐκείνου καὶ ἄλλον τρόπον οὐ παρόντος.

Comments. Although it is difficult to detect from these complex and elliptical lines what a human existent is and in what its individuality consists, some features are clear. A human soul in both its lower and higher states is distinguishable from the All-Soul. The latter by reason of its multiple and, in fact, infinite contents (all souls and intellects) is all-perfect but also is intrinsically and essentially one because its contents, manifold and explicated though they be, are not actually separated but are all-together and so always remain in unity (#1).

An individual soul entails two manners of existing inasmuch as it remains within the Soul or departs from It. Within the Soul an individual soul and intellect also contains and contemplates all reality from its own more limited perspective and is quiet, at peace and one with the Soul. Nonetheless, it is not totally identical with Soul or with other individual souls There: although not actually isolated from them, it is divisible and distinguishable from them and, thereby, is *individual* in an analogous but authentic sense. This individuality, when combined There with its other dimension of all-perfections-in-unity, constitutes the "higher man" (#3). The "lower man" is the same soul but now as in time and enmeshed in an encompassing body (#5). Any individual soul is, then, a couple (*to synampho*): it is at once the higher man and the lower man, although on occasion its higher aspect predominates, on other occasions its lower (#6).

If we now reflect more in detail on human individuality, it becomes clear that an "individual" in Plotinus' texts commonly signifies that which is somehow other than or different from something else. That otherness can consist, as here, in a soul's distinguishability or divisibility from other souls and Soul while yet remaining within Soul and associated with its psychic companions There. A further otherness and, hence, individuality arises when a soul "departs from" Soul and is enmeshed in a body. It is of this second individuality that Plotinus speaks in VI, 5 (23), 12, 16 sqq., where he directly addresses a human soul to explain how it acquires and also frees itself from such individuality:

> [In ascending back to Intellect] you have come to the All and not stayed in a part of it, and have not said even about yourself, "I am so much." By rejecting the "so much" you have become all—yet you were all before. But because something else other than the All added itself to you, you became less by the addition, for the addition did not come from real being (you cannot add anything to that) but from that which is not. When you have become an individual by the addition of non-being, you are not all till you reject the non-being. You will increase yourself then by rejecting the rest, and by that rejection the All is with you.

Ἦ ὅτι παντὶ προσῆλθες καὶ οὐκ ἔμεινας ἐν μέρει αὐτοῦ οὐδ' εἶπας οὐδὲ σύ « τοσοῦτός εἰμι », ἀφεὶς δὲ τὸ « τοσοῦτος » γέγονας πᾶς, καίτοι καὶ πρότερον ἦσθα πᾶς· ἀλλ' ὅτι καὶ ἄλλο τι προσῆν σοι μετὰ τὸ « πᾶς », ἐλάττων ἐγίνου τῇ προσθήκῃ· οὐ γὰρ ἐκ τοῦ παντὸς ἦν ἡ προσθήκη — οὐδὲν γὰρ ἐκείνῳ προσθήσεις — ἀλλὰ τοῦ μὴ ὄντος. Γενόμενος δέ τις καὶ ἐκ τοῦ μὴ ὄντος ἐστὶν οὐ πᾶς, ἀλλ' ὅταν τὸ μὴ ὂν ἀφῇ. Αὔξεις τοίνυν σεαυτὸν ἀφεὶς τὰ ἄλλα καὶ πάρεστί σοι τὸ πᾶν ἀφέντι·

By liberating itself from the body, then, a soul discards the individuality which physical existence had put upon it and which prompted it to say: "I am so much," "I am this definite human being distinct from all else," "I am this individual." Thereby the soul regains its place within the Soul and, eventually, within the Intellect, where nonetheless it retains its other sort of individuality—its distinguishability or divisibility from Intellect, Soul and other souls.

But even this individuality is set aside when a soul ascends beyond Soul and Intellect to become one with the One and thereby achieves happiness above being. In that beatifying union, Plotinus states in VI, 9 (9), 11, 4 sqq., there were not two, but the seer himself was one with the Seen (for It was not really seen but united to him). . . . He was himself then, with no distinction in him either in relation to himself or anything else; for there was no movement in him, and he had no emotion, no desire for anything else when he made the ascent, no reason or thought; his own self [= what he was on a lower level: soul] was not there for him, if we should say even this (lines 4–12: Ἐπεὶ τοίνυν δύο οὐκ ἦν, ἀλλ' ἓν ἦν αὐτὸς ὁ ἰδὼν πρὸς τὸ ἑωραμένον, ὡς ἂν μὴ ἑωραμένον, ἀλλ' ἡνωμένον, ὃς ἐγένετο ὅτε ἐκείνῳ ἐμίγνυτο εἰ μεμνῷτο, ἔχοι ἂν παρ' ἑαυτῷ ἐκείνου εἰκόνα· Ἦν δὲ ἓν καὶ αὐτὸς διαφορὰν ἐν αὐτῷ οὐδεμίαν πρὸς ἑαυτὸν ἔχων οὔτε κατὰ ἄλλα — οὐ γάρ τι ἐκινεῖτο παρ' αὐτῷ, οὐ θυμός, οὐκ ἐπιθυμία ἄλλου παρῆν αὐτῷ ἀναβεβηκότι — ἀλλ' οὐδὲ λόγος οὐδέ τις νόησις οὐδ' ὅλως αὐτός, εἰ δεῖ καὶ τοῦτο λέγειν).

In fact, his contemplation of God was perhaps "not a contemplation but another kind of seeing, a being out of oneself [= what one is as a distinct and lower existent], a simplifying, a self-surrender [a surrender of what one is as a distinct, less real being], a pressing toward contact, a rest, a sustained thought directed to perfect conformity" (lines 22–25: Τὸ δὲ ἴσως ἦν οὐ θέαμα, ἀλλὰ ἄλλος τρόπος τοῦ ἰδεῖν, ἔκστασις καὶ ἅπλωσις καὶ ἐπίδοσις αὐτοῦ καὶ ἔφεσις πρὸς ἁφὴν καὶ στάσις καὶ περινόησις πρὸς ἐφαρμογήν). Those lines apparently explicate the identity between man when fully real and primal Reality: man then is one with the One.

Plotinus then recapitulates (l. 36 sqq.) the entire process of descent and ascent.

When a soul goes down it comes to evil and so to non-being. . . . When it travels the opposite way it comes, not to something else but to itself; and so when it is not in anything else it is in nothing but itself. But when it is in itself alone and not in being, it is in That, for one becomes oneself not as being but beyond being by that intercourse. . . . When a man falls from that vision [and union with the One], he wakes again the virtue in himself and considers himself in all his order and beauty, and is lightened and rises through virtue to Intellect and through wisdom to the Divine. This is the life of gods and divine and blessed men, deliverance from the things of this world, a life which takes no delight in the things of this world, escape in solitude to the Solitary.

Inspiring and consoling as that text is, it leaves little doubt but that an individual human soul is most truly real when it is no longer individual at all. This occurs when it has shed all particularity, uniqueness, distinction, otherness by rising above not only the physical universe but also the psychic and intelligible realms, by transcending thereby being and knowledge, by losing itself in the One, by somehow literally becoming the One. Consequently, individuality is (as with Plato but even more radically) unreality, nonbeing, negation, evil almost, since it is equated with otherness, distinction, separateness, all of which are inimical to unity, wherein alone reality resides.[45]

Hence, although Plotinus wrote no *Republic* or *Statesman* or *Laws*, wherein his devaluation of the individual might be disclosed in political theory, still his metaphysics is enough to consistently exclude all value from the individual as individual. This exclusion seems to guarantee that contemporary theories of individualism have not arisen from his or any other version of Neoplatonism.[46]

Aristotle

With respect to individualism, then, Plotinus is similar to Plato, who however antedates him by five centuries. What of Aristotle (384–321 B.C.), who was a younger contemporary of Plato and in fact a student of Plato for twenty years (367–347)? Are their theories on the nature and value of the individual also similar?

---

[45] See Danièle Letocha, "Le statut de l'individualité chez Plotin ou le miroir de Dionysos," *Dionysius* 2 (1978), 76: "Chez Plotin individualité n'est rien du point de vue ontologique, elle manifeste la distance à l'Un, le non-être, l'exil." *Ibid.*, p. 78: "Les grandes hypostases du *Nous* et de la *Psychê*, le multiplicité progressive qui semble submerger la perception première, c'est l'Un lui-même fragmenté par cette illusion du regard." The entire article deserves attention. Also see Pierre José About, *Plotin* (Paris: Editions Seghers, 1973), especially pp. 63–88. But see Appendix B below.

[46] However much Porphyry, Iamblichus, Proclus and other Neoplatonists may differ from Plotinus in their conceptions of soul and intellect, in their eschatologies, epistemologies and logics (see ch. 16 below, "Are Plotinus and Albertus Magnus Neoplatonists?" paragraphs corresponding to notes 1–12), they seem to agree with him in viewing metaphysics as a henology: for all of them to be real is to be one. If so, they would consider an individual as individual unreal, individuality as negation and nonbeing—a consideration which would eliminate them as sources of modern individualisms.

Individuality: Positive Entitative State

However alike they may be in other areas,[47] Plato's and Aristotle's positions on the individual diverge rather radically. Consider the interpretation each would give to (say) two beautiful, blooming cherry trees. Both philosophers agree that tree #a is other than tree #b, that #a is not #b: they are two individual trees. But, as we have suggested earlier, that otherness and, hence, individuality is, for Plato, simply a negation and unreal because the reality of each tree resides in what they have in common (the immanent perfections of beauty, treeness, color, etc.) through participating in the subsistent Forms of Beauty, Treeness, Color and the rest. Those immanent participated perfections are not received, literally and permanently, by and in their participants and are not entitatively affected by them: in brief, those perfections are not individuated (in any positive sense) by the participants.

The situation is quite different in an Aristotelian approach. The otherness, distinction, uniqueness—in a word, individuality—of the two trees is a positive factor in them. Why so? Because it arises when the forms (accidental and substantial) which help constitute them are educed by efficient causes from the potency of the substance and of prime matter, which also are real constituents of the trees and which entitatively affect the forms (perfections, acts) thus brought forth and continuing on within them for at least some duration. Those forms do not subsist apart from actual cherry trees, but they actually are and are what they are only as present and concretized in those trees. In a word, those forms (both accidental and substantial) are *real* only when *individuated* by the substance or matter within which they are present.

But are not those forms the perfections that the two trees have in common? Yes, but they have that commonness only as known: only as the content of our awareness of them and, hence, only as specifically alike; only, therefore, as universals (both direct and reflexive). In the actual trees such forms are not common but individual: their being is itself permeated by the distinctiveness, uniqueness, individuality issuing from the components from which they have been

---

[47] One position they have in common is that knowledge in one of its aspects is a *pathêma* inasmuch as the object known is its content-determining-cause. See Plato, *Phaedo*, 79D4–7; *Republic*, VI, 511D6–E2; *Symposium*, 210E2–211B5; Aristotle, *On the Soul*, III, ch. 2, 425b26–27 and 426a8–10 (where *energeia* means "actuation" and not "activity," as it is generally translated); ch. 21 below, paragraphs corresponding to notes 16–24.

educed, which are limiting and thereby determining them and which are formally perfected and thereby determined in turn.

For Aristotle, then, individuality of forms and of the existents they help constitute is the positive entitative state of uniqueness and differentiation in which all material things find themselves.

But does that affirmative conception of individuality automatically mean that Aristotle also gives primacy to the individual as individual, that (especially) each individual human being is of value and significance in and of himself? We could answer yes with greater conviction if his political theory turns out to be an individualism. But can it be correctly so interpreted? Is it marked by the three traits Hall finds within contemporary individualism (see paragraph above corresponding to note 27)—namely, supremacy of the human individual, freedom and equality? Answering such questions is crucial for our chapter,[48] but there are other preliminary questions to be raised if we are to understand Aristotle more adequately.

Preliminary Questions

Having seen the prominence Aristotle gives substance/accidents and prime matter/substantial form in his explanation of how material existents are individual, let us now inquire how he establishes that there are such components. As technically taken they are not directly perceived. He must, then, infer their presence, but how? Why does an Aristotelian affirm that they make up an individual cherry tree or a human being? Because from start to finish of his philosophical enterprise he concentrates upon concrete cases of (say) human existents who, while remaining to some degree what they are, go through two sorts of changes.[49] In the first of these someone like Russian president Boris Yeltsin reflects on the crises confronting him, announces a nationwide referendum for April 25, and yet remains essentially the same sort of existent he was two months, two years, two decades previously—namely, human.[50]

---

[48] These issues we shall face in the section below, "Political Theory."

[49] In this concentration Aristotle diverges from Plato, for whom concrete cases furnish common characteristics and names but who then turns within himself to find the Forms causing them by awakening the awareness he had gained of Forms when contemplating them in his preexistence. See *Phaedo*, 65D–E, 74A–77A, 78D–79D; *Republic*, 518C and 533C; also above, n. 39.

[50] I am revising this portion of the chapter in early spring 1993, when the news media are filled with reports on the political situation in Russia.

This combination of specific continuity with accidental perfective changes is evidence of the presence within of two imperceptible but actually present constituents:

substance—that by which he is and remains the specific sort of being he is, while simultaneously undergoing various nonessential perfective processes;

accidents—that by which he, while remaining the specific sort of being he is, is actually being thus perfected.

But physical existents go through another and much more radical change, which affects the very sort of being they are and yet which also witnesses to an underlying continuity. For example, on February 26, 1993, six persons were killed in the terrorist bombing of the World Trade Center in New York City. Each of the six had been human and living but, as a result of the explosion, became nonhuman and dead: a conglomerate of chemicals.[51] This radical change with underlying continuity indicates that before death the substance of each such person was itself made up of constituents:

substantial form—that by which he is the specific sort of being he is;

prime matter—that by which he receives that substantial form but in such a way as to be capable, through substantial change, of receiving other substantial forms.[52]

Of those two sets of components (substance/accidents and prime matter/substantial form) prime matter is the basic substantial cause of individuation in an existent: once a substantial form is educed (or created) within matter, individuation has so thoroughly marked every fiber of its being, as well as that of its faculties, the operations and operative habits they efficiently cause, that the nature it specifies will develop thenceforward in a singular, never-to-be-reduplicated fashion.

But there are difficulties in this Aristotelian theory, as this new series of inquiries reveals.[53]

---

[51] The same media carry daily accounts of the terrorist attack and its aftermath.

[52] On both sets of components see my *AM*, pp. 50–53 and 56–64; on calling them acts/potencies see *ibid.*, pp. 53–54 and 102–6. Also see Joseph Owens, *An Elementary Christian Metaphysics* (Milwaukee: Bruce, 1963), pp. 147–64; Alan D. Code, *Aristotle on Changing Individuals* (Ph.D. diss., University of Wisconsin-Madison, 1976), ch. 3; C.-H. Chen, *Sophia: The Science Aristotle Sought* (Hildesheim: George Olms, 1976), pp. 174–88, 304–7, 341–49.

[53] Subsequent paragraphs are excerpted from my *AM*, pp. 190–93.

First: "Is prime matter the sole principle of individuation? If so, how can that which is itself pure potency accomplish such a feat?" *Answer:* Prime matter is only the ultimate principle of individuation. The proximate principle is quantified matter— matter at its lowest degree of essential perfection, matter in such a state that besides whatever other perfections it may have it has extended parts outside of parts. The result is that this parcel of matter is other than that parcel and, hence, what happens in and develops from this parcel is necessarily other than what happens in and develops from that parcel.

Second: "But is not matter quantified only when substantial form is present in the composite? If so, is not form the principle of individuation? Or how can substantial form somehow be genuinely necessary and yet matter remain the individuating principle?" *Answer:* Substantial form is necessarily present as conferring the specific perfection which inevitably carries along with it the generic perfection of corporeity—that by which the existent is of such a nature as to have extended parts outside of parts, as to have quantity as a property. In and through its proper function of specifying, then, form is also that by which a composite is of such a nature as to have extended parts outside of parts. The composite as so consti- tuted individuates the additional perfections of life, sensitiv- ity, and rationality by receiving them in a unique way. This it can do because, by reason of the quantity, it is physically sep- arate from and is thus other than any other composite receiving its own set of essential perfections. The intrinsic cause which is directly responsible for individuation, then, is the composite itself in that initial stage of composition—the composite as being of such a nature (whatever specifically it may be) as to have extended parts outside of parts, as to have quantity as its property. And this is what we call "quantified matter."

Third: "But such an answer only suggests a new difficulty. Either those essential perfections are really distinct from one another (and then one has as many really different substantial forms as there are such perfections; thus man is no longer an intrinsic unity). Or they are solely mentally distinct (and, in that case, they are merely arbitrary disjunctions and theoreti- cal constructs—just different synonyms for one and the same reality); if so, they cannot be real factors in causing individua- tion within actual existents." *Answer:* There is a third possibil- ity: their mental distinction is not arbitrary but is such as to be objectively grounded in actual existents, as this evidence shows. Although rationality, sensitivity, and the rest are only mentally distinct in this human existent, they are sources of faculties and other properties which are really distinct—for example, his intellect and will (which flow from rationality) differ really from his sense faculties (which flow from sensitivity), from his vegetative operative powers (which come from life), and so forth. Again, even though such perfections are not really distinct in this man, they show themselves to be genuinely different when those in a man are contrasted with those in a dog, a plant, or a chemical compound. The lower perfections are actually found to exist without the higher ones and thus they cannot be totally identical—for instance, a dog has sensitivity but not rationality, a geranium lives but is not sentient, water has various chemical properties but is without life. Moreover, when found within one and the same nature, the higher perfections are never found without the lower (no rationality without sensitivity, no sensitivity without life, no life without an apt chemical constitution in the body), and the higher depends on the lower, which receives, affects and influences the higher. Accordingly, although various essential perfections are only mentally distinct when considered in any one nature, that distinction is not merely constructural but has a real basis in actual existents. Among these perfections the higher depends upon the lower, and in this sense the lower is to the higher as the prior is to the posterior. Because of this atemporal dependence and priority, quantified matter can individuate the further essential perfections, which it receives and from which it is genuinely and objectively (although mentally) distinct.

Fourth: "But a problem remains. If substantial form is the source of the essential perfection of corporeity (as was indicated in the answer to the second question) and hence is the reason why matter is quantified, then form still seems to be the principle of individuation." *Answer:* This might be true were it not for the fact that prime matter is more directly the cause of corporeity and quantity than is the substantial form. True enough, quantity is property of the composite and thus comes from both. Nonetheless, it flows more proximately from matter than from form. The latter is the proximate principle of specific perfection and properties; but "quantified body" is not a species—nothing actually exists simply as "quantified body" but always as such-and-such a body—as a hydrogenous body, a geraniaceous body, a canine body, a human body; consequently, the substantial form is not the proximate principle of body or quantity. This role must be filled by its partner-component in the nature or essence—prime matter. Accordingly, quantity is a property of the composite itself and yet is more directly the result of prime matter than of form because it is a nonspecific and generic perfection. Prime matter is pure potency, yes, but it is not merely a negation. It is an actually existing and hence real component, now revealing itself to be capable of more immediately causing quantity than does substantial form, provided the latter is informing it and specifying the existent. True enough, substantial form, because it is autodetermining, individuates itself through prime matter, since this latter can individuate only if it is in an existent which is specifically such-and-such, which has been formally and essentially perfected. Still, as the more direct cause of quantity prime matter performs a function which the form could itself take over only at the price of no longer being substantial form.[54]

Let the preceding paragraphs suffice as a presentation of how prime matter and substantial form cooperate as intrinsic causes in individualizing material existents. Granted they are lengthy and intricate[55] but they seem useful for more precisely understanding

---

[54] On substantial form as autodetermining and thereby individuating itself through prime matter, see Appendix C below.

[55] On why an Aristotelian explanation of individuality is intricate see my *AM*, p. 193, which comes at the end of the paragraphs reproduced above from *ibid.*, pp. 190–93 and corresponding to notes 53 and 54: "Such, then, is the intricate answer to the question of what causes the otherness of individuality which issues from the natures or essences of material existents. The intricacy of the solution is proportioned to the intricacy of the problem. No principle of individuation is needed at all if with Plato one says there are no individuals but only Natures, or with Ockham or Sartre one says there are no natures but only individuals. In the first case there is only unity, in the second sheer multiplicity."

Why (we may ask parenthetically) are there no individuals for Plato? Because for him an individual as individual is unreal. Why are there only individuals for Ockham and Sartre? Because in Ockham's eyes nature is nothing but a name, a term, whereas Sartre explicitly eliminates natures: "There is no human nature, since there is no God to conceive it" (*Existentialism*

Aristotle and for attending to current secondary literature on his theory of individuation.[56] Now let us take up his political theory.

Political Theory

In this area I shall rely on an author whose firsthand acquaintance with Aristotle's *Politics*, ethical writings and other treatises recommends him as a guide worthy of respect. He attributes some sort of genuine individualism to the Stagirite.

Max Hamburger concludes his book *Morals and Law: The Growth of Aristotle's Legal Theory* (1st ed., 1951; New York: Biblo and Tannen, 1965) with an informative section on "Happiness and Individualism" (pp. 167–75).[57] There he makes a summary of eleven

---

[New York: Philosophical Library, 1947], p. 18). Accordingly, a "principle of individuation is demanded only when unity mingles with multiplicity, when individuals share a common specific nature. Each is truly and equally human, although one is this man, the other that man. All are specifically alike, although individually different. How can these disparate characteristics arise from the single, concrete natures they have? Because that nature is itself composed of two components. Substantial form is that by which this man is human and thus specifically similar to all other men; prime matter, because the more immediate source of quantity, is that by which he is ultimately this man and thus is unique and singular. Embedded within the concrete and composite nature itself is the intrinsic cause not only of specific perfection, similarity, unity, but also of individuation, dissimilarity, and multiplicity" (*AM*, p. 193).

[56] For a survey of such literature see Appendix D below.

[57] In previous sections of the book Hamburger treated voluntary action and choice (pp. 12–43), which grounds Aristotle's treatment of culpability in the section on law and justice (pp. 43–110), which then leads to a section on friendship (pp. 111–66), which furnishes general principles that govern contracts. One of the author's main aims is (with H. von Arnim) to challenge Werner Jaeger's interpretation of *Great Ethics* (= *Magna Moralia*) as a late epitome of *Eudemian Ethics* and *Nicomachean Ethics* by seeking to show that the *Great Ethics* precedes the other two as an "Urethik." Reviews of his book have been rather favorable on the validity of his challenge—see A. R. Lacey, *Philosophy* 43 (1968), 290: "Cumulatively his case is a formidable one." Also see E. N. Garlan, *Journal of Philosophy* 49 (1952), 528–32; Eric Weil, *Revue de Métaphysique et de Morale* 57 (1952), 465–66. Only Lacey expresses reservations on Hamburger's viewing Aristotle as espousing individualism—see *Philosophy*, p. 291: "Hamburger is very kind to Aristotle, sometimes too kind. . . . He sees nothing wrong with Aristotle's paternalistic legislation for morality. . . ; no evidence is brought to show that Aristotle had really advanced in this respect beyond the Sophists at their best, however much he may be responsible for integrating equity into justice and the law."

points (always based directly and abundantly on Aristotle's own texts). (a) Happiness, which is activity in accordance with complete virtue, with sufficiency of external goods and throughout a complete life, is the goal of each individual (pp. 167–68). (b) Happiness is also the goal of the state, which is "a moral institution which aims at educating its citizens in goodness and righteousness" (pp. 168–69). (c) The happiness which "the state provides is not restricted to any particular class of citizens. . . . 'It must be a political organization which will enable all sorts of men to be at their best and live happily'" (*ibid.*).[58]

(d) Rejecting Plato's total unification of the state, Aristotle insists "that the individual must not be totally merged with the state." In fact, " 'a state which goes on and on and becomes more of a unity, will eventually cease to be a state at all' " (pp. 169–70). (e) Nonetheless, a citizen is not "an individual completely independent of the state and only belonging to himself." No, he is "a member, a part of the state which must shape him into a useful member of the community by an appropriate system of equal education" (p. 170).

(f) But this dependence on the state is not the totalitarianism implied in Plato's *Republic* and *Laws*—namely, "the total submergence of the individual beneath the flux of state influence." Rather, Aristotle's "insistence on the close tie between the citizen and the state" is coextensive "with a true, ethical individualism," because only in a state "where the members are not merely relatively good but absolutely the best can the good man and the good citizen be absolutely identical" (pp. 170–71). (g) The backbone of such a state is its middle class, wherein lies the very essence of Aristotle's individualism.

A straight line leads from Aristotle's concept of happiness to its realization in the state. Happiness is the end of the state. All members should have a share in this end. The best way of life, consisting in a mean attainable by every individual, secures this happiness for the greater part of the citizens. The middle class, representing the mean between the rich and the poor, is in its way of life an embodiment of this mean. Thus the middle class is essential for the well-being of the state and its citizens. The middle class unites the qualities of the class extremes. Hence, the middle class represents individualism and safeguards it against oppression either by the poor or the rich (p. 172).

---

[58] Single quotation marks indicate that Hamburger is quoting Aristotle.

(h) But, more precisely, what is "the best possible life which confers happiness"? The first best form of happy life is practice of intellectual virtues (science, practical wisdom, intuitive reason, theoretical wisdom, etc.) and perfect happiness consists in contemplation. The second best form of happy life consists in the practice of moral virtues (justice, courage, temperance; pp. 172–173). (i) This twofold state of well-being for a citizen should be mirrored in the state too: "In principle there is no difference in the essence of state happiness and the individual happiness, both consisting in the activity of goodness" (pp. 173–74).

(j) For both state and citizen a central role is accorded to leisure, "which does not mean inactivity but rather implies the most sublime activity, thought." As Aristotle himself writes, "The final end of man is the same whether they are acting individually or acting collectively; and the standard followed by the best individual is thus the same as the standard followed by the best political constitution. It is therefore evident that the qualities required for the use of leisure must belong to the state as well as the individual; for . . . peace is the final end of war, and leisure the final end of occupation" (p. 175).

(k) And what qualities are required for contemplation and action? Wisdom, courage, endurance, temperance and justice. "Here we have the final synthesis of Aristotelian ethics and politics culminating in the ideal of felicity in the sense of good activity, the activity being one of leisure and peace, based upon and secured by such virtues as courage, endurance, temperance and justice. One can scarcely conceive of a more striking synthesis of the ideals of humanitarianism, humanism" (*ibid.*) and, one may add, individualism.

Conclusions

Accordingly, Hamburger interprets Aristotle's political theory as a bona fide individualism. But is his exegesis correct? Donald J. Allan, "Individual and State in the *Ethics* and *Politics*" (*La "Politique" d'Aristote* in *Entretiens sur l'Antiquité Classique* 11 [1965], 55–85), formulates conclusions similar to Hamburger's. Even though Aristotle claims in the *Politics* "that the *polis* is 'by nature prior' to the household and the individual man, that the State is a whole of which every man is a part" (pp. 83–84), nonetheless "the enlightened 'politikos' is one whose paramount aim is to make the citizens happy" by "giving them a chance to perform good actions." Because of this goal he will ensure either directly or through their parents that "they obtain the indispensable discipline of the emotions from infancy" to adulthood, that through laws he will help them abstain from morally wrong action. Moreover, he will recognize that he can encourage but not manufacture morally good activity and that "there are human activities which, judged metaphysically, are higher," which are pursued during the time of leisure and over which he has no control (p. 83). Hence, Aristotle's position, while excluding "any naive form of political liberalism," is not a commitment "to a severe form of totalitarianism" (p. 84). Granted that no ancient thinker arrived at our Western view "of the dignity of the individual human being as such"—a development "in which a predominant part falls to Christianity"—but "Aristotle's careful analysis of choice would have put him on the path towards political liberalism if he could have discarded certain social prejudices" (p. 85).

By and large, then, Allan's interpretation agrees with Hamburger's. In opposition to both stand Ernest Baker, Alexander Grant, J. A. Stewart and René Antoine Gauthier, names Allan himself furnishes.[59] In opposition, too, is the implication in Aristotle's own theory of the preservation of species that the individual's good is subordinated to the good of the species.[60] Also, Aristotle's metaphysics and philosophy of nature can only with difficulty be transformed into a genuine humanism as long as the human soul is taken to be mortal and man's highest cognitive faculty, the agent

---

[59] "Individual and State," pp. 55, 63, 64. Allan finds that Wilhelm Oncken, *Die Staatslehre des Aristoteles* (first published 1870–1875; Aalen: Scientia Verlag, 1964), to some extent anticipated his views: according to Oncken, although "Aristotle does not call in question the ominpotence of the state over the entire life of the citizens," still "he does not sacrifice to it, like Plato, all personal and individual life. . . . [Rather] Aristotle mediates between the unity of the State and the freedom of the citizens. . . . He is the first thinker of the ancient world to make the attempt to determine the limits of state activity" (Allan, "Individual and State," p. 82). For an opposing view see D. Badareu, *L'Individuel chez Aristote* (Paris: Boivin, n.d.), pp. 15–20 and *passim*. For a different approach see Manfred Riedel, *Metaphysik und Metapolitik: Studien zu Aristoteles und zur politischen Sprache der neuzeitlichen Philosophie* (Frankfurt am Main: Suhrkamp Verlag, 1975).

On Aristotle's educational theory, see Carnes Lord, *Education and Culture in the Political Thought of Aristotle* (Ithaca: Cornell University Press, 1982).

[60] See D. M. Balme, *Aristotle's "De Partibus Animalium" and "De Generatione Animalium"* (Oxford: Clarendon Press, 1972), pp. 96–97, where he refutes that implication; Joseph Owens, *The Doctrine of Being in the Aristotelian Metaphysics*, 3d ed. (Toronto: Pontifical Institute of Mediaeval Studies, 1978), p. 388, n. 55.

intellect, is considered to be separate from him.[61] Yet a humanism they must be if preeminence is to be given to human beings in general and to each individual human being in particular.

But despite such considerations that militate against finding an individualism in Aristotle's philosophy, one must recall that individuality for him is not negation or nonbeing (as they are for Plato and Plotinus). No, it is a positive state of reality within material existents which arises when substance receives accidents and prime matter receives substantial form. When that substantial form is a human soul, conceived as spiritual and immortal, then a structure within which the infinite value and dignity of each individual human person reside can be built upon the speculative foundation Aristotle has at least in part laid.[62]

Appendix A: The Good in Plato's *Republic*

In the *Republic* the movement of Plato's thought on the Good can be charted as follows.

505D–E: The Good is that which every soul pursues and is that for the sake of which a soul does everything; hence, one must try to grasp what it is.

---

[61] On the soul's tight connection with matter because it is its actuation, see *On the Soul*, II, ch. 1, 412a18 sqq. (also see J. Owens, *The Doctrine of Being in the Aristotelian Metaphysics*, p. 381, n. 18); on the agent intellect as alone separable from the body (and, we may infer, immortal) see *On the Soul*, III, ch. 5, 430a18. For other references concerning the agent intellect see Sir David Ross, *Aristotle "De Anima"* (Oxford: Clarendon Press, 1967), pp. 41–48 and 214; D. W. Hamlyn, *Aristotle's "De Anima"* (Oxford: Clarendon Press, 1977), pp. 141–42; H. G. Apostle, *Aristotle "On the Soul"* (Grinnell, Iowa: Peripatetic Press, 1981) p. 159 sqq.

Aristotle's conception of the human soul as mortal and of the agent intellect as separate from man, numerically one and immortal was developed most fully by Averroës (1126–1197) and by Christian Averroists at the University of Paris in the thirteenth century—a development which culminated in the 1270 and 1277 condemnations of Aristotelian doctrines. On Averroës see Beatrice H. Zedler, "Averroës on the Possible Intellect," *Proceedings of American Catholic Philosophical Association* 25 (1951), 164–78; Roland J. Teske, "The End of Man in the Philosophy of Averroës," *New Scholasticism* 37 (1963), 431–61; E. Gilson, *History of Christian Philosophy in the Middle Ages* (New York: Random House, 1955), pp. 216–25; on the Paris condemnations see *ibid.*, pp. 387–410.

[62] On the primal role the Judeo-Christian Scriptures and the ecumenical councils and creeds of the Church played in building that structure, see paragraphs corresponding to notes 5–9 above.

506D–E: But let us leave aside for another time what the Good in itself is and instead speak of it by setting up an analogy with its offspring, the sun.

507B–508E: Through this comparison one realizes that the Good is the cause

> directly:
>> of the intelligibility, truth and being of whatever is intelligible (i.e., the other Forms);
>> of our intellection, which it illuminates and the content of which it also determines;
>
> indirectly (i.e., through the sun, which the Craftsman of *Timaeus* makes efficiently but which the Good causes as goal and model):
>> of being and growth of physical things and of their visibility;
>> of our seeing them.

508E–509B: the Good is more powerful, beautiful and real than all other Forms—in fact, it is beyond being (*ousia*), which it exceeds in dignity and power.

509D–511E: If we set up a divided line to show the relationship between the intelligible and visible realms, the Good is its apex: grasped by the power of dialectics, it is the absolute beginning of all else and is itself without beginning—it is *anhypostheton*.

514A–517C (also see 518C, 527E, 533D): In the allegory of the cave, which aims at illuminating how citizens are to be educated, items within the cave (the fire, people carrying artifacts but not themselves seen, the artifacts themselves, their shadows cast on the wall and seen by prisoners facing the wall) are matched by existents outside the cave (the sun, other heavenly bodies, individual animals and other things, their reflections on water and mirrors), which in turn correspond to the Good, other Forms, visible things as their participants, the reflections and images of the visible things.

521C–532B: The entire course of education is thereupon geared to usher suitably talented men and women to contemplation of the Form of the Good that they may be philosopher-kings—first through military training, gymnastics and music; then through the mathematical sciences of arithmetic, geometry, astronomy and harmonics; finally, through dialectics, by which one attempts through intellection to attain to the very essence of each thing and does not desist until he apprehends that which is the Good itself and thus comes to the very end of the intelligible realm (532A–B:

οὕτω καὶ ὅταν τις τῷ διαλέγεσθαι ἐπιχειρῇ ἄνευ πασῶν τῶν αἰσθήσεων διὰ τοῦ λόγου ἐπ' αὐτὸ ὃ ἔστιν ἕκαστον ὁρμᾶν, καὶ μὴ ἀποστῇ, πρὶν ἂν αὐτὸ ὃ ἔστιν ἀγαθὸν αὐτῇ νοήσει λάβῃ, ἐπ' αὐτῷ γίγνεται τῷ τοῦ νοητοῦ τέλει).

532D–533A: Yes, the power of dialectics is such as to "lead us at last toward that place which is for the one who reaches it a haven from the road, as it were, and an end of his journey." There one would "no longer be seeing an image [of the Good] but rather the truth itself, at least as it looks to me. Whether it is really so or not can no longer be insisted on. But that there is some such thing to see must be insisted upon" (Greek for 533A:

οὐδ' εἰκόνα ἂν ἔτι οὗ λέγομεν ἴδοις, ἀλλ' αὐτὸ τὸ ἀληθές, ὅ γε δή μοι φαίνεται — εἰ δ' ὄντως ἢ μή οὐκέτ' ἄξιον τοῦτο διισχυρίζεσθαι· ἀλλ' ὅτι μὲν δὴ τοιοῦτόν τι ἰδεῖν, ἰσχυριστέον).

For all practical purposes Plato has come to the end of his investigation of the Good. If we take the last passage literally, he seems to have terminated with what in effect amounts almost to a denial that the philosopher can know what the Good is, although he may know that It is. If so, Plato's conception of the Form of the Good in the *Republic* is indeed sketchy and incomplete. Perhaps, though, this denial helped prompt him in the *Timaeus* to study goodness and beauty in existents other than the Forms but made by the divine Craftsman as their images, a study which enabled him to decide in the *Philebus* (65A) not only *that* the Form of the Good is but also *what* it is: a combination of Beauty, Proportion and Authentic Reality (*alêtheia*).

For chronological ordering of the dialogues see Leonard Brandwood, *A Word Index to Plato* (Leeds: W. S. Maney, 1976), pp. xvii sq.; *idem, The Chronology of Plato's Dialogues* (Cambridge University Press, 1990), pp. 249–52 and *passim;* G. R. Ledger, *Re-counting Plato* (Oxford University Press, 1989).

Appendix B: Rist on Plotinus

John M. Rist in *Human Value: A Study in Ancient Philosophical Ethics* (Leiden: E. J. Brill, 1982), pp. 99–113 and 145–52, affirms that Plotinus gives positive value to human existents in their individuality and uniqueness. As he reads the *Enneads*, each person is considered to be of little value when he is conscious merely of physical things. But when he chooses (see *Enneads*, VI, 8) to be conscious of himself as soul and, especially, as intellect he is highly valuable. Thus he is aware of the intelligible All and, in fact, each of us thereby is an actually intelligible world. Each then is at his best— namely, when he has achieved "the integration of his levels of activity, and the 'completion' of the 'we' by this kind of integration would suggest that man in his highest 'version' is more than any of his 'parts'. . . . It would also imply that each individual man is in some sense unique, not merely a man with the characteristics of men, but a man whose specifically integrated personality is somehow 'greater' than would be the case were he merely an *example* of the form of Man" (p. 101). And when the "we" is raised "to the level of the upper soul and the vision of the Forms . . . 'personality' does not disappear." In fact, even at "the level of the union of the self with the One," the "I" remains. "It is not the Form of Man that attains union with the One; it is I who attain to such a union" (p. 102).

According to Rist, then, a human individual attains value from increasingly integrated levels of consciousness until he becomes one with the One. What can be said in response? Does his exegesis of Plotinus establish that a human individual has value in his/her very individuality?

First of all, the integration he speaks of is apparently equivalent to the growing unification which a human soul undergoes and which constitutes its reality. Would not this be a sign that Plotinus' system is monistic (to be real is to be one and all things are real insofar as they are the One-on-a-lower-level)? If so, even Rist grants that a monism deals "with a reassimilation of the self in which all individuality is lost" (p. 102); "each being would lose its individuality, or rather would abandon the semblance of individuality which it appeared to possess, at the moment of union with the One" (p. 151).

But even prescinding from whether or not Plotinus is a monist, one finds other problems. When human souls become (Rist observes) aware of the intelligible All, they thereby are each an actually intelligible world, presumably because each knows all reality. The difference between the content of such knowledge in multiple knowers is not in the content itself (since each soul contemplates the identical All) but in the perspective from which each knower views the All. But what is that perspective? Is it anything positive in the individual knower? Or is it not merely that the vantage point from which one soul contemplates the All *is not* the same as that of another soul? If this latter alternative is correct, individuality remains a negation (as I maintain) and is nothing positive.

Finally, Rist's basing his position at least in part (see pp. 106–13) on *Enneads,* VI, 8, is risky, since most likely Plotinus does not express his own mind in that treatise but intends it rather as a pedagogical ploy to safeguard his students against a "presumptuous discourse" (as he describes it) put forth by some or other sect of Gnostics (see Curtis L. Hancock, "*Energeia* in the *Enneads* of Plotinus" [Ph.D. dissertation, Loyola University of Chicago, 1984], pp. 220–26; Georges Leroux, *Plotin: Traité sur la liberté et la volonté de l'Un* [Paris: J. Vrin, 1990], reviewed by Dominic J. O'Meara, *Review of Metaphysics* 45 [1991], 407–8). Consequently, the treatise gives no solid support to Rist's interpretation on the positive nature of individuality or, for that matter, on the aligned doctrine that the One is infinite *Being* and efficient cause and thus creates all other existents (pp. 103–4, 107–9, 112). This last doctrine is no more compelling now than when Rist previously proposed it in *Plotinus: The Road to Reality* (1967)—for my critique see *Classical Journal* 64 (1969), 180–83, and ch. 4 above, "Plotinus' Conception of Neoplatonism," three paragraphs before "Conclusion."

Appendix C:
Substantial Form as Autodetermining

Understanding the autodetermination of a component such as substantial form requires reflection on these three points: why autodetermination is twofold, what decides whether a component actually is autodetermining and, finally, why substantial form but not prime matter is autodetermining.

First of all, the verb "determine" can have at least two distinct but complementary meanings: to confer a perfection (let us refer to this as sense #1) and to limit a perfection (sense #2; for examples from everyday life see *AM*, pp. 119–20). Hence, self- or auto-deter-mination is also twofold: by conferring a perfection (#1) something would also limit itself (#2) through that upon which the perfection is conferred and, second, by receiving and limiting a perfection (#2) something also perfects itself (#1) through that very perfection received. Let us illustrate this through act/potency: what would self-determination mean there? That an act would not

only confer a perfection (and thus, as we would expect, deter-mine the existent in sense #1 of the term), but would also limit itself through its partner-component (and thus determine it-self in sense #2 of the term). Likewise, a potency would not only limit a perfection (and thereby, as one would expect, determine that perfection in sense #2 of the term), but would also perfect itself through that act (and thus determine itself in sense #1 of the term).

Second, what decides whether a component, be it an act or a potency, actually is autodetermining?

The fact that the intrinsic causality it exercises upon its part-ner-component within the existent (conferring or limiting a perfection) is of such a nature that the latter relies absolutely upon the former in order to exercise its own intrinsic causality (limiting or conferring a perfection). If such is the case, if the former necessarily helps the latter in carrying out its own causality, if the former in the function it uniquely performs is absolutely necessary for the latter's function, then the former determines itself through the latter. If the former is an act, it limits itself through the potency it actuates ("determine" in sense #2). If a potency, it perfects itself through the act it receives ("determine" in sense #1).

Finally, why is substantial form but not prime matter auto-determining? Because substantial form individuates itself through prime matter, which however does not specify itself through the form. Let us start with prime matter. Is prime matter self-deter-mining? Does the prime matter

of (say) this man specify itself through his human soul? Does it even mediately humanize itself? It does if each proposition of the following line of argumentation turns out to be true.

Substantial form determines [sense #1] prime matter by specifying it;

But substantial form is specifically such-and-such only because it is individuated, because it is in this individual, because it is this individual substantial form—for example, a human soul is human only because it is *this* human soul;

But prime matter is ultimately that by which the substantial form is individuated, that by which it becomes *this* form;

Therefore, prime matter is mediately self-specifying through the substantial form, and thus is autodetermining [sense #1].

Is prime matter, then, mediately self-determining? Obviously not, for the second proposition of the argument is false. No substantial form is specifically such-and-such because of the individuation it receives from prime matter, for if this were the case, the substantial form could be found only in this individual. The species would be confined to him or her alone. Rather, the substantial form is what it is specifically *from itself*, from its own nature. A human soul is human rather than canine proximately because its very nature is to be human. Accordingly, the individuation which prime matter exercises upon a human soul does not make that soul be human or contribute directly to the humanization which the latter carries out in the existent. The result is that prime matter is not self-specifying, even through the substantial form it receives and limits.

But is substantial form autodetermining? Does it mediately individuate itself? Once again, it does if each proposition of the following argument is true.

Prime matter determines [sense #2] substantial form by receiving and individuating it;

But prime matter can receive and individuate the substantial form only if it is in an existent which is specifically such-and-such;

But that by which an existent is specifically such-and-such is the substantial form;

Therefore, the substantial form is mediately self-individuating through prime matter, and thus is self-determining [sense #2].

Is substantial form, then, mediately self-determining? Yes, since the crucial second proposition of the argument is true. That is to say, prime matter is the basic cause of individuation, because quantity, although a property of the composite and not of either form or matter taken alone, flows more directly in the composite from prime matter than from substantial form because it is a generic rather than a specific property of material things. But prime matter cannot *by itself* be the more immediate source of quantity because of itself it is only pure potency. Quantity can issue from it only when it is informed, only inasmuch as it is a component within an existent which is material, which is of such a nature as to be extended, as to have physical parts outside of parts. But an existent has such a nature only insofar as it is also aqueous or geraniaceous or canine or human, for we never find any actual existent which is *only* material, which is without some or other specific perfection. In brief, what makes a nature to be specifically such-and-such is the substantial form. Hence, the substantial form, in carrying out its own function of specifying the existent, also enables prime matter to carry out its function of individuation. Accordingly, through prime matter the substantial form individuates itself, and thus is self-determining (sense #2). (Excerpts from *AM*, pp. 120–23)

Appendix D:
Secondary Literature on Aristotle's Texts

Scholars have concentrated upon at least two textual areas in Aristotle on "individual," in the first of which he applies the word to nonsubstantial characteristics (e.g., grammar, whiteness), in the second to substances (e.g., the man who is grammatical and white). In our survey of each area let us first list Aristotle's texts, comment briefly upon them, and finally refer to some relevant secondary literature.

A. Aristotle on Nonsubstantial Individuals
(1) *Categories*, ch. 2, 1a20 (Ackrill translation, p. 4):

1a20. Of things there are: (a) some are *said of* a subject but are not *in* any subject. For example, man is said of a subject, the individual man, but is not in any subject. (b) Some are in a subject but are not said of any subject. (By 'in a subject' I mean what is in something, not as a part, and cannot exist separately from what it is in.) For example, the individual knowledge-of-grammar is in a subject, the soul, but is not said of any subject; and the individual white is in a subject, the body (for all colour is in a body), but is not said of any subject. (c) Some are both said of a subject and in a subject. For example, knowledge is in a subject, the soul, and is also said of a subject, knowledge-of-grammar. (d) Some are neither in a subject nor said of a subject, for example, the individual man or individual horse—for nothing of this sort is either in a subject or said of a subject. Things that are individual and numerically one are, without exception, not said of any subject, but there is nothing to prevent some of them from being in a subject—the individual knowledge-of-grammar is one of the things in a subject.

(2) *Comments.* (a) Here Aristotle expresses "individual" *re* both nonsubstantial characteristics and substances by *tis* (see especially 1a26: *hê tis grammatikê kai to ti leukon;* 1b4: *ho tis anthropos kai ho tis hippos*). (b) Such nonsubstantial individuals apparently show up only in the *Categories*—see Barrington Jones, "Individuals in Aristotle's *Categories*," *Phronesis* 17 (1972), 107. (c) Although an introductory text, the *Categories* is itself "a mature rather than a juvenile production" of someone who has "a deep and exact comprehension of Aristotelian metaphysics" and hence must be Aristotle himself—Montgomery Furth, "Transtemporal Stability in Aristotelian Substances," *Journal of Philosophy* 75 (1978), 632, note 8 (the entire article is an admirable and informative study of Aristotle's metaphysics and philosophy of nature). (d) Such nonsubstantial characteristics as knowledge-of-grammar and whiteness are, in my view, rendered individual by their presence in a human existent, who radically is himself substantially individuated by matter—see above, "Individuality: Positive Entitative State" and "Preliminary Questions"–see nn. 47–56 above.

(3) *Secondary Literature.* G. E. L. Owen, "Inherence," *Phronesis* 10 (1965), 97–105; R. E. Allen, "Individual Properties in Aristotle's *Categories*," *ibid.*, 14 (1969), 31–39 (see p. 32, n. 4, for references to W. D. Ross, G. E. M. Anscombe, J. L. Ackrill and K. von Fritz); B. Jones, "Individuals in Aristotle's *Categories*," *ibid.*, 17 (1972), 107–123; Julia Annas, "Individuals in Aristotle's *Categories*: Two Queries," *ibid.*, 19 (1974), 146–52.

B. Aristotle on Substantial Individuality

(1) Here one finds at least two series of texts, the first of which locates the cause of individuation in matter, the second in form. For convenience I am reproducing them from Edward Regis, "Aristotle's 'Principle of Individuation,'" *Phronesis* 21 (1976), 158 and 162.

Series One from *Metaphysics*:

(1) things are one in number whose matter is one, in species whose form is one: ἀριθμῷ μὲν ὦν ἡ ὕλη μία, εἴδει δ' ὦν ἡ λόγος εἷς (1016b32–3, cf. 1054a34);

(2) 'man' and 'horse' and what applies to individuals in this way, but universally, are not substance but a composite of this formula and this matter taken universally; an individual is composed of the last matter (τῆς ἐσχάτης ὕλης), Socrates for example, and similarly in other cases (1035b27–31);

(3) those things which are many in number have matter (for one and the same formula is of many, for example 'man,' whereas Socrates is one) (1074a33–5);

(4) when the whole has been generated, such a form in this flesh and in these bones, this is Callias or Socrates; and they are different on account of their matter (for it is different) (καὶ ἕτερον μὲν διὰ τὴν ὕλην [ἑτέρα γὰρ]), but the same in species (for the species is indivisible). (1034a5–8).

Series Two:

(1) things whose substance is one have also one essence (τὸ τί ἦν εἶναι) and are themselves one (*Meta.* 1038b14–15);

(2) the causes and elements are distinct for things not in the same genus . . . and they are distinct even in the same species, not distinct in species, but numerically distinct, as in the case of your matter and your form (ἥ τε σὴ ὕλη καὶ τὸ εἶδος) and your moving cause, on the one hand, and mine, on the other, although universally and in form they are the same (*Meta.* 1071a24–9, Apostle tr.; cf. 14–15);

(3) shape or form is that in virtue of which a thing is said to be a *this* (*De An.*, 412a8–9; cf. *Meta.* 1042a26–30);

(4) an individual has a form and shape peculiar to it (ἕκαστον ἴδιον ἔχειν εἶδος καὶ μορφήν, *De An.*, 407b23–24);

(5) we are seeking the cause (and this is the form) through which the matter is a thing (*Meta.* 1041b7–8).

(2) *Comments.* (a) As studying the publications listed below reveals, one of the main objections to prime matter as the principle of substantial individuation is that it is pure potency and, hence, incapable of producing something so precious as individuality and, accordingly, that function must be reserved for substantial form. But as I interpret Aristotle, prime matter is the *ultimate* principle of individuation inasmuch as it is the immediate source of quantity (which is not a specific perfection in any material existent and hence can come directly from no substantial form but must issue from the only other component in the substance—namely, prime matter). (b) Moreover, substantial form, because it is autodetermining, actually is also a principle of individuation: it individuates itself (and the substance it informs) but only mediately—that is, through prime matter. (c) Finally, when a substantial form is educed or created within matter, individuation marks every fiber of its being, as well as that of its faculties, the operations and operative habits they efficiently cause—so thoroughly, indeed, that the substance it specifies (and the accidents inhering therein) will develop thenceforth in a singular, never-to-be-reduplicated way through its own efficient causality and through the influences upon it of environment, culture and other external forces (see above, "Individuality: Positive Entitative State" and "Preliminary Questions," as well as notes 54 and 55). (d) Such is the background of my previous remark in this Appendix (*Categories*, "Comments" #d above) that non-substantial characteristics are rendered individual by their presence within an existent substantially individuated by matter.

C. Secondary Literature

Harold Cherniss, *Aristotle's Criticism of Plato and the Academy* (Baltimore: Johns Hopkins University Press, 1944; New York: Russell and Russell, 1962), pp. 351–52 and 506–12; Jan Lukasiewicz, "The Principle of Individuation," *Proceedings of Aristotelian Society*, supplementary vol. 27 (1953), pp. 69–82 (because the ground of the Aristotelian metaphysics is not intelligible enough, one must rely on the ontology of Stanislaw Lesniewski and conclude that "the unity [and hence individuality] of any composite thing requires, . . . a non-materialistic principle, a form or a functor" (p. 81); G. E. M. Anscombe, *ibid.*, pp. 83–96 (the principle of individuation is matter); R. Albritton, "Forms of Particular Substances in Aristotle's *Metaphysics*," *Journal of Philosophy* 54 (1957), 699–708 (commentary on Wilfrid Sellars' thesis that for Aristotle the form of a material substance is not the universal form of its species but a particular instance of that form, informing the thing's particular matter); A. C. Lloyd, "Aristotle's Principle of Individuation," *Mind* 79 (1970), 519–29 (when individuation is equated with numerical difference, its principle is matter); W. Charlton, "Aristotle and the Principle of Individuation," *Phronesis* 17 (1972), 239–49 (form, not matter, is the principle of individuation); Edward Regis, "Aristotle's 'Principle of Individuation,'" *ibid.*, 21 (1976), 157–66 (after formulating seven questions to make the problems *re* the principle of individuation more precise, Regis notes that A. C. Lloyd, Whitney J. Oates, G. R. G. Mure and W. D. Ross consider matter to be that principle, whereas W. Charlton, J. Owens and H. Cherniss consider form to perform that role; he then concludes that neither matter nor form is the principle and that there is no need of such a principle: an existing composite exists and it is just its nature to exist as individual); M. Furth, "Transtemporal Stability in Aristotelian Substances," *Journal of Philosophy* 75 (1978), 624–48 (the principle of "diachronic individuation" is form—see p. 644); Joseph Owens, *The Doctrine of Being in the Aristotelian Metaphysics*, pp. 386–95: form, because it is a *tode ti*, an Entity and is separate in notion, is neither singular nor universal but is prior to both singularity and universality; it is not made singular in the composite, which alone is singular, although known by its form; because form is not a universal and because the question of a "principle of individuation" arises only when form is considered to be universal, the problem of determining such a principle does not arise in Aristotelian metaphysics. As a matter of fact, Owens has no discussion on the "principle of individuation" in his *Elementary Christian Metaphysics* (Milwaukee: Bruce, 1963), although see his "Matter and Predication in Aristotle" in John R. Catan (ed.), *Aristotle: Collected Papers of Joseph Owens* (Albany, N.Y.: SUNY Press, 1981), p. 39, n. 6, found on p. 193: prime matter "when actuated, differentiates by its very nature in making possible the spread of the same form in parts outside parts and the multiplication of singulars in a species. In that way it is an individuating principle without being of itself individual."

6

Mani's Twin and Plotinus: Questions on "Self"

Some autobiographical data will help to indicate the occasion of my interest in Mani's Twin and the limited scope of this chapter. Since that occasion concerns the *Cologne Mani Codex* (hereafter: *CMC*), let me first speak briefly of it. The *CMC* is a miniature parchment of the fifth century A.D. and is a biography of Mani up to his twenty-fifth year.[1] A Greek translation of a Syriac ori-

---

[1] Its title is "Concerning the Origin of His Body," where the last word refers not so much to Mani's physical body as to his Church (after the manner in which St. Paul calls the Christian Church the "Mystical Body of Christ"). See Ludwig Koenen, "Augustine and Manichaeism in Light of the *Cologne Mani Codex*," *Illinois Classical Studies* (hereafter: *ICS*) 3 (1978), 164–66. On the Coptic Manichaean Codex, which was probably part of the same work as the *CMC* and was a history of the Manichaeans from the death of Mani up to ca. A.D. 300, see *ibid.*, pp. 164–65 and n. 37.

Although biographical in content and even autobiographical in appearance, the *CMC* is formally an anthology. It consists of excerpts from Mani's own works and from the writings of Mani's immediate disciples (Baraies is one whose name will show up in our translations or paraphrases below), which an unknown editor collected and arranged in a roughly chronological sequence and according to five thematic units (Mani's childhood, his first revelation, his break with the baptists, his second revelation and separation from the baptists, his first missionary activities). See Albert Henrichs, "Literary Criticism of the *Cologne Mani Codex*" (hereafter: "Literary Criticism"), in B. Layton (ed.), *The Rediscovery of Gnosticism*, vol. 2 (Leiden: E. J. Brill, 1981), pp. 724–33. On the *CMC* as "neither genuinely biographical nor always historical, but theological and, more specifically, ecclesiastical," see *idem*, "Mani and the Babylonian Baptists: Historical Confrontation," *Harvard Studies in Classical Philology* (hereafter: *HSCP*) 77 (1973), 41.

ginal,[2] it was rendered legible in 1969 by A. Fackelmann[3] and its 192 pages were edited with a German translation and commentary by Albert Henrichs and Ludwig Koenen in ZPE 19 (1975), 1–85; 32 (1978), 86–199; 44 (1981), 201–318; and 48 (1982), 1–59.[4] An English translation of pages 1–99 of CMC has been made by Ron Cameron and A. J. Dewey. [5]

According to its English translators the importance of the CMC

cannot be overestimated for the history of religions. For the Codex provides the only Greek primary source for Manichaeism. Now we have not only new reports and accounts of the early life of Mani, but even additional evidence for a Gospel of Mani. Indeed, many of the excerpts resemble a proto-gospel in a raw state, along with apocalypses and aretalogical material. Moreover, the origin of Manichaeism becomes quite complex, since we now possess convincing evidence of the connection of Mani's baptists with Elchasai, the alleged founder of a predominantly Jewish-Christian sect. And, most of all, we are privy to new and unparalleled information on the organization, ritual practices, and theology of the baptist sect in which Mani was reared.[6]

---

[2] The original compilation was "very likely . . . made soon after Mani's death in 276 from sources written [in an Eastern Aramaic dialect] during his lifetime"—A. Henrichs, "The Cologne Mani Codex," HSCP 83 (1979), 352; also see idem, HSCP 77 (1973), 35–36.

[3] When acquired by the University of Cologne, the CMC consisted of some badly damaged lumps of parchment—see photographs at the end of "Ein Griechischer Mani-Codex" by H. Henrichs and L. Koenen in Zeitschrift für Papyrologie und Epigraphik (hereafter: ZPE) 5 (1970), 96–216; A. Henrichs, HSCP 83 (1979), 342–52.

[4] Still to appear is the commentary on pp. 121–92 of the Codex, as well as Indices and "Tafelband"—see ZPE 48 (1982), 1.

[5] The Cologne Mani Codex, "Texts and Translations," no. 15 of "Early Christian Literature Series," no. 3 (Missoula, Mont.: Scholars Press, 1979). Although only a partial translation (with accompanying Greek text), still it does translate the pages which are most important philosophically and religiously. The pages of the Codex which Cameron and Dewey have not yet translated are pp. 99–116, which Henrichs describes as less metaphysical and more pragmatic, and pp. 116–92, which are "more monotonous, less informative, and more concerned with legendary material than any other part of the codex" (see "Literary Criticism," pp. 730 and 731).

[6] For other high evaluations of the CMC see A. Henrichs, "Literary Criticism," p. 724: "Anyone who wishes to find out about the historical origins of Manichaeism, about Mani's view of himself or about the central role of books,

Now let me turn to autobiography. Aware of the importance of the *CMC*, Dr. James G. Keenan of the Department of Classics, Loyola University of Chicago, invited Drs. Henrichs and Koenen to give papers on the Codex at a colloquium in March, 1977. Dr. Henrichs spoke on "Mani's Elchasaites: Manichaeism and Jewish Christianity" and Dr. Koenen on "Manichaeism and Judeo-Christian Gnosticism." As commentators on their papers Dr. Keenan chose John Baggarly and myself.[7] In my commentary I concentrated upon Mani's Twin for two reasons. I had little prior acquaintance with Mani's positions (other than as the founder of the sect to which Augustine belonged and then rejected after nine years) but initial reading suggested that there might be a possible parallel between what Mani wrote on his Twin and what his contemporary, Plotinus, remarked on man as entailing higher and lower levels of existence.[8] Secondly, Henrichs and Koenen themselves gave considerable attention to Mani's Twin both in their Loyola University papers and in their publications (as will be clear later).

My current chapter is, obviously, a return to that suggested parallel and the methodology used will be similar to that in my presentation at Loyola, where I attended primarily to Henrichs' and Koenen's descriptions of Mani's Twin and, more precisely, to the questions which their exegesis raised when they identified "twin" with "self" in seemingly some contemporary sense. Here, then, I shall also concentrate upon their identification of "twin" and "self." The second part of my chapter will be devoted to Plotinus'

---

and of Mani's own words, in the propagation of his religion" will want to peruse the *CMC*. In summary, "the *CMC* is a rich repertory of Manichaean history, beliefs, and literary skill. . . . As a religious anthology of multiple authorship it has no parallel outside Manichaean literature" (*ibid.*, pp. 732–33). Also see K. Rudolph, "Die Bedeutung des Kölner Mani-Codex" in *Mélanges d'histoire des religions offertes à H.-Ch. Puech* (Paris: Presses Universitaires de France, 1974), pp. 471 sqq.; for a digest of contents of *CMC*, see A. Henrichs, *HSCP* 83 (1979), 340–42.

[7] John Baggarly, S.J., in 1977 was teaching in the Department of Theology at Loyola University Chicago and then librarian at the Pontificio Istituto Orientale in Rome; he is now working on a critical edition of the Greek text of the Byzantine author, Athanasius of Sinai.

[8] Plotinus (205–270) was slightly older than Mani (216–276). On the latter's dates see G. Haloun and W. B. Henning, "The Compendium of the Doctrines and Styles of the Teaching of Mani, the Buddha of Light" (hereafter: "Compendium"), *Asia Minor* 3 (1953), 197–201; Mary Boyce, *A Reader in Manichaean Middle Persian and Parthian* (hereafter: *A Reader*) (Teheran-Liège: Bibliothèque Pahlavi, 1975), pp. 1–3.

conception of the human person and to the questions which result when some scholars find a doctrine of "self" also in Plotinian texts.

The Twin of Mani

Let me, then, attend primarily to the questions which Henrichs' and Koenen's description of Mani's Twin as "self" suggests, since their understanding of Mani on other doctrinal points is basically accurate, as one would expect and can verify from their intelligent editing, translating and commenting upon the *CMC*. But I am puzzled on what "self" means when applied to Mani's Twin. This application may prove correct but it needs (in my opinion) to be discussed.

But before starting that discussion let me reproduce (in translation or paraphrase and with commentary reduced to footnotes) key passages from the *CMC* on the Twin,[9] which may serve as the context within which to appreciate and evaluate Henrichs' and Koenen's exegesis. [A] Twice (Mani states early in *CMC*) the voice of the Twin (*hôs syzygos phônê*) said to me: "Strengthen your power, make your mind strong and submit to all that is about to come upon you" (13.2).[10] [B] In order that he might free souls (*tas psychas*) from ignorance [as the Father of Greatness intended],[11] Mani became paraclete and leader of the apostleship in this generation.[12]

---

[9] Mani mentions the Twin in treatises other than the *CMC*, but less frequently and with little information. See G. Henrichs and L. Koenen, ZPE 5 (1970), 161. Besides the *CMC* there are seven other canonical writings. See G. Haloun and W. B. Henning, "Compendium," pp. 204–11; Mary Boyce, *A Reader*, pp. 12–13.

[10] References are given to the *CMC* according to the following rubric: the first number indicates the page of the Greek text, the second number the initial line of the passage translated or paraphrased. I have inserted capital letters in brackets to render subsequent referrals easier.

[11] Father of Greatness, who is the supreme God and is opposed to the Prince of Darkness, is the ultimate source of Mani's mission and leadership. But God works through intermediaries, such as the Messenger, Jesus the Splendor, etc. For a helpful diagram, which is based on the *Kephalaia* but which also represents many of the emanations mentioned in the *CMC*, see A. Henrichs and L. Koenen, ZPE 5 (1970), 183, reproduced below, Appendix A.

[12] "Paraclete" is the word used in John's Gospel, 14:16, and 16:17, to refer to the Holy Spirit and is here applied to Mani. On this application, see L. Koenen, *ICS* 3 (1978), 170–74, quoted and discussed below in the paragraphs corresponding to notes 25–27.

Then [Baraies now purports to quote Mani][13] "at the time when my body reached its full growth, immediately there flew down and appeared before me that most beautiful and greatest mirroring of [who I really am—namely, my twin][14] (17.1); the Greek for lines 12–16: ὤφθη ἔμπροσθέν μου / ἐκεῖνο τὸ εὐειδέστα / τον καὶ μέγιστον κά / τοπτρον τ[οῦ προσώ] / που μ[ου] . . .

[C] Yes, at the time I was twenty[-four] years old, the most blessed Lord was greatly moved with compassion for me, called me into his grace, and immediately sent to me [from there my] Twin, who appeared in great glory and who is mindful of and informer of all the best counsels from our Father (18.1 and 19.2; also see 72.20–73.7). [D] Baraies continues to quote Mani: "When my Father was pleased and had mercy and compassion on me, to ransom me from the error of the Sectarians [the Elchasaite baptists], he took consideration of me through his very many revelations and sent to me my Twin" (19.8), who "delivered, separated and pulled me away from the midst of that [Elchasaite] Law in which I was reared" (20.8).

[E] Baraies now quotes Mani on the instruction given him by the Twin on "how I came into being; and who my Father on high is; or in what way, severed from him, I was sent out according to his purpose; and what sort of commission and counsel he has given to me before I clothed myself in this instrument and before I was led astray in this detestable flesh, and before I clothed myself with its drunkenness and habits, and who that one is, who is himself my ever-vigilant Twin" (22.1).[15] [F] Yes, the Twin showed Mani "the secrets and visions and the perfections of my Father; and concerning me, who I am, and who my inseparable Twin is; moreover,

---

[13] Baraies is "a Manichaean apologist of the first generation after Mani"— L. Koenen, *ibid.*, p. 165; A. Henrichs, *HSCP* 83 (1979), 354. Also see note 1 above.

[14] In order to avoid the questionable use of "self," my translation differs from Cameron-Dewey's (". . . greatest mirror-image of [my self]"—see *The Cologne Mani Codex*, p. 19) and Henrichs-Koenen (". . . machtvolle Spiegelbild [meiner Gestalt]"—see *ZPE* 19 [1975], 19).

[15] Also see 21.10 on how Mani "was begotten into this fleshly body, by what woman I was delivered and born according to the flesh, and by whose [passion] I was engendered." The pessimistic view of body here and in 22.10 must be juxtaposed to earlier statements that the body is designed as "the holy place for the glory of the mind (*nous*), as the most holy shrine for the revelation of its wisdom" (15.8). This juxtaposition discloses the paradox in Mani's thought: the body is evil and yet good, it is enslaving but salvific.

concerning my soul, which exists as the soul of all the worlds, both what it itself is and how it came to be" (23.1).[16]

[G] The result was (Mani continues to speak) "that I acquired (the Twin) as my own possession. I believed that he belongs to me and is mine and is a good and excellent counselor. I recognized him and understood that I am that one from whom I was separated. I testified that I myself am that one who is unshakable"[17] (24.4); the Greek for lines 6 sqq.:

> ἐπίστευσα δ' αὐτὸν
> ἐμὸν / ὑπάρχοντά τε καὶ ὄν / τα
> καὶ σύμβουλον ἀγα / θὸν καὶ χρηστὸν ὄντα. /
> ἐπέγνων μὲν αὐτὸν
> καὶ / συνῆκα ὅτι ἐκεῖνος ἐ / γώ εἰμι
> ἐξ οὗ διεκρίθην. /
> ἐπεμαρτύρησα δὲ
> ὅτι ἐ / γὼ ἐκε[ῖ]νος αὐτός εἰμι /
> ἀκλόν[ητο]ς ὑπάρχων . /..."

The Codex continues in the same vein,[18] but enough samples have been taken to illustrate how prominent a role the Twin plays

---

[16] The fact that Mani's soul is a portion of the World Soul is not surprising in light of his monistic tendency—see Appendix A below, second paragraph, and the quotation from H.-Ch. Puech. On the formation of the physical universe, see 65.12: the Father "disclosed to me how I was before the foundation of the world, and how the groundwork of all the works, both good and evil, was laid, and how everything of [this] aggregation was engendered [according to its] present boundaries and [times]." On Mani's cosmogony and cosmology see J. Ries, "Manichaeism," *New Catholic Encyclopedia,* IX, 156D–157C; H.-Ch. Puech, *Le Manichéisme,* pp. 74–85; Hans Jonas, *The Gnostic Religion* (publishing data given below), ch. 9.

[17] For Henrichs-Koenen's translation of the last two sentences, see ZPE 19 (1975), 27: "Ich habe ihn erkannt und ich habe verstanden, dass ich jener bin, von dem ich getrennt wurde. Ich habe bezeugt, dass ich selbst jener bin und dass ich daher unerschütterlich bin." This corrects their earlier translation in ZPE 5 (1970), 68. On the monism which the two sentences suggest, see n. 16 above and Appendix A below. Also see the sentences from "The Hymn of the Pearl," quoted below in the paragraph corresponding to n. 28.

[18] See, for instance, such texts as these: the Twin, all-glorious and all-blessed, disclosed to Mani exceedingly great mysteries (26.8), which are hidden to the world and which are not permitted for anyone to see or hear (43.4). The Twin is a good counselor (32.14), an ally and protector at all times (33.4), "my unfailing Twin," the "entire fruit of immortality," that Mani might be

in Mani's life, as well as what the nature of the Twin himself is. He prepares Mani for the revelations which will establish him as an original religious leader by advising him to be strong and yet receptive (#A).[19] Sent by the Father that Mani might save souls from ignorance and darkness, the Twin—the most beautiful and greatest duplication of who Mani really is (#B)—brought counsels from the Father to Mani in his twenty-fifth year (#C). Through the many revelations the Father entrusted to him, the Twin freed and separated Mani from the errors of the Elchasaites (#D).[20] The information the Twin communicated opened up to Mani not only who the Father is and what his mission for Mani is, but also what Mani's soul is, how it came into being and how it came to be associated with body, as well as the fact that the Twin is an ever-vigilant and inseparable factor in his life (#E and #F). The Twin belongs to Mani as a good and excellent adviser—in fact, Mani *is* the Twin, from whom he was separated when his soul entered into matter but whom he has now rejoined through the initiative of the Father (#G).[21]

The Twin as "Self"

But important as the preceding key-texts are on the Twin's function and nature, they also serve as the context within which to evaluate Henrichs' and Koenen's identification of "twin" with "self." Although this identification occurs within their commentary upon the German translation of *CMC*,[22] let us for the sake of convenience turn to their other publications.

---

redeemed and ransomed from the Elchasaite error (69.15). Also, 101.13: "mein allerseligster *Syzygos*—mein Herr und Helfer"; 104.11: "der Allerherrlichste;" 105.17: the beauty of "meines allerseligsten *Syzygos*, jenes Allerherrlichsten und Erhabensten."

[19] This contrast between strength and submission is deliberately paradoxical: to receive the divine messages Mani must be intellectually robust. But thereby he shows himself to be a religious leader worthy of credence: his salvific message is divine because it comes from above, but it coexists with Mani's personal strength.

[20] This baptist sect, founded by Elchasai in the early second century A.D., had a predominantly Jewish-Christian, rather than Gnostic, basis. When Mani's father joined the sect, Mani was four years old and hence grew up in it. See A. Henrichs, *HSCP* 77 (1973), 44–45; L. Koenen, *ICS* 3 (1978), 187–90; Henrichs and Koenen, *ZPE* 5 (1970), 141–60; A. Henrichs, *HSCP* 83 (1979), 360–67.

[21] On the identity between Mani and the Twin see also the excerpt from the "Hymn of the Pearl" quoted below in Hans Jonas' translation and in n. 28.

[22] For example, see *ZPE* 19 (1975), 76.

According to Albert Henrichs, "Mani and the Babylonian Baptists: A Historical Confrontation," *HSCP* 77 (1973), 24, a duplication of Mani was an essential factor in his theory of salvation.

In terms of Manichaean soteriology, the notion of a duplicate Mani was, in fact, not at all unheard of, but was a well-established doctrine, propagated time and again by Mani himself. Mani's double, though his steady companion on earth, his counselor and helper in times of hardship, and his consoler in moments of despair, was not a creature of flesh and blood, but an incorporeal and celestial being, not subject to the terrestrial limitations of time and space. As the preexistent and eternal Twin of Light, he is the mirror-like reflection of Mani's inner self, the heavenly embodiment of his spiritual essence, his true identity, from whom he was separated when his soul put on the garment of a mortal body and with whom he was reunited at his death.

Here Henrichs appears to be making these relevant points. Mani's existence entails two main levels, one of which is his status as a creature of flesh and blood, subject to limitations of space and time and separated from his true identity when his soul put on the garment of a mortal body. The second level is occupied by his double—steady companion, counselor, helper and consoler—who is not material, spatial and temporal. Rather, he is an incorporeal and celestial being—namely, the preexistent and eternal Twin of Light, who mirrors, reflects, duplicates Mani's inner self and is the embodiment of his spiritual essence and is his true identity. *Comments*: On the first level Mani consists of body and *of soul*, which is his inner self and spiritual essence, reflected and duplicated by his Twin on the second level. This latter, then, is Mani's true identity, from which he was separated when his soul became incarnate and which he will regain at death by escaping from the body. *Question:* Mani's soul is his spiritual essence, yes, because it makes him be what he really is and continues to be even in matter. But what exactly is meant by saying Mani's soul is his inner *self*? What exactly does the italicized word express?

But let us turn to another passage from Henrichs, now commenting upon the stress Mani puts on his uniqueness as the final god-sent messenger to the world.

Mani's awareness of, and insistence on, his own singularity is the basis of his self-conception, and any attempt to penetrate into Mani's complex personality has to start from that point. But . . . Mani's self-understanding has little to do with the awareness of one's own individuality or terrestrial historicity, notions which would have been much less meaningful and important to Mani than they are to us. The fact that Mani possessed an alter-ego in the form of the Twin of Light makes him a split personality in the literal sense of that term rather than an individual: his human existence was nothing but a briefly reflected image of its true and eternal counterpart (*ibid.*, pp. 39–40).[23]

What is Henrichs saying here? Mani's awareness of his singularity allows him to understand himself and lets us penetrate the complexity of his personality. His true self-understanding consists not in his being aware of himself as an individual existing in history (i.e., in such-and-such a place, at such-and-such a time) but of his personality as split: his existing here and now contrasts with his true and eternal counterpart—namely, the alter-ego who is his Twin. His human status of mortal body clothing immortal soul or self separates him from his true self—the Twin. That separation results in his split personality: one self (Mani's soul in matter) is apart from the other self (the Twin). Psychological wholeness and religious salvation are achieved when the two come together and become one, either on earth when the Twin visits Mani or in heaven. *Question:* Is the contemporary notion of "split personality," if taken technically, applicable to Mani's situation?[24] Again, what does "self" signify when predicated of Mani and the Twin?

---

[23] The conception of Mani as a split personality comes to Henrichs from G. Haloun and W. B. Henning, "Compendium," p. 208: because of the Twin of Light "Mani possessed a split mind; he realized his condition and invented this striking term for his second personality: the 'Twin.'" See Henrichs and Koenen, *ZPE* 5 (1970), 182, n. 215: after quoting Henning they then add: "Wir habe zu zeigen versucht, in welchem Sinne man tatsächlich von einem 'split mind' Manis sprechen kann: Seine irdische Seele is ein Teil seines transzendentalen ichs und gleichsam von diesem abgespalten. In der Inspiration vereinigen sich die beiden Teile seines Ichs." Also see n. 27 below.

[24] Information on the hysterical neurosis of a dissociative kind, which Drs. Cornelia Wilbur, Malcolm Graham, William Rothstein, Frank Putnam and other contemporary psychologists call "multiple personalities," can easily be found in daily newspapers—see *Chicago Tribune* for February 5, 1979 (*re* "Sybil," a young woman with sixteen personalities, and "William," a twenty-two-year-old man with ten); October 4, 1982 (*re* "Eric"); April 18, 1983 (*re* "Natasha"). For more technical treatments see *Diagnostic and Statistical Manual*

Let us turn now to Ludwig Koenen, "Augustine and Manichaeism in the Light of the Cologne Mani Codex," *ICS* 3 (1978), 170, who speaks of Mani's Twin while discussing the larger question of identifying the "paraclete" mentioned in John's Gospel, 14:16 and 16:17. For Baraies (see *CMC*, 17.1) Mani's *Nous* is the paraclete. "His *Nous*, like that of all men, descended from the heavenly realm of Light and was imprisoned in the body. The real Mani was the *Nous* of Mani" and is identified with the paraclete. But according to other evidence the paraclete was identical with Mani's "*alter-ego* who brought him the revelation. This is the *syzygos*, the 'Twin,' a gnostic term" (*ibid.*). Koenen then sums up the discussion (pp. 173–74): "Mani identified (1) himself or rather his *Nous* and (2) his 'Twin' with the paraclete of *John.*" Despite what some scholars (G. Quispel, K. Rudolph, P. Nagel) think, there is no contradiction here. The contradiction disappears upon

consideration of the gnostic concept of the Twin. When Mani, i.e., the *Nous* of Mani, was sent into the world, a mirror image of the *Nous*, i.e., his *alter-ego*, remained in heaven. The one ego, the *Nous*, was imprisoned in the body and, consequently, forgot his mission. Then the Twin, the *alter-ego*, was sent to him from heaven. He brought Mani the revelation by reminding him of his divine nature and mission and, like an angel, protected him. The *Nous* of Mani and his Twin are the two complementary aspects of Mani's identity. The first represents him as incorporated in the body; the second represents his being as it is outside the body. Together they are the one complete Mani. When Mani looked into himself, he found his Twin approaching him from heaven; or, *vice versa*, when he looked at his Twin, he found himself. The story of the Twin bringing him the revelation relates what in abstract terms may be called the rediscovery of his identity and mission.[25]

In this passage Koenen offers considerable information. Every human being consists of body and of intellect.[26] This last consti-

---

of Mental Disorders (3d edition; American Psychiatric Association) and relevant articles in the journal *Archives of General Psychiatry*.

[25] Also see L. Koenen, "From Baptism to the Gnosis of Manichaeism," *The Rediscovery of Gnosticism*, vol. 2, pp. 741–43 and 750.

[26] "Intellect" or *nous* in Koenen expresses what Henrichs calls "soul" in *HSCP* 77 (1973), 24 (quoted above).

tutes his divine nature, reality, *ego*. Mani is no exception: he too consists of body and of intellect or *ego*. But in addition he also has another *ego*, called his "Twin," who mirrors and duplicates his real and divine nature (= intellect and *ego*) and who is sent to Mani to recall his authentic nature and mission and to guard him. Consequently, the single and complete reality of Mani consists of his terrestrial intellect or *ego* and of his celestial *ego*, the Twin. By awareness of his intellect imprisoned in matter, he knows his Twin and thereby his true identity as a complete self and, also, as the paraclete of John's Gospel. The account of his Twin's bringing him heavenly messages is merely a figurative and concrete way of expressing the fact that he rediscovered his identity and mission. *Questions:* In light of the last comment should one conclude that the Twin, as well as other emanations and factors in Mani's doctrine, is a figure within a story that is not literally true? Should one infer that the Twin is not an actually existing intellect and *ego* (whatever the last term may mean) but the projection of Mani's belief in his divine call, coupled with an awareness of his needing help in gaining freedom from his sinful material condition and from his previous religious adherence and in promulgating his gospel?[27]

---

[27] The accuracy of one's inference that the Twin is such a projection is guaranteed by Henrichs and Koenen, *ZPE* 5 (1970), 182: "Die Aufgaben, die in dem gnostischen Perlenlied auf Kleid, Bruder, Gefährte und Brief verteilt sind, übernimmt bei Mani der Gefährte oder Zwilling. Gefährte und brief des Perlenliedes ermöglichen es der Seele, ihre Sendung in dieser Welt zu erfüllen; das Gleiche tut Manis Gefährte. Das Kleid aber ist das himmlische Urbild der Seele, das mit ihr identisch ist und in dem die Seele sich selbst erkennt; genauso ist Manis Zwilling das geistige, vom Körper freie Ich Manis, das in eine konkrete Gestalt projiziert ist. Die vier transzendentalen Projektionen der Seele des Perlenliedes sind bei Mani in der einen Gestalt des Gafährten zusammengefasst. Der Gefährte ist von aussen herantretender Schützer und Mahner, und er ist doch zugleich mit Manis innerem Selbst identisch.

"Soeben wurde der Begriff der Projektion benutzt, um Manis Verhältnis zu seinem Gefährten verständlich zu machen. Uns ist aus der Psychologie bekannt, dass der Mensch dazu neigt, sein eigenes Seelenleben nach aussen in andere Personen und Personengruppen zu projizieren und dann sich selbst im anderen zu betrachten. Manis Denkweise was umgekehrt und lässt sich eher so umschreiben: Seine Lichtseele brachte aus sich die Seele hervor, die in den Körper hinabging, um ihr Erlösungswerk zu vollenden; so kannte sie in ihrem Ursprungswesen im Lichtreich bleiben und als geistige Wesenheit zugleich der in den Leib gefesselten Seele Manis jederzeit nahe sein. Dieses Über-Ich hatte keine Gemeinschaft mit dem Leib und trieb daher das im Leib gefangene Ich zu seiner Aufgabe an und beschützte es vor den Gafahren der Welt."

Before moving on, let me turn to another respected scholar, whose book antedates Henrichs' and Koenen's papers and who also gives great prominence to the Twin as "self": Hans Jonas, *The Gnostic Religion. The Message of the Alien God and the Beginnings of Christianity*, 2d ed. (Boston: Beacon Press, 1967). The crucial sentences occur when Jonas is commenting upon this passage from "The Hymn of the Pearl" (p. 115):[28]

On "The Hymn of the Pearl," which Henrichs and Koenen mention in the initial sentence of the quotation, see n. 28 below.

Concerning the influence which psychology and, especially, Jungian psychology wield on the exegesis of Gnostic and Manichaean texts see Gilles Quispel, "Gnosis and Psychology" in B. Layton (ed.), *The Rediscovery of Gnosticism*, vol. 1 (Leiden: E. J. Brill, 1980), pp. 17–31—pages 22 and 23 are specially noteworthy: "The discovery of the Self is the core of both Gnosticism and Manicheism. Even before Nag Hammadi this psychological approach was already a necessary supplement to the purely historical or unilaterally existentialistic interpretation of Gnosis which prevailed in other quarters. There is no question that psychology in general is of great help, an auxiliary science, for history in general, which otherwise tends to become arid and pedantic. And more specifically the Jungian approach to Gnosticism, once decried as a soul-shaking spectacle concocted by decadent psychologists and vain students of Judaic mysticism, turned out to be adequate when the *Gospel of Truth* was discovered. For then it became clear to everybody that Gnosis is an experience, inspired by vivid and profound emotions, that in short Gnosis is the mythic expression of Self experience. . . .

"So Jungian psychology has already had a considerable impact on Gnostic research. The term Self is used by practically everyone; the insight that Gnosis in the last analysis expresses the union of the conscious Ego and the unconscious Self is commonly accepted; nobody, not even the fiercest existentialist, can deny that Jung is helpful in discerning the real meaning of myth."

Also see Hans-Rudolf Schwyzer, "The Intellect in Plotinus and the Archetypes of C. G. Jung," in J. Mansfeld and L. M. de Rijk (eds.), *Kephalaion: Studies in Greek Philosophy and Its Continuation Offered to Professor C. J. de Vogel* (Assen: Van Gorcum, 1975), pp. 214–22; G. Quispel, "Hesse, Jung und die Gnosis," *Gnostic Studies*, vol. 2, pp. 241–58.

[28] What modern translators call "The Hymn of the Pearl" is entitled "Song of the Apostle Judas Thomas in the Land of the Indians" in its original source, the apocryphal *Acts of the Apostle Thomas*. Extant in both Syriac and Greek versions, the "Hymn" is a poetic composition "which clothes the central part of the Iranian doctrine [of gnosis] in a garment of a fable"—see Hans Jonas, *The Gnostic Religion*, p. 112. For another English translation see Robert M. Grant, *Gnosticism: A Source Book of Heretical Writings from the Early Christian Period* (New York: Harper, 1961), pp. 116 sqq. (the poem "reflects late Valentinian doctrine, perhaps that of Bardaisan—A.D. 154–222"); for a German translation see Raimund Kobert, "Das Perlenlied," *Orientalia* 38 (1969),

My robe of glory which I had put off and my mantle which went over it, my parents . . . sent to meet me by their treasurers who were entrusted therewith. Its splendor I had forgotten, having left it as a child in my Father's house. As I now beheld the robe, it seemed to me suddenly to become a mirror-image of myself: myself entire I saw in it, and it entire I saw in myself, that we were two in separateness, and yet again one in the sameness of our forms.

Jonas' commentary runs as follows.

The garment has become this figure itself [of light] and acts like a person. It symbolizes the heavenly or eternal self of the person, his original idea, a kind of double or *alter ego* preserved in the upper world while he labors down below. . . . The encounter with this divided-off aspect of himself, the recognition of it as his own image, and the reunion with it signify the real moment of his salvation. Applied to the messenger or savior as it is here and elsewhere, the conception leads to the interesting theological idea of a twin brother or eternal original of the savior remaining in the upper world during his terrestrial mission. Duplications of this kind abound in gnostic speculation with regard to divine figures in general wherever their function requires a departure from the divine realm and involvement in the events of the lower world (pp. 122–23).

Next comes a section to which Jonas gives a striking title.

The Transcendental Self

The double of the savior is as we have seen only a particular theological representation of an idea pertaining to the doctrine of man in general and denoted by the concept of the Self. In this concept we may discern what is perhaps the profoundest contribution of Persian religion to Gnosticism and to the history of religion in general. The Avesta word is *daena*, for which the orientalist Bartholomae lists the following mean-

---

447–56—his translation from the Syriac version (as is Jonas') of the last sentence of the lines excerpted from the poem is: "Doch plötzlich, als ich ihm begegnete, glich mir das Kleid wie mein Spiegelbild. Ich sah und erkannte es ganz in mir ganzen, und auch ich begegnete mir ganz in ihm. Wir waren zwei in der Trennung und wiederum eins durch dieselbe Gestalt" (p. 454).

ings: "1. Religion; 2. inner essence, spiritual ego, individuality; often hardly translatable."

In the Manichaean fragments from Turfan, another Persian word is used, *grev*, which can be translated either by "self" or by "ego." It denotes the metaphysical person, the transcendent and true subject of salvation, which is not identical with the empirical soul. In the Chinese Manichaean treatise translated by Pelliot, it is called "the luminous nature," "our original luminous nature," or "inner nature," which recalls St. Paul's "inner man"; Manichaean hymns call it the "living self" or the "luminous self." The Mandaean "Mana" expresses the same idea and makes particularly clear the identity between this inner principle and the highest godhead; for "Mana" is the name for the transmundane Power of Light, the first deity, and at the same time that for the transcendent, non-mundane center of the individual ego (pp. 123–24).[29]

The parallels between the Twin of "The Hymn of the Pearl" and that of *CMC* which stand out from Jonas' exegesis are so clear now from our previous pages as to need no explanation: The Twin remaining above and its counterpart descending below; the identity nonetheless between the Twin and its counterpart; the Twin as the eternal self, original idea, alter-ego contrasted with the selfhood in its terrestrial duplicate. Yet puzzlement still persists. "Perhaps the profoundest contribution to Gnosticism and to the history of religion in general" (to repeat Jonas) is "the concept of the Self" (p.

---

[29] Pertinent information on proper names within Jonas' paragraphs is as follows. *Avesta:* the canon of Zoroastrian writings as redacted in the Sassanian period. C. Bartholomae: the author of *Altiranisches Worterbuch* (Strassburg, 1904), which is the standard lexicon for Avestan and Old Persian. The fragments found at Turfan in Eastern Turkistan have been most recently edited by W. B. Wenning, *Nachricht. Gött. Ges. Wiss.* (Göttingen, 1933), pp. 217 sqq.; for an English translation (from text edited in 1904 by F. W. Müller) with commentary see A. V. Williams Jackson, *Researches in Manichaeism with Special Reference to the Turfan Fragments* (New York: Columbia University Press, 1932). On the Mandaeans, a southern Babylonian baptist sect, see H.-Ch. Puech, *Le Manichéisme*, pp. 40–44 and n. 147 (pp. 123–25); H. Jonas, *The Gnostic Religion*, ch. 3, which ends with a glossary of Mandaean terms (pp. 97–99); Henrichs and Koenen, *ZPE* 5 (1970), 133–40; A. Henrichs, *HSCP* 83 (1979), 367. On "the Chinese Manichaean translation by Pelliot," see G. Haloun and W. B. Henning, "Compendium," pp. 184–85; Williams Jackson, *Researches in Manichaeism*, "Bibliography," p. xxxvi.

124), which he illustrates by "daena," "grev" and terms from other sources. But what meaning are these words attempting to express in the original? Is "self" a helpful translation of them? Is "self" synonymous with "inner essence," "metaphysical person," "transcendent subject of salvation," "luminous, inner nature," "inner man"? Or does not Jonas intend it to be taken as in contemporary philosophical and psychological writings?

This last question explicates what is for me the problem underlying all else: the contemporary notion of "self" is multiple and ambiguous. In fact, it has no commonly accepted meaning. In order to realize this, let us look at the article on "Self" in the *New Catholic Encyclopedia*. I choose this not from any sectarian motive, but because of the surprising fact that among recent philosophical encyclopedias in English it alone provides such an article. The *Dictionary of the History of Ideas* has none, nor has the *Encyclopedia of Philosophy*, which gives the topic a single, short paragraph in its article on "Personal Identity" (V, pp. 95–107), where indeed "self" is set aside, because of its restriction to the mental and spiritual, as misleading in a discussion of the problem of personal identity.

Also, the *Encyclopedia Britannica* offers no full-scale paper on "self" but only a definition in its *Micropaedia*, IX, p. 41:

> Self is the subject of successive states of consciousness. In modern psychology the notion of the self has replaced earlier conceptions of the soul. According to Carl Jung the self is a totality comprised of conscious and unconscious contents that dwarfs the ego in scope and intensity. The coming-to-be of the self is sharply distinguished from the coming of the ego into consciousness, and is the individuation process by which the true self emerges as the goal of the whole personality.

Obviously, that brief description discloses mainly that "self" has largely become an area of study for empirical psychologists. And the impression given there, as well as in the paragraph from the *Encyclopedia of Philosophy*, is that "self" in contemporary literature has varied and divergent meanings.

That impression deepens when we open the *New Catholic Encyclopedia* to Margaret Gorman's article (XIII, pp. 56–60). Descartes is there credited with introducing "the word *self* as it is currently used" and with identifying it with "spiritual substance" (p. 57A). Disagreeing with him, Locke doubted that the self always thinks or that it is substantial: the self, understood as one's consciousness of continuing the same now as in the past, is distinct from soul or spiritual substance. By analyzing consciousness Hume challenged the view that any permanent self exists in the human person, who may be merely a "congeries of perceptions" (p. 57C). To Spinoza self is the substance which is at once the world and God; for Leibniz it is a thinking substance, where "thinking" includes "little perceptions" also. Kant speaks of "self" in several senses: phenomenal, noumenal, transcendental, ethical (pp. 57D-58A). Fichte opposed self (whose reality consists in its action of self-positing) to nonself, thereby laying the foundation for the dialectics of Hegel and Marx (p. 58A). In America Josiah Royce distinguished between the phenomenal self (a group of ideas) and the metaphysical self (a group of ideals; p. 58B). Husserl speaks of both an empirical and a transcendental self, the second of which constitutes the meaning of the world (58D). To Kierkegaard self is the right relationship one has to God a... to himself; for Gabriel Marcel it is incarnate consciousness (p. 59B). A modern psychologist such as Jung believes that self comprises both the conscious and the unconscious (p. 59C).

Although one could excerpt other examples from the article in the *New Catholic Encyclopedia*, the above suffice to suggest how complex and divergent "self" is among modern philosophers and psychologists. That complexity is mirrored in Gorman's conclusions from the historical survey.

> The term *self* does not supplant the older concept of soul, nor is it the same as ego, mind, or person. It is a concept used to designate functions that philosophers felt were not included in soul . . . [which] had become for them a term designating the static thinking substance revealed by the *Cogito* of Descartes [and which was replaced by "mind."] With the advent of the philosophers of the will, mind became inadequate to represent the human person in his dynamic growth and development. Person referred to the individual substance of a rational nature—a definition that . . . seemed to ignore the concrete individual development in the world. . . . Self then began to be used to suggest all those aspects of man thought to be left out by the terms soul, mind, person, and nature—and to designate the unifying, purposeful, growing, and interacting aspect of man's activities. It included also the notions of alienation and of encounter (pp. 59D–60A).[30]

---

[30] Also see B. B. Wolman (ed.), *Dictionary of Behavioral Sciences* (New York: Van Nostrand Reinhold, 1973), p. 342, which gives one-half column and seven

What has been our purpose in surveying what "self" signifies in modern literature? To realize that it is an extremely ambiguous notion and, thus, that one can use it to translate or interpret Mani only after carefully reflecting on whether it helps or hinders getting at *what he himself had in mind* in *CMC* and other canonical or semicanonical treatises (see note 10 above). Part of that reflection must be that each interpreter decide for himself what exactly "self" signifies in his own position before inquiring whether it is applicable to Mani's.

Let me illustrate by setting forth what "self" has come to mean within my own philosophical position, which is influenced mainly by Aristotle and Thomas Aquinas and which is (I hope) an authentic existentialism. Within a unique and individual human existent what constitutes "self"? It is not solely my soul, which is merely a part of me; nor does it consist solely in individuation, which comes from matter, nor in my state of being a supposit, which issues from existence. Rather, self is my entire unique and individual being but especially and precisely as I am conscious of who and what I am, as I freely determine who I am and yet as I am also determined by outside forces (other human existents, environment, culture, etc.). Thus, my selfhood concerns me in my uniqueness and individual-

---

definitions to "self." As examples of "self" taken less technically see Virginia Woolf, *To the Lighthouse* (New York: Harcourt Brace and World, Inc., 1927), p. 95: "*She could be herself, by herself.* And that was what now she often felt the need of—to think; well, not even to think. To be silent, to be alone. All the being and the doing, expansive, glittering, vocal, evaporated; *and one shrunk,* with a sense of solemnity, *to being oneself, a wedge-shaped core of darkness,* something invisible to others" (emphasis added). Also, Patrick Hart, "The Contemplative Vision of Thomas Merton," *Notes et Documents de l'Institute International Jacques Maritain,* no. 19 (avril–juin 1982), who quotes and interprets Merton's unpublished manuscript, "The Inner Experience": "Merton laid down a few basic notes on contemplation, which bear quoting: 'the first thing that you have to do before you start thinking about such a thing as contemplation is to try to recover a coordinated and simple whole, and learn to live as a unified human person. This means that you have to bring back together the fragments of your distracted existence so that when you say "I" there is really something present to support the pronoun you have uttered.' Therefore, we must know who we are, from whom we originated and where we are going. In Merton's words: 'Before we can realize who we really are, we must become conscious of the fact that the person we think we are, here and now, is at best an impostor and a stranger.' The false self, or the empirical ego, as Merton refers to it, is illusory, really a mask for our true identity, our true self, which is the deepest in which we stand naked before God's love and mercy" (p. 6).

ity as a psychological agent. In sum, my self is my-soul-actually-existing-within-this-body but considered not so much entitatively (i.e., in the parts which constitute me) as operationally (i.e., as dynamic, as active and passive, as the source and recipient of unique and singular activities).[31]

Manifestly, "self" interpreted in this fashion cannot validly be predicated either of Mani's Twin (who is soul or mind solely) or of Mani in his earthly state (whose true reality consists also of intellect or soul only). But one may also doubt whether "self" in other contemporary philosophical settings may be legitimately predicated of Mani and of his counterpart. At least such predication should (I am proposing) occur only after the meaning of "self" in those contemporary positions is clearly isolated and after Mani's writings are studied on his own terms, within his own third-century cultural and religious milieu.

Perhaps studying Plotinus on the human existent will give further insights.

Plotinus on the Human Existent

If we are to successfully compare Mani with Plotinus, at least two points need to be recalled. For the former the true reality of a human existent on earth—whether he be Mani or someone else—consists solely of intellect, or soul.[32] Second, Mani, as specially designated by the Father of Greatness (see note 11 above) to be a new channel of revelation, also involves another and higher dimension—a Twin, who is a more powerful intellect or soul, sent on occasion by the Father to communicate knowledge to Mani, to advise and console him, to free him from errors. Mani, then, entails two levels of reality—one higher, the other lower.

Does a human existent as Plotinus conceives him entail similar levels of reality? If so, might the higher level serve as his "Twin"? Let us reflect on some texts in the *Enneads*.

---

[31] On individuation, individuality, supposit and subject, see Leo Sweeney, S.J., *Authentic Metaphysics in an Age of Unreality* , 2d ed. (New York/Bern: Peter Lang Publishing, Inc., 1993), "Actual Existence and the Individual," pp. 181–93 and 197); chapter 22 below, "Existentialism: Authentic and Unauthentic," prgrs. corresponding to notes 22–33.

[32] The two nouns are interchangeable. Also see n. 26 above.

Mani's Twin and Plotinus: Questions on "Self"   147

Text A: IV, 2 (21), 1

In the single chapter which constitutes this entire treatise of *Enneads* IV, Plotinus investigates the nature of souls and, thereby, their relationship to Intellect.[33]

[1] "True being is in the intelligible world and *Nous* is the best of it. But souls are There too, for they come here from There. [2] That world contains souls without bodies; this one contains souls which have come to be in bodies and are divided by their bodies. [3] Each *nous* There is all-together, since it is neither separated nor divided. All souls in that eternal world also are all-together and without spatial separation. Accordingly, *Nous* is always without separation and is undivided, and soul There is likewise not separated or divided but it does have a nature which is divisible. [4] [But what does 'division' mean *re* souls?] Division for them is their departure from the intelligible world and their coming to be in bodies. Hence, a soul is reasonably said to be divisible with reference to bodies because in this fashion it departs from There and is divided. [5] How, then, is it also undivided? The whole soul does not depart: something of it does not come to this world and by nature is not such as to be divided. (Lines 12–13: Οὐ γὰρ ὅλη ἀπέστη, ἀλλ' ἔστι τι αὐτῆς οὐκ ἐληλυθός, ὃ οὐ πέφυκε μερίζεσθαι.) To say that the soul consists of what is undivided and of what is divided in bodies is the same as saying that it consists of what is above, upon which it depends, and of what reaches as far as the things down here, like a radius from a center [reaches the circumference of the circle]. [6] But when it has come here it sees with the part of itself in which it preserves the nature of the whole. Even here below it is not only divided but is undivided as well, for its divided part is divided in such a way as to remain undivided. It gives itself to the whole body and is undivided because it gives itself as a whole to the whole and yet it is divided by being present in each part." (Lines 20–22: Εἰς ὅλον γὰρ τὸ σῶμα δοῦσα αὐτὴν καὶ μὴ μερισθεῖσα τῷ ὅλη εἰς ὅλον τῷ ἐν παντὶ εἶναι μεμέρισται.)

Comment. In this passage Plotinus describes the two states in which souls find themselves. The first is their existence in the intelligible world (#1), where they are without bodies and, thus, are undivided (#2) and where their having all perfections present at once makes them similar to Intellect (#3). Yet even There a soul

---

[33] That single chapter is a commentary on Plato, *Timaeus*, 34C–35A.

The numbers in brackets here and in Texts B and C are added to make references easier in my "Comments."

by nature is divisible. The second state arises when soul comes from There to a body and thus is divided (#4). But even here a soul remains indivisible to an extent because of that part of it (*ti autēs*) which continues to be There (#5)[34] and through which it depends in its earthly career upon Intellect and knows reality (#6). In the intelligible world, then, a soul is undivided as aligned with Intellect and yet remains divisible because of its nature too; in the sensible world it is divided by the body it enters, within whose parts it is present;[35] but it is undivided because it is wholly present there (#6) and because of its continuing link with and dependence on Intellect (#5).

Is Plotinus' anthropology similar to Mani's? Yes, insofar as for each a human existent entails two levels of reality, the higher of which perfects, illumines and controls the lower.[36] For each there is an identity of sorts between the lower and the higher: according to Plotinus a soul's intellect is one with Intellect, from which it never departs; Mani proclaimed that "I am that one from whom I was separated. . . . I myself am that one who is unshakable" (*CMC*, 24. 9 sqq., quoted above). Yet there are differences. Mani's Twin is (as I interpret the *CMC*) more distinct from Mani himself than a soul's intellect is, in Plotinus' text, from the soul—the Twin seems almost an hypostasis with its own independent reality and function. Moreover, in the Manichaean worldview each human being is an intellect/soul but only Mani as the new and final prophet has a Twin, whereas every Plotinian human soul has an intellect, which remains There.

Perhaps more information will issue from subsequent pages of the *Enneads*.

---

[34] "That part of it" which remains There is its intellect, as will be clear from Texts B and C and *passim*.

[35] That body is not identical with matter solely, see H. J. Blumenthal, *Plotinus' Psychology: His Doctrines of the Embodied Soul* (The Hague: Martinus Nijhoff, 1971), p. 9: "We have already found it necessary to define soul in a special way. Coming to body we find that it is already a complex entity (IV. 7. 1. 8–10), as are even simple bodies in so far as they consist of both matter and form (*ibid.*, 16f; cf. V. 9. 3. 16–20): only pure matter is completely devoid of any of the form which all sensible substances have (II. 4. 5. 3f). Such form comes from the lower powers of the world soul sometimes called *physis* (nature). So when we ask how soul is in the body we must remember that that body already has soul in a certain way (cf. VI. 4. 15. 8ff)."

[36] Provided, of course, that a soul-in-body allows the Intellect to do so by a soul's using its intellect to turn away from matter, to contemplate, etc.

Text B: VI, 4 (28), 14

Just as Text A is a commentary on a Platonic dialogue (*Timaeus*, 34C sqq.), so this passage is excerpted from Plotinus' comments on Plato's *Parmenides*, 131B sqq.[37] There Plato inquires whether a single Form is present to multiple sensible participants in its entirety or only partially. Plotinus poses that question in three ways: how Intellect and Being can be omnipresent to lower existents; how the spiritual can be omnipresent to the corporeal; finally, how soul is omnipresent to body.[38] While replying to the third question, he offers a conception of the human existent which perhaps may parallel to some extent Mani's statements on himself and his Twin.

Plotinus begins chapter 14 by tracing the relationship between a human soul and Soul. [1] The latter contains all [individual] souls and intellects, and yet in spite of its distinguishable, multiple and, in fact, infinite contents it is one, since all such existents are there in an unseparated fashion and all-together, springing from but always remaining in self-identical unity (ch. 14, lines 1–15). [2] "But *we*—who are we? Are we that All-Soul[39] or, rather, are we that which drew near to it and came to be in time? [3] Before this sort of birth came about we were There as men different from those we now are—some of us as gods, pure souls, intellects united with all reality, since we were parts of the intelligible world, not separated or cut off, but belonging to the whole—indeed we are not cut off even now. [4] But now there has come to that higher man another man who wishes to be and who finds us, for we were not outside

---

[37] *Enneads*, VI, 4 and 5, are also commentaries on *Parm.*, 142B sqq. See E. Bréhier, *Plotin: Ennéades* (Paris: "Les Belles Lettres," 1954), VI, i, "Notice," pp. 160 and 165–67.

[38] See *ibid.*, pp. 161–63.

[39] Obviously, *ekeino* in line 17 refers to the Soul, on which attention had centered in the opening portion of the chapter. See E. Bréhier, *ibid.*, p. 194: "cette âme-là"; V. Cilento, *Plotino Enneadi* (Bari: Laterza, 1949), III, i, p. 265: "quell'Essere."

In *Plotinus* (London: Allen and Unwin, 1953), p. 125, A. H. Armstrong's translation is "that higher self," which is (in my view) questionable. Also see *idem*, "Form, Individual and Person in Plotinus," *Dionysius* 1 (1977), 51; Plato S. Mamo, "The Notion of the Self in the Writings of Plotinus" (Ph.D. diss., University of Toronto, 1966), p. 161: "that infinite spiritual life"; G. J. P. O'Daly, *Plotinus' Philosophy of the Self* (New York: Barnes and Noble, 1973), p. 25: " 'the higher primal,' within which we existed in the transcendent and thus "our 'real self' is located in a transcendent phase, prior to 'our' existence here on earth."

the All. [5] He wound himself round us and fastened himself to that
man that each one of us was There (as if there was one voice and
one word, and someone else came up from elsewhere and his ear
heard and received the sound and became an actual hearing, keeping present to it that which made it actual). [6] Thus we became a
couple and [we were no longer] the one [= higher man] we were
before. Sometimes we even became the other [= lower man], which
had fastened itself to us, when the first man is not active and is in
another sense absent.[40]

Comments. Before considering VI, 4, 14, 1 sqq. themselves, let us
note the general remarks of Dominic J. O'Meara (Plotinus: An Introduction to the "Enneads" [Oxford: Clarendon Press, 1993]) on "the
problem of presence," which he finds central to treatises 4 and 5 of
Enneads VI. That problem arises "from a mental confusion which
consists (1) in thinking of immaterial being as subject to the same
restrictions, in particular local restrictions, as bodies, and consequently (2) not seeing how an immaterial being can be present as a
whole throughout body." Its therapy consists in "accustoming oneself to thinking of immaterial being in another way. . . in the light of
its proper, non-quantitative, non-local characteristics. Much of VI,
4–5 is devoted to this therapy" (ibid, p. 24). Still further: "presence"
when spoken of in "regard to immaterial being" involves singling
out "its unchangingness, its independence from any particular place
of body 'in' which it would exist, a perfection of existence that
excludes its 'going away' from itself to be in another, a self-dis-
persal such as marks corporeal nature." Accordingly, "the totally
unified and stable nature of the intelligible constitutes a kind of
complete presence to itself." Finally, "the relation between immaterial and material reality" issues from the fact that "in Greek 'in' can
mean to be 'in' someone's or something's power. In this sense
immaterial being is 'in' nothing as not depending on any body for
its existence. On the other hand body, as dependent on soul, can be

---

[40] In this lower man body "acquires a trace of soul, not a piece of soul but a
kind of warming or enlightenment coming from it" (VI, 4, 15, 14–16; Armstrong
translation, Plotinus, p. 126). The coming (and, thus, presence) of the higher
man to the lower "does not mean that the soul departs from itself and comes
to this world but that the bodily nature comes to be in soul and participates in
it . . . by giving body something of itself, not by coming to belong to it; and
'departure' [and absence] means that body has no share in it" (VI, 4, 16, 7–17;
Armstrong translation, Plotinus, pp. 134–35); also see idem, Loeb translation,
VI, p. 317). For the Greek text see Ch. 5 above, prgr. corresponding to n. 44

said to be 'in' soul, just as material reality depends on, or is 'in', immaterial being" (*ibid.*, p. 26).

After that general introduction let us now turn to VI, 4, 14, 1 sqq. so as to detect from those complex and elliptical lines what a human existent is. A human soul in both its lower and higher states is distinguishable from the All-Soul. The latter by reason of its multiple and, in fact, infinite contents (all souls and intellects) is all-perfect but also is intrinsically and essentially one because its contents, manifold and explicated though they be, are not actually separated but are all-together and so always remain in unity (#1).

An individual soul entails two manners of existing inasmuch as it remains within the Soul or departs from It.[41] Within the Soul an individual soul and intellect also contains and contemplates all reality from its own more limited perspective, and it is quiet, at peace and one with Soul. Nonetheless, it is not totally identical with Soul or with other individual souls There: although not actually isolated from them, it is divisible and distinguishable from them and, thereby, is *individual* in an analogous but authentic sense.[42] This individuality, when combined There with its other dimension of all-perfections-in-unity, constitutes the "higher man" (#3). The "lower man" is the same soul but now as in time and enmeshed in an encompasssing body (#5). Any individual soul is, then, a couple (*to synampho*): it is at once the higher man and the lower man,

---

[41] Departure from Soul is described in VI, 4, 14, 11–12, as a "springing (*arxamenas*) from unity and yet remaining in that from which they sprang; or rather they never did spring from it but were always in this state" (Armstrong translation, *Plotinus*, p. 123).

[42] An "individual" in Plotinus' texts commonly signifies that which is somehow other than or different from something else. That otherness can consist, as here, in a soul's distinguishability or divisibility from other souls and Soul while yet remaining within Soul and associated with its psychic companions There. A further otherness and, hence, individuality arises when a soul "departs from" Soul and is enmeshed in a body (see notes 40 and 41 above). It is of this second individuality that VI, 5 (23), 12, 16 sqq., speaks (both *re* how one acquires it and how one frees himself from it): "[In ascending back to Intellect] you have come to the All and not stayed in a part of it, and have not said even about yourself, 'I am so much.' By rejecting the 'so much' you have become all—yet you were all before. But because something else other than the All added itself to you, you became less by the addition, for the addition did not come from real being (you cannot add anything to that) but from that which is not. When you have become an individual by the addition of non-being, you are not all till you reject the non-being. You will increase

although on some occasions its higher aspect predominates, on others its lower (#6).

Accordingly, who are *we*? What constitutes *us*? What makes us be who we are? Where do we find ourselves? No one of us is the All-Soul as such but each is (so to speak) one area of Soul, one participation in It, one portion or dimension of Its contents. And that area, participation, portion, dimension (call it what you will) either rests quietly within Soul (then I am the "higher man" and am more fully real) or it has gone forth to movement, time, body (and I am the "lower man" and am less real).[43] Consequently, "we" in Text B is the combination of the two, even though at times we are more one than the other to correspond with which "man" is more active and in control.

Thus far our attempt to decipher Plotinus' clues on what a human existent is. Now our question: does his triad of Soul, higher

---

yourself then by rejecting the rest, and by that rejection the All is with you." For Greek text see ch. 5, p. 104.

By liberating oneself from matter, then, one regains his place within Soul and, eventually, within Intellect, where nonetheless he retains his first sort of individuality—his distinguishability or divisibility from Intellect, Soul and other souls. Even this individuality is set aside when a soul ascends beyond Soul and Intellect to become one with the One and thereby achieves well-being (*eudaimonia*) above being. See VI, 9 (9), 11, 4 sqq., discussed below.

On problems which VI, 4 and 5, raise *re* "individual" (especially *re* the Idea of Individual), see H. J. Blumenthal, *Plotinus' Psychology*, pp. 123 sqq.

[43] Blumenthal states (*Plotinus' Psychology*, p. 110), "we" are "a focus of conscious activity that can shift as such activity shifts." He quotes with approval E. R. Dodds' view: "Soul is a continuum extending from the summit of the individual *psyché*, whose activity is perpetual intellection, through the normal empirical self right down to the *eidôlon*, the faint psychic trace in the organism; but the *ego* is a fluctuating spotlight of consciousness" (*ibid.*, n. 25; see references there also to J. Trouillard, P. Hadot and W. Himmerich).

The value of conferring such mobility on "we" is that it allows one to understand how Plotinus can variously state that the "we" is multiple, that it is twofold, that it is found only at the level of reason, that it is found at the level of *nous* (see Blumenthal, *ibid.*, pp. 110–11, for references to the *Enneads*). One must conclude, then, that "'we' is not bound to any particular level or to a restricted range," even though it is usually to be found at the level of reason, which is "directed both towards the processing of sense-data, for which it may use the knowledge that it derives from above, and to the consideration of such knowledge in itself. It may thus be regarded as the meeting place of the sensible and intelligible worlds. And this is where we would expect to find Plotinus' man, a being who must live in this world but whose thoughts and aspirations are directed beyond it" (*ibid.*, p. 111).

man and lower man parallel Mani's conception of himself and his Twin? Mani also speaks of a triad of Light-Intellect (see note 11 above), Twin and terrestrial soul.[44] Consequently, there is a parallel of sorts, which nonetheless entails the same differences as noted in our "Comments" on Text A. Mani's Twin seems entitatively less one with him than does Plotinus' higher man with lower man. Second, the latter's schema of Soul, higher man and lower man fits every human existent, whereas Mani's apparently is restricted to himself as founder of the Manichaean church.[45]

Text C: II, 9 (33), 2

Let us take up another passage from Plotinus, this time from the treatise he wrote against the Gnostics of his time.[46] [1] "One must not posit more existents There than these [the Good-One, the Intellect and the Soul—see previous chapter of II, 9] nor make superfluous distinctions in such realities [e.g., between an Intellect which thinks and an Intellect which thinks that it thinks—see *ibid.*] No, we

---

[44] For Mani the hierarchy of reality above Light-Intellect consists (in ascending order) of Jesus the Splendor, the Envoy, the Father of Greatness. In Plotinus' hierarchy the One-Good and Intellect precede Soul.

[45] Mani's acceptance of Buddha, Zoroaster and Jesus as prior prophets, as well as his own role as the ultimate prophet and savior, would be abhorrent to Plotinus, for whom each human being can save himself and needs not divine intervention, since each has an intellect which always remains above and needs only be actuated in order that he attain salvation. On Mani's conception of Jesus see M. Boyce, *A Reader*, p. 10; F. C. Burkitt, *The Religion of the Manichees* (Cambridge University Press, 1925), pp. 37–43.

On Plotinus *vs.* Christianity, see *Enneads*, III, 2 (47), 9, 10–12: "It is not lawful for those who have become wicked to demand others to be their saviors and to sacrifice themselves in answer to their prayers"—for A. H. Armstrong "this looks as if it might be directed against the Christian doctrine of Redemption. If so, it is the only reference which I have detected to orthodox Christianity in the *Enneads*" (*Plotinus*, p. 167, n. 9; also see *idem*, Loeb III, 221–22; *idem*, *Introduction to Ancient Philosophy* [Totowa, N.J.: Rowman and Allanheld, 1983], p. xvi). Also see E. Bréhier, *Plotin: Ennéades*, VI, i, 168.

[46] Besides "Against the Gnostics," Porphyry also gives the title "Against those who say that the maker of the universe is evil and the universe is evil" (see Armstrong, Loeb II, 220). On who these Gnostics were see *ibid.*, pp. 220–22; E. Bréhier, *Plotin: Ennéades*, "Notice," II, pp. 96–110; Harder *et al.*, *Plotins Schriften* (Hamburg: Felix Meiner, 1964), III *b*, pp. 414–18; H.-Ch. Puech, "Plotin et les Gnostiques," in *Entretiens sur l'Antiquité Classique*, V: *Les Sources de Plotin* (Vandoeuvres-Genève: Fondation Hardt, 1960), pp. 161–90; Francisco García Bazán, *Plotino y la Gnosis* (Buenos Aires: Fundación para la Educación, la Ciencia y la Cultura, 1981), pp. 199–340; Richard T. Wallis, "Soul and Nous in

must posit that there is one Intellect, which remains unchangeably the same and without any sort of decline and which imitates the Father [= the Good-One] as far as it can. [2] One power of our soul is always directed to realities There, another to things here, and one is the middle between them. [3] Since the soul is one nature in multiple powers, sometimes all of it is carried along with its best part and with being. At times its worst part is dragged down and drags the middle part with it—not, to be sure, the whole of soul because that would be unlawful. [4] This misfortune befalls [a soul's middle part] because it does not remain There among the fairest realities (where nonetheless soul stays which is not such a part—nor indeed is the distinctive 'we' such a part) but rather allows the whole of body to hold whatever it can hold from it. [5] Even so, soul [in its highest part] remains unperturbed itself: by discursive thinking it does not manage body or set anything right but it orders things with a wonderful power by contemplating that which is before it. [6] The more it is directed to that contemplation, the fairer and more powerful it is. And receiving from There, it gives to what comes after it, and it illumines [what is below] in accordance as it is illumined [from above]." (Chapter 2 in its entirety:

Οὐ τοίνυν οὔτε πλείω τούτων οὔτε ἐπινοίας περιττὰς ἐν ἐκείνοις, ἃς οὐ δέχονται, θετέον, ἀλλ᾽ ἕνα νοῦν τὸν αὐτὸν ὡσαύτως ἔχοντα, ἀκλινῆ πανταχῇ, μιμούμενον τὸν πατέρα καθ᾽ ὅσον οἷόν τε αὐτῷ. Ψυχῆς δὲ ἡμῶν τὸ μὲν ἀεὶ πρὸς ἐκείνοις, τὸ δὲ πρὸς ταῦτα ἔχειν, τὸ δ᾽ ἐν μέσῳ τούτων· φύσεως γὰρ οὔσης μιᾶς ἐν δυνάμεσι πλείοσιν ὁτὲ μὲν τὴν πᾶσαν συμφέρεσθαι τῷ ἀρίστῳ αὐτῆς καὶ τοῦ ὄντος, ὁτὲ δὲ τὸ χεῖρον αὐτῆς καθελκυσθὲν συνεφελκύσασθαι τὸ μέσον· τὸ γὰρ πᾶν αὐτῆς οὐκ ἦν θέμις καθελκύσαι. Καὶ τοῦτο συμβαίνει αὐτῇ τὸ πάθος, ὅτι μὴ ἔμεινον ἐν τῷ καλλίστῳ ὅπου ψυχὴ μείνασα ἡ μὴ μέρος, μηδὲ ἧς ἡμεῖς ἔτι μέρος, ἔδωκε τῷ παντὶ σώματι αὐτῷ τε ἔχειν ὅσον δύναται παρ᾽ αὐτῆς ἔχειν, μένει τε ἀπραγμόνως αὐτὴ οὐκ ἐκ διανοίας διοικοῦσα οὐδέ τι διορθουμένη, ἀλλὰ τῇ εἰς τὸ πρὸ αὐτῆς θέᾳ κατακοσμοῦσα δυνάμει θαυμαστῇ. Ὅσον γὰρ πρὸς αὐτῇ ἐστι, τόσῳ καλλίων καὶ δυνατωτέρα· κἀκεῖθεν ἔχουσα δίδωσι τῷ μετ᾽ αὐτὴν καὶ ὥσπερ ἐλλάμπουσα ἀεὶ ἐλλάμπεται.)

Plotinus, Numenius and Gnosticism," in Richard T. Harris and J. Bregman (eds.), *Neoplatonism and Gnosticism* (Norfolk, Va.: International Society for Neoplatonic Studies, 1991), ch. 20, pp. 459–80.

Comments. After restricting the primal existents to three (the One-Good, Intellect and Soul)[47] and positing a threefold power in a human soul (#2), Plotinus pays considerable attention to its highest and intellectual power. The lowest power tends to the physical world (#2) and is dragged down by the body ensnaring it (#3) and the second power is marked by discursive reasoning, through which it endeavors to manage the body (#5), and by its vulnerability to being misled by the power beneath it (#3). But the highest power of an individual soul always tends (#2) to the realm of most beautiful realities (#4), where it remains at peace (#5) and which are the objects of its contemplation (#6). From the illumination issuing from this contemplation, it becomes more beautiful and strong and thus can enrich and illumine the middle and even the lowest portions of the soul (#6). [48]

If we related the tripartite soul in Text C to Mani's position, what information can be drawn? The steadfast link of the highest power in the nature of the human soul with the realm of the really real, whence comes its illumination and power, would be congenial to Mani's view of his soul as enlightened by the Father of Greatness and as the channel of salvific knowledge to members of his church. And, of course, that supreme psychic power could be made to correspond with his Twin. But the basic dissimilarity between the two authors remains: Plotinus sketches a view embracing all human existents, Mani a view confined to himself as divinely commissioned savior, a commission which is repugnant to the Neoplatonist (see note 45 above).

Summary and Conclusions

Texts other than the three so far discussed are relevant but they do not provide radically different information. One such is V, 3 (49), 3, in which Plotinus speaks of a soul as consisting of three powers—highest, middle and lowest, of which the first is aligned with intellect, the second with reason, the third with sense-perception—and thus it is similar to our Text C above.[49] Hence, such a passage does not need separate exegesis.

---

[47] See II, 9, 1, 1–19.

[48] Would not "we" (see #4) be here identical with intellect, which is the highest power of a soul and which is not dragged down to body with soul's middle power? See n. 43 above.

[49] But it is dissimilar too: in Text C "we" is identified with intellect (see n. 48 above), in V, 3 (49), 3, with reason, the middle power of soul. See Blumenthal,

Accordingly, let us list briefly the relevant information of Texts A to C. In the first, Plotinus describes an individual soul as existing in two states, the first of which is the intelligible world, the second the physical world. In each state it is marked with attributes of the other. For instance, when existing on the level of Intellect, it is undivided from other souls and intellects and yet its nature is such as to be divisible. When existing within a body, it is isolated from other living beings but also remains united with the higher level because of its part which continues to be There and through which it still depends upon Intellect and knows reality. In Text B Plotinus continues the contrast between the higher and lower states in which human souls exist but tries to locate their distinctive individuality by asking "Who are we?" His answer: no one of us is the All-Soul but each is one portion or participation of its contents, which either rests immutably within It (then I am the "higher man") or has been immersed in motion, body and time (then I am the "lower man"). Join these together and one has the couple (*to synampho*) that each of us distinctively is. Text C portrays an individual soul entailing the triple powers of intellect, reason and sensation, the first of which rests steadfastly on the level of Intellect, from its contemplation of which comes the illuminations that enrich its middle and lowest powers.

What, now, would Mani's reaction be if he were to read Plotinus? He would find himself both agreeing and disagreeing. He would agree that he himself involves higher and lower levels of existence, the first of which is occupied by his Twin (a more powerful and immutable intellectual being, destined to be his helper and guide), the second by his intellect or soul within a body. He would concur also that salvific knowledge and illumination come from the higher levels to him as the terrestrial conduit to those open to his divine message and leadership. But he would disagree that human individuals other than himself would entail a Twin as a transcendent

---

Plotinus' Psychology, p. 110, for a comparison of V, 3, with other texts; Armstrong, *Plotinus*, p. 166, considers "the doctrine of this very late treatise to represent a rethinking and an attempt to arrive at greater precision about the relationship between soul and *Nous*. Elsewhere Plotinus says without qualification that we at our highest are, and remain eternally, *Nous*."

Denis O'Brien has kindly alerted me to two additional texts: I, 1 (53), 12, 21–39 (especially relevant because of the possible parallel between Heracles' unique status and Mani's) and III, 4 (15), 3–6 (the entire treatise, however, seems no more consistent and clear than is Plato's position on *daimon* set forth in *Phaedo*, *Republic* and *Timaeus*, upon which Plotinus is commenting).

Intellect to be their consoler and guide: Mani himself is to perform those functions for them. Neither would he agree that human individuals need no outside help in achieving ultimate well-being: the intellect of no one existing here in matter resides immutably in the upper realms of light so as to serve as instrument of salvation—no one, that is, except Mani's, who is to administer the divine help all others need.

But despite those disagreements Mani concurs with his contemporary sufficiently to prompt our wondering what the source of their concurrence may be. Why are their positions parallel in certain important aspects, even though it is very unlikely that either read or met the other?

This fact, at least, seems obvious: each formulated a monism which is dynamic rather than static.[50] That is, all existents are real insofar as they consist of the same basic stuff (unity for Plotinus, light for Mani). All existents other than the First proceed from higher existents, of which the ultimate source is the One-Good for Plotinus and the Father of Greatness for Mani. For both authors that process is a movement downward from the more to the less perfect.[51] And the higher existents, which are the causes of whatever reality a lower existent may have, automatically and structurally are (so to speak) concerned with and care for their effects. This entitative concern and care explain why Mani's Twin comes from

---

[50] This dynamism contrasts them with Parmenides, whose monism of Being eliminates all change and movement from reality. See Leo Sweeney, S.J., *Infinity in the Presocratics: A Bibliographical and Philosophical Study* (The Hague: Martinus Nijhoff, 1972), pp. 93–110, especially 107–10.

[51] This direction of their dynamic monism contrasts them with Hegel, in whose monism Absolute Spirit moves from the less to the more perfect: from Categories (Being, Essence, Notion) through Nature to Spirit (Art, Religion, Philosophy).

Hans Jonas, "The Soul in Gnosticism and Plotinus," in *Philosophical Essays from Ancient Creed to Technological Man* (University of Chicago Press, 1974), pp. 325–28, considers what I call "dynamic monism" to be a speculative system common to Plotinus and Mani, as well as to Valentinus and Ptolemaeus, the anonymous authors of the *Poimandres* and the *Apocryphon of John*, and Origen. W. R. Schoedel, "Gnostic Monism and the Gospel of Truth," in B. Layton (ed.), *The Rediscovery of Gnosticism*, vol. 1: *The School of Valentinus*, pp. 379–90, describes the theology of the Valentinian "Gospel of Truth" as a monism, which, however, means "that everything arises directly or indirectly from one source" (p. 390). Such a definition does not do justice to monism in Plotinus and Mani, which demands also that all existents consist of the same basic stuff and not be fully distinct from one another.

the Father to him as counselor and consoler and why for Plotinus the Intellect furnishes a steadfast and safe haven from which individual intellects never depart and to which individual souls can thereby return.

If one were asked to locate such worldviews within the history of Western thought, one would have to say they are Platonic—a Middle Platonism which is influenced by Stoic monism, by Neopythagoreanism and by Aristotelian ontology, epistemology and ethics, but which radically originates with Plato. Plotinus' indebtedness to Plato and to Middle Platonism is beyond question.[52] But what philosophical influences (if any) directly or even indirectly influenced Mani? Such a question has, as far as I know, yet to be answered adequately.[53]

"Self" and Plotinus?

Just as several interpreters find Mani to espouse a doctrine of "self" (see the section above, "The Twin as 'Self'"),[54] so some scholars think that Plotinus has a doctrine of "self." For instance, Plato Salvador Mamo describes Plotinus as apparently "the first philosopher explicitly concerned with the notion of the individual consciousness or ego." The last term should be defined, he adds, "not in static but in dynamic terms; not as individual substance but as striving, attention, direction of consciousness."[55]

Gerard J. P. O'Daly has written an entire book with the significant title of *Plotinus' Philosophy of the Self* (New York: Barnes and Noble, 1973; Ph.D. dissertation, 1968). Moreover, O'Daly lists an impressive number of contemporary authorities to back up his

[52] For helpful studies of Middle Platonism see R. T. Wallis, *Neoplatonism* (New York: Charles Scribner's Sons, 1972), pp. 29–36 (bibliography p. 187); John Dillon, *The Middle Platonists: A Study of Platonism 80 B.C. to A.D. 220* (London: Duckworth, 1977), bibliography pp. 416–21 (p. 420 *re* Gnosticism and Christian Platonism); *idem*, "Descent of the Soul in Middle Platonic and Gnostic Theory," in B. Layton (ed.), *The Rediscovery of Gnosticism*, vol. 1, pp. 357–64.

[53] On the philosophical background of Mani, see Appendix B below.

[54] For example, A. Henrichs, *HSCP* 83 (1979), 340: "Mani's 'twin companion' (*syzygos*) is the personification of a typically Gnostic concept, the transcendent projection of one's soul" and is his celestial alter ego or self.

[55] "The Notion of the Self in the Writings of Plotinus" (Ph.D. diss., University of Toronto, 1966), initial "Summary," p. 1.

position. Emile Bréhier, Jean Trouillard, Richard Harder, E. R. Dodds and Wilhelm Himmerich all observe "that this concept [of "self"] plays an original and important part in Plotinus' thought" (pp. 4–5). Still others "have recognized the importance of the concept" —Pierre Hadot, E. von Ivanka, E. W. Warren, H. J. Blumenthal, J. M. Rist, P. S. Mamo, A. H. Armstrong (p. 98, note 8). The last named, A. H. Armstrong, has in fact published an important article in 1977 on "self" and entitled "Form, Individual and Person in Plotinus" (*Dionysius* 1 [1977], 49–68).

But despite those explicit affirmations that "self" is to be found in Plotinus' *Enneads,* some of the same authors speak also in such a way as to raise questions about the accuracy of their affirmative statements. In the Preface to his dissertation, Mamo says that "it can be argued that a doctrine of the nature and destiny of the self must occupy a central position in any mystical system. But in Plotinus' case we have neither an explicit doctrine contained in his writings, nor a comprehensive study by a commentator. Scholars, who have given us little beyond scattered remarks, seem to be divided in their interpretations of the texts. It is held, on the one hand, that there is no room for the ego in Plotinus' heaven. On the other hand, we are told that Plotinus was so impressed by the uniqueness of each ego that he wanted to maintain a distinction between it and the One even within the *union mystica*" (*op. cit.*, p. ii). Even O'Daly grants toward the end of his book *Plotinus' Philosophy of the Self* that Plotinus has "no fixed word—hence, no *concept,* strictly speaking—for 'self': as P. Henry has pointed out, there is no word for 'person' or 'self,' in Greek" (p. 89).

But in the light of O'Daly's admission, how can one discover a philosophy of "self" in the *Enneads*? What does one look for?

Perhaps it will be instructive to observe how O'Daly develops Plotinus' philosophy of "self." After noting (as just mentioned) that Plotinus has "no fixed word—hence, no *concept,* strictly speaking— for 'self' . . . there is no word for 'person' or 'self' in Greek," the Irish scholar states that Plotinus uses *autos* or *hêmeis* or the reflexive *hauton* to express the concept of "self." He continues: even "if the word, and the explicit, canonized concept are missing, . . . adequate testimony . . . [is] given of Plotinus' clear awareness of the importance of a concept of self . . . to account for the identity of a human subject at the several levels of existence possible to man" (pp. 89–90).[56]

---

[56] H. J. Blumenthal, after affirming that "a person's identity . . . is a concept for which Greek had no word" (*Plotinus' Psychology*, p. 109), adds that "the

That identity on the level of man in history involves the empirical or historical self (man as image [*eidolon*], as exterior and individual, soul as embodied; pp. 26–30). But it consists mainly in soul when reasoning and thinking and, thus, at its highest (p. 43): it becomes aware of itself as derived from *nous* as secondary image and as a repository of Forms (p. 44). "Self," then, is "essentially a faculty of conscious self-determination, a mid-point which can be directed towards the higher or the lower" (p. 49; also see p. 43). On the next level self continues to be soul but now as more closely linked with *nous*: through wisdom and virtue a soul "has a capacity for the divine by reason of its kinship and identical substance with the divine" (p. 52). Despite its divinization, though, the soul remains human (pp. 56–58, 62–63): "the human self, reverting to the intelligible, remains itself, while at the same time being one with the totality of Being" (p. 65). On the highest level self is soul as above being and *nous* and as one with the One (pp. 83–84) and, thereby, it is transcendent and absolute (p. 91). Yet it is not annihilated in that union: although its "everyday" or historical selfhood is transformed, it truly has become itself: "the self is a *reality* . . . in the moment of *union*, and not merely afterwards—despite the fact that one is *not aware* of the distinction at that moment" (p. 85).

O'Daly is obviously intelligent, industrious and thoroughly acquainted with the *Enneads*. Nonetheless, his book makes me uneasy. That uneasiness does not issue primarily from any one of his individual conclusions (e.g., that the human self on the highest level is soul, which There is one with the One and yet remains itself—soul—in that very union) so much as from the conviction which underlies the book: that Plotinus has an authentic philosophy of "self," that he was aware of "self" in some sort of technical meaning, even though O'Daly admits (as we have seen) that Plotinus has "no fixed word—hence, no *concept*, strictly speaking—for 'self'" (p. 89).

But in the light of this admission, how (to repeat our earlier questions) can one discover a *philosophy* of "self" in the *Enneads*?

---

lack of suitable terms need not mean that the concept did not exist" (*ibid.*, n. 21). But when reviewing O'Daly's book (*Gnomon* 50 [1978], 407–10) he observed that Plotinus' using such words as *autos* or *hêmeis* or *anthrôpos* does "not imply that he set himself the philosophical task of formally defining the 'self.' Even less does it mean that when he uses these terms he must be taken to be talking about the 'self' as such . . . [O'Daly] is perhaps too prone to see references to the self when Plotinus is using words in their normal sense." Also see my review in *Review of Metaphysics* 30 (1977), 533–34.

What does one look for? Why bother, even? But suppose someone would say, "Perhaps Plotinus anticipated 'self' in its contemporary significance." Then I become increasingly puzzled because there *is* no commonly accepted notion. As we previously concluded from studying Margaret Gorman's article on "self" in the *New Catholic Encyclopedia* (XIII, 56–60), "self" is an extremely ambiguous notion in both philosophical and psychological literature. Accordingly, it can help us discover a philosophy of self in the *Enneads* only with great difficulty. Yet, unless I am mistaken, we need some such aid if Plotinus himself has "no fixed word—hence, no *concept*, strictly speaking—for 'self' " (O'Daly, p. 89).

Another Approach?

Is there another way of reading those passages of the *Enneads* in which O'Daly believes their author is speaking of "self"? Yes, by refusing to translate *autos* or *hauton* or *hêmeis* as "self" (except, of course, when the meaning of the English word is not technical, as in the statement, "No one helped me—I did it myself") but in some such fashion as "what someone really is," "what we really are," "what the human person is essentially" and so on; or second, by coupling "self" with a bracketed phrase to indicate what is meant. Then, perhaps, Plotinus will more easily reveal what he was intending.

Let us now apply this methodology in some detail to *Enneads*, I, 6, upon which O'Daly (in part, at least) bases his interpretation and which is interesting as the first treatise Plotinus wrote. We shall first present our own paraphrase and/or translation of its relevant lines with comments, which will then be contrasted with O'Daly's.[57]

I, 6: "On Beauty"

In explaining what the primary beauty in bodies is, Plotinus observes that [A] our soul, upon becoming aware of such beauty, welcomes it and as it were adapts itself to it. [B] But upon encountering the ugly, it shrinks back and rejects it and is out of tune and alienated from it (lines 1–6). [C] Why so? Because soul "is by nature what it is and is related to the higher sort of entity among beings, and thus, when seeing what is akin to it—or even a trace of what is akin to it—[in bodies], it is delighted and thrilled and [by turning from the body's beauty] it returns to itself [as soul] and remembers

---

[57] I have inserted bracketed capital letters in my paraphrase/translation to facilitate references.

its true nature and its own possessions" (ch. 2, lines 7–11: Φαμὲν δή, ὡς τὴν φύσιν οὖσα ὅπερ ἐστὶ καὶ πρὸς τῆς κρείττονος ἐν τοῖς οὖσιν οὐσίας, ὅ τι ἂν ἴδῃ συγγενὲς ἢ ἴχνος τοῦ συγγενοῦς, χαίρει τε καὶ διεπτόηται καὶ ἀναφέρει πρὸς ἑαυτὴν καὶ ἀναμιμνήσκεται ἑαυτῆς καὶ τῶν ἑαυτῆς).

Comments. Plotinus is here intent on illumining the human soul's reaction to corporeal beauty and ugliness. It flees from the latter (#B) and welcomes the former (#A). Confronted with beauty in bodies, our soul initially opens up to it (#A) but next turns away and within to its own nature and contents (#C). The contrast is between soul and body, with stress put upon what the soul essentially is. Thus, there is little likelihood that *hautê* in its three occurrences in lines 10–11 has to do technically with "self."

Shortly after, Plotinus speaks of the beauty to be found within soul. [D] What do you feel (he asks) about virtuous activities and dispositions and the beauty of souls (lines 2–5)? In fact, "what do you feel when you look at your own souls and the beauty within them? How are you wildly exalted and stirred and long to be with yourselves by gathering yourselves [= your souls, what you really are] together away from your bodies?" (ch. 5, lines 5–8: Καὶ ἑαυτοὺς δὲ ἰδόντες τὰ ἔνδον καλοὺς τί πάσχετε; Καὶ πῶς ἀναβακχεύεσθε καὶ ἀνακινεῖσθε καὶ ἑαυτοῖς συνεῖναι ποθεῖτε συλλεξάμενοι αὐτοὺς ἀπὸ τῶν σωμάτων;). [F] You feel, no doubt, what true lovers feel. But what is it which makes them feel like this? Not shape or color or any size, which are linked with beauty in bodies but soul, which possesses a moral, colorless order and all the other light of the virtues. [G] This you feel when in yourselves [= your souls] or in someone else you see greatness of soul, righteous life, pure morality, courage, dignity, modesty, calmness, upon all of which the godlike Intellect shines and all of which we love and call beautiful. Why so? Because they are genuinely real beings (*ta ontôs onta*) and, thereby, are beautiful (lines 8–20).

Comments. Chapter 5 gives information on a human soul's reaction to psychic beauties. It is enraptured and deeply moved (#D) by seeing moral virtues (whether its own or someone else's), their high ontological status and consequent fairness (#G), the illumination bestowed upon them by the Intellect (#G). Such a soul desires to withdraw from body and to be solely what it truly is: soul. Accordingly, an emphasis continues to be put upon contrasting soul with body and, thus, *heautous* and *heautois* in lines 5 and 7 need not refer to "self" as such.

In chapter 7 Plotinus begins to depict how we are to attain the Good and Beautiful. [H] We must ascend to the Good, which every soul desires but which only those attain who go up to the higher world, are turned around and [I] "strip off what we put on in our descent . . . until passing in the ascent all that is alien to God, one sees only with what he truly is That which is alone, simple, pure and from which all depends and to which all look and in which all are and live and think. (Ch. 7, lines 4–10: Ἐφετὸν μὲν γὰρ ὡς ἀγαθὸν καὶ ἡ ἔφεσις πρὸς τοῦτο, τεῦξις δὲ αὐτοῦ ἀναβαίνουσι πρὸς τὸ ἄνω καὶ ἐπιστραφεῖσι καὶ ἀποδυομένοις ἃ καταβαίνοντες ἠμφιέσμεθα . . . ἕως ἄν τις παρελθὼν ἐν τῇ ἀναβάσει πᾶν ὅσον ἀλλότριον τοῦ θεοῦ αὐτῷ μόνῳ αὐτὸ μόνον ἴδῃ εἰλικρινές, ἁπλοῦν, καθαρόν, ἀφ' οὗ πάντα ἐξήρτηται καὶ πρὸς αὐτὸ βλέπει καὶ ἔστι καὶ ζῇ καὶ νοεῖ·).

But, more precisely, [J] what method can we devise (Plotinus asks in chapter 8) to see the inconceivable Beauty? His answer in brief from the end of the chapter: Give up all hope in material or mechanical means, disregard your physical vision. Then change to and make another way of seeing (ch. 8, lines 24–27). [K] And what does this inner sight see? The soul must be trained to see, first of all, beautiful ways of life, then good and virtuous works and, next, the souls which produce them (ch. 9, lines 1–6). [L] "How, then, can you see the sort of beauty a good soul has? Go back to your own and look. [M] If you do not see yours is beautiful, then just as someone making a beautiful statue cuts away here and polishes there, . . . so you too must cut away excess and straighten the crooked and clear the dark and make it bright, and never stop 'working on your statue' till the divine glory of virtue shines out on you . . . [N] If you have become beautiful and see it, and you are at home with your pure state, with nothing hindering you from be-coming in this way one, with no inward mixture of anything else but wholly what you really are—namely, nothing but pure light, not measured by dimensions, or bounded by shape into littleness, or expanded to size by unboundedness but everywhere unmeasured . . . —[O] when you see that you have become this, then you have become sight. You can trust what you are then; you have already ascended and need no one to show you. Concentrate your gaze and see . . . the enormous Beauty."

Πῶς ἂν οὖν ἴδοις ψυχὴν ἀγαθὴν οἷον τὸ κάλλος ἔχει; Ἄναγε ἐπὶ σαυτὸν καὶ ἴδε· κἂν μήπω σαυτὸν ἴδῃς καλόν, οἷα ποιητὴς ἀγάλματος, ὃ δεῖ καλὸν γενέσθαι, τὸ μὲν ἀφαιρεῖ, τὸ δὲ ἀπέξεσε,

τὸ δὲ λεῖον, τὸ δὲ καθαρὸν ἐποίησεν, ἕως ἔδειξε καλὸν ἐπὶ τῷ
ἀγάλματι πρόσωπον, οὕτω καὶ σὺ ἀφαίρει ὅσα περιττὰ καὶ
ἀπεύθυνε ὅσα σκολιά, ὅσα σκοτεινὰ καθαίρων ἐργάζου εἶναι
λαμπρὰ καὶ μὴ παύσῃ τεκταίνων τὸ σὸν ἄγαλμα, ἕως ἂν
ἐκλάμψειέ σοι τῆς ἀρετῆς ἡ θεοειδὴς ἀγλαΐα, ἕως ἂν ἴδῃς
σωφροσύνην ἐν ἁγνῷ βεβῶσαν βάθρῳ. Εἰ γέγονας τοῦτο καὶ εἶδες
αὐτὸ καὶ σαυτῷ καθαρὸς συνεγένου οὐδὲν ἔχων ἐμπόδιον πρὸς
τὸ εἰς οὕτω γενέσθαι οὐδὲ σὺν αὐτῷ ἄλλο τι ἐντὸς μεμιγμένον
ἔχων, ἀλλ᾽ ὅλος αὐτὸς φῶς ἀληθινὸν μόνον, οὐ μεγέθει
μεμετρημένον οὐδὲ σχήματι εἰς ἐλάττωσιν περιγραφὲν οὐδ᾽ αὖ
εἰς μέγεθος δι᾽ ἀπειρίας αὐξηθέν, ἀλλ᾽ ἀμέτρητον πανταχοῦ, ὡς
ἂν μεῖζον παντὸς μέτρου καὶ παντὸς κρεῖσσον ποσοῦ· εἰ τοῦτο
γενόμενον σαυτὸν ἴδοις, ὄψις ἤδη γενόμενος θαρσήσας περὶ σαυτῷ
καὶ ἐνταῦθα ἤδη ἀναβεβηκὼς μηκέτι τοῦ δεικνύντος δεηθεὶς
ἀτενίσας ἴδε· οὗτος γὰρ μόνος ἢ ὀφθαλμὸς τὸ μέγα κάλλος βλέπει
(lines 6–25).

Comments. One finds in the final three chapters just paraphrased
that Plotinus has returned to a methodology similar to that disclosed in the passages paraphrased above (#A–#G), but with a
difference. There the soul turned away from matter so as to see and
be captivated by the beauty of its own moral virtues. Here, though,
the Greek author is concerned with how the soul, disregarding
whatever is lower, is eventually to ascend to the Good (#I and ch. 9,
lines 37 sqq.) and the Beautiful (#K).

Plotinus' explanation is complex, though, inasmuch as he first
gives general directions (#H–#I), which then become more specific
(#J–#O). But in each case they consist in setting aside impediments
so as to arrive at what the soul really is and, thereby, to be capable
of attaining primal reality.

His general advice is, then, to discard matter and whatever vices
we have succumbed to in departing from the higher realms so that
each of us, relying solely on what he truly is, might behold the
divine Good in its solitude, simplicity and purity (#I). Here, rather
obviously, the crucial words in line 9 (*autô monô*) do not pertain to
"self" as such but to a man's own reality as contrasted with the
unreality of matter and vice and with the supreme reality of God.

In its more exact formulation, though, his advice comes in several stages. Let one wishing to see Beauty (#J) refuse to be drawn
toward external and bodily beauties, which are mere shadows and
can ruin him (ch. 8, lines 3–16, left unparaphrased above). Rather,

let him journey back to his origin There not on foot or by carriage or boat (lines 16–24). No, let him put hope in no material or mechanical means but close his physical eyes and activate his spiritual vision (#J), with which he should attend to the beauties of virtues and of the souls they perfect (#K). If someone finds no beauty in his soul, let him work upon his soul (as a sculptor upon a statue) to replace the ugliness of vice with the beauty and divine refulgence of virtue (#M). This done, and no hindrances remaining to pureness and unity and no internal composition, he has become wholly what he really is: authentic and immeasurable light (#N) and vision itself (#C). Having thus achieved his own true reality, he has arrived too at Beauty itself: let him look and see (#C).

Here, again, the words in lines 7 (*anage epi sauton*), 8 (*sauton*) and 15 sqq. of chapter 9 occur when Plotinus contrasts what a man truly is with matter and evil (then he is soul) and with Beauty (then he is light and vision). In neither contrast may (at least: must) one replace them with "self" technically taken.

O'Daly's exegesis puts the crucial lines into a different and (I think) misleading focus, as this quotation shows (*Plotinus' Philosophy of Self*, p. 83).[58]

At I, 6 (1), 9 the self (*autos*, 18) *is* the "only veritable light," and "when you perceive that you have grown to this, you are now become very vision" (22). A transformation of the "everyday" self is in question: at chapter 9, 7 ff. it is said that man can work upon this transformation. Plotinus . . . has subtly rewritten the image of the *Phaedrus* (252d), so that the "statue" (*agalma*) becomes the self . . . Thus at chapter 5 Plotinus can speak to the "lovers" (9) who "when you see that you yourselves are beautiful within . . . long to be one with your self," 5 ff. Similarly, at ch. 9, 15 ff., "you have become this perfect work [i.e., the *agalma*], and have had vision of it and you are self-gathered in the purity of your being." . . . For Plotinus . . . it is in a heightening of *self-possession*, of *self-concentration*, carried to its extreme, that vision occurs; if the self experiences unification (17), it is *entirely as itself* (18) (italics in the original).

---

[58] In the quotation the first number in parentheses indicates that I, 6, is chronologically Plotinus' first treatise. Subsequent numbers, with the exception of those which are designated as references to its chapters, refer to lines in those chapters.

Before proceeding to other texts let me offer these brief tentative conclusions. In *Enneads* I, 6, Plotinus primarily is a metaphysician and, thus, is intent also and especially on two questions which underlie the explicit discussion of what beauty is—namely, "What is reality? What does it mean to be real?" and, concomitantly, "In what does man's genuine reality consist?" The answer to this second question differs when man is compared to what is lower (then he is soul) and to what is primal reality (then he is light and vision).

Other Treatises

When that comparison to what is below man is made in subsequent treatises, the same reply is given. But when he is compared to primal reality, the reply changes somewhat inasmuch as Plotinus increasingly realized that reality is unity and, hence, man insofar as he is genuinely real must basically and ultimately be *one*. This radical state of unity and reality is disclosed when, having transcended not only evil and matter but even soul and intellect, he is united to the One *seu* the Good *seu* God. In that union, Plotinus states in VI, 9, (9), 11, 4 sqq. (as we have seen above in chapter 5, which also provides the relevant Greek text), "there were not two, but the seer himself was one with the Seen (for It was not really seen but united to him). . . . He was one himself then, with no distinction in him either in relation to himself or anything else; for there was no movement in him, and he had no emotion, no desire for anything else when he had made the ascent, no reason or thought; his own self [= what he was on a lower level: soul] was not there for him, if we should say even this." In fact, his contemplation of God was perhaps "not a contemplation but another kind of seeing, a being out of oneself [= what one is as a distinct and lower existent], a simplifying, a self-surrender [a surrender of what one is as distinct, less real being], a pressing towards contact, a rest, a sustained thought directed to perfect conformity." Those lines apparently explicate the identity between man when fully real and primal Reality: man then is one with the One.

The same explication continues in III, 8 (30), 9, 19 sqq., where Plotinus asks: "Since knowledge of other things comes to us from intellect, . . . by what sort of simple intuition could one grasp this which transcends the nature of intellect?[59] We shall say . . . that it is

---

[59] On *epibolê* as "intuition" and its ancestry in Epicurus, see John Rist, *Plotinus: The Road to Reality* (Cambridge University Press, 1967), pp. 47–52; G. O'Daly, *Plotinus' Philosophy of the Self*, pp. 93–94.

by the likeness in ourselves. For there is something of it in us too; or rather there is nowhere where it is not, in the things which can participate in it. For, wherever you are, it is from this that you have that which is everywhere present, by setting to it that which can have it" (lines 19–26: Καὶ γὰρ αὖ τῆς γνώσεως διὰ νοῦ τῶν ἄλλων γινομένης καὶ τῷ νῷ νοῦν γινώσκειν δυναμένων ὑπερβεβηκὸς τοῦτο τὴν νοῦ φύσιν τίνι ἂν ἁλίσκοιτο ἐπιβολῇ ἀθρόᾳ; Πρὸς ὃν δεῖ σημῆναι, ὅπως οἷόν τε, τῷ ἐν ἡμῖν ὁμοίῳ φήσομεν. Ἔστι γάρ τι καὶ παρ' ἡμῖν αὐτοῦ· ἢ οὐκ ἔστιν, ὅπου μὴ ἔστιν, οἷς ἐστι μετέχειν αὐτοῦ. Τὸ γὰρ πανταχοῦ παραστήσας ὁπουοῦν τὸ δυνάμενον ἔχειν ἔχεις ἐκεῖθεν·).

The next chapter helps to explain that omnipresence of God. The One *is* the "power of all existents (*dynamis tôn pantôn*): if it did not exist," neither would they (ch. 10, lines 1 sqq.). "Everywhere, then, we must go back to *one*. And in each and every existent there is some *one* to which you will trace it back, and this in every case to the *one* before it, which is not simply one, until we come to the simply one; and this cannot be traced back to something else. But if we take the *one* of the plant . . . and the *one* of the animal and the *one* of the soul and the *one* of the universe, we are taking in each case what is most powerful and really valuable in it; but if we take the *one* of the beings which truly are, their origin and spring and power, shall we lose faith and think of it [the One] as nothing? [By no means]" lines 20–28: Διὸ καὶ ἡ ἀναγωγὴ πανταχοῦ ἐφ' ἕν. Καὶ ἐφ' ἑκάστου μέν τι ἕν, εἰς ὃ ἀνάξεις, καὶ τόδε τὸ πᾶν εἰς ἓν τὸ πρὸ αὐτοῦ, οὐχ ἁπλῶς ἕν, ἕως τις ἐπὶ τὸ ἁπλῶς ἓν ἔλθῃ· τοῦτο δὲ οὐκέτι ἐπ' ἄλλο. Ἀλλ' εἰ μὲν τὸ τοῦ φυτοῦ ἕν — τοῦτο δὲ καὶ ἡ ἀρχὴ ἡ μένουσα — καὶ τὸ ζῷου ἓν καὶ τὸ ψυχῆς ἓν καὶ τὸ τοῦ παντὸς ἓν λαμβάνοι, λαμβάνει ἑκαστανοῦ τὸ δυνατώτατον καὶ τὸ τίμιον· εἰ δὲ τὸ τῶν κατ' ἀλήθειαν ὄντων ἕν, τὴν ἀρχὴν καὶ πηγὴν καὶ δύναμιν, λαμβάνοι, ἀπιστήσομεν καὶ τὸ μηδὲν ὑπονοήσομεν). The fact that man, as well as existents on every level, is somehow one with the One is so clearly suggested in those lines as to need no comment.

The same suggestion emerges in a still later treatise, VI, 7 (38): "The soul must not keep by it good or evil or anything else, that it may alone receive Him, the Only One . . . [When] His presence becomes manifest [to the soul], when it turns away from the things present to it and prepares itself, making itself as beautiful as possible, and comes to likeness with Him, . . . then it sees Him suddenly appearing in itself (for there is nothing between, nor are they still two, but both are one; while He is present, you could not distinguish them)" (ch. 34, lines 6–18; the Greek for lines 12–14:

ἰδοῦσα δὲ ἐν αὐτῇ ἐξαίφνης φανέντα — μεταξὺ γὰρ οὐδὲν οὐδ᾽ ἔτι δύο, ἀλλ᾽ ἓν ἄμφω· οὐ γὰρ ἂν διακρίναις ἔτι, ἕως πάρεστι).

Then in chapter 36: after purifying and adorning the soul with virtues, after gaining a foothold in the world of Intellect and settling firmly there, after contemplating what he really is and everything else, a man then "is near: the Good is next above him, close to him already shining over the whole intelligible world." Now "letting all study go, . . . he raises his thought to that in which he is, but is carried out of it by the very surge of the wave of Intellect and, lifted high by its swell, suddenly sees without knowing how; the Sight fills his eyes with Light but does not make him see something else by it, but the Light is That Which he sees. There is not in It one thing which is seen and another which is Its Light" (lines 8–22; the Greek for lines 19–20: ἀλλ᾽ ἡ θέα πλήσασα φωτὸς τὰ ὄμματα οὐ δι᾽ αὐτοῦ πεποίηκεν ἄλλο ὁρᾶν, ἀλλ᾽ αὐτὸ τὸ φῶς τὸ ὅραμα ἦν).

With this affirmation that the One is light, we have come full circle. In I, 6, 9, man is light upon achieving God; VI, 7, 36 asserts that God is light. Therefore, man *is* God—or, at least, becomes God during that state of mystical unification.

Our interpretation of the previous three passages intimates that Plotinus' metaphysics has become increasingly monistic.[60] This, I grant, is a thorny question, which, however, needs to be touched upon in any discussion of "self." But, at least, this seems comparatively certain: his discussion of man's relationship to primal and other reality is primarily *metaphysical* (i.e., knowledge of the real as real):[61] how man actually exists; what he is on the physical, psychic, noetic and mystical levels of reality; to what extent he is real there. Yes, Plotinus' discussion is primarily metaphysical, even though he often describes man in terms of his operations—physical, psychic, noetic, mystical. But even then Plotinus is intent on the data these operations give on man's ontological and henological status of reality—*re* what he actually is as he exists on those four levels, *re* the degree to which he attains or loses the reality uniquely his of being one with the One.

---

[60] The monistic character of Plotinus' position flows from the fact that to be real is to be one. See L. Sweeney, S.J., *Divine Infinity in Greek and Medieval Thought* (New York/Bern: Peter Lang Publishing, Inc., 1992), ch. 11: "Basic Principles in Plotinus' Philosophy," pp. 243–56; ch. 16 below, "Are Plotinus and Albertus Magnus Neoplatonists?" prgrs. corresponding to notes 14–21.

[61] On what "metaphysics" means in Plotinus see *ibid.*, n. 13.

But if Plotinus' discussion of man's relationship to primal and lower reality is primarily metaphysical, this is another reason to rethink whether *autos* and so on do mean "self." The latter notion, when it came to prominence in modern times, appears to have arisen often within discussions of a psychological (both philosophical and empirical) nature. If Plotinus' investigations of man are metaphysical in essence, finding "self" there may put them out of focus.

Suggested Methodology

Let me terminate with a suggested methodology for reading Plotinus' *Enneads*.[62] First, when reading his Greek do not translate *autos* or *hauton* or *hêmeis* or *ekeino* as "self" but in some such fashion as "what someone really is," "what we really are," "what man is essentially" and so on (as illustrated earlier *re* I, 6, 1 sqq.). Second, try to understand Plotinus on his own terms (what he had in mind when writing such and such a passage). Third, reflect anew to see if the application to Plotinus of some or other modern notion of "self" may be helpful.[63] That reflection should cover these points. (a) Does the application of such a conception of "self" to Plotinus' *Weltanschauung* help in understanding *him* better, more richly, more authentically? (b) Does it reveal him perhaps to have anticipated contemporary theories on "self"? (c) Does it help us understand what the notion of "self" itself entails, whether in some modern

---

[62] The same approach is also suitable for reading Manichaean documents, *mutatis mutandis*, as we have indicated above, "The Twin as 'Self, '" ad finem.

[63] The notions Plotinian literature provides are less flamboyant and chronologically determined than those furnished in secondary literature on Gnosticism and Manichaeism (see n. 27 above) and, hence, may prove less anachronistic. For example, G. O'Daly, *Plotinus' Philosophy of the Self,* p. 90: self is "the identity of a human subject at the several levels of existence possible to man"; P. S. Mamo, "The Notion of the Self," initial "Summary," p. 1: self is defined "not as an individual substance but as striving, attention, direction of consciousness" and p. 190: the ego "is a focus capable of infinite extension"; A. H. Armstrong, "Form, Individual and Person in Plotinus," p. 65: "Person [is] that in us which is capable of free decision, true thought, and the passionate love of God [which for Plotinus is] so open that its only bounds are the universe and God"; E. R. Dodds (quoted with approval by H. J. Blumenthal, *Plotinus' Psychology,* p. 110, n. 25): in contrast to soul "the ego is a fluctuating spotlight of consciousness." Or one might apply to Plotinus the description M. Gorman gathered from her historical survey (*New Catholic Encyclopedia,* XIII, p. 60A): self suggests "all those aspects of man thought to be left out by the terms soul, mind, person and nature and to designate the unifying, purposeful, growing and interacting aspect of man's activities."

and contemporary author or in our own philosophical position? In following this threefold methodology we have certainly lost nothing, since we do take into account "self," *ego,* person with respect to Plotinus. But his own texts control the contemporary notions rather than the other way round.

Appendix A

This diagram, which is based on the *Kephalaia* but which also represents many of the emanations mentioned in the *CMC,* is taken from A. Henrichs and L. Koenen, *ZPE* 5 (1970), 183.

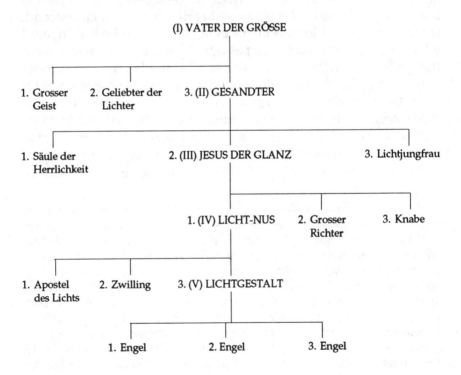

For a more detailed presentation of the Manichaean hierarchy, see M. Boyce, *A Reader,* pp. 8–10.

One must keep in mind that Mani's position is, philosophically, a monism of light and that anything on any level is real to the extent that it is light and, thereby, is one with all else. Hence, Mani's attributing his call to (say) Jesus the Splendor in some passages is not to deny its coming also from the Father of Greatness, with whom Jesus is one. Henri-Charles Puech stresses that God and souls are consubstantial and that human souls are parts of the World Soul, which also is God's soul (this consubstantiality corresponds to what I call "monism"). See H.-Ch. Puech, *Le Manichéisme. Son Fondateur. Sa Doctrine* (Paris: Civilisations du Sud, 1949), p. 71 and n. 275 (pp. 154–55): "Il y a consubstantialité entre Dieu et les âmes; les âmes ne sont que des fragments de la substance divine. Ce qui revient à dire que c'est une partie de Dieu qui est ici-bas déchue, liée au corps et à la Matière, mêlée au Mal. . . . Dans le manichéisme, les âmes humaines sont . . . des parties ou des parcelles de l'Âme universelle (c'est-à-dire de l'âme même de Dieu) englouties dan les Ténèbres à la suite de la défaite de l'Homme Primordial et avec l'Homme Primordial lui-même. Celui-ci est l'âme, . . . le 'moi' de Dieu . . . une 'projection' ou une 'emanation' de la substance divine. . . . A noter que le 'consubstantiel' manichéen a joué son rôle dans les débats trinitaires suscités par l'arianisme. . . . Mais le mot [consubstantiel] indique plutôt l'identité de forme que l'identité de substance."

On Albert the Great and Bonaventure as two medieval theologians whose positions tend to be monistic because reality is light, see chapter 16 below, "Are Plotinus and Albertus Magnus Neoplatonists?"; also see chapter 3 above, "Augustine and Bonaventure on Christian Philosophy."

Appendix B

To date I am unaware of much literature on the possible philosophical background of Mani. Besides H. Jonas' article already cited in note 51 above, see the following, which attend at least to the speculative influences (whether philosophical or religious) on Manichaeism: Dmitri Obolensky, *The Bogomils: A Study in Balkan Neo-Manichaeism* (Cambridge University Press, 1948), ch. 1: "The Manichaean Legacy," pp. 1–27 (especially p. 3 *re* dualism in Plato); L. J. R. Ort, "Mani's Conception of Gnosis" in Ugo Bianchi (ed.), *Le Origini dello Gnosticismo* (Leiden: E. J. Brill, 1967), pp. 604–13; H.-Ch. Puech, "The Concept of Redemption in Manichaeism" in Joseph Campbell (ed.), *The Mystic Vision: Papers from the Eranos Yearbooks* (Princeton University Press, 1968), pp. 247–314 (especially pp. 266–88: "The Theoretical Foundations of Redemption: The Cosmological and the Anthropological Myth"); P. W. Van der Horst and J. Mansfeld, *An*

*Alexandrian Platonist Against Dualism: Alexander of Lycopolis' Treatise
"Critique of the Doctrines of Manichaeus"* (Leiden: E. J. Brill, 1974);
Gilles Quispel, "Mani the Apostle of Jesus Christ," *Gnostic Studies,*
vol. 2 (Istanbul: Nederlands Historisch-Archaeologisch Institute,
1975), pp. 230–37 (mainly *re* Mani's influence upon St. Augustine).

During the Oklahoma conference of 1984 on Neoplatonism and
Gnosticism, at which portions of this chapter were presented, Mi-
chel Tardieu alerted me to the philosophical influence of Bar-
daisan upon Mani. On that topic see these studies: Saint Ephraim
the Syrian, *St. Ephraim's Prose Refutations of Mani, Marcion and
Bardaisan,* transcribed by C. W. Mitchell, 2 vols. (London: C. W.
Mitchell, 1912 and 1921), Text and Translation Society; F. C. Burkitt,
Religion of the Manichees, pp. 82–86; H. J. W. Drijvers, *Bardaisan of
Edessa* (Assen: Van Gorcum, 1966); *idem,* "Bardaisan of Edessa and
the Hermetica. The Aramaic Philosopher and the Philosophy of
His Time," *Jaarbericht Ex Oriente Lux* 21 (1969–70), 190–210; *idem,*
"Mani und Bardaisan. Ein Beitrag zur Vorgeschichte des Mani-
chäismus" in *Mélanges H.-Ch. Puech,* pp. 459–69; *idem, Cults and
Beliefs at Edessa* (Leiden: E. J. Brill, 1980)—see "Index" and bibliog-
raphy, pp. xviii–xix, for complete list of Drijvers' works; *idem,* "Bar-
daisan, die Bardaisaniten und die Ursprünge des Gnostizismus"
in Ugo Bianchi (ed.), *Le Origini dello Gnosticismo,* pp. 307–14; Ugo
Bianchi, "Le Gnosticisme: Concept, Terminologie, Origines, Délimitation" in Barbara Aland (ed.), *Gnosis: Festschrift für Hans Jonas*
(Göttingen: Vandenhoeck und Ruprecht, 1978), pp. 48–50; Geo
Widengren, "Der Manichäismus" in *ibid.,* pp. 311–13 (*re* F. C. Burkitt
and H. H. Schaeder); Michel Tardieu, *Le Manichéisme* (Paris: Presses
Universitaires de France, 1981), ch. 1–2.

What of philosophical influences upon Gnosticism itself? Birger
A. Pearson, "The Tractate *Marsanes* (*NHC* X) and the Platonic Tradition" in Barbara Aland (ed.), *Gnosis: Festschrift für Hans Jonas,* p.
373, sets forth (with Willy Theiler) the "three basic options" on the
relationship between Gnosticism and Greek Philosophy as "(1) the
philosophy of the Empire is disguised Gnosis [held by H. Jonas, C.
Elsas]. (2) Gnosis is debased philosophy, oriental mythology over-
laid with formal elements derived mainly from Platonism. (3) Im-
perial philosophy and Gnosis are to be explained out of similar
social and spiritual currents of late antiquity." Pearson gives a good
résumé of Jonas' position with references to his publications (*ibid.,*
notes 5–8): Hans Jonas has argued "that the 'mythological' gnostic
systems described by the church fathers and the major philosophical and theological systems of late antiquity, from Philo Judaeus on,

express a common 'gnostic' understanding of existence. Particularly important are his observations on later Platonism, especially Plotinus. Jonas poses the question 'whether in the final analysis Gnosis, transformed gnostic myth, provided the innermost impulse' to the philosophy of Plotinus, rather than Plato. He provides a brief but powerful positive answer."

In the same volume one finds three other helpful papers: Ugo Bianchi, "Le Gnosticisme: Concept, Terminologie, Origines, Délimitation," pp. 33–64; especially A. H. Armstrong, "Gnosis and Greek Philosophy," pp. 87–124; Hans Martin Schenke, "Die Tendenz der Weisheit zur Gnosis," pp. 351–72.

In addition the following are worthy of note: J. Zandee, *The Terminology of Plotinus and of Some Gnostic Writings, Mainly the Fourth Treatise of the Jung Codex* (Istanbul: Nederlands Historisch-Archaeologisch Institute, 1961), especially pp. 38–41; R. M. Grant, *Gnosticism and Early Christianity* (New York: Columbia University Press, 1966), ch. 5: "From Myth to Philosophy?" pp. 120–50 (see p. 147: "Gnosticism is not a form of philosophy"); several papers in U. Bianchi (ed.), *Le Origini dello Gnosticismo*—for example, H. Jonas, "Delimitation of the Gnostic Phenomenon—Typological and Historical," pp. 90–108; E. von Ivánka, "Religion, Philosophie und Gnosis: Grenzfälle und Pseudomorphosen in der Spätantike," pp. 317–22; R. Crahay, "Éléments d'une mythopée gnostique dans le Grèce classique," pp. 323–39; P. Boyancé, "Dieu cosmique et dualisme: les archontes et Platon," pp. 340–58; Gilles Quispel, "Gnostic Man: The Doctrine of Basilides," in Joseph Campbell (ed.), *The Mystic Vision*, pp. 210–46 (especially pp. 215–27: "The Frame: Platonist Philosophy"); S. R. C. Lilla, *Clement of Alexandria: A Study in Christian Platonism and Gnosticism* (Oxford University Press, 1971); H. B. Timothy, *The Early Christian Apologists* [Irenaeus, Tertullian, Clement of Alexandria] *and Greek Philosophy* (Assen: Van Gorcum, 1973); René Nouailhat, "Remarques méthodologiques à propos de la question de 'L'Hellénisation du Christianisme,' " in F. Dunand and P. Lévêque (eds.), *Les syncrétismes dan les religions de l'antiquité* (Leiden: E. J. Brill, 1975), pp. 212–32; C. Elsas, *Neuplatonische und gnostische Weltablehnung in der Schule Plotins* (Berlin: Walter de Gruyter, 1975); Pheme Perkins, *The Gnostic Dialogue: The Early Church and the Crisis of Gnosticism* (New York: Paulist Press, 1980), especially ch. 1: "Gnosticism in Its Context," pp. 1–22; Carsten Colpe, "Challenge of Gnostic Thought for Philosophy, Alchemy and Literature," in B. Layton (ed.), *The Rediscovery of Gnosticism*, vol. 1, pp. 32–56 (see pp. 34 sqq. for the four ways in which "the complex subject of 'Gnosis and philosophy' can conventionally be dealt with"); H. Chadwick, "Domestication of Gnosticism," *ibid.*, especially pp. 11–13 *re* Plato's influence on Valentinus and other Gnostics; G. C. Snead, "The Valentinian Myth of Sophia," *Journal of Theological Studies,* n.s. 20 (1969), pp. 74–104— see Armstrong, *ibid.,* p. 103, n. 23: "A very well documented and careful article" *re* Hellenic influence on Valentinus is R. van den Broeck, "The Present State of Gnostic Studies," *Vigiliae Christianae* 37 (1983), 41–71 (a survey of papers in the Proceedings from conferences on Gnosticism at Quebec, Yale and Halle, as well as in *Gnosis: Festschrift für Hans Jonas* and in G. Quispel's *Gnostic Studies);* K. Rudolph, *Gnosis: The Nature and History of Gnosticism* (New York: Harper and Row, 1983).

7

Was Augustine a Christian or a Neoplatonist? Old Question, New Approach

The question to which the title of this chapter refers has to do with whether Augustine was intellectually a Neoplatonist or a Christian when baptized in April 387 and in the years immediately subsequent. That question has been at the center of controversy among scholars since G. Boissier first raised it in 1888,[1] Prosper Alfaric repeated it in 1918[2] and Pierre Courcelle asked it anew in 1950.[3]

What is the basis of that controversy? The fact that two groups of Augustine's writings draw different pictures of what happened between 386 and (say) 391. In the Cassiciacum dialogues (e.g., *Contra Academicos, De Ordine, De Beata Vita, Soliloquias*) Augustine appears as a philosopher amid a coterie of students and friends aiming at achieving philosophical wisdom, whereas in the *Confessions* (written 397) Augustine is portrayed as a penitent. The dialogues present the causes of his resigning his position as teacher of rhetoric in Milan and retiring to Cassiciacum as an onset of respiratory illness and a desire for leisurely pursuit of study, while in the *Confessions* he is shown as intent on preparing for and receiving the

---

[1] G. Boissier, "La conversion de S. Augustin," *Revue des Deux Mondes* 85 (1888), 43–49; reprinted in *La fin du paganisme* (Paris: Hachette, 1891, I, pp. 339–79.

[2] *L'Evolution intellectuelle de S. Augustin. I. Du Manichéisme au Néoplatonisme* (Paris: E. Nourry, 1918).

[3] *Recherches sur les Confessions du Saint Augustin* (Paris: E. de Boccard, 1950).

Sacrament of Baptism and as undergoing a moral conversion upon reading St. Paul after hearing children chanting, "Tolle, lege!" in a garden scene of which the dialogues make no mention.[4] Because of these and other discrepancies in the two sorts of treatises, the authors mentioned in the previous paragraph conclude that between the mid-eighties and 391 Augustine was a Neoplatonist and that only after a doctrinal evolution did he become truly a Christian.

Such, then, is the "old" controversy to which the title of this chapter refers. What is the "new approach" it advocates? Previously scholars often sought to solve the controversy by comparing the dialogues and *Confessions* so as to isolate what were taken to be Neoplatonic and Christian (often as interpreted in Augustine's own era) elements in each and thereby to determine whether Augustine showed himself inclined more to one set of elements than to the other in his earlier and later writings. Without in any way disparaging that attempted solution, what this chapter seeks is to isolate the essence of the Christian religion not as it might show itself in the final decades of the fourth century and the initial ones of the fifth, when Augustine *floruit*, but as it is expressed in the epistles of Paul, the four Gospels, the *Acts of Apostles* and other canonical documents. These, together with tradition, furnish the divine revelation which all those calling themselves authentic Christians must believe and which all subsequent authors, if they are genuinely Christian, endeavor to interpret, explicate and transmit. So conceived, the essence of Christianity is prior to that explication, interpretation and development which theologians as early as Justin Martyr and as late as David Tracy in our own day engage in, often with the help of philosophical theories. And that essence is the criterion as to whether their theology is authentically Christian.[5] Augustine's speculation throughout his career fits within that saga and can also be judged therein.

---

[4] For a survey of the controversy see Eugene TeSelle, *Augustine the Theologian* (New York: Herder and Herder, 1970), pp. 25–43; Peter Brown, *Augustine of Hippo: A Biography* (Berkeley: University of California Press, 1969), pp. 113–14 and *passim*; Robert J. O'Connell, S.J., *St. Augustine's Early Theory of Man, A.D. 386–391* (Cambridge: Harvard University Press, 1968), pp. 1–28 and *passim*.

[5] Of course, the Gospel of John contains theological speculation, which however is directly under the inspiration of the Holy Spirit and thus is divinely revealed. For studies on the philosophical and religious influences upon John see Raymond E. Brown, *The Gospel According to John* (Garden City, N.Y.: Doubleday Image Books, 1966 and 1970); *idem, The Community of the Be-*

New Approach

What, then, does the essence of the Christian religion consist in? At least three factors can be suggested. In charting the differences between philosophies and Christianity, Patrick Verbraken, *The Beginnings of the Church: The First Christian Centuries* (New York: Paulist Press, 1968), p. 56, finds their most radical divergence to be that the initiative for salvation in merely human wisdom comes from below, in Christianity it comes from above.

It must be strongly emphasized that a radical difference existed and always will exist between philosophies and Christianity. However sincere, however religious they may have been, the former were in spite of everything only *human wisdom*, of very noble inspiration doubtless, but only human. They guided the groping, and the efforts, praiseworthy as they may have been, of minds and hearts preoccupied with saving themselves, with marking out for themselves the way which according to their point of view should forward their own salvation. In a word, the initiative came from below; it was like a great cry of appeal directed towards heaven and borne by the fragile hope of not having been uttered in vain. But for Christians the perspective was quite different. They knew that the salvation of men and of the world came from on high, that it was the gift of the Father through his Son in the Holy Spirit; they knew that their faith was not an appeal, but a *response*, a response to the word of truth, and their love a response to the Love who first loved them; they knew that an abyss separated human hope and Christian hope. For them, the initiative came from God, from the time of Abraham who was called by Yahveh up to the invitation given to all in the Apocalypse to

loved Disciple (New York: Paulist Press, 1979); Rudolf Schnackenburg, *The Gospel According to John*, vols. 1–3 (New York, London, Montreal: Herder and Herder, 1968; New York: Seabury Press, 1980; New York: Crossroad, 1982); C. A. Evans, "On the Prologue of John and Trimorphic Protennoia," *New Testament Studies* 27 (1980), 397–401; Thomas Tobin, *Creation of Man: Philo and History of Interpretation*, "Catholic Biblical Quarterly Monograph Series," 14 (Washington, D.C.: Catholic Biblical Association of America, 1983); George W. MacRae, *Invitation to John* (Garden City, N.Y.: Doubleday Image Books, 1978); J. L. Martyn, *History and Theology in the Fourth Gospel* (New York: Harper and Row, 1968).

come to the wedding of the bridegroom and the bride. The divergence was so fundamental that it was quickly seen to be irreducible.

For Verbraken, then, the essence of the Christian religion is that we achieve salvation by responding to the triune God's initiative and that Christianity thus stands in contrast with merely philosophical wisdom and its stress on the need that each person has of developing and saving himself.

Peter G. van Breemen is of a similar mind in *As Bread That Is Broken* (Denville, N.J.: Dimension Books, 1974), p. 66: the radical distinction between the Christian religion and all other world religions is that in the latter man reconciles himself to God, in the former it is God who reconciles man to Himself.[6] But later in the same book (pp. 143 and 144) van Breemen locates the heart of Christianity also in the central place it gives to Christ and the cross.

Christianity does not spare us pain. The Gospel does not promise that we will not suffer. Indeed the Gospel makes it very clear that we do have to lose our lives, to take up our cross and follow Christ. And that is unique! All other religions either try to avoid pain or make one immune to it so that it will no longer be felt. This is not the Gospel approach. The cross remains a human reality but the Gospel gives meaning to it, and that fact makes a difference. Once we know that suffering has a purpose, or at least once we can believe that there is a meaning to it, we can endure much more. That is the Gospel message—that suffering need not be a loss. . . . Pagan theology says, "If you are the Son of God, come down from the cross." The Gospel says, "Because I am the Son of God, I remain on the cross."

---

[6] Page 66: "The experience of guilt has always been one of the most excruciating problems in the history of mankind. . . . All the great world religions have a substantial message about guilt and reconciliation; otherwise they would not have achieved their status. Christianity, too, addresses itself to this question. However, it is unique in its approach. In all other religions, it is man who reconciles the godhead to himself by penance, atonement, sacrifice (even as far as sacrifice of children). In Christianity it is *God* who reconciles. Justification is a free gift of God's grace (*Romans* 3:24) offered to us with the urgent appeal to be kind enough to accept this gift of reconciliation from the silver plate on which it is offered. It is God's initiative, God's longing."

Accordingly, a religion is uniquely Christian to the extent that Christ's cross is at its very center.[7]

Still a third conception is that the Christian religion essentially consists also in the value given to an individual existent *precisely as individual*.[8] This stress on the value and reality of each individual was begun in the Jewish Scriptures. Take as an example *Psalm* 139:1 sqq.:[9]

---

[7] Pope Paul VI explicitly adds the resurrection to the cross in discussing two sorts of Christians: those who empty the name "Christian" as far as possible "of its original religious and theological content" and those who "acknowledge a character of considerable commitment to important realities in Christianity," among which are "a personal relationship of faith, hope and love with Christ, with the historical Christ of the Gospels, with Christ the Savior, . . . with the Christ of Easter, who associates every authentic believer with the *palingenesis* of His resurrection" (*Who Is Jesus?* [Boston: St. Paul Editions, 1972], pp. 21–22).

[8] On this dimension of Christianity, see Bede Griffiths, *The Cosmic Revelation: The Hindu Way to God* (Springfield, Ill.: Templegate, 1983), pp. 126–27, where he contrasts the Hindu and Christian attitudes to a human individual: "God's revelation in historic time and place, God entering into human history . . . changes one's whole attitude to the world, and it changes one's attitude to material things. . . . [For the Hindu] the body is conceived of as an appearance: you take on the appearance of a body, but you will lose that. All this world is passing away, and only the spirit will remain. The idea that the body itself is to be transformed, as the body of Jesus was transformed in the resurrection, and that the material universe is also to be transformed—that there is to be a 'new creation'—this is something unique in the Biblical Revelation. The divine life penetrates history, time, suffering and death and then raises history and time and suffering and death into a new creation, a new order of being in which these things are not lost, not destroyed, but transfigured. This gives a value to every human person. With the doctrine of karma human persons get mixed up: you may have been Cleopatra in a past life, or somebody else. You are not yourself any longer, and in the end everything merges into one. You will enjoy the absolute bliss of the one. But 'you' are really no longer there. In the Christian view, each individual person, body and soul has a unique character, is a unique image of God, and that person will not dissolve."

[9] In reproducing *Psalm* 139 I have italicized "me" and "my" in the first three lines to emphasize that God attends to each human person. One should read all subsequent lines in it and other quotations from Scripture as though such personal pronouns and adjectives were similarly italicized. For additional instances of passages from the Old Testament, see *Psalm* 147:3–4: "God heals the brokenhearted and binds up their wounds. He tells the number of the stars; he calls each by name." If God calls each star by name, how much more so each individual man or woman. Also see *Isaiah* 43:1 sqq., which speaks of God calling Jacob and Israel by name as nations but terminates by attending

O Lord, you have probed *me* and you know *me;*
    you know when *I* sit and when *I* stand;
    you understand *my* thoughts from afar.
My journeys and my rest you scrutinize,
    with all my ways you are familiar.
Even before a word is on my tongue,
    behold, O Lord, you know the whole of it.
Behind me and before, you hem me in
    and rest your hand upon me.

And why do you know me so well, O Lord?

Truly you have formed my inmost being;
    you knit me in my mother's womb. . . .
My soul also you knew full well;
    nor was my frame unknown to you
When I was made in secret,
    when I was fashioned in the depths of the earth.
Your eyes have seen my actions;
    in your book they are all written;
    my days were limited before one of them existed.

The same concern for each human individual shows up in the New Testament. For instance, read of St. Paul's conviction that Christ's redemption affects him as an individual person: "Christ is living in me. I still live my human life, but it is a life of faith in the Son of God, who loved me and gave himself for me" (*Galatians* 2:20). Or consider Matthew's portrayal (*Mt.* 26:31 sqq.) of Christ's coming at the end of the world, when everyone will be judged in accordance with whether or not he has fed, welcomed, clothed, comforted, visited other individual human beings, each of whom is one with Christ: "As often as you did it for one of my least brothers, you did it for me. . . . As often as you neglected to do it for one of

---

to each son and daughter within those nations: "Thus says the Lord, who created you, O Jacob, and formed you, O Israel: fear not, for I have redeemed you; I have called you by name: you are mine. When you pass through the water, I will be with you. . . . I will say to the north and to the south: 'Bring back my sons from afar and my daughters from the ends of the earth: everyone who is named as mine, whom I created for my glory, whom I formed and made.'"

Many texts cited here in notes 9–12 appear also in ch. 5 above, prgrs. corresponding to notes 6–9.

these least ones you neglected to do it to me." Thus, each individual human person is of value in Christ's eyes. Earlier Matthew had made it clear that individuals of any sort are valuable: although "two sparrows are sold for next to nothing, yet not a single sparrow falls to the ground without your Father's consent." Yet much more valuable is each human individual: "As for you, every hair of your head has been counted. . . . You are worth more than an entire flock of sparrows"[10] and thus you need be afraid not of physical but of spiritual harm (*Mt.* 10:28–31). Yes, John amplified, anyone who "practices evil hates the light and does not come near it [to his own detriment]. . . . But he who acts in truth comes into the light, to make clear that his deeds are done in God" (*Jn.* 3:20–21). "He who hears my word and has faith in Him who sent me possesses eternal life" (*Jn.* 5:24). "No one who comes to me shall ever be hungry, no one who believes in me shall ever thirst. . . . No one who comes will I ever reject. . . . I myself am the living bread come down from heaven. If anyone eats this bread, he shall live forever" (*Jn.* 6:35–38 and 51).

Such texts from the canonical Scriptures can be multiplied almost indefinitely, but those quoted disclose adequately that Christ attends to each individual human person.[11] Hence, the religion He founded must have as one of its essential characteristics an appreciation of the individual precisely as such.[12]

---

[10] *Luke* 12:22 sqq. explicates the greater worth in God's eyes of human individuals over ravens and lilies and grasses of the field. Also see *Matthew* 6:26 sqq.

[11] As Søren Kierkegaard observed in an entry of his diary for 1850: "In the eyes of God, the infinite spirit, all the millions that have lived and now live do not make a crowd: He only sees each individual." Two years earlier (1848): "Each human being has infinite reality." See G. M. Anderson (trans.) and P. P. Rohde (ed.), *The Diary of Søren Kierkegaard* (New York: Philosophical Library, 1960), pp. 106 and 103.

[12] Even its enemies recognized that characteristic. According to Karl Marx, "Political democracy is Christian in the sense that man, not merely one man but every man, is there considered a sovereign being, a supreme being—"On the Jewish Question," in R. C. Tucker (ed.), *Marx-Engels Reader,* 2d ed. (New York: W. W. Norton, 1978), p. 39. German text: *Karl Marx-Friedrich Engels Werke,* Band 1 (Berlin: Dietz Verlag, 1970). Or Adolph Hitler: "To the Christian doctrine of the infinite significance of the individual human soul . . . I oppose with icy clarity the saving doctrine of the nothingness and insignificance of the human being"—Quoted by Hermann Rauschning, *The Voice of Destruction* (New York: G. P. Putnam's Sons, 1940), p. 25.

In the light of those Scripture passages, then, the essence of the Christian religion is found in its concern with the individual *exactly as individual*. When coupled with its insistence that salvation is initiated from above (Verbraken) and with the central position it gives to Christ's cross and resurrection (van Breemen and Paul VI), one is in a position to conceive of it in its primal revelation in the inspired canonical writers and thus in its authentic and essential state.[13]

This conception also is at the center of our "new approach" to studying whether Augustine is authentically Christian or Neoplatonist. Does he consider each individual human person *precisely as individual* to be valuable and thus real in and of himself?[14] If so, he obviously is Christian; if not, his Christianity is less clear in this area.

But before beginning this approach, let me note that my aim here is not directly to answer definitively the question of the authenticity of Augustine's Christianity—that must wait for another time and place. It is rather to develop a technique of reading his *Confessions* attentively so as to detect his attitude on human individuality as such and only subsequently to appreciate how it may have affected his more general doctrinal state.

But before beginning that reading, let me sketch the basic metaphysics of Plotinus, which apparently makes it impossible for him

---

[13] No doubt other constituents of the core of the Christian religion can and will be suggested. The three listed are at least a start.

[14] We shall postpone approaching him with the other two conceptions in mind until more time and space are available. Besides, deciphering Augustine's understanding of Christ upon reading the Platonist books is puzzling. According to *Confessions*, VII, 19, 25, to Augustine Christ was then "only a man of surpassing wisdom," an authoritative teacher, a man complete with body, soul, mind and will. But he admits he could not conceive "what mystery was contained within the words 'The Word was made flesh,'" even though he realized from those books that the Word is God (see *ibid.*, 9, 13–15). This failure meant that he was then unaware that Christ also is truly God, that He is the Word-made-flesh. According to E. TeSelle, *Augustine the Theologian*, pp. 146–47, Augustine did not have a well-worked out Christology until shortly before Easter 391. See TeSelle's entire section, pp. 146–56. Also see P. Courcelle, "Saint Augustin 'Photinien' à Milan (*Conf.*, VII, 19, 25)," *Ricerche di Storia Religiosa* 1 (1954), 63–71, where he surveys the literature on the problem and believes Porphyry's *La Philosophie des Oracles* to be the source of the position Augustine had personally accepted and attributes to Photinus. On this problem in Augustine's Christology, see ch. 8 below, "Augustine on Christ as God and Man."

to conceive of individuality except as nonbeing and unreality[15] and which is one of the main philosophical influences upon Augustine from 386 on.[16] If for Plotinus individuality is indeed nonbeing, Augustine may perhaps have been thereby inclined to conceive of individuality in a similar fashion.

Let us look, then, at Plotinus himself—more precisely at the core of his metaphysics. What does he mean by "to be real"?[17]

---

[15] This impossibility he inherits, in my opinion, from Plato himself, for whom individual things are constituted by the perfections they participate in from the Forms and by their distinction from one another. The former are positive and common to all of them and to the Forms; the latter is negative and consists simply in the fact that this thing *is not* that one. See ch. 5 above, "The 'Individual' in Plato, Plotinus and Aristotle."

[16] For a brief but informative history of the "sources" of Augustine, see R. J. O'Connell, *St. Augustine's Early Theory*, pp. 6–20 (on Plotinus), pp. 20–26 (on Porphyry, whose influence is championed by W. Theiler, John J. O'Meara, Pierre Courcelle, Aimé de Solignac but is denied by O'Connell until after the year 400). See pp. 25–26, where he claims that for the period 386–391 "the most rewarding procedure is that of considering the *Enneads* [of Plotinus] as the dominant Neo-Platonic influence on his thinking, so dominant that any competing influence from Porphyry can be safely ignored." But see E. TeSelle, *Augustine the Theologian*, pp. 49–54, a section which ends with the evaluation (in agreement with O. du Roy and Pierre Hadot) that after 387 "Augustine can be said to be more Porphyrian than Plotinian where the two differed." John J. O'Meara, "The Neoplatonism of Saint Augustine," in Dominic J. O'Meara (ed.), *Neoplatonism and Christian Philosophy* (Norfolk, Va.: International Society for Neoplatonic Studies, 1982), pp. 34–41, has again reaffirmed that Porphyry, as well as Plotinus, influenced Augustine. But for our purposes deciding whether Porphyry in addition to Plotinus affected Augustine's thinking is not crucial, because the radical metaphysics of each would be identical: reality is unity. See ch. 16 below, "Are Plotinus and Albertus Magnus Neoplatonists?"

[17] In Plotinus metaphysics is contrasted with ethics, philosophy of man, cosmology and religion, all of which are to be found in the *Enneads* but will receive little or no direct attention. We shall attend rather to Plotinus' position on the real precisely as real and, thus, on unity wherever found. Plotinian metaphysics is then the knowledge of the real as real and not (as Aristotle expresses it) of beings as being, since reality for Plotinus is not being but unity. Were Aristotle's formula taken literally, metaphysics would be restricted to reflection on *Nous*, Soul and the physical world, because the One transcends being.

I shall indicate the chronological place of each treatise of the *Enneads* cited below by a number in parenthesis—for example, "VI, 9 (9), 1, 1–8" means "Sixth *Ennead*, Treatise 9, ninth treatise chronologically, ch. 1, lines 1 to 8." The Greek text used is that of P. Henry and H.-R. Schwyzer, *Plotini Opera*, vols. 1–3 (Paris: Desclée de Brouwer, 1951, 1959 and 1973). Unless otherwise indicated, translations are my own.

Plotinus on Reality

In VI, 9 (9), 1, 1–8, the Greek author gives his reply. To be real is
to be one; that which constitutes the value and worth of an existent
is its unity.

All beings [he begins] are beings by the One, both those which
are primarily so [= the Nous and the Soul] and those which are
in some way classed among beings [= sensible things]. For
what could *be* if it were not one? If beings are deprived of what
we call unity, they *are not*. For instance, an army or a choir or a
flock no longer *is* if it is not one. In fact, neither a house nor a
ship *is* if it has not unity, for a house is one and a ship is one and
if it loses its unity, a house is no longer a house or a ship a ship.

Πάντα τὰ ὄντα τῷ ἑνί ἐστιν ὄντα, ὅσα τε πρώτως
ἐστὶν ὄντα, καὶ ὅσα ὁπωσοῦν λέγεται ἐν τοῖς οὖσιν εἶναι.
Τί γὰρ ἂν καὶ εἴη, εἰ μὴ ἓν εἴη; Ἐπείπερ ἀφαιρεθέντα
τοῦ ἓν ὃ λέγεται οὐκ ἔστιν ἐκεῖνα. Οὔτε γὰρ στρατὸς
ἔστιν, εἰ μὴ ἓν ἔσται, οὔτε χορὸς οὔτε ἀγέλη μὴ ἓν
ὄντα. Ἀλλ᾽ οὐδὲ οἰκία ἢ ναῦς τὸ ἓν οὐκ ἔχοντα, ἐπείπερ
ἡ οἰκία ἓν καὶ ἡ ναῦς, ὃ εἰ ἀποβάλοι, οὔτ᾽ ἂν ἡ οἰκία ἔτι
οἰκία οὔτε ἡ ναῦς.

In a later treatise—III, 8 (30), 10, 14 sqq.—Plotinus continues to
equate reality with unity when he aligns the One with the onenesses found in other existents. We must, he advises,

go back everywhere to the one [in each existent]: in each there
is some one to which you reduce it and this in every case to the
one before it, which [however] is not simply one, until we
come to the simply one, which cannot be reduced to something else. [For example,] if we take the one of the plant—this
is its source remaining within it[18]—and the one of the animal
and the one of the soul and the one of the physical All, we are
taking in each case that which is most powerful and valuable

---

[18] This source would be the individual plant's share of what Plotinus had
earlier in the same chapter spoken of as "the life of a huge plant, which goes
through the whole of it while its origin remains and is not dispersed over the
whole, since it is, as it were, firmly settled in the root. So this origin gives to the
plant its whole life in its multiplicity, but remains itself not multiple but the
origin of the multiple life" (lines 10–14; Armstrong's translation).

in it. But if we take the one of the beings which truly are—that one which is their origin and spring and power—shall we lose faith and think of it as nothing? [By no means: that One is truly real, even though] it is certainly none of the things of which it is the origin: it is such, though nothing can be predicated of it—neither being nor entity nor life—as to be above all such existents (lines 20–31; for Greek text see ch. VI above p. 167).

Comments. As was the case in VI, 9, 1, 1 sqq. (see above), here Plotinus also proceeds inductively: he moves from the oneness we perceive in plants, animals, our souls and the physical universe to truly real beings (Soul and Intellect) and then to the One, who is fully real because of His sheer unity and transcendence of being. Second, the One gives them oneness and, thereby, also reality because their being one is what makes each of them worthy of esteem. And the oneness which the One furnishes also is that which is most powerful in them (see lines 25–26: *to dynatôtaton kai to timion*) and which constitutes their power to contemplate and thereby to make themselves and subsequent existents.[19] In fact, the power in them *is* the One—He is power[20]—just as the oneness in them *is* the One (see lines 26–27): each of them *is* the One-on-a-lower-level, each is a *logos* of the One.[21] This basic identity of each lower existent with the One balances Plotinus' other paradoxical statements that the One is other than all else (see ch. 9, lines 39–54; ch. 10, line 10): yes, God is

---

[19] See *ibid.*, chs. 3 sqq., where Plotinus sets forth his position on contemplation. *Theoria* is found on all levels of reality except the highest (the One transcends contemplation) and the single word expresses both (say) the Intellect's operative state of contemplating and its content (i.e., what is contemplated, what is caused by the contemplating). This content itself is in turn an operative state producing its own content, until one comes to the *logoi* of plants, which are the content of Nature's operative state of contemplation but do not themselves contemplate. One may with profit consult John J. Deck, *Nature, Contemplation and the One: A Study in the Philosophy of Plotinus* (University of Toronto Press, 1967).

[20] After concluding the previous chapter of *Enneads*, III, 8, 9, by observing that the One is other than all things and is before all of them, Plotinus initiates chapter 10 with the statement that the One is "the power of all" (*dynamis tôn pantôn*): not only can the One produce all of them but He is in all as their *dynamis*.

[21] On *logos* meaning "a higher existent on a lower level," see Donald L. Gelpi, "*Logos* as a Cosmological Principle in Plotinus" (Master's thesis, St. Louis University, 1958); *idem,* "The Plotinian *Logos* Doctrine," *Modern Schoolman* 37 (1960), 301–15.

other than all His products inasmuch as God Himself is not totally identical with God-on-a-lower-level, but this otherness does not eliminate the fact that whatever reality (oneness, *dynamis*) is found on any subsequent level *is* God and, consistently, Plotinus' position is a monism. To be real is to be one.[22]

This equation of reality with oneness furnishes us with the primal principle of his metaphysics: "Whatever is real is one" or "Any existent is real because of its unity," with the result that the more unified something is, the more real it is.

Consequently, that which is totally simple is also the Primal Reality—namely, the One, which is the absolutely first and highest hypostasis.[23] On the other hand, an existent's lapse into multiplic-

---

[22] Do Plotinus' texts themselves underwrite this conclusion? Yes, provided one realizes that, although they disclose existents to be both distinct from and yet one with another, the unity there disclosed overshadows their distinctness. (For a listing and discussion of texts see L. Sweeney, *Divine Infinity in Greek and Medieval Thought* (New York/Bern: Peter Lang Publishing, Inc., 1992), ch. 11, "Basic Principles in Plotinus' Philosophy," prgrs. corresponding to notes 12–15.) The most apt comparison of this relationship between the One, Intellect, Soul and all other existents is that of a man and his integral parts. "Every man is both other than his hands and feet and the like and yet is physically joined to them all, each of which is really different from any other part and is less than the man in his entirety. In such a living being one finds a sort of real distinction but immersed in genuine unity, which overshadows it. The parts are really but, let us say, inadequately and only virtually distinct from one another and from the whole, but they are vitalized by a single soul and thus coalesce into an essential unity or *unum per se*. The distinction is, so to speak, accidental; the unity is essential. . . . Something like that sort of inadequate real distinction seems to exist" between the One and all other existents without eliminating their radical unity and the basic monism which marks his metaphysics (*ibid.*, p. 246). Also see A. H. Armstrong, "The Apprehension of Divinity in the Self and Cosmos in Plotinus," in R. Baine Harris (ed.), *The Significance of Neoplatonism* (Norfolk, Va.: International Society for Neoplatonic Studies, 1976), pp. 187–98; Plato Mamo, "Is Plotinian Mysticism Monistic?" *ibid.*, pp. 199–215 (*vs.* Zaener, Arnou, Rist); for references to studies by Trouillard, Carbonara, Bréhier and de Gandillac, see L. Sweeney, *Divine Infinity in Greek and Medieval Thought*, ch. 11: "Basic Principles in Plotinus' Philosophy," n. 13; *idem*, "Are Plotinus and Albertus Magnus Neoplatonists?" ch. 16 below, prgrs. corresponding to notes 13–43.

[23] See John P. Anton, "Some Logical Aspects of the Concept of *Hypostatis* in Plotinus," *Review of Metaphysics* 31 (1968), 258–71 (with references to studies by Armstrong, Rist, Deck, Wallis); Heinrich Dörrie, "Hypostasis: Wort und Bedeutungsgeschichte," *Nachrichten der Akademie der Wissenschaften in Göttingen* (1955), pp. 35–92 (on Plotinus: pp. 68–74).

ity is equated with a lapse into unreality—an equation which is equivalent to saying that the emanation of Intellect, Soul and Nature from the One is a movement of what is increasingly less perfect from what is more perfect. To go forth from a cause is to proceed from the perfect to the imperfect. And by this process lower existents become increasingly determined and, thereby, less real. For example, VI, 9 (9), 11, 36 sq.: "When [the human soul] goes down, it comes to evil and so to nonbeing." VI, 5, (23), 12, 16–25:

> [In ascending back to God] you have come to the All and not stayed in a part of it, and have not said even about yourself, 'I am so much.' By rejecting the 'so much' you have become all— yet you were all before. But because something else other than the All added itself to you, you became less by the addition, for the addition did not come from real being (you cannot add anything to that) but from that which is not. When you have become a particular person by the addition of non-being, you are not all till you reject the non-being. You will increase yourself then by rejecting the rest, and by that rejection the All is with you. (For Greek text see ch. V above.)

Determination so conceived helps preserve Plotinus' monism because what alone is real in any existent is the oneness it has from and with the One and not the apparent additions and individuation it has put on. Hence, we arrive at the crucial realization that for Plotinus an individual existent *precisely as individual* is unreal, valueless, worthless.[24]

This realization has great significance for our understanding the Christian religion in relation to Augustine, but first let us summarize what Plotinus' basic metaphysics has shown itself to be. It is a monism in which the primal reality is an actually existing, divine One-Good, whose existence does not exclude but rather guarantees (through its spontaneous and necessary emanative causality of procession) that Intellect and intellects, Soul and souls, the physical world and its contents also actually exist, but in such a manner that whatever genuine reality they have is the One on a lower level. To

---

[24] But see John Rist, *Human Value: A Study in Ancient Philosophical Ethics* (Leiden: E. J. Brill, 1982), pp. 101 sqq.: an individual man *qua individual* is of value and individuality and is the necessary mark of the perfected self. His interpretation of Plotinus appears inaccurate and misleading. See ch. 5 above, "The 'Individual' in Plato, Plotinus and Aristotle," especially Appendix B.

participate more fully in reality they must return (a second sort of causality operative in Plotinus) to the One-Good through contemplation and, eventually, through some sort of full identification with Him. In that return they gradually put off the multiplicity, unreality, determination and *individuality* they had put on in their going forth from Him.

If such, then, is Plotinian metaphysics in a nutshell, it differs from the Christian religion in its devaluation of the individual. For Plotinus individuality or individuation is what an existent puts on in descending from the One. It is a descent into multiplicity. It is negation, nonbeing, unreality. An individual existent *precisely as individual* is unreal, valueless, insignificant. How different is the stance that the Christianity found in Paul, Mark, Matthew, Luke and John takes. There each individual lily or sparrow or human person is of value in and of itself. God the Son became incarnate in history as an individual human existent that He might save individual men and women. God freely causes all individual creatures to exist and, as the efficient and creative cause, is thereby present to them but also is really distinct from them (hence, His simultaneous immanence and transcendence).

This is not to deny that the Neoplatonism initiated by Plotinus has aided Christianity in explicating itself in some areas. Its negative theology has enabled Christians to stress the otherness and uniqueness of God. The place it gives in reality to the spiritual, the intellectual and the immortal has reminded Christians that those dimensions are also properties of human individuals. Neoplatonic versions of divine causality in its extensiveness and intensity have been translated by Christians into theories of creation. But where Neoplatonism cannot help Christianity is, I submit, in the area of basic metaphysics. If a Christian author is so influenced by Neoplatonism as to equate reality with unity, to identify creatures with the Creator, to conceive of an individual existent qua individual as unreal, his position is no longer authentically Christian.

St. Augustine: Plotinian or Christian?

Where does St. Augustine fit? Does he view individuals qua individuals as real? Everyone would want to answer affirmatively. But there are some texts in the *Confessions* that recommend caution. For instance, take his description of time and related issues. Here let me first reproduce his statements and then add brief commentaries on some of them.

(a) Present time *is* only because it tends not to be (XI, c. 14, #17):

What, then, is time? If no one asks me, I know; but, if I want to explain it to a questioner, I do not know. Yet I say with confidence that I know that, if nothing were to pass away, there would be no past time; if nothing were coming, there would be no future time; and if nothing were existing, there would be no present time.

These two times, then, past and future, how *are* they, seeing the past now is no longer, and the future is not yet? But the present, should it always be present and never pass into the past, indeed it would not be time but eternity. So if the present (if it is to be time) only comes into existence because it passes into the past, how can we say that it *is* whose cause of being is that it shall not be; so, namely, we cannot truly say that time *is* but that it is tending not to be?

Quid est ergo tempus? Si nemo ex me quaerat, scio; si quarenti explicare velim, nescio; fidenter tamen dico scire me, quod, si nihil praeteriret, non esset praeteritum tempus, et si nihil adveniret, non esset futurum tempus, et si nihil esset, non esset praesens tempus. Duo ergo illa tempora, praeteritum et futurum, quomodo sunt, quando et praeteritum iam non est et futurum nondum est? Praesens autem si semper esset praesens nec in praeteritum transiret, non iam esset tempus, set aeternitas. Si ergo praesens, ut tempus sit, ideo fit, quia in praeteritum transit, quomodo et hoc esse dicimus, cui causa ut sit illa est, quia non erit, ut scilicet non vere dicamus tempus esse, nisi quia tendit non esse?

(b) Time is, moreover, a kind of distention (*ibid.*, c. 23, #30: "Video igitur tempus quamdam esse distentionem") of the very mind itself (*ibid.*, c. 26, #33: "Inde mihi visum est nihil esse aliud tempus quam distentionem. Sed cuius rei, nescio, et mirum si non ipsius animi").

(c) But the individual human person *is* the mind (X, c. 6, #9: "I, the inner man, knew these sensible things—I, I the mind, by means of my bodily sense"—"Homo interior cognovit haec per exterioris ministerium; ego interior cognovi haec, ego, ego animus per sensum corporis mei").

(d) Therefore, time *is* the individual human person.

Comments on #c: Augustine here contrasts the individual human person or *ego* with "man" (lines 8–10: "Et direxi me ad me et dixi mihi: 'Tu quis es?' Et respondi: 'Homo.' Et ecce corpus et anima in me mihi praesto sunt, unum exterius et alterum interius"). "Man" is soul and body but in the Platonic sense of soul using a body but not as forming an Aristotelian entitative unit. The "inner man" or "ego" *is* the soul or mind.

Comments on #b: Why is time a distention of the human mind itself? Because present time is my actual current transient conscious state, whereas the past and future times "are" only insofar as I *now* am consciously remembering what happened previously or as I *now* am consciously expecting what will come about (*ibid.*, XI, c. 28, #37). In my present state of consciousness, then, I am living in the past or in the future; I am being stretched, pulled, distended toward what is not. In this state I am myself that tending to non-being and unreality, and time is that tendency (#a); thus, I am time (#d).

If we integrate those comments with the previous texts of the *Confessions*, we come up with this syllogism: time is that whose being is solely a tendency to nonbeing; but the individual human person is time; therefore, the human individual is that whose being or reality is a tendency to nonbeing and unreality. If so, how can an individual human existent qua individual and in itself be real? Do not you and I become eternal, immutable and thereby real only by participating in God through contemplating Him by our *rationes superiores*?

But when I do contemplate God (someone may argue) and thus participate in His truth, permanence, eternity and reality, do not *I* thereby become (to some degree, at least) true, immutable, eternal and real? Yes, but only provided that such perfections become *mine*, that they genuinely are a part and constituent of me and are not merely transient and (literally) superficial perfections which do not enter into my makeup as an individual (as for Plato participated perfections are solely on the surface [and fleetingly, too] of the Receptable in the *Timaeus* and never enter into it). Otherwise, I myself remain merely the *mutabilitas* which then wholly constitutes me: the *prope nihil*, the *nihil/aliquid*, the *ens/nonens* of which Augustine speaks in *ibid.*, XII, c. 6, #6. And undoubtedly this is the condition of any sinner, who turns from God and refuses to participate in His reality. Such an individual in his mutability and "almost nothingness" would be sheerly unreal because without divine illumination, truth and stability.

In fact, would this not be Augustine's status during the years prior to his intellectual, moral and religious conversion, as well as after that *metanoia*, if we are to judge by his concluding remarks (with obvious Neoplatonic echoes) in *ibid.*, XI, c. 29, #39, which (one should add) are applicable to any human person in his struggle to achieve salvation, well-being, reality.

> Behold, my life is distention. But Your right hand has upheld me in my Lord, the Son of man, mediator between You, the One, and us, the many, who are [dissipated] in many ways upon many things, so that . . . I may be gathered together again from my former days, to follow the One . . . and not distended but opened wide ("non distentus sed extentus"), but not to things that shall be and shall pass away but to those things which transcend them. . . . But now my years are wasted away in sighs, and You, O Lord, my comfort, my Father, are eternal. But I am distracted amid times, whose order I do not know, and my thoughts, the inmost bowels of my soul, are torn asunder by tumult and change until being purged and melted clear by the fire of your love, I may flow together into you.

> Sed quoniam melior est misericordia tua super vitas ecce distentio est vita mea, et me suscepit dextera tua in Domino meo, mediatore filio hominis inter te unum et nos multos, in multis per multa, ut per eum apprehendam, in quo apprehensus sum, et a veteribus diebus colligar sequens unum, praeterita oblitus, non in ea quae futura et transitura sunt, sed in ea quae ante sunt non distentus, sed extentus, non secundum extentionem, sed "secundum intentionem sequor ad palmam supernae vocationis," ubi audiam vocis laudis et contempler delectationem tuam nec venientem nec praetereuntem. Nunc vero anni mei in gemitibus, et tu solacium meum, Domine, pater meus aeternus es; at ego in tempora dissilui, quorum ordinem nescio, et tumultuosis varietatibus dilaniantur cogitationes meae, intima viscera animae meae, donec in te confluam purgatus et liquidus igne amoris tui.

What should one make of that passage? Is Augustine's God identical with Plotinus' One? Is not Christ the mediator conceived as the

One/many—i.e., God/man? Is each of us precisely in ourselves anything more than multiplicity, mutability, time? In my individual self am I anything more than the stretching-out of disordered times, the tumult of transient thoughts in the inmost recesses of my soul, deliverance from which will come only when "I flow together into You"?

If I answer *yes* to those questions, am I not, in Augustine's eyes, unreal, valueless, worthless *in and of myself* as an individual human existent?

In fact, am I capable of acting on my own? Granted that I appear to efficiently cause my own seeing, knowing, speaking and the like, but the prayer Augustine addresses to God toward the very end of the *Confessions* (XIII, c. 31, #46) might suggest that it is really God who causes such operations in me.

> Whoever sees these things ["the fabric of the heavens and the arrangement of the stars, . . . all things of flesh, all very minute living beings, and whatsoever things cling to earth by roots"] through Your Spirit, You see in them. Therefore, when they see that they are good, You see that they are good, and whatsoever things are pleasing because of You, in them You Yourself are pleasing, and such things as are pleasing to us because of Your Spirit are in us pleasing to You. "For what man knows the things of man but the spirit of man that is in him? So the things also that are of God no one knows but the Spirit of God. Now we have received not the spirit of this world, but the Spirit that is of God, that we may know the things that are given us of God." (I *Cor.* 2, 11–12) I am admonished to say: Truly, no one knows "the things that are of God but the Spirit of God." How then do we also know "what things are given us of God?" The answer is made to me that likewise the things that we know by his Spirit "no one knows, but the Spirit of God." Just as it was rightly said to those who would speak in the Spirit of God, "It is not you who speak," so it is rightly said to those who know in the Spirit of God, "It is not you who know." Therefore, no less rightly is it said to those who see in the Spirit of God, "It is not you who see," so that whatsoever in the Spirit of God they see to be good, it is not they but God who "sees that it is good."

> Qui autem per Spiritum tuum vident ea, tu vides in eis. Ergo cum vident quia bona sunt, tu vides, quia bona sunt, et

quaecumque propter te placent, tu in eis places, et quae per Spiritum tuum placent nobis, tibi placent in nobis. *Quis enim scit hominum quae sunt hominis nisi spiritus hominis, qui in ipso est? Sic et quae Dei sunt nemo scit nisi spiritus Dei. Nos autem,* inquit, *non spiritum huius mundi accepimus, sed spiritum, qui ex Deo est, ut sciamus quae a Deo donata sunt nobis.* Et admoneor ut dicam: Certe nemo scit quae Dei nisi spiritus Dei. Quomodo ergo scimus et nos *quae a Deo donata sunt nobis?* Respondetur mihi, quoniam quae per eius Spiritum scimus etiam sic nemo *scit nisi spiritus Dei.* Sicut enim recte dictum est: *non enim vos estis, qui loquimini,* eis qui in Dei spiritur loquerentur, sic recte dicitur: *Non vos estis, qui scitis,* eis, qui in Dei spiritu sciunt. Nihilo minus igitur recte dicitur: *Non vos estis qui videtis,* eis, qui in spiritu Dei vident: ita quidquid in spiritu Dei vident, quia bonum est, non ipsi, sed Deus videt, quia bonum est.

This sort of text is in line with E. Gilson's interpretation of Augustine's philosophy as a "metaphysics of conversion." The experience of his own moral weaknesses and incapacity in the supernatural order perhaps led Augustine to overemphasize God's part and devaluate creatural efficiency in human knowledge and physical causality.[25]

But I have played the role of "advocatus diaboli" long enough. Such a sampling of texts is one-sided and can be more than matched by texts that show the individual as individual to be of significance and of value and, thus, to be real.[26] But locating the status of an individual existent qua individual in Christianity and in Plotinus'

---

[25] See E. Gilson, *The Spirit of Mediaeval Philosophy* (New York: Charles Scribner's Sons, 1936), p. 132: "From the deepest roots of its inspiration down to the details of its technical structure the whole doctrine of St. Augustine is dominated by one fact: the religious experience of his own conversion.... His philosophy is essentially a 'metaphysic of conversion.'" Also see his *Introduction à l'étude de S. Augustin* (Paris: Vrin, 1949), p. 316.

[26] Some of those texts would be Augustine's emphasis (against Manichaeism) that all things are good because divinely created. See *Confessions*, VII, chs. 12–15, of which the following two passages are especially significant.

Ibid., ch. 12, 18: "As long as things are, they are good. Therefore whatsoever is is good"—*Quamdiu sunt bona sunt. Ergo quaecumque sunt bona sunt.*

Ibid., ch. 15, 21: "I looked back over things other than You and I saw that they owe their being to You and that everything finite is in You—not as though in a place but in a different fashion, because You contain all things in Your hand by Your truth. All things are true insofar as they are, nor is there

metaphysics seems to help one read and reflect upon Augustine much more attentively than previously. This approach to his *Confessions*, as well as to other writings, may eventually aid also in testing the authenticity of his Christianity.

---

any falsity except when that is thought to be which is not"—*Et respexi alia et vidi tibi debere quia sunt et in te cuncta finita, sed aliter, non quasi in loco, sed quia tu es omnitenens manu veritate, et omnia vera sunt, in quantum sunt, nec quicquam est falsitas, nisi cum putatur esse quod non est.*

8

Augustine on Christ as God and Man: Exegesis of *Confessions*, VII, 19

In 1954 Pierre Courcelle declared[1] that chapter 19 of Book VII of Augustine's *Confessions* merits special attention ("une attention particulière") since Augustine, while speaking of his reading of the Platonic books and their influence upon his conversion to the Catholic faith, there admits that he thought of Christ as fully human but not as God.

I conceived my Lord Christ only as a man of surpassing wisdom, whom no other man could equal. Above all, because he was born in a wondrous manner of the Virgin, to give us an example of despising temporal things in order to win immortality, he seemed by the godlike care that he had for us, to have merited such great authority as a teacher. But what mystery was contained within those words, "The Word was made flesh," I could not conceive. But of what has been handed down in writing concerning him, namely, that he ate and drank, slept, walked about, was joyful, grew sad, and preached, I had learned only that that flesh did not cleave to your Word except together with a human soul and mind. Any man who has knowledge of the immutability of your Word knows this:

[1] "Saint Augustin 'Photinien' à Milan (*Conf.*, VII, 19, 25)"[hereafter: "Saint Augustin"], *Ricerche di Storia Religiosa* 1 (1954), 63. I am grateful to Roland Teske, S.J., for this reference.

I knew it at that time, as far as I could know it, and had no
doubt whatsoever concerning it. Now to move one's bodily
members at the command of the will, and now not to move
them; now to be affected by some emotion, and now not to be
affected; now to utter wise judgments by means of signs, and
now to remain silent—such things belong to a soul and a
mind that are subject to change. If these things were written
falsely of him, then all else would be in danger of being false,
and no saving faith for mankind would remain in those Scriptures. But since the things written are true, I acknowledged
that in Christ there was a complete man: not merely a man's
body, nor an animating principle in the body but without a
mind, but a true man. I accounted him a person to be preferred above all other men, not as the person of Truth, but
because of some great excellence of his human nature and a
more perfect participation in wisdom.

Ego vero aliud putabam tantumque sentiebam de Domino
Christo meo, quantum de excellentis sapientiae viro, cui nullus
posset aequari, praesertim quia mirabiliter natus ex virgine ad
exemplum contemnendorum temporalium prae adipiscenda
immortalitate, divina pro nobis cura tantam auctoritatem
magisterii meruisse videbatur. Quid autem sacramenti haberet
Verbum caro factum, ne suspicari quidem poteram. Tantum
cognoveram ex his, quae de illo scripta traderentur, quia
manducavit et bibit, dormivit, ambulavit, exhilaratus est, con-
tristatus est, sermocinatus est, non haesisse carnem illam
verbo tuo nisi cum anima et mente humana. Novit hoc omnis,
qui novit incommutabilitatem Verbi tui, quam ego iam nov-
eram, quantum poteram, nec omnino quicquam inde dubita-
bam. Etenim nunc movere membra corporis per voluntatem,
nunc non movere, nunc aliquo affectu affici, nunc non affici,
nunc proferre per signa sapientes sententias, nunc esse in
silentio, propria sunt mutabilitatis animae et mentis. Quae si
falsa de illo scripta essent, etiam omnia periclitarentur men-
dacio, neque in illis litteris ulla fidei salus generi humano remaneret. Quia itaque vera scripta sunt, totum hominem in
Christo agnoscebam, non corpus tantum hominis aut cum
corpore sine mente animum; sed ipsum hominem, non persona veritatis, sed magna quadam naturae humanae excellen-
tia et perfectiore participatione sapientiae praeferri ceteris
arbitrabar.

After describing Alypius' misconception of the Catholic belief regarding Christ (He is God with a human body but without a soul and mind),[2] Augustine concludes chapter 19 by remarking that "it was somewhat after this, I admit, that I learned how, with regard to those words, 'The Word was made flesh,' Catholic truth is distinguished from the false teachings of Photinus."[3]

---

[2] "Alypius, on the other hand, thought that Catholics believed that God was clothed in flesh in such wise that in Christ there was no soul, in addition to his divinity and his body. Nor did he think that a human mind was attributed to him. Because he was firmly convinced that the deeds recorded of him could only be done by a creature possessed of life and reason, he moved more slowly towards the Christian faith. However, he learned later that this was the error of the Apollinarian heretics, and he was pleased with the Catholic faith and better disposed towards it."

Alypius autem Deum carne indutum ita putabat credi a catholicis, ut praeter Deum et carnem non esse in Christo animam, mentemque hominis non existimabat in eo praedicari. Et quoniam bene persuasum tenebat, ea quae de illo memoriae mandata sunt, sine vitali et rationali creatura non fieri, ad ipsam christianam fidem pigrius movebatur. Sed postea haereticorum apollinaristarum hunc errorem esse cognoscens, catholicae fidei conlaetatus et contemperatus est.

Unless otherwise noted, the English translation is that of John K. Ryan (Doubleday Image Books, 1960); the Latin text is that critically edited by Angel Custodio Vega, *Obras de San Agustín* (Madrid: Biblioteca de Autores Cristianos, 1963), Tomo II: *Las Confesiones*.

On Alypius, a lifelong friend of Augustine and eventually bishop of Thagaste, see Peter Brown, *Augustine of Hippo* (Berkeley: University of California Press, 1969), pp. 67–68 and *passim*. On Apollinarius (ca. 300–390), bishop of Leodicea, see A. de Solignac, Commentary on *Confessions* (publishing data given below), XIII, p. 698; Jaroslav Pelikan, *The Christian Tradition: A History of the Development of Doctrine*, vol. 1: *Emergence of the Catholic Tradition (100–600)* (University of Chicago Press, 1971), pp. 238–41; F. L. Cross (ed.), *Oxford Dictionary of the Christian Church* (London: Oxford University Press, 1966), p. 70: "The objects of Apollinarianism, the first great Christological heresy, were (1) to assert the unity of Godhead and manhood in Christ, (2) to teach the full Deity of Christ, and (3) to avoid teaching that there was a moral development in Christ's life. To gain these ends, Apollinarius asserted that in man there coexist body, soul and spirit. In Christ, however, were to be found the human body and soul, but no human spirit, the spirit being replaced by the Divine Logos. Thus while he possessed perfect Godhead, He lacked complete manhood."

[3] On Photinus see F. L. Cross, *Oxford Dictionary*, p. 1069: Photinus was a pupil of Marcellus of Ancyra and became bishop of Sirmium ca. 344, condemned together with Marcellus by a Council of Antioch ca. 345 but retained his see until 351, when he was deposed and exiled for his version of Sabellianism.

Ego autem aliquanto posterius didicisse me fateor, in eo, quod *Verbum caro factum est*, quomodo catholica veritas a Fotini falsitate dirimatur.

Although scholars other than Courcelle have subsequently shed light on chapter 19, it seems good to reopen the question of Augustine's Christology. This I shall do by examining Courcelle's 1954 article, Aimé de Solignac's 1962 Commentary on the *Confessions*, Eugene TeSelle's *Augustine the Theologian* (1970) and William Mallard's "The Incarnation in Augustine's Conversion" (1980). That examination will terminate with an inquiry into the sources of Augustine's Christology.

Pierre Courcelle

Before giving his own interpretation of *Confessions*, VII, 19, 25, Courcelle surveys previous reactions to that passage.[4] According to that survey Prosper Alfaric ignored chapter 19 because he considered Augustine to have firmly believed not only in the existence of God and of providence but also in the divinity of Christ before he read Plotinus and Porphyry. Jean-Marie Le Blond granted that, although Augustine erred gravely on the matter of Christ's divinity, "he was an authentic Christian and his faith was genuine," whereas Pierre de Labriolle considered him only to have partially ignored that basic article of Catholicism.

On the other hand, Charles Boyer was astonished that Augustine (like Photinus) did not believe Christ to be divine if interpreted strictly ("à la divinité proprement dite de Jésus-Christ")—an attitude he later realized was an unrecognized heresy alienating himself from orthodoxy. Had not (Boyer asked) Monica instructed him as a child in this fundamental point of Christianity? Was Augustine unaware of the Nicene Creed (formulated in 325)? What did he understand by the words "Christ is the Word" and "The Word was made flesh"? For J. Nörregaard chapter 19 shows Augustine's long-standing alienation from orthodoxy prior to and unrelated to his reading the Neoplatonic books.

In expressing his own interpretation Courcelle starts by characterizing Nörregaard's position as a "gratuitous conjecture": it fails

---

[4] See Courcelle, "Saint Augustin," pp. 64–66, where he gives exact references to those scholars surveyed.

to take into account the context of chapter 19, which consists of how Augustine became acquainted with those Neoplatonic writings and what they did or did not disclose to him on God and His creatures. In fact, those writings furnish the key to Augustine's problem, consisting as they do of several treatises of Plotinus' *Enneads* and Porphyry's *De Regressu Animae* ("Saint Augustin," p. 66). The latter philosopher (rather than Photinus) is the source of Augustine's conception of Christ as perfect man but not as God, as one can gather (Courcelle avers) by consulting Augustine's *De Consensu Evangelistarum* (written in 399 or 400 and hence shortly after the *Confessions*) and the later *City of God*, which relies on Porphyry's *De Philosophia ex Oraculis Haurienda*. And Simplicianus' function in Augustine's life was to replace Porphyry's position (Christ was a man of superior wisdom but not God) with the orthodox belief that Christ was both man and God ("Saint Augustin," pp. 66–71).[5]

Aimé de Solignac

Eight years after Courcelle's article Aimé de Solignac commented upon Augustine's *Confessions* as edited by M. Skutella (1934) and published as volumes 13 and 14 of *Bibliothèque Augustinienne* (Paris: Desclée de Brouwer, 1962). In his commentary on chapter 19 of Book VII, entitled "La christologie d'Augustin au temps de sa conversion" (vol. 13, pp. 693–98), he disagrees with Courcelle on the source of Augustine's misconception of Christ: it was not Porphyry but Photinus. Why so? Because in both *Confessions*, VII, 19, and *De agone christiana* (written ca. 396–97) Augustine affirms that Christ's wisdom was so supreme as to surpass all other human participants of wisdom because of His virgin birth from Mary. But locating the supremacy of His wisdom in the fact that "he was born in a wondrous manner of the Virgin" (*Conf.*, VII, 19, 25) does not appear to

---

[5] On Plotinus, see R. T. Wallis, *Neoplatonism* (New York: Charles Scribner's Sons, 1972), pp. 47–93. On Porphyry see *ibid.*, pp. 94–137; Eugene TeSelle, *Augustine the Theologian* (publishing data given below), pp. 49–54, 124–26, 241–42, 257–58 and *passim*; F. L. Cross, *Oxford Dictionary*, pp. 1091–92. On Simplicianus, see Eugene TeSelle, *Augustine the Theologian*, pp. 36–37; F. L. Cross, *Oxford Dictionary*, p. 1259: Simplicianus was heard of between 350 and 360 at Rome, where he helped convert Marius Victorinus (translator of Plotinus into Latin) and, later, Augustine, and in the 370s tutored St. Ambrose, whom he succeeded as bishop of Milan in 397; he died in 400. Also see n. 20 below.

come from Porphyry, who would not have accepted that fact. Rather, that conception of Christ's wisdom seemingly came from the influence of Photinus and/or his followers at Milan ("La christologie," pp. 693–95).[6]

Whatever may be the origin of Augustine's misunderstanding of Christ's divinity at this time in his life, though, a crucial aspect of it is that he was thereby ignorant of the Incarnation: "What mystery was contained within those words, 'The Word was made flesh,' I could not conceive." Instead he conceived of Christ (Solignac continues) as *totus homo*—that is, he was not only a body animated by a soul but also a spirit: an intellectual principle and will ("il voit dans le Christ 'un homme tout entier,' c'est-à-dire non pas seulement un corps humain ou même une âme animant un corps, mais également un 'esprit,' un principe d'intelligence et de volonté"; *ibid.*, pp. 695–96). And it is this *totus homo* (Augustine will at a later date affirm in *Sermo* 237, IV, 4) which the person of the Word will assume: "totum redemit qui totum creavit, totum suscepit, totum liberavit Verbum. Ibi mens hominis et intellectus, ibi anima vivificans carnem, ibi caro vera et integra; peccatum solum non ibi" (*ibid.*, p. 696).

Eugene TeSelle

Eugene TeSelle in *Augustine the Theologian* (New York: Herder and Herder, 1970) grants that Solignac has disposed of Courcelle's identifying the source of Augustine's misconception as Porphyry. Rather, "it must be an echo of a Photinian brand of Christianity in Milan" (*Augustine*, p. 146, n. 14). Granted, also, that Augustine "thought of Christ as a complete man, but in such fashion that he could be only a wise man participating in the Word, not the Word incarnate." Moreover,

---

[6] Olivier du Roy, *L'Intelligence de la foi en la Trinité selon Saint Augustin: Genèse de sa théologie trinitaire jusqu'en 391* (Paris: Études Augustiniennes, 1966), pp. 90–92, agrees with Solignac that Porphyry is not the source of Augustine's unorthodox view of Christ, which does parallel Photinus', but that parallel need not mean that Augustine personally knew the followers of Photinus at Milan or took his Christology from them. Rather, identifying his views with theirs may have come later when he was writing the *Confessions*: "Ce peut être une identification postérieure de l'évêque d'Hippone" (p. 91). See *ibid.*, pp. 92–95: what separated Augustine from the full truth of Christianity was not his errors in Christology taken abstractly but rather his lack of humility and his unappreciation of the need of the incarnate Word's grace in his religious life.

Augustine's closing comment [in *Conf.*, VII, 19, 25] should not be overlooked. "Surely it is the process of refuting heretics," he says, "that brings to light the mind of your Church and the content of sound teaching. There must be heresies, in order that those who are tested and proved genuine might be manifested in the midst of the weak." This is not, I think, merely a moral added at the end but a comment on the actual situation of that day. In 386 the doctrinal controversies with the Photinians and the Apollinarians had just come to a resolution; tendencies toward the one side or the other were still present, and the positive doctrine had not been made entirely clear (*Augustine the Theologian*, p. 147).

Nonetheless, by Easter 391 Augustine already had a well-worked-out Christology, as is evident in his first venture in preaching.

A complete man, that is, a rational soul and a body, was assumed by the Word, in such fashion as to be one Christ and one God the Son of God, not the Word alone, but the Word *and* the man [or as he puts it more explicitly in the next paragraph, Word and soul and flesh], and this whole [*totum hoc*] is the Son of God the Father according to the Word and the son of man according to the man. . . . He is not only man, but Son of God, but according to the Word, by whom the man is assumed; and he is not only the Word but the son of man, but according to the man, who is assumed by the Word (*Sermo* 214, 6—quoted by TeSelle, *ibid.*, pp. 147–48).[7]

---

[7] Also see Augustine's *Enarratio in II Psalmum*, 6 (*Ancient Christian Writers*, vol. 1, p. 27): "*The Lord hath said to me: Thou art my son, today have I begotten thee.* It is possible to see in the word *today* a prophecy of the day on which Jesus Christ was born in His human nature. Yet as the word *today* denotes the actual present, and as in eternity nothing is past as if it had ceased to be, nor future as if it had not yet come to pass, but all is simply present, since whatever is eternal is ever in being, the words *Today have I begotten thee* are to be understood of the divine generation. In this phrase, orthodox Catholic belief proclaims the eternal generation of the Power and Wisdom of God who is the only-begotten Son."

Also *Enarratio in III Psalmum*, 3 (*ibid.*, p. 33): "*But thou, O Lord, takest me up.* Christ speaks to God in His human nature, since God's taking of human nature is the Word made flesh. *My glory.* He even calls God His glory, this Man whom the Word of God has so taken upon Himself that God and He are One. A lesson for the proud, who close their ears when asked: *What hast thou*

William Mallard

In an illuminating article, "The Incarnation in Augustine's Conversion" (*Recherches Augustiniennes* 15 [1980], 80–98), William Mallard surveys the previous three studies, as well as many others (e.g., those by H. I. Marrou, Michele Pellegrino, T. Van Bavel, R. J. O'Connell, Goulven Madec), and concludes that in various ways and to varying degress they tended to discuss whether Augustine did truly affirm the Incarnation in 386 and not what he intended in that affirmation: "that he affirmed the Incarnation does not tell us what mingling of dogma and Neoplatonist philosophy took place in that affirmation. *That* he confessed the Incarnation does not tell us *how* he understood it" (p. 81).

Mallard himself stresses the latter question: What does the fact that the divine Word became flesh mean and entail? Relying on *De Ordine*, II, 5, 16, which previous scholars had utilized, and the *Contra Academicos*, III, 19, 42, which they had passed over (see pp. 85–88), he detects that a major change had occurred in Augustine's conception of Christ between the "Photinianism" he held in the

---

that thou hast not received? And if thou hast received, why dost thou glory as if thou hadst not received it? And the lifter up of my head. Here, I think, is denoted Christ's human mind, not without reason termed the head of the soul; and this soul was so united, so inextricably part of the surpassing excellency of the Word Incarnate, as it were, that it was not surrendered even in the deep humiliation of the passion." These two *Enarrationes* were written ca. 392 and hence are dated at approximately the same time as *Sermo* 214.

TeSelle himself interprets Augustine's orthodox Christology of 391 and subsequent years as "Origenist"—the "soul of Christ is the medium of union between the Word and the flesh and it is inseparably united to the Word with such an intensity of affection and immediacy of intuition that it becomes like the Word in every respect" (*Augustine the Theologian*, p. 148). The value of this conception is that it shows "how the Word can remain free from the desires and fears of the body even while assuming a human life into unity with himself" (*ibid.*, p. 149). Again: this sort of Christology "can keep the integrity of both the divine and the human, to the extent of speaking unabashedly of 'the Word' and 'the man,' and still bring them so closely together that it is possible to speak of 'one person.' This can be achieved only by placing the emphasis upon *mind* or *spirit* as the medium of union, for it can be at once active and closely conjoined to another. What is asserted here is not any less a theory of 'real' or 'hypostatic' union; but the reality involved is mind, and its actuality is gained through enactment, not through bare subsistence alone" (*ibid.*, p. 156), as will happen presumably in the theories of the Medieval and Renaissance Schoolmen on "person" and "supposit."

years from 382 to 386 and expressed in *Confessions,* VII, 19, 25 (Christ is man only) and the orthodox view of the Cassiciacum dialogues composed after August 386 (Christ is man/God). That change is disclosed in how Augustine conceives of "participation" in the two sets of writings. In the preconversion account of the *Confessions* "the excellence of this real human being, this whole human being [who is Christ] is by participating in wisdom, i.e., in ultimate, divine truth" and not by being identified with wisdom and truth. But in the postconversion dialogues

> the picture is not of a man rousing himself to excellence by participating in divine authority, but rather the opposite: God is acting to participate downward in bodily human life. The agency, and thereby presumably the initiative, has completely shifted around. This shift in agency from the man participating "upward" to God participating "downward" is quite enough to say that a cornerstone of thought has changed for Augustine. A unique "downward" initiative of singular divine agency could not emerge within Augustine's strictly philosophical milieu. Undoubtedly, these passages are evidence that Augustine has affirmed the essential outline of "verbum caro factum est," the Catholic biblical teaching on the Incarnation (pp. 88–89).

But despite this accurate affirmation and his conception, in some sense, of what the Incarnation meant, he still lacked "full understanding of the content of the Christian faith," which however will surely be "cast along Neoplatonic lines" (p. 90).

> God submitted the authority of the divine intellect to the human body. The Incarnation thereby serves as God's gracious self-humbling means to an end that is Neoplatonist—or better, an end on whose general nature Neoplatonist principles and Christianity do not contradict. In fact, the Incarnation is the manifestation on earth, in a human body, of the Neoplatonic *nous,* i.e., "the authority of the divine intellect."

And in writings later than *Contra Academicos,* III, 19, 25, Augustine "will continue, as is well known, to see in the Christian faith an authoritative means to a philosophical-Christian end through the divine intellect self-humbled and incarnate" (p. 91).

In summary, then, "the young Augustine saw the Eternal Truth articulate in both Neoplatonist books and Christine doctrines, even if in different words (*Confessions*, VII, 9, 13)." And the Church's insistence on the Incarnation was no stumbling block, as he discovered at the heart of his conversion, once he realized that the

> Word made flesh was a self-humbling Word because God is by essence a self-abasing, merciful God. God's mercy in humility is indeed a divine perfection, not inconsistent with his nature as immutable and eternal. For God forever disposes himself graciously and mercifully towards the world. Thus one may reflect on God in a platonizing manner without contradicting his self-giving nature in the Incarnation. The "God is One" of the platonizing books fits into the richer, more complex and typically Augustinian scheme, "God is Love" (pp. 95–96).

Whence Augustine's Christology?

In the light of all four exegetes studied, one cannot doubt that Augustine misconceived Christ up to the time of his conversion, as he himself makes clear in *Confessions*, VII, 19, 25, where he characterizes his conception of Christ as Photinian. No less certain is the fact that this Photinian phase in his Christology was replaced sometime later by the orthodox view of Christ as God-and-man. Mallard's distinguishing between the fact *that* Augustine accepted the Incarnation and *how* he understood it seems especially helpful. But neither he nor the other three scholars sufficiently discuss the origin of Augustine's twofold interpretation of Christ. What or who influenced him to think of Christ as only human and, later, as human/divine?

Let us turn now to that question.

First of all, no one need be surprised at Augustine's ignorance of orthodox Christology. In 1945 Vernon Bourke observed:[8]

> At the end of the Cassiciacum period, Augustine was still far from being a well-informed Christian. In fact, he had as yet received no formal religious instruction, except for the scattered information gleaned from the sermons of St. Ambrose.

[8] *Augustine's Quest of Wisdom* (Milwaukee: Bruce Publishing Co., 1945), p. 80.

His first works give no indication of anything like a thorough grasp of the mysteries of the Incarnation and the Redemption, of the role of divine grace in the salvation of man, of the important functions of the Holy Spirit, of the sacraments of the Church, or even of the true destiny of man. He still had much to learn.

And twenty-five years later Eugene TeSelle echoed Bourke's observations:

Augustine's intellectual furniture at the time of his conversion, let us remember, was that of classical philosophy. He knew nothing about Christian theology except the little he might have gleaned from Ambrose's sermons. He was as much at the 'beginnings' of theological reflection as, say, Justin Martyr or Clement of Alexandria long before him (*Augustine the Theologian*, p. 55).

Moreover, Augustine may not have been greatly helped by contemporary churchmen. Auxentius, whom Ambrose replaced as bishop of Milan in 374, was Arian—in fact, "the most prominent supporter of Arianism in the West." And despite condemnations for heresy at councils at Ariminum (359) and Paris (360) and attacks on him by Hilary of Poitiers (364–365) and Athanasius (369), he continued in possession of the bishopric of Milan from 355 until 373 or 374—a period of nineteen years.[9]

Ambrose, his replacement, had been a practicing lawyer in Rome and then a governor of Aemilia-Liguria but was elected bishop by the Catholic laity in Milan while as yet unbaptized. After baptism and ordination he first devoted himself to the study of theology under the guidance of the Platonist Simplicianus (see n. 5 above).[10] How much theology did Ambrose, thus tutored, communicate to Augustine in his sermons? Certainly this seems true: Augustine did not realize that Christ was God-man from his contacts with Ambrose, and this because either Ambrose himself was without that realization or Augustine did not listen well.

Again, Milan appears then to have been infiltrated by followers of Photinus, bishop of Sirmium (ca. 344–351),[11] whose position on

---

[9] On Auxentius, see F. L. Cross, *Oxford Dictionary*, pp. 112–13.

[10] On Ambrose, see *ibid.*, pp. 41–42.

[11] See *ibid.*, p. 1069.

Christ as man but not God Augustine later saw as parallel to his own and who was himself a pupil of Marcellus (d. ca. 374), bishop of Ancyra. Deposed from his see in 336, restored in 337, expelled again in 339, Marcellus "taught that in the unity of the Godhead the Son and the Spirit only emerged as independent entities for the purposes of Creation and Redemption. After the redemptive work is achieved they will be resumed again into the Divine Unity and 'God will be all in all.' The clause in the Nicene Creed, 'whose kingdom shall have no end,' was inserted to combat his teaching."[12] This teacher of Photinus, whose followers lived in Milan, may indirectly at least have contributed to the doctrinally turbulent milieu in which Ambrose for many years and Augustine for a shorter period found themselves.

Yet we still have to face the question of what caused Augustine to move from his misconception of Christ as mere man to an orthodox conception in line with the Nicene Creed: "We believe in one Lord Jesus Christ, the Son of God, begotten from the Father, God from God, light from light, true God from true God, begotten not made, of one substance with the Father . . . Who came down and became incarnate, becoming man"—see F. X. Murphy, "Creed," *New Catholic Encyclopedia* (hereafter: *NCE*), VI, p. 435A. But was this creed the origin of his orthodoxy? Although it was operative in the East at the synods of Sirmium (357 and 359), Rimini (359) and Constantinople (360), it "was unknown in the West until Hilary of Poitiers [ca. 315–367], who confessed that he had not heard of it until leaving for exile" (*ibid.*, p. 435C) in 356, where he remained until 361. Its restatement at the Council of Constantinople (381) "seems to have been established as a baptismal creed in the capitol [Constantinople] and its environs [only] during the mid-5th century," and it appears "to have been adopted in Rome during the 7th century." It came to be recited in the eucharistic liturgy in the East in the sixth century; "in the West the Council of Toledo III (589) ordered that the creed be chanted aloud before the Lord's prayer in all Churches of Spain and Gaul" (*ibid.*, p. 436B–D).[13]

---

[12] See *ibid.*, p. 853.
[13] On the Nicene Creed see J. N. D. Kelly, *Early Christian Creeds* (London: Longmans, Green and Co., 1950), chs. 7 and 8—the latter's concluding section "After Nicea" (pp. 254–62) is especially striking; see p. 261: "Whatever the position and status of the Nicene creed [in the West], there was no occasion to set it up as a standard of orthodoxy, since the particular doctrines it sought to maintain seemed in no danger of being compromised in the West. St. Augus-

In view of those statements, one may wonder how much influence the Nicene Creed had on Augustine's interpretation of Christ as God-man. Whence came that more accurate interpretation? Was he enlightened by Ambrose (see paragraph corresponding to note 10 above)? by Hilary of Poitiers?[14] To what extent was he influenced by Simplicianus? by his own more mature reflection on the Prologue to John's Gospel and St. Paul?

Let us pause briefly on these last two questions, beginning with the second.

---

tine, for example, who wrote much about the Trinity and cannot be accused of disinterest in the Nicene theology, scarcely ever referred to the creed in his treatises"; J. Pelikan, *Christian Tradition*, vol. 1, pp. 200–210.

Also see Charles Piétri, "Les lettres nouvelles et leurs témoignages sur l'histoire de l'Église romaine et de ses relations avec l'Afrique" in *Les Lettres de Saint Augustin découvertes par Johannes Divjak. Communications presentées au colloque des 20 et 21 septembre 1982* (Paris: Études Augustiniennes, 1983), pp. 343–54; B. Studer, "Augustin et la foi de Nicée," *Recherches Augustiniennes* 19 (1984), 133–54.

[14] On Hilary of Poitiers, who "was the first Latin writer to acquaint Western Christendom with the vast theological treasures of the Greek Fathers," see S. J. McKenna, *NCE*, VI, pp. 1114–16; especially see p. 1115: "Hilary's primary purpose in all his writings was to prove that the nature of the Son was consubstantial with that of the Father, and therefore he made no careful study of Christ's human nature. He teaches clearly the two essential doctrines of the Incarnation: that Jesus was only one divine person and that He had both a divine and a human nature."

Note this interesting text from Hilary's *De Trinitate*, Book II, 1, 33 and 35: "Our Lord commanded us to baptize in the name of the Father and of the Son and of the Holy Spirit. In baptism, then, we profess faith in the Creator, in the only-begotten Son and in the gift which is the Spirit. There is one Creator of all things, for in God there is one Father from whom all things have their being. And there is one only-begotten Son, our Lord Jesus Christ, through whom all things exist. And there is one Spirit, the gift who is in all. So all follow their due order, according to the proper operation of each: one power, which brings all things into being, one Son, through whom all things come to be, and one gift of perfect hope. Nothing is wanting to this flawless union: in Father, Son and Holy Spirit, there is infinity of endless being, perfect reflection of the divine image, and mutual enjoyment of the gift." He then adds: "Since our weak minds cannot comprehend the Father or the Son, we have been given the Holy Spirit as our intermediary and advocate, to shed light on that hard doctrine of our faith, the incarnation of God."

On Hilary see J. M. McDermott, "Hilary of Poitiers: The Infinite Nature of God," *Vigiliae Christianae* 27 (1973), 172–202; R. P. C. Hanson, *Search for Christian Doctrine of God* (Edinburgh: T. and T. Clark, 1988), pp. 459–506.

John, Paul and Platonist Books

In *Conf.*, VII, 9, 13–15, Augustine compares John's *Prologue* and Paul's *Letter to Philippians* with the Platonist books. Although "not indeed in these words but much the same thought, enforced by many arguments," these latter reveal "that 'in the beginning was the Word, and the Word was with God, and the Word was God,'" that all things were made by Him, that "the Word, God Himself, is 'the true light which enlightens every man that comes into the world,'" that "the Word, God, 'was born not of the flesh nor of blood' but of God," that "the Son, 'being in the form of the Father, thought it not robbery to be equal with God,' for by nature he is the same with Him." But (Augustine observes) "I did not read there that 'the Word was made flesh and dwelt among us,'" or "that 'he emptied himself, taking the form of a servant, being made in the likeness of men . . . or that he humbled himself, becoming obedient unto death, even to the death of the cross. For which cause God also has exalted him' from the dead . . . 'so that every tongue should confess that the Lord is in the glory of God the Father.'"

Augustine continues the contrast, but enough has been cited to indicate that what was absent from Plotinus (and Porphyry?) was what was then absent in Augustine's own Christology, as he confesses in chapter 19. Yes, Christ was fully human but was not God. Yes, He was body, soul and spirit but was not the Word. And his realization of the Word *as incarnate* was expressed briefly in the *De Ordine* and *Contra Academicos*, composed at Cassiciacum between August 386 and March 387, and more fully in his Easter homily of 391 (see TeSelle, *Augustine the Theologian*, pp. 147–48, quoted above).

But one more issue arises from Augustine's chapter 9. He there affirms that the Platonic writings deal with God the Word as found in John's Gospel and in Paul. In the last two authors the Father and the Word or Son are equally God. But in Plotinus the *Nous* or *Logos* or Word is inferior to the One: the *Nous* is the One but on a lower level. Hence, we are faced with the alternatives: either Augustine misinterpreted Plotinus' *Enneads* or Augustine himself is guilty of some sort of subordinationism. The first alternative is (I hope) more likely to be true.[15]

---

[15] See A. de Solignac's commentary on *Confessions*, VII, 9 (XIII, pp. 682–89), where he juxtaposes passages of Augustine and Plotinus. On the *Nous* in Plotinus as lower than the One, see ch. 16 below, "Are Plotinus and Albertus Magnus Neoplatonists?" prgrs. corresponding to notes 13–43.

Simplicianus

But what of Simplicianus—did he instruct Augustine on the incarnation of the Son of God?

As we learn from F. L. Cross (see note 5 above), Simplicianus was first heard of at Rome between 350 and 360, where he helped convert Marius Victorinus (translator of Plotinus into Latin) and in the 370s tutored St. Ambrose, whom he succeeded as bishop of Milan in 397 until his death in 400. Pierre Courcelle (we will recall) considers Simplicianus to have been instrumental in Augustine's replacing Porphyry's position on Christ as mere man with the orthodox belief that He is also God. Just as Simplicianus had helped Marius Victorinus to become a Christian, so he performed the same function for Augustine, who visited him after reading the Neoplatonic books: he taught him the Catholic doctrine of the incarnate God.

> Le cas d'Augustin, en ces semaines [of Augustine's visit], était identique [as with Victorinus]; pour le déloger de sa position "photinienne" (entendons par là désormais: porphyrienne), Simplicien lui enseigne longuement la doctrine catholique du Dieu incarné ("Saint Augustin," p. 70).

In his article Courcelle makes no further mention of Simplicianus except for the reference in its note 23 to his *Recherches sur les Confessions de S. Augustin* (1950),[16] which contains a section "Simplicien et la confrontation des *Ennéades* avec le Prologue Johannique." There Courcelle credits Simplicianus with revealing the Catholic belief in Christ's twofold nature (He is both human and divine) to Augustine, who thereupon realized with astonishment that up till then he had shared the heretic Photinus' view that Christ was only a perfect man.

> Par l'exégèse du 'Verbe fait chair,' Simplicien révéla à Augustin la doctrine catholique de la double nature du Christ; celui-ci s'aperçut alors avec stupeur qu'il avait, sans s'en douter, partagé jusque-là les idées de l'hérétique Photin sur le Christ, homme parfait (*Recherches*, p. 173).

---

[16] *Recherches sur les Confessions de Saint Augustin*, 2d ed. (Paris: Éditions E. de Boccard, 1968), pp. 168–73. In his article "Saint Augustin," p. 70, n. 23, Courcelle also quotes Augustine's *De agone Christiano*, which gives an orthodox version of Christ as God-man. But this treatise was written in 397 and hence is not directly relevant to Augustine's position in the 380s.

When did that revelation and realization occur? After Augustine read the Platonic books (June 386) and before departing for Cassiciacum (ca. 23 August 386),[17] where Augustine already expresses the Catholic doctrine of the Word in *De Ordine*. And this chronology alone (Courcelle adds) invites us to think that Augustine owes this discovery to Simplicianus (p. 173, n. 4: "La chronologie seule inviterait donc à penser qu'il doit cette découverte à Simplicien").

Accordingly, Courcelle's crediting Simplicianus with ushering Augustine to the orthodox understanding of the incarnate Word rests upon the two passages from *De Ordine* to which he refers: I, 10, 29, and II, 5, 16.[18] The first is sandwiched between Augustine's inquiring of Licentius what order is (Russell, p. 266, #28) and his scolding him and Trygetius for immaturely and unbecomingly trying to score points at each other's expense (*ibid.*, p. 267, #29). The intervening lines are what is relevant.

After Licentius had replied that "order is that by which are governed all things that God has constituted" ("Ordo est per quem aguntur omnia quae Deus constituit"), Augustine initiated this dialogue:

Augustine: What about God Himself? Does He not seem to you to be governed by order?

Licentius: Of course He does.

Trygetius: Therefore, God is governed?

Licentius: What of it? Do you not admit that Christ is God, who came to us by way of order and says that He was sent by God the Father? If, therefore, God sent us Christ by way of order, and we admit that Christ is God, then God not only governs all things but is Himself governed by order.

Trygetius, somewhat perplexed: I know not how I should take that. But when we say 'God,' it is not Christ that occurs to the mind, so to speak: it is the Father. On the other hand, Christ occurs when we say 'Son of God.'"

---

[17] Courcelle infers that Augustine visited 'Simplicianus in July 386. See *Recherches*, p. 602.

[18] The English translation (entitled "Divine Providence and the Problem of Evil") of *De Ordine* is that by Robert P. Russell in *Fathers of the Church* (New York: CIMA Publishing Co., 1948) [hereafter: Russell], vol. 5, pp. 235–332. The Latin text is that of *Patrologia Latina* as reproduced by R. Jolivet in *Oeuvres de S. Augustin*, vol. 4 of *Dialogues Philosophiques* in *Bibliothèque Augustinienne* (Paris: Desclée de Brouwer, 1948).

Licentius: A fine thing you're doing. Shall we, therefore, deny that the Son of God is God?

Trygetius, uneasy at this turn of the conversation, forced himself to reply: "Yes, He is God, but properly speaking we call the Father 'God.'"

Augustine: Control yourself better, for the Son is not improperly called God. (*ibid.*, p. 266, #29)

Quid ipse Deus, inquam, non tibi videtur agi ordine? Prorsus, inquit, videtur. Ergo agitur Deus, ait Trygetius. Et ille: Quid enim, inquit, Christum Deum negas, qui et ordine ad nos venit, et a Patre Deo missum esse se dicit? Si igitur Deus Christum ordine ad nos misit et Deum Christum esse non negamus, non solum agit omnia, sed agitur ordine etiam Deus. Hic Trygetius addubitans: Nescio, inquit, quomodo istuc accipiam. Deum enim quando nominamus, non quasi mentibus ipse Christus occurrit, sed Pater. Ille autem tunc occurrit, quando Dei Filium nominamus. Bellam rem facis, inquit Licentius. Negabimus ergo Dei Filium Deum esse? Hic ille, cum ei respondere periculosum videretur, tamen se coegit atque ait: Et hic quidem Deus est, sed tamen proprie Patrem Deum dicimus. Cui ego: Cohibe te potius, inquam; non enim Filius improprie Deus dicitur.

For our purposes that exchange makes clear that Augustine is aware that Christ is God as the Son of God. But nothing explicitly is said as to the fact that the Son of God, who is Christ, is also incarnate. That explication occurs in the second reference Courcelle gives: *De Ordine*, II, 5, 16.

Having noted that the disorders encountered in human life lead some impiously to believe "that we are not governed by any order of Divine Providence" and others, "upright and good and endowed with splendid mentality," to be "confused by the great obscurity and maze of affairs," Augustine advises them to "provide for themselves a stronghold of faith, so that He, who suffers no one that rightly believes in Him through the mysteries to perish, may by this bond draw them to Himself and free them from these dreadful, entangling evils" (II, 5, 15; Russell, p. 291).

Yes, Augustine continues,

When the obscurity of things perplexes us, we follow a two-fold path: reason, or at least, authority. Philosophy sends forth reason, and it frees scarcely a few. By itself it compels these not only not to spurn those mysteries, but to understand them insofar as they can be understood. The philosophy that is true—the genuine philosophy, so to speak—has no other function than to teach what is the First Principle of all things— Itself without beginning—and how great an intellect dwells therein, and what has proceeded therefrom for our welfare, but without deterioration of any kind. Now, the venerated mysteries, which liberate persons of sincere and firm faith— not indiscriminately, as some say; and not harmfully, as many assert—these mysteries teach that this First Principle is one God omnipotent, and that He is tripotent, Father and Son and Holy Spirit. Great, indeed, though it be that so great a God has for our sake deigned to take up and dwell in this body of our own kind, yet, the more lowly it appears, so much the more is it replete with clemency and the farther and wider remote from a certain characteristic pride of ingenious men.

Duplex enim est via quam sequimur, cum rerum nos obscuritas movet, aut rationem, aut certe auctoritatem. Philosophia rationem promittit et vix paucissimos liberat, quos tamen non modo non contemnere illa mysteria, sed sola intelligere, ut intelligenda sunt, cogit. Nullumque aliud habet negotium, quae vera, et, ut ita dicam, germana philosophia est, quam ut doceat quod sit omnium rerum principium sine principio quantusque in eo maneat intellectus quidve inde in nostram salutem sine ulla degeneratione manaverit, quem unum Deum omnipotentem cumque tripotentem, Patrem et Filium et Spiritum sanctum, docent veneranda mysteria, quae fide sincera et inconcussa populos liberant, nec confuse, ut quidam, nec contumeliose, ut multi praedicant. Quantum autem illud sit, quod hoc etiam nostri generis corpus tantus propter nos Deus assumere atque agere dignatus est, quanto videtur vilius, tanto est clementia plenius et a quadam ingeniosorum superbia longe lateque remotius (*De Ordine*, II, 5, 16).

The relevant information this passage furnishes is threefold. It discloses Augustine's understanding of God as origin of this universe, as triune and as incarnate. Let us look at each of those points. God, Who is without beginning and is intelligent, is the first principle of all things and of our salvation, without Himself undergoing any diminution. Second, this first principle is the omnipotent

God, who is one and nonetheless is triune: Father, Son and Holy Spirit. Third, this great God has deigned for our sakes to assume and dwell in a human body so that His humility and fullness of mercy would distance Himself from the pride characteristic of certain "ingenious men."[19]

Having inspected the two passages of *De Ordine* to which Courcelle referred, what conclusions can we draw? When engaging in the conversations at Cassiciacum with Licentius and Trygetius which that treatise records, Augustine shows himself aware that Christ is both man and God: the Son of God became incarnate to save us. If so, the Latin author had apparently overcome the Photinian heresy of which he speaks in *Confessions*, VII, 19 (Christ is fully human but not divine) and had distanced himself from the Platonists whose books he mentioned in *ibid.*, chapter 9, and who were aware of the Word as God but not of the Word as made flesh.

Had his visits to Simplicianus in July 386 before coming to Cassiciacum in August effected that orthodox realization? In *De Ordine* he does not explicitly attribute it to his elderly mentor. In his subsequent account of those visits (*Conf.*, VIII, 1, 2 and 5) he does not indicate that he went there for intellectual enlightenment—"It was not to be more certain concerning You but to be more steadfast in You that I desired. . . . I wished he [Simplicianus] would show me the proper manner for one affected like me to walk in Your way" (*ibid.*, VIII, 1, 1). And Simplicianus exhorted him "to accept Christ's humility" by disclosing how Marius Victorinus had determined to become a Catholic and to submit to baptism (*ibid.*, ch. 2). The result of this disclosure? Augustine's own answer: "When Simplicianus your servant related to me all this concerning Victorinus, I was on fire to imitate him, and it was for this reason that he had told it to me" (*ibid.*, chs. 5, 10). But the actual resolve to imitate Victorinus occurred only after the garden scene (*ibid.*, chs. 8 and 12), where under God's command he read *Romans* 13:14: "Put on the Lord Jesus Christ and make no provision for the flesh in its concupiscences," and Augustine was baptized by Ambrose in Milan on April 23, 387 (*ibid.*, IX, 6).

If the previous exegesis of *De Ordine* and *Confessions* is basically accurate, Augustine's understanding of Christ would have devel-

---

[19] These "ingenious men" (*ingeniosorum*) would in Russell's opinion probably be "certain Platonists, some of whose teachings are openly antagonistic to revealed truths of Christianity. One such [would be] . . . that God does not mingle with man" (Russell, p. 292, n. 4).

oped in at least five stages. As a child he gained a deep and lasting awareness from Monica that Christ was, in some sense, his savior, an awareness that even in his late teens tempered his otherwise boundless enthusiasm for Cicero's *Hortensius:* "In so great a blaze only this checked me, that Christ's name was not in it [Cicero's treatise]. For this name, O Lord, according to your mercy, this name of my Savior, your Son, my tender heart had holily drunken in with my mother's milk and kept deep down within itself. Whatever lacked this name, no matter how learned and polished and veracious it was, could not wholly capture me" (*Conf.,* III, 4, 8). Second, as a Manichaean he imagined Christ to be some sort of emanation from God, a luminous mass of body, so as to be our savior. But He was not truly incarnate or born of the Virgin Mary (*ibid.,* V, 10, 20).

Sometime between his break with Manichaeism in 382 and his reading the Neoplatonic writings, he conceived Christ as described in *Conf.,* VII, 19: He was "born in a wondrous manner of the Virgin"; He was fully human because He "ate and drank, slept, walked about, was joyful, grew sad and preached" and engaged in other activities which come from will, "soul and mind that are subject to change." But because of such changes He could not be God, whose nature is totally immutable. And this conception he later saw to be identical with Photinus' heresy.

But (in Courcelle's and Mallard's view) by the time of the Cassiciacum dialogues it was replaced by the orthodox position that Christ is both man and God because He is the Word made flesh who dwells amongst us. Finally, by 391 (in TeSelle's interpretation) Augustine had moved from the paragraphs in *De Ordine* and *Contra Academicos* to the explicit and fuller elaboration of Christ's incarnation in his first Easter homily.

Such are the five stages in Augustine's Christology. What induced him to shift from the heretical view of Photinus (third stage) to the next and orthodox stages of affirming Christ as the incarnate Word? Was it Simplicianus? Courcelle infers that it was. But no explicit evidence exists for that affirmation in either the *Cassiciacum Dialogues* or the relevant passages of the *Confessions.* The source of that shift remains, in my opinion, puzzling, and part of the puzzle is Simplicianus himself.[20]

---

[20] For a summary of what is definitely known about Simplicianus see Almut Mutzenbecher (ed.), *Sancti Aurelii Augustini de Diversis Quaestionibus ad Simplicianum,* "Corpus Christianorum, Series Latina," vol. 44 (Turnholti:

If he wrote any treatises, none is extant. There is no knowledge of where or when he was born. In 386 he was at least sixty years old and thus was born in the first quarter of that century. By 354 he had lived in Rome for some time if he was present at Marius Victorinus' baptism in that year; he was present in Milan at Ambrose's baptism in November 374 and was visited there by Augustine in 386. By August 28, 397, he was bishop of Milan (it is unknown whether he was already a priest). He died sometime between September 400 and June 16, 401. He considered Neoplatonism by reason of its doctrine on God and His Word to be a preparation for Christianity (Mutzenbecher, p. xxii: "war auch der Überzeugung, dass der Neuplatonismus wegen seiner Lehre von Gott und seinem Wort als eine Vorbereitung auf das Christentum anzusehen sei.")[21] He may possibly have become acquainted with Neoplatonism by traveling to the East (recall Clement of Alexandria and Origen's roles there).[22]

But even after this review of data on Simplicianus, the question returns: was he responsible for Augustine's more orthodox view of Christ also as God? Could it not have been also Augustine's own prayerful reflection on John and Paul (see section above), triggered by contrasting them with the Platonic writings as described in *Confessions*, VII, 9?

Final Words

But whatever the origin of that shift may be, it remains beyond controversy that Augustine's Christology did evolve from several

---

Typographi Brepols Editores Pontificii, 1970), pp. xx–xxiv. I am grateful to Joseph T. Lienhard, S.J., for this reference.

For studies on other relevant issues see C. Basevi, *Alle fonti della dottrina agostiniana della incarnatione, l'influenza della cristologia di Sant'Ambrogio* (Pamplona: Eunsa, 1975); M. Lods, "La personne du Christ dans la 'conversion' de saint Augustin," *Recherches Augustiniennes* 11 (1976), 3–34; A. Verwilchen, *Christologie et spiritualité selon saint Augustin. L'Hymne aux Philippiens*, "Theol. hist." 72 (Paris: Beauchesne, 1985).

[21] See Augustine, *Conf.*, VIII, 2, 3: "In the works of the Platonists God and His Word are introduced in all manners"—*in istis [libris] autem omnibus modis insinuari deum et eius verbum.*

[22] Besides Mutzenbecher see also Aimé de Solignac, Commentary on *Conf.*, VIII, 1, 1 (XIV, pp. 530–33); Pierre Hadot, *Marius Victorinus. Traits théologiques sur la Trinité* (Paris: Editions du Cerf, 1960), "Sources Chrétiennes," vol. 68, pp. 12–18.

inaccurate stages into the orthodox Catholic view. And this need to develop his theology, coupled with his honest admission of misconceptions replaced by more accurate understandings and formulations (recall his *Retractiones:* how few bishops—or even theologians!—write such a treatise) add to his attractiveness.[23] This appeal is as great perhaps as are his confessions of moral lapses in his earlier years or, even, his admission as a bishop in *Conf.*, X, 28 and 29 of how difficult he finds human life to be. The first of those chapters is aptly entitled "Life Is a Warfare":

> When I shall cleave to You with all my being, no more will there be pain and toil for me. My life will be life indeed, filled wholly with You. But now, since You lift up him whom You fill with Yourself, and since I am not yet filled with You, I am a burden to myself. Joys that I should bewail contend with sorrows at which I should rejoice, but on which side victory may rest I do not know. My evil sorrows contend with my virtuous joys, and on which side victory may rest I do not know. Alas for me! Lord, have mercy on me! Alas for me! See, I do not hide my wounds. You are the physician; I am a sick man. You are merciful; I am in need of mercy. Is not "the life of man upon earth a trial"?

> What man wants trouble and hardship? You command that they be endured, not that they be liked. No man likes what he endures, although he likes to endure it. Yet, even though he may rejoice that he endures hardship, he prefers rather that there be nothing to endure. In the midst of adversities, I desire prosperous days; in the midst of prosperity, I dread adversity. Between these two, is there no middle ground where the life of man is not a trial? Woe to the prosperity of this world, once and again, both from fear of adversity and from corruption of joy! Woe to the adversities of this world, once and again, and a third time, from desire for prosperity, and because adversity itself is hard, and because it can make wreck of endurance! Is

---

[23] Augustine is miles apart from current "dissenting theologians." Once he became aware of what the *magisterium* of the Church put forth, he subscribed to it completely and faithfully. See *Contra Academicos*, III, 20, 43: "No one doubts that we are impelled toward knowledge by a twofold force: the force of authority and the force of reason. And I am resolved never to deviate in the least from the authority of Christ, for I find none more powerful."

not the life of man upon earth a trial, without any relief whatsoever?

Cum inhaesero tibi ex omni me, nusquam erit mihi dolor et labor, et viva erit vita mea tota plena te. Nunc autem quoniam quem tu imples sublevas eum, quoniam tui plenus nondum sum, oneri mihi sum. Contendunt laetitiae meae flendae cum laetandis maeroribus, et ex qua parte stet victoria nescio. Contendunt maerores mei mali cum gaudiis bonis, et ex qua parte stet victoria nescio. *Ei mihi! Domine, miserere mei!* Ei mihi! Ecce vulnera mea non abscondo; medicus es, aeger sum; misericors es, miser sum. Numquid non *temptatio est vita humana super terram?* Quis velit molestias et difficultates? Tolerare iubes ea, non amari. Nemo quod tolerat amat, etsi tolerare amat. Quamvis enim gaudeat se tolerare, mavult tamen non esse quod toleret. Prospera in adversis desidero, adversa in prosperis timeo. Quis inter haec medius locus, ubi non sit *humana vita temptatio?* Vae prosperitatibus saeculi semel et iterum a timore adversitatis et a corruptione laetitiae! Vae adversitatibus saeculi semel et iterum et tertio a desiderio prosperitatis, et quia ipsa adversitas dura est, et ne frangat tolerantiam! Numquid non *temptatio est vita humana super terram* sine ullo interstitio? (*Conf.*, X, 28, 39)

Augustine terminates this line of thought in the opening two lines of chapter 29, 40: "All my hope is found solely in your exceedingly great mercy. Give what you command and command what you will" (*Et tota spes mea non nisi in magna valde misericordia tua. Da quod iubes et iube quod vis*).

In God's mercy, then, lies Augustine's and our hope. And my hope also is that this chapter enables us to read Augustine more attentively, to hear better the overtones and undertones of what he is saying.[24]

---

[24] Traditionally Augustine is thought to have written the *Confessions* between 397 and 401. But James J. O'Donnell, *Augustine: Confessions* (Oxford: Clarendon Press, 1992), Vol. One, p. xli, n. 62, has shown on the basis of *Epistle* 38, written in 397, that Augustine dictated the *Confessions* in that year of illness. O'Donnell concludes: "Rhetorical and stylistic unity and the intensity that runs through the book like an electric current makes it easiest to read as a work written entirely in 397."

Together with chapter 7 above and chapters 9 and 10 below, may this chapter illustrate also why Augustine is authentically a Christian philosopher and that he compares favorably with Bonaventure (see ch. 3 above)[25] and, in chapters still to come, with Albert (chs. 14–16) and Thomas (chs. 17–26).

Bibliography

Babcock, W. S. "The Christ of the Exchange. A Study in the Christology of Augustine's *Enarrationes in Psalmos.*" Ph.D. diss., Yale University, 1971.

Bailleux, E. "La christologie de saint Augustin dans le *De trinitate.*" *Recherches Augustiniennes* 7 (1971), 219–43.

———. "La sotériologie de saint Augustine dans le *De trinitate.*" *Mélanges de Science Religieuse* 23 (1966), 149–73.

———. "Histoire du salut et foi trinitaire chez S. Augustin." *Revue Thomiste* 75 (1975), 533–61.

Basevi, C. "Alle fonti della dottrina agostiniana della incarnazione, l'influenza della cristologia di Sant'Ambrogio." *Scripta Theologica* 7 (1975), 489–529.

Bavaud, G. "Un thème augustinien, le mystère de l'Incarnation, à la lumière de la distinction entre le verbe intérieur et le verbe proféré." *Revue des Etudes Augustiniennes* 9 (1963), 95–101.

Bavel, T. J. van, and B. Bruning. "Die Einheit des *Totus Christus* bei Augustinus." In *Festschrift A. Zumkeller zum 60,* pp. 43–75. Edited by C. P. Mayer and W. Eckerman. Würzburg: Augustinus-Verlag, 1975.

Bernard, R. "La prédestination du Christ total selon saint Augustin." *Recherches Augustiniennes* 3 (1965), 1–58.

Cantalamessa, R. "Tertullien et la formule christologique de Chalcédoine." *Studia Patristica* 9 (1971), 139–50.

Desjardins, R. "Une structuration de mots chez saint Augustin: Le thème de l'incarnation." *Bulletin de Littérature Ecclesiastique* 71 (1970), 161–73.

---

[25] Also see L. Sweeney, "Monism and Distinct Sciences? Plotinus and Bonaventure," *The Journal of Neoplatonic Studies,* IV (Fall, 1995)

Eijkenboom, P. "*Christus Redemptor* in the Sermons of St. Augustine." In *Mélanges offerts à Chr. Mohrmann*, pp. 233–39. Edited by L. J. Engels, H. W. Hoppenbrouwers and A. J. Vermeulen. Utrecht: Spectrum Ed., 1963.

Fleteren, F. van. "Augustine's Ascent of the Soul in Book VII of the *Confessions:* A Reconsideration." *Augustinian Studies* 5 (1974), 29–72.

Geerlings, W. "Der manichäische Jesus patibilis in der Theologie Augustins." *Theologische Quartalschrift* 152 (1972), 124–31.

———. *Christus Exemplum. Studien zur Christologie und Christusverküngigung Augustins.* Mainz: Matthias-Grünewald-Verlag, 1978.

Hevia, B. A. "La Pascua de Cristo, acontecimiento de salvación, en la predicación de San Agustín." *Studium Ovetense* 5 (1977), 155–72.

Lods, M. "La personne du Christ dans la 'conversion' de saint Augustin." *Recherches Augustiniennes* 11 (1976), 3–34.

Madec, G. "Christus, scientia et sapientia nostra: Le principe de cohérence de la doctrine augustinienne." *Recherches Augustiniennes* 10 (1975), 77–85.

———. "Une lecture de *Confessions* VII, ix, 13–xxi, 27 (Notes critiques à propos d'une thèse de R. J. O'Connell)." *Revue des Etudes Augustiniennes* 16 (1970), 79–137.

Mallard, W. "The Incarnation in Augustine's Conversion." *Recherches Augustiniennes* 15 (1980), 80–98.

———. *Language and Love: Introducing Augustine's Religious Thought Through the Confessions Story.* University Park, Penn.: Pennsylvania State University Press, 1994.

McCallin, J. A. "The Christological Unity of Saint Augustine's *De Civitate Dei.*" *Revue des Etudes Augustiniennes* 12 (1966), 85–109.

Newton, J. T. "Neoplatonism and Augustine's Doctrine of the Person and Work of Christ. A Study of the Philosophical Structure Underlying Augustine's Christology." Ph.D. diss., Emory University, 1969.

———. "The Importance of Augustine's Use of the Neoplatonic Doctrine of Hypostatic Union for the Development of Christology." *Augustinian Studies* 2 (1971), 1–16.

O'Connell, R. J. "*Confessions* VII, ix, 13–xxi, 27: Reply to G. Madec." *Revue des Etudes Augustiniennes* 19 (1973), 87–100.

O'Donnell, James J. *Augustine: Confessions.* 3 vols. Oxford: Clarendon Press, 1992.

Remy, G. *Le Christ médiateur dans l'oeuvre de saint Augustin.* 2 vols. Paris: Champion, 1979.

Studer, B. "Zur Christologie Augustins." *Augustinianum* 19 (1979), 539–46.

———. "Augustin et la foi de Nicée." *Recherches Augustiniennes* 19 (1984), 133–54.

Turrado, A. "El carácter según san Agustín." In *El Sacerdocio de Cristo y los Diversos Grados de su Participación en la Iglesia,* pp. 213–34. Madrid: Ed. Augustinus, 1969.

———. "Le teología trinitaria de san Agustín en el Mysterium salutis." *Revista Agustiniana de Espiritualidad* 12 (1971), 445–59.

Vega, C. "Cristo en la vida de san Agustín." In *Strenas Agustinianas* V. Capanaga Oblatas, pp. 423–32. Edited by I. Oroz-Reta. Madrid: Ed. Augustinus, 1967.

Verges, S. *La Iglesia esposa de Cristo. La encarnación del Verbo y la Iglesia en san Agustín.* Barcelona: Ed. Balmes, 1969.

Verhees, J. "Heiliger Geist und Inkarnation in der Theologie des Augustinus von Hippo, Unlöslicher Zusammenhang zwischen Theologie und Ökonomie." *Revue des Etudes Augustiniennes* 22 (1976), 234–53.

Verwilghen, A. *Christologie et Spiritualité selon Saint Augustin. L'Hymne aux Philippiens.* Paris: Beauchesne, 1985.

9

Augustine and Gregory of Nyssa:
Is the Triune God Infinite in Being?

Seemingly one may appropriately study Augustine (354–430) and Gregory of Nyssa (ca. 331–395) in a single chapter, in the light of Bernard C. Barmann's remarks: Nyssa deserves "to be ranked among the truly leading Christian philosophers and . . . as one of the greatest minds produced by the Christian East. . . . The Christian philosophy of Nyssa in the East marks an achievement as significant as that of Augustine in the West."[1]

Let us begin with the Greek author, who antedates the Latin Father by a couple of decades and whose answer as to whether God's very being is infinite is clearly *yes*—a clarity arising from the manner in which the Arians had formulated the question. Both Arius and Eunomius discussed the Trinity in terms of "being": the divine Being consists, they said, in Unbegottenness, and thus, only the Father is God. In replying, Gregory had to speak in terms of "being" too—God, although triune in really distinct persons, is also one Being, with which the three persons are identical: they are *homoousioi*. Within the parameters of debate drawn by the Arians, then, a Neoplatonic God who is nonbeing because beyond being obviously would not do.[2] Nor would anything less than an infinity

---

[1] *The Cappadocian Triumph over Arianism*, revised Ph.D. diss., Stanford University, 1966 (Ann Arbor, Mich.: University Microfilms), pp. 323 and 441.

[2] On the important but complicated question of Gregory's relationship to Plotinus and, more generally, to Neoplatonism, Jean Daniélou's remarks appear accurate: "Grégoire ne se rattache donc à aucune école néo-platonicienne

consonant with God as supreme Being suffice: in His very entity
He is infinitely perfect.

The Arian formulation of the problem in terms of "being" or
"essence" (*ousia*) and Gregory's reply in similar terms will set the
stage for investigating Augustine, who might be expected to reply
in a similar fashion in his *De Trinitate*.

First let us consider one of the many texts in which Gregory sets
forth his understanding of how the triune God of Father, Son and
Holy Spirit is infinite in being, as well as in goodness, wisdom,
power, love and truth: *Contra Eunomium*, Book I, chapter 19. But let
us momentarily postpone considering it in order to set down what
can be called "the metaphysical basis of infinity."

---

définie. Il utilise Plotin pour sa mystique, Porphyre pour la logique et
l'ontologie, Jamblique pour la cosmologie. Il est d'ailleurs très indépendant
dans cette utilisation. *Il n'est pas un néo-platonicien.* Mail il connaît bien les
courants du néo-platonisme" ("Orientations actuelles de la recherche sur
Grégoire de Nysse" in M. Harl [ed.], *Ecriture et culture philosophique dans la
pensée de Grégoire de Nysse* [Leiden: E. J. Brill, 1971], p. 6 [italics added to the
quotation]). For a helpful summary of the contrast between Daniélou's and H.
Cherniss' assessments of Gregory and Platonism, see W. Jaeger, *Two Re-dis-
covered Works of Ancient Christian Literature: Gregory of Nyssa and Macarius*
(Leiden: E. J. Brill, 1954), p. 71, n. 1: "Cherniss [*The Platonism of Gregory of Nyssa*]
finds in Gregory much that is Platonic but thinks that Gregory has not im-
proved Platonism by applying and adjusting its ideas to Christian problems.
Daniélou [*Platonisme et théologie mystique*], on the other hand, believes that
Gregory's 'Platonism' is no longer Platonic and that it must be judged on the
basis of its Christian motifs rather than its original philosophical intention—
in other words, there has been a complete metamorphosis of its traditional
meaning." J. Quasten, *Patrology* (Utrecht/Antwerp: Spectrum Publishers, 1966),
vol. 3, pp. 284–86, sides with Daniélou over Cherniss. Also see David Balás,
Metousia Theou (publishing data given below, n. 16), pp. 163–64; E. Mühlenberg,
"Die philosophische Bildung Gregors von Nyssa in den Buchern *Contra
Eunomium*," in M. Harl (ed.), *Ecriture et culture*, pp. 230–52; all the articles in
Heinrich Dörrie *et al.* (eds.), *Gregor von Nyssa und die Philosophie* (Leiden: E. J.
Brill, 1976), with special attention given to Jean Daniélou, "Grégoire de Nysse
et la philosophie," pp. 3–18 (especially p. 17: "L'élément le plus remarquable
est que Grégoire, s'il depend pour une part du néoplatonisme, est aussi
l'expression d'une reaction antiplatonicienne et d'un renouveau du moyen
stoicisme") and to T. Paul Verghese, "*Diastêma* and *Diastasis* in Gregory of
Nyssa," pp. 243–60 (especially p. 257: "Gregory's view of the relation of God
and the world is fundamentally different from that of Plotinus or others of the
so-called Neoplatonic School, [so] that it is not correct to class Gregory among
Neoplatonists or Christian Platonists. There is no theory of emanation in Gregory, no ontological continuity between the One and the Many. Etc."

The Metaphysical Basis of Infinity

Infinity turns out to be a much more intricate and diversified topic than expected when referred to the divine reality itself and not merely to divine power or duration and other such relational aspects. So understood, infinity is not found in the Jewish, Islamic or Christian Scriptures. Some medieval authors (e.g., Hugh of S. Cher) also are silent on it. Others (e.g., Guerric of S. Quentin, Albert the Great) deny it. Still others (e.g., Alexander of Hales, Bonaventure) answer yes but intend thereby only divine immensity. Thomas Aquinas, as well as Richard Fishacre apparently, replies affirmatively, grounding it in God's total freedom from matter and potency. But Plotinus and Proclus consider God to be above being and form, which are confined to His effects, and thus to be *apeiros* or *aoristos* as nonbeing (as well, of course, in power).[3]

But however disparate such attitudes to divine infinity may be, they apparently have in common these convictions: infinity is equivalent to indeterminateness, finiteness to determinateness; second, determination arises either solely from form and act upon matter and potency,[4] or, in addition, from matter and potency upon form and act.[5] Consequently, a philosopher or theologian grounds his position on divine infinity upon what he takes "determination" to mean, which in turn rests upon his basic metaphysics of what "real" signifies. If "to be real" (= to be objectively of value, significance, worth) consists solely in form, act and being, then God to be real must be Being, which can itself be infinite provided matter and potency are also positive determinants within created reality and He is totally free of them as subsistent act. [6] But if "to be real" is not to be form or being but (say) "to be one," as in Neoplatonism, then

---

[3] On all these authors see Leo Sweeney, S.J., *Divine Infinity in Greek and Medieval Thought* [hereafter: *Divine Infinity*] (New York/Bern: Peter Lang Publishing, Inc., 1992).

[4] Plato, Plotinus and other Neoplatonists would restrict determination to form and being (see *ibid.*, chs. 3, 4, 9–12). Would this restriction also be made by authors who are silent on infinity as a property of divine Being (e.g., Hugh of S. Cher) or deny it or reduce it to immensity (e.g., Alexander of Hales)? See *ibid.*, chs. 19 and 20.

[5] Aquinas, as well as Fishacre probably and Bonaventure on two occasions, adds this second determination. See *ibid.*, chs. 19 and 23.

[6] Any author who hesitates to assert that God is infinite in being may also be found denying that matter is real and considering it instead as nonbeing, evil, unreal.

God can be described as infinite in power, in His transcendency of beings and their knowledge and in other such relational terms but not as being, which He rises above.[7]

Will conceiving infinity as based upon a more fundamental metaphysics prove helpful in reading Gregory of Nyssa? As a test case let us turn to his *Contra Eunomium*, Book I, chapter 19, where we shall first outline its context, to be followed by its translation or paraphrase, which in turn issues into a commentary.

Contra Eunomium, Book I, Chapter 19 (W. Jaeger edition, vol. I, pp. 94–96)

Context for this capital text will be twofold: remote (historical facts on the Trinitarian heresies Gregory faced and on relevant documents) and proximate (the movement of thought in Gregory's response to Eunomius).

Remote context. (a) Arianism, which takes its name from Arius of Alexandria (ca. 256–336), has as its fundamental tenet "that the Son of God is a creature" and receives the title "God" only in a moral sense and by participation; the Son was not begotten out of the substance or entity (*ousia*) of the Father but was made out of nothing. The Holy Spirit is subordinate to the Son.[8]

(b) Eunomius, who was bishop of Cyzicus for a short time (ca. 360) and died in 394, held a theory describable as neo-Arianism: the very essence or being (*ousia*) of God is unbegottenness (*agenne-*

---

[7] Would the One as hyperbeing for Plotinus be infinite in Its very reality? That is at least a possibility, which however must contend with the fact that no one can know what that reality comprises and, second, it may transcend both infiniteness and finiteness. See *ibid.*, ch. 10, "Another Interpretation of Plotinus' *Enneads*, VI, 7, 32."

[8] See R. Williams, *Arius: Heresy and Tradition* (London: Darton Longman and Todd, 1987), pp. 82–91, 95–116 and 230–32 (helpful references throughout to Abramowski, Opitz, Kannengiesser, Gregg, Groh, Meijering, Simonetti); R. J. Deferrari (trans.), *Saint Basil: The Letters* (London: William Heinemann, 1926), "Loeb Classical Library," vol. 1, pp. xxv–xxxii, is still helpful on the complex history of the Arian controversy, which had both religious and political dimensions. Also see G. L. Prestige, *God in Patristic Thought* (London: SPCK, 1959), ch. 7: "Subordinationism," pp. 129–56, as well as subsequent chapters on the history of the Trinitarian and Christological controversies; R. P. C. Hanson, *The Search for the Christian Doctrine of God: The Arian Controversy 318–381* (Edinburgh: Clark, 1988), especially chs. 1–4, pp. 3–128.

tos) and thus only the Father is God: His operation (*energeia*) begot the Son (*ergon*), who is less than the Father; the Son's operation or *energeia* produced the Holy Spirit (*ergon*), who is less than the Son and, of course, the Father. Neither Son nor Spirit is identical in *ousia* with God the Father.[9]

(c) The stages of debate between Eunomius and the Cappadocians and the relevant documents are as follows:

(1) Eunomius, *Apologia*, written ca. 360 to explain and defend his position;[10]

(2) Basil of Caesarea, *Adversus Eunomium* (Books I–III), ca. 363;

(3) Eunomius, *Apologia Apologiae* (Books I and II), ca. 378;

(4) Gregory of Nyssa, *Contra Eunomium* (Books I and II), ca. 380–381;

(5) Eunomius, *Apologia Apologiae* (Book III), ca. 382;

(6) Gregory, *Contra Eunomium* (Book III), ca. 383.

(d) The text of Gregory about to be investigated is taken from *Contra Eunomium* named above in #c4 and edited by Werner Jaeger.[11]

---

[9] R. P. Vaggione (ed. and trans.), *Eunomius: The Extant Works* (Oxford: Clarendon Press, 1987), "Liber Apologeticus" [Vaggione prefers this title to "Apologia"], pp. 3–12 and (especially) chs. 7–9 and 23–28 of the "Liber" itself. Also see B. Barmann's ch. 1, pp. 13–62 and ch. 5, section 4: "*Energeia* and the New Metaphysics," pp. 306–17.

[10] This treatise can be divided as follows: Introduction (chs. 1–6) culminating in a Symbol of Faith, Father (chs. 7–11), Son (chs. 12–24) and Spirit (ch. 25), Summary and Conclusion (chs. 26–27) and Appendix (ch. 28). For a textual division which Vaggione considers to give "a more satisfactory understanding of Eunomius' meaning" and which is based on Eunomius' "two methods of doing theology, the one a priori . . . the other a posteriori," see Vaggione, *Eunomius: The Extant Works*, pp. 11–12.

For the Greek text and French translation of Eunomius' *Apologia* see B. Sesboüé, G.-M. de Durand and L. Doutreleau, *Basil de Césarée: Contre Eunome* (Paris: Les Éditions du Cerf, 1983), tome II, pp. 235–99, of "Sources Chrétiennes," no. 305. For the Greek text and Latin translation see *Patrologia Graeca* [hereafter: *PG*] 30, cols. 835–68.

Eunomius' *Apologia Apologiae*, listed below as Stage #3, is no longer extant and is known through Gregory's quotations of it in his *Contra Eunomium* [hereafter: *CE*]—see R. P. Vaggione, *Eunomius: The Extant Works*, pp. 79–127.

[11] For this list of stages and dates, see Barmann, pp. 9–10. The Greek text used will be that established by Werner Jaeger (Leiden: E. J. Brill, 1960), vol. I. In my paraphrases and translation of *CE* I have consulted the English translation of W. Moore and H. Wilson in *Select Library of Nicene and Post-Nicene Fathers of the Christian Church* [hereafter: *NPN*] (New York: Christian Literature

Proximate context. (e) Gregory's chapter 19 depends upon chapter 13, where he quotes Eunomius: "The whole account of our doctrines is summed up thus. There is the supreme and absolute being (*ousia*), and another being (*ousia*) existing by reason of the first but after it, though prior to all others; and a third being (*ousia*) not ranking with either of these but inferior to the one [the Father] as to its cause, and to the other [the Son] as to the operation which produced it" (J, I, p. 71, l. 28; *PG* 45, 297A; *NPN*, p. 50a).[12]

(f) He begins chapter 19 by again turning to Eunomius: "Each of those beings (*ousiai*) [Father, Son, Holy Spirit] is absolutely simple and totally one when considered according to its own proper worth [and nature]; and since operations are circumscribed by their products, which in turn are commensurate with the operations, one must conclude that the operations which are consequent upon each being are greater and lesser—the former pertain to beings of first rank, the latter to those of second rank" (J, I, p. 90, l. 20; *PG* 45, 317C; *NPN*, p. 56b).[13]

(g) What Eunomius proposes, Gregory adds, is to establish that the Father has no connection (*synapheian*) with the Son or the Son with the Spirit; rather, they are *ousiai* which are separate from one another and possess natures foreign and unfamiliar to each other. Besides this, they differ in the magnitude and unequal ranking of [the perfections which constitute] their worth and in other such ways (J, I, p. 92, l. 2; *PG* 45, 317D; *NPN*, pp. 56b–c).

(h) Accordingly (Gregory warns), let us not be taken in: by his words Eunomius makes the underlying being (*ousia*) of each [person] be different from that of the others, with the result that he is speaking of several entities (*ousiai*), each with its own unique differences which alienate them from one another (J, I, p. 93, l. 17; *PG* 45, 320C; *NPN*, p. 56d).

Co., 1893; reprinted 1994), vol. 5; the Latin translation in *PG* 45. For an explanation of why the books of *CE* as found in *PG* are ordered differently than in Jaeger's volume, see Quasten, vol. 3, pp. 257–58.

[12] The last portion of the third clause in the quotation from Eunomius is translated in *PG* 45, 297A, thus: "Sed illi quidem ut causae, huic vero ut operationi qua facta est subjicitur."

[13] For additional information on the Arian position see R. C. Gregg (ed.), *Arianism: Historical and Theological Re-assessments* (Cambridge, Mass: Philadelphia Patristic Foundation, 1985); also see n. 8 above.

Key Text[14]

[1] But let us again examine Eunomius' words, "Each of those entities or beings (*ousiai*) is simple and totally one." Of course they are: the divine and blessed nature is simple—how can anyone conceive of that which is formless, entirely structureless and separate from quantified mass to be multiform and composite? (J, I, p. 94, lines 20–22:

. . . τὴν γὰρ ἀειδῆ τε καὶ ἀσχημάτιστον
πηλικότητός τε πάσης καὶ τῆς ἐν τῷ μεγέθει ποσότητος
κεχωρισμένην πῶς ἄν τις πολυειδῆ καὶ σύνθετον ὑπολάβοι;)

[2] In fact, this description of the supreme Being as "simple" is inconsistent with the rest of his system. Who does not realize that simplicity with reference to the Holy Trinity does not admit of more or less? There one does not think of a mixture or confluence of qualities but rather we intellectually grasp there power which is without parts and is incomposite—how can one be aware there of any differentiation of more and less? [3] For to mark differences somewhere one must be aware of qualities in a subject underlying them—e.g., differences of largeness and smallness *re* quantity or differences through abundance and lessening of goodness, power, wisdom or other such factors worthy of application to God. [4] But in neither case [i.e., of quantitative or of qualitative differences] can one escape the notion of composition, for nothing which possesses wisdom or power or any other good by reason of what it is by nature and not as a gift from outside can allow a lessening in such perfections. [5] The result is that if anyone says he detects smaller and greater beings in the divine nature, he is surreptitiously making what is divine be composed of dissimilar parts in such a way that he conceives of the subject as one constituent, what is participated as another—by participating in the latter that which was not good before becomes so now.

[6] If he had been thinking of Being which is really simple and entirely one and of Being which is good as it is itself and not by becoming so through acquisition, he would not be computing it in terms of more or less.

---

[14] Here, paragraphs will be marked by bracketed arabic numbers to facilitate references and to distinguish them from paragraphs in the "Context" marked by bracketed lower-case letters.

[7] As we said above,[15] the good can be lessened only by the presence of evil and where there is a nature incapable of deteriorating, there is no conceivable limit to its goodness, [8] for the unlimited (*to aoriston*) is not such because of a relationship to anything else but rather, considered precisely in itself, it escapes limit. How can anyone reflect accurately and think one infinity to be greater or less than another infinity? [9] Consequently, if he acknowledges that the supreme Being is simple and self-consistent, then let him also grant that it combines and associates simplicity and infinity. [10] But if he divides and estranges the Beings from each other so that the Only Begotten is an *ousia* other than the Father's and that of the Spirit is other than the Only Begotten's inasmuch as he attributes a more and less to them, then let his hidden snares not deceive us: he verbally attributes simplicity, but in reality he fraudulently inserts composition into God. (J, I, p. 94, l. 15–p. 96, l. 12; *PG* 45, 321A–324A; *NPN*, pp. 57a–c.) The Greek for #5–#6 and # 8–#9 of the key text (J, I, p. 95, lines 15–23; p. 95, l. 26–p. 96, l. 6):

. . . ὥστε ἢ λέγων ἐλάττους τε καὶ μείζους ἐν τῇ
θείᾳ φύσει καταλαμβάνειν τὰς οὐσίας λέληθεν ἑαυτὸν σύνθετον ἐξ ἀνομοίων κατασκευάζων τὸ θεῖον, ὡς ἄλλο μέν
τι νοεῖν εἶναι τὸ ὑποκείμενον, ἕτερον δὲ πάλιν τὸ μετεχό-
μενον, οὗ κατὰ μετουσίαν ἐν τῷ ἀγαθῷ γίνεσθαι τὸ μὴ
τοιοῦτον ὄν. εἰ δὲ ἀληθῶς ἁπλῆν καὶ πάντη μίαν
ἐνενόει τὴν οὐσίαν, αὐτὸ ὅπερ ἐστὶν ἀγαθὸν οὖσαν, οὐ γινο-
μένην ἐξ ἐπικτήσεως, οὐκ ἂν τὸ μεῖζον καὶ τὸ ἔλαττον
περὶ αὐτὴν ἐλογίζετο. . . .

. . . τὸ δὲ ἀόριστον οὐ τῇ
πρὸς ἕτερον σχέσει τοιοῦτόν ἐστιν, ἀλλ' αὐτὸ καθ, ἑαυτὸ
νοούμενον ἐκφεύγει τὸν ὅρον. ἄπειρον δὲ ἀπείρου πλέον
καὶ ἔλαττον λέγειν οὐκ οἶδα πῶς ἢ λελογισμένος συνθή-
σεται. ὥστε εἰ ἁπλῆν ἡμολογεῖ τὴν ὑπερκειμένην οὐσίαν
καὶ οἰκείως ἔχειν αὐτὴν πρὸς ἑαυτήν, συντιθέσθω τῇ κατὰ
τὸ ἁπλοῦν καὶ ἄπειρον κοινωνίᾳ συναπτομένην. . . .

Commentary

Having established through his quotations from Eunomius (#c–#f) that the Arian was intent on disconnecting the Father from the Son and the Son from the Spirit because they are all separate beings

---

[15] See J, I, p. 77, l. 7; *PG* 45, 310D; *NPN*, pp. 51d–52a.

differing in perfections and rank (#g–#h), Gregory begins his refutation in the key text.

As Eunomius himself proclaims, each of those three *ousiai* is simple and absolutely one—why? Because each is without form, structure and extension (#1). But their simplicity excludes their being compared as more and less (whether in goodness, power, wisdom or any other divine attribute; #2–#3). Why? Because each divine person is good, wise and powerful by and in what it is by nature and not by receiving such perfections from some outside source (#4–#6). Otherwise one has introduced into each a composition of recipient and perfection received, of participant and perfection participated in [and a process] whereby what was not good before [= the participant] is made good [by the perfection received; #5] and [whereby the perfection itself is limited by and to the participant]. But the divine Being is goodness and completely transcends evil (#7) and, thus, He is unlimited in and of Himself and, as infinite, rises above any comparison of more or less (#8). If, then, Eunomius grants that the supreme Being is simple, then let him also concede that He is infinite in unlimited perfection (#9). Otherwise, we have unmasked him as injecting composition into God by denying that the Father, Son and Holy Spirit are identical in being because the Father is greater than the Son, who is greater than the Spirit (#10).

Such is the refutation, from which we shall extricate Gregory's position on divine infinity. For the Cappadocian, the Father, Son and Holy Spirit are one and the same God, who *is* being, goodness, wisdom, power and, thus, is subsistently so. He also is infinitely so because those perfections are not participated or received in a participant [which would thereby determine them]. They are identical with the divine Being (itself identical with the three divine persons). Therefore, the divine Being is itself infinite as without the determination that would arise were participation to occur.[16]

---

[16] In this conclusion Gregory anticipates Aquinas, for whom also the divine Being is infinite as free from determination. But even though the Latin author often uses the theory of participation to express other doctrines (for instance, see *S.T.*, I, 3, 4 ["Utrum in Deo sit idem essentia et esse"], resp.), he uses act/potency instead of participated perfection/participant to set forth his view on God as infinite. For example, see *In I Sent.*, 43, 1, 1 resp.; *De Veritate*, 2, 2, ad 5; *De Potentia*, 1, 2 resp.; *S.T.*, I, 7, 1 resp.; *ibid.*, III, 10, 3 ad 2; *S.C.G.*, I, 43, where ten proofs for divine infinity are given, only in the seventh of which participation is mentioned once: "Omne quod habet aliquam perfectionem tanto est perfectius quanto illam perfectionem plenius partici-

In Gregory, then, we presumably come upon the twofold determination needed (see above, "The Metaphysical Basis of Infinity")
if an author is to propose God as infinite in His very being: that
which goodness, wisdom and other perfections exercise upon their
recipients or participants and, second, that which the recipients or
participants exercise upon the perfections themselves.

Such a theory of determination fits neatly within the theology
that resulted when Gregory was confronted with Arius' (see above,
#a and #b) and Eunomius' (#c –#h) discussion of the Trinity in
terms of being: the divine Being consists (so they say) in
Unbegottenness and thus only the Father is God. In replying, Gregory had to speak in terms of being too—God, although triune in
really distinct persons, is also one Being, with which the three
persons are identical: they are *homoousioi*. Within the parameters of
debate drawn by the heretics, then, a Neoplatonic God who is
nonbeing because beyond being obviously would not do. Nor would

---

pat." On Aquinas' theory of infinity, see my *Divine Infinity*, chs. 19 and 23, and
my doctoral dissertation, "Divine Infinity in the Writings of Thomas Aquinas"
(University of Toronto, 1954), with introductory chapters on infinity in
Aristotle, Plotinus, Proclus, Pseudo-Dionysius and *Liber de Causis*.

On the other hand and as far as I currently know, Gregory shows no awareness of an Aristotelian doctrine of act/potency. True enough, he speaks often of
energeia (as do Basil and Eunomius) but solely, it seems, as "operation" or "activity" and, often, linked with the *ergon* it produces. So too he mentions *dynamis*
frequently but as operative power rather than a constitutive and ontological
factor within substance or essence. Moreover, if B. Barmann (pp. 368–70) is right,
hypokeimenon comes to the Cappadocian from Stoicism and not from Aristotle.

Note, too, that for Nyssa (and Basil) matter is not physical but is the intersection of purely "intelligible universal forces" and nothing else—see A. H.
Armstrong, "The Theology of the Non-Existence of Matter in Plotinus and the
Cappadocians," in F. L. Cross (ed.), *Studia Patristica* (Berlin: Academie-Verlag,
1962), V, 427–49; David L. Balás, *Metousia Theou: Man's Participation in God's
Perfections According to Saint Gregory of Nyssa* (Rome: Herder, 1966), pp. 41–42.

Finally, Gregory apparently does not speak of God as subsistent Act, even
though he thinks of the divine reality as being, goodness, beauty and other
perfections free of any determination which might come from a participant or
recipient. In contrast, Thomas constantly conceives and speaks of God as subsistent act of being, and Aristotle in *Meta.*, Lambda, c. 7, of the Unmoved Mover
as subsistent act of intellection. Perhaps Gregory's silence is evidence of his
not being fully acquainted with Aristotelian metaphysics. All agree that he
knows Aristotle's *Categories*—for instance, see D. Balás, *Metousia Theou*, p. 133;
E. Mühlenberg, *Die Unendlichkeit Gottes*, pp. 123 and 160; B. Barmann, p. 227.
Also see S. Lilla, "Aristotelianism." *Encyclopedia of the Early Church* (New York:
Oxford University Press, 1992), pp. 73–76.

anything less than an infinity consonant with God as supreme Being suffice: in His very entity He is infinitely perfect. Such apparently is the Cappadocian's message in the key text just studied.

Augustine of Hippo

Do we find a similar message in Augustine's *De Trinitate*, "composed over a long period of years from 400 to 416"?[17] Although this work in Oates' view "was not written against any antagonist, nor indeed was it precipitated, as were so many of his works, by the heat of controversy,"[18] still Augustine explicitly mentions Arius himself (*De Trin.*, VI, 1, 10), distinguishes between his earlier and later followers (VI, 1, 15) and in the final book of the treatise explains and refutes Eunomius' view that the Son of God is Son not by nature (that is, not born of the substance of the Father) but by His will (XV, 20, 1).[19]

Another similarity Augustine has with Gregory is that he, following the Nicene and other *symbola*,[20] can be interpreted as speaking of the Trinity in terms of "being" inasmuch as he applies "substance" and "essence" to God. For example, the Father, the Son and the Holy Spirit are rightly said, believed and understood to be of one and the same substance or essence" (I, 2, 4: "unius eiusdemque substantiae vel essentiae"). In fact, all previous Catholic expounders of the divine Scriptures have taught that "the Father, Son and Holy Spirit entail a divine unity of one and the same substance in an indivisible equality" (I, 4, 5: "unius substantiae inseparabili aequalitate divinam insinuent unitatem"). Two chapters later, Augustine relies upon the Prologue to John's Gospel to stress that the incarnate Word not only is God but also is of the same

---

[17] Whitney J. Oates (ed.), *Basic Works of Saint Augustine* (New York: Random House, 1948), II, p. 666. Also see W. J. Mountain, *Sancti Aurelii Augustini De Trinitate* (Turnholti: Typographi Brepols Editores Pontificii, 1968), vol. 50, pp. vii–x.

[18] Oates, *Basic Works*, II, p. 666.

[19] Noteworthy too is Augustine's own initial description (*De Trin.*, I, 1, 1) of his treatise as a guard "against the sophistries of those who disdain to begin with faith and are deceived by a crude and perverse love of reason" and he describes three classes of such "calumniantes."

References to Augustine's treatise here and subsequently will be to book, chapter and initial line in the Mountain edition cited above in n. 17.

[20] For documentation see Mountain *passim*.

substance with the Father and thus is not a creature (I, 6, 10: "declarat non tantum deum esse sed etiam eiusdem cum patre substantiae"; also see VI, 3, 35).

Finally, in his lengthy discussion of how the Greek Catholic authors speak of the Trinity as involving "una essentia, tres substantiae" in contrast to the Latins, whose language is "una essentia vel substantia, tres personae" (VII, chapters 4–6), Augustine pauses midway to consider whether and how "subsistere" may be predicated of God. A body subsists and thus is a "substance," whereas its color and shape are not substances but are in a substance. Hence, only mutable and composite things are properly called "substances." From this perspective "substance" is only improperly said of God ("deum abusive substantiam vocari"), who truly and rightly is "essence." Why? He is immutable, and hence only He *is* truly. Thus "essence" is the name God revealed to Moses (*Exodus* 3:14): "I am who am" and "Say to them: He who is has sent me to you" (VII, 5, 19: "Fortasse solum deum dici oporteat essentiam. Est enim vere solus quia incommutabilis est, idque suum nomen famulo suo Moysi enuntiavit cum ait: 'Ego sum qui sum' et 'Dices ad eos: Qui est misit me ad vos'"). But (Augustine continues) whether "essence" is properly and "substance" improperly said of God, what matters is that each expresses God as such and not the persons. Accordingly, for God to be is for Him to subsist and, thus, if the Trinity is one essence, it is also one substance. Hence, the Latin manner of describing the Trinity as "tres personae" is perhaps better than "tres substantiae" (VII, 5, 22).

Rather obviously, Augustine has tentatively sided with the Latins rather than the Greeks in expressing the Trinity. Would this preference coincide with a distance between his and Nyssa's conceptions of the triune God as infinite being?

Let us reflect on the two instances so far found of Augustine's applying "infinitum" to the Trinity. Each is found in the final paragraph of the last chapter of Book VI, which discusses what Hilary of Poitiers intended by stating, "Aeternitas in patre, species in imagine, usus in munere."[21] In this complicated and rather contrived discussion Augustine speaks of "aeternitas," "species" and "usus" with reference first to the Trinity, then to creatures and

---

[21] In Hilary's own *De Trinitate*, II, 1, 1, the initial noun is "infinitas" and not "aeternitas"—see Mountain, p. 241. On Hilary's position on infinity see my *Divine Infinity*, ch. 15: "Divine Infinity: 1150–1250," prgrs. corresponding to notes 30–44.

finally to the Trinity again. In this last section he classifies the three persons both as determined and as infinite. Let us follow him in that threefold movement of thought.

[a] "Eternity" signifies that the Father does not himself have a father, whereas the Son is from the Father and thus is coeternal: as perfect image the Son is coequal to the Father (VI, 10, 2).

[b] The Son is named "species"[22] to designate the beauty issuing from His primal equality, likeness and identity with the Father in being, life and intellection. This is to be expected in Him who is the perfect Word and exemplar (filled with all immutable, living and unified *rationes*) of the omnipotent and wise God ("ars quaedam omnipotentis atque sapientis dei plena omnium rationum viventium incommutabilium"), who thereby knows everything He has made (lines 10 sqq.).

[c] The Holy Spirit is named "usus" to indicate the love, joy and happiness which exists between the Father and the Son and which allows all creatures to achieve their order and proper rank (lines 29 sqq.).

[d] All these created existents manifest an inner unity, beauty ("speciem") and order: unity in the natures of their bodies and in the abilities of their souls; beauty in their physical shapes and qualities and in their knowledges and skills; order in their physical juxtapositions and in their loves and delights (lines 17 sqq.).

[e] Consequently, from creatures so disposed to be signposts ("vestigia") we should know the Trinity, which is the supreme origin of all things, most perfect beauty and most blessed delight.

[f] [Now come the key lines]: Thus those three [origin, beauty, delight or, by reduction, Father, Son and Holy Spirit] are seen to be mutually determinate [as persons] but to be infinite in themselves [as God]. (Lines 47 sqq.: "In illa enim Trinitate summa origo est rerum omnium et perfectissima pulchritudo et beatissima delectatio. Itaque illa tria et a se[23] invicem determinari videntur et in se infinita sunt").

---

[22] What does "species" mean? It is hard to pin down in Hilary and Augustine, as well as in Bonaventure, Aquinas and other medievals, who use it often. In origin it apparently is a translation of *eidos*, which comes from the Greek verb "to see" and thus which first means "that which is seen or appears." The connotation is that what one sees in an object is the beauty it puts across to the viewer. Consequently, "species" can mean "beauty" and Augustine uses it here in this sense.

[23] Here Migne (*PL* 42, 932B) reads "ad se." But the difference in meaning between "ad se" and "a se" appears slight: "ad se invicem determinari" sig-

[g] But in corporeal things one is not as much as three, and two is more than one. In the Trinity, though, one is as much as three, and two is not more than one, and the three [persons] are mutually infinite [because they are the same God]. (Lines 52 sqq.: "In summa trinitate tantum est una quantum tres simul, nec plus aliquid sunt duae quam una, et in se infinita sunt.")

[h] Thus, any one person is individually in each of the other two, and all three are in any one, and each is in all and all in all and each is all (lines 54 sqq.: "Ita et singula sunt in singulis et omnia in singulis et singula in omnibus et omnia in omnibus et unum omnia").

[i] May whoever glimpses this truth, either partially or darkly as in a mirror, rejoice in that he knows God, whom he should honor and thank. But anyone without such a glimpse should strive to attain it, since God is one and yet triune (lines 56 sqq.).

Thus far Augustine's *De Trinitate*, VI, 10, translated or paraphrased. Manifestly he speaks of the three persons as somehow "infinita" (see #f and #g) but the term is not applied to God as such or to the divine essence and substance. Accordingly, one might infer that Augustine differs from Nyssa in this application.

Etienne Gilson

But such an inference must contend with the interpretation of none other than the eminent historian of philosophy, Etienne Gilson, who has located *De Trinitate*, VI, 10, among passages in which Augustine is developing a doctrine of divine infinity where the "future speculations of theologians are contained in germ" and which makes a definitive contribution to the Christian theologians of the Middle Ages and, specifically, to Thomas Aquinas.[24] What is

---

nifies that the divine persons are distinct with reference to one another; "a se invicem determinari" that they are distinct from one another as persons.

One should note that Augustine uses "ad se" elsewhere. See *De Trin.*, VII, 6, 8, where "ad se invicem" expresses relation and person: "Nam si esse ad se dicitur, persona vero relative. Sic dicamus tres personas Patrem et Filium et Spiritum sanctum, quemadmodum dicuntur aliqui tres amici aut tres proponqui aut tres vicini quod sint ad invicem, non quod unusquisque eorum sit ad se ipsum."

[24] E. Gilson, "L'infinité divine chez saint Augustin," *Augustinus Magister* (Paris: Etudes Augustiniennes, 1954), I, p. 570: ". . . des spéculations futures des théologiens sont ici en germe . . ." *ibid.*, p. 572: "En revanche, il est vrai de dire que ce qu'apporta sur ce point saint Augustin est resté dans la théologie chrétienne du Moyen Age comme une acquisition définitive. Saint Thomas

that doctrine? Basically, this: Because He is immaterial and, thus, is not contained in place and has no direct connection with anything corporeal or quantitative, God is Himself infinite and without limitation.[25] Such is Augustine's message, Gilson maintains, in the lines from *De Trinitate:* although the divine persons are three, still, number here does not imply limitation because the persons are infinite in their absolute immateriality.

Sa position favorite est celle que nous avons vue, et il y revient spontanément lorsque l'occasion l'invite à s'expliquer sur ce point. Par example, les personnes divines sont trois, mais elles n'en sont pas moins infinies pour cela, parce qu'elles sont incorporelles. Il s'agit de refuser que le nombre entraîne en Dieu aucune limite; donc l'infinité entre en jeu.[26]

What should one's reaction be to Gilson's exegesis? The question of whether or not God's freedom from matter and place is ground for inferring Him to be infinite being and reality must be postponed until later, but rereading chapter 10 of *De Trin.*, VI, discloses no direct mention of matter or place. Rather, that chapter conveys a meaning of infinity very different from that proposed by Gilson, as is evident from consulting three thirteenth-century commentaries on Peter Lombard's twelfth-century *Sentences,* Book I, Distinctions 19 and 31, who quotes the key text from Augustine's *De Trinitate.*[27]

Three Medieval Commentators
The first of these commentators is Stephen Langton (d. 1228). Coming upon Augustine's statement "Itaque illa tria et a se invi-

---

d'Aquin construit sa démonstration de l'infinité de grandeur spirituelle en Dieu sur la conclusion préalablement établie que Dieu est incorporel. La même notion d'infinité spirituelle, établie dans la *Summa contra Gentiles,* est reprise dans la *Summa theologiae,* non d'ailleurs sans y être fondée sur des raisons beaucoup plus profondes."

[25] "Le principe que l'immatériel est par essence soustrait à la limite, se trouve donc clairement dégagé dans ces textes de saint Augustin" (*ibid.,* p. 570). "Ici [in *Contra Faustum Manichaeum,* XXV, 1–2] encore l'élimination de la matière ouvre la voie à la notion d'un être infini parce que sans limite" (*ibid.,* p. 570–71). It is an infinity "qui suit d'une simple absence de limites corporelles" (*ibid.,* p. 571).

[26] *Ibid.,* p. 572.

[27] On Lombard's position, see my *Divine Infinity,* ch. 15: "Divine Infinity: 1150–1250," prgrs. corresponding to notes 21–53, and ch. 17: "Lombard, Augustine and Infinity," upon which the second half of this current chapter is based.

cem determinari videntur et in se infinita sunt," he restricted his explanation to one word. "'Infinite,'" he asserted, "means 'indistinct according to essence.'"[28]

Some years later Hugh of S. Cher, teaching at the University of Paris between 1230 and 1235, was more generous. "The word, 'three,' in the phrase, 'Itaque illa tria,'" he began, "stands for Father, Image and Gift" (the last two terms refer, as we have seen, in Hilary's and Augustine's texts to the Son and the Holy Spirit). "The word, 'determinari,'" he added, "means, are distinguished by eternity, beauty, and joy," which also Hilary and, after him, Augustine set up as properties of the Father, Son and Holy Spirit. "The word, 'infinita,' in the phrase, 'In se infinita sunt,' can be understood in a twofold manner. If applied to the divine persons qua *persons*, it is synonymous with 'incomprehensible.' If applied to them [qua *divine*—inasmuch as they have identically one and the same divine nature] it means 'not-finite, that is, not-different in their nature.'"

"*Itaque quia illa tria,* id est, tres: Pater, Imago, Munus.

"*Determinari,*" id est, distingui per haec alia tria, scilicet eternitatem, speciem, usum.

"*In se infinita sunt,*" id est, respectiva vel incomprehensibilia vel non finita, i.e., in natura sua indifferentia.[29]

Approximately a decade later Richard Fishacre wrote comments which are in many respects similar to those of Hugh. "The word, 'three,' in the phrase, 'illa tria,'" he began, "stands for Father, Image and Gift," an explanation which exactly reproduces what Hugh had said. "'Determinari,'" he continues, "signifies 'are distinguished.'" Finally, "the word, 'infinita,' in the phrase, 'et in se infinita sunt,' indicates one of two things. Either the three persons are not-different in nature [which is one and the same for all three]. Or each of the

---

[28] "'Infinita' et indistincta secundum essentiam" (*Der Sentenzen-kommentar des Kardinals Stephen Langton*, Band 27, Heft 1 of *Beiträge zur Geschichte der Philosophie und Theologie des Mittelalters* [Münster i. W.: Aschendorffsche Verlagsbuchandlung, 1952], p. 40). He bypasses Augustine's other sentence "Et in se infinitae sunt," quoted in Distinction 19, without any comment. See *ibid.*, pp. 21–22.

[29] *Commentarium in I Sent.*, d. 31 (Cod. Vat. lat., 1098, 29vb). Hugh makes no comment upon Augustine's sentence in Distinction 19—see *ibid.*, d. 19, c. 12 (Cod. Vat. lat., 1098, 21r).

three persons, who are distinct from one another qua persons, is incomprehensible or, even, is infinite in power and magnitude."

"Illa tria," id est, tres: Pater, Imago, Munus.

"Determinari," id est, distingui.

"Et in se infinita sunt," id est, incomprehensibilia vel [in] natura indifferentia.

Quod dicit: illi tres sic distinguuntur, et tamen in se incomprehensibilis est unusquisque eorum.

"Vel infinita" secundum potentiam et magnitudinem.[30]

What interpretation, then, of the key sentence in *De Trinitate*, VI, 10, can be gathered from those three medieval commentators? First of all, Augustine intends to speak of the three divine persons, to whom "tria" in the phrase "Itaque illa tria" refers. In the next words, "et ad se invicem determinari videntur," he says that qua persons they are distinct from one another. In the final portion, "et in se infinita sunt," however, he reminds us that they are nonetheless indistinct with reference to the divine essence—they are one and the same God and have identically one and the same divine nature.[31] Putting the phrases together, then, we learn that accord-

---

[30] *Commentarium in I Sent.*, d. 31, c. 4 (Cod. Ottob. lat., 294, 57va). Earlier Richard had commented upon two sentences of Augustine in Distinction 19: "In rebus corporeis non est tantum una quantum tres simul" and "Et in se infinitae sunt." With regard to the first, he explains that Augustine is not speaking of bodies which can interpenetrate, such as light and air or fire and iron. But even if he were, any two such bodies are more than one both "naturally" and numerically. *"Non est tantum una quantum tres simul.* [Marg.: Quaestio] Contra. Posito quod lux sit corpus, eadem est magnitudo infinitorum corporum, quia luminum quotlibet et aeris, eadem est linea longitudinis, latitudinis et spissitudinis. Similiter est de ferro et igne. [Marg.: Solutio] Sed Augustinus intelligit quod hic dicitur de talibus corporibus quae non possunt esse simul in eodem loco. Item licet sint in eodem loco, tamen duo sunt maius uno naturaliter, quia plus in eis est de natura; et numeraliter, quia maiorem numerum faciunt" (*ibid.*, d. 19, c. 20, 38vb). As regards the second sentence, his comment is that infinity there refers to magnitude and not to number: *"Et in se infinitae sunt* magnitudine non numero" (*ibid.*).

[31] Actually, as their previously reproduced texts make clear, both Hugh and Richard suggest two interpretations—the one which we have chosen to retain, and the other in which infinity is equivalent to incomprehensibility and is referred to divine power and magnitude. Our choice seems better suited to Augustine's aim and to the immediate context of his sentences.

ing to Augustine the three divine persons are distinct qua persons
but are indistinct in the divine nature, with which each is identical.
They are three qua persons but are one qua divine or, to say the
same thing, God is one and yet triune.

Notice how neatly the sentence, when so understood, fits into
the immediate context. Beginning with chapter 6, Augustine aims
at establishing God's absolute simplicity.[32] Truly, God is great,
good, wise, happy, true and the like. Nevertheless, His magnitude
of power is the same as His wisdom, His goodness the same as His
wisdom and magnitude, His truth the same as all three.[33] In fact,
even divine trinity, the bishop continues in chapter 7, is no obstacle
to divine simplicity. God is triune, not tripartite, since the Father or
Son or Holy Spirit alone is as much as the Father, Son and Holy
Spirit together.[34] The Son is equal to the Father, we read in chapter
8, and the Holy Spirit is equal to both. Perfect is the Father, perfect
is the Son, perfect is the Spirit, and a perfect God is the Father, Son
and Holy Spirit. Accordingly, there is a trinity, not a triplicity.[35]
"Having, then, demonstrated that the three persons are equal and
are one and the same substance," Augustine concludes in chapter
9, "nothing should prevent us from acknowledging the supreme
equality of the Father, Son and Holy Spirit."[36]

Chapter 10 immediately follows. Let us with St. Hilary apply
eternity, Augustine begins, to the Father as the sourceless source
even of the Son. Let us characterize the Word as beauty, the Holy

---

[32] "Si autem quaeritur quomodo simplex et multiplex sit illa [divina] substantia . . ." (*De Trin.*, VI, 6, 1).

[33] "Deus vero multipliciter quidem dicitur magnus, bonus, sapiens, beatus,
verus, et quidquid aliud non indigne dici videtur. Sed eadem magnitudo eius
est quae sapientia (non enim mole magnus est sed virtute); et eadem bonitas
quae sapientia et magnitudo, et eadem veritas quae illa omnia. Et non est ibi
aliud beatum esse et aliud magnum aut sapientem aut verum aut bonum esse,
aut omnino ipsum esse" (*ibid.*, VI, 7, 1).

[34] "Nec quoniam Trinitas est ideo triplex putandus est. Alioquin minor erit
Pater solus aut Filius solus, quam simul Pater et Filius" (*ibid.*, VI, 7, 8).

[35] "In ipso igitur Deo cum adhaeret aequali Patri Filius aequalis, aut Spiritus
sanctus Patri et Filio aequalis, non fit maior Deus quam singuli eorum, quia
non est quo crescat illa perfectio. Perfectus autem sive Pater sive Filius sive
Spiritus Sanctus, et perfectus Deus Pater et Filius et Spiritus Sanctus, et ideo
Trinitas potius quam triplex" (*ibid.*, VI, 8, 13).

[36] "Nunc autem aequalitas Trinitatis et una eademque substantia, quantum
breviter potuimus, demonstrata est, . . . nihil impediat quominus fateamur
summam aequalitatem Patris et Filii et Spiritus Sancti" (*ibid.*, VI, 9, 47).

Spirit as subsistent joy. Let us even recognize the Trinity in creatures, all of whom bear its imprint to some degree, for in that Trinity one discovers the ultimate source of all things, as well as most perfect beauty and maximal joy. And its three divine persons are distinct as persons and yet are not distinct from one another with respect to the divine essence, with which each is identical ("illa tria et ad se invicem determinari videntur et in se infinita sunt"). In material things one is not as much as three such items taken together, and two are more than one. But in the august Trinity one person is as much as all three together, nor are two any more than one, for qua divine they are not distinct from one another ("et in se infinita sunt") but are one and the same God. For this reason, each person is in each other and all in each and each in all and all in all, and one is all. Whoever even partially understands this doctrine should rejoice in his knowledge and should give thanks. But should someone not understand it, let him be brought through piety to understand and not through blindness to calumniate, for truly God is one and yet is triune.[37]

Conclusions

If we follow the lead of such medieval commentators as Stephen Langton, Hugh of S. Cher and Richard Fishacre, and if we then reread the key sentences from Augustine's *De Trinitate*, VI, 10, in the light of their immediate context, what else can we conclude but that "infinity" there is a technical trinitarian term? It is synonymous with "absence of distinction" or, expressed positively, "complete identity" in nature. As "infinite" the divine persons are not distinct from the divine nature they all have in common or, in that sense, from one another. They are, in short, one and the same God.

In this passage Augustine is not dealing with whether or not the divine being is itself infinite and, thus, is not comparable here with Gregory's refutation of the Arians by stressing that the Son and the Spirit, as well as the Father, are the same divine and *infinite being* and thus are equal and are equally God.

What does Augustine say elsewhere? Let us answer that question in our immediately following chapter, which considers why Augustine does not list "infinity" among the divine attributes in *De Doctrina Christiana*.

---

[37] *Ibid.*, VI, 10, 1. See my prgrs. above, #a–#i.

10

Divine Attributes in
De Doctrina Christiana: Why Does
Augustine Not List "Infinity"?

Despite first appearances, Augustine's *De Doctrina Christiana* is carefully structured.[1] Any study (*tractatio*) of Sacred Scripture (Augustine begins) involves a method of discovering what is to be understood in and from its pages and then a method of setting forth what is learned (I, 1, 1, 180: "modus inveniendi quae intelligenda sunt et modus proferendi quae intellecta sunt"). Postponing the second method until Book III, Augustine immediately begins the process of discovery in Book I by separating the *doctrina* it discloses into that which one learns from signs (this will constitute the topic of Book II) and from things (*res*), which is the topic of Book I.[2]

---

[1] On the makeup of *De Doctrina Christiana* [hereafter: *DC*], the date of its composition and a general introduction to its contents, see M. G. Combès and M. Farges (trans.), *Le magistère chrétien* (Paris: Desclée de Brouwer, 1949), *Oeuvres de Saint Augustin*, vol. 11, pp. 152–63 [hereafter: Combès-Farges]—for sake of convenience I shall use their Latin text, checked however with Green's critical edition noted immediately below; references to the Combès-Farges text are to book, chapter, section and page—thus, I, 1, 1, 180 = Book I, ch. 1, sec. 1, p. 180); William M. Green, *De Doctrina Christiana* (Wien: Hoelder-Pichler-Tempsky, 1963) [hereafter: Green], *Sancti Aurelii Augustini Opera*, Sect. VI, Pars VI of *Corpus Scriptorum Ecclesiasticorum Latinorum*, vol. 8, pp. vii–xiii; John J. Gavigan, "Christian Instruction" [hereafter: Gavigan] (Washington, D.C.: The Catholic University of America Press, 1947), *Fathers of the Church*, II, pp. 3–8. Also see Joseph Martin, *Sancti Aurelii Augustini De Doctrina Christiana* (Turnholti: Typographi Brepols Editores, 1962), pp. vii–xix.

[2] "Signs" are "those things which are employed to signify something. Therefore, every sign is also a thing, for whatever is not a thing is absolutely

Res means that which is not used to signify something (I, 2, 2, 182: "Proprie autem tunc res appelavi quae non ad significandum aliquid adhibetur").

Such *res* are in turn divided into those which are to be enjoyed, those which are to be used and others which are enjoyed and used (I, 3, 3, 182: "Res ergo aliae sunt quibus fruendum est, aliae quibus utendum, aliae quae fruuntur et utuntur"—for explanation see Combès-Farges, pp. 558–61). The first make us happy; the second are means to achieving happiness; the third, if we enjoy what is solely to be used, can cause problems by impeding or even canceling our movement toward true goods of the first sort (*ibid.*, p. 182).

In the next chapter our author further comments on "enjoy" and "use." The former is clinging to something with affection for its own sake, the latter is employing something so as to obtain what we want, provided the object desired is right and lawful for us. Otherwise to employ something in order to obtain what is wrong is not "use" but "abuse" (I, 4, 4, 184). For example, if we are traveling home and we so enjoy the journey itself as to want to continue traveling rather than to arrive, we are wrongly enjoying what we should only use. So too, as wanderers from God on the road of mortal life, we must use this world and not enjoy it so that the "invisible attributes" of God may be clearly seen, "being understood through the things that are made" [*Rom.* 1:20]—that is, that through what is corporeal and temporal we may comprehend the eternal and spiritual (I, 4, 4, 184: ". . . utendum est hoc mundo, non fruendum; ut invisibilia Dei, per ea quae facta sunt, intellecta conspiciantur, hoc est ut de corporalibus temporalibusque rebus aeterna et spiritualia capiamus").

Divine Attributes

Up to now we have traced the careful outline which Augustine will follow throughout *De Doctrina Christiana* and which also pro-

---

nothing, but not every thing is also a sign." I, 2, 2, 182: "Omne signum etiam res aliqua est: quod enim nulla res est, omnino nihil est; non autem omnis res etiam signum est." Again: "A sign is a thing which, apart from the impression it makes upon the senses, causes of itself something else to enter into our thinking"—examples: footprints, smoke, living voice, trumpet sounding. II, 1, 1, 238: "Signum est enim res, praeter speciem quam ingerit sensibus, aliud aliquid ex se faciens in cogitationem venire."

vided the setting for his listing the divine attributes. What are those "'invisible attributes' of God" he has just mentioned?[3] Before listing them Augustine speaks again of the *res* we should enjoy—it is the Trinity of Father, Son and Holy Spirit, which is one supreme *res* common to all who enjoy it—or (he stops to ask) *is* it a *res* or, better, is it not the cause of all things or, even better, is it not both *res* and cause (I, 5, 5, 186: "una quaedam res, communisque omnibus fruentibus ea; si tamen res et non rerum omnium causa sit, si tamen et causa")? What term might aptly fit such great excellence? Perhaps it is better to say that this Trinity is the one God from whom, through whom and in whom are all things [*Rom.* 11:36]. Thus there are Father, Son and Holy Spirit, each of whom is God and simultaneously all are one God. Each of them individually is full substance and simultaneously all are one substance (*ibid.*: "et singulus quisque horum plena substantia, et simul omnes una substantia"). All of them is the same eternity, the same immutability, the same majesty, the same power (*ibid.*: "Eadem tribus aeternitas, eadem incommutabilitas, eadem majestas, eadem potestas"), even though unity characterizes the Father, equality the Son, perfect harmony of unity and of equality the Holy Spirit.

If we pause to synthesize the information Augustine has just given on the divine attributes, what list emerges? The triune God is both the *res* to be enjoyed by all and the cause of all. Perfect substance, the three divine persons are identically one and the same eternity, changelessness (this will turn out to be the primal attribute),[4] majesty, power.

So far have I (Augustine continues in chapter 6) spoken or given utterance to anything worthy of God? Not really, because God is ineffable and one should be silent before Him. But He wishes us to rejoice in His praise in our own language. Thus, we call Him "Deus," a two-syllable Latin word which doesn't disclose Him but which, when heard, causes us to reflect upon His most excellent and immortal nature (I, 6, 6, 188: "[iste sonus] movet ad cogitandam excellentissimam quamdam immortalemque naturam"). The result is that we attempt to conceive of something which is more excellent and more sublime than all else (I, 7, 7, 188: "ut aliquid quo nihil melius sit atque sublimius illa cogitatio conetur attingere")

---

[3] Such is Gavigan's translation (p. 30) of *invisibilia*, which Combès-Farges translate (p. 185) as "les perfections invisibles de Dieu."

[4] See I, 6, 6, 188; I, 7, 7, 188; I, 8, 8, 190; I, 32, 35, 224—all of which are quoted below.

and which is above not only all visible and corporeal natures but even all intellectual and spiritual natures—in a word, above all changeable things. Hence, everyone agrees that God is that which is worthy of esteem above all other things (*ibid.*). Also, all think of God as something living—in fact, as Life itself (I, 8, 8, 190: "vivum aliquid cogitant . . . vitam ipsam cogitant")—as unchangeable life, as wisdom itself, as the unchangeable wise life ruled over by unchangeable Truth, which contrasts with their own changeable lives and by which they know that the unchangeable life is better (*ibid.*). Unchangeable Truth it is we are to enjoy to the full, once our minds are cleansed by holy desire and lofty morals, and in which the triune God as author and founder of the universe takes counsel for the things He has created (I, 10, 10, 192).

In subsequent chapters Augustine speaks of Christ's incarnation (chapters 11–14), His resurrection and ascension (chapter 15), and His Church (chapters 16 sqq.). In chapter 32 he begins anew to contrast enjoyment with use. In that renewed discussion he discloses two further attributes of God when explaining how God uses rather than enjoys us. His use of us differs from our using something inasmuch as by using us He increases the good He confers upon us.

> Since God is good, we are. Insofar as we are, we are good. . . . He is supremely and primally who is entirely unchangeable and who could most fully say: "I am who am" and "You shall say to them: 'He who is sent me to you'" [*Exod.* 3:14]. Other existents could not be except by Him and they are good inasmuch as they have received the ability to be. Therefore, God's using us redounds not to His but to our benefit, and this solely because of His goodness (I, 32, 35, 224: "Quia enim bonus est sumus; et in quantum sumus, boni sumus. . . . Ille enim summe ac primitus est qui omnino incommutabilis est, et quia plenissime dicere potuit: 'Ego sum qui sum' et 'Dices sic: Quis est, misit me ad vos'" . . . Ut cetera quae sunt, et nisi ab illo esse non possint, et in tantum bona sint in quantum acceperunt ut sint. Ille igitur usus qui dicitur Dei, quo nobis utitur, non ad ejus sed ad nostram utilitatem refertur ad ejus autem tantummodo bonitatem").[5]

---

[5] In the initial sentence "Quia enim [Deus] bonus est sumus," *sumus* is best rendered not as "exists" (see Gavigan, p. 52) but simply as "are" in the sense of "are real." Existence as such for human persons and other creatures con-

In light of this passage, God is primal Being—and this because He is total immutability—and primal goodness.

If we add these two divine properties of supreme being and goodness to those discovered earlier, what do we have? The triune God is full substance. He is eternity, changelessness, majesty and power (chapter 5). He is ineffable in His most excellent and immortal nature, which is higher and more sublime than all else, even than intellectual and spiritual natures, all of which are changeable (chapter 6). He is Life itself, unchangeable Truth and Wisdom (chapter 7), which became incarnate in Christ (chapters 11–14). Primal goodness, He is also primal Being because of His absolute changelessness (chapter 32).

God Infinite Being?

But nowhere in those passages does Augustine predicate infinity of the divine being itself, and the question is, Why not? Unlike his earlier contemporary, Gregory of Nyssa (331–395),[6] why does he not list infinity among God's attributes?

The answer may be found in the *Confessions*, which was written in 397, the year after he had written the first portion of *De Doctrina Christiana*, but which recounts the stages of his intellectual and religious conversion occurring between autumn of 384 and August 386 and thus preceding his writing *De Doctrina Christiana* by a decade.[7]

---

notes mutability and unreality. What God properly does in us is to cause us to be immutable by our sharing in His immutability and reality. The same understanding of the verb *esse* should be applied to the other quoted clauses here and in similar situations.

[6] On Gregory of Nyssa see my volume *Divine Infinity in Greek and Medieval Thought* [hereafter: *Divine Infinity*] (New York/Bern: Peter Lang Publishing, Inc., 1992), ch. 21, "Gregory of Nyssa on God as Infinite Being"; also ch. 9 above, "Augustine and Gregory of Nyssa: Is the Triune God Infinite in Being?"

[7] For J. O'Donnell's assigning 397 as the date for *Confessions*, see ch. 8 above, n. 24. For its traditional dates 397–401, the nature of the book, the intellectual and religious conversion described in Books VII–VIII occurring from 384 to 386, see Peter Brown, *Augustine of Hippo* (Berkeley: University of California Press, 1969), pp. 74–183 sqq.; Eugene TeSelle, *Augustine the Theologian* (New York: Herder and Herder, 1970), pp. 12, 59–89, 185–223. As to when *De Doctrina Christiana* was started (ca. 396), see references given in n. 1 above.

What information does the *Confessions* provide? Influenced by Manichaeism and then by Stoicism,[8] Augustine thought of God, although incorruptible and immortal (VII, 1, 1), as a corporeal reality which indefinitely extends throughout space and penetrates the entire universe and all its parts—as though God is an immense ocean, in the middle of which the world is immersed like a large sponge. Thus all things are finite because located in God, Who is Himself infinite in His limitless physical extension and, second, in His freedom from any extrinsic location—because of His material greatness and surpassing size, He extends beyond all space and, thus, nothing contains Him.[9]

But at the time of his intellectual conversion, which God brought about on the occasion of his reading some Neoplatonic literature (VII, chapters 9 and 20), what happened to Augustine's conception of infinity? He then saw that creatures are finite not because they are physically located in divine reality but because God conserves their being and truth (VII, 15, 21: ". . . in te cuncta finita sunt sed aliter, non quasi in loco, sed quia tu es omnitenens manu veritate, et cuncta vera sunt inquantum sunt"). Second, he realized that God is completely immaterial because He is the unchangeable Light far

---

[8] See Robert J. O'Connell, *St. Augustine's Early Theory of Man, A.D. 386–391* (Cambridge: Harvard University Press, 1968), pp. 88–99; Peter Brown, *The Body and Society: Men, Women, and Sexual Renunciation in Early Christianity* (New York: Columbia University Press, 1988), pp. 196–202; Marianne Djuth, "Stoicism and Augustine's Doctrine of Human Freedom after 396," in Joseph C. Schnaubelt and Frederick Van Fleteren (eds.), *Collectanea Augustiniana* (New York/Bern: Peter Lang Publishing, Inc., 1990), I, pp. 387–401 (where she gives helpful references to G. Verbeke and M. Colish).

[9] *Conf.*, VII, 1, 2: ". . . corporeum tamen aliquid cogerer per spatia locorum, sive infusum mundo sive etiam extra mundum per infinita diffusum. . . . Ita etiam te, vita vitae meae, grandem per infinita spatia undique cogitabam penetrare totam mundi molem, et extra eam quaquaversum per immensa sine termino, ut haberet te terra, haberet caelum, haberent omnia et illa finirentur in te, tu autem nusquam." *Ibid.*, VII, 5, 7: [Augustine first pictured the entire universe with all its visible and invisible creatures as a huge mass; then] et eam feci grandem, non quantum erat, quod scire non poteram, sed quantum libuit, undiqueversum sane finitam; te autem, domine, ex omni parte ambientem et penetrantem eam, sed usquequaeque infinitum; tanquam si mare esset, ubique et undique per immensa infinitum solum mare, et haberet intra se spongiam quamlibet magnam, sed finitam, plena esset utique spongia illa ex omni sua parte ex immenso mari; sic creaturam tuam finitam, te infinito plenam putabam."

different from all physical lights: He is Eternity, Love and Truth. But Augustine asked,

> "Is truth nothing because it is diffused neither through finite nor infinite space?" From afar you cried to me, "I am who am." I heard as one hears in his heart; there was no further place for doubt, for it would be easier for me to doubt that I live than that there is no truth, which is "clearly seen, being understood by what is made" (VII, 10, 16).

Through *Exodus* 3:14 God thus assures Augustine that He is Truth and that He is entirely nonspatial. But because God then is totally incorporeal, He is infinite in a way other than he had earlier imagined (VII, 14, 20: "et evigilavi in te et vidi te infinitum aliter"). God is infinite, yes, but not as physically diffused through space, whether finite or infinite (VII, 20, 26: "certus esse te et infinitum esse, nec tamen per locos finitos infinitosve diffundi").

One may conclude, then, that the divine incorporeal and immutable being is infinite, not however through physical extension but in some way different from what Augustine had previously thought. What is that different fashion? Nowhere in the *Confessions* does he answer. Apparently no reply occurred to him in the years covered by that treatise (the conversion itself in Books I–IX; his reflection on memory, time and eternity, form and matter, the creation of the world in Books X–XIII).[10]

Consequently, no one need be surprised that in *De Doctrina Christiana* he omits infinity from among the divine attributes: by the time of his composing its Book I (ca. 396), he seemingly was still no more certain then as to what infinity might mean when applied to the incorporeal existent who is God than when he was writing the *Confessions*.[11]

---

[10] See Brown, *Augustine of Hippo*, pp. 158–81; prgrs. *re* nn. 25–27 below.

[11] For E. TeSelle (*Augustine the Theologian*, p. 185), "at sometime in 396 or 397 ... [Augustine] broke off *De Doctrina Christiana*" and began to write the *Confessions*. Actually, *DC*, I, chapter 7, anticipates (although very briefly) some of the stages we have seen set forth in *Conf.*, VII. On the occasion in *DC*, I, 7, 7, of interpreting *Psalm* 50:1 and *Joshua* 22:21–22, he discussed those polytheists who "have surrendered to the bodily senses and think that the sky, or what they see most radiant in the sky, or the world itself is the God of gods. Or, if they attempt to go beyond the world, they visualize something luminous and conceive it as infinite or of that shape which seems most pleasing in their vague imagining.

Infinity in Subsequent Writings

Does that uncertainty persist in his later writings? In *De Trinitate*, VI, 10, he twice uses "infinity" as a technical trinitarian term to express the fact that the three divine persons are distinct as persons and yet are not distinct from one another in respect to the divine essence, with which each is identical ("illa tria [= the divine persons] et ad se invicem determinari videntur et in se infinita sunt"). Qua divine they are not distinct from one another ("et in se infinita sunt") but are one and the same God. Manifestly, Augustine here is not dealing with whether or not the divine being is itself infinite and thus does not directly deal with the question raised in the *Confessions* as to how the incorporeal God is Himself infinite.[12]

What does Augustine say elsewhere? In commenting on *Psalm*, 144, 3, "God is exceedingly worthy of praise for there is no end to His greatness," he links the nonfiniteness of God's spiritual greatness or magnitude with our inability to comprehend Him.

Reflect in thought as much as you want, but when can that be thought of which cannot be captured in thought? For, as the Psalmist says, "He is exceedingly worthy of praise for there is no end to His greatness." . . . Indeed [although] there is no end to His greatness, yet we must praise Him whom we cannot capture in thought (for if we so capture Him, there would be an end to His greatness; but even if there is no end to His greatness, we can by thought capture something of Him, al-

---

Or they think of it in the form of the human body, if they prefer that to other things" (I, 7, 7, 188: ". . . aliquid lucidum imaginatur, idque vel infinitum").

Who thought of the "God of gods" as having the form of a human body? No answer is given there, or in *Conf.*, VII, 1, 1, where Augustine mentions that identification twice: "Yet from the time that I first began to learn anything of wisdom I did not think of you, O God, as being in the shape of the human body. Such a conception I always shunned." In the next paragraph: "Although I did not think of you as being in the shape of a human body, I was forced to think of you as something corporeal."

Linking God to the shape of a human body originated with the Audians, "a rigorist sect of the 4th century founded by Audius, a Mesopotamian" (R. B. Eno, *Encyclopedic Dictionary of Religion* [Washington, D.C.: Corpus Publications, 1979], p. 308): since humans are images of God, He too would have a human shape; L. G. Müller, *ibid.*, p. 196.

[12] On *De Trin.*, VI, 10, see ch. 9 above, "Augustine and Gregory of Nyssa: Is the Triune God Infinite in Being?" prgrs. corresponding to notes 17–37.

though we cannot capture Him wholly). Granted we only deficiently measure up to His greatness, but we are refreshed by His goodness; hence, let us look at His effects and praise Him as working in them, and thus we praise Him as producer from His products, as creator from His creatures.[13]

In light of this passage Augustine advises moving from effects to cause, with the result that we know and praise God, working within His effects, as *conditor* and *creator*. But we can never comprehend Him because His greatness is without end ("magnitudinis eius non est finis"). This endlessness or nonfiniteness of His spiritual magnitude seemingly resides in us—it is directly a description of our inability to cope with it and its surpassing perfection. God is said to be infinite and incomprehensible, then, with reference to us and thus through extrinsic denomination.

Another relevant text occurs in Augustine's commenting on the initial verses of John's Gospel: "In the beginning was the Word, and the Word was with God, and the Word was God." There Augustine contrasts the transient words we speak with the immutable word God the Father speaks. What kind of Word is it, he asks, which is "both spoken and does not pass away"? Or take the word "God"—"how short it is: three letters and one syllable. Is this

---

[13] "Cogita quantumvis. Quando autem potest cogitari qui capi non potest? *Laudabilis* est *valde; et magnitudinis eius non est finis.* . . . Verumtamen, quia *magnitudinis eius non est finis,* et eum quem non capimus laudare debemus (si enim capimus, magnitudinis eius est finis; si autem magnitudinis eius non est finis, capere ex eo aliquid possumus; Deum tamen totum capere non possumus); tamquam deficientes in eius magnitudine, ut reficiamur eius bonitate, ad opera respiciamus et de operibus laudemus operantem, de conditis Conditorem, de creaturis Creatorem" (*Enarratio in Psalm.* 144, 3 [vol. 40 of *Corpus Christianorum* (Turnholti: Typographi Brepols Editores Pontificii, 1956)], nos. 5 and 6, p. 2091). See *Enarratio in Psalm.* 146, 5 (vol. 40 of *Corpus Christianorum,* no. 11, p. 2129). "Intelligentiae eius non est numerus. Conticescant humanae voces, requiescant humanae cogitationes; ad incomprehensibilia non se extendant quasi comprehensuri sed tamquam participaturi."

On spiritual or virtual magnitude in God see *De Trin.,* VI, 7, 1: "Deus vero multipliciter quidem dicitur magnus, bonus, sapiens, beatus, verus, et quidquid aliud non indigne dici videtur. Sed eadem magnitudo eius est quae sapientia (non enim mole magnus est sed virtute); et eadem bonitas quae sapientia et magnitudo, et eadem veritas quae illa omnia. Et non est ibi aliud beatum esse et aliud magnum aut sapientem aut verum aut bonum esse, aut omnino ipsum esse."

actually the whole reality that God is, three letters and one syllable? Or is this as trifling as what is understood in this is precious?" The crucial lines follow.

> What happened in your heart when you had heard "God"?
> What happened in my heart when I said "God"? A certain
> great and perfect substance was in our thoughts, which transcends every changeable creature of flesh and soul. And if I
> should say to you, "Is God subject to change or is he immutable?" you will immediately answer, "Far be it from me either to believe or to imagine that God is subject to change.
> God is immutable." Your soul, although small, although perhaps still carnal, could only reply to me that God is immutable. But every created being is changeable. How were you
> able, therefore, to have a spark of understanding of that which
> is above every created being so that you, with certainty, reply
> to me that God is immutable? What, then, is in your heart
> when you think of a *certain substance that is living, eternal,*
> *omnipotent, infinite, everywhere present, everywhere whole, no-*
> *where confined?* When you think of these attributes, this is the
> word about God in your heart.

This inner word,[14] Augustine adds, is not the sound of the exterior word "God." No, "what the sound has signified and what is present in the thought of the one who said it and in the understanding of

---

[14] The inner word is that which is the content of an awareness and which is expressed either orally or mentally (in my case) in English. For example, when confronted by this dog, I am aware of what a dog is (in contrast to what a cat is) and I express the content of that awareness by the English word "dog," someone else in Latin by "canis" or in French by "chien." But what all those different external words are expressing is the same: the interior word— namely, what a dog is. It is the intelligibility which a dog puts across to a knower. It is the content of one's awareness thus produced and can be expressed in various languages and which all people, no matter what their language, understand a dog to be and have in common when they know what dogs are. And Augustine is amazed that the Latin word "Deus" (or, in translation, the English word "God") is expressing an inner word whose content is (as he will say) "a great and perfect substance which transcends every mutable creature and which is life, eternity, omnipotence, infinity, omnipresence, completeness, nonconfinement." His amazement is completely understandable.

the one who heard it, *this* remains when the sounds have passed away."[15]

In this rich and complex passage the bishop of Hippo is trying to communicate the awe he experiences in the contrast between the content of the Word as spoken by God the Father and the content of the words we speak. This contrast remains even when we humans try to express the divine reality itself: our exterior word "God" is as transient and trifling as what we thereby are trying to signify (the interior word—see note 14 above) is precious—namely, a great and perfect substance which transcends every creature ("magna et summa quaedam substantia cogitata est, quae transcendat omnem immutabilem creaturam").

Even granting that contrast, a further question arises for Augustine: how can your soul,[16] narrow as it surely is and carnal as it may be, realize that God is not changeable but immutable,[17] since every creature we experience is changeable and, besides, the divine being transcends all creatures? If the origin of that realization is puzzling, how much more so is this: what your and my external word "God" is expressing is the content of our inner awareness—namely, that the great and highest substance which is God is aligned with life, eternity, omnipotence, infinity, omnipresence, completeness, nonconfinement. And that content remains within our hearts when the one-syllable word "God" is no longer sounding.

In that eloquent *tour de force* what does Augustine intend by speaking of the divine substance as "infinite"? That the adjective is predi-

---

[15] *In Joannis Evangelium*, tract. I, c. 1, no. 8 (*Corpus Christianorum*, XXXVI, 5). The Latin for the italicized English words in the indented quotation: "Quid est ergo illud in corde tuo, quando cogitas quamdam substantiam, vivam, perpetuam, omnipotentem, infinitam, ubique praesentem, ubique totam, nusquam inclusam? Quando ista cogitas, hoc est verbum de Deo in corde tuo." The English translation used is by John W. Rettig, *St. Augustine: Tractate on the Gospel of St. John 1–10* (Washington, D.C.: The Catholic University of America Press, 1988), *Fathers of the Church* 78, pp. 48–49, who also furnishes a helpful introduction (pp. 3–33) to Augustine's tractate.

This tractate was written 406–408—see Rettig, pp. 28–31. Thus it precedes *Epistle* 118, analyzed below and dated 410–411.

[16] Augustine was addressing an audience: his tractates on John's Gospel were sermons or homilies given as part of a liturgy—see Rettig, pp. 7–10 and 31–32.

[17] Augustine is speaking from experience: even in his "carnal" days as a Manichean he considered God, albeit corporeal, to be immutable—see *Conf.*, VII, 1, 1.

cated of God's substance through intrinsic denomination—i.e., His subsistent reality is *itself* without limit (as in the interpretation of Gregory of Nyssa and of Thomas Aquinas—see *Divine Infinity*, chapters 21 and 19)? Or is it predicated through extrinsic denomination—i.e., the divine being is so perfect as to be capable of causing infinitely numerous and varied creatures, of being present to them and uncircumscribed by them? In that case infinity would apply directly to creatures and not to God, who would be describable as infinite in view of them. This application appears probable in light of the fact that in Augustine's list of divine attributes infinity is associated with omnipotence, omnipresence and nonconfinement.[18]

Perhaps the last set of sentences to be studied will clarify the situation of what Augustine means. In his *Epistle* 118, which is even more complex than *Tractatus in Johannis Evangelium*, I, 1, 8, just analyzed, he is answering questions proposed by Dioscorus, a young student in Carthage about to travel in Greece and Asia Minor and desiring an initial understanding of Greek philosophers to complement his reading of Cicero, Virgil and other Latin authors.

Sections 23 and 24 of that *Epistle* are most relevant.[19] There Augustine is criticizing Anaximenes' theory that God is air and Anaxagoras' theory that God is mind. In that critique Augustine uses Cicero's *De natura deorum*, I, secs. 26–27 (Loeb edition, pp. 28–30), a review of which will help us understand Augustine better. [1] Anaximenes held, Cicero begins, that air is god, that it began in time and that it is immense and infinite ("aera . . . inmensum et infinitum"). [2] But air is formless ("aer sine ulla forma") and hence cannot be god, who not only possesses a form but the most beautiful form of all ("deum non modo aliqua sed pulcherrima specie deceat esse").

---

[18] Even the predication of the attributes of eternal life and completeness ("substantiam . . . perpetuam . . . ubique totam") may connote an extrinsicism in duration or in total presence to creatures. See *Epistle* 118, #23, p. 686: "deum . . . totum ubique praesentem sicut veritatem"; also last sentence of prgr. corresponding to n. 29 below.

[19] The Latin text is that edited by Al. Goldbacher, *Corpus Scriptorum Ecclesiasticorum Latinorum* [hereafter: *CSEL*] (Vindobonae: F. Tempskey, 1898), XXXIV, ii: *S. Aurelii Augustini Epistulae*. The English translation is by Sr. Wilfred Parsons, *St. Augustine: Letters* (Washington, D.C.: The Catholic University of America Press, 1953), "The Fathers of the Church," XVIII.

Numbers added in brackets to subsequent sentences of Cicero and of Augustine are to facilitate references.

[3] His successor is (Cicero continues) Anaxagoras, who was the first to hold that the orderly disposition of the universe is designed and perfected by the rational power of an infinite mind ("primus omnium rerum discriptionem et modum mentis infinitae vi ac ratione dissignari et confici voluit"). [4] "But in saying this he failed to see that there can be no such thing as sentient and continuous activity in that which is infinite ("non videt neque motum sensui iunctum et continentem in infinito ullum esse posse") and that sensation in general can only occur when the subject itself becomes sentient by the impact of what is sensible" ("neque sensum omnino quo non ipsa natura pulsa sentiret").

[5] Moreover, if he intended his infinite mind to be a definite living being ("si mentem istam quasi animal aliquod voluit"), it must have an inner principle of life to justify the name of "living being." But what would that inner principle be except the mind itself ("quid autem interius mente")? [6] Therefore, mind will be clothed with an outer body ("cingetur igitur corpore externo"). [7] But Anaxagoras will not allow mind to be associated with body, and so it eludes the capacity of our understanding that mind itself, naked and simple and without that material adjunct, should be capable of sensation.

So far Cicero's account. The helpful points it makes are: (a) form—in fact, form which is most beautiful—may be predicated of God (#1–#2); (b) that which designs and produces our well-distributed and orderly universe is the rational power of an infinite mind (#3); (c) but in order to produce and control such a material universe, such a mind would itself need to be sentient (#4) and a definite living being (#5), which (d) because engaging in sensation would need to entail sense-faculties and, thereby, a body also (#6), an entailment which Anaxagoras refuses to allow (#7).

Keeping Cicero in mind will, I hope, aid in clarifying Augustine, who first takes up Cicero's sections 26–27 (outlined above) in a commentary which is as long as Cicero's on Anaximenes and Anaxagoras is short. Let me isolate its salient points, the first of which is an admonition to Dioscorus to humbly seek genuine learning and Christian wisdom: "Our Lord Jesus Christ was humbled in order that He might teach this most beneficial humility, and it is directly opposed . . . to that sort of ignorant knowledge ("imperitissima scientia")—if I may use that expression—which makes us take pleasure in knowing" what various pre-Socratics thought "for the sake of appearing learned and well informed. In reality, that is far removed from true learning and erudition."[20] In fact, [8] whoever has truly learned that God is not extended or diffused through space, whether limited or unlimited, . . . but that He is wholly present everywhere, knows that truth is the same. [9] No one in his sane mind would say that part of truth is in this place and part of it in that, since truth is God.

Next Augustine turns directly to Anaximenes' position [10] Nor would such a sane and humble person be at all impressed by what anyone thinks about the unbounded air, in case anyone thinks that is God (see #1 above). [11] It is of no importance to that person if he does not know what bodily shape they assign to God—and they do indeed assign one which is limited on all sides—or whether it was for the purpose of refuting Anaximenes that Cicero spoke as an Academic in protesting that God must necessarily have form and beauty, thinking in terms of physical appearance, because the former [Anaximenes] said that God was a corporeal being and that His body was the air (#2). [12] Or did he [Cicero] himself think that truth had form and is the incorporeal beauty which gives form to the mind and through which we judge that all the actions of a wise man are beautiful and, in that case, did he say with perfect truth— and not just to refute the other—that God must necessarily have an appearance of absolute beauty, because nothing is more beautiful than intelligible and unchangeable truth?

[13] But when Anaximenes says that the air, which he thinks is God, came into being, he does not convince this person who truly understands, for He is not produced like air—that is, brought into being by any cause—for then He would not be God at all. [14] And it is God by whom the air is created and who cannot be created by any other being. [15] Anaximenes' saying that air in motion is God will not upset someone into thinking such a view is true if he knows that all bodily activity ("motus") is inferior to the activity of the human mind ("animus") and that such human activity ("motus") is far more sluggish than the activity of the supreme and unchangeable wisdom ("motus summae atque incommutabilis sapientiae").

[16] Likewise if Anaxagoras, or anybody else, says that the mind itself is truth and wisdom ("si mentem dicit ipsam veritatem atque sapientiam"), why should I quarrel with him about a word?

---

[20] *Epistle* 118, sec. 23; *CSEL*, p. 686.

[17] For it is evident that "the orderly disposition of the universe comes about through a mind, which can be appropriately called infinite, not in reference to spatial locations but to a power which cannot be understood by human thought."[21] [18] But divine wisdom is not infinite as though it were something formless, which is a characteristic of bodies so that those of them which are infinite are also formless.

"Manifestum est enim omnium rerum descriptionem et modum ab illa [divine wisdom and truth] fieri eamque non incongrue dici infinitam, non per spatia locorum sed per potentiam, quae cogitatione humana comprehendi non potest. Neque quod informe aliquid sit ipsa sapientia; hoc enim corporum est ut, quaecumque infinita fuerint, sint et informia."

[19] But Cicero, using the language of the opponents he was refuting [Anaximenes, Anaxagoras], overzealously asserts that nothing can be added to the infinite if this latter is a body because bodies necessarily have limits (*CSEL*, sec. 24, p. 687, lines 20 sqq.). [20] Yet the intellect or mind cannot be infinite (as Anaxagoras would want) because it also must sentiently know (and thus be a soul) if it is to be the "ordinatrix et moderatrix rerum omnium" (p. 688, line 6). Why? Because the soul,[22] wherever it senses, does so throughout its whole nature (line 8: "totam sentire animam") since any body perceived does not escape the soul's entire attention (line 9: "totam . . . non latet"). But if the whole nature of the soul is engaged in the sensation (line 11: "totam naturam sentire"), it cannot be infinite since any sense of the body it animates starts at a particular spot and then terminates at its own proper origin—characteristics excluded from what is infinite. Then come key lines again (p. 688, lines 16–19):

[21] That which is incorporeal is in another fashion called a whole because it is conceived without limitations from places: it is whole because of its completeness, it is infinite because it is not surrounded by spatial limits. "Aliter dicitur totum quod incorporeum est, quia sine finibus locorum intellegitur, ut et

---

[21] The words within double quotation marks are from Cicero—see #3 above.
[22] Augustine interprets Cicero's reference to the mind as "animal aliquod" (see #5 above) to mean "soul."

totum et infinitum dici possit: totum propter integritatem, infinitum quia locorum finibus non ambitur."

Thus end what seem to be the most relevant sentences from Augustine's answer to Dioscorus in *Epistle* 118 on how he might best approach understanding Greek philosophers. Let me first list attributes other than infinity which Augustine there applies to God, to be followed by reflection upon divine infinity.

God is truth (#9)—in fact, He is intelligible and unchangeable truth and thereby is absolute beauty (#12). He is supreme and immutable wisdom (#15). He is the cause of air (and all else) and is Himself uncaused (#13, #14). He is subsistent form and incorporeal beauty, which inform human minds and beautify our morally good actions (#12).

But God also is infinite, as Augustine indicates in two key places. Building upon the prominence Anaxagoras gave to mind as some sort of cause, which the Latin author translates into mind as subsistent truth and wisdom (#16), he concludes that the mind which designs and produces our well-distributed and orderly universe is infinite, not because it is in space and is contained within places but because its power is so great as to escape human comprehension (#17).

The divine mind is, as Augustine confirms in the second key passage, known to be infinite because it is not surrounded and limited by places because it is incorporeal (#21). But (to revert to the first passage) no one should infer from the fact that divine wisdom is infinite that it is formless (as are infinite bodies; #18)[23]— no, God is subsistent form (#12). Accordingly, He would, as such, be determinate and determinately perfect in and of Himself. Would He also be infinitely perfect as incorporeal, as free of matter, which if present would determine and thereby limit Him? Let us postpone that question momentarily so as to stress that infinity would,

---

[23] See #19 above: actual bodies necessarily have limits or boundaries; hence, if a body is thought of as without boundaries and thus as infinite, it would be as matter without form and thus as formless. This conception had been anticipated by Aristotle, for whom any actually extended line is definite in length and thus is terminated by points, which serve as its limits, whereas that line considered without those limits is indefinite (either by bisection or addition) and without limits. Accordingly, the relation of definiteness to indefiniteness, of limit to limitlessness, of finitude to infinity is that of form to matter, of perfection to imperfection, of presence to lack, of intelligibility to unintelligibility. See *Divine Infinity*, ch. 8: "Aristotle's Infinity of Quantity."

everything else being equal, be predicated of His power through extrinsic denomination—i.e., He is powerful enough to cause the endlessly numerous and varied effects (and thus be incomprehensible) to which infinity is directly and intrinsically applied.[24]

Infinity: Intrinsic or Extrinsic?

Let us repeat Augustine's two sentences given above.

[17] It is evident that "the orderly disposition of the universe comes about through a mind, which can be appropriately called infinite, not in reference to spatial locations but to a power which cannot be understood by human thought." [18] But divine wisdom is not infinite as though it were something formless, which is a characteristic of bodies so that those of them which are infinite are also formless.

"Manifestum est enim omnium rerum descriptionem et modum ab illa [divine wisdom and truth] fieri eamque non incongrue dici infinitam, non per spatia locorum sed per potentiam quae cogitatione humana comprehendi non potest. Neque quod informe aliquid sit ipsa sapientia; hoc enim corporum est ut, quaecumque infinita fuerint, sint et informia."

The first of those sentences joins the incomprehensibility (already applied to God's greatness in his commentary on *Psalm*, 144, 3—see above) more precisely to God's power. But in its second sentence Augustine warns that infinity applied to divine wisdom does not indicate that the latter is formless but rather (by implication) that it is subsistent form and thus would be totally determinate in and of itself. Would, then, God's wisdom be also indeterminate and thus infinite because, as incorporeal, it is free of matter, which if present would determine and thereby limit Him? The answer would be yes if Augustine would be aware that matter determines the form it receives and, thus, God's wisdom as subsistent and incorporeal would be indeterminate because without matter and thereby infinite (here his position would anticipate Aquinas'—see *Divine Infinity*, chapter 19).

Let us test that hypothesis by considering Augustine's conception of matter. In *Confessions*, XII, chapter 3, he begins his reflec-

---

[24] See paragraph corresponding to n. 18 above.

tions on *Genesis*, 1, 1–2: "When God created the heavens and earth, the earth was a formless wasteland, and darkness covered the abyss." There "darkness" is to be identified with "the absence of light and light with form (*Conf.*, XII, 3, 3).[25] [22] Thus, the darkness covering the earth created by God was an "unformed matter," which was not "any sort of thing, or color or shape or body or spirit. And yet it was not absolutely nothing but there was a certain formlessness devoid of form" ("Nonne tu, Domine, docuisti me quod, priusquam istam informem materiam formares atque distingueres, non erat aliquid, non color, non figura, non corpus, non spiritus? Non tamen omnino nihil; erat quaedam informitas sine ulla specie"). [23] It was, in fact, a formless matter, which was divested utterly of every remnant of every form. It was something between form and nothing, neither formed nor nothing, a formless near-nothing (*ibid.*, ch. 6, 6: "Et suadebat vera ratio, ut omnis formae qualescumque reliquias omnino detraherem, si vellem prorsus informe cogitare, et non poteram; citius enim non esse censebam quod omni forma privaretur, quam cogitabam quiddam inter formam et nihil nec formatum nec nihil, informe prope nihil").

[24] Moreover, matter was the mutability of mutable things and a capacity for all the forms into which mutable things are changed. [25] What is it? Neither mind nor body but a "nothing/some-thing," an "is/is-not," which already existed somehow (because God had created it) so that it might receive these visible and composite forms (*ibid.*, 6, 6 *ad finem*: "Mutabilitas enim rerum mutabilium ipsa capax est formarum omnium, in quas mutantur res mutabiles. Et haec quid est? Numquid animus? Numquid corpus? . . . Si dici posset *nihil aliquid* et *est non est*, hoc eam dicerem; et tamen iam utcumque erat ut species caperet istas visibiles et compositas").[26]

In those passages from his exegesis of *Genesis*, 1, 1–2, what does Augustine reveal matter to be? Matter does actually exist (#25) but not as a body, spirit, color, shape or any definite sort of thing (#22): rather it is a near-nothing which of and in itself has no form (#23). It is the mutability which gives all mutable things their ability to change (#24) by its receiving forms (#25). Although neither mind nor body (and thus not a "something"), it is a something-which-is-

---

[25] The bracketed numbers 22 to 25 continue the sequence of such numbers in previous paragraphs.

[26] On matter in Augustine as good but also as "mutabilitas," "nihil aliquid" and "est non est," see Eugene TeSelle, *Augustine the Theologian*, pp. 139–44, with helpful references to E. Gilson, Jules Chaix-Ruy, Jean-Marie Le Blond.

a-nothing and a being-which-is-a-nonbeing (#4). Augustine's understanding of matter in physical things as the actually existing formless recipient of the forms they receive can thus be interpreted as a parallel to matter in Aristotle.[27] But he shows no awareness that matter as the formless factor in mutable things enabling them to receive their forms also determines those forms by limiting them—that is, he shows no realization of the twofold determination (matter determines by limiting the form, form by perfecting the matter) needed for him to be explicitly aware of form without matter as indeterminate and thereby infinite—no more, in fact, than Aristotle himself (see *Divine Infinity,* chapters 8 and 23). Hence, Augustine would not explicitly be a forerunner of Aquinas (see *ibid.,* chapter 19).

But if we return to Augustine's second sentence (#18) quoted at the beginning of this section ("Infinity: Intrinsic or Extrinsic?"), might not one consider divine wisdom as subsistent word to be infinite because it would be unparticipated? That is, it is free of any participant which might limit it. The answer would be affirmative if Augustine would show an awareness that a participant determines the perfection it receives and, thus, divine wisdom as subsistent and unparticipated would be indeterminate and thereby infinite (thus his theory would run parallel to Gregory of Nyssa's—see chapter 9 above; also *Divine Infinity,* chapter 21). Augustine, however, seems not to show an awareness that a participant limits and determines its participated-in perfection (at least in texts so far examined). Moreover, in #18 he makes no mention of participation but simply warns that, although divine wisdom is infinite, it is so not because it is formless.

Might not, however, Augustine's explicit conception in #21 of God as incorporeal and thus infinite because free of the boundaries which affect all bodies signal that He is free from their limitation and determination? Physical place contains and thereby determines an object within it and thus an object which escapes place is not so contained and determined and, in that sense, is indeterminate; but God is such an object—He is not contained by place; consequently, He thereby is indeterminate and infinite. What can be said to such an argument?

The relationship of container/contained apparently need not illumine the intrinsic nature itself of what is contained. Let me

[27] See my *Authentic Metaphysics in an Age of Unreality,* 2d ed. (New York/ Bern: Peter Lang Publishing, Inc., 1993), ch. 3: "Lessons from Aristotle."

explain. The relationship of container/contained differs from that of matter/form (or, more generally, potency/act) and of participant/participated perfection. These last are intrinsic constituents of existents and, thus, when potency or participant is absent, the existent free of them is infinite act or is perfection by nature and not by participation and thus is infinite. The situation is dissimilar between container and contained. For example, the pail containing milk is not a part of the milk, it does not make milk be milk. Hence, whether the container be a bucket or a glass or a bowl—in fact, whether there is any container at all—the milk remains milk. Likewise, God is not contained by place and thus the divine being is termed infinite because He transcends place. This infinitude of transcendence, this absence of containment, however, does not intrinsically depict the divine being as such (whether God's essence is infinite or not must be decided elsewhere and otherwise).[28] It simply describes God's independence of space and thus of this physical world, in which nonetheless He is present, not physically but as working in it and in what it contains: He produces and creates them so that not only do they actually exist but also (and especially) that they are real by becoming to some extent immutable through His illumining them with truth and goodness.[29]

However acceptable the previous reflections may or may not be, at least this is true: much research and reflection remain to be done on Augustine's theory of infinity.[30] Moreover, no one need be surprised if he did not list infinity among the divine attributes in his early treatise, *De Doctrina Christiana*, Book I, chs. 5–32. Put quite simply: he was not yet certain as to what divine infinity might

---

[28] See my *Divine Infinity*, p. xvii, n. 9; also *ibid.*, ch. 17: "Lombard, Augustine and Infinity," prgrs. corresponding to notes 48–52, which touch on many of the same texts studied here at greater length.

[29] See *Enarratio in Psalm.*, 144, 3, 3, quoted in n. 13 above: "ad opera respiciamus et de operibus laudemus operantem, de conditis conditorem, de creaturis creatorem"; *Epistle* 118, 23 (see #8 above): "deum . . . totum ubique esse praesentem veritatem." Perhaps it is better to say not that God is present in creatures but that they are present in Him: creatures are finite because they are in God, not as in a physical place but as in Him who is conserving their being and truth—"in te cuncta finita sunt . . . non quasi in loco sed quia tu es omnitenens manu veritate, et cuncta vera sunt inquantum sunt" (*Conf.*, VII, 15, 21).

[30] For texts on "infinity" and "participation" see *Augustine Concordance* residing in the VAX computer at Villanova University and efficiently administered by Allan Fitzgerald, O.S.A., to whom I express thanks.

mean in the light of his discovery, set forth in *Confessions*, Book VII, of God as completely incorporeal and thus as "infinite in a way different" from how Augustine as a Manichean conceived Him to be an infinite body endlessly extended throughout space.[31]

---

[31] On *De Doctrina Christiana* and *Confessions* read as "literary pragmatics" and biblical conferences, see Mark Vessey, "Conference and Confession: Literary Pragmatics in Augustine's 'Apologia contra Hieronymum,'" *Journal of Early Christian Studies* 1 (1993), 175–213.

11

Boethius on the "Individual": Platonist or Aristotelian?

From chapters 5 and 6 above we learn the answers to several questions concerning individuality. First of all, what "individual" expresses is that someone (whether prominent or not) personally matters, is different from all others and is, literally, irreplaceable.[1] But how did that appealing notion arise? What is its source in the history of ideas? Certainly one major origin is the Judeo-Christian Scriptures, which emphasize that God knows and loves each human person.[2] Another ultimate source of contemporary individualism is the stress put on "person" and "supposit" *vs.* "essence" and "nature" in early ecumenical councils and creeds of the Church.[3]

Plato, Plotinus

But still another inquiry may be raised: how early in the history of thought did the conception of "individual" described above as "someone (whether prominent of not) [who] personally matters, is different from all others and is, literally, irreplaceable" arise? That conception is not to be found, apparently, in Plato (428–347 B.C.) or

---

[1] See ch. 5 above, "The 'Individual' in Plato, Plotinus and Aristotle," prgrs. corresponding to notes 1–4. For secondary literature on "individual," see *ibid.*, n. 1.

[2] See *ibid.*, prgrs. corresponding to notes 5–9.

[3] See *ibid.*, n. 9.

Plotinus (A.D. 205–270) but is so (to an extent) in Aristotle (384–321 B.C.), if our remarks in chapter 5 ("The 'Individual' in Plato, Plotinus and Aristotle") on those three Greek philosophers are accurate.

As we concluded in chapter 5,[4] what each beautiful thing has in common through participation in the Form of Beauty with that Form and, what is especially relevant, *with other participants* is the participated perfection of beauty. But what distinguishes one participant from other participants (and, of course, from the Form itself), that which is uniquely its own, that which makes it other than them is its "individuality." And what does that consist in? It is aligned with unreality because the reality of this individual participant is whatever participated perfection it has in common with other participants transiently and, so to speak, on loan. But a participant's individuality is linked with negation: beauty (for example) in participant #a *is not* the beauty in participants #b and #c. It is other than their beauties. But that otherness is not something positive but simply the observable fact that somehow and for some inexplicable reason beauty in #a *is not* beauty in #b or in #c. [5]

Accordingly, the outcome of Plato's metaphysics is that individuality *as such* is not a perfection: in and of itself it is merely negation, unreality, nonbeing. An individual existent *qua* individual is unreal, worthless, insignificant. Consistently, then, Plato's position cannot have been a precursor of our current dedication to the "infinite reality" (Kierkegaard) of each individual. Even if he had never written the *Republic,* with its subordination of all ranks of citizens to philosopher-kings, themselves subordinate to the Form of the Good, his metaphysics would locate whatever reality individual human souls have in the perfections they have in common and not in their individuality.

---

[4] See *ibid.,* prgrs. corresponding to notes 37–40.

[5] Apparently what corresponds in the realm of the Forms to this negation ("beauty in #a *is not* beauty in #b or in #c") is the Form of Otherness and Nonbeing in *Sophist,* 255C–E and 256D–258C, a Form which accounts for the fact that the Form of Rest is *other than* and, thus, *is not* the Form of Motion by their participating in Otherness and Nonbeing. More relevantly: the Form of Otherness and Nonbeing accounts for the fact that the Form of Justice is other than and is not the Form of Courage by their participating in Otherness and Nonbeing. So too Plato's justice is other than Socrates' by their participating in the Form of Otherness or Nonbeing. But their being other than one another constitutes their individuality. Hence, the Form of Otherness and Nonbeing in the *Sophist* can be called the Form of Individuality, by participating in which individual existents are individual, even though their individuality as such is negation, unreality, absence.

This is the metaphysics which helped produce the downgrading of individuality which we meet in Plotinus' *Enneads* VI, 5 (23) 16 sqq., and which rests upon the equation of reality with unity. Unity is found primally and fully in Plotinus' highest hypostasis (the One-Good, who is God and who is sheer and subsistent unity) and derivatively in all other existents—the Intellect (and the intellects it contains) and the Soul (and its contents: the World Soul, astral souls, human souls, subhuman souls). The Intellect and intellects come about by the One overflowing and by that overflow (which is intelligible matter and power) turning back to contemplate its source; the Soul and souls come about when the Intellect in turn overflows and the resultant overflow looks back at the Intellect and the One and fashions itself. In all those existents other than the One, reality is unity and nothing else: each is real to the extent that *it is the One on a lower level.*[6]

But each existent is individual to the degree that it is *other than* the One and, thus, each is thereby unreal. Take as an example an individual human soul: when embodied it is distinct and separate from other human souls and intellects, from the Soul and the Intellect and, of course, from the One. Even when it puts off matter and ascends to the higher realms of reality, it is not separate from the Soul, Intellect and One, but it is at least distinguishable from (and thus other than) them and, hence, remains individual. It puts off even this individuality by becoming one with the One and, thus, is truly real but only when no longer what it was as a distinct existent.

Aristotle

But what of Aristotle (384–321 B.C.)? On the "individual" has Plato influenced him as he did Plotinus?

However alike Plato and Aristotle may be in other areas,[7] their positions on the individual diverge rather radically. Consider the

---

[6] On reality as identified with unity, which is primally found in God as the One-Good, who is the source of all other existents, see VI, 9 (9), 9, 1–8; III, 8 (30), 10, 14–31; V, 2 (11), 1, 10–21. For translation and commentary on those texts see ch. 16 below, "Are Plotinus and Albertus Magnus Neoplatonists?" prgrs. corresponding to notes 14–35; on monism as the essence of Plotinus' metaphysics, see *ibid.*, prgrs. corresponding to notes 36–43.

[7] One position they have in common is that knowledge in one of its aspects is a *pathêma* inasmuch as the object known is its content-determining-cause. See ch. 5 above, Appendix C: "Plato and Aristotle on Knowledge."

interpretation each would give to (say) two beautiful blooming cherry trees. Both philosophers agree that tree #a is other than tree #b, that #a is not #b: they are two individual trees. But, as we have suggested earlier, that otherness and, hence, individuality is, for Plato, simply a negation and unreal, because the reality of the two trees resides in what they have in common (the immanent perfections of beauty, treeness, color, etc.) through participating in the subsistent Forms of Beauty, Treeness, Color and the rest. Those immanent participated perfections are not received, literally and permanently, by and in their participants and are not entitatively affected by them: in brief, those perfections are not individuated (in any positive sense) by the participants.

The situation is quite different in an Aristotelian approach. The otherness, distinction, uniqueness—in a word, individuality—of the two trees is a positive factor in them. Why so? Because it arises when the forms (accidental and substantial) that help constitute them are educed by efficient causes from the potency of the substance and of prime matter, which also are real constituents of the trees and which entitatively affect the forms (perfections, acts) thus brought forth and continuing on within them for at least some duration. Those forms do not subsist apart from actual cherry trees, but they actually are and are what they are only as present and concretized in those trees. In a word, those forms (both accidental and substantial) are *real* only when and *as individuated* by the substance or matter within which they are present.

But are not those forms the perfections which the two trees have in common? Yes, but they have that commonness only *as known:* only as the content of our awareness of them and, hence, only as specifically alike; only, therefore, as universals (both direct and reflexive). In the actual trees such forms are not common but individual: their being is itself permeated by the distinctiveness, uniqueness, individuality issuing from the components from which they have been educed, which are limiting and thereby determining them and which are formally perfected and thereby determined in turn.

For Aristotle, then, individuality of forms and of the existents they help constitute is the positive entitative state of uniqueness and differentiation in which all material things find themselves.[8]

---

[8] See ch. 5, prgrs. corresponding to notes 41–46. For a detailed presentation of how prime matter and substantial form cooperate as intrinsic causes in individualizing material existents, see *ibid.*, prgrs. corresponding to notes 53–56; *ibid.*, Appendix C.

Boethius

After sketching what "individuality" means to Plato, Plotinus and Aristotle, we now can profitably study Boethius' attitude on the topic.

Living more than seven centuries after Plato and Aristotle and even a full two and a half centuries after Plotinus, how does Anicius Manlius Severinus Boethius (ca. 480–525) view the "individual"?[9] Apparently he holds individuality in high esteem—at least he uses the term in his very definition of "person" as "naturae rationabilis *individua* substantia" (*Contra Eutychen et Nestorium,* Sec. 3, 4–5). This definition he applies not only to humans but to angels and even to God[10] and hence "individua" therein would seem to imply perfection.

Let us set that definition within the context provided by the theological tractate itself. As its title indicates, the tractate aims at answering criticisms against the position put forth in the Council of Chalcedon in 451 that Christ consists of two natures (divine and human) and one person.[11] In contrast, Nestorius saw in Christ two

---

[9] For a general introduction to the thought of Boethius see E. Gilson, *History of Christian Philosophy in the Middle Ages* (New York: Random House, 1955), pp. 97–106 plus notes 82–92 (pp. 603–5); Hans von Campenhausen, *Men Who Shaped the Western Church* (New York: Harper and Row, 1960), ch. 7: "Boethius" (pp. 277–313); Edmund Reiss, *Boethius* (Boston: Twayne Publishers, 1982); Margaret Gibson (ed.), *Boethius: His Life, Thought and Influence* (Oxford: Blackwell, 1981). On specific topics see Michael Masi, *Boethian Number Theory* (Amsterdam: Editions Rodopi, 1983); Seth Lerer, *Boethius and Dialogue* (Princeton University Press 1985); John Magee, *Boethius on Signification and Mind* (Leiden: E. J. Brill, 1989); Ralph McInerny, *Boethius and Aquinas* (Washington, D.C.: Catholic University Press, 1990)—for a challenge to McInerny's interpretation see my "Aquinas and Gilson" (forthcoming): for Aristotle "existence" expresses a fact but not an actuation; for Aquinas existence is a fact, evidence and actuation.

[10] See *ibid.,* Sec. 2, 25–28 and 36–37, quoted below in prgr. corresponding to n. 12. In our references to Boethius' tractate the final numbers indicate the relevant lines of the section as found in the Loeb edition first put out by E. K. Rand and H. F. Stewart and revised by S. J. Tester in 1973. In my translations or paraphrases brackets will indicate the interpolations needed to explicate the movement of Boethius' thought so as to clarify his meaning.

[11] See Henry Chadwick, *The Consolations of Music, Logic, Theology and Philosophy* [hereafter: Chadwick] (Oxford: Clarendon Press, 1981), p. 190: Boethius' "prime objective is to reconcile the critics of Chalcedon by assuring the hesitant that Chalcedon's 'two natures' is both necessary to avert Eutychianism

natures and two persons, Eutyches one nature and one person.[12] In
his reply Boethius elaborates what "natura," "substantia" and other
key Latin terms in the definition mean. "Natura" means "the specific difference which informs anything": "natura est unamquamque
rem informans specifica differentia" (*ibid.*, Sec. 1, 57–58).[13] Both
Catholics and Nestorius agree (Boethius adds) on "nature" so defined: in Christ there are two such natures because the specific
difference which makes Him be God cannot be the same as that
which makes Him be human (*ibid.*, 59 sqq.: "Tam Catholici quam
Nestorius secundum ultimam definitionem duas in Christo naturas
esse constituent; neque enim easdem in deum atque hominem
differentias convenire").

[But in the face of this agreement why do Catholics not also
agree with Nestorius that He is two persons? Because of the meaning they give to "persona"], a topic which is (Boethius concedes) a
"matter of very great perplexity" (*ibid.*, Sec. 2, 1–2: "Sed de persona
maxime dubitari potest quaenam ei definitio possit aptari"). Nonetheless, these points are clear: "Natura" is a substrate of "persona"
and thus is always involved whenever "persona" is predicated
(*ibid.*, 9–12: "Nam illud quidem manifestum est personae subjectam
esse naturam nec praeter naturam personam posse praedicari").
But unlike "natura," which is applicable to substances and to accidents (e.g., whiteness, blackness, largeness), "persona" is said only

---

and is altogether distinct from Nestorianism." Chadwick's discussion of *Contra
Eutychen et Nestorium* (pp. 180–202) is helpful and informative, as is his bibliography, pp. 261–84.

[12] This simplified statement is drawn from Boethius' own tractate, corrobo-
rated however by Chadwick, who sees it as filling the then current need of a
"middle way between Nestorius and Eutyches" (p. 182).

[13] Boethius illustrates "nature" here with gold and silver: it is that form
which specifically and properly differentiates the two metals (*ibid.*, 54–56).
This definition of "natura," based on Aristotle's *Physics*, 193a28–31 (see
Chadwick, p. 191), is contrasted with several other meanings, the first of
which appears in Syrianus, Ammonius and other Neoplatonists and is applicable to anything that exists: "Nature is a term for those things which, insofar
as they exist, can in some way be apprehended by the intellect (*ibid.*, 8–10):
"Natura est earum rerum quae, cum sint, quoquo modo intellectu capi
possunt"). In another sense, based on Plato's *Phaedrus*, 270d and *Sophist*, 247e,
nature is "that which can act or can be acted upon" (*ibid.*, 25–26: "Natura est
vel quod facere vel quod pati possit"). In still a third sense, based on Aristotle's
Physics, 192b20, nature is "the principle of movement *per se* and not acciden-
tally" (*ibid.*, 41–42: "Natura est motus principium per se et non per accidens").

of substances (*ibid.*, 17–18: "Relinquitur ergo ut personam in substantiis dici conveniat").

But one can take substances in a twofold manner—either as they are found in actual existents [this let us call Schema One] or according to our way of predicating them [Schema Two]. According to Schema One actually existing substances are twofold insofar as they are either corporeal or incorporeal.[14] Corporeal substances are either living or nonliving (e.g., a stone); living substances are either rational [a human as a composite of soul and body] or irrational (e.g., a horse or an ox).[15] Let us now return to the second component of Schema One and subdivide it. Some incorporeal substances are rational, others not so (e.g., the life-giving principles in subhuman animals; *ibid.*, 23–24: "[substantiae incorporeae irrationales] ut pecudum vitae"). Rational substances are either by nature immutable and impassible (e.g., God) or, because of their status as creatures, mutable and passible except through grace (e.g., angels and human souls):

> Sed substantiarum aliae sunt corporeae, aliae incorporeae. Corporearum vero aliae sunt viventes, aliae minime; viventium aliae sunt sensibiles, aliae minime; sensibilium aliae rationales, aliae irrationales. Item incorporearum aliae sunt rationales, aliae minime, ut pecudum vitae; rationalium vero alia est inmutabilis atque inpassibilis per naturam ut deus, alia per creationem mutabilis atque passibilis, nisi inpassibilis gratia substantiae ad inpassibilitatis firmitudinem permutetur ut angelorum atque animae (*ibid.*, 18–28).

These last alone (God, angels and human souls) are "personae" (*ibid.*, 36–37: "At hominis dicimus esse personam, dicimus dei, dicimus angeli").

But what if we understand "substance" precisely as a predicable (Schema Two)? Then substances are either universal or particular.

---

[14] The methodology which initiates and constitutes Schema One, as it will Schema Two also, Chadwick relates to "the so-called Porphyrian tree" (p. 192). It also could easily be reduced back to the dialectics of division/collection Plato introduced in *Phaedrus*, 265e sqq., and utilized not only in that dialogue but also in *Sophist, Statesman* and *Philebus*.

[15] Boethius gives no example of a rational corporeal substance, but one may infer it to be a composite of human soul and body from his instancing a human soul itself as a rational incorporeal substance.

Universal substances are such as can be predicated of many individuals and thus are genera and species. For instance, the genus
"animal" can be said of several individual [sorts of] animals (e.g.,
horses, oxen, snakes), "stone" of individual [sorts of] stones (e.g.,
pieces of granite, diamonds, limestones), "wood" of individual
[sorts of] sticks of wood (e.g., oak, maple, walnut), the species
"man" of individual humans:

> Rursus substantiarum aliae sunt universales, aliae particulares.
> Universales sunt quae de singulis praedicantur ut homo, ani-
> mal, lapis, lignum ceteraque huiusmodi quae vel genera vel
> species sunt; nam et homo de singulis hominibus et animal de
> singulis animalibus lapisque ac lignum de singulis lapidibus
> ac lignis dicuntur (*ibid.*, 37–44).

On the other hand, particular substances are such as not to be
predicable of things other [than what each is but only of itself]—
e.g., "Cicero" is said only of this Roman citizen, "this rock" only of
this marble statue of Achilles, "this wood" solely of this oaken
table.

Accordingly (Boethius now draws his first conclusion), "persona" can never be said of "substance" taken universally (e.g.,
genus, species) but solely of particulars and individuals (e.g., Cicero,
Plato and any other single rational existent):

> Particularia vero sunt quae de aliis minime praedicantur ut
> Cicero, Plato, lapis hic unde haec Achillis statua facta est,
> lignum hoc unde haec mensa composita est. Sed in his omni-
> bus nusquam in universalibus persona dici potest, sed in
> singularibus tantum atque in individuis; animalis enim vel
> generalis hominis nulla persona est, sed vel Ciceronis vel
> Platonis vel singulorum individuorum personae singulae
> nuncupantur (*ibid.*, 44–52).

Second, "persona" is definable as "naturae rationabilis individua
substantia" because "persona" belongs to rational substances solely
and because "substantia" here entails a nature that is individual:[16]

---

[16] In the rest of Sec. 3 Boethius discusses the Greek terms *prosôpon, ousia,
hypostasis* and *ousiôsis* and their Latin equivalents. In Sec. 4, 6–9, he reaffirms
his definitions in Sec. 3, 4–5 of "natura" and "persona." According to Chadwick
a comparison of *Contra Eutychen et Nestorium* "with Boethius' other writings

Quocirca si persona in solis substantiis est atque in his rationabilibus substantiaque omnis natura est nec in universalibus sed in individuis constat, reperta personae est definitio: "naturae rationabilis individua substantia" (*ibid.*, Sec. 3, 1–5).

But what does "individua" in the definition indicate? That the nature or substance so described is such as to be in a single and unique existent (see *ibid.*, Sec. 2, 44 sqq.), which moreover is either divine or angelic or human (*ibid.*, 24–28). This last fact—namely, that "individua" applies not only to humans but to angels and God as well—guarantees that for Beothius individuality is a perfective and positive factor of such existents and that he thereby differs from Plotinus (see above). Hence, in this area he is not Platonic but Aristotelian.

Conclusions

In our exegesis of Boethius' definition of "persona" as "naturae rationabilis individua substantia," we inferred that individuality there is a perfection and expresses a positive state of reality within the divine, angelic and human existents of which it is predicated. Second, the Latin author's position is thereby akin to Aristotle's rather than to Plato's.

This kinship becomes even clearer if one turns to Section 6 of *Contra Eutychen et Nestorium*, where Boethius deals with Eutyches' contention that even if Christ's body was taken from Mary, the human and divine natures did not last (and, thus, Christ consists of one nature and is one person; *ibid.*, Sec. 6, 3–8) because His humanity was transformed into divinity.[17] But (Boethius replies) such a

---

shows that his treatment of 'person' varies according to the degree to which Aristotelian language about primary or individual substance is enfolded within a Platonic metaphysic of universals" (p. 194). On Maxentius of Constantinople, theological leader of a group of monks known as "Scythian" and influential at Rome also in the early sixth century, see Chadwick, pp. 186–88: Maxentius' definition of "persona" is "una res individuae naturae," the last word signifying the substrate of person. For reactions to Boethius' definition of "persona" beginning with his own century and extending up to Aquinas see Chadwick, p. 195.

[17] This reason is the second of three, the first of which is that the divinity is changed into humanity, the third that divinity and humanity are both so

transformation is impossible because Christ's human substance consists of a human soul and body and thus is corporeal; but no corporeal substance can be changed into an incorporeal one or *vice versa*, because change or transformation can occur only if the two substances share a common subject that is matter (*ibid.*, 24–26: "Sola enim mutari transformarique in se possunt quae habent unius materiae commune subjectum").[18] Obviously, what is human and what is divine have nothing entitative directly in common and thus cannot be transformed into one another (*ibid.*, 66–77).

What interests us is not the validity of Boethius' reply to Eutyches but his positing matter as a necessary principle of change and, by implication, as also involved in individuating the human soul. Giving matter that function is what Aristotle explicitly does. As we have stated above, individuality arises when forms (substantial or, for that matter, accidental) that constitute physical existents are educed by efficient causes from the potency of prime matter and of substance, which as real components of such existents entitatively affect the forms thus brought forth. The latter are what they are solely as present and concretized in those existents. In brief, those forms are real only when and as individuated by the matter or substance within which they are present. Thus, the individuality of forms and of the existents they help constitute is a positive entitative state of uniqueness, differentiation and perfection, in which all physical things find themselves by reason of matter and substance.

Such is Aristotle's position on individuality. Such also is perhaps implied in Boethius' description of "persona" as "naturae rationabilis individua substantia" when joined with his characterizing matter as the subject which renders possible the change of one physical thing into another.[19] I make this suggestion even

---

modified that neither retains its proper reality. But only the second reason is directly relevant for our purposes.

[18] Boethius adds a second requirement for such transformation: the two substances must also have the ability to act upon and be acted upon by each other. Examples of substances which do not have this reciprocal ability are bronze and grass, whereas wine and water do. Hence, even if two things have a common matter, they still need this additional characteristic in order to be transformed (*ibid.*, 26–65). The second requirement is not immediately relevant and hence I give it no special attention.

[19] According to J. Gracia, "Boethius and the Problem of Individuality" (see ch. 5, n. 1), the Latin author speaks of "individual" "in his two editions of the

though James Shiel has rather convincingly shown that Boethius
had no other Aristotelian Greek text than the *Organon* and this in a
single codex, which however did contain marginal quotations from
Aristotle's other treatises.[20] If my reading of Boethius on individuality as a positive perfection in an existent is accurate, Aristotle's
Physics, 190a13 and 226a10, and *De Generatione et Corruptione*, 329a24,
must have been among the passages quoted.[21]

Commentary of Porphyry's 'Isagoge,' the two editions of the *Commentary on
Aristotle's 'De Interpretatione'* and the theological tractate commonly known as
De Trinitate. . . . None of these five works contains a systematic treatment of
individuality. . . . The comments pertinent to our discussion are scattered
throughout the texts and contain little to suggest that Boethius had a clear and
comprehensive view of individuality." But see Gracia's summary, pp. 180–82.
Unfortunately, he does not attend to *Contra Eutychen et Nestorium*. Likewise
Gracia appears to pay little attention to that tractate in his *Introduction to the
Problem of Individuation in the Early Middle Ages* (Washington, D.C.: The Catholic University of America Press, 1984)—references seem to occur only on p. 55,
n. 7; p. 155 (this as well as the next two references are to Gilbert of Poitiers'
commentary on the tractate); p. 184, n. 80, and p. 189, n. 114; p. 257. Although
Gracia's book deserves more study, it seems clear that his beginning it by
discussing twentieth-century approaches to the problem of individuation so
as to secure a framework for early medieval authors (see ch. 1, pp. 17–63) is
questionable methodology, which he follows also in the two articles cited also
in *ibid.*, n. 1, prgr. 2. Nonetheless, his chapter on Boethius (pp. 65–121) is
significant—see especially pp. 109–10 on the contrast between metaphysical
and logical approaches to individuality; also see p. 259: Plato "downgraded
individuality to the realm of the unreal and, concerned as he was with the
realm of the real, paid little attention to it. And even Aristotle, whom one
would have expected to have paid more attention to it, was so concerned to
attack his former teacher's views that he seems often to have forgotten about
this fundamental feature of the world. There are only a handful of passages in
his works in which individuality is discussed, and then only incidentally and
briefly."

[20] "Boethius' Commentaries on Aristotle," *Medieval and Renaissance Studies*
4 (1958), 217–44. Also see J. Shiel, "A Recent Discovery: Boethius' Notes on the
Prior Analytics," *Vivarium* 20 (1982), 128–41. For a list of his other articles, see
Chadwick, p. 280.

[21] See Chadwick, p. 199: "Change is possible only to entities that share a
common substrate of the same matter, a proposition Boethius has learnt from
Aristotle's treatise 'On coming to be and passing away' (226a10) [*read*: 329a24].
. . . Boethius' argument . . . presupposes that in matter lies the root of all
mutation, an opinion which Augustine once records as maintained by 'some'
(*City of God*, VIII, 5). Among late Neoplatonists it is the general view, as, for
example, in Simplicius' commentary on Epictetus."

Finally, Boethius is both philosopher and theologian. His philosophical interests and talents are disclosed by *De Consolatione philosophae*, which E. Reiss claims

> is not only Boethius's masterpiece but one of the most significant books ever written. In its Latin original and its several translations into virtually every European language, it represented a best seller in the Western world for more than a thousand years. Along with providing the definitive word for the next millenium on such perplexing matters as the role of fortune in this world and man's free will in relation to God's foreknowledge, it also affected subsequent literature so much that its influence is virtually impossible to measure.[22]

His talent and interest in philosophy are also indicated by his translation of and commentaries on Aristotle's *Categories, De Interpretatione, Prior* and *Posterior Analytics, Sophistical Arguments,* and Porphyry's *Isagoge,* as well as by original treatises on topics in logic and mathematics.[23]

His expertise in theological issues is clear from what have come to be called his four "theological tractates"—"Quomodo trinitas unus Deus ac non tres Dii," "Quomodo substantiae in eo quod sint bonae sint cum non sint substantialia bona," "De fide christiana," and the tractate studied above on Christ as divine/human: "Liber contra Eutychen et Nestorium."[24]

Since his philosophy arises from his knowledge of Greek authors (e.g., Plato, Aristotle, Stoics, Plotinus, Porphyry) and since his Christian theology will strongly influence the medieval authors of the West, Maurice de Wulf rightly called him "the principal chan-

---

[22] *Boethius*, (Boston: Twayne Publishers, 1982), Preface, p. x. E. K. Rand, *Founders of the Middle Ages* (Cambridge: Harvard University Press, 1928), pp. 135–36, also praises Boethius: "[He] was the most thoroughgoing philosopher, and, with the exception of St. Augustine, the most original philosopher that Rome had ever produced. . . . Boethius' *Consolation of Philosophy* was one of the hundred best books—one of those books no educated man left unread. That was still the case in the eighteenth century and had been so since the Middle Ages, in which period his influence was sovereign."

[23] One finds a convenient list of translations and commentaries in F. Copleston, *A History of Philosophy* (London: Burns Oates and Washbourne, 1951), I, 485; Maurice de Wulf, *Histoire de la Philosophie Médiévale* (Paris: J. Vrin, 1934), pp. 112–13.

[24] On the Latin text see n. 10 above.

nel by which Aristotelianism was transmitted to the West: he established doctrines, he initiated how translation and commentary were to be made."[25] He was indeed the "last of the Romans, the first of the scholastics," as the humanist Lorenzo Valla in the fifteenth century described him.[26] Obviously, then, Boethius serves as a good transition to our Part Three on "Medieval Scholasticism" immediately following, the first chapter of which presents an overall view of scholasticism.

---

[25] M. de Wulf, *Histoire*, p. 114: "Jusqu'à la fin du XIIe siècle, il est le principal canal par lequel l'aristotélisme se déverse en Occident: il fixe des doctrines, il inaugure des méthodes de traduction et de commentaire."

[26] For the quotation see Chadwick, p. xi. On Valla (1407–1457) see F. Copleston, *History*, III, 217 and 436.

III

Medieval Scholastics

12

Scholasticism

Scholasticism is a term describing the intellectual climate in which Catholic teachers and writers have worked since the Middle Ages. The term is etymologically derived from *schola*, the Latin word meaning "school." In early Christian educational centers the *scholasticus* was the master in charge of such schools as the Church then had and, accordingly, scholasticism came in time to refer to factors within the intellectual life of (mainly) the Roman Catholic Church over several centuries. These centuries fall into five periods of differing length.

The Five Periods of Scholasticism

What is found in the first of these periods is not so much scholasticism in a strict sense as its preparation. This period begins roughly in the ninth century with John Scotus Erigena (ca. 810–878) and terminates at the close of the twelfth, having included such prominent authors as St. Anselm of Canterbury (1033–1109), Gilbert of La Porrée (1076–1154) and others connected with the school of Chartres, Hugh of St. Victor (1096–1141) and others at the abbey school of St. Victor, Peter Abelard (1079–1142), St. Bernard of Clairvaux (1091–1153), Peter Lombard (ca. 1100–1160) and others. What marks this initial time is a growing intellectual ferment and interest within all social classes, a sudden mushrooming in the number of students, and a consequent growth of cathedral and abbey schools until the groundwork for the universities of the thirteenth century began to be laid.

The second period is coterminous with the thirteenth century and can be called the golden age of scholasticism for reasons to be discussed later. In this era there appeared, among others, such intellectual giants as St. Albertus Magnus (1206–1280), St. Bonaventure (1221–1274) and St. Thomas Aquinas (1225–1274). The third is a time of decadence in the quality of intellectual activity and runs from ca. 1300 to the Renaissance. The latter initiates the fourth period, which produced such important thinkers as Jacopo Cajetan (1468–1534), Francis Silvester of Ferrara (d. 1526), Francisco de Vitoria (d. 1546), Domingo Báñez (d. 1604), Luis Molina (d. 1600), St. Robert Bellarmine (1542–1621), Francisco de Suárez (1548–1617) and others. Eventually, though, the influence of René Descartes (1596–1650) and of succeeding modern philosophers greatly reduced the number and importance of scholastic authors until the resurgence of interest in scholasticism that appeared in the latter half of the nineteenth century and that continues up to the present day. This final period, commonly called neo-scholasticism, received an important impetus from the encyclical "Aeterni Patris" of Pope Leo XIII in 1879, which asked for a return to the authentic doctrine of medieval scholastics (especially that of Thomas Aquinas), and from more recent papal documents.

The Diversity of Scholasticism

But the question still remains: What is scholasticism itself? That question is hard to answer for the very reason that the term is applied to so many authors over such a span of years. Moreover, these authors greatly differ in doctrine. Although they all agree on points of faith that are clearly contained in divine revelation and that have been formally defined by the Roman Catholic Church, within that area each scholastic develops and, so to speak, understands those truths in the light of his own philosophic background and by his own efforts of reflection. Outside that area of faith one finds deep and almost constant diversity of positions, approaches, etc. For example, in the thirteenth century many of Aquinas' positions differed radically from those of his teacher, Albertus Magnus, as well as from Bonaventure's. In the following century the group which called themselves Thomists disagreed with the followers both of Duns Scotus (ca. 1275–1308) and of William of Ockham (ca. 1285–1349), each of whom was in frequent conflict with the other. Even in the twentieth century, one finds a similar diversity of attitudes. Besides Scotists, Ockhamists and Suarezians, there are Thomists who are essentialists, Thomists who are "transcendental" and Thomists who are "authentic" existentialists (in opposition to the "radical" brand of existentialism espoused by Jean-Paul Sartre and others).

In every period, then, individual scholastics have held rather widely divergent positions on many questions. Accordingly, scholasticism does not point so much to common doctrines (except, as previously mentioned, in matters of strict faith) as to a common intellectual milieu in which the scholastics have worked.

Scholasticism's Golden Age

In what does that milieu consist? Perhaps that question can best be answered if we turn to the thirteenth century, the golden age of scholasticism. In that era the intellectual milieu was generally marked by the primacy given to faith and, second, by a definite methodology in classroom procedure.

The Primacy of Faith

How this primacy of faith arose is easily understood if we recall that the medieval university grew directly out of cathedral and abbey schools, which were staffed and conducted by the Church. Not so readily apparent, though, is what such a primacy involved in practice and what its results were. First of all, medicine and law (both canon and civil) were faculties of a medieval university and thus were under ecclesiastical supervision in their own way. Second and much more important, the faculty of arts (philosophy) came under similar supervision. At times this consisted in condemnations by local bishops (acting with the advice and often at the instigation of the faculty of theology) of philosophical conclusions which were in opposition to truths of faith. An example is the condemnation in 1270 of thirteen propositions, among which were the following: "That the will of man wills or chooses from necessity. . . . That the world is eternal. . . . That the soul is corrupted when the body is corrupted. . . . That God does not know things in particular. . . . That human actions are not ruled by divine Providence." Such directives were a benefit to scholastic philosophy in pointing out that philosophers must reinvestigate thought-processes they had previously considered accurate.

Much more helpful, though, was the use theologians made of philosophy within their own science. Their task centered around divinely revealed truths, which must not only be defended against heretical interpretations but must also be explained, developed and, in their own way, understood. A tool the theologians frequently relied upon to accomplish that development and understanding was the work of previous thinkers, including philosophers. And that reliance resulted not only in their deeper awareness of individual theological dogmas but also in the development of various philosophical notions. For example, because theologians had worked out what "person" and "nature" mean with reference to the Trinity and to Christ, we can derive from their writings a philosophy of person and of nature which is more profound than anything found in philosophers who were not also trained as theologians. Again, because they investigated what "being" signifies when predicated of God and of creatures, we find implied in their treatises various metaphysics of being which utilize but far surpass the previous philosophical treatises.[1] It is within the theological writings of the thirteenth century that one finds tremendous advances in metaphysics, natural theology, psychology, epistemology and the other philosophical disciplines. Paradoxically enough, philosophy at its best was found not in the faculty of arts but in that of theology, even though its members gave primacy to faith and considered philosophy its handmaid and servant.

The theologians' conception of theology also produced another and final result—a twofold attitude which came rather generally to characterize intellectual life within the golden age. As previously mentioned, theologians conceived their function to be the defense, development and understanding of truths assented to by faith. As one means of achieving this goal, they eagerly turned to earlier thinkers. As one would expect, these included Christian authors— St. John Damascene and other Greek Fathers; St. Augustine, St. Hilary of Poitiers, Boethius, Venerable Bede, St. Isidore of Seville and others of the Latin writers. But they also avidly read and, wherever possible, utilized all available writings of Plato, Aristotle, Proclus and other pagans, as well as those of the Arabians (al-Farabi, al-Ghazzali, Avicenna, Averroës) and the Jews (ibn-Gabirol, Moses Maimonides). In brief, they were energetic in their intellec-

---

[1] See ch. 2 above, "Can Philosophy Be Christian? Its Relationship to Faith, Theology and Religion?" prgrs. corresponding to notes 12–30 and "Concluding Questions," prgrs. 1–6.

tual efforts and open to truth wherever found. It is this combination which forms a significant part of the intellectual milieu of scholasticism.

Classroom Methodology

Aside from the primacy of faith, that milieu also involved a definite methodology in classroom procedure, the predominant feature of which was perhaps the constant use each teacher made of the problem-method in teaching (then called the "question"-method because every topic was approached in the form of a *quaestio* or question: "*Quaeritur utrum . . .*" ["Now the question arises whether . . ."]).

Broadly characterized, this approach aimed at formulating a conclusion on some topic or other only after many other possible answers had been examined and evaluated. Accordingly, its purpose was not only to attain as accurate a conclusion as possible but also to guide the students in thinking, evaluating and then deciding as intelligently as possible. Therefore, after the teacher had proposed the question to be discussed, that process ordinarily consisted of four main parts. The first of these presented as many and as cogent considerations as possible in support of, say, an affirmative answer to a question. In the next portion arguments supporting the negative side were marshaled. Then, after the master and students were sufficiently aware of the question at issue, the problems involved, and the merits and demerits of each side, the master next indicated and then explained his own definitive view in the third and main portion. In the final section he took up the arguments previously given so as to answer those he opposed, and so amplify and further clarify his own position.

This problem-method was found effective both in conveying fundamental, universally accepted doctrines and in investigating new and controversial points (and this, incidentally, not only in the faculties of philosophy and theology but also in those of medicine and law). Accordingly, it provided the format for most of the various kinds of scholarly treatises issuing from the medieval universities. For example, *Disputed Questions* (*quaestiones disputatae*) are nothing more than the written account of actual classroom discussions, held weekly or biweekly and covering an enormous span of controverted points. Thomas Aquinas' *Disputed Questions on Truth* covers his teaching activity at Paris from 1256 to 1259 and comprises 253 individual questions on truth and goodness, each consisting of the four parts described above. *Quodlibetal Questions* (*quaestiones quodlibetales*) are written reports of discussions concerning contemporary issues held by various masters twice a year and open to the entire city. The *Summae* are systematic and organic developments of philosophy or theology in its entirety (hence the term *summa*) through the question-method. Even commentaries on Peter Lombard, Aristotle, Boethius, the *Liber de Causis,* etc., used the question-method once the letter of the text had become clear.

The problem-method, then, was one of the chief features of medieval classroom methodology and resultant publication. Another and complementary feature was the constant effort teachers and students made, presumably as a result of their training in Aristotelian logic, to think and then to express themselves clearly, precisely and in an orderly manner. No term was to be used unless precisely defined, no argument to be advanced except in syllogisms and these as logically impeccable as possible, no solution unfolded except coherently and systematically, no objection refuted unless *in forma* (that is, by distinguishing its premises one by one). The end result was that the thirteenth century was not only intellectually alive to a rather extraordinary degree but also formulated the outcome of that mental activity clearly, precisely and systematically.

Scholasticism in Later Periods

The intellectual atmosphere of succeeding centuries was marked by the same two general characteristics, though affirmation of the primacy of faith and the established pedagogy never again appeared to the same degree or in exactly the same way. In the fourteenth century the primacy of faith came to be accompanied by a considerable distrust of reason and speculation (because of the condemnation at Paris in 1277 of Aristotle as interpreted by Christian Averroists), with a consequent divorce of theology and philosophy. The problem-method was still operative, but many teachers tended to turn it away from genuine problems and to concentrate upon defending Thomas Aquinas from Scotus or Scotus from the disciples of Thomas and from Ockham. In the Renaissance, though, thinkers within the Church rather generally realized that an intelligent primacy afforded to faith need entail no skeptical attitude toward philosophy. Moreover, they addressed themselves to authentic problems within the department of political theory. For example, what is the relation of church and state? of pope and king? What is the origin and nature of political society? Can there be a community of nations? On such questions their speculation contributed to the theory behind Western democracy itself. They also studied the relationship between man's freedom and God's foreknowledge—an area in which, despite tremendous effort and innumerable words, they were not entirely successful. In spite of this healthy return to genuine problems, though, much effort and time were still wasted in partisan bickering between Jesuits, Dominicans and Franciscans. Moreover, in time the problem-method degenerated into the thesis-method. The latter begins with the teacher's announcing the position or thesis he wishes to defend. He proceeds to explain the point at issue, followed by proofs that the position he has taken is correct and, then, by answers to objections offered. This approach is pedagogically much inferior to the problem-method, for now no vivid awareness of the question at hand need arise because there is no previous investigation or evaluation of various possible answers. One should note also that the sixteenth and seventeenth centuries saw a scholasticism under Calvinist auspices: a philosophy admitting the primacy of faith (although not the ecclesiastical supervision of Rome) and using the thesis-method.

How do the two general characteristics show up in neo-Scholasticism? In certain ways and in some locales, the present era of Scholasticism reproduces some of the best features of its golden age. Through an objective and firsthand study of previous theologians and philosophers, many Scholastics have again become aware that the primacy of faith does not destroy but rather enhances and advances Christian philosophy. Again, following the lead of their thirteenth-century predecessors, many have opened themselves up to truth wherever found—whether in ancient, medieval, modern or contemporary authors, whether Christian or non-Christian. They are addressing themselves to authentic and important contemporary problems. Panel discussions which occasionally are initiated between scholastics and non-scholastics are close facsimiles of authentic medieval disputations. Even in the classroom many teachers are adopting slightly altered versions of the problem-method and are putting aside the thesis-method, while preserving the tradition of thinking and expressing themselves in as clear, accurate and orderly a manner as possible.

In conclusion, let it be stressed that the various periods of scholasticism have never been identical but only analogously the same. That fact makes scholasticism difficult to describe and to understand. In summary, though, one may say that the term points to the common intellectual milieu in which Catholic authors have worked since the thirteenth century and which arises from a primacy given to faith and, second, from a unique methodology in classroom procedure.

13

Human Knowledge According to
Guerric of St. Quentin

Although Guerric of St. Quentin's *Quaestiones Quodlibetales* transcribed below directly concern angelic rather than human knowledge, they do speak often enough about human cognition to show Guerric's epistemology to be in part an independent Aristotelianism.[1] This disclosure is especially welcome on a medieval author in a period as yet opaque because of scarcity of published texts: the years 1230–1245.[2] Such is the era to which Guerric belongs, since as the replacement of John of St. Giles he taught theology at the University of Paris from 1233 until 1242, when he was himself

---

[1] Besides the *quaestiones de quolibet*, Guerric also authored commentaries on Scripture, *quaestiones disputatae*, sermons and a commentary on Lombard's *Sentences*. See F. M. Henquinnet, O.F.M., "Les écrits du Fr. Guerric de S. Quentin, O.P.," *Recherches de théologie ancienne et médiévale* 6 (1934), 184–214, 248–312, 394–409; 8 (1936), 369–88.

In my chapter on Guerric, Marvin Kessler (see n. 3 below) has furnished the transcription of Guerric's texts, as well as biographical and bibliographical data, which I gratefully acknowledge. This chapter first appeared under both our names in *Arts Libéraux et Philosophie Médiévale* (Montréal: Institut d'Études Médiévale; Paris, J. Vrin, 1969), pp. 1129–41.

[2] As an example of the opacity of those years, recall how little is known on the theories of divine infinity held then. See L. Sweeney, S.J., *Divine Infinity in Greek and Medieval Thought* (New York/Bern: Peter Lang Publishing, Inc., 1992), ch. 15: "Divine Infinity: 1150–1250." For Guerric's position on infinity see *ibid.*, ch. 19: "Bonaventure and Aquinas on the Divine Being as Infinite," pp. 416–20.

replaced by Albert the Great. It was most likely that he conducted the *Quaestiones* during his teaching career at Paris.[3]

On the strength of these remarks, then, let us turn to Guerric. Our procedure will be this. After transcribing the two *quaestiones* in which the Dominican theologian discusses knowledge, we shall study each separately. At the end of the chapter we shall formulate general conclusions.

Transcription of Text A

Codex Vaticanus Latinus 4245, Folios 62ra–62va:[4]

Tertio quaeritur communiter circa bonos et malos angelos. Et primo quaeritur si habent cognitionem rerum per species innatas vel acquisitas; secundo, de differentia animae et angeli.

Ad primum sic.

5   Angeli habent duplicem cognitionem de rebus, scilicet matutinam et vespertinam, hoc est, in Verbo et in genere proprio rerum. Et hanc duplicem habuerunt a principio. Sed quod vident res factas sive in genere suo non fuit per naturam superadditam, ut patet. Ergo per naturam habent cognitionem rerum actualem [*read:* actualium?].

10   Item. Intellectus angelicus dignior est quam humanus. Et intellectus angeli mali [dignior est quam humanus], quia, sicut dicit Augustinus, Deus sic punit naturam quod non aufert. Ergo et intellectus angeli mali dignior est intellectu humano. Sed anima habet potentiam ad omnia quae sunt naturaliter cognoscenda. Ergo angelus actu se extendit ad omnia, alioquin

15   quid amplius haberet angelus quam anima?

---

[3] Guerric became a Dominican in 1225; after teaching at Paris (1233–1242), he went to Bologna but died in Paris in August 1245. For these and other biographical facts, see P. Féret, *La faculté de théologie de Paris et ses docteurs les plus célèbres* (Paris: Picard et Fils, 1894), tome I, p. 340 sq.; P. Mandonnet, O.P., "Thomas d'Aquin, novice prêcheur," *Revue Thomiste* 30 (1925), 502–7; P. Glorieux, "Répertoire des maîtres en théologie de Paris au xIIIᵉ siècle," *Études de philosophie médiévale* 17 (1933), 54–58; *idem*, "La littérature quodlibétique," *Bibliothèque Thomiste* 21 (1935), 106–7; Marvin Kessler, "Union of Body and Soul According to Guerric of Saint Quentin, O.P., in his *Quaestiones de Quolibet*" (Master's thesis, Department of Philosophy, St. Louis University, 1962), pp. 3–18 (for transcription of the *Quaestiones*, see pp. 64–144).

For bibliographical data, see n. 26 below.

[4] In the transcription any departure from the text of the Vatican MS will be indicated by brackets, plus the correction or addition. No notice, however, will be given of such innocuous corrections as (when context requires it) changing verbs from singular to plural, making adjectives agree in gender with nouns, etc.

Item. Non haberet secundum hoc intellectum deiformem, sed esset possibilis eius intellectus. Ergo eorum habet actualem cognitionem quorum anima potentialem.

Contra. Magister in *Sententiis* non dicit quod habeat innatam cognitionem
20 nisi trium, scilicet [1] Dei sui et creaturarum secum sicut materiae primae, [2] et caeli empyrii, [3] et temporis. Non ergo habet omnium cognitionem actualem a creatione.

Item. Noscit omnia in particulari aut in universali. Non in particulari quia particularia sunt infinita; cognitio autem ipsius finita est.
25 Item. Generatio successiva est. Nec est determinatum in natura quot debebant esse singularia sub unaquaque specie quia infinita potest esse multiplicatio individuorum sub una specie. Unde in solo divino arbitrio est determinatum quod [*read:* quot] debeant esse individua secundum quamlibet speciem. Nullus autem intellectus creatus potest in id quod solo divino
30 arbitrio est determinatum. Non ergo in particulari cognoscit. Ergo in universali.

Quaeritur in quo universali, cum nullum sit universale sive commune omnium. Et si est, quaeritur quid est illud.

Item. Cognitio in universali est cognitio imperfecta. Ergo imperfectius
35 cognocit quam anima.

Quaeritur postea quae sit differentia inter animam et angelum. Dicebat quod anima est intellectus possibilis, angelus intellectus agens.

Contra. Perfectum et imperfectum non diversificantur [*read:* diversificant] speciem. Possibile autem dicit imperfectum; plenum sive agens dicit
40 perfectum. Ergo per hoc non differunt anima et angelus secundum speciem.

Item. Si possibile est differentia specifica animae, ergo ubique et semper concomitatur ipsam. Ergo, etiam cum est separata, est possibilis.

Contra. Novit omnia quae naturaliter fiunt et multa quae fiunt per gratiam, et loquitur de anima sancta vel beata. Ergo non est illud differentia
45 specifica ipsius. Quod autem non sit possibilis, patet, quia in futuro, sicut dicit Augustinus, non erunt cogitationes volubiles, quod quidem essent si anima esset intellectus possibilis.

Item. Esto quod anima sit creata a principio exuta corpore sicut posuerunt aliqui, secundum hoc haberet cognitionem actualem omnium sicut
50 et angelus. Ergo possibile non est eius differentia secundum quam differt ab angelo.

Respondeo. Angelus creatus est actu intelligens omnia quae naturaliter fiunt. Intelligentia autem plena est formis. Anima autem potentia [intelligens]. Unde est quasi tabula rasa nihil habens picturae, possibilis
55 tamen pingi.

Item, [anima] dicitur possibilis intellectus respectu eorum quae fiunt per naturam, secundum quod possibile dicit capacitatem et operationem ut scilicet cooperetur aliquo modo ut actu ea habeat respectu quorum est [in] potentia. Respectu autem eorum quae per gratiam fiunt non dicitur possibilis
60 intellectus, quia respectu eorum non habet operationem etsi habeat capacitatem, quia ex se nullo modo potest disponi ut cognoscat ea quae fiunt per gratiam.

In intellectu angelico est aliter quia est quasi tabula plena. Ideo non est possibilis sed in actu, et ideo deiformis, et, licet sit capax eorum quae per
65 naturam fiunt, non tamen dicitur possibilis respectu illorum quia respectu eorum non habet comparationem [*read:* cooperationem]. Non enim acquisivit eas sibi sed innatae sunt ei. Respectu eorum quae per gratiam fiunt operationem non habet, licet capacitatem. Unde nec respectu eorum dicitur possibilis.
70 Plenus igitur est intellectus angelicus habens innatam actualem sibi cognitionem omnium naturalium, in universali scilicet, non in particularibus, quia hoc est solius Dei in cuius arbitrio determinatum est quot singularia debeant exire et produci secundum unamquamque speciem.
    Sed quomodo cognoscit in universali?
75 Respondeo, in causis universalibus. Habet enim causas universales particularium per naturam, et in eis tanquam in universali intelligit particularia quae fiunt per naturam, non tamen omnia.
    Nec illa cognitio particularis ut particulare est innata sed accepta. Nec tamen dicitur intellectus eius possibilis, quia non habet cooperationem
80 respectu eius. Sed, quia jam cognoverat in causa universali, cum [particulare] ostenditur ei in propria ratione, cognoscit sine alia operatione vel immutatione facta in ipso; sicut, si sciam omnem mulam esse sterilem, quamsi [*read:* quando] ostenditur mihi haec vel illa, scio ipsam esse sterilem de qua tamen non sciebam de propria ratione.
85 Quod objicitur, cognitio in universali est imperfecta omnino, respondeo, imperfectum est respectu cognitionis Dei qui cognoscit omnia non solum in universali sed etiam in particularibus. Perfecta vero est respectu animae quae nec in universali nec in particulari omnia scit.
    Quod quaeritur, in quo differat angelus ab anima, respondeo, secundum
90 possibile et plenum.
    Et quod objicitur, perfectum et imperfectum non diversificant speciem, etc., respondeo, perfectum et perfectum [*read:* imperfectum] possunt considerari dupliciter: vel secundum quod respiciunt statum rei vel ipsam rem in se. Verbi gratia, caritas dicitur perfecta et imperfecta non secundum
95 essentiam suam sed secundum statum. Similiter, iste homo est perfectae qualitatis vel imperfectae, quod quidem non est quia homo, sed quia homo in tali statu. Unde patet quod perfectum et imperfectum non sequuntur rem secundum se sed secundum statum rei, et isto modo non faciunt differentiam secundum speciem. Alicubi tamen respiciunt rem ipsam, non statum, et tunc
100 faciunt differentiam secundum speciem. Et sic est hic quia intellectus hominis secundum se dicitur possibilis vel imperfectus. Intellectus autem angeli dicitur secundum se plenus et perfectus.
    Quod objicitur, si possibile est differentia specifica intellectus humani, ergo sequitur ipsam, etc., respondeo, anima separata per naturam habet
105 intellectum possibilem.
    Quod autem objicitur de anima sancta quod habet plenum, dicendum quod habet plenum per gratiam sed possibilem per naturam.
    Quod objicitur, si anima esset creata separata, haberet actualem cognitionem omnium sicut angelus, etc., ergo possibile accidit illi, respondeo,

110 qui posuerunt animas creatas separatas, posuerunt quod [animae] habuerunt omnium scientiam in sua creatione, et in conjunctione cum corpore obliviscebantur. Unde bene concedebant isti quod, sicut angelus actualem cognitionem, ita et animae; et secundum hoc bene esset verum quod possibile non esset differentia specifica animae sed accideret. Sed illud erat 115 heresis, et ideo dicendum quod possibile est differentia specifica animae.

Comments

Text A begins by listing two questions concerning angels (lines 2–3): do they know material things through innate or through acquired species? Second, what is the difference between an angel and a human soul? Guerric undertakes to answer the first by noting the *pro* and *con* arguments presented presumably by those attending the *quaestio de quolibet*. Angelic knowledge occurs through innate species because angels know things through a *cognitio vespertina* which they have had from the very beginning (lines 5–9); because an angelic intellect is more perfect than a human intellect and therefore must actually and not just potentially extend to everything (lines 10–15); because an angel's intellect is godlike and not merely possible (lines 16–18).[5] On the other side, though, angels would seem to know through acquired species because Peter Lombard omits mention of material things when listing objects of which they do have innate cognition (lines 19–22);[6] because angels know material things only universally and not individually, and this for two reasons: individuals are infinite, whereas angelic knowledge is finite (lines 23–24); the number of individuals in any one specific class of beings is not determined by nature but by divine decision, which is beyond the range of any created intellect (lines 25–31).

This last point (namely, that angels do not know material existents individually but only universally—"non in particulari; ergo

---

[5] Characterizing an angelic intellect as godlike or deiform comes (ultimately, at least) from Pseudo-Dionysius, *De divinis nominibus*, c. 7, sectio 2 (Romae: Marietti, 1950), no. 319, p. 270: "Angelos scire dicunt eloquia ea quae sunt in terra, non secundum sensus ita cognoscentes sensibilia quidem existentia, sed secundum propriam deiformis mentis virtutem et naturam."

[6] As yet we have not been able to find this list in Lombard, although we have checked the following places in *Liber IV Sententiarum* on divine knowledge: Book I, distinction 35 (Quaracchi ed.), pp. 220–24; distinctions 38–39, pp. 240–48; on angels: Book II, distinctions 2–7, pp. 312–40; on human knowledge: Book II, distinctions 19 and 23, pp. 393–97 and 416–19.

in universali") prompts both a further question and a comment
(lines 32–35). The question: what would that *universale* be? The
comment: knowledge *in universali* is imperfect and, accordingly, an
angel's knowledge is less perfect than a soul's. Guerric will face
both the question and the comment later on (lines 74–88), but now
he turns to the second of the two initial inquiries (what differentiates a soul and an angel?) and, more pointedly, to the opinion
voiced by someone (line 36: *dicebat*) that the difference consists in
the fact that a soul is a possible intellect but an angel an agent
intellect (lines 36–37).[7] Several arguments showing that opinion to
be inadequate are noted: agent [intellect] is related to possible
[intellect] as perfect to imperfect, but perfect and imperfect are not
specific differences (lines 38–40); if such were what specifically
differentiates soul and angel, they would be their inseparable characteristics and, hence, a soul when separated by death from the
body and dwelling in heaven would be a possible intellect, which
is false (lines 41–47); a soul created apart from matter (as some
have held) and an angel would equally know all material things,
would equally be agent intellects and, thus, be specifically differentiated by some means other than the contrast between agent and
possible intellects (lines 48–51).[8]

---

[7] The contrast between possible and agent intellects finds its remote origins, of course, in Aristotle, *On the Soul*, III, ch. 5, 430a10–19. Which Christian
first identified the agent intellect with an angel? The history of that identification is, as far as I know, not yet written. One of its chapters would necessarily
concern Avicenna (and, for that matter, other Arabians too), who conceived of
the agent intellect as the separate intelligence of the lowest heavenly sphere.
See Ján Bákos, *Psychologie d'Ibn Sînâ (Avicenne) d'après son oeuvre As-Sifâ* (Prague:
Éditions de l'Acad. Tchécoslovaque des Sciences, 1956), vol. II, pp. 166–77; F.
Rahman, *Avicenna's Psychology* (Oxford: Clarendon Press, 1952); Soheil M.
Afnan, *Avicenna: His Life and Works* (London: George Allen and Unwin, 1958),
especially pp. 160–61, 185–86. On the psychologies of various Christians, see
E. Gilson, *History of Christian Philosophy in the Middle Ages* [hereafter: HCP]
(New York: Random House, 1955), *passim*. As a sample see *ibid.*, pp. 321–22,
on Peter of Spain, who is a late representative (d. 1277) within Christianity of
someone who views the agent intellect "as Intelligence of the last and lowest
order which, being intimately present to the intellectual soul, reveals to it, by
its illumination, the intelligibles so that its relation to the intelligible forms is
the same as that of light to colors."

[8] Later (lines 108–14) Guerric will concede that this line of arguing would
be legitimate provided a soul were created without the body. But such a
conception, he adds, is heretical: "Sed illud erat haeresis, et ideo dicendum
quod possibile est differentia specifica animae" (lines 114–15). His charge of

Thus far Guerric has surveyed various considerations given in support of one or other side of the two initial questions. Next he sketches his own position in a *respondeo* (lines 52–74) directed to both questions simultaneously. The specific difference between a soul and an angel can be expressed by the two words "possible" and "plenary." A soul's state of possibility is anchored in two facts. Of itself it only potentially knows things, for it is a "tabula rasa nihil habens picturae, possibilis tamen pingi" (lines 53–55).[9] Second (lines 56–62), it actually knows solely when influenced by and cooperating with things in the sensible universe: with respect to them it has both *capacitas* and *operatio*, from them it receives the *species* necessary for its knowledge-process. With respect to what happens in the realm of grace, a soul has a *capacitas* but no *operatio* and, hence, is not termed even a "possible intellect."

But on the other hand, an angel is "plenary."[10] Each angelic existent has been created in a state of actually knowing everything which occurs in nature. Each is full of forms (lines 52–53), each is a *tabula plena* (line 63) by reason of *species* which are innate and not acquired (line 67). Hence, each is godlike, each knows actually and cannot be described as "possible" (line 64). With respect to things

---

heresy could refer to *Canones adversus Originem*, issued in 543: "Si quis dicit aut sentit, praeexsistere hominum animas . . . anathema sit." H. Denzinger and C. Bannwart, *Enchiridion Symbolorum* (Friburgi Brisgoviae: Herder, 1953), no. 203, p. 95. Most likely, though, his charge is based on an ecclesiastical pronouncement closer to his own era.

One may add that our Dominican theologian shows a frequent sensitivity to the *magisterium* of the Church on topics other than the one just given. For example: "Although the bodies of infants dying without baptism are capable of suffering, still they will not suffer. . . . This we say without prejudice to the Faith because we are not aware of any authoritative statement on this matter" ("hoc autem dicendum sine praejudicio, quia expressam auctoritatem ad hoc non vidimus") (fol. 64rb). Again: "For the soul to be essentially in every part of the body is unintelligible and is not demanded by any article of Faith. Hence, such is not my position, but rather I say with Aristotle that the soul is essentially in man's heart" ("Non intelligo quomodo anima sit in qualibet parte sui corporis per essentiam, nec hoc est de articulis fidei. Ideo hoc non dico, sed dico quod est in corde per essentiam, ut dicit Philosophus") (fol. 70rb).

[9] See Aristotle, *On the Soul*, III, ch. 4, 429b30–430a2.

[10] One should notice that, although Guerric has called the human soul "possible intellect" (e.g., lines 56, 60), he does not call an angel "agent intellect" but contents himself with such language as *tabula plena* (line 63), *in actu* (line 64), *deiformis* (line 64), *plenus* (lines 70, 90). See n. 7 above.

in nature, then, as well as to what occurs through grace, an angel has *capacitas* but no *operatio* and, thus, should not be described as "possible" in either area.

Guerric's reply to the twofold initial inquiry is, then, that an angel knows material things through innate rather than acquired species and that an angel differs from a human soul inasmuch as the former's intellect is plenary whereas the latter's is possible solely.

While ending his *respondeo* Guerric turns to a subtopic previously noted (lines 32–33) but left undiscussed. An angelic intellect, he concludes, is full by having innate actual knowledge of all things in nature inasmuch as it knows them not in particular but in universal (lines 70–71): "plenus igitur est intellectus angelicus habens innatam actualem sibi cognitionem omnium naturalium, in universali scilicet, non in particularibus"). But how does this *cognitio in universali* occur? Our author explains the occurrence through universal causes of particular things an angel has of its very nature (lines 75–76: "habet enim causas universales particularium per naturam"). Seemingly, he even allows an angel to have knowledge of a particular precisely as particular, which would not, however, be innate but received (line 78: "Nec illa cognitio particularis ut particulare est innata sed accepta"). He makes little or no attempt to explain such allowance,[11] but he does make clear that such

---

[11] One puzzling aspect of the knowledge an angel has of a particular qua particular is that it is not innate but acquired (line 78: "Nec . . . est innata sed accepta"). Acquired from the particulars themselves? If so, how? No data for an answer has been so far discovered in the MS.

Guerric is not alone in granting angels knowledge which is acquired rather than innate. The authors of the *Summa theologica* attributed to Alexander of Hales make a similar grant, first of all, to demons: "Non recipiunt species rerum intelligibilium a phantasmatibus, licet sumant ab ipsis rebus, et non sumunt per modum intellectus possibilis, sed per modum agentis, qui sibi sufficit ad species accipiendas." Alexandri de Hales *Summa theologica* (Quaracchi: Ex Typographia Collegii S. Bonaventurae, 1924), I, p. 152c. In fact, any angel (good or bad) has a possible intellect with reference to *inferiora*, but differently than does a human: "Habet etiam intellectum possibilem ad capiendum notitiam istorum inferiorum, sed non illo modo quo intellectus possibilis humanus: intellectus enim possibilis humanus indiget ministerio sensus praeambulo et ministerio virtutum sensibilium quod non est in angelo. . . ." *Ibid.*, p. 165c. His intellect also can be called an "agent intellect" if the phrase is not used strictly: "Sumendo autem communius intellectum agentem, prout agentis est educere potentiam intelligendi in actum per acceptionem quamdam specierum, intellectus angeli potest dici agens." *Ibid.*,

knowledge does not justify one in characterizing the angelic intellect as possible. The angel achieves such cognition without submitting to, cooperating with, being modified by particular things (lines 78–82: "nec tamen dicitur intellectus eius possibilis quia non habet cooperationem respectu eius . . . cognoscit sine alia operatione vel immutatione facta in ipso").

---

p. 165d. Accordingly, an angel does know material things *in universali* through innate species: "Cognitio naturalis rerum naturalium aut fuit quantum ad formas universales quae fuerunt omnes primitus creatae: et secundum hoc potuit esse per similitudines innatas vel a principio conditionis datas." *Ibid.*, p. 184d. Nevertheless, his knowledge of material things as singular is through acquired species: "Cognitio autem singularium est per similitudines quas sibi capit ex rebus existentibus." *Ibid.*, p. 185a. Whence and how acquired? From things but not by things: "Res non faciunt suas similitudines in intellectu, sed intellectus angelicus sua virtute capit a rebus. Nec oportet ibi esse receptionem ad modum sensus vel speculi, cum non sit acceptio per modum rei sensibilis, sed rei intelligibilis." *Ibid.*, p. 185c. One angel even knows another by acquired rather than innate species: "Dicimus quod unus angelus cognoscit alium angelum et per speciem, non innatam sed potius acquisitam, quia ipse eam sibi facit in se. . . . Dicimus ergo quod unus angelus cognoscit alium per speciem sive similitudinem suam et accipit speciem illam a specie alterius angeli, quoniam similitudinem illius speciei accipit. . . . E contra est quoad hoc in intellectu angelico et in intellectu animae potentiali: quoniam in intellectu angeli non fit proprie abstractio, cum sic unus alium intelligit, et hoc est quia fit abstractio ut res fiat spiritualior; sed angelus non facit illam speciem spiritualiorem nec indiget ut sit spiritualior, sed hoc tantum indiget ut ipsi cognoscenti coniungatur, et hoc est quia iam est abstracta a materia sensibili." *Ibid.*, p. 178a–b.

Aquinas is aware that some have thus attempted to explain an angel's knowledge of individual existents by species originating from the existents themselves. See *In II Sent.*, d. 3, q. 3, a. 3, resp. (Mandonnet ed.), pp. 119–20. But he rejects such an explanation as "non . . . conveniens." After canvassing several other positions, he sets forth his own: an angel knows singulars solely through innate *rationes* because they are modeled on divine ideas, which reveal each thing both in its form and in its matter, whence comes individuation. "Deus est causa rei, non solum quantum ad formam sed etiam quantum ad materiam, quae est principium individuationis; unde idea in mente divina est similitudo rei quantum ad utrumque, scilicet materiam et formam; et ideo per eam cognoscuntur res non tantum in universali sed etiam in particulari. Formae autem quae sunt in mente angeli sunt simillimae rationibus idealibus in mente divina. . . . Unde per eas angeli cognoscere possunt rerum singularia, quia sunt similitudines rerum etiam quantum ad dispositiones materiales individuantes, sicut et rationes vel ideae rerum existentes in mente divina." *Ibid.*, p. 121.

Finally (lines 85–115), he endeavors to refute several *sed contra* arguments previously given. All of these refutations except one we can omit here, since they provide little additional relevant information. One of them does, though. Reply to lines 34–35: Cognition *in universali* (such as angels have of material things) is less perfect than the knowledge of God, who knows all existents both universally and individually. It is more perfect than that of a soul, who is not aware of all things either universally or individually.

We have accompanied Guerric through these two *quaestiones de quolibet* so as to observe their general structure. What information have we found on the nature and genesis of human knowledge? Rather more than one might expect in light of the fact that Guerric himself is primarily interested in angels (line 1: "quaeritur . . . circa . . . angelos") and uses the human soul mainly as a foil for them. (1) From one point of view the human knower is quite respectable. Granted that his knowledge is not as good as God's or an angel's (lines 85–88), granted that he does not know all existents either universally or individually (*ibid.*), granted that he needs to be complemented and determined from without. Nonetheless, he does know intellectually. He does have an intellect, which must at least be an ability of somehow helping to efficiently cause intellection. He does have the *capacitas* (lines 57, 61) to respond to external determinants, he does have a tablet dynamically responsive to what is written thereon (lines 54–55: "tabula . . . possibilis tamen pingi").[12]

(2) From the point of view of what is to be known, though, the human knower is marked by emptiness (line 54: "est quasi tabula rasa nihil habens picturae"), by passivity, determinability, potentiality—in a word, by possibility (lines 54, 56, 57, 90, 101, 105, 107, 115). (3) When the material thing to be known establishes contact with the human intellect, which despite its emptiness and indetermination (#2) is a power for producing intellection (#1), there occurs what Guerric calls *operatio* (lines 57, 60, 68, 81) or, with equal frequency, *cooperatio* (lines 58, 66, 67, 79). (4) The result can be described in several ways. It is an actuation: the intellect actually possesses the cognoscibles which before it had only potentially (lines 58–59: "cooperetur aliquo modo ut actu ea habeat respectu

---

[12] One should note that Guerric makes no explicit mention of an agent intellect in man. This omission is remedied possibly by the way he speaks in Text B, lines 123–25. Also see n. 10 above.

quorum est [in] potentia"). It is a disposition, a readiness for knowledge (lines 60–62: "non habet operationem . . . quia ex se nullo modo potest disponi ut cognoscat ea quae fiunt per gratiam").[13] It is an acquirement of species (lines 64–67: the angelic intellect, "licet sit capax eorum quae per naturam fiunt, non tamen dicitur possibilis respectu illorum quia respectu eorum non habet cooperationem. Non enim acquisivit eas sibi sed innatae sunt ei"). It is the intentional change which the intellect undergoes under the influence of the cognoscible (lines 78–82: in knowing a particular as particular, an angelic intellect "non habet cooperationem respectu eius" because it knows the particular *in causa universali* and, thus, "cognoscit sine alia operatione vel immutatione facta in ipso"). (5) When thus actuated, disposed, specified and changed, the intellect then produces the operation itself of intellection.

Transcription of Text B

Codex Vaticanus Latinus 4245, Folio 66ra:

Ex hoc quaeritur an [angeli] habeant illam [scientiam inferiorum] innatam vel acquisitam. Et videtur quod innatam dicendum.

Angeli existentia non secundum sensum sed secundum deiformem intellectum cognoscunt. Sed in Deo est cognitio, non autem a rebus sed ad res
120 quia ejus cognitio habet quemdam respectum ad res. Ergo, cum in angelo sit respectus [*read:* intellectus] deiformis, est in eo cognitio non a rebus sed ad res, et ita non est acquisita sed innata.

Item. Intellectus humanus, quia permixtus est sensui, accipere potest speciem spoliatam quia adjunctus est aliis viribus interioribus et exterioribus
125 mediantibus quibus potest spoliare species. Sed in angelo non est hoc. Ergo non potest habere cognitionem acquisitam rerum sensibilium.

Contra. Apostolus [*read:* Angelus] potest alii revelare justitiam hujus hominis. Ergo cognoscit non per praesentiam quia non habet justitiam hujus hominis in se ipso, ut puta fidem. Ergo, cum non sit nisi duplex modus
130 cognoscendi rem, scilicet per praesentiam et per speciem, cognoscit per speciem; et ita habet de ea scientiam acquisitam.

Sed similiter hic quaeritur quomodo potest cognoscere justitiam per speciem cum justitia et hujusmodi formae spirituales non habeant aliam

---

[13] This is an inference from what Guerric says concerning angels. Angels have no *operatio* because they cannot of themselves be disposed with respect to what occurs through grace; but if they could be so disposed, they would have *operatio*; therefore, *operatio* is a disposition and readiness for knowledge in an intellect. A similar inference is beneath the two subsequent sentences.

speciem a se ipsis. Non ergo cognoscit per speciem nec per praesentiam.
135 Quomodo ergo [cognoscit], cum intellectus angelicus abundet ab humano, et
   intellectus humanus etsi non sit creatus sciens scibilis [*read:* scibilia?], tamen
   necesse est quod intellectus angelicus creatus sit sciens?

   Et hoc videtur velle Philosophus, qui dicit quod intelligentia est plena
   formis, et Ezechielis, xxviii, dicit de Lucifero: plenus sapientia, etc.
140   Unde dico quod habent innatas eorum [quae] tamen tantum fiunt
   secundum naturam et species universales non particulares. Et ex universali
   cognoscunt particularia, sicut ex hoc universali quam scio, scilicet omnem
   mulam esse sterilem, quam cito video hanc mulam esse sterilem. Eorum
   autem quae sunt secundum liberum arbitrium vel ex gratia Dei non habent
145 cognitionem nisi per revelationem vel per effectus et signa, quia horum non
   habent praesentiam nec habent eorum species apud se cum ipsa non habeant
   species alias ab ipsis.

Comments

In Text B Guerric raises identically the same question as the first
asked in Text A: is the knowledge angels have of material things
innate or acquired (lines 116–17)? His procedure is similar also,
since he first notes *pro* and *con* arguments. Angelic knowledge of
things is innate because an angel resembles God, Whose knowledge of things is innate: His knowledge is of things but not from
things (lines 118–22). Again, angelic knowledge cannot be acquired
from sensible things because this would demand what is not true:
that an angelic intellect is like a human intellect, which can receive
species despoiled [of matter] by reason of the internal and external
sense-powers with which it is linked (lines 123–26).

On the other hand, though, an angel's knowledge would seem
acquired, since he can be aware of a man's justice, which is known
not through presence but rather through an acquired species (lines
127–31). The mention of justice raises a counter-question: how *can*
justice be known? If not through presence, then neither through a
species, since justice, as well as any other spiritual form, furnishes
no species other than itself (lines 132–37).

With line 138 Guerric starts his own *respondeo.* An angel's knowledge is through innate species, and this I say on the strength of
Aristotle's statement that an intelligence is full of forms[14] and of

---

[14] The statement is from the *Liber de Causis,* Prop. IX, which was commonly
considered to be Aristotle's until William of Moerbeke's translation of Proclus'

Ezechiel's that Lucifer is full of wisdom.[15] Such innate knowledge is limited in a twofold way. It extends only to those things which occur through nature and, even so, an angel knows any one such thing only universally—in somewhat the same way as I realize this mule is sterile by knowing that all mules are sterile (lines 140–44). As far as what occurs through free choice or under the influence of divine grace, an angel is ignorant unless he achieves cognition through divine revelation or by inference from effects and signs. Why so? Because such occurrences provide no species (a concession to the point made previously in lines 132–37) and, thus, are unknowable through either species or presence (lines 144–47).

Such is an outline of Text B. Does it offer any relevant information? Yes, in two areas, the first of which concerns a diversity within knowledge itself. There are, Guerric explains, two ways of knowing a thing: through presence and through a species (lines 129–30: "cum non sit nisi duplex modus cognoscendi rem, scilicet per praesentiam et per speciem"). The *species* mentioned is not innate but acquired, since it enables an intellect to achieve acquired science (lines 130–31: "cognoscit per speciem; et ita habet de ea scientiam acquisitam"). According to our author, would knowledge through presence involve innate species? Perhaps, although

---

Elementatio theologica from Greek to Latin in 1268 revealed its doctrine to be largely Procline in origin. Whether its compiler was a ninth- or tenth-century Arabian working in Baghdad or the twelfth-century Jewish author David (Ibn Daoud, Avendauth) working in Spain is still controverted. See Adriaan Pattin, O.M.I., "Le *Liber de Causis*: Édition établie à l'aide de 90 manuscrits avec introduction et notes," *Tijdschrift voor Filosofie* 28 (Maart 1966), 90–98. Also see L. Sweeney, S.J., *Divine Infinity in Greek and Medieval Thought*, ch. 13: "Doctrine of Creation in the *Liber de Causis*," pp. 289–90 and n. 2; see ch. 14 below, n. 20.

[15] Chapter 28 of Ezechiel is the last in a series of three prophecies against Tyre. The Prince of which it speaks is the embodiment of the country of Tyre itself. Verse 12, as well as the verses immediately preceding and subsequent, is an elegy of the Prince, enumerating the gifts lost when he sinned: "You were the seal of perfection, full of wisdom, and complete in beauty." See B. Orchard *et al.*, *Catholic Commentary on Holy Scripture* (New York: Thomas Nelson and Sons, 1953), pp. 602, 613–15, especially 614.

Guerric applies verse 12 to Satan, as do other medieval authors. For example, St. Bonaventure, *In II Sent.*, d. 3, a. 2, qu. 1 (Quaracchi ed.), p. 109a: "Videtur sacra Scriptura velle, Ezechielis 28, 12: *Tu plenus sapientia et perfectus decore*—dicitur ad diabolum." Much earlier Peter Lombard had made the same application (referring, besides, to Gregory the Great). See *Liber IV Sententiarum*, II, d. 6, c. 1 (Quaracchi 3d ed.), vol. 1, pp. 354–55.

conceivably it might entail no species at all. Not much light is shed on this point by another text in which Guerric uses similar language. In discussing whether or not the vision of faith differs from the vision of God which saints have in heaven ("utrum visio fidei differat a visione patriae"), he answers affirmatively. The vision of faith specifically differs from vision in heaven because faith is not a vision. Why so? Because vision is either through presence (then we have vision in its strictest sense) or through a similitude (then we have vision in a less strict sense): "Visio vel est per praesentiam, et haec est propriissima, vel est per similitudinem, et haec non est ita propria." But faith is not a vision in either sense, because it is "per speculum et in aenigmate."[16]

The second and more important area in which Text B provides data concerns the role which man's sense faculties play in human cognition. By its link with sense, the human intellect (unlike an angelic intellect) can receive species despoiled [from matter presumably] because it is joined to internal and external sense-powers. Through them the intellect can strip species [from matter] and, thereby, have knowledge acquired from things.

> Intellectus humanus, quia permixtus est sensui, accipere potest
> speciem spoliatam quia adjunctus est aliis viribus interioribus
> et exterioribus mediantibus quibus potest spoliare species.
> Sed in angelo non est hoc. Ergo non potest habere cognitionem
> acquisitam rerum sensibilium (lines 123–26).

The powers of sense cognition are, then, a crucial medium between intellect and things. Things work upon and influence the intellect through the senses: through them things are the cause determining the content of the intellect, determining what the intellect is to think about. Equally important, the intellect works upon things through the senses: through them it can strip and separate the intelligible species ("viribus ... mediantibus quibus potest spoliare species") from (presumably) the individuating material conditions represented in the phantasm and, ultimately, located in sensible existents themselves. Through the senses the intellect is able to transfer a thing from potential intelligibility to actual intelligibility. Seemingly, one and the same intellect prepares the intelligible spe-

---

[16] Folio 63rb.

cies and receives them once prepared ("intellectus humanus . . . accipere potest speciem spoliatam . . . potest spoliare speciem"). One and the same intellect performs the functions which later thirteenth-century authors will divide between agent intellect and possible intellect.[17]

Whether or not this interpretation of agent and possible intellects is correct, at least this can be said safely: the current text fills in some details of how the *cooperatio* mentioned in Text A comes about. The material thing to be known establishes contact with man's intellect through his senses, and there ensues the *cooperatio* in which intellect and thing work together and by which intellect is actuated, disposed, specified and intentionally modified through intelligible species so that he can then produce the activity itself of intellection.

General Conclusions

If we join Text A to Text B, what do we get? A fairly clear and adequate picture, despite the fact that neither is an *ex professo* treatment of human knowledge. Man's intellection has two sources, one of which is material things, which determine its content by working upon and through the senses. The other is the intellect itself, which works through the senses to help produce the intelligible species acquired from things, which also receives them once produced, and which then efficiently effects intellection.

Is this version of cognition Aristotelian? Yes, to the extent that intelligible species are not innate but acquired, that sensible existents are the content-determining cause of our directly intellecting them.[18] No, if intellect both produces and receives intelligible spe-

---

[17] For example, see Thomas Aquinas, *In II Sent.*, d. 17, q. 2, a. 1, resp. (Mandonnet ed.), pp. 427–28; *idem, Summa theologiae*, I, 79, articles 3 and 4, resp. (Leonine manual ed.), pp. 384–85; St. Bonaventure, *In II Sent.*, d. 24, a. 2, qu. 4, resp. (Quaracchi ed.), pp. 586–89. On Albert the Great, see E. Gilson, *HCP*, pp. 284–87; also see L. A. Kennedy, "The Nature of the Human Intellect According to St. Albert the Great," *The Modern Schoolman* 37 (January 1960), 121–37; on Roger Bacon, *HCP*, pp. 303–4.

[18] See Aristotle, *On the Soul*, III, ch. 4, 429a13–18, which reads in part: "If thinking is like perceiving, it must be either a process in which the soul is acted upon by what is capable of being thought, or a process different from

cies. Although Aristotle is ambiguous as to whether the agent intellect is a constitutive part of man or whether (a more likely interpretation) it is an intelligence separate from him, still he clearly posits two intellects: one by which man becomes all things, the other which makes all things.[19] One and the same faculty cannot perform the two functions. The intellect producing species cannot receive them.

That Guerric's conception of the human knower is not totally Aristotelian is borne out also by his view of the human soul. A soul can be viewed in two ways: as what it is in itself and, second, as animating the body. According to the first view, soul is a spirit and is essentially present only in man's heart. According to the second, it is virtually present everywhere in the body.

> Potest dici quod anima potest considerari ut est quaedam essentia in se, et sic est spiritus, et hoc modo essentialiter est in corde. Item, potest considerari ut est animans, et sic, cum totum animet, tota est in toto, et hoc est virtualiter.[20]

But why does such a passage reveal non-Aristotelian dimensions in Guerric? Does not the Dominican claim Aristotle himself as his authority when locating the soul essentially in the heart? Granted that he does make such a claim.

> Concedimus [quod anima non est in toto corpore integraliter per essentiam] dicentes cum Philosopho quod anima est in corde solum per essentiam, in cerebro per manifestationem, in toto corpore per operationem. [21]

Granted also that Aristotle does seem to state that the soul is present in the heart.[22] But the agreement between the Greek and the Latin stops there. Aristotle's statement concerns the soul as

---

but analogous to that. The thinking part of the soul must therefore be, while impassible, capable of receiving the form of an object." See ch. 21 below.

[19] *Ibid.*, ch. 5, 430a10–17.

[20] Paris: *Bibl. Nat. Lat., Nova Acquisita, Codex 1470*, folio 153b.

[21] *Ibid.*, lines preceding text cited in n. 20. Also see see *ibid., Codex 16417*, folio 67c.

[22] See *De motu animalium*, chs. 9–10, 702b13–703a30, especially 702a4–16; A. S. L. Farquharson, trans., and J. A. Smith and W. D. Ross, eds., *The Works of Aristotle* (Oxford: Clarendon Press, 1912).

source of motion and not in its essence as specifying principle and substantial form of the body.[23] Nor does he speak of the soul itself as spirit.[24]

Moreover, Guerric's conception of the soul as essentially a spirit entails a consequence Aristotle would hardly accept. If it is a spirit, a soul would be composed of form and spiritual matter, as are angels and all other spirits.

> Diverse sunt opiniones de hoc [utrum esset omnium creaturarum communis materia]. Quidam enim dicunt quod angeli et omnes spiritus sunt ex materia spirituali, non quidem [increata] sed creata simul cum ipsi creantur. Alii dicunt quod non habent materiam omnino sed quasi materiam seu *quod est.* Contra quos supra diximus quod habent materiam spiritualem et binarium in esse, non solum in fieri.[25]

If it is itself composed of form and matter, the human soul can scarcely be the substantial form of matter (at least not in a strictly Aristotelian sense). If so, we find in Guerric an early version of the doctrine of a plurality of forms, which will have such an illustrious

---

[23] What Guerric says in *Codex Vat. Lat. 4245*, folio 70rb, *respondeo*, is closer to Aristotle's own doctrine: "Dico quod est in corde per essentiam, ut dicit Philosophus, quia principaliter ibi operatur. Et est fons centrum [*read:* centralis] vitae et, existens ibi, per operationem movet quamlibet partem. Unde in corde per essentiam, et principaliter operatur, et, sicut centrum vitale, movet omnes alias partes corporis."

[24] He describes mind (*nous*) rather than soul as spiritual: "Mind in this sense [as the cause which is *poiêtikon* because it makes all things] is separable [from matter], impassible, unmixed, since in its *ousia* it is activity. . . . When mind is set free from its present conditions it appears as just what it is and nothing more: this alone is immortal and eternal." *On the Soul*, III, ch. 5, 430a17–18 and 22–23. The soul itself is the substantial form of matter: "The soul must be an *ousia* in the sense of the form of a natural body having life potentially within it." *Ibid.*, II, ch. 1, 412a20–22; also see *ibid.*, ch. 2, 414a4–28.

[25] *Codex Vat. Lat. 4245*, fol. 62vb. The *binarium in esse, non solum in fieri* of the last sentence is found explained a few lines earlier: "Primus recessus ab unitate est binarius. Angelus autem recedit ab unitate prima quae est summa et prima unitas, id est, a Deo. Ergo habet binarium. Binarius autem duplex: in esse et in fieri. Angelus non solum est sed fit. Ergo habet binarium utrumque, scilicet et binarium in esse, qui quidem est formae et materiae ex quibus est substantia; et binarium in fieri, qui quidam est finis et efficiens quibus fit res, res."

history in later medieval authors whose psychology also departs from Aristotle.[26]

Did Guerric's rather strange amalgam of Aristotelianism and plurality of forms affect Albert the Great's positions? This question arises because Guerric taught his fellow Dominican for one if not two years (1243 or 1244 to 1245) when the latter first came to Paris.[27]

Let us now turn to Albert himself.

---

[26] Among those holding (in some sense) a doctrine of plurality of forms are Roger Bacon (see E. Gilson, *HCP*, pp. 301–3), Bonaventure (*ibid.*, pp. 339–40), Peter John Olivi (*ibid.*, pp. 344). On the condemnation of 1277 and the doctrine, see *ibid.*, pp. 416–20, and D. A. Callus, O.P., "The Problem of the Unity of Form and Richard Knapwell, O.P.," in *Mélanges offerts à Étienne Gilson* (Paris: J. Vrin, 1959), pp. 123–60. Also see *idem*, "The Origins of the Problem of the Unity of Form," *The Thomist* 24 (1961), pp. 257–85.

Bibliographical data on Guerric of St. Quentin. Besides Henquinnet's two articles (see n. 1 above) and the references given there, the following studies may be consulted with profit: H. Fr. Dondaine et B. G. Guyot, "Guerric de Saint-Quentin et la condamnation de 1241," *Revue des sciences philosophiques et théologiques* 44 (avril 1960), pp. 225–42; B. G. Guyot, "Quaestiones Guerrici, Alexandri et aliorum magistrorum parisiensium (Praha, Univ. IV. D. 13)," *Archivum Fratrum Praedicatorum* 32 (1962), pp. 5–119; Beryl Smalley, "A Commentary on Isaias by Guerric of Saint-Quentin, O.P.," *Miscellanea Giovanni Mercati (Studi e testi* 122) (Citta del Vaticano: Biblioteca Apostolica Vaticana, 1946), pp. 383–97.

Unlike those three entries, the following are not devoted mainly to Guerric but study him together with several other medieval authors and only in reference to a general problem or topic (but often newly edited texts are furnished): Z. Alszeghy, S.J., *Nova Creatura. La nozione della grazia nei commentari medievali di S. Paolo (Analecta gregoriana* 81) (Romae: Universitas Gregoriana, 1956); H. Fr. Dondaine, "L'objet et le 'medium' de la vision béatifique chez les théologiens du XIIIe siècle," *Recherches de théologie ancienne et médiévale* 19 (1952), pp. 60–130; Odon Lottin, *Psychologie et morale aux XIIe et XIIIe siècles* (Louvain: Abbaye du Mont César, vol. II, 1948), especially pp. 557–64; vol. IV (1954) pp. 137–38; K. F. Lynch, O.F.M., *The Sacrament of Confirmation in the Early–Middle Scholastic Period* (Franciscan Institute Publications, Theology Series, 5) (St. Bonaventure, N.Y.: Franciscan Institute, 1957); A. McDevitt, O.F.M., "The Episcopate as an Order and Sacrament on the Eve of the High Scholastic Period," *Franciscan Studies* 20 (1960), pp. 96–148; V. Natalani, O.F.M., *De natura gratiae sacramentalis juxta S. Bonaventuram (Studia Antoniana* 17) (Romae: Pontificium Athenaeum Antonianum, 1961); Beryl Smalley, "Some Thirteenth Century Commentaries on the Sapiential Books," *Dominican Studies* 2 (1949), pp. 318–55, especially pp. 325–55: "From Alexander Nequam to Guerric of S. Quentin."

[27] See J. A. Weisheipl, *Albertus Magnus and the Sciences* (for publishing data see ch. 14 below, n. 2), p. 23. See ch. 14, n. 61, below *re* Guerric and Albert.

14

The Meaning of *Esse* in Albert the Great's Texts on Creation in *Summa de Creaturis* and *Scripta Super Sententias*

On September 2, 1959, Etienne Gilson wrote a gracious letter to acknowledge a paper, "Doctrine of Creation in the *Liber de Causis*," that I had contributed to the volume his North American students published in his honor.[1] In the course of that letter he said:

> One cannot ask a philosopher to conceive creation at a deeper level than that of his own notion of being. If God is the cause of that which being is, then God is a creator and being is a created being. . . . The progress achieved by Thomas Aquinas concerns less the notion of creation than that of being.

Gilson's statements merit serious consideration. If creation causes something to *be* which before *was not* at all, then understanding what an author means by "being" should help disclose how he conceives creation.

In this chapter on Albert the Great's texts on creation in two of his early theological writings, I shall investigate what he intends by *ens* or, more precisely, by *esse* so as to discover his stand on *creare*.

---

[1] C. J. O'Neil, ed., *An Etienne Gilson Tribute Presented by His North American Students* (Milwaukee: Marquette University Press, 1959), pp. 274–89.

Secondary Literature

Consulting bibliographies on Albert reveals that relatively little
attention has been given to his doctrine on creation.[2] In 1913 Anselm
Rohner published in *Beiträge zur Geschichte der Philosophie des Mittelalters* a study of the topic in Moses Maimonides, Albert and
Thomas Aquinas.[3] This is mainly concerned with their responses
to such questions as: Can one philosophically prove that our universe was created? How does one know it was created in time?
How disprove the Peripatetic arguments that the universe is eternal?[4] In a still unpublished Louvain dissertation of 1948, J. R. Losa
compared the treatises on creation by Albert, Aquinas and
Bonaventure in their commentaries on Lombard's *Sentences*.[5] Four
years later Joseph Hansen's contribution to *Studia Albertina*, a
Festschrift honoring Bernhard Geyer, focused again on how one
knows, according to Albert, that the world was created in time.[6]
Three years later J. F. Kiley presented a master of arts thesis entitled "The Doctrine of Creation in St. Albert the Great," which is
weakened by Kiley's tendency to read Albert in the light of Aqui-

---

[2] See M. H. Laurent and J. Congar, "Essai de bibliographie Albertinienne,"
Revue Thomiste 36 (1931), 422–68; Fernand van Steenberghen, "La littérature
albertino-thomiste (1930–1937)," *Revue néoscolastique de philosophie* 41 (1938),
126–61; Francis J. Catania, "A Bibliography of Albert the Great," *Modern
Schoolman* 37 (1959–60), 11–28; Roland Houde, "A Bibliography of Albert the
Great: Some Addenda," *Modern Schoolman* 39 (1961–62), 61–64; M. Schooyans,
"Bibliographie philosophique de S. Albert le Grand (1931–1960)," *Revista da
Universidade Católica de São Paulo* 21 (1961), 36–88; J. A. Weisheipl. "Bibliogra-
phy," *Albertus Magnus and the Sciences* [hereafter: Weisheipl] (Toronto: Pon-
tifical Institute of Mediaeval Studies, 1980), pp. 585–616; J. Schöpfer,
"Bibliographie" in G. Meyer and A. Zimmerman (eds.), *Albertus Magnus—
Doctor Universalis* [hereafter: Meyer/Zimmerman] (Mainz: Matthias-
Grünewald-Verlag. 1980), pp. 495–508.

[3] *Das Schöpfungsproblem bei Moses Maimonides, Albertus Magnus und Thomas
von Aquin.* Band 11, Heft 5 of *Beiträge zur Geschichte der Philosophie des Mittelalters*
[hereafter: *BGPM*] (Münster: Aschendorff, 1913).

[4] The section on Albert is found on pp. 45–92; for a comparison of Albert
with Moses Maimonides and Aquinas, see pp. 135–38.

[5] "Étude comparée du Traité de la Création dans les *Commentaires des Sentences* de S. Albert, S. Bonaventure et S. Thomas d'Aquin" (Dissertation
dactylographiée; Louvain, 1948).

[6] "Zur Frage aufanglosen und zeitlichen Schöpfung bei Albert dem
Grossen," *Studia Albertina*, Supplementband 4 of *BGPM* (1952), 167–88.

nas.[7] Finally, William Dunphy touched *passim* upon creation in his valuable paper "St. Albert and the Five Causes,"[8] as is clear from his concluding remarks:

Aristotle and the Peripatetics, proceeding by way of demonstrations *quia* and starting from the world of motion, could not philosophically arrive at an efficient cause that is not in any way a moving cause, namely one that creates everything *ex nihilo*. And what Plato held concerning an efficient cause not related to motion, while resting on merely probable grounds, can now be explained and held by theologians on the strength of principles derived from revelation and the inspiration of the Spirit (pp. 20–21).

In light of my survey, then, not much secondary literature has been devoted to Albert's doctrine of creation.[9] Have scholars been more concerned with what he said on *esse*? The answer is again somewhat negative. Apart from a few remarks by Peghaire, Pollet, de Solages and Pelster while treating other topics,[10] only four appear to have studied it in any detail. In his 1926 edition of Aquinas' *De Ente et Essentia*,[11] Roland-Gosselin wrote several chapters on the real distinction between essence and *esse*, one of which concerns the

---

[7] "The Doctrine of Creation in St. Albert the Great" (Master's thesis, St. John's University, 1955).

[8] *Archives d'Histoire Doctrinale et Littéraire du Moyen Âge* 33 (1966), 7–21.

[9] In "Création: La synthèse scolastique," *Dictionnaire de Théologie Catholique* (Paris: Letouzey et Ané, 1938), cols 2084–2092, H. Pinard mentions Albert only three times, attending mostly to Aquinas and implying that the position of all medieval authors is pretty much the same. In *General Doctrine of Creation in the Thirteenth Century with Special Emphasis on Matthew of Aquasparta* (München: F. Schöningh, 1964), Zachary Hayes gives no extended treatment to Albert's position.

[10] See J. Péghaire, "La causalité du bien selon Albert le Grand," *Études d'Histoire Littéraire et Doctrinale du* XIIIe *Siècle* (Ottawa: Institut d'Études Médiévales, 1932), pp. 59–89; V.-M. Pollet, "L'union hypostatique d'après S. Albert le Grand," *Revue Thomiste* 38 (1933), 505–32 and 689–724; Bruno de Solages, "La cohérence de la métaphysique de l'âme d'Albert le Grand," *Mélanges Cavallera* (Toulouse: Bibliothèque de l'Institut Catholique, 1948), pp. 367–400; F. Pelster, "Die *Quaestio* Alberts des Grossen über das Ein Sein in Christus nach Cod. Vat. Lat. 4245; Ein Beitrag zur Geschichte des Problems," *Divus Thomas* (Fribourg) 26 (1948), 3–25. Also see E. Gilson, *History of Christian Philosophy in the Middle Ages* [hereafter: *HCP*] (New York: Random House, 1955), p. 669, n. 5.

[11] M.-D. Roland-Gosselin, *Le "De Ente et Essentia" de S. Thomas d'Aquin* (Kain: Le Saulchoir, 1926; 2d ed., 1948).

stance Albert took on the problem. In twelve pages (pp. 172–84) Roland-Gosselin presents a sampling of texts from the *Summa de Creaturis, In Sententiarum,* the commentaries on Aristotle's treatises (*Categories, Metaphysics, De Anima, Liber de Causis*), *De Unitate Intellectus* and *Summa Theologiae.* The passages sampled reveal that "la pensée d'Albert le Grand sur la composition de l'être crée a beaucoup varié" (p. 172) and also that *esse* has several different meanings. For example, it is the *forma totius* or essence taken either concretely (*re* material existents) or abstractly (*re* spiritual existents; pp. 173–75, 181–82); *re* Christ it is aligned, from one point of view, with hypostasis but, from another, with essence or *quod est* and linked with existence (pp. 178–79, 180).[12]

Four decades later Léonard Ducharme published an important article, "*Esse* chez saint Albert le Grand. Introduction à la métaphysique de ses premiers écrits," the subtitle of which indicates its restriction to the two early treatises: *Summa de Creaturis* and *In Sententiarum.*[13] In them Albert at times does use *esse* (as Ducharme establishes) to express "existence" as the situation in which things find themselves when efficiently caused by external agents (p. 4). Existence thus understood has to do with the *fact* that various things *are* and *are caused* by God or (say) a carpenter, and Albert uses *esse* in stating that fact. But the fact that things exist is never considered by him to be a perfection, let alone their supreme perfection, and hence *esse* never designates existence as an ontological constituent and perfection of anything (p. 8; also see pp. 11–12, 16, 37). Rather, *esse* most frequently and properly signifies essence or specific nature— namely, the *quo est* by which a *quod est* is that which it specifically is, the reality and definition which the *forma totius* gives to whatever is (pp. 11–13, 18–19). In the phrases "esse essentiae" or "esse ut actus

---

[12] In *ibid.,* pp. 180–83, Roland-Gosselin notes that in the *Summa Theologiae* Albert uses *id quod est* and *esse* equivocally. His attempts on pp. 183–84 to eliminate that equivocation terminate thus: "Il semble plus conforme à la vérité historique de laisser à la pensée d'Albert la Grand l'indétermination que nous avons constatée. . . . Albert le Grand semble avoir été de ces esprits vastes, ouverts à toutes les influences, d'une mémoire tenace, incapables d'oublier ou d'abandonner une idée, et qui se trouvent empêchés par leur étendue même, et leur fidélité, d'unifier leur pensée." A. Hufnagel's solution is to question whether the *Summa Theologiae* is rightly attributed to Albert as author—see "Zur Echtheitsfrage der *Summa Theologiae* Alberts des Grossen," *Theologische Quartalschrift* 146 (1966), 8–39. Also see E. Gilson, HCP, p. 671, n. 12.

[13] *Revue de l'Université d'Ottawa* 27 (1957), 1–44.

essentiae," the first noun points to the very effect and reality an essence causes within its concrete subject (pp. 24 sqq. and 32 sqq.).[14]

Five years after Ducharme's publication there appeared Geiger's long study in the Canadian annual *Études d'histoire littéraire et doctrinale* entitled "La vie, acte essential de l'âme [et] l'*esse*, acte de l'essence d'après Albert-le-Grand."[15] Basically agreeing with Ducharme's interpretation that *esse* is linked chiefly with essence,[16] Geiger parallels the relationship of essence to *esse* with that of soul to life. Life is the formal effect of the soul within the living body. *Vivere* is the animation or vivification effected by the soul's presence within matter: it is what the soul formally causes as an intrinsic constituent of a living existent. It emanates from the soul as the latter's essential and continuous act and is, thereby, a sort of intermediary between soul and body (see pp. 56–97, especially pp. 59–62, 85–87, and the résumé on pp. 92–97). Similarly, *esse* is the formal effect of a concrete essence within a being. It is the specification of matter by the *forma totius*. It is the essentialization, the essential determination effected by the presence of a definite nature within an individual *quod est*. It is the act emanating from essence; it is diffused (*diffunditur*) by the form. It is a quasi-intermediary between the principle (the essence or *quo est*) and the recipient (the *quod est* or matter; see pp. 97–111, especially pp. 97–98, 100–108, 110–11).

Even the tightly abridged and simplified version of Geiger's reading just presented shows it to be profound and helpful. But one negative comment on his methodology seems called for. On page 50, note 9, he states that

> Albert presents the same doctrine, often expressed in the same terms, in his first as well as his last treatises, both philosophical and theological in nature. Hence, one may abstract from questions of chronology and from the distinction between philosophical and theological writings.

That statement makes me uneasy. One can know that the same position on *esse* is presented in philosophical or theological treatises from different temporal periods of Albert's career only if one

---

[14] See *ibid.*, p. 33: "l'*esse* est l'effet de l'essence dans le sujet concret."

[15] *Études d'histoire littéraire et doctrinale* 17 (1962), 49–116.

[16] Geiger also grants (with Ducharme) that *esse* on occasion does point to existence as a fact but not as a perfection—see *ibid.*, pp. 62, 104, 106.

has first arranged and then read them in the chronological order they were written. But if they are read in that fashion, why not present the results of that reading in a chronological order?

The fourth and final study of *esse* is Georg Wieland's *Untersuchungen zum Seinsbegriff im Metaphysikkommentar Alberts des Grossen.*[17] He accepts Geiger's exegesis of *esse* as act of form or essence but complements it with *esse* as the *primum creatum* from Albert's *De Causis et Processu Universitatis.*[18] Let us speak briefly on those two points.

Form or essence gives *esse*, which is in fact the "diffusio formae." In that phrase "forma" stands for "forma totius" and not "forma partis"[19] because the latter, even though the act of matter, is potential with respect to *esse*, which issues into the individual thing from form-and-matter as its act and completion and which accordingly needs as source the form (= *forma totius*), which is, to some extent, over and beyond that composite of matter/form. In support of that interpretation Wieland quotes these lines from Albert's *Metaphysica*, I, tr. 4, c. 9 (Geyer edition, p. 60, lines 27–30 and 33–35):

> Forma est quasi foris manens dicta, et quanto plus manet foras materiam substantia et esse et operatione, verius habet nomen formae. . . . Illae autem formae quae in materia sunt imagines vocantur, eo quod sunt formarum verarum resultationes et imitationes, quantum permittunt materiae, ut dicit Plato.

Hence the form, the diffusion of which is *esse*, the form which has *esse* as its essential and proper act, is the *forma totius*—namely, "forma, quae est totum esse et est species" (*Meta.*, II, c. 9; p. 100, lines 77 sq.; quoted by Wieland on p. 67, n. 4, and *passim*). Consequently, *esse* is the formal effect of the essence or form which makes a being be *what it is* (p. 93). It is the intermediary between essence and the

---

[17] Münster: Aschendorff, 1972. Wieland first submitted this as a doctoral dissertation in 1969 to Ruhr-Universität Bochum. It now appears as Band VII in the new series of *BGPM*.

[18] This is Albert's commentary on the *Liber de Causis*, which is Neoplatonic in its philosophical positions (see n. 20 below) but was considered by Albert as belonging to the Aristotelian *Metaphysics*. Hence, Wieland justly includes it in his study of Albert's commentary on the *Metaphysics*.

[19] This phrase Wieland believes (see pp. 72–90, especially pp. 75–76) Geiger left ambiguous and hence seeks to dispel the ambiguity. On "forma totius," see pp. 28 sqq., 39.

individual (pp. 90, 103), which it also makes one, intelligible, definable and nameable (pp. 94 sqq.). Just as accidents are products of substance, so *esse* is the product of essence (p. 70), from which however it is only virtually distinct through a "distinctio rationis rationcinatae cum fundamento in re" (p. 93, n. 136).

As so conceived, *esse* belongs to the Aristotelian dimension of Albert's thought and answers the question *quid sit res*. But one must, Wieland continues, ask also *an sit res*, the answer to which Albert finds in Proposition 4 of the Neoplatonic treatise *Liber de Causis:* "Prima rerum creatarum est esse, et non est ante ipsum creatum aliud."[20] Considered as *primum creatum, esse* pertains to the relationship that all created existents have to the first cause: in each of these *esse* is His effect and allows one to say that the thing *is, exists* (pp. 108–9). It is the "prima effluxio dei" and, thus, involves an "Aktivität von einem vorgeordneten Prinzip," just as "esse ut actus essentiae" entails an activity from a principle too— the form which "dat esse" (p. 109). *Esse* as *primum creatum* and as act of form has, then, two distinct sources, but the relationship between the two conceptions of *esse* and between its two principles is not clearly set forth by Albert.[21] Despite that lack of clarity,

---

[20] The treatise is Neoplatonic in its philosophy (basically, that of Plotinus and Proclus), but whether its author is Arabian, Jewish, or Christian is still not clear. For surveys of authorship, see H. Bédoret, "L'auteur et le traducteur du *Liber de Causis,*" *Revue néoscolastique de philosophie* 41 (1938), 519–33; H.-D. Saffrey, *Sancti Thomae de Aquino Super Librum de Causis Expositio* (Fribourg: Société Philosophique Louvain, 1954), pp. xv sqq.; G. C. Anawati, "Prolégomènes à une nouvelle édition du *De Causis* arabe," *Mélanges L. Massignon* (Paris: A. Maisonneuve, 1957), pp. 73–85 (he favors a ninth-century Arabian Neoplatonist as author); H.-D. Saffrey, "L'état actuel des recherches sur le *Liber de Causis* comme source de la métaphysique au moyen âge," in P. Wilpert, ed., *Miscellanea Mediaevalia* (Berlin: Walter de Gruyter, 1963), 267–81 (see especially p. 274: "Il nous est impossible de décider si le *Liber* a été compilé par un ancien philosophe arabe, ou si déjà avant lui un original grec ou syriaque existait, qu'il se serait contenté de traduire"); A. Pattin, "Le *Liber de Causis,*" *Tijdschrift voor Filosofie* 28 (1966), 90–98; A. Badawi, *La transmission de la philosophie grecque au monde arabe* (Paris: J. Vrin, 1968), pp. 60–72; also see my *Divine Infinity in Greek and Medieval Thought,* (New York/Bern: Peter Lang Publishing, Inc., 1992) ch. 13, pp. 289–90. I shall use the Latin text as found in Otto Bardenhewer, *Die pseudo-aristotelische Schrift Ueber das reine Gute bekannt unter dem Namen Liber de Causis* (Freiburg im Breisgau: Herder, 1882), pp. 163 sqq.; for a German translation of the Arabic text, see *ibid.*, pp. 58–118.

[21] Wieland also finds a similar lack of clarity in whether creation is a necessary or a free act—see *op. cit.*, p. 60, n. 67. But see n. 46 below.

though, his grafting a Neoplatonist version of creation (wherein *esse* is *primum creatum*) upon an Aristotelian theory of *ousia* (within which *esse* is *actus essentiae*) to answer the double question of *an sit res* and *quid sit res* discloses Albert's commentaries on Aristotle to be no mere compilations of disjointed materials but a genuine contribution to medieval philosophy and theology (pp. 111–12).

Obviously Wieland's rather spectacular conclusions are directly relevant to this chapter on *esse* in Albert's texts on creation. Undoubtedly, too, they are attractive. Whether or not they are valid cannot be decided until one has independently studied Albert, especially his *Liber de Causis et Processu Universitatis*. But one negative note can be sounded now on Wieland's methodology. On occasion he tends to excerpt short portions (sometimes a single sentence) of the same text and to repeat them in connection with various topics throughout his book.[22] This tendency can lead one to assess an excerpt apart from its context and also to impart to his interpretation a higher degree of textual strength than is merited.

The previous survey of the attempts four scholars made to cope with *esse* in Albert's writings is helpful by illustrating procedural flaws to be avoided and, second, by stressing questions which need reflection. We should read Albert's treatises in a chronological order (*vs.* Geiger) and, also, study key texts in them not piecemeal but each in its entirety within its context (*vs.* Wieland). Among questions meriting attention within the two general areas of *esse* and creation are whether *esse* is linked with existence (if so, as a mere fact or as a perfection?) or only with essence; what essence means: whether it is synonymous with form and, if so, in what sense; how *esse* fits into the Boethian scheme of *quo est/quod est*; what connection *esse* has with prime matter; whether and how it is the *primum creatum*; whether God creates freely; what creation strictly taken entails.[23]

Let us now reflect upon such questions in Albert's own treatises, chronologically ordered.

---

[22] One such is: "forma, quae est totum esse et est species" (*Meta.*, II, c. 9) quoted by Wieland on p. 67, n. 4, and referred to on pp. 74, 76, 78 and *passim*.

[23] On this last question see the prgr. corresponding to n. 45 below.

Text A: *Summa de Creaturis,* Pars I, Tr. 1, q. 2, a. 1: "An materia sit," ad 1 and ad 2

The first key-text is from his *Summa de Creaturis,*[24] which (in the Jammy edition and for our purposes) consists of two parts. The second of these is "De homine"; the first is "De coaequaevis": the four *creata* which God made simultaneously and which are all equal inasmuch as each is a principle of further creation: matter, the "caelum empyreum," angelic nature and time (Pars I, Tr. 4, c. 69, *solutio; XIX,* 215A). Our text concerns the first of these *coae-quaeva*—matter—in a *quaestio* which comes after Albert had in an

---

[24] Written between 1240 and 1243 in the judgment of F. J. Catania, "Divine Infinity According to Albert the Great's Commentary on the *Sentences*" (Ph.D. diss., St. Louis University, 1959), p. 9, who gives a helpful survey of the views of Lottin, Doucet and Brady (*ibid.,* pp. 8–10). Also see J. A. Weisheipl, "Life and Works of Albert the Great," pp. 22–23: *Summa Parisiensis,* of which the *Summa de Creaturis* is a section, was composed at Paris before his commentary on the *Sentences* and apparently as a result of his disputations as master. For A. Maurer, *Medieval Philosophy* (New York: Random House, 1962), p. 403, n. 1, it was composed 1236–43; for Etienne Gilson (with M. H. Laurent), 1228–33— see *HCP,* p. 668, n. 2. This much seems clear: the *Summa* is among Albert's earliest works and is earlier than *In Sententiarum.*

On the plan of the complete *Summa,* see P. G. Meersseman, *Introductio in Opera Omnia B. Alberti Magni* (Brugis Apud Carolum Beyaert, 1932), pp. 107–10: the *Summa* consists of four books, each with subdivisions—*De Deo Uno et Trino; De Creatione et Creaturis; De Bono et de Virtutibus; De Incarnatione, Sacramentis, Resurrectione.* "De Coaequaevis" is the first part of Book Two. For a different and chronological arrangement, see B. Geyer, *Alberti Magni Opera Omnia,* Tomus XXVIII: *De Bono* (Monasterii Westfalorum in Aedibus Aschendorff, 1951), Prolegomena," p. XIX: (1) *De Sacramentis,* (2) *De Incarnatione,* (3) *De Resurrectione,* (4) *De IV Coaequaevis,* (5) *De Homine,* (6) *De Bono.*

Vol. XXVII of the Cologne critical edition, which will contain "De IV Coaequaevis," has not yet been published (only vol. XXVI [1958], which contains *De Sacramentis, De Incarnatione, De Resurrectione,* and vol. XXVIII, containing *De Bono,* have so far appeared). Consequently, my references to the "De IV Coaequaevis" portion of the *Summa* are to the seventeenth-century edition: Petrus Jammy, *Opera B. Alberti Magni* (Lugduni Sumptibus Claudii Prost, 1651, vol. XIX: *Summa de Creaturis Divisa in Duas Partes.* Its Latin text I use without change except for occasional simplification of punctuation and modernized spelling, as well as a few corrections required to make sense of a passage (which however are always indicated). Also, references in the "Index Tractatuum . . ." of the volume are occasionally inaccurate and have been corrected.

initial question of eight articles discussed creation itself ("an creatio
sit; quid sit; cuius sit proprius actus creare; utrum creatio sit communicabilis alii; utrum sit opus naturae vel voluntatis; utrum creatio
sit actus separatus ab opere naturae et propositi; utrum actus
creationis plus sit ostensivus potentiae vel sapientiae vel bonitatis;
utrum actus creationis sit naturalis vel miraculosus"). In the first
article of question 2, "De Materia," Albert asks whether prime
matter exists ("an materia sit") and answers through the familiar
technique of four *videtur quod non*s, five *sed contra*s (drawn from
Glossa super Genesim, Augustine's *Confessions*, XII, and Aristotle's
Physics), a *solutio* (which consists of two words *re* those *sed contra*s:
"Quod concedimus") and, finally, replies to the four *videtur quod non*s
(Pars I, Tr. 1, q. 2; XIX, 7C–8C).

Let us turn to the first of those replies, which confronts this
endeavor to show that prime matter does not exist. Since form
gives *esse*, since to lack *esse* is to be nothing, and since prime matter
entirely lacks form, matter is entirely without *esse* and thus, precisely as prime matter, is nothing [and, hence, does not exist].

Forma dat esse; ergo quod caret omni forma caret omni esse;
sed materia prima secundum rationem primae materiae accepta caret omni forma; ergo caret omni esse; et quicquid
caret omni esse nihil est; ergo materia prima nihil est secundum rationem materiae primae accepta, quia caret omni
forma; ergo caret omni esse. [*Ibid.*, *videtur quod non* 1; p. 7D]

Albert's reply to that argumentation is indeed interesting but puzzling. Although prime matter has of itself the *esse* which properly
belongs to what is a subject and potency, this is *esse secundum quid*
and not *esse simpliciter*, which however form gives to matter; [hence,
prime matter does exist].

Dicentes ad primum quod forma dat esse; materia autem habet
esse subjecti et potentiae, et hoc habet a seipsa, et hoc non est
esse simpliciter sed secundum quid. [*Ibid.*, ad 1; p. 8B]

Puzzlement issues from several sources. In the sentence just
quoted, the *esse* which "forma dat" is no doubt "esse simpliciter,"
which amounts to "existence" in light of the problem at hand:
whether or not prime matter exists. But if so, how can both Geiger
and Wieland so confidently refer the clause to the formal causality
form or essence exercises within an existent—the diffusion of the

form, the specification by which a form makes the existent be *what he is* and not *be* simply?[25] Second, must not the first noun in the clause "forma dat esse" stand for "forma partis" rather than "forma totius," since the form at issue is the counterpart of prime matter? If this should be the case, though, what of Wieland's claim that "forma" in this formula is "forma totius"?[26] Third, the "esse subjecti et potentiae," which prime matter has of itself, is "esse secundum quid" and pertains to *what* matter is, to its very nature.[27] But if (with Geiger and Wieland; see note 25 above) the *esse* which form is responsible for as an intrinsic cause is the specific determination of the existent, might not the *esse* which matter has by reason of its very status as subject and potency be the effect it exercises in that existent as intrinsic cause and, thus, be the limitation and individuation of the individual existent?[28] But no matter what one's reaction is to that, this seems obvious: the *esse* in the single sentence

---

[25] On Geiger, see *art. cit.*, pp. 103–5 and 108 sqq. (where he attends mainly to *De Anima* and *De Unitate Intellectus*); on Wieland see *op. cit.*, pp. 26–27 and 72 sqq. (where he attends solely to *Meta.*). Also see the previous portions of my chapter corresponding to notes 15–16 and 17–21.

[26] On "forma" *re* "materia" as "forma substantialis" and, hence, "forma partis," see *ibid.*, a. 2 ("Quid sit Materia"), ad 1 (p. 9D): "Prima potentia materiae est ad formam substantialem"; *ibid.*, ad [3] (p. 10A): "Et primum dicit etiam ante quod nihil est: potentia enim materiae primo est ad substantialem formam et ad alias per accidens, scilicet propter illam"; *ibid., ad illud quod objicitur contra quartam* [*definitionem materiae*] (p. 11A): "Inter materiam autem primam et formam substantialem non est medium." For Wieland's position see above, n. 19.

[27] On the essence of matter as subject and potency see also *ibid.*, a. 1, ad 4 (p. 8C): "Unumquodque dicitur perfectum quando est in debito statu sui esse; et ideo materia perfecta est, quando habet rationem subjecti ad formas generabilium et corruptibilium"; *ibid.*, a. 2, *solutio* (p. 9C): "substantia et entitas materiae in se considerata non est intelligibilis proprio intellectu sed intelligitur secundum privationem, scilicet quod hoc est materia quod praeter formas accidentales et substantiales invenitur in ente"; *ibid.*, a. 3, ad 3 (p. 11D): "materia prima in ratione materiae accepta non potest abstrahi a ratione potentiae, quia ipsa secundum seipsam habet rationem potentiae: secundum seipsam enim subjectum est, et ratio potentiae et ratio subjecti in ipsa sunt idem, et sic habet formam quandam rationis."

Question: what link, if any, is there between the "esse secundum quid" which matter has of itself (see key text A, under discussion) and "incohatio formae" in matter? On this last see Geiger, *art. cit.*, pp. 23–25, 105–7, especially p. 105 and n. 214; G. Wieland, *op. cit.*, pp. 84–87 with notes.

[28] On matter as the principle of individuation in sensible existents, see *ibid.*, a. 5, *solutio* (p. 15C): "Dicendum quemadmodum dicit Aristoteles in primo *de*

which constitutes Albert's *ad primum* has a twofold meaning: existence (the *esse simpliciter* which "forma dat") and nature or essence
(the *esse secundum quid* which matter has on its own).

What information does Albert give on those (and other) points
in *ad secundum*, which concludes our Text A and in which Albert
answers this *videtur quod non? Esse* is what is created first (as Aristotle says in *Liber de Causis*) and nothing else is created before it;
accordingly, whatever is prior to *esse* is not created; but whatever is
prior to form is also prior to *esse;* hence, whatever is prior to form is
not created; but prime matter is prior to form and, thus, is not
created; but whatever is not created is nothing; therefore, prime
matter is nothing [and, accordingly, does not exist].[29]

> Dicit Philosophus in *libro de causis* quod prima rerum creatarum
> est esse, et non est ante ipsum creatum aliud. Ergo quod est
> ante esse non est de numero creatorum; sed quicquid est ante
> formam est ante esse; ergo quod est ante formam non est de
> numero creatorum; materia autem prima est ante formam;
> ergo non est de numero creatorum; et quicquid non est de
> numero creatorum, nihil est; ergo materia prima nihil est.
> [*Ibid., videtur quod non* 2; p. 7D]

Albert's response to that impressive line of argumentation is equally
impressive but not without problems, as will be evident from this
paraphrase.

When *esse* is said in the *Liber de Causis* to be the first of created
things, *esse* stands for *ens* (as the one commenting there on Prop. 4
and Blessed Dionysius both make clear)[30] and "first" by nature

---

caelo et mundo quod cum dico hoc caelum, dico materiam; sed cum dico caelum, dico formam"; *ibid.,* Tr. 4, q. 28, a. 1, *solutio* (p. 97D): "Notandum quod
quoddam facit personam et aliquid ostendit eam esse discretam. Hoc autem
facit personam quod facit per se unam eam; nihil autem facit eam per se unam
nisi particulatio formae super hanc materiam. . . . Individuantia autem
ostendunt personam distinctam esse et in materialibus quidem materialiter
sunt individuantia, in intellectualibus spiritualiter." See Roland-Gosselin, *op.
cit.,* pp. 89–103, especially pp. 89–94 for exegesis and texts from *Summa de
Creaturis* and *In Sententiarum.*

[29] I omit in my paraphrase and Latin quotation the two proofs why what is
before *esse* is what is before form because Albert is silent in *ad secundum* on
those proofs, which also are not directly relevant to our topic. But see n. 33
below.

[30] See Dionysius, *De Divinis Nominibus,* ch. 5, #266 of the Latin translation
found in C. Pera, *Thomae Aquinatis in Librum Beati Dionysii de Divinis Nominibus*

refers to that which is not [entirely] convertible with subsequent subsistents. In this sense *ens* is absolutely first. Why so? Because the process of resolving what is posterior to what is prior comes to a halt in *ens*. Consequently, "first" here has to do with a principle of cognition. But when matter is said to be "first," "principle" is understood with respect to generation and time. Obviously, then, "first" is used equivocally, because when applied to *ens* it is a principle of cognition with reference to what can be fitted into predicaments, but when applied to matter it is a principle of generation with respect to the existents generated.

Ad aliud dicendum quod cum dicitur prima rerum creatarum est esse, ponitur esse pro ente, sicut dicit ibi Commentator in expositione illius propositionis. Et idem dicit beatus Dionysius in *libro de divinis nominibus*, cap. 5 de ente. Et dicitur ibi primum natura a quo non convertitur consequentia subsistendi, et sic ens est absolute primum, quia in ipso stat resolutio posteriorum in prius. Et ibidem hoc primum ponit principium cognitionis. Cum autem dicitur materia prima, ponitur principium secundum rationem generationis et temporis. Et sic patet quod primum hinc inde ponitur aequivoce, quia cum dicitur de ente est principium cognitionis respectu eorum quae ordinabilia sunt in praedicamento. Cum autem dicitur de materia, est principium generationis respectu generatorum. [*Ibid., ad secundum;* p. 8B]

Where are the problems areas of which we spoke in that important reply? One consists in how to translate and interpret the sentence "Et dicitur ibi primum natura a quo non convertitur consequentia subsistendi, et sic ens est absolute primum, quia in ipso stat resolutio posteriorum in prius." My paraphrase reads: "*first* by nature refers to that which is not [fully] convertible with subsequent subsistents. In this sense *ens* is absolutely first. Why so? Because the process of resolving what is posterior to what is prior comes to a halt in *ens*." That is an endeavor to make Albert intelligible and not to translate the precise wording of his Latin. But what

---

Expositio (Turin: Marietti, 1950), p. 230: "Et ante alias ipsius participationes esse propositum est"; *ibid.,* #267: "Et quidem principia existentium omnia esse participant et sunt et principia sunt et primum sunt, postea principia sunt. . . . Per se participationes invenies ipso esse primum illas participantes et ipso esse quidem primum existentes, postea huius aut huius principia existentes et participare esse et existentes et participatas."

data is elsewhere provided to ground that endeavor? The author of the *Liber de Causis*, Prop. 1, states: "Quando removes virtutem rationalem ab homine, non remanet homo, et remanet vivum, spirans, sensibile. Et quando removes ab eo vivum, non remanet vivum, et remanet esse, quoniam esse non removetur ab eo sed removetur vivum. . . . Remanet ergo homo esse. Cum ergo non est individuum homo, est animal, et si non est animal, est esse tantum." The process thus described could be what Albert intends by "in ipso [ente or *esse*] stat resolutio posteriorum in prius," since he had already referred in the *Summa de Creaturis* (q. 1, a. 1, arg. 3; p. 1D sq.) to Prop. 1.[31] Second, in a portion of our next key-text (*In II Sent.*, d. 1, a. 1, ad "id quod objicitur de tertia expositione"; XIV, p. 5A), we read: "Secundum rationem formae et simplicitatis nihil est ante esse, quia omnia aliquo modo se habent ex additione ad ens, etiam unum et verum et bonum." These last three "convertuntur cum ente," which nonetheless retains its prior status as that to which the others are added. Accordingly, it makes some sense to understand Albert as meaning: *ens* or *esse* is first as that at which stops the resolution of humanity, animality and life, and as that to which *bonum* and the other convertibles are added. Hence, my paraphrase: "*esse* or *ens* as 'first' refers to that which is not [fully] convertible with subsequent subsistents. In this sense *ens* is absolutely first. Why so? Because the process of resolving what is posterior to what is prior comes to a halt in *ens*."

---

[31]On "resolutio" see *In I Sent.*, d. 8, a. 24 ad 1 (Jammy ed., XIV, 155D–156A): "Quod objicitur de ente dicendum quod id in quo stat resolutio nostri intellectus est simplex secundum quid et simpliciter compositum. Intellectus enim resolvens abstrahit universale a particulari et ulterius magis universale a minus universali, et ideo non aufert nisi differentias coarctantes, et verum est quod secundum ablationem illarum differentiarum ens simplex est et ideo stat in ipso resolutio." To date the only information found in the *Summa de Creaturis* on "subsistere" comes from *ibid.*, tr. 1, q. 2, a. 2, *ad id quod objicitur contra tertiam definitionem* (XIX, 10C–D): "Sic se habet informe et materia ad substantiam et hoc aliquid et quod est. Et intelligit per informe rationem privationis in materia, per materiam autem naturam subjecti, per substantiam autem intelligit formam, per hoc aliquid determinatam ac compositam substantiam: hoc aliquid enim est forma contracta per materiam. Per hoc quod est intelligit rationem subsistentiae, quam habet composita substantia a compositione materiae et formae. Unde quod est idem quod nunc est apud naturam. Per formam autem intelligitur materia secundum quod accipit esse a forma: secundum Philosophum enim in 7 *metaphysicae*, idem est esse subjecti et formae in composito, quia subjectum non habet esse nisi a forma."

But Albert's *ad secundum* contains another and more serious difficulty. The *videtur quod non* it is answering is explicitly directed at showing that prime matter does not exist, since it is (to reverse the order of points made there) nothing, not created, prior to form, prior to *esse*. But in his reply Albert explicitly sets down only why *esse* (= *ens*) and matter are "first" in an equivocal sense and leaves the reader to infer that the priority of *esse* neither excludes that of matter nor prevents matter from existing, because *esse* can also mean "existere." More fully stated: the priority of *esse* in the *Liber de Causis* has to do with cognition, whereas that of prime matter has to do with generation and time: it is prior to form inasmuch as of itself it is not form but the potency to receive form; accordingly, prime matter precedes form and yet *is*—because the *esse* spoken of in the *Liber* pertains directly to knowledge and not to the temporal world where generation and other changes occur and where *esse* as "existence" is operative—and is created.

If our reading of *ad secundum* is accurate, then, Albert applies *esse* explicitly to the intramental world, where *ens* is contrasted with such other conceptions as *verum, unum* and *bonum* or, again, with "man," "animal," and "life" (as in *Liber de Causis*) or, again, with the predicaments. Implicitly, though, he applies *esse* to the extramental world of actual existents, where prime matter is an ingredient in their coming to be through generation but itself exists as that "quod praeter formas accidentales et substantiales invenitur in ente" (*ibid.*, a. 2, *solutio;* XIX, p. 9D) through divine creation.[32]

And if these results (i.e., *esse* points to *ens* as concept and to existence as fact) are joined with those attained earlier in our exegesis of *ad primum*, we have a third meaning for *esse*, which matter has of itself: its nature as subject and potency, which is *esse secundum quid*. Nowhere (at least in the portions of *Summa de Creaturis* so far studied) does *esse* point to the form itself or its essential act.[33] In *ad*

---

[32] On matter as created see *ibid.*, a. 3, *solutio* (p. 11C), which consists in Albert's saying, "Quod concedimus," where *quod* refers to this *sed contra* (p. 11B–C): "Augustinus in 12 *confessionum:* Tu Domine fecisti mundum de materia informi, quam fecisti de nulla re pene nulla [*read:* nullam] rem. Item, Augustinus in libro *de trinitate* dicit quod omne ens est ab ente primo quod est Deus. Materia prima est ens. Ergo est ab ente primo, et non nisi per creatum; ergo est creata." Also see n. 47 below.

[33] One comes closest to this in the first of two proofs in *videtur quod non* 2 of a. 1 ("An materia sit") why whatever is prior to form is also prior to esse: "Quod autem hoc sit ante esse quod est ante formam patet ex hoc quod esse

primum, in fact, "forma dat esse" appears to link existence with form.

But perhaps the picture will change in the key text we now take up.

Text B: *In II Sent.,* d. 1, a. 1, ad objectionem de tertia explicatione[34]

The passage at hand is occasioned by Lombard's quotation from *Genesis* 1:1: "In principio creavit Deus caelum et terram," and, more exactly, by his triple explanation of that verse, the first two of which concentrate on "principium" (which is taken to refer to the Son and, second, to time; XV, pp. 3D–4A), the third on "caelum et terram" (which stands for "angelicam naturam et materiam quatuor elementorum"; *ibid.,* p. 4C). The key text is Albert's reply to this objection against the third interpretation. According to Aristotle, *esse* is what is created first, and no other creature is created before it; therefore, the angelic nature and prime matter are not first.

> Objicitur autem: sicut dicit Philosophus prima rerum creatarum est esse et non est ante ipsum creatura alia; ergo angelica natura et materia prima non sunt prima, ut videtur. [*Ibid.,* p. 4C]

What is Albert's response? The objection is solved (he comments) inasmuch as "first" is used with reference either to the intelligibility of form and simplicity or to the order substance has in *esse.* According to the intelligibility of form and simplicity nothing is prior to *esse* because everything—even *unum, verum* and *bonum,* as was established above *(In I Sent.,* d. 46)—is in some sense an addition

---

non est nisi individui vel speciei vel generis vel principii, et omne tale est a forma; ergo omne tale est a forma individui vel speciei vel generis vel principii" (p. 7D). But, as noted above (n. 29), Albert in *ad secundum* takes no notice of that proof.

[34] Albert's *Scripta Super IV Libros Sententiarum* (to give its full title—see P. G. Meersseman, *op. cit.,* p. 106) is to be dated after the *Summa de Creaturis* (1249 is its *terminus ad quem*): see F. J. Catania, *op. cit.* [see n. 24 above], p. 9. According to W. Kübel, *Alberti Magni Opera Omnia,* Tomus XXVI: *De Sacramentis* . . . (1958), "Prolegomena," p. X, it is almost certain that Albert was writing *In II Sent.* in 1246; similarly Weisheipl, p. 22. Since the Cologne critical edition is not yet published, we shall use the Jammy edition (see above, n. 24, last paragraph), vol. XV.

to *ens*. But according to the order of substance in nature and *esse* all philosophers hold that the first intelligence is what the creator of the universe created first. What they call "intelligences" we call "angels." Thus, the explanation that "in the beginning God created the angelic nature first" holds because creation has to do with *esse* rather than with simplicity, which comes about by abstraction through the intellect.

> Ad id quod objicitur de tertia [expositione] dicendum quod soluta est objectio, quia primum dicitur duobus modis, scilicet secundum rationem formae et simplicitatis, et secundum ordinem substantiae in essendo. Secundum rationem formae et simplicitatis nihil est ante esse, quia omnia aliquo modo se habent ex additione ad ens, etiam unum et verum et bonum, ut in penultima distinctione primi libri est ostensum. Sed secundum ordinem substantiae in natura et esse opinio omnium philosophorum est quod intelligentia prima sit primum causatum a creatore universitatis. Quod autem illi intelligentias nos vocamus angelos; et tunc stat expositio illa quia creatio potius respicit esse quam ordinem simplicitatis. In abstractione autem fit per intellectum. [*Ibid., ad objectionem* . . .; p. 5A]

In the objection Judeo-Christianity confronts pagan Aristotelianism (Neoplatonism, actually) on what God created first. According to the Old Testament, as interpreted by Lombard, it was angels and prime matter; for the author of the *Liber de Causis* it was *esse*. In his reply Albert tries (unsuccessfully, I would say) to defuse the explosive situation by distinguishing two levels on which "first" is applicable. One of them has to do with actual substances or natures: intelligences [human souls, animals and plants]. Here "first" pertains to the existents which are highest hierarchically: intelligences or angels. These *Genesis* 1:1 described as created first, since creation concerns *esse* or existence.[35] The other level consists of intelligibilities, forms, quiddities achieved through intellectual abstraction,

---

[35] *Ibid.*, ". . . creatio potius respicit esse quam ordinem simplicitatis."

In his defense here of the third explanation, Albert has so far said nothing of the last word in the phrase: "angelica natura et materia." But see the subsequent two paragraphs ("Si autem" and "Ad aliud"), the pertinent lines of which are these: "Etiam secundum philosophos materia ponitur primo antequam aliquid fiat ex ipsa. . . . [Deus] intelligit omnia simul in materia creata et non in formis distinctis."

and here one intelligibility is prior to another if it is more simple. Which intelligibility is first, then? *Ens* because it is less complex than *verum, unum and bonum,* which are additions to it: for example, *verum* is "being-as-*related-to-intellect.*"[36]

Such is Albert's explicit message, which at first hearing seems sound enough. Why, then, is it deficient? Because he has not directly faced the objection that God first created *esse* and not the angelic nature. In his answer he removes the *esse* of the *Liber de Causis,* Prop. 4, from the actual universe, in which alone creation takes place, by reducing it to an intelligibility (*ens*). Because of simplicity in its content or comprehension this may have priority over other intelligibilities (true, good, one), but it is not something capable of being created: no concept can, strictly speaking, be created, but only thought of, analyzed, reflected upon. Yet Prop. 4 of the *Liber* reads: "Prima *rerum creatarum* est esse." Despite his clear acknowledgment that *esse* can signify existence in creationist contexts, then, Albert apparently excludes that meaning from Prop. 4, where it stands rather for the intelligibility or ratio of "ens" with only a conceptual priority.

Perhaps, though, the reference he gives in his reply to his commentary on distinction 46 of Lombard's *Sentences,* Book I, will remedy the situation. Beginning with article 11 of d. 46, his remarks there concern truth (for example, "quid sit; quot modis dicatur veritas; de conversione ipsius cum bono et ente et uno; secundum quem ordinem habent se adinvicem unum, verum, bonum et ens") and contain two relevant passages, each entailing a discussion of *Liber de Causis,* Prop. 4.

In the first he takes issue with this objection against Augustine's statement "verum est id quod est": If the true is that which is, then truth is a thing's entity and, thus, its *esse* and *quod est* are the same—

---

[36]See *In I Sent.,* d. 46, a. 14 [*solutio*] (XIV, p. 669B): "Verum autem dicit relationem ad formam ad minus exemplarem per quam habet rationem manifestationis; et ideo dicit Hilarius quod verum est declarativum entis: oportet enim in quolibet esse principium intelligendi aliquod per quod ordinetur ad intellectum. Bonitas autem et bonum dicunt respectum ad finem extra a quo est et ad quem est, quia enim bonus est sumus, et inquantum sumus boni sumus." On abstraction see *ibid.,* d. 8, a. 18 ad 4 (p. 153A); *ibid.,* a. 24, ad 1 (p. 155D), quoted in n. 31 above; U. Dähnert, *Die Erkenntnislehre des Albertus Magnus gemessen an den Stufen der "abstractio"* (Leipzig: G. Gerhardt, 1933); E. Gilson, *HCP,* pp. 286–87 and p. 671, n. 11; H. Johnston, "Intellectual Abstraction in St. Albert," *Philosophical Studies* 10 (1960), 204–12.

an identity found only in God; therefore, any truth would be God—
a conclusion which is false, and, hence, Augustine's definition is
null and void.

> Verum est id quod est; ergo a conjugatis veritas est rei entitas;
> ergo esse suum et quod est idem habet; ergo ipsum est quod
> habet; et hoc non convenit nisi Deo; ergo omnis veritas esset
> Deus, quod falsum est; ergo diffinitio est nulla. [*In I Sent.*, d.
> 46, a. 11; XIV, p. 665A]

Albert begins to defend Augustine by distinguishing between a
thing's "entitas vel id quod est" as in itself and as found in a
concrete nature or subject.[37] Grant that distinction, and it is not
always accurate to say that "a thing's truth is its entity" or "the true
is that which is." Why so? If "entity" is understood precisely as
such and in itself [and if "truth" is affirmed to be "entity" in this
sense], then truth (because entity) would be (*esset*) the first creature, according to Aristotle's statement "*esse* is what is created first
and nothing else is created before it"; also, "that which is" will be
described (*dicetur*) as "that which has *esse*," which then is the act of
entity or essence so understood. [In this case one should not define
a thing's truth as its entity or the true as that which is.] But if one
takes "entity" and "that which is" in their concrete natures ("supposita natura quaedam"), he views them with reference to determinate species ("secundum modum determinationis ad speciem"),
and thereby truth is the entity by which something or other truly is
and "true" is that which truly is, as exemplified in the phrases *true
gold, true color, true body, true science.* Yet one should note that the
determination of "that which is" to a nature is not properly to a
species as such [because "being" transcends species, genus and
other predicaments]. But conceding that, one may say "that which
is" is "that which truly is in nature" and, thus, that the "true"
equals "that which is." Consequently, neither truth and entity nor
the true and what-is are entirely identical, as will be clearer later.

> Ad id quod quaeritur de diffinitione Augustini, dicendum
> quod rei entitas vel id quod est accipitur dupliciter, scilicet in

---

[37] A difficulty in interpreting Albert's response lies in the fact that he
simultaneously distinguishes "entitas" and "id quod est" each in two ways:
"in se vel ut supposita natura quaedam." Once one is aware of that fact, what
he says is comparatively clear.

se vel ut supposita natura quaedam; et sic, ut opinor, non bene
diceretur veritas rei entitas esse vel verum esse id quod est.
Accipitur etiam [*read:* enim] entitas secundum modum
determinationis ad speciem, et sic veritas est entitas qua res
vere est et verum est id quod vere est. Si vero entitas accipiatur
prout supponitur per nomen entitatis, tunc in veritate entitas
esset prima creatura, secundum quod dicit Philosophus quod
prima rerum creatarum est esse, et non est ante ipsam creatum
aliud; et id quod est dicetur id quod habet esse, quod est actus
sic intellectae entitatis vel essentiae. Si autem accipiatur id
quod est prout dicit quandam determinationem circa esse,
tunc non trahitur ad speciem, et tunc vere est quia unumquodque tunc vere est quando trahitur ad speciem sibi propriam ex natura determinata, sicut dicimus verum aurum et
verum colorem et verum corpus et veram scientiam. Et hoc
sonare videtur id quod est, quia id quod est est id quod vere
est in natura. Et sic patet quod non omnino idem sunt veritas
et entitas. Et hoc infra magis patebit. [*Ibid., ad objectionem de
definitione Augustini;* p. 665C]

Despite the demands Albert makes upon one's intelligence and
patience because of his elliptical and disjointed Latin, a couple of
relevant points are clear. Unlike his silence in *In II Sent.*, d. 1, a. 1,
ad objectionem de tertia explicatione (which we are still trying to cope
with) on creation with respect to *Liber de Causis*, Prop. 4, and unlike
his taking *esse* there as the concept of *ens* rather than as "existence,"
Albert talks about creation (truth if entity would be the first creature) and, second, he explicates *esse* as the act of entity or of essence
taken as such and in itself ("id quod est dicetur id quod habet esse,
quod est actus sic intellectae entitatis vel essentiae"). As "act of
entity or essence," would not *esse* be (as Geiger and Wieland wish)
the act which essence or entity gives to an *id quod est*? If so, it is
neither a mere intelligibility nor existence but a third and, literally,
essential factor in a created existent. But if Albert is already aware
of *esse* in this sense, he is in the passage from *In II Sent.* no less silent
on it than he is on existence. Before returning to *In II Sent.*, though,
let us study another discussion on truth where he utilizes *Liber de
Causis*, Prop. 4.

That utilization is found in the *solutio* of *In I Sent.*, d. 46, a. 13:
"Utrum verum convertatur cum ente, uno et bono." One may (he
acknowledges) grant their convertibility in direct predication if *ens,
verum, bonum* and *unum* are taken concretely; thus, one may say

that "a being is good, true and one." But considered abstractly, they are not convertible or directly predicable except of God, and in creatures it is wrong to say that essence *is* truth or goodness or unity.[38] Nor should one affirm that essence is true, truth is being or goodness is true. But it is even more improper to say that "essence is being or good" than to say that "truth is being and one." Whence the impropriety? From the fact that *esse* or essence is what is created first, according to Aristotle's *Liber de Causis*, Prop. 4, and no other creature is prior. Consequently, essence has nothing to serve as its foundation or subject,[39] of which it would in turn serve as form; the result is that essence as essence cannot be in nature unless created from nothing. Everything other than essence comes about, as one reads there in the commentary on Prop. 4, through formation of essence—for instance, in the order of nature the good presupposes the concept of essence as that in which it is. Therefore, the intelligibility of essence is based upon [no substrate but upon] nothingness and thereby is prior to all else. Hence, too, one will not say that essence "*is* truth" but "entails truth" as predicable of it; similarly, not: "essence *is* goodness" but "entails goodness."[40] But

---

[38] "Concretive sumpta" and "abstractive sumpta" correspond to "supposita natura quaedam" and "in se" of the previous text (a. 11, *ad objectionem de definitione Augustini*; p. 665C), which ended up with: "infra magis patebit."

In the third sentence of the current text (*ibid.*, a. 13, *solutio*) *ens* is not a noun but an adjective so as to be parallel with *verum, bonum* and *unum*—for example, "veritas est *ens* ... essentia est *ens* vel bona ... veritas est *ens* vel veritas est una" (italics added).

[39] *Ibid.*, a. 14 [*solutio*] (p. 669B) makes "substrate" be a synonym for "foundation" and "subject": "Sic generaliter considerando ista [ens, unum, verum, bonum] ut consideraverunt Sancti, dicemus quod inter ista essentia et ens est primum natura, circa quod ut substratum sibi ponuntur alia." From the fact that *esse* or *ens* or *essentia* serves as substrate, foundation, subject for subsequent determinations or "forms" one may infer that it is like matter (intelligible or spiritual). See E. Gilson, *HCP*, pp. 279–80.

[40] In the Latin text Albert promises to touch on unity later ("De unitate autem est alia ratio, quae infra patebit"), a promise which he kept in the final paragraph of the *solutio* and which contains this relevant information: unity, truth and so on add to essence not another nature but a relationship to the First Cause—"Si autem tu quaeras utrum unum se habeat ex additione ad alterum, dico quod si intelligatur additio alterius naturae, sicut forma et materia sunt alterius naturae et substantia et accidens sunt alterius naturae, tunc unum non addit super alterum. Si autem intelligatur additio secundum rationem respectus ad attributum causae primae, tunc unum addit super alterum rationem respectus, quia tunc essentia dicetur fluens ab essentia

someone may inquire why essence cannot be termed "true" and
"good" if truth and goodness can be predicable of it. The answer is
that essence as such is not conceivable as formed upon any other or
prior *ratio*; this is in line with Boethius: "that-which-is involves
something over and beyond itself but *esse* has no such addition."
Again, one properly says not that "truth *is* essence" but "entails
essence." Nonetheless, essence, truth, goodness and unity are convertible when taken concretely because everything is being, true,
good and one.

Solutio. Ad hoc sine praejudicio potest dici quod ista quatuor
convertuntur concretive sumpta, scilicet ens, ur. im, verum,
bonum, in recto, scilicet quod ens est bonum et verum et
unum, et sic de omnibus. Si autem sumantur abstractive, non
credo quod [convertuntur] secundum rectam praedicationem
nisi in Deo; in creaturis autem non, quia non credo quod haec
sit vera: essentia est veritas vel bonitas vel unitas. Hoc autem
est impropria: essentia est vera et veritas est ens et bonitas
vera; tamen haec est magis impropria: essentia est ens vel
bona, quam haec: veritas est ens vel veritas est una. Cuius
ratio sic patet per Philosophum in *libro causarum*, qui dicit quod
prima rerum creatarum est esse vel essentia et non est ante
ipsum creatura alia; ergo non est in quo fundetur essentia
sicut id circa quod sit ut forma subjecti alicuius; et ideo etiam
secundum ordinem naturae non potest essentia in ratione
essentiae esse nisi creata de nihilo. Omnia autem alia, ut dicit

prima, veritas fluens a sapientia et bonitas fluens a bonitate; et ideo omne ens
est verum et unum et bonum" (p. 668A).
In those lines note the frequency of "fluens" as a description of divine
causality, which incidentally separates the position of the "sancti" in *ibid.*, a.
14, from Aristotle's: "Si autem quaeritur secundum quem ordinem se habeant
adinvicem unum, verum, bonum, et ens, dicendum quod secundum Philosophum ante omnia sunt ens et unum. Philosophus enim non ponit quod
verum et bonum sint dispositiones generalitur concomitantes ens; nec divisio
entis secundum quod est ens est per verum et bonum, quia Philosophus non
considerat ens secundum quod fluit ab ente primo et uno et sapiente et bono,
sed ipse considerat ens secundum quod stat in ipso intellectus resolvens
posterius in prius et compositum in simplex et secundum quod ipsum per
prius et posterius colligit omnia; et ideo de vero et bono non determinat per
hunc modum, sed de bono quod est finis ad quem est motus" (669B; Albert
immediately thereafter contrasts Aristotle's view with that of the "sancti" in
the sentence already quoted in n. 39 above).

Commentator ibidem, sunt per informationem circa essentiam; et dat exemplum de bono quod secundum ordinem naturae praemittit sibi intellectum essentiae in qua est; ergo patet quod essentia dicit intellectum suum super nihil fundatum, et in omnibus priorem. Unde loquendo sic de essentia non dicetur veritas sed veritatis, quia veritas ponitur circa ipsam; et non dicetur bonitas sed bonitatis. . . .

Si autem tu queras quare non dicatur vera et bona, ex quo veritas et bonitas ponuntur circa ipsam, dico quod loquendo de simplici essentia non potest dici quod illa non intelligitur [*read:* illa intelligitur] informata secundum rationem. Unde Boetius in *libro de hebdomadibus:* quod est habet aliquid praeter id quod ipsum est, esse vero nihil habet admixtum. Eodem modo veritas non dicetur essentia sed essentiae proprie loquendo. Eodem modo est de bonitate. Tamen secundum supposita concretive dicta convertuntur, quia quodlibet est ens, verum, bonum, et unum. [*Ibid.*, a. 13, *solutio;* pp. 667D–668A].

In that long paraphrase and quotation what interests us is how Albert explains the excerpt from the *Liber.* One is inaccurate (so his comments run) in stating that essence "is truth" or "is true"[41] because such statements might incline us to think that the awareness of essence comes after that of truth, that essence is based upon, and received in, truth as a form in a subject or substrate. But as Aristotle makes clear in Prop. 4 of the *Liber, esse* or essence is what is first created and no other creature (*sic*) comes before it. Consequently, essence as essence cannot *be* unless it is created from nothing, which alone (except for God as creator) precedes it ("secundum ordinem naturae non potest essentia in ratione essentiae esse nisi creata de nihilo"). Everything else (e.g., truth, goodness, unity) comes about as a form or determination or addition[42] received in essence as in its subject ("omnia autem alia . . . fiunt per informationem circa essentiam") and, thereby, is subsequent to essence.

---

[41] For convenience I shall illustrate Albert's point through truth solely. Also, my paraphrase omits what he believes is the worst statement of all, since I suspect the accuracy of the italicized word: "Essentia est *ens* vel bona." Why could not *ens* be predicated of *essentia?* Perhaps we should read: "Essentia est una vel bona"—not "vera," which appeared earlier in the sentence.

[42] On "addition," see *ibid.*, final paragraph of *solutio,* which is quoted in n. 40 above (first paragraph) and which explains that what is added is not a second nature but a relationship to the First Cause.

Several points are noteworthy in Albert's explanation. On one occasion *esse* apparently means existence and this with reference to creation; "secundum ordinem naturae non potest essentia in ratione essentiae *esse* nisi creata de nihilo." Second, *esse* in Prop. 4 of the *Liber* is nonetheless viewed as *essentia:* ("Prima rerum creatarum est esse vel essentia"), as also in Boethius' *De Hebdomadibus:* "Esse vero nihil habet admixtum. Eodem modo veritas non dicetur *essentia sed essentiae.*" Third, the essence which God creates from nothing and thereby causes to exist serves as the basis, subject, substrate of subsequent realities, which function as its forms or determinations. Finally, essence, truth, goodness and unity involve concepts, intelligibilities, *rationes* also: "[bonum] praemittit sibi *intellectum* essentiae in qua est; ergo . . . essentia dicit *intellectum suum* super nihil fundatum et in omnibus priorem. . . . [Simplex essentia] non potest dici quod . . . *intelligitur* informata secundum *rationem.*" That is, we are *aware of* essence before goodness and the others; again, the very intelligibility of goodness rests upon and presupposes that of essence, the intelligibility of which however presupposes nothing.

Summary
From *In II Sent.*, d. 1, a. 1, we moved back to *In I Sent.*, d. 46, articles 11 and 13, in the hope that these might unloosen the knot Albert had tied in the former: even though Prop. 4 of the *Liber de Causis* has plainly to do with creation ("prima rerum *creatarum* est esse") and, presumably, with existence, he transferred *esse* (= *ens*) from the actual world of creatures to that of intelligibilities, where *ens* precedes *verum, bonum* and *unum* in virtue of its greater simplicity. That hope is fulfilled somewhat. In article 11 (*ad objectionem* . . .) of *In I Sent.*, d. 46, Prop. 4 is discussed in the light of creation (truth if entity would be the first creature), and, also, *esse* is explicated as the act of entity or essence and no longer as solely the intelligibility of *ens*. In *ibid.*, a. 13 (*solutio*), he again places the *esse* of Prop. 4 within a creationist setting, where it is linked again with essence ("prima rerum creatarum est esse *vel essentia*), which however exists because created from nothing (hence, *esse* means "existere" also) and which receives all subsequent determinations as their subject. But there is another and intramental dimension to *esse* or essence, as well as to truth, goodness and unity: the fact that they are intelligible and predicable. And article 13 inquires precisely into the sort of intelligibility and predicability *ens, verum* and so on entail: whether they are synonyms, whether they are convertible with one another, which of them comes first in our awareness, how the others are added to it.

This dimension it is which Albert in Text B (*In II Sent.*, d. 1, a. 1, *ad objectionem* . . .) isolated in view of the problem at hand: did God first create angelic nature and prime matter, as Lombard interprets *Genesis*, or was it *esse*, as we read in the *Liber*? Confronted with different questions, as in *In I Sent.*, d. 46, he gave other and complementary exegeses of the *Liber*, Prop. 4.

Conclusions

But we are mainly interested in what *esse* means in Albert's texts on creation. In the key passages so far studied, it turns out to be a many-splendored thing. *Esse* is entity, as in *In I Sent.*, d. 46, a. 11, *ad objectionem* . . . : "in veritate entitas esset prima creatura, secundum quod dicit Philosophus quod prima creatarum est esse." It is essence, as in *ibid.*, a. 13, *solutio:* "esse vel essentia." Once it is even designated as the act of essence or entity—*ibid.*, a. 11, *ad objectionem* . . . : "esse quod est actus sic intellectae entitatis vel essentiae."[43] It is the nature of matter as subject and potency—*Summa de Creaturis*, Pars I, Tr. 1, q. 2, a. 1, ad 1: "Materia autem habet esse subjecti et potentiae, . . . et hoc [est esse] secundum quid." It is the intelligibility, *ens* (*ibid.*, ad 2), which functions as the principle of our cognition of the predicaments (*ibid.*: "cum [primum] dicitur de ente, est principium cognitionis respectu eorum quae ordinabilia sunt in praedicamento"); that at which the resolution of posterior to prior intelligibilities stops (*ibid.*: "in ipso [ente] stat resolutio posteriorum in prius"); that to which subsequent *rationes* are added that also arise through intellectual abstraction (*ibid.*: "[ens] a quo non convertitur consequentia subsistendi, et sic ens est absolute primum"; also *In II Sent.*, d. 1, a. 1, *ad objectionem* . . . : "secundum rationem formae et simplicitatis [*vs.* secundum ordinem substantiae in essendo] nihil est ante esse, quia omnia aliquo modo se habent ex additione ad ens, etiam unum et verum et bonum . . . [ordo simplicitatis qui] in

---

[43] See also *ibid.*, a. 16 ("An veritas est simplex et incommutabilis?"), *solutio* (p. 672B): "Non credo aliquam illarum [veritatis, bonitatis, unitatis, entitatis] esse compositam ex quo est et esse, secundum quod [id quod] est dicit aliquid ens in se, in quo diffunditur esse quod est actus essentiae."

Meyer/Zimmermann contains these relevant and informative studies: I. Craemer-Ruegenberg, "Die Seele als Form in einer Hierarchie von Formen. Beobachtungen zu einem Lehrstück aus der De anima–Paraphrase Alberts des Grossen," pp. 59–88; P. Hossfeld, "'Erste Materie' und 'Materie im allgemeinen' in den Werken des Albertus Magnus," pp. 205–34; A. Zimmermann, "Albertus Magnus und der lateinische Averroismus," pp. 465–94.

abstractione autem fit per intellectum"); that which if taken precisely *qua* abstract is not convertible with good, true and one *re* creatures, since the concept of (say) "good" presupposes the concept of "essence," which however presupposes no prior *ratio* (*In I Sent.*, d. 46, a. 13, *solutio*: "Si autem [ens, unum, verum, bonum] sumantur abstractive, non credo quod [convertuntur] secundum rectam praedicationem . . . in creaturis . . .; [bonum] secundum ordinem naturae praemittit sibi intellectum essentiae in qua est . . . essentia dicit intellectum suum super nihil fundatum et in omnibus priorem").

Finally, *esse* also expresses existence when it is the *esse simpliciter* which a *forma partis* gives to prime matter and which makes it exist (*Summa de Creaturis*, Pars I, tr. 1, q. 2, a. 1, ad 1); the *esse* which pertains to the temporal world where generation brings about existents (implied in *ibid.*, ad 2); the *esse* which creation results in (*In II Sent.*, d. 1, a. 1, *ad objectionem* . . . .: "creatio potius respicit esse quam ordinem simplicitatis"); the *esse* by which an essence as essence *is* inasmuch as it is created from nothing (*In I Sent.*, d. 46, a. 13, *solutio*: "secundum ordinem naturae non potest essentia in ratione essentiae esse nisi creata de nihilo").

This last signification of *esse* as *existere* helps guarantee that *creatio* has an authentic ring even in these early treatises of Albert.[44] In order to realize this, let us first describe "creation" in its authentic and technical sense. Put more precisely: what factors does a genuine doctrine of creation necessarily entail? There appear to be three. The producer himself must undergo

> . . . no change in the act of producing, neither losing nor acquiring any perfection, and the implication is that he is both all-perfect and entirely free. Next, what is produced must be really distinct from the producer and, finally, must be *wholly* produced. For the causality ascribed by an author to his First Principle to be authentically creationist, it must include all those factors. Obviously, that inclusion need only be implicit, provided the writer somehow indicates his mind. For example, one can be sure that the product is *wholly* produced if the author states that God made it from nothing or that He pro-

---

[44] But *esse* signifies *existere* only as expressing the *fact that* things exist and not as an act or component by which they exist, as L. Ducharme has convincingly argued (see the paragraph above corresponding to notes 13 and 14; *re* Geiger, see n. 16).

duced even its prime matter or that He does not cause the item merely to be such and such but actually to exist. Obviously, too, the clear presence of one factor can imply another. For instance, if divine causality makes something actually exist which before was not, one can infer that such an effect is really distinct from its cause.[45]

If those factors are applied to Albert's doctrine, how does he fare? Very well. God is (he explicitly notes) immutable, all-perfect and entirely free and, thus, He undergoes no change in creating.[46] Also, every creature is really distinct from the Creator because he makes that which before was not now actually exist. Moreover, what is created is, as such, wholly produced by God, since He not only makes it from nothing and produces even its prime matter but also causes it actually to be.[47]

---

[45] L. Sweeney, *Divine Infinity in Greek and Medieval Thought*, ch. 13: "Doctrine of Creation in the *Liber de Causis*," pp. 305–6. This conception of creation is based upon statements from the Fourth Lateran Council (H. Denzinger, *Enchiridion Symbolorum*, 32d edition [Friburgi Brisg: Herder, 1963], no. 800) and the Vatican Council (*ibid.*, nos. 3024 sq.). For an analysis of these statements, see Pinard, "Création," cols. 2081 and 2181–95.

Interestingly enough, creation was not explicated in conciliar documents as a production *ex nihilo* until the Lateran Council of 1215: "[Deus] qui sua omnipotenti virtute simul ab initio temporis utramque de nihilo condidit creaturam, spiritualem et corporalem" (Denzinger, *op. cit.*, no. 800). That explicit description had, though, been given much earlier by such authors as Hermas (whose *The Shepherd* is dated ca. A.D. 140), Origen, Chrysostom, Leo, Tertullian, Lactantius and Augustine. For references and discussion see A. Solignac, *Les Confessions*, vol. 14 of *Oeuvres de S. Augustin* (Paris: Desclée de Brouwer, 1962), pp. 603–6.

[46] On God as immutable, see *In I Sent.*, d. 8, a. 16 (pp. 150 sqq.); as all-perfect, see *ibid.*, d. 34, a. 4 *solutio* (p. 498D); *Super Dionysium de Divinis Nominibus*, c. 13: "Utrum hoc nomen 'perfectum' deo conveniat" (Cologne critical edition, XXXVII, pp. 433, line 32–p. 435, line 42); as free, see *In I Sent.*, d. 30, a. 3 *solutio* (p. 448D); *ibid.*, d. 45, a. 1 ("An in Deo sit voluntas"; pp. 640–41); *In II Sent.*, d. 1, a. 2 ad [6] (p. 6B); *ibid.*, a. 3 ad [3] and ad [4] (p. 7B); *ibid.*, a. 5, *ad hoc quod quaeritur* (p. 10D); *ibid.*, a. 6 *solutio* (p. 11C). For Wieland's comments on divine freedom in creating, see n. 21 above.

[47] On prime matter as divinely created, see n. 32 above; *In II Sent.*, d. 1, a. 3 in entirety (XIV, pp. 6C sq.). On creation as causing something to exist by making it from nothing, see *ibid.*, ad 1 (p. 7A): "Creatio non dicit actum vel passionem quae media sit inter Deum agentem et id quod educitur de non esse, sed potius relationem consequentem ipsum quod nunc primo de nihilo est et ante non fuit. . . . Et huius haec est ratio, quia perfecti agentis est agere

But granted that Albert's position on creation is sound and that his viewing *esse* as existence helps to account for that soundness (to create is to cause something to exist which before was in no way), still his God does not *properly* cause existence if to be real is for him (as Ducharme, Geiger and Wieland suggest) to be essence rather than to exist.[48] And if to create is to cause things to exist, then to create is not an exercise of proper causality for God, Who properly causes what things are and not that they are.[49]

Let me explain by speaking first of a "proper *effect*" without direct reference to creation and God.

Whenever a single effect is produced by two or more different agents (for example, by principal and instrumental causes), *each agent makes a unique contribution to that effect* because each acts according to what it is if it is to act at all, and what each is makes it unique and diverse from everything else. *The unique contribution which an agent makes by acting according to what it is is called its "proper effect."* No matter what other effects it may have, then, *every agent has a proper effect, since an agent always acts according to what it is.*

---

non actione media, in qua res prius sit in fieri quam in esse. . . . Vere creantis nihil aliud est quam quod esse faciat rem postquam non fuit sine mutatione media"; *ibid.*, ad 4 (p. 7B): "Materia non est ante omne fieri si fieri dicatur actio creantis, quia cum illa nihil sit nisi facere ex imperio suo rem nunc esse postquam non fuit de ea aliquid nec potentia nec actu, illud fieri non praesupponit sibi potentiam aliquam, quia nec est proprie fieri." Also see *Summa de Creaturis*, Pars I, Tr. 1, q. 1, a. 2, *argumentum* 1 (XIX, p. 2D); *ibid.*, a. 3, *argumenta* 2 and 3 (p. 3D); *ibid.*, ad *sed contra* 4 (p. 4B); *ibid.*, a. 4, *sed contra* 1 (p. 4C); *ibid.*, a. 5, *solutio* (p. 5A); *ibid.*, a. 7, ad *sed contra* (p. 6D); *In II Sent.*, d. 1, a. 3 ad 1 (XIV, p. 7A); *ibid.*, ad 4 (p. 7B); *ibid.*, a. 6, ad 2 (p. 11D); *ibid.*, a. 7, *sed contra* 2 (p. 12A); *ibid.*, d. 3, a. 7, [*solutio*] (p. 58D); *ibid.*, d. 30, a. 1, ad 1 (p. 446D); *ibid.*, a. 2, *solutio* and ad 1 (p. 447D).

[48] That reality for Albert is not existence, see n. 44 above with its references. That reality is some or other essence follows from the fact which Ducharme, Geiger and Wieland have stressed (see prgrs. corresponding to notes 13–21 above) that *esse* is *actus essentiae*—*In I Sent.*, d. 46, a. 11, *ad objectionem* . . . (p. 665C): "Esse quod est actus sic intellectae entitatis vel essentiae"; *ibid.*, a. 16, *solutio* (p. 672B): "[id quod est dicitur] aliquid ens in se, in quo diffunditur esse quod est actus essentiae" (quoted above, n. 43).

[49] At least not "proper causality" in the sense Thomas Aquinas gives to the phrase—see next paragraph with texts cited in n. 50 below. But Albert has his own understanding of the phrase, as will be clear below, last two paragraphs.

By way of example, consider a teacher using a piece of red chalk to write "dog" upon the blackboard. The effect produced is composite and yet one. It is composite inasmuch as it is a symbol which is both meaningful and colored. It is one insofar as it is a single symbol where the color expresses the meaning, which in turn determines the precise position of chalk particles on the board. That effect is wholly caused by both the principal and instrumental agents, since each causes both meaning and color, but differently. The teacher causes the color through the chalk, but the meaning directly and of himself; the chalk causes the meaning only as moved by the teacher, and the color directly in virtue of its own nature. By directly causing the meaning, then, the teacher also causes the color; by directly causing the color, the instrument also causes the meaning. What is the *proper effect* of each cause? For the teacher it is the meaning, because by nature he is an intelligent being and agent. For the chalk it is the color, because by nature it is a piece of red chalk.

Whatever an agent causes in virtue of what it itself is, then, is its proper effect.[50]

To state the same from the point of view of "proper cause": the agent properly causes that in the effect which corresponds to what he is, to his nature.

Now, if God's very nature is existence (as it is for Aquinas), then He properly causes all things to exist; but to cause something to exist which before was not at all is to create; therefore, a God who *is*

---

[50] L. Sweeney, *Authentic Metaphysics in an Age of Unreality*, 2d ed. (New York/Bern: Peter Lang Publishing, Inc., 1993), p. 247. See Aquinas, *S.T.*, I, 8, 1 resp.: "Cum autem Deus sit ipsum esse per suam essentiam, oportet quod esse creatum sit proprius effectus eius; sicut ignire est proprius effectus ignis"; *ibid.*, I, 45, 5, resp.: "Creare non potest esse propria actio nisi solius Dei. Oportet enim universaliores effectus in universaliores et priores causas reducere. Inter omnes autem effectus universalissimum est ipsum esse. Unde oportet quod sit proprius effectus primae et universalissimae causae, quae est Deus. . . . Producere autem esse absolute, non inquantum est hoc vel tale, pertinet ad rationem creationis. Unde manifestum est quod creatio est propria actio ipsius Dei. . . . Videmus quod securis scindendo lignum quod habet ex proprietate suae formae producit scamni formam, quae est effectus proprius principalis agentis. Illud autem quod est proprius effectus Dei creantis est illud quod praesupponitur omnibus aliis, scilicet esse absolute." Also see *ibid.*, I, 105, 5 resp.; *S.C.G.*, III, c. 68, "Adhuc."

existence properly creates: creation is (so to speak) merely an exercise of proper causality for Him, through which an existent universe replaces nothingness and by which beings are produced *precisely as beings*, since "being" here is "that which actually exists." Gilson's words quoted above describe Aquinas' position so well that they merit repetition:

> One cannot ask a philosopher to conceive creation at a deeper level than that of his own notion of being. If God is the cause of that which being is, then God is a creator and being is a created being. . . . The progress achieved by Thomas Aquinas concerns less the notion of creation than that of being.

Thomas conceived creation on the very level of being itself, since God properly causes *being* in all beings. Thus the achievement of this student of Albert was first to have modified the notion of being, which then harmonized perfectly with that of creation.

That harmony seems lacking in the texts of his teacher. For if God's very nature is not existence but some or other essence—for instance, immutability, as Augustine holds[51]—then He properly causes things to be immutable, whereas secondary agents (parents,

---

[51] See *Confessions*, VII, c. 11, #17 (John K. Ryan [trans.], *The Confessions of St. Augustine* [New York: Doubleday Image Books, 1960], p. 171): "That truly is which endures unchangeably. . . . [God] abides in himself" (Skutella Latin text: "Id enim vere est quod inconmutabiliter manet. . . . Ille autem in se manens innovat omnia"); *ibid.*, c. 17, #23 (Ryan trans., pp. 175–76), where his awareness that to be real is to be immutable leads him to realize that God is and is immutability, truth, eternity (these last two are so closely linked with immutability as to be interchangeable with it): "[From reflecting upon sound judgments I had made,] I found that immutable, true, and eternal Truth which exists above my changeable mind." Moving from bodies to within the soul and its multiple powers, all of which are variable, Augustine finds the light which enables his soul to assent that "beyond all doubt the immutable must be preferred to the mutable. Hence it might come to know this immutable being, for unless it could know it in some way, it could in no wise have set it with certainty above the mutable. Thus in a flash of its trembling sight it came to That Which Is" (Skutella edition: "Hoc ergo quaerens unde iudicarem cum ita judicarem, inveneram inconmutabilem et veram veritatis aeternitatem supra mentem meam conmutabilem. . . . ut inveniret quo lumine aspargeretur cum sine ulla dubitatione clamaret inconmutabile praeferendum esse mutabili, unde nosset ipsum inconmutabile—quod nisi aliquo modo nosset, nullo modo illud mutabili certa praeponeret—et pervenit ad id quod est in ictu trepidantis aspectus").

carpenters, etc.) properly cause them to exist. But in order that there *be* secondary agents, God must cause them to exist—i.e., He must create them. This He does but not properly: even in creating them He properly causes them not to exist but to be immutable. If Albert is an essentialist (as Ducharme, Geiger and Wieland intimate),[52] then to be real is, for him, to be essence of some sort or other, and, second, God's reality is Essence. Accordingly, his God in creating properly causes a thing not to exist but to be essence. That is, creation is not an exercise of proper causality (see note 49 above). Creation does not account for the very being of beings. It is not aligned fully and directly with being itself.

Significantly enough, this distinction between nonproperly causing something to *be* and properly causing it to be *what it is* helps one understand why creation is difficult for an essentialist to cope with and, also, why in Neoplatonism production of existents occurs in two moments or stages: procession and reversion. In the first the primal cause overflows, and thereby the existence of the effect is accounted for; in the second that which has overflowed and now exists (e.g., Plotinus calls it intelligible matter, otherness, *dynamis*) turns back to the cause, contemplates it, completes itself and thereby becomes what it is. A Neoplatonist who believes in creation (e.g., the author of the *Liber de Causis*) retains those two stages but interprets them thus.[53] In the first, creation replaces emanation: the Creator causes intelligible matter (the author of the *Liber* calls this *esse* in Prop. 4) to exist, which in the second moment and under continued divine but noncreational influence is completed and perfected through information so as to be what it is. The Creator properly causes the creature thereby to be what it is but not that it is, because the Creator is not existence but the One or the One-Good or some other Essence.

Here, though, a question arises: can the One or the One-Good rightly be called "essence"? Yes, provided the word is not restricted to the level of being (as it usually is) but is taken to mean whatever can serve as a predicate in a sentence. "One," "good" and "true" can be predicated of an existent and, thus, are "essences," no less than are "immutable," "eternal," "simple" and so on. Hence, if the Creator for a theologian or philosopher is the One or the One-Good or Immutability or Eternity or (as perhaps is the case with

---

[52] See n. 48 above.

[53] See L. Sweeney, ch. 13: *Divine Infinity,* "Doctrine of Creation in the *Liber de Causis*," pp. 299–303.

Albert) Simplicity,[54] then He properly causes creatures to be one or good or immutable or eternal or simple but not to exist. Only He Who *is* Existence properly causes them to exist.

In this connection it is intriguing to note that Albert computes the perfection of a cause not from *what* it causes (properly or otherwise) but from its *manner of causing:*

> Ad aliud dicendum quod haec propositio est falsa: causatum primae causae verius est ens quam causatum secundae causae. Et si quis probet eam sic: sicut se habet causa prima ad secundam, ita causatum primae causae ad causatum secundae causae, dicendum quod propositio falsa est. Si ergo quaeritur in quo attenditur nobilitas causae primae respectu secundae, dicendum quod in modo causandi, quia causa prima causat per seipsam et non causa secunda, sed secunda causa non causat nisi supposita prima.[55]

This computation results in Albert's using "proper effect" or "proper cause" differently than was explained above (see paragraphs corresponding to notes 49–52), as is disclosed in these lines from his commentary on the *Liber de Causis:*

> Primae autem causae quae causat non causante quodam alio proprius actus creare est. Quod enim causat non causante

---

[54]See E. Gilson, *HCP,* pp. 291–92. These texts on simplicity from Albert should be taken into account: *In I Sent.,* d. 8, a. 4 *solutio* (XIV, pp. 138D–139B); *ibid.,* a. 15, *solutio* (p. 149B); *ibid.,* a. 22, ad 1 and ad 2 (p. 155A); *ibid.,* a. 24, *solutio* and *ad ultimum* (pp. 155D and 156D); *ibid.,* a. 28, [*solutio*] (p. 161A); *ibid.,* d. 34, a. 1 *solutio* (p. 495B). Also *S.T.,* Pars I, Tr. 4, q. 19, membrum 1, *solutio* (vol. XVII, p. 68C); *ibid.,* q. 20, membra 1–5 (pp. 73–80); *Liber de Causis et Processu Universitatis,* Bk. I, tr. 2, c. 5 (Cologne ed., XVII, ii, p. 31c); *ibid.,* tr. 3, c. 1, p. 36a; *ibid.,* tr. 4, c. 1, p. 43d; *ibid.,* tr. 4, c. 3, p. 46a; *ibid.,* Bk. II, tr. 1, c. 17, p. 81c; *ibid.,* c. 18, p. 82c; *ibid.,* tr. 4, c. 11, p. 165a; *ibid.,* tr. 5, c. 12, p. 178c.

[55] *Summa de Creaturis,* Pars I, Tr. 1, q. 2, a. 3 ad 2; p. 11D. In the text quoted Albert is answering this argumentation that matter is not created: "Item, causatum causae primae verius est ens quam causatum causae secundae; sed creatum est causatum causae primae; ergo [creatum] verius erit ens quam causatum causae secundae. Inde ulterius: effectus formae verius est ens quam materia; sed effectus primae causae, ut habitum est, verius est ens quam effectus secundae; ergo materia non erit effectus primae causae; sed creatum est effectus primae causae, ut probatum est in primo syllogismo; ergo materia non est creatum" (*ibid., videtur quod non* 2; p. 11B).

quodam alio ante se, ex nihilo facit omne quod facit. Si autem praesupponeret aliud ante se causans, non ex nihilo faceret, sed id quod jam est formaret in id quod facit et causat. Actus igitur primae causae proprie creatio est. Esse autem quo res est primum est, quod ante nihil praesupponit; esse igitur in omnibus quae sunt primae causae proprius effectus est.[56]

God properly causes *esse* because as the absolutely First Cause He causes solely through and of Himself: such is His unique manner of causing. The causality exercised by every other agent is subsequent to His, based upon His, presupposes His because He is supreme and primal. Therefore, He properly creates, and *esse* is His proper effect, which secondary agents then form and determine.

Can anyone conceive of how greater similarity in language can be combined with greater diversity in meaning than that found in Albert's theory on *esse* and creation when compared with that of his star pupil, Aquinas?[57] For the latter, *esse* is God's proper effect because His very nature is to exist, and, thus, existence in an effect is that which corresponds directly to what He is. It is that which He causes by acting in accord with what He Himself essentially is. It is the perfection *par excellence* of an existent, the intrinsic source of its other perfections, the actuation of its forms and, in general, of its essence.[58] But for Albert *esse* is the proper effect of God because He alone causes it: no other agent precedes Him, the activity of all

---

[56] *De Causis et Processu Universitatis,* Book II, Tr. 1, c. 13 (Cologne ed.,p. 75d); also see *ibid.,* tr. 2, c. 17, p. 110a; *ibid.,* tr. 3, c. 10, p. 147c–d.

[57] On Aquinas see texts listed in n. 50 above and the portions of this chapter corresponding to notes 48–50.

[58] *De Potentia,* q. 7, a. 2 ad 9 (Marietti ed., p. 192): "Hoc quod dico esse est actualitas omnium actuum, et propter hoc est perfectio omnium perfectionum"; *S.C.G.,* I, c. 28 (Leonine Manual ed., p. 29d): "Omnis enim nobilitas cuiuscumque rei est sibi secundum suum esse. . . . Sic ergo secundum modum quo res habet esse est suus modus in nobilitate"; *S.T.,* I, 3, 4 resp. (Leonine Manual ed., p. 17b): "Esse est actualitas omnis formae vel naturae"; *ibid.,* I, 4, 1, ad 3 (p. 21d): "Ipsum esse est perfectissimum omnium: comparatur enim ad omnia ut actus. Nihil enim habet actualitatem nisi inquantum est; unde ipsum esse est actualitas omnium rerum et etiam ipsarum formarum. Unde non comparatur ad alia sicut recipiens ad receptum; sed magis sicut receptum ad recipiens. Cum enim dico esse hominis vel equi vel cuiuscumque alterius, ipsum esse consideratur ut formale et receptum"; *ibid.,* I, 8, 1 resp. (p. 36c): "Esse autem est illud quod est magis intimum cuilibet et quod profundius omnibus inest, cum sit formale respectu omnium quae in re sunt."

other agents presupposes His. They determine and complete the *esse* which He creates and which then serves as universal substrate and subject for the perfections which they add.[59]

At the beginning of his book on Alfred North Whitehead "which includes destructive criticism of Whitehead," Nathaniel Lawrence nonetheless claimed that his "major indebtedness is to Whitehead himself." He admitted that "there may seem to be an irony in [that] claim." But Whitehead himself

> summarized his critique of Einstein with the remark that "the worst homage we can pay to genius is to accept uncritically formulations of truths which we owe to it." A student who does not differ from his teacher has learned little from him.[60]

The differences which set Aquinas' position so widely apart from Albert's show how much he had learned from him. Judged by Lawrence's criterion, Albert must have been a superb teacher, as well as excellent scholar and impressive thinker.[61]

---

[59] Yet *esse* is not potency but act—in fact, the act which contains *vivere* and other acts and from which they emerge. At least, such is Albert's position in his commentary (written between 1264 and 1267) on the *Liber de Causis*. See ch. 15 below: "*Esse Primum Creatum* in Albert the Great's *Liber de Causis et Processu Universitatis.*"

[60] *Whitehead's Philosophical Development* (New York: Greenwood Press, 1968), p. ix. On Whitehead see ch. 25 below: "Whitehead's Cosmology: A Monism of Creativity?"

[61] For recent studies focusing on "Albert's philosophy of nature, understanding that discipline as comprising work relating not only to Aristotle's *Physics* but also to his *De Anima*, together with the logical and epistemological underpinnings such work requires," see the Winter 1996 issue of *American Catholic Philosophical Quarterly* (vol. 90), edited by William A. Wallace and entitled *Albert Magnus*.

The article by Steven Baldner, "St. Albert the Great on the Union of the Human Soul and Body" (*ibid.*, pp. 103–20), allows one to detect a parallel between Guerric of St. Quentin's and Albert's positions on the soul: the human soul moves the body inasmuch as the soul is "essentially united only to the heart" (see pp. 108–17, especially p.113). For Guerric's similar position see ch. 13 above, pp. 302–3. Thus Guerric may have influenced his student, Albert, on this point (see *ibid.*, p. 304).

15

Esse Primum Creatum in Albert the Great's *Liber de Causis et Processu Universitatis*

That Albert the Great (ca. 1200–1280) was interested in the conception in *Liber de Causis,* Proposition 4, of *esse* as *primum creatum*[1] is attested to by his commenting upon it in his earliest down to his latest treatises.[2] For example, in *Summa de Creaturis,* composed before 1243, Albert interprets Prop. 4 of the *Liber* ("Prima rerum creatarum est esse, et non est ante ipsum creatum aliud") in such a way that *esse* pertains to cognition rather than to the actual world:

---

[1] See Otto Bardenhewer (ed.), *Die pseudo-aristotelische Schrift Ueber das reine Gute bekannt unter dem Namen Liber de Causis* (Freiburg im Breisgau: Herder, 1882), p. 166: "Prima rerum creatarum est esse, et non est ante ipsum creatum aliud." For Bardenhewer's translation of the Proposition from Arabic, see *ibid.,* p. 65: "Das erste der geschaffenen Dinge ist das Sein; ein anderes Geschaffenes vor ihm gibt es nicht." The anonymous *Liber de Causis* is Neoplatonic in its philosophy (basically, that of Plotinus and Proclus), but whether its author is Arabian, Jewish or Christian is still not clear. For a survey *re* its authorship see ch. 14 above: "The Meaning of *Esse* in Albert the Great's Texts on Creation in *Summa de Creaturis* and *Scripta Super Sententias,*" [hereafter: "The Meaning of *Esse*"], n. 20.

[2] For the chronology of Albert's life and writings, see J. A. Weisheipl, "Albertus Magnus and the Oxford Platonists," *Proceedings of American Catholic Philosophical Association* 32 (1958), 124 sqq.; *idem,* "Life and Works of St. Albert the Great," *Albertus Magnus and the Sciences:* [hereafter: Weisheipl] (Toronto: Pontifical Institute of Mediaeval Studies, 1980), pp. 13–51; the "Prolegomena" to the volumes of the Cologne critical edition (e. g. see nn. 7 and 14 below).

esse or *ens* is first in the sense that it is the concept beyond which the resolution of other concepts cannot go and, accordingly, *ens* is not entirely convertible with *bonum, verum* or *unum* (*Summa de Creaturis*, Pars I, Tr. 1, q. 2, a. 1, ad 2; XIX, 7d).[3] When writing the slightly later *Scriptum Super I Librum Sententiarum*,[4] Albert used Prop. 4 of the *Liber de Causis* to prove the impropriety of saying that "essence is being or good." Since *esse* or essence is what is created first and no other creature is prior, essence has nothing to serve as its foundation or subject, of which it would in turn serve as form; the result is that essence as essence cannot *be* unless created from nothing. Everything other than essence comes through formation of essence—for instance, in the order of nature the good presupposes the concept of essence as that in which it is. Therefore, the intelligibility of essence is based upon no subject or substrate[5] but upon nothingness, and thereby is prior to all else (*ibid.*, a. 13, *solutio*; XIV, 667D–668A).[6]

Fifteen years later Albert was still concerned with the exegesis of *Liber de Causis*, Prop. 4.[7] In chapter 2 of *Metaphysica*, Liber IV, tr. 1, he first proves that metaphysics is the science of being *qua* being and then faces opposing views, one of which is this: *ens* is what is caused first and thus there is nothing caused prior to it; accordingly, it is in no way a subject ("igitur nulli subicibile esse videtur") but is predicable of all else (XVI, 163, lines 3–5). *Ens* is (Albert replies) a subject in which all subsequents come about through information (*ibid.*, lines 12–15)—thus, life, substance, sensibility, reason and intellect are all added as forms to *ens* (lines 16–17). As

---

[3] Since the Cologne critical edition of this *Summa* is not yet available, my references are to the Jammy edition: Petrus Jammy, *Opera B. Alberti Magni* (Lugduni Sumptibus Claudii Prost, 1651), vol. XIX: *Summa de Creaturis Divisa in Duas Partes*. On its date as prior to 1243, see L. Sweeney, "The Meaning of *Esse*," n. 24.

[4] On dating the *Scriptum* ca. 1245 and, thus, as somewhat later than the *Summa de Creaturis*, see L. Sweeney, *ibid.*, n. 34. My references will be to the Jammy edition, vol. XIV.

[5] On *esse* as substrate, see *In I Sent.*, d. 46, a. 14 [*solutio*]; XIV, 669B.

[6] For other comments on Prop. 4 see *ibid.*, a. 11, *ad objectionem de definitione Augustini*; XIV, 665C; *In II Sent.*, d. 1, a. 1, *ad objectionem de tertia explicatione*; XV, 5A; for interpretation of those texts, see L. Sweeney, "The Meaning of *Esse*," prgrs. corresponding to notes 34 sqq.

[7] That Albert wrote his *Metaphysica* between 1260 and 1263, see B. Geyer, *Alberti Magni Opera Omnia* [hereafter: Cologne edition] (Monasterium Westfalorum in Aedibus Ashchendorff, 1960), Tomus XVI, Pars I, p. VIII; Weisheipl, p. 32, n. 67.

subject it is that which is presupposed in all subsequents and stands under them all (lines 20–22). Accordingly, all subsequent existents are shown to be in being in the same way that beings which have *esse* through information are present in being which has *esse* solely through creation. Why this? Because being has absolutely nothing prior to it, whereas whatever comes after it presupposes being itself. Such is the meaning of the statement in the *Liber de Causis:* "*esse* is what is created first and no other creature precedes it." All else (e.g., good, etc.) comes about through informing [and determining] it (*ibid.*, lines 25–34).

As a final instance of Albert's attention to Prop. 4, consider how he solves one of the *problemata* given him in 1271 by the Dominican master general John of Vercelli[8] as to whether the angelic movers of the heavenly bodies thereby mediately help produce whatever arises on earth through natural causes and, thus, educe them from potency to act (*Problemata Determinata*, qu. 14; XVII, 45, lines 44–47). Even if angels should (Albert responds) move the heavenly bodies—a philosophical impossibility, though—it would not follow that they would cause whatever comes about on earth through nature by also educing them from potency to act (*ibid.*, p. 53, line 69–p. 54, line 5). This eduction they would do not by their own power but by that of the first cause within them; hence, their function will be to make others be apt recipients of the causality of the first cause (*ibid.*, p. 54, lines 5–8). Otherwise one would infer that *esse* is not what is caused first and is not the proper effect of the first cause—a position most effectively disproved in the *Liber de Causis* (lines 9–12).[9]

Those four passages are sufficient witnesses to the fact that Albert attended to Prop. 4 of the *Liber de Causis* from start to finish of

---

[8] On 1271 as the date of composition, see P. Simon's "Prolegomena" to J. A. Weisheipl's edition of *Problemata Determinata*, Cologne edition (1975), Tomus XVII, Pars I, pp. XXVII–XIX.

[9] Also see *Summa Theologiae*, I, tr. 13, q. 53, m. 1 *ad ultimum sed contra;* Jammy edition, XVII, 308A. A. Hufnagel doubts, however, that this *Summa* is rightly attributed to Albert—see "Zur Echtheitsfrage der *Summa Theologiae* Alberts des Grossen," *Theologische Quartalschrift* 146 (1966), 8–39; but see R. Kaiser, "Die Benutzung proklischer Schriften durch Albert den Grossen," *Archiv für Geschichte der Philosophie* 45 (1963), 14, n. 33: Part I of the *Summa* is certainly Albert's; Part II may have been finished by Gottfried von Duisburg. Albert also comments on *Liber de Causis*, Prop. 4, in *Super Dionysium De Divinis Nominibus*, c. 11, ad 2; Cologne edition XXXVII, 423, lines 26 sqq.; *De Bono*, tr. 1, q. 1, a. 6, *Praeterea; ibid.*, XXVIII, 10, line 88.

his writing career.[10] They also disclose one of the major speculative problems *esse primum creatum* entailed for him as a professed Aristotelian: how does *esse* so conceived fit into Aristotle's theory of act and potency?[11] Although this question is muted in Text A, it is rather blatant in the other three. According to Texts B and C *esse primum creatum* serves as foundation, subject, substrate for everything else which is consequent upon *esse* and functions as form or determinant added to it. But in an Aristotelian worldview, subject or substrate is aligned with potency, form with act. Therefore, is not *esse primum creatum* on the side of potency and not of act? But Text D intimates that *esse primum causatum* is act, as this line of argumentation indicates. The power which secondary causes such as angels have over *esse* is their share of the divine power resident within them and is exercised by their helping subsequent agents fittingly receive the divine causality; but God causes not by educing act from potency but by creation; therefore, His first effect—*esse*—is an act not issuing from a potency but resulting from His creative *fiat*.[12]

The relationship of *esse primum creatum* to Aristotle's act/potency is, then, a genuine problem. Has Albert faced it squarely in any of his treatises? Yes, in *Liber de Causis et Processu Universitatis*, composed betwen 1264 to 1267 and after his commenting on other books of Aristotle's *Metaphysics*.[13]

---

[10] For greater convenience we shall refer to the key passage in *Summa de Creaturis* as Text A; *In I Sent.* as Text B; *Metaphysica* as Text C; *Problemata* as Text D.

[11] On Albert's claim to be Aristotelian and on his aim to explain the *corpus aristotelicum* to his contemporaries, see R. Kaiser, "Zur Frage der eigenen Anschauung Alberts d. Gr. in seinen philosophischen Kommentaren," *Freiburger Zeitschrift für Philosophie und Theologie* 9 (1962), 53 sqq.; L. A. Kennedy, "The Nature of the Human Intellect According to St. Albert the Great," *Modern Schoolman* 37 (1960), 121–23; J. A. Weisheipl, "Albert's Disclaimers in the Aristotelian Paraphrases," *Proceedings of the PMR Conference* 5 (1980), 1–28. On the meaning Albert gives to "Peripatetic," see below, n. 23, last prgr.

[12] The intimation that *esse* is act arises from Albert's contrasting God's causality with that of natural causes, which are "de potentia in actum eductores . . . [et] productores" (*Problemata Determinata*, q. 14; Cologne ed., XVII, p. 45, line 47, and p. 54, lines 4–5). *Esse*, whether created by God or educed from potency by creatures, is act.

[13] I say "other books of Aristotle's *Metaphysics*" because Albert considered what we know as the anonymous and Neoplatonic *Liber de Causis* to be the concluding portion of Aristotle's *Metaphysics*—see R. Kaiser, "Versuch einer

Problem Revisited

On first reading *Liber de Causis et Processu Universitatis* one might be tempted to conclude that Albert intensifies rather than solves the problem since he appears in some places to equate *esse primum creatum* with act, but in others with potency.[14]

Why (Albert asks in an instance of the first sort of passage) does the First Principle cause life in all living existents? Because *esse*, as well as *vivere* and *intelligere*, is an *actus continuus* issuing from the First Being, First Life and First Intelligence (*PU*, 1, 2, 2; XVII, ii,

---

Datierung der Schrift Alberts des Grossen *De Causis et Processu Universitatis*," *Archiv für Geschichte der Philosophie* 45 (1963), 129.

Kaiser dates Albert's *Liber de Causis et Processu Universitatis* as not earlier than 1265 and not later than 1272 (he prefers this last date)—see *ibid.*, where he lists and evaluates the arguments of those who posit Albert's *De Causis* to be written as early as 1244 (e.g., Mandonnet, Endres, von Hertling, Feigl) and as late as 1272 (e.g., Pelster, Geyer, Bach, Bardenhewer, Scheeben).

In an article in the same volume of the *Archiv* and entitled "Die Benutzung proklischer Schriften durch Albert den Grossen," pp. 1–22, Kaiser refutes the claim of Ernst Degen in his 1902 Munich dissertation "Welches sind die Beziehungen Alberts des Grossen *Liber de Causis et Processu Universitatis* zur *Stoicheiôsis Theologikê* des Neuplatonikers Proklos?" that in his commentary on the *Liber* Albert uses not only the *Liber de Causis* itself but also Proclus' *Elements of Theology* in a Latin version of an Arabic translation (*ibid.*, pp. 1–14). As a result of Albert's seeming unawareness of William of Moerbeke's translation (finished 1268) of Proclus' *Elements*, Kaiser concludes that either Albert's commentary on the *Liber* was before 1268 or that Moerbeke's translation was not available to him personally. Albert does refer (although somewhat sporadically and arbitrarily) to Proclus' *Elements* in his *Summa Theologiae*, which is subsequent to his commentary on the *Liber* (*ibid.*, pp. 14–21).

[14] References to Albert's *Liber de Causis et Processu Universitatis* will be to the Cologne critical edition: *Alberti Magni Opera Omnia* W. Fauser, ed. (Monasterii Westfalorum in Aedibus Aschendorff, 1993), Tomus XVII, Pars ii. Hereafter I shall abbreviate the title of Albert's commentary as *PU*, which he divides into books, tractates and chapters, and I shall refer to them in that order. Hence, this reference—*PU*, 1, 2, 2; XVII, ii, 28a—means *Liber de Causis et Processu Universitatis*, Book I, tractate 2, ch. 2; Cologne Vol. XVII, Part ii, upper half of the first column on p. 28. The Cologne editor also numbers the lines on each page, but to make transferring the references from the Jammy and Borgnet editions (which I used when first writing my chapters on Albert) to the Cologne edition, I generally do not list the line-numbers. Since Albert' *PU* does not extend beyond Vol. XVII, Part ii, of the Cologne edition, references will generally omit the Volume and Part numbers.

28a). Again, the termini of an *esse* in time are its potency and act—
such an *esse* starts in potency and finishes in act ("in potentia enim
esse inchoatur et in actu terminatur"); the *esse* of the First Cause
starts neither from without nor from within and, thus, is fully
eternal; but the *esse* which the First Cause produces and which
belongs to intelligence and soul has a start from without (the First
Cause) but not from within: although produced by God, it is so
comprehended by His light as to be immutable and, accordingly,
exists entirely in act and without any potency ("totum existens in
actu, nihil sui habens in potentia"; 2, 1, 8, 69d–70a). On one occasion when speaking of the simplicity characterizing a self-standing
substance, Albert even describes *esse primum creatum* as "pure act":
whereas a substance which comes about through *fieri* has an *esse*
which is not pure but mixed and multiple because of many potencies, a self-standing and immutable substance possesses an *esse*
which is a simple and pure act without any mixture of nonbeing
("esse enim est simplex actus et purus, nihil habens admixtum de
non esse") and which has flowed from the First Cause into an *id
quod est* marked by immobility (2, 5, 12, 178b–d).

In other passages, though, Albert links *esse primum creatum* with
potency. For example, why is such an *esse* less simple than its First
Cause? Because it is distant from that Cause; because according to
that-which-it-is it has come from nothing and is, of itself, in potency. Thus it is concrete through the relationships it has to the nothingness from which it came and to the power of its First Cause, in

---

That Albert wrote PU sometime between 1264 and 1267, see *ibid.*,
"Prologomena, " p. v, lines 55–56 and 73–80.

On the nature of Albert's *PU* see *ibid.*: "De indole huius operis eiusque
fontibus, " pp. vi–vii. Albert divides *PU* into two parts, the first of which
treats of natural thology and consists of Book I, tractates 1–3. These offer a
"sectio historica" (tractate 1, chs. 1–6: Epicureans, Stoics, materialists, volun-
tarists) and a "sectio systematica" based on Algazeli's *Metaphysics*, as well as
on Alfarabi and Avicenna, all of whom Albert calls "posteriores Peripatetici"
(tractate 1, chs. 7, to tractate 3). Part Two of *PU* treats "de processu universitatis
a causa prima." It begins with an explanation of Neoplatonic emanation Book
I, tractate 4: "de fluxu causatorum a causa prima" and continues (Book II,
tractates 1–5) with a commentary on the *Liber de Causis* itself: "Liber secundus
operis Alberti tractans de causis primariis est commentum super anonymum
Librum de causis a Gerardo de Cremona ex Arabico in Latinum translatum,
qui videtur seaculo IX in Bagdad ortum esse cuiusque ultimi fontes sunt
imprimis Procli Elementatio theologica, sed etiam Plotini Enneades."

which it existed intelligibly before it came to be (2, 1, 17, 81c).[15] Again: even though simple, *esse primum creatum* entails relationships and powers (*potentias*) and, thereby, is a composite of finiteness and infiniteness. Finite because of its origin as form and light from the First Intellect, it is infinite with respect to what follows upon it through division: potentially it is in and of that infinitude. It also is infinite in itself because of the goods, powers and other *potentiae* which flow out from it to subsequent realities. But these goods and powers do not make the *esse primum creatum* a composite: it remains a simple concept or intelligence, which however involves a diversity because of the relationships and potencies underlying them. This diversity in turn causes the subsequent intellects to be diverse: the *esse* is potentially each subsequent ("potentia est sequens"), which comes to be when that potency is brought into act by determination replacing the state of confusion [and of indetermination in which the subsequents exist in that *esse*] (2, 1, 19, 83c–d and 84a–b; see key text H below). This connection which Albert puts between *esse primum creatum* and *potentia* no doubt results, we may note, from his conviction that everything except the Necessary Being is in potency and, thus, nothing has *esse* from what-it-is, which is rather in potency and from nothing (2, 1, 14, 77b).

The paraphrases so far offered are rather lengthy, but they seem warranted as a restatement of the problem encountered above in Texts A to D: how is *esse primum creatum* related to Aristotle's theory of act/potency? Is it act or potency or both or neither? Second, they illustrate that Albert was very much aware of that theory and often tried to deal with how *esse* could be best situated within it. In order better to understand and evaluate his efforts let us study separately and in context several key passages.[16]

---

[15] Also see *ibid.*, c. 18, 82b.

[16] These will be lettered as "E" and so forth (see n. 10 above) to facilitate reference. Numbers in brackets will also be added to them for the same reason.

PU, 1, 2, 8, 34a–c, speaks informatively of *esse primum creatum* but not explicitly in connection with act/potency; hence *PU*, 2, 1, 5, 65c sqq., is instead chosen as Text E.

Text E: *PU*, 2, 1, 5 (Cologne ed., XVII, ii, 65a–66c): "Qualiter causa primaria universalis plus influit in causatum quam secundaria universalis"

In Book I Albert discusses the First Cause (its status of *Necesse Esse*;[17] its knowledge, freedom, will and omnipotence; Tr. 1 to 3) and *fluxus* as the manner of its causing effects (Tr. 4). At the beginning of Book II he speaks of the four primary causes: the First Cause, who is efficient, formal and final source of all realities; Intelligence, which moves all subsequents through the desire it instills in them; Soul, which moves the first heavenly body by the desire it conceives for the Intelligence; Nature, the form and power diffused through all the heavens as their innate principle of motion and life (2, 1, 2, 62a–63a). Those are the causes with which Albert concerns himself in Text E on this point: in a situation in which an effect arises from primary and secondary causes, the primary cause literally "influences" (= flows over into, pours into) the effect more than does the lower cause.[18] The gist of his discussion follows.

[1] That a primary cause's flowing over into the effect is greater than that of a secondary cause is based upon four reasons. [a] The first cause flows into the effect even when the secondary cause does not. [b] The latter cause is set up as a substance (*substantificatur*) only through the former, which gives it its power of flowing-into (*virtutem influendi*). [c] Whatever a secondary cause does, the primary cause does more eminently and more perfectly, but not *e converso*. [d] A secondary cause is in the primary virtually, potentially, substantially and (so to speak) influentially or outgoingly, as some philosophers say, for it goes out from the primary cause

---

[17] Designating God as *Necesse Esse* comes from Avicenna, whom Albert took to be one source of the original *Liber de Causis*—see *PU*, 1, 2, 1, 59a and 60d–61a. On Avicenna, see P. Morewedge, *The Metaphysics of Avicenna* (New York: Columbia University Press, 1973), pp. 206 sqq., 298–99 and 324; S. M. Afnan, *Avicenna: His Life and Works* (London: Allen and Unwin, 1958), pp. 130–35; M. M. Anawati, *Avicenna: La Métaphysique* (Paris: J. Vrin, 1978); G. Verbeke, "Introduction," in S. van Riet (ed.), *Avicenna Latinus: La Métaphysique* (Leiden: E. J. Brill, 1978). Also see n. 22 below on *dator formarum*, which likewise is Avicennian in origin.

[18] In his discussion Albert contrasts the four primary causes not only with secondary ones but also among themselves, as the chapter shows. The quotation marks around the words "influence," "inflow" and "flow" on subsequent pages indicate that they are to be understood literally.

according to its entire reality. But a primary cause is not present in a secondary cause in any way. Hence, a primary cause pours more into the effect than does a secondary cause, which in fact is an effect of the primary.

[2] Accordingly, the primary cause is said to be *in* many (*in multis*) because its causality extends to all secondary causes and, second and to some extent, to be *of* many (*de multis*), since as a sort of univocal cause it shares form, name and meaning (*rationem*) with those secondary causes.[19] In this sense, then, the primary cause is called "universal" (2, 1, 5, 65c–d).

[3] If with Aristotle we take a universal to be a one in and of many, what is more universal is in and of more ("in pluribus . . . et de pluribus") and, consequently, a primary cause is more universal and more "influential" than a secondary one. Moreover, not every primary cause is the first cause but only that one cause which has neither equal nor contrary. Again, a secondary cause, although it receives "influence" from antecedent causes, is of itself and sub- stantially a cause; yet it does not pour more into the effect than the prior causes, even though its pouring-into combines its own cau- sality with that from above: all the resources that the "influence" of a secondary cause calls upon, it has from its prior cause, where they are in a more potent and strong state (p. 65d).

[After settling an objection that a secondary cause has the greater "influence" because what it pours into an effect grounds the effect's definition and demonstration (p. 66a), Albert summarizes what has preceded and sets down conclusions.]

[4] From what has been said previously it is clear that a primary cause pours more into an effect than a secondary cause, for it inflows more intensely and extensively ("intensius . . . et in pluri- bus"), more eminently and powerfully, and its "influx" adheres more tenaciously to the effect than that from a secondary cause. [5] True enough, the latter flows into the effect in a more determinate fashion than does the former, for that which the secondary cause

---

[19] The explanation here of *in multis* and *de multis* helps clarify *PU,* 2, 1, 19, 83d (which has been cited above, "Problem Revisited," and below as Text H, #3b): if "esse comparatur . . . ad id quod post ipsum est . . . infinitum est: potentialiter enim in infinitis et de infinitis est." On univocal cause see next note.

On #1d, second last sentence ("But a primary cause is not present in a secondary cause in any way"), see 2, 2, 29, 122d., for an apparently different doctrine ("Causa agens formaliter est in eo quod agit et constituit").

pours into the effect determines it as to its form more than does that coming from the primary cause (p. 66b).

[6] Accordingly, some attack the position just presented by saying that the "influx" from a secondary cause when compared with that from a primary cause is as act to potency—thus *vivere* with respect to *esse* is act to potency, and likewise *sentire* with reference to *vivere*. Since, then, an act contributes more to reality (*esse*) than potency, they conclude that a secondary cause pours more into the effect than does a primary one.

[7] But that is an error, for no act is a potency except inasmuch as it is imperfect, but an act is imperfect not of itself but from the fact that it is an act of what is imperfect. [8] But with reference to efficient and to formal causes, every act is perfect because it is an act of what is perfect ("Nullus enim actus potentia est nisi per hoc quod imperfectus est. Imperfectus autem est non ex se sed ex eo quod est imperfecti. Comparatus autem ad efficientem et formalem causam, omnis actus perfectus est propter quod est actus perfecti"). Thus, motion is a perfect act with reference to the mover from which it proceeds but is an act of what is imperfect by being in what is moved. [9] But the going-forth or "flux" from a primary cause is a perfect act insofar as it issues from that cause, and accordingly it is an imperfect act only inasmuch as it is received in the effect ("Processus autem sive fluxus a primaria causa secundum quod est ab ipsa actus perfectus est, et accidit illi actum imperfectum esse secundum quod est receptus in causato"). [10] But truly the perfection of the effect is present more simply and eminently in a primary rather than in a secondary cause and, thus, the objection is invalid. Hence, a universal primary cause clearly flows more into an effect than does a universal secondary cause (p. 66b–c).

Comments. Of the many texts in *PU* which touch on *esse primum creatum* this one serves as a good introduction since 2, 1, 5 is a clear affirmation that *esse* is not potency with reference to *vivere* and other subsequents but is, of itself and as from the First Cause, a perfect act and, second, it sets forth the basis (in part, at least) upon which that affirmation rests: the crucial notions of *influere* and *fluere*. Let us begin with these last two words.

In order to understand *influere* we must first investigate *fluere*, since the former entails the latter: "Influere . . . est fluxum talem [the sort of *fluere* Albert had discussed in the previous chapter] alicui innectere receptibili" (1, 4, 2, 44a). What, then, is *fluere*? It is not synonymous with *causare* but is restricted to analogous causality[20] and is exemplified in the art (p. 42c) of an architect's building a house or of a doctor's inducing health (p. 42c), as well as in a ray of light from the sun (p. 42c) or in water of a creek from a spring (p. 42b). What those instances have in common is that one and the same causative factor is in the source (architect, doctor, sun, spring) and in the effect (house, healthy organism, illumined surface, creekbed); consequently, that factor (the perfections of "house," "health," light, water) is said to "flow" from cause to effect.[21] Thus, only that factor "flows" which is of the same sort both in cause and in effect: "non enim fluit nisi id quod unius formae est in fluente et in eo in quo fit fluxus" (p. 42b).

Accordingly, a "flux" (the translation of *fluxus*, the noun formed upon *fluere*) is the form emanating from the First Source, which Plato calls the "Giver of Forms" (p. 43a).[22] "Flux" is not an eduction of act from potency (as Peripatetic authors describe the process)

---

[20] Albert first states that *fluere* is similar to (note that he does not say: identical with) univocal *vs.* equivocal causality (p. 42b: "Similiter enim idem est fluere quod univoce causare"). A bit later (*ibid.*, c. 6) he calls it analogous: the "flow" from the First to the last existent occurs neither "in genere causae efficientis aequivocae omnino" nor "inter ea quae omnino univoca sunt." Rather, it occurs "inter ea quae per analogiam dicuntur, in quibus secundum quasi instrumentale est ad primum. Et forma qua fluit primum magis ac magis coarctatur et determinatur secundum quod fluit in secundo vel in tertio et sic deinceps. . . . In omnibus enim his idem est quod fluit, licet secundum aliud esse sit in primo et secundum aliud in secundo, et sic deinceps" (pp. 49d and 50a). On causes as univocal, analogous and equivocal see L. Sweeney, *Authentic Metaphysics in an Age of Unreality*, 2d ed. [hereafter: *AM*], 2nd ed. (New York/Bern: Peter Lang Publishing, Inc., 1993), pp. 244–47.

On *esse* or "being" as analogous when applied to God and creatures, see below, Text F, #16–#19; L. Sweeney, *AM*, pp. 151–60 and 194–96.

[21] The first two examples are truly analogous, since the same factor is in cause and in effect but differently: the house-as-planned *vs.* the house-as-built-of-bricks, health-as-envisioned-by-the-doctor *vs.* health-as-achieved-in-the-patient. The other two examples are not analogous but univocal: the same factor is in both cause and effect and in the same way: the light is physically in both its source (the sun) and on the surface of the wall, the water is physically in both the spring from which it flows and in the riverbed. On causes as analogous, see preceding note.

[22] The conception of *dator formarum* is, of course, not Plato's but Avicenna's— see E. Gilson, *History of Christian Philosophy in the Middle Ages* (New York: Random House, 1955), pp. 195–96, 204–5, 213–15; A.-M. Goichon, *Lexique de la langue philosophique d'Ibn Sīnā* (Paris: Desclée de Brouwer, 1938), p. 440, #784; S. M. Afnan, *Avicenna*, pp. 112 and 130. On the active intelligence as *plena formis*, see *PU*, 2, 2, 21, 115a–d, where Albert mentions both Plato and Avicenna.

but the coming of act from act ("dici potest quod fluat secundum quod est actus ab actu")[23] by the First Origin's communicating itself without lessening its own perfection (1, 4, 2, 43a). It is an incessantly ongoing process ("fluxus semper est in fieri"; p. 43c) issuing from the generosity of the First, Who is always in act ("ipsa communicabilitas primi cum semper sit in actu . . . hanc facit emanationem"; p. 43b) and Who is the Agent Intellect (literally) illumining and thus constituting whatever He effects ("intellectus agens, qui lumine quod sibi est de se, sic semper formas emanat quibus constituit ea quae agit"; p. 43c). It is the intelligible and simple emanation from that First Source, Who thereby penetrates everything and is everywhere present (p. 43d).

Next, what is *influere*? Before answering, though, let us note that *fluere* is not confined to efficient causes, as one might think from the chapter just analyzed, but applies also to formal (= exemplary) and to telic causes (see 1, 1, 4, 46d–48b).[24] Now the First Cause simultaneously exercises all three causalities: He is the efficient, formal and final source containing everything (2, 1, 2, 62a: "Et causa . . . prima est in qua sicut in fonte effectivo et formali et finali sunt omnia"). Therefore, the "flux" from Him is an efficiently pro-

---

[23] An example of an act coming from act is, Albert adds, that of a house built to conform with its design in its architect's mind or of a patient's health resulting from his doctor's awareness of what constitutes health. These instances Albert next admits finding in Aristotle's *Meta.*, VII, c. 7, 1032b1 sqq. On act from act see also below, Text I, #4; notes 33, 70 and 75.

At times Albert is content (as here) to mention the *Peripatetici* without naming them—e.g., 2, 2, 9, 102b, where he contrasts them with *theologi* such as Dionysius. Elsewhere he also names them—e.g., 1, 2, 7, 32c: *antiqui Peripatetici* are Theophrastus, Porphyry and Themistius; *posteriores Peripatetici* include Avicenna, Algazel and Alfarabi; 1, 3, 2, 36d: Peripatetics who deny a will to the First Principle are Theophrastus, Porphyry, Avicenna and Averroës; 1, 3, 5, 40c: *posteriores Peripatetici* are Avicenna, Alfarabi and Algazel. At times he names only Aristotle among them (or, at least, lists one of his treatises): e.g., 2, 2, 1, 92a and 92c–d; *ibid.*, c. 33, 127b–c.

On Albert and Averroës see A. Zimmermann, "Albertus Magnus und der lateinische Averroismus," in G. Meyer and A. Zimmermann (eds.), *Albertus Magnus—Doctor Universalis 1280–1980* (Mainz: Matthias-Grünewald-Verlag, 1980), pp. 465–93.

[24] *Fluere* is, in fact, the causality exercised by each sort of cause: the activity itself of an agent, the direction given by an exemplar, the attraction issuing from a goal. Can the grounding, limitation, individuation and multiplication which matter effects in something be described as a *fluere*? Yes, although not strictly and only *per accidens*—1, 4, 4, 46d and 47a–b; 2, 1, 3, 63c.

duced emanation exemplarily directed by omniscience and telically aimed at freely communicating divine riches to creatures.[25]
Esse primum creatum is, if we anticipate what will be documented
later,[26] that "flux" in its initial but enduring moment.

If the above paragraphs successfully re-present what Albert intends by *fluere*, we are now ready for *influere*: what is the force of
the preposition "in" in that infinitive? It reminds us that anything
flowing must be flowing *into* something which contains, encloses,
borders it. Even though a flowing liquid of itself is just that—a
liquid—it involves something over and beyond itself—the bottle,
bucket—into which it is poured and which is its container. The
"flux" which is the *esse primum creatum* is no exception. It is itself
a single and simple emanating form or light[27] and remains so
throughout its development into *vivere* and *intelligere*.[28] Nonetheless it connotes compositeness when "part" of a composite: the
existents (Intelligence, Soul, heavenly bodies, bodies on earth) which
receive, contain, curtail it and which are themselves the fonts of the
possibility or potency (1, 4, 2, 44c: "[continentia est] in possibilitate

---

[25] On divine omniscience, will and freedom see Book I, Tractates 2 and 3,
pp.25a–42c.

[26] See 2, 1, 15, 78d and 79b; Text F, #10 (= 2, 1, 17, 81c); Text H, #6 (= 2, 1, 19,
83c); Text I, #4 and #8b (= 2, 1, 20, 85a and b); 2, 3, 10, 147d.

[27] Elsewhere Albert designates *esse* as "simplex conceptus mentis" (Text F,
#4; 2, 1, 17, 81a); as "intelligentia simplex," which he explains as "forma a
lumine intellectus agentis in esse producta et in simplici illo lumine per
intentionem accepta" (Text H, #2; 2, 1, 19, 83c). See n. 56 below.

One should keep in mind that "to be real" for Albert means "to be light"—
see 1, 2, 1, 26b: "Omnis res ab illo est in quod resolvitur sicut in suae constitutionis
principium. Ex quo ergo omne quod est, sive sit per se sive per accidens, sive sit
per naturam sive per animam, sive corporeum sive sit incorporeum, resolvitur
in tale lumen intellectus agentis, et id ad aliud resolvi non potest; constat ergo
quod primum efficiens est sicut intellectus universaliter agens"; 1, 4, 8, 55d:
"Dum ergo primus intellectus universaliter agens hoc modo intelligit se,
lumen intelligentiae quod est ab ipso prima forma est et prima substantia
habens formam intelligentis in omnibus." In fact, God *is* pure light (2, 1, 25,
91a). In and through that light He pre-possesses the forms of all things and,
then, establishes and distinguishes all of them (1, 3, 6, 42a). Because the divine
light extends everywhere, God is omnipresent (1, 2, 5, 31a).

[28] As will be clear from Text F, #6 (= 2, 1, 17, 81b), *esse primum creatum* is the
actus entium, whereas *vivere* and *intelligere* are, respectively, *esse viventium* and
esse intelligentium. The latter two are acts within the act which is *esse primum
creatum*: they are that *esse* in a more explicated and less perfect state—see below,
Text H, #11 (= 2, 1, 19, 84b); Text I, #3 (= 2, 1, 20, 85a–b); notes 31, 72 and 76.

rei cui fit fluxus, quae possibilitas rei est ex seipsa") whereby the light (= *esse*) flowing from the primal Agent Intellect is gradually reduced from bright to dim, from spiritual to physical, as it moves from the intellectual to terrestrial levels (pp. 44a–45a).[29]

Influere, is, then, to link *fluere* with some recipient: "influere autem est fluxum talem alicui innectere receptibili"; p. 44a). This link occurs whenever a cause (efficient, paradeigmatic, telic) transmits the "flow" (which at its first stage is *esse primum creatum* and, then, is *vivere* and *intelligere* as *esse* evolves further) into the receptacle that contains and limits it. As the "flow" is transferred, it becomes more determinate intrinsically (e.g., *esse* becomes *vivere*) or is limited or terminated extrinsically by its recipient (e.g., *esse* becomes *hoc esse*). Obviously, the "flow" is more perfect, both intrinsically and extrinsically, on a higher level in the cascade of causality and, second, the higher the cause, the more powerful and "influential" it is.

The preceding comments are relevant because Text E deals with the situation in which higher and lower causes are cooperating in that "influx" and, thereby, in producing the effect. Here Albert first draws the conclusion that a primary cause's responsibility for the "influx" (with its two dimensions of "flux" and reception) constituting an effect is greater than that of a secondary cause,[30] and this for reasons now so manifest (see #1) as to need no further explanation. He then (#2) discusses how a first cause is universal (*in* all secondary causes through its causality and *of* them because its causality is analogous; see note 19 above). Next he contrasts it with a secondary cause: the latter's influence is less than the former's, from which it has received all its resources (#3) and which accordingly "inflows" more intensely, widely, eminently and powerfully into what is caused than does a secondary cause (#4); second, the latter's "inflow" forms the effect more determinately (#5). This second contrast gives occasion for the objection that the "flux" (e.g., *vivere*) from the secondary cause is act, whereas that (e.g., *esse*)

---

[29] For additional information on the production of the heavens and on terrestrial existents (a topic to which little explicit attention will be given in this chapter) see 1, 4, 4, 47a–b; 2, 1, 2, 62c; 2, 1, 3, 63d; 2, 1, 21, 85d; 2, 2, 1, 94a–c; 2, 2, 19, 113a; 2, 2, 37, 130b; 2, 4, 2, 157a–b; 2, 4, 12, 165b–166c.

[30] Although "influx" entails both those dimensions, he stresses now one (as in Text E), now the other.

from the first cause is potency and, thus, a secondary cause inflows more into an effect than does the first (#6).[31]

Albert already had the data needed for responding in previous sections of the text: formal determination of *esse* is due to the primary cause, since whatever a secondary cause does, it does more perfectly and transcendently (#1c); a secondary cause is an effect of the first (#1d); all the resources which the "influence" of a secondary cause uses in formally determining the effect come to it from the prior cause, where they are present more powerfully and strongly (#3). Eventually, that is his response (see #10): the perfection of the effect is present more simply and eminently in its prior rather than in its secondary cause.

But his first attempt at replying is based on analyzing the notions of act/potency (see #7–#9), an analysis which the very wording of the objection (#6) triggers: the "flow" (e.g., *vivere*) from the secondary cause when compared with that (*esse*) from the first cause is as act to potency; but act contributes more to reality than potency; therefore, a secondary cause "inflows" more than does a primary. Albert handles its major premise in an elliptical and rather puzzling line of argumentation (#7–#9):

an act is potency only if it is itself imperfect;

but an act is imperfect not of itself but from the fact that it is an act *of* something imperfect;

but with reference to efficient and to formal (= exemplary) causes an act is perfect because it is an act of what is perfect [although it may be imperfect if it is in an effect which is imperfect]—e.g., motion is a perfect act with reference to the mover from which it proceeds but is an act of what is imperfect by being in what is moved;

but [*esse* as] the "flux" or going-forth from a primary cause, precisely as from that cause, is a perfect act [and, thus, not a potency], although it may be an imperfect act [and thereby a potency] inasmuch as it is received in the effect [and is *hoc esse*].

The flaw which makes Albert's argument puzzlingly irrelevant to the objection is clearer if we express its last proposition in this fashion:

---

[31] In #6 the objector also speaks of *sentire* compared to *vivere* as act to potency, but for our purposes we need report Albert's discussion only on *vivere* and *esse* as act and potency. On *esse, vivere, intelligere, sentire,* see notes 28 and 72.

esse as "flux" is act, *hoc esse* as "influx" is limited by its recipient, which serves as potency.

But as "influx" *esse*, though limited and received by potency, is not itself a potency, which is the recipient rather. Second, *esse* can be in the state of "influx" (i.e., can be *hoc esse*) without the presence of any secondary cause—e.g., the primal Agent Intellect is solely responsible for the first created Intellect, which consists of *esse* and *id quod est* and wherein *esse* has become *hoc esse*.[32] But the objection dealt with primary *and* secondary causes and, more precisely, it made the point that the latter contributes more to the effect than does the former because the latter makes *esse* be *vivere* (not: *esse* be *hoc esse*) by changing potency to act.

The thrust of that more precise point Albert seems not to have met here. I say "here" because what he said earlier on "flux" in *PU*, 1, 4, 1, 43a, does counteract their position. As noted above, the "flowing" of a form (read: *esse*) from the First Source is not an eduction of act from potency but the creative emanating of act from Act (p. 43a: "dici potest quod [forma] fluat secundum quod est actus ab actu") by that Source's communicating itself without lessening its own perfection.[33] If one may describe the "flowing" of *esse primum creatum* from God as the coming of act from Act, may one not validly describe the development of *esse* into *vivere* as the coming of act (*vivere*) from act (*esse*)? The relationship of *esse/vivere* would then be not that of potency/act but of act/act and, accordingly, the objection discussed has no foundation and is thereby invalid.

Conclusions. Although Text E concentrates on relationships between primary and secondary causes (efficient, exemplary, final)

---

[32] On God as immediately causing the first intellectual substance, see 1, 2, 1, 26a–b; 2, 2, 19, 112c. On the significance of capitalizing "Intellect" or "Intelligence," see n. 56 below.

[33] On God's status as Act, see 1, 2, 3, 28d–29a: God knows all creatures, even though these be potentially infinite, because "sui nulli habet in potentia sed totum quod in ipso est, actus purus est et simplex"; 1, 4, 1 and 2, 43a–b and 44a: the "flow" or emanation of reality from God is accounted for by the fact that He is always in act ("cum semper sit in actu") and in no way is in potency ("cum nullo modo in potentia sit"); 2, 2, 4, 97b–c: as the "intelligentia universaliter activa" God "nihil in potestate habet . . . intelligentia est actus purus." Incidentally, on "intellectus universaliter agens" as the best name for God, see 2, 1, 24, 90c–d; also see n. 27 above.

On "act flowing from Act," see below, Text I, #3, and "Comments" corresponding to n. 75.

and between their "influences," it also furnishes important data on *esse primum creatum*. When fitted into an Aristotelian framework, it is act and not potency. It is act flowing *from* the Act Who is First Cause and *into* the subsequent acts of *vivere* and of *intelligere*. Limited by recipients and thereby linked (but not identified) with potency, it becomes *hoc esse, hoc vivere, hoc intelligere*.

The next key text will, we hope, illumine dimensions of *esse* which still remain obscure.

Text F: *PU,* 2, 1, 17 (XVII, ii, 80d–82c): "Quid sit primum causatum in rebus et entibus"

Having earlier in this tractate contrasted primary and secondary causes as to causality (chapters 2–6; see above, Text E, for chapter 5) and as to the *esse* which characterizes each (chapters 7–10) and having discussed the nature and origin of Soul (chapters 11–16),[34] Albert next takes up the crucial question of what God causes first (chapters 17–20). Let us begin with chapter 17.

[1] *Esse* is what God causes first or, more precisely, creates first, since He causes it from nothing: His causality does not presuppose anything else preexisting (p. 81a). [2] Another reason for the priority *esse* has over other effects is that no intelligibility is prior to *esse*. If the composite should be resolved into the simple, or effect into formal cause, or the posterior into what is prior either in nature or in intelligible content, or the particular into the universal, that resolution will always stop at *ens*. [3] But whatever is last in a resolving process is necessarily first in a composing process. Therefore, *esse* is the *first* of all the effects proceeding from the First Cause, for they go forth from Him by a process of composition inasmuch as everything is constituted in its reality as a composite (p.81a).

[4] Consequently, *esse* is created and is first, for it is the simple mental concept ("simplex conceptus mentis") which is not formally determined at all and which enables one to reply *yes* whenever asked whether some or other thing exists.[35] [5] This question of *an*

---

[34] The discussion of "anima nobilis" in *ibid.* ch. 13–15, is complex—see L. Sweeney, "A Controversial Text on 'Esse Primum Creatum' in Albert the Great's *Liber de causis et processu universitatis*" in J. A. Schnaubelt (ed.) *Proceedings of the PMR Conference,* 5 (1980),137–49.

[35] On *esse* as "simple concept," see the portion of this chapter corresponding to n. 27 above and its first prgr.

sit only the First Cause can definitively settle,[36] for only He can create *esse*, which is a simple concept and at which ultimately the resolution stops. Why so? *Esse* is not educed from anything in which it might have a formal start, as indeed *vivere* is educed from *esse*, *sentire* from *vivere*, and the rational from the sensible (p. 81b). That is, whatever is rational is sensible, whatever is sensible is living, whatever is living is being, but not conversely.

[6] And *esse* "inflows" its power upon all subsequents and, accordingly, just as it is the act of beings ("esse actus est entium"), so *vivere* is *esse* for living existents, *sentire* is *esse* for sentient ones, *ratiocinari* is *esse* for rational ones, as Aristotle says (*ibid.*).[37]

[7] This power—that *vivere*, *sentire* and *ratiocinari* should be the *esse* in living, sentient and reasoning existents—they can have only from *esse primum* ("et hanc virtutem, quod scilicet quodlibet istorum sit esse quorum est, sequentia non possunt habere nisi a primo quod est esse"). Why? Because each of those subsequents' intelligibilities presupposes something preceding and, consequently, is not produced from nothing but from that in which its *esse* is inchoate; [8] therefore, none of them can come about through creation, since what is subsequent is related to what precedes as to that which informs and determines it and, thus, the subsequent is produced not through creation but through information (p. 81b).

[9] The result is that *esse* is what is created first, that all other effects are not created, and that no effect can be before *esse*. [10] But *esse* is not called "being" or "entity," for it proceeds first from the First Cause as the simple process and act causing anything which is to be.[38] Since, then, *esse* signifies that process as the act of being, it

---

[36] On *an est* Albert refers to "what had been shown in Book I"—see 1, 1, 8, 16d: "Quod autem esse habeat in effectu ex se non est sibi sed potius ex primo esse, ex quo fluit omne esse quod est in effectu. Hoc ergo quod est, ab alio habet esse et illud quod est, et sic esse hoc modo accidit ei, quia ab alio sibi est; et ideo in ipso quaeri potest an est an non est; et quaestio determinabilis est per causam ejus quod est esse. In primo autem propter hoc quod esse non habet ab alio, esse per se est, et quaestio an est locum nullum habet."

[37] In referring to Aristotle Albert most likely has in mind *On the Soul*, II, c. 4, 415b13, where *to zên* is identified with *to einai*. For a discussion of *esse* and *vivere*, see L. B. Geiger, "La vie, acte essentiel de l'âme—l'*esse*, acte de l'essence d'après Albert-le-Grand," *Études d'histoire littéraire et doctrinale* (Paris: J. Vrin, 1962), pp. 49–116; for an evaluation of Geiger's article, see my ch. 14 above: "The Meaning of *Esse*," pages corresponding to notes 15–16.

[38] On the Latin here ("processus enim simplex prius a causa prima procedit ut actus in esse constituens omne quod est"), see 2, 1, 13, 76b–c: "Tale ergo esse et constitutionem in esse a prima causa accipit anima nobilis."

is better that the *primum creatum* be called *esse* rather than "being" or "entity" (p. 81c).

[11] From its being first, one can infer that *esse* is simpler than all else: that is most simple which cannot be resolved into something else; but *esse* is that at which the resolution of beings stops, for if *esse* were to be resolved into anything else, this latter would necessarily be prior to the first and subsequent to the last—a situation which is unintelligible.

[12] But *esse*, even though more simple than all other effects, is not as simple as the First Cause for the reason that it is second and, thus, is distant from that Cause. Hence, according to its what-is, it is from nothing and of itself is in potency and, thus, is concretized through relationships (p. 81c: "et hoc [its not being as simple as the First Cause] est propter hoc quia est secundum [et] distans a causa prima, et secundum id quod est ex nihilo est, et secundum seipsum in potentia est, et sic est concretum habitudinibus").[39] [13] For example, it has a relationship to the nothingness from which it came and to the power of the First in which it was intelligibly before it existed actually: it exists not of itself but by the active power of the First. [14] Of itself *esse* is nothing and, accordingly, its reality is not nothing-but-*esse* to the extent that the *esse* of the First Cause is so (p. 81c–d).

[While next answering the objection that, if *esse* is the first process from the Cause, it can be neither first nor created, Albert furnishes some relevant data.] [15] *Esse* is "first" by its not presupposing that anything *of* itself is preexistent which might furnish essential and intrinsic constituents. It does presuppose its Creator, Who however is no part of it or of any effect. Hence, the resolution of beings into their essential parts does not go back as far as the First Principle. [16] Accordingly, the *esse* predicated of that Principle and the *esse* predicated of His effects is not univocal[40] and, second, *esse* predicated of both God and creatures is neither one genus (since then the divine *esse* would be an essential constituent of created beings) nor is it in one genus (since then something would be prior to and simpler than the First Principle). [17] Ac-

---

[39] Derived from *concrescere*, the past participle, *concretum*, means literally "that whch has been congealed or hardened" and, thus, that which is fashioned and made definite by the relationships it has to the divine power and to nothingness.

[40] Not univocal, Albert adds, because "univocum . . . in omnibus his est essentialiter de quibus praedicatur" (pp. 81d–82a). On *fluere* as analogous and not univocal, see n. 20 above.

cordingly, whenever the First Principle and an effect are each said
to be, "being" is common to them through analogy and belongs to
God directly and properly but to the effects as His images. [18]
Therefore, the esse which is first when existents are being assembled
and is last when they are being disassembled is not that which is
absolutely First but that which is created first. [19] And when
"first" is applied to this effect, it is referred to subsequents not as
their genus but as their principle. Why? Because every genus is a
composite so as to be distinguishable from another genus; but
whatever is first is simple also and becomes the first constituent of
a composite—none of which characteristics esse would have were it
itself a composite; therefore, esse is related to subsequents as their
principle but not as their genus. Hence, esse is what is created first
(pp. 81d–82b) and [20] creation is the First Agent's simple action
upon no preexisting subject (p. 82b–c).

   Comments. Albert structures this text into three clear parts, the
first of which (#1–#8) establishes that esse is primum creatum, the
second (#9–#14) draws inferences from that fact and the third
(#15–#20) faces an objection. In them we shall concentrate upon his
remarks on act/potency.

   In his initial attempt to establish that esse is primum creatum
Albert does not disclose why it is esse rather than something else
which is first but rather why esse is not merely caused but is created: the First Agent's causality presupposes nothing preexisting
(#1). His second attempt settles on the former question. Esse it is
which is created first because no other intelligibility precedes it, as
witnessed by the fact that (note the word he now substitutes) ens
terminates the resolution of all other intelligibilities. But ens or esse
is not entirely intramental since Albert also makes it the terminus
of the reduction of such extramental items as composites, effects
and subsequents in nature (#2) and, thus, esse as their term would
be something simple, a formal cause, and that which is first. Granted
that shortly afterward he speaks of esse as "simplex conceptus
mentis," the content of which is unformed and undetermined ("ad
nihil formatus et determinatus") and enables one to reply affirmatively when asked whether anything whatsoever exists (#3). But
this statement is sandwiched between his affirming that esse proceeds from God prior to all else (#2) and his remark that the esse
[which corresponds actually to] the initial simple concept can only
be created by the First Cause (#5).[41] His proof for this last calls his
attention to esse as act, to which we now turn.

41 See n. 35 above.

Why, then, is *esse* created by the First Cause? Because it is not educed from anything in which it might have a formal start and, thus, it is unlike *vivere, sentire* and *ratiocinari*. The argument that these last are educed from something prior in which they are inchoate is that every rational existent is sentient, every sentient thing is living, every living thing is *ens*, but not conversely (#5).[42] This issues from everyday experience and amounts to a resolution of what is composite to what is simple. To its four grades (rational, sentient, living, being) there correspond in reverse order the four processes from the First Cause of *esse, vivere, sentire* and *ratiocinari*, the last three of which are educed from an inchoate state in its predecessors. Are these three, then, in potency in what precedes? In Text E (#6–#7) Albert had firmly denied that *vivere* is related to *esse* as act to potency or, again, that *sentire* and *vivere* have that relationship. If, then, Text F is to be consistent, Albert does not mean that (say) *vivere* is educed from *esse* (#5) as act from potency but eduction is equivalent to a development, disclosure, articulation by which act comes from act (see Text E, portion of "Comments" corresponding to note 33).

In fact, he applies "act" to *esse* three times in immediately subsequent lines. *Esse* is the act of beings ("actus est entium"), and the "inflowing" of its power upon *vivere, sentire* and *ratiocinari* enables them to be *esse* [and acts] in their respective recipients (Text F, #6).[43] A bit later when drawing inferences from the fact that *esse* is the *primum creatum: esse* should not be called *ens* (but see #2) or *entitas* because it is the simple process flowing from the First Cause as the act causing that whatever is *is* ("processus enim simplex . . . procedit ut actus in esse constituens omne quod est"; #10). No, the *primum*

---

[42] The transition from rational to sensible to living to being appears to leave out the stage of chemical, which should fit between living and being— unless, of course, being stands for chemical. This seems doubtful in view of the fact that *ens* or *esse* is *primum creatum*, which could hardly be a composite of chemicals. The same omission and/or difficulty occurs in Prop. 1 of the *Liber de Causis* itself, which moves from *virtus rationalis* to *vivum* to *esse* (see Bardenhewer ed., p. 163, lines 13 sqq.).

[43] On *esse* as *actus entium*, see L. Ducharme, "*Esse* chez S. Albert le Grand. Introduction à la métaphysique de ses premiers écrits," *Revue de l'Université d'Ottawa* 27 (1957), 1–44, especially pp. 19–23 and 32–38; G. Wieland, *Untersuchungen zum Seinsbegriff im Metaphysikkommentar Alberts des Grossen* (Münster: Aschendorff, 1972), "Beiträge zur Geschichte der Philosophie und Theologie des Mittelalters," Neue Folge, Band VII, especially pp. 47–112. For an evaluation of Ducharme and Wieland, see my ch. 14 above: "The Meaning of *Esse*," pages corresponding to notes 13–14 and 17–22.

creatum should (Albert continues) be called *esse* and not *ens* or *entitas* because *esse* designates that initial process precisely as the act of being ("esse illum processum nominat in actum entis").

Those three clear affirmations of *esse* as act should make the exegesis of ambiguous texts easier, one of which we encounter in the paragraphs which directly follow #10 and which set forth inferences drawn from the status of *esse* as *primum creatum*. Although this status indicates that *esse* is simple, it is not as simple as God because it is distant from Him and, thereby, its what-is is from nothing and *of itself it is in potency* ("et secundum seipsum in potentia est") and, thus, it is concretized by relationships (#12). The italicized words juxtaposed so closely to his previously affirming *esse* to be act makes one wonder whether Albert is contradicting himself. Apparently not, in view of that very juxtaposition and, especially, by reason of the explanation he gives directly after the puzzling words: *esse* is related to the nothingness from which it came and to the divine power in which it was in an intelligible manner before it was actually—it exists not of itself but by virtue of the power of the First Cause: "habet enim habitudinem ad potentiam primi in qua fuit antequam esset secundum intellectum. Non enim secundum seipsum est sed a potentia et virtute primi" (#13). Here *esse* is not said to be potential itself but solely with reference to the active power of God as exemplary cause in which it previously existed and by which it is now created. In this active and paradeigmatic sense *potentia* is applied intrinsically and properly to God and extrinsically to the *esse primum creatum*: this is the effect of God's creative *potentia* and, thus, is dubbed *potentia* through extrinsic denomination.[44] But in itself it properly deserves the title Albert bestowed on it earlier of *actus entium* (#6, #10).

Will the subsequent chapter in *PU* favor this exegesis? Let us see.

---

[44] This predication of *potentia activa* to *esse primum creatum* through extrinsic denomination is matched by the status of *esse* as container of divine, intellectual and psychic powers, which result in subsequent existents and which are in *esse* as active powers and not as complete essences—see 2, 1, 15, 79a: Soul "divinam habet operationem eo quod esse suum processus divinus est: . . . in processu manet virtus divinitatis causae primae"; *ibid.*, p. 79b: on the level of Soul *esse* is one numerically but causes diverse multiple existents inasmuch as it operates through the power of God, Intelligence and Soul ("causat . . . prout est in potentia virtutis divinae et virtutis intelligentiae et virtutis animae"; *ibid.*, p. 79c: why is *esse* one? Because in Soul it contains three active *potentiae* (creative, intellectual, psychic) but not as complete essences,

Text G: *PU,* 2, 1, 18 (Cologne ed. XVII, ii, 82c–83c): "Quod esse simplicius et universalius est omnibus aliis entibus"

[1] From what has preceded one realizes [Albert begins] that *esse* is more one[45] and simpler and, thereby, more universal and of greater extension than all subsequent beings. [2] This realization is based upon the fact that although *esse creatum* is a simple concept, and, as created, is second after the First and is essentially distant from Him, nonetheless it is made concrete by its relationships to the nothingness from which it came and to the First's power in which it was before it actually existed (p. 82c). [3] But those relationships do not constitute in it an essential composition, for they are not different constitutive essences but a single relationship with different terms, which reside in reason rather than in nature.

[4] But the First Principle has the greatest number of relationships, which however come about when the multitude of His effects are viewed in reference to Him; but these relationships, because based not in Him but in the effects, do not diminish His simplicity.

[5] On the other hand, the relationships of the *esse primum creatum* are based in it; accordingly, although they induce in it no essential composition, they do diminish its simplicity. [6] Therefore, *esse* is simple (though not absolutely so) and, thus, is more strongly one than all other divine effects. The reason is that all those other effects are composites and, thus, involve a number of natures or essences, which are their components and [which make] some [composites] prior, some posterior;[46] but *esse,* though rendered concrete through relationships, is not a composite and, hence, is more one and simpler than all of them (pp. 82c–d).

---

since the powers which ground its causality are its contents, and content and container are, despite a conceptual distinction, one and the same. Also see n. 79 below.

[45] "More one" translates *unicius,* which elsewhere might mean "more unique" but which the context indicates has to do with oneness rather than singularity. Also see below, #7, which has to do with how God is one: "Primum principium est et pure unum . . . vere est unum et non unitum": He is truly one and not merely united as though from parts.

[46] The prior and posterior composites mentioned here are those spoken of below, #11c–d.

[7] But the First Principle is absolutely one ("pure *unum*") and entails (as Boethius says) no number, for it is neither composed of essences nor concretized by any relationships with a basis in Him; therefore, He is truly one and not merely united (p. 82d).

[8] But *esse primum creatum* is more one than all subsequent divine effects by its proximity to God through imitating His unity but it is not genuinely nothing-but-one. [9] Everything subsequent to it has no unity except through a composition of potency and act, which would not be a genuine unity but a mere aggregation [exemplified in #10 and #11d below by substance and accidents] if it were not one and the same existent which is in potency and in act. That is, it is one and the same existent whose [specific] reality as inchoate is in potency and as perfect is in act (pp. 82d–83a: "Sequentia autem unitatem non habent nisi compositionis potentiae et actus, quae unitas non esset sed congregatio, si idem et unum non esset in potentia et actu. Idem enim et unum est cujus esse secundum inchoationem est in potentia et secundum perfectionem est in actu").

[10] Moreover, whatever is composed of substance and accident is one in subject and by aggregation and, hence, is not strictly one at all.

[11] Accordingly, "one" is fourfold: [a] He Who is truly and absolutely one and in Whom there is no number; [b] *unum essentialiter* [and *primum creatum*], which is one in such a way as to involve a number of relationships but not of essences; [c] a composite of potency and act, which is one by involving a number of natures, one of which contains the other ("unum ex potentia et actu compositum, in quo est numerus naturarum, quarum una continetur in altera");[47] [d] that which is one as the subject in which a number of essences reside, no one of which causes the other except improperly ("nisi per accidens"), as happens when a subject is said to cause the reality of an accident ("esse accidentis"), which however is not other than the subject's nature or essence (p. 83a).

[12] [Now, an existent on a lower level possesses its unity from the immediately higher level. Thus] what is one as a composite of potency and act [#11c] derives its ability to be one from that which is one without composition—namely, *esse* [#11b], which contains everything within its power and from which a genus gets its ability to contain species: these are one because they are in a unity and are

---

47 Also see above, 2, 1, 15, 79a–c: that which is present in another is identical with that in which it is present (see n. 44 above); 2, 2, 28, 122b (quoted below in n. 72).

reduced to a unity [i.e., the genus]. [13] That which is one because it is not a composition of essences [and is the *esse primum creatum;* #11b] has its capacity to be one from Him [#11a] Who is truly and purely one. That is, because He is one and because only unity can immediately flow from unity, that "flow" is one. [14] That which is one as a subject [#11d] has its ability to be one from that which is one as potency and act [11c] inasmuch as such a unified and yet composite subject causes diverse dispositions and properties: act terminates potency diversely—sometimes perfectly, sometimes imperfectly ("tale enim unum compositum in subjecto diversas causat dispositiones et proprietates propter hoc quod actus potentiam diversimode terminat, aliquando perfecte aliquando imperfecte")— so that different dispositions emanate and occasionally occur ("emanant et occasionantur") and, thus, are accidents inhering in a single subject (p. 83a–b).

[15] Finally, from the fact that *esse* is more stringently one than all subsequent effects, it is more extensively universal than any of them. Why? Whatever is composed of a constitutive form or of a restrictive difference is thereby set apart from others. [This is true even of] the highest genus, which does not have any external or antecedent constitutive difference but does have something which serves as a difference (as is clear when one says: "Substance is being which exists of itself": "Substantia est ens per se existens") and which contrasts it with accidents. Therefore, "being" as determined by such a quasi-constitutive difference cannot be predicated of absolutely everything (p. 83b)..

[16] But *esse primum creatum* is determined by no difference and, consequently, the scope of its predication is in no way curtailed. Hence, its universality is most extensive, which nonetheless is not that of a genus, species, specific difference, property or accident. Rather it is that of a first principle which enters into the reality of all things and which is analogously referred to beings (p. 83c: "universalitatis . . . principii primi ingredientis in esse rerum omnium, quod per analogiam refertur ad entia"). Therefore, *esse primum creatum,* which is simply one, is a universal of the widest possible universality.[48]

---

[48] Would not God be an exception, since He would be most universal as the principle and cause even of *esse?* See 1, 1, 10, 24a: "Primum quod est necesse esse fundamentale erit ad omnia, et si ipsum contineat emanationem esse, nihil erit ens vel esse in tota existentium universitate"; Text F, #15.

Comments. The present key-passage deals directly with why *esse primum creatum* is simpler and more universal than all other creatures: it is more simple because it is not a composite of essences, as all subsequent beings are (#6); it is more universal because it is the first intrinsic source of the reality of all things (#16). But the text also is informative on *esse primum creatum* in itself, as these reflections show.

Why is *esse*, despite its greater simplicity with respect to whatever is subsequent, less simple than God? Because it is made concrete by the relationships it has to nothingness and "to the First's power in which it was before it actually existed" ("habitudinibus . . . ad potentiam primi in qua fuit antequam esset"; #2). Note that here *potentia* is not ascribed to it but solely to God, who contained *esse* prior to creation and then created it as His first effect.[49] This corroborates our interpretation of Albert's description of those relationships in Text F above—namely, that his statement, "et [esse] secundum seipsum est in potentia et sic est concretum habitudinibus" (see Text F, #12) should be read in the light of what he immediately adds there: "habet enim . . . habitudinem ad potentiam primi in qua fuit antequam esset secundum intellectum. Non enim secundum seipsum est sed a potentia et virtute divini" (#13). That is, "[esse] secundum seipsum est in potentia" is equivalent to "[esse] secundum seipsum est . . . a potentia et virtute primi." *Potentia* is applied to *esse primum creatum* itself only in reference to the divine power knowing, containing and creating it. The fact that in his subsequent discussion of Text G on why *esse* is concrete through relationships Albert is silent on *esse*'s being "secundum seipsum in potentia" and simply repeats "[esse] concretum est habitudinibus . . . ad potentiam primi in qua fuit antequam esset" (#2) is a reassurance of the validity of our previous exegesis in Text F.

Text G illumines other dimensions of *esse* and of subsequent effects. For example, *esse primum creatum* is concrete through relationships but is simple. All other divine effects are composed of natures or essences (#6), which function as potencies and acts (#9). Here, though, one must distinguish between two sorts of compositions. In the first sort the same item is in potency inchoately and then in act perfectly; nonetheless, it is genuinely one inasmuch as the natures or essences which it entails are contained one in another. Thus, the generic essence "animal" is, as genus, potentially

---

[49] On God's power see 1, 3, 3, 37d–38a; 2, 2, 17, 110a–d sq. Also see n. 54 below.

"rational" but also is actually "rational" when determined by someone defining "man."[50] Despite the presence in it of the potential
determinations of "rational," "canine," "equine" and so forth, "animal" is one because it *contains* those determinations (Text G, #9,
#11c, #12): that which is contained is one with its container, that
which is in another is one with that other.[51]

But in the second sort of composition the same item is not first in
potency and then in act; moreover, it is not a genuine unity but an
aggregation. Thus, substance is potency and remains in potency
even when perfected by the accidents it causes and receives; the
accidents themselves are acts. Although these inhere in and are not
really distinct from the substance, accidents and substance are not
strictly one in being (Text G, #10, #11d, #14). [52]

Esse transcends both types of composition and, by inference,
potency/act also. Granted it involves relationships, but these are
mental rather than actual and, strictly speaking, are a single *habitudo* with several terms (e.g., nothingness, divine power, as well as
all subsequent effects that *esse* helps set up as an intrinsic constituent; #3, #5–#6, #11b). [53]

Furthermore, *esse* transcends all logical categories: the five predi-
cables (#16) and *ens* even (#15). And yet it is universal, but its
universality is analogous to God's: each is a first source, but God
functions extrinsically as efficient, exemplar and final cause of all
existents (2, 1, 2, 62a), *esse primum creatum* intrinsically as their
essential and radical component (#16).[54] Thence they derive not

---

[50] Genus and species are the sole instances Albert gives in #12 of the unity
he described in #11c (a composite of several natures related to one another as
act/potency, which nonetheless is one because those natures contain one
another), but would Intelligence, Soul and Nature fit into #11c also? The
answer apparently is affirmative, since if genus and specific difference are
there, *a fortiori* Intelligence, Soul and Nature would be also. See 2, 1, 15, 79b,
for another reference to genus and specific difference.

[51] See also *ibid.* and n. 44 *re* inchoate presence of active powers.

[52] Are there any other instances of #11d besides substance/accidents? See
n. 50 above.

[53] On the relationships between *esse* and subsequent realities, see below,
Text H, #2 and #6 sqq.

[54] An intrinsic source or cause differs from an extrinsic cause inasmuch as
the former is a constitutive part of the product, the latter is not. See L.
Sweeney, *AM*, p. 235, n. 3.

On God's causality as unfolding from *esse* whatever perfections it contains
(e.g., *vivere, intelligere*) see *PU*, 2, 2, 14, 107a sqq.; 2, 2, 17, 110a; 2, 3, 5, 143c; 2, 3,
6, 144b–c; 2, 3, 10, 147c; 2, 3, 13, 150b; 2, 4, 11, 164b.

only existence but also such specific perfections as *vivere, sentire*
and *intelligere*, all of which are present in *esse* as acts,[55] whence they
emerge as *actus ab actu* (1, 4, 1, 43a; see above, Text E, "Comments,"
second last paragraph).

Let us look for more data in chapter 19.

Text H: *PU,* 2, 1, 19 (Cologne ed. XVII, ii, 83c–84d): "Quod quamvis esse sit simplex, tamen compositum est ex finito et infinito"

In this chapter immediately following Text G Albert makes the
point that the simplicity of *esse primum creatum* does not prevent its
being composed of the finite and the infinite.

[1] Despite the fact that *esse primum creatum* is a simple intelligence, it is a composite of finiteness and infiniteness by reason of
the relationships and powers it has (p. 83c: "per habitudines et
potentias quas habet"). [2] By affirming that *esse* is a "simple intelligence" one does not mean that it is an intellectual substance such
as are the ten involved with the heavenly spheres[56] but that it is a
form caused to be by the light of the Agent Intellect and received
intentionally in that simple light[57]—thus, we call *esse* the first intel-

---

[55] On the presence of *vivere*, etc., in *esse* as acts and *potentiae activae*, see n. 44
above; Text G, #2, and "Comments." On *esse* accounting for the fact that
things exist, as well as its other significations (e.g., entity, essence, act of
essence, intelligibility of *ens*), see my ch. 14 above: "The Meaning of *Esse*,"
especially its sections of "Summary" and "Conclusions" corresponding to
notes 42 sqq.

[56] See 1, 4, 8, 56c–d. On Intelligence as a "causa primaria," see 1, 4, 7, 54b–
55c; 1, 4, 8, 55c–58d; 2, 1, 2, 62a–b.

As one can easily gather from Text H, #2, *intelligentia* can mean the intellectual substance which is a primary cause (see references given in first prgr. of
this note) and, second, the simple procession or "flow" from the First Cause
which in its first stage of development is the *esse primum creatum* with which
#2 deals. For another clear statement of both meanings see 2, 1, 21, 85d. In this
chapter I distinguish the two meanings by capitalizing the English word to
express the intellectual substance (thus: Intelligence) and by using lower case
to express the simple "flow" from the Cause (thus: intelligence).

[57] The italicized words from p. 83c, ". . . intelligentia, hoc est, forma a
lumine intellectus agentis in esse producta et in simplici illo lumine *per
intentionem accepta* . . . ," perhaps suggest Avicenna's influence. On "intentio"
in the Latin Avicenna, see E. Gilson, *History of Christian Philosophy*, pp. 190–91;
A.-M. Goichon, *Lexique*, p. 253, #469.

ligence, *vivere* the second, sensibility the third, and so forth.[58] [3] [*Esse* as] such an intelligence is composed of the finite and of the infinite because of the twofold relationships it has, for [a] when compared to that whence or by whom it is, *esse* is finite and is terminated by the light of the First Intellect; [b] when compared to that which is after it, *esse* is infinite: it is potentially in and of the infinite [multitude of existents][59] which go forth from it through its being divided into *ens per se* and *ens in alio*—a division which proceeds into an endless multiplicity because what is infinite can be divided only because it is potentially infinite (p. 83d).

[4] But one must realize that [its being infinite with reference to the infinite series of subsequent existents is also equivalent to] its being infinite of itself, since it is distant from the First of itself and this distance brings about the infinite multitude it entails (p. 83d).

[5] But it is finite not of itself but from the First Principle, for as being it stands in the light of the Intellect producing it: unless it were finite in this way, it could neither be the term of resolution nor the beginning of composition for all beings.

[6] In this fashion, then, *esse* is the intelligence which is not only finite but also infinite by reason of the perfections, capabilities and other powers which it contains and "inflows" upon everything subsequent to a degree unsurpassed by any other power—"unsurpassed" is its power because no other power is so rich and extensive in "inflowing"[60] ("Est ergo hoc modo intelligentia complexa ex finito et infinito in bonitatibus et virtutibus et in reliquis potentiis, quas habet influere super sequentia ultima. Dico autem ultima

---

[58] Here Albert quotes Aristotle, *On the Soul*, III, c. 6, 430a26 sqq.: "Intelligentia ergo indivisibilium est, in quibus non est verum et falsum. In quibus autem verum et falsum est jam compositio quaedam intellectuum est." For the more authentic import of the quotation (*re* error and truth in our intellection) in Aristotle's own thought, see the following commentaries: D. W. Hamlyn, *Aristotle's De Anima* (Oxford: Clarendon Press, 1968), pp. 142–44; P. Siwek, *Aristotelis Tractatus De Anima* (Roma: Desclée, 1965), pp. 335–36; D. Ross, *Aristotle: De Anima* (Oxford: Clarendon Press, 1961), pp. 299–300.

[59] Its being *in* and *of* infinitely many existents constitutes one aspect of its universality—see above, Text E, #2, and Text G, #16.

In 2, 1, 23, 87c–d, *esse* is contrasted with Intelligence, Soul and sensibles as "ens secundum se acceptum" with "ens in parte."

[60] A more literal translation of the Latin would be: ". . . 'inflows' upon subsequent things down to their very last, and this it does because no other power. . . ." On *esse* as intelligence, see 2, 1, 23, 88b: "esse quod est creatum primum secundum totum sui est intelligentia in lumine intellectus agentis [= God] constituta."

quia ultra illa nulla potentia adeo ampla et lata est ad influendum quemadmodum sua"). [7] Why? Because other intelligible forms such as *vivere, sentire* and *ratiocinari* are more expansive and more strongly universal when present in *esse* than in themselves. [8] Granted that in themselves they are intelligences,[61] but they are inferior to the intelligence which is *esse* and are beneath it in fullness, goodness and power to "inflow." This inferiority is due to their being less spread out [when existing formally] as themselves than when they are virtually present in the intelligence which is *esse* (p. 84a: "Quia non sunt ita dilatatae in seipsis sicut sunt quando virtute accipiuntur intelligentia quae est esse"): a restrictive difference diminishes a thing's power of expansion, as indicated above.[62]

[9] The perfections and powers which *esse* "inflows" into its subsequents are caused by its relationships and thus do not make it a composite, although they do render it necessarily concrete. [10] Therefore, the whole which is *esse primum creatum* is a simple intelligence or concept, which nevertheless entails a diversity of relationships and powers (p. 84a). And this causes the diversity of the intelligences coming after *esse:* [11] its power [allows it to be] · the subsequent[63] and, hence, the reduction of that power to act is at once [the development of] *esse* from a state of indetermination to one of determination and the production of the subsequent.[64] When this last's indetermination is likewise determined as a further act, a still additional effect is produced; when this third's indetermination is similarly determined still further, the fourth effect is produced, and so the process goes until one reaches infinity ("Quia enim potentia est sequens, in ipso, ideo deducta ad actum in quo confusio esse determinatur [et] efficitur sequens, cujus confusio si iterum determinetur ad actum ulteriorem, efficitur tertium. . . .").

---

[61] But not Intelligences—i.e., intellectual substances—see above, #2, and notes 27 and 56.

[62] On restrictive difference, see Text G, #15. On the fact that the lower is more perfect when present in the higher than on its own level, see 1, 4, 2, 45a; 2, 1, 1, 60a; 2, 2, 28, 121d; *ibid.*, 122b; 2, 2, 37, p. 130b.

[63] Perhaps the Latin ("potentia est subsequens") should be translated: "by its power *esse* is the subsequent," especially in view of the later parallel text— 2, 1, 23, 87d–88a: *esse* "secundum seipsum est potentia quodlibet sequentium" (ch. 23 in its entirety is a helpful summary of preceding pages).

[64] This product would not be *vivere* but the first intellectual substance since production goes on indefinitely.

[12] This process is akin to what happens in this lower world. Here form is divided by matter and, thereby, it gives reality (*esse*) to a multitude of individuals: its potency can be divided [into an infinity of individuals] but in such a way [a] that it is itself present in each one as a whole in quiddity, activity and power [b] and yet as it exists in one and in another it is distinct (p. 84b).

[13] But *esse* or first [created] intellect is joined to the next intellect without undergoing corruption, since "joining" for it consists in its going from indetermination to determination, whereas its being apart from a subsequent is not through any local or essential separation (as is the case in material things) but through its being indefinite and undetermined (p. 84b–c).[65]

[14] But for a lower form to be joined to matter is to corrupt it, since to generate a material composite is simultaneously to do away with the [independent reality of] what brought it about; on the other hand, a material form severed from an individual is entirely apart from it and is present in it in no manner.

After affirming that simple forms when taken in light of the intelligence causing them have a superior reality ("esse superius") and are eternal and universal, Albert restates his conclusion that] *esse primum creatum* is a complex of the finite and the infinite (p. 84c).

Comments. For our purposes this text is important because of the data it gives on the *potentia* which *esse* entails, as this survey shows. *Esse primum creatum* is describable as infinite with reference to the infinite effects subsequent to it: by its power it is present in them and is part of them (#3: "potentialiter enim in infinitis et de infinitis est"). Why so? Because *esse* is their primary intrinsic cause and, as the "principium primum ingrediens in esse rerum omnium" (see Text G, #16), its causality permeates theirs and brings to them form, name and meaning analogously the same as its own (see Text E, #2).

Again: what makes *esse* both finite and infinite is the "bonitates et virtutes et reliquae potentiae" it pours forth until they reach the very lowest existents. The causality of nothing else extends so far

---

[65] In the lines directly following, Albert continues to contrast *esse* and other intelligences (#13) with physical forms (#12): the former have *esse superius,* the latter *esse inferius;* the former are eternal and universal, the latter temporal and particular (*ibid.*, p.84c).

In #13, proceeding from indetermination (e.g., *esse*) to determination (e.g., *vivere* or, as the case may be, the first Intelligence) is from the more to the less perfect. See n. 76 below.

since no other power is comparable in richness and extension (Text H, #6). In fact, *vivere* and other intelligible forms are more expansive and more strongly universal when they exist in and as *esse* than formally in and as themselves (#7), where their "complementum et bonitas et virtus influendi" are inferior because more restricted (#8).

Furthermore: whence arise the "bonitates et virtutes" of *esse?* From its relationship (#9) to God's power, where it originally existed and which eventually made it actual (see Text G, #2).[66] These *potentiae* of *esse* are diverse and this diversity causes diverse intelligences to arise subsequently (p. 84a: "Et haec diversitas causa est diversitatis sequentium primum creatum"; Text H, #10), for by its *potentia* it *is* the subsequent (see note 63 above) and to reduce that *potentia* to act is to determine *esse* further and thereby to produce a subsequent existent, and this process continues on down the line (#11) until the *potentiae* of *esse primum creatum* have all been unfolded and developed. The last level of this explication is, of course, the visible world, where the *potentia* of a form is divided by matter into many individuals but in such a way that the quiddity, operation and *virtus* of the form is wholly present in each particular thing (#12).

The conclusion which reflection upon these statements on *potentia* and *esse* suggests seems obvious. *Potentia* here has an active sense: because *esse primum creatum* contains *vivere, sentire* and so on,[67] it *can cause* them. Its *potentiae* are those perfections *present within it as acts*, which come forth as an issuance of acts from act and not as an eduction of acts from potency.

The last key-text will further illumine how acts issue from act.

---

[66] This portion of Text G also speaks of the relationship *esse* has to nothingness. But this *habitudo* is irrelevant in our locating the source of the perfections and powers *esse* has, but not so in our understanding the source of recipiency and potentiality in an existent. On its *habitudo* to nothingness, also see Text F, #12–14; notes 54 and 79.

[67] See Text G, #12: *esse* "potestate continet omnia"; notes 28, 44 and 55 above.

Text I: *PU,* 2, 1, 20 (Cologne ed. XVII, ii, 84d–85c): "De solutione quaestionis: [Unde veniat actus determinans esse primum creatum ad intellectum secundum et tertium et sic deinceps]"

In this chapter immediately subsequent to Text H Albert explicitly deals with the extrinsic cause of how *esse* is further determined, although simultaneously he illuminates also the intrinsic factors in that determination.

[1] To ask whence comes the act determining *esse primum creatum* to be the second, third or other subsequent intellects is to seek the actually existing agent which causes *esse* to be living and which thereby must itself be living and possess sensible light and other such qualities. Why so? Because anything which goes from potency to some or other act does so under the efficacy of an agent having that act (p. 84d: "Quaeritur autem . . . unde veniat actus determinans ipsum [esse primum creatum] ad intellectum secundum et intellectum tertium et sic deinceps. Omne enim quod efficitur in actu de potentia veniens ad actum non potest effici in actu nisi per id quod est in actu").[68]

[2] Answering that question is not difficult if we recall points previously made. The First Principle is absolutely perfect: all perfections and excellences are in Him but are completely one and cause no multiplicity in Him at all, for privations, motions and compositions are in Him immaterially, nondeficiently, immutably and simply—the manner in which lower existents are present through their *rationes* in what is higher. [3] Hence, the Principle Who as uncreated *Esse* produces *esse* also makes *esse* be *vivere* inasmuch as He is life and also causes *vivere* to be *sentire* inasmuch as He is the Light of sensibles (p. 84d–85a).[69]

---

[68] Although Albert's Latin is awkward, the thought is clear. Despite the initial word, *quaeritur,* of the paragraph, he is expressing the difficulty (see #13: "in hoc stat solutio dubitationis propositae") that if *esse* becomes *vivere* and *sentire,* its extrinsic cause must not only *be* and be living but also be sentient.

[69] On God as cause of *esse, vivere* and *intelligere,* see 2, 3, 5, 143e sq.; 2, 3, 13, 150b; 2, 3, 14, 151b–c; 1, 2, 2, 27b–c (the entire chapter is informative); also n. 54 above.

[4] Accordingly, Aristotle says that act is from act:[70] the act of that which is caused is from the act of its cause. For example, the house made of stones and wood is from the house which is in its builder's soul (p. 85a: "actus est ab actu: actus ejus quod fit, ab actu ejus quod facit, sicut domus quae est in lapidibus et lignis, a domo quae est in anima architecti") and which is the *ratio* or *species* of the house existing in the light of his practical intellect: this *ratio* is related to the house of logs and stones as art is related to the matter of artifacts.

[5] Plato too posited ideal forms in the light of the universally Agent Intellect, forms which are imprinted upon material things as is a seal upon wax and which subsist and are incorruptible and more perfect in every way there [than they are in things] inasmuch as in that light they are present in an *esse* higher than their own. [6] These forms are, he says, "universals existing prior to things" and serve as source for the forms of all things, since the light of the First Agent Intellect goes forth to everything which is and carries them to all things (p. 85b). [7] But they are not affected when their "parts" [i.e., the things they cause] are corrupted because their source or principle is not those "parts" and nothing is destroyed so long as its principles remain intact. Consequently, they too remain intact in the principles which constitute them and which are the processions of lights and the light of the Agent Intellect, which is the universal cause of all: since they are the light of that First Agent Intellect, they are the light and *rationes* of all things, with the result that the forms of things are intelligible and that whatever is intellectually known is known through its form.

[8] But such forms can be taken in a threefold way, [a] the first of which [consists in our viewing them] in the principle itself whence they proceed; so considered, they are all one. [b] Second, [one may view them] in the light in which they proceed from the First; so considered, they differ in their *rationes*. [c] Third, [we may view them] in the light as it terminates at [and constitutes] the things themselves; so taken, they are actually diverse, for the light of the First Cause gives form to every secondary cause, which then acts [under the influence] of the form and power of that First Agent. [9] Thus a soul "forms" digestive heat, which thereby acts according to the form not of fire but of the living organism nourishing itself: not fire but the soul imprints upon that heat the forms which

---

[70] See *Meta.*, VII, c. 7, 1032b1 sqq.; also n. 23 (first prgr.) above and n. 75 below.

make it living and animated. It is in this fashion that the action of the First stretches from first to last (p. 85b–c).

[10] Since Plato looked on the ideal forms within the light in which they proceed from above (see #8b above) and, thus, as differing from one another in their *rationes* as the rays proceeding from a single point in the sun differ from one another, he also stated that they cannot be compared with material things. [a] Each of these latter is, in its reality, one solely and stands in itself lethargic and unproductive, [b] whereas the reality of a form viewed in the procession of light [from the First Cause] is, because of its power, a principle of infinite subsequents by continuously sending forth forms to produce the reality of things and yet stands in itself immutable and eternal ("esse autem formae in processu luminis acceptum virtute principium est infinitorum, continue emittens formas ad esse rerum, et est stans in seipso fixum et aeternum").

[11] [Because they are thus the source of an infinitude of existents] these forms have for Plato a relationship even to the "smallest perfections"—namely, the forms enmeshed in matter, which are perfections only as byproducts and images of genuine perfections. [12] The latter are, Plato concludes, separate substances, which differ generically and specifically among themselves insofar as they are viewed now indeterminately, now determinately within the "flowing" of light from the First Agent (p. 85c).

[13] [Let this suffice as a solution to the difficulty proposed of how the actually existing agent which causes *esse* can also cause it to be *vivere, sentire* and so on.]

Comments. This key passage consists of four parts, in the first of which Albert states the problem (#1), in the second he sketches a broad outline of his solution (#2–#3), in the last two he fills in that sketch by calling upon Aristotle (#4) and, at greater length, Plato (#5–#12).

The problem he is here concerned with is at the bull's-eye of our topic. As *esse primum creatum* moves from an initial and relatively indeterminate stage, it becomes *vivere*, then *sentire* and so on; but *vivere, sentire*, etc., are acts with reference to *esse* and one must search for their source; but that source must be an agent who possesses those acts if he is to cause them in *esse*, since whatever comes from potency to act achieves act only by the efficacy of that which is in act; accordingly, one must discover an agent who is a living and sensitive existent (#1).[71]

---

[71] See n. 68 above; 2, 2, 2, 95b.

The way in which the problem is stated even in paraphrase discloses at least two pitfalls Albert must avoid: that *esse* is in potency to *vivere* and to *sentire* and, second, that the agent causing *esse* to be *sentire* must itself exist with senses and therefore be physical. Hence, in answering he must emphasize that *esse* is act and restate that God (and, hence, *esse primum creatum* too as His first effect) does contain (and, thus, causes) sensible and other physical perfections but in a nonphysical fashion.

Albert presents his reply with broad strokes and, even so, rather indistinctly (#2–#3).

> All perfections are in God—e.g., *esse, vivere, sentire,* [*intelligere*], as well as those which privation, motion and composition entail;[72]

> all those perfections are there in their *rationes* (since such is the way in which the lower is present in the higher), and yet each is completely one with God and with the others, each is there according to the divine manner of being rather than its own (thus privations are there nondeficiently, motions

---

[72] I insert *intelligere* because it is higher than *sentire* and is its source. *Intelligere* is listed with *esse* and *vivere* in the following: 1, 2, 2, 27b–c (see n. 69 above); 2, 2, 28, 121c–d; *ibid.*, ch. 29, 122d; 2, 3, 5, 143a (see n. 28 above). In 2, 1, 17, 81b (= Text F, #6), he inserts *sentire* as third member in the list between *vivere* and *rationale* or *ratiocinari*; in 1, 4, 4, 47a, the list is *ens, vivum, sensus, ratio, intellectus*; 2, 1, 4, 64d: *esse, vivere, sentire, intelligere*; 2, 1, 19, 84a: *esse, vivere, sentire, ratiocinari*. See 2, 3, 5, 143c, for an explanation of how *esse, vivere* and *intelligere* "complectuntur omnia quae sunt: vivere enim per nutrimentum et incrementum vegetabilibus est esse, vivere autem per sensum sentientibus est esse, et vivere per intellectum intelligentibus est esse."

On the triad of *esse, vivere* and *intelligere* in other authors see P. Hadot, "Être, vie, pensée chez Plotin et avant Plotin," *Les sources de Plotin* (Genève: Fondation Hardt, 1960), pp. 105–57; A. H. Armstrong, "Eternity, Life and Movement in Plotinus' Account of *Nous*," *Le Néoplatonisme* (Paris: Centre National de la Recherche Scientifique, 1971), pp. 67–76; R. T. Wallis, *Neoplatonism* (New York: Charles Scribner's Sons, 1972), pp. 66–67, 124–25, 130, 132–33; Stephen Gersh, *KINÉSIS AKINETOS: Spiritual Motion in the Philosophy of Proclus* (Leiden: E. J. Brill, 1973), pp. 20–22 and 78–80; *idem, From Iamblichus to Eriugena: An Investigation of the Prehistory and Evolution of the Pseudo-Dionysian Tradition* (Leiden: E. J. Brill, 1978), pp. 47, 87–88, 143 sqq.; E. R. Dodds, *Proclus: Elements of Theology*, p. 252–54; L. J. Rosan, *The Philosophy of Proclus* (New York: Cosmos, 1949), pp. 97–98; Pierre Hadot, *Porphyre et Victorinus* (Paris: Études Augustiniennes, 1968), ch. 4: "La triade intelligible: être, vie et pensée," pp. 213–46; *ibid.*, pp. 260–71; J. Rist, "Mysticism and Transcendence in Later Neoplatonism," *Hermes* 92 (1964), 218.

immutably, compositions simply, matter immaterially, sensibility nonsensibly);

moreover, all those perfections are there as acts, since an agent must be in act the acts which he causes and God is the agent causing those acts in subsequent existents;

consequently, because God is uncreated *Esse,* He causes the act which is *esse primum creatum;* because He is Life, He causes *esse* to be the act which is *vivere;* because He is Light, He causes *vivere* to be the act which is [*intelligere* and its offshoot], *sentire.*

If our re-presentation of Albert's solution is accurate, he has cleverly sidestepped the two traps set in #1 insofar as he conceives of *esse, vivere* and other intelligences as acts and, second, of the divine nature as containing the perfections even of His effects in the visible world but in an invisible and spiritual way.[73]

But he still must account for *how* God's causality works. This account he finds partially in Aristotle's dictum that act comes from act because an effect's act arises from the act of its cause (#4). Take the case of an architect's designing and building a house, which results from its blueprint in his mind directing his activity of building. The finished product *is* the perfection or act of the blueprint of "this house" as concretized and realized in materials. Its act has come from its agent's act existing in the light of his intellect (p. 85a). Its act "flows" from him, its analogous cause (1, 4, 2, 44b; see above, Text E, "Comments," paragraphs 2 and 3).[74]

To apply this reflection to *esse:* the acts which are *esse primum creatum, vivere* and so on are caused by the acts of *esse, vivere,* etc., existing as paradeigmatic *rationes* in the light of the divine intellect.

---

[73] On this point Albert differs from such a Neoplatonist as Plotinus, according to whom the One causes all precisely because He transcends all and contains nothing: "How then do all things come from the One, which is simple and has in It no diverse variety or any sort of doubleness? It is because there is nothing in It that all things come from It. ... The One, perfect because It seeks nothing, has nothing and needs nothing, overflows, as it were, and Its superabundance makes something other than Itself" (*Enneads,* V, 2 [11], 1, lines 3–5 and 7–9). See L. Sweeney, *Divine Infinity in Greek and Medieval Thought* (New York/Bern: Peter Lang Publishing, Inc., 1992), ch. 11: "Basic Principles in Plotinus' Philosophy."

[74] Albert often utilizes an artist and his art in his commentary, as this partial list of texts indicates: 1, 2, 1, 25d–26a; *ibid.,* 26c; 1, 2, 5, 31a; 1, 4, 1, 42b sq.; 1, 4, 2, 44b; 1, 4, 8, 56b; 2, 1, 1, 60b; 2, 1, 20, 85b; 2, 2, 1, 94b; 2, 2, 2, 95b; 2, 2, 3, 96d–97a; 2, 2, 9, 101c; 2, 2, 28, 122b; 2, 2, 29, 123c; 2, 2, 37, 130b; 2, 3, 5, 143d.

An actual *esse* is the act of its exemplar but as concretized and realized in an existent. It is an act "flowing" from the Act Who is God, the analogous cause of all things.[75]

But Albert still must explain more precisely how He causes effects in the sensible world. For help he turns to Plato, whom he finds locating forms in three places: in God, where their *rationes* are all united; in the light in which they proceed or "flow" from their divine source and where they differ *ratione;* in the light as it terminates and constitutes existents, where they differ actually (#8). But how do these three levels illumine how an immaterial and incorruptible divine cause can even produce material and corruptible things? What is common to all three is the fact that each entails forms. Those in material things (#8c) are separated from one another and are each lethargic and unproductive (#10a); those in the flow of light from the First Cause (#8b) are endlessly productive and yet are immutable and eternal (#10b); those in God (#8a) are there in a divine manner: simply, transcendently, eminently, immaterially (#10b). Yet transcendent, eminent, simple, immaterial as they are in the divine light which is the First Agent Intellect (#7, #8) and in the light emanating from Him, those forms are the means by which God causes all subsequent existents. His light goes forth and carries the forms to whatever is—constituting existents in their reality (#6), rendering them cognoscible (#7), and also giving them causal power (#8) as the channels through which God's action reaches from on high down to the bottom of reality in the physical universe (p. 85b: "lumen enim causae primae omnem causam secundariam format ut agat ad formam virtutis agentis primi. . . . Et hoc modo actio primi pertingit a primo usque ad ultimum"— (#9); also see note 54 above).

And in that light issuing from the divine Agent Intellect those forms are (to revert to Aristotelian terminology) acts which come from Act. Since they are also present in *esse primum creatum*, God's first effect, as the acts and *potentiae activae* of further effects (see above, Text H, "Comments"), they also emerge as acts from the act which is *esse* as this becomes increasingly determined.[76]

---

[75] Other texts on "actus ex actu" are 2, 2, 23, 117a; 2, 5, 15, 181b. Also see 2, 2, 2, 95c, which speaks of "fluxus formae super formam."

[76] This increasing determination is a transition from the more to the less perfect, as can be inferred from texts cited above in n. 62: if the lower is more perfect when present in what is higher than on its own level and if going from presence on the higher to its own level is to move from indetermination to

Conclusions

The key text just commented upon suffices to bring our entire chapter to a close, for it is an unambiguous answer to the question with which we began of how *esse primum creatum* could be fitted into Aristotle's theory of act and potency.[77] Despite earlier statements which were ambiguous (Text F, #13) or elliptical (Text E, #7–#9), Albert here clearly responds that *esse primum creatum* is *act.*[78] In fact, its contents (*vivere, intelligere, sentire*) are acts too. These, then, are related to *esse* as acts to act and not as acts to potency. Hence, their coming forth from *esse* is not an eduction of acts from potency but an unfolding of acts from act through the three-fold extrinsic causality (efficiency, exemplarity, finality) of the Act Who is *esse increatum* and *intellectus universaliter agens.* Together with *esse primum creatum*, they are simultaneously the *potentiae activae* within the procession or "outflow" of light by which He causes all creatures to be and to be what they are in the cascade of reality reaching from God down to matter (see notes 27, 33, 54 above).

Albert's identifying *esse primum creatum* and its contents with lights or forms, which "flow" into, and thereby constitute, created existents, discloses him to be a Platonist (= Neoplatonist). But his calling them acts also reveals an Aristotelian strain in his position.

His adherence to Aristotle's theory of act and potency is, though, less than wholehearted when we realize that potency for the German Dominican often seems to point not so much to an intrinsic state of potentiality in an existent as to some sort of relationship to an outside cause. This realization can be gained from many texts. Passive potency is equivalent to receptivity, which however arises

---

determination, that transition to greater determination reduces it from a more to a less perfect state. See n. 28 above.

[77] See the section above of our chapter corresponding to n. 11.

[78] On *esse* as act see also 1, 1, 8,17b: "esse . . . est actus ejus quod est"; 1, 1, 10, 19c: "non autem est causans nisi actum illum qui est esse"; 1, 2, 2, 27c: "esse, vivere et intelligere actus continui sunt"; 1, 4, 7, 54c: "forma . . . actus et esse eorum est . . . [intelligentia] caelo dat actum et esse"; 2, 1, 8,69d: "esse intelligentiae et animae nobilis . . . totum existens in actu, nihil sui habens in potentia"; 2, 1, 17, 81b and 81c (= Text F, #6, #10): "esse actus est entium . . . [esse est] processus . . . a causa prima . . . ut actus in esse constituens omne quod est. . . . Esse processum illum nominat in actum entis"; 2, 2, 11, 103d: "intellectuale enim esse est . . . intelligentiae substantialis ejus actus"; 2, 4, 12, 165b: "potentia non in esse alicujus est"; 2, 5, 12, 178c: "esse enim est simplex actus et purus." Also see n. 33 above *re* God as Act.

from an existent's distance from the First Cause (2, 1, 14, 78b).[79] In
an earlier passage: what is second is in potency to what is first,
what is third is in potency to what is second, and so on down the
line. Why? Because the second is distant from the first, the third
from the second, and so forth (1, 4, 5, 49b–c).

A bit later: the difference in grade between the existents (e.g.,
Intelligence, Soul, the heavens, things on earth) which constitutes
the natural order of the universe arises in this manner. Whatever is
from another has a threefold comparison: to the higher existent
which is its cause, to itself with respect to what it is and to the
potency it involves inasmuch as it came from nothingness—before
it existed, it was in potency because whatever is from another is
caused by that other and was in a state of potency before it came to
be (1, 4, 8, 55d–56a: "In hoc quod ab alio est . . . habet comparationem
. . . ad hoc quod in potentia est secundum hoc quod ex nihilo est:
antequam esset, in potentia erat quia omne quod ab alio est, factum
est et in potentia erat antequam fieret"). Nearly forty-five pages
later: an intelligence of lower rank is in potency both to the First
Cause and to an intelligence of higher rank—to the First Cause
because it is His creature and to the higher intelligence because it is
formed and perfected by the light flowing thence (2, 2, 5, 98c).

Subsequently: the *id quod est* of an intelligence entails potency
and privation: potency because it is in potency to the cause producing it; privation inasmuch as it has arisen from nothingness (2, 2,

---

[79] According to 2, 1, 21, 86b, Dionysius is the source of this emphasis on
distance. See 2, 3, 7, 145b, for a comparison of the distance which dissimilarity
causes in immaterial existents with that which diversity of place causes in
bodies; 2, 4, 2, 157a–b: the relationships and active powers which a being
receives are proportioned to its distance from the First Cause.

Although 1, 4, 2, 44c, states that the possibility which enables something to
receive and contain an "inflowing" perfection arises from the thing itself
("possibilitas rei est ex seipsa"), still 2, 4, 12, 165b, portrays God as the
producer of a being's receptive potency: "Causa enim prima non tantum est
producens res sed gradus et ordinem rerum praedeterminat . . . ; et ideo sub
actu producto producit potentiam susceptivam, quae quia sub umbra actus
producitur, necesse est quod imperfecta sit."

On active powers, see 2, 1, 15, 79a–b: distance of Soul from God accounts
also for the efficacy of its intellectual and divine *potentiae activae*. In *ibid.*, ch.
14, p. 78c, Albert explains that *potentia activa* is linked with distance not *qua*
distance but *qua* involving a process in and through which the power of
higher causes travels to the effect and is operative there. Also see n. 44 above
and the prgrs. corresponding to notes 66 and 67.

14, 107b: "'Id autem quod est'" permixtum est potentiae et privationi secundum illud 'quod est.' Potentiae dico quia ipsum est in potentia ad causam constituentem: sic enim non est necesse esse. Permixtum est etiam privationi in quantum ex nihilo est"). Its *esse,* although it is the pure goodness flowing from the First Cause and is without impurity insofar as it is from and in that Cause, is at a distance from that Cause, and thus an intelligence is neither caused nor produced except in a state of potency and privation because of its distance from the First.

A final passage: the First Cause and a creature differ in their manner of acting because they differ in their manner of being. In God *esse* and *id quod est* are identical and, hence, He acts through that which He is (2, 4, 1, 156a). But every creature is in potency and, according to that which each is, is nothing and from nothing; therefore, it engages in activity not according to what it is but in accordance with its *esse.* Not so with God, Whose *id quod est* is not from nothing or in potency: according to what He is, He is self-subsistent and has absolutely no cause in comparison to which He might be in potency (p. 156b: "secundum id quod est, non ex nihilo est nec in potentia est. Secundum enim id quod est, in seipso est, nullam penitus habens causam ad quam comparatum sit in potentia").

In the light of those texts *potentia* in at least one of its meanings (see note 79 above) indicates primarily the openness of an existent to extrinsic causes rather than the intrinsic constituent which receives and limits an intrinsic act and which is more characteristic of Aristotelianism as traditionally understood.[80] And if one adds this

---

[80] Aquinas' approach to potency/act in his early treatises seems marked by a similar sort of "extrinsicism"—see ch. 19 below: "Existence/Essence in Thomas Aquinas' Early Writings," section "Act and Potency," especially prgr. b: "One realizes that *esse*/essence are act/potency not by what they are in themselves but by the relationship the existent has to God."

Incidentally, some contemporary Thomists interpret Aquinas' texts on *esse* in such a way that in an existent it solely is real and essence is reduced to "pure possibility" or "pure potency of being" or, even, a negation almost (e.g., if *esse* is the line drawn on a blackboard, essence would be the point terminating it). Thus, *esse* contains and is the source of all perfections whatsoever in an existent. See Maurice Holloway, "Towards the Fullness of Being," *Proceedings of Twenty-Fourth Convention of Jesuit Philosophical Association* (Woodstock, Md.: Woodstock College Press, 1962), p. 22: "The act of existing then is the source of the reality of the individuality [of a being] . . . [and] of its total intelligibility"; *ibid.,* p. 26: "Diverse acts of existing are responsible for diverse essences"; *ibid.,* p. 28: "Our act of existing . . . pre-contains the fullness of being"; *ibid.,*

non-Aristotelian conception of *potentia* to Albert's identifying *esse* and its contents (as already noted) with lights and forms "inflowing" into existents from the divine *intellectus universaliter agens* and *plenitudo formarum* (see note 22 above), he is much more Platonic

---

p. 34: "Our act of existing is all of these at once [namely, material and immaterial, physical and intentional, substantial and accidental] on the level of human existence, just as God is all existence infinitely"; *ibid.*, p. 37: our act of existence is "the total reality of what we are and . . . the very intrinsic content of all our perfections." Also W. Norris Clarke, "What Cannot Be Said in St. Thomas' Essence-Existence Doctrine," *New Scholasticism* 38 (1974), 36: "All perfection resides in the act of existence itself. Existence is now seen . . . as the whole inner core of all the perfection the being contains" (see *ibid.*, n. 9, for references to G. Phelan and W. E. Carlo); W. J. Hoye, *Actualitas Omnium Actuum: Man's Beatific Vision as Apprehended by Thomas Aquinas* (Meisenheim am Glan: Anton Hain, 1975), p. 78: "If *esse* is taken as intensive act, . . . [it contains] all acts and perfections whatsoever"; *ibid.*, p. 79, where he quotes with approval W. E. Carlo's statement that "as all creatures flow from God, so all other principles flow from *esse* in the creative act"; *ibid.*, p. 80: "There is nothing in an existent which is not existence"; Fran O'Rourke, *Pseudo-Dionysius and the Metaphysics of Aquinas* (Leiden: E. J. Brill, 1992), especially pp. 117–87 (on O'Rourke's indebtedness to C. Fabro, see p. 155).

However unfavorably one reacts to those authors' statements as an interpretation of Aquinas, they would be right on target if directed at Albert's conception of *esse primum creatum* as the act which contains all subsequent perfections (e.g., *vivere, intelligere, sentire*) precisely as acts and his understanding of passive potency (= essence) as merely a being's distance from its Cause (see n. 79 above).

On Albert in relationship to Aquinas see the studies listed in the following: M. H. Laurent and Y. Congar, "Essai de Bibliographie Albertinienne," *Revue Thomiste* 36 (1931), 460, nos. 548–55; F. J. Catania, "Bibliography of St. Albert the Great," *Modern Schoolman* 37 (1959), 24–27; M. Schooyans, "Bibliographie Philosophique de Saint Albert le Grand—1931–1960," *Revista da Universidade Católica de São Paulo* 21 (1961), 83–84. The following have appeared since 1960: Guy Allard, "Réactions de trois penseurs du xiiie siècle vis-à-vis de l'alchimie (T. d'Aquin, Albert le Grand, Roger Bacon)," *Cahiers d'Études Médiévales* 2 (1974), 97–106; D. González, "El legado intelectual de San Alberto Magno," *Studium* 5 (1965), 127–35; P. Montané, "Algunos precedentes Albertinos del tomismo," *Espíritu* 24 (1975), 5–26; A. Pelzer, "Le cours inédit d'Albert le Grand sur la *Morale à Nicomaque* recueilli et rédigé par St. Thomas d'Aquin," *Études d'Histoire Littéraire sur la Scolastique Médiévale* (Paris: Nauwelaerts, 1964), 272–325; F. Ruello, *La notion de verité chez Saint Albert le Grand et Saint Thomas d'Aquin* (Louvain: Nauwelaerts, 1969).

than Aristotelian.[81] This conclusion stands firm, despite the fact that on almost every possible occasion he speaks of *esse primum creatum* as act.

---

[81] On Albert with reference to his predecessors (e.g., Plato, Aristotle, Greek Neoplatonists, Arabians, etc.) see the studies listed in the following: Laurent and Congar, "Essai de Bibliographie," pp. 457 sqq., nos. 514–41; Catania, "Bibliography," pp. 24–27 (in those pages studies referring to Albert's predecessors are not separately listed from those referring to Aquinas); Schooyans, "Bibliographie," pp. 66–69. Since 1960 the following studies have been published: Bernard Burke, *Das neunte Buch (Theta) des Lateinischen Grossen Metaphysik-Kommentars von Averroes* (Bern: Francke Verlag, 1969); see especially section 3: "Einfluss des Averroes auf Albert den Grossen und Thomas von Aquinas," pp. 119–52; F. J. Catania, "Albert the Great, Boethius and Divine Infinity," *Recherches de Théologie Ancienne et Médiévale* 28 (1961), 97–114; A. Cortabarria, "Literatura algazeliana de los escritos de San Alberto Magno," *Est. Filos.* 11 (1962), 255–76; J. Dunbabin, "The Two Commentaries of Albertus Magnus on the *Nichomachean Ethics*," *Recherches de Théologie Ancienne et Médiévale* 30 (1963), 232–50; H. Gätje, "Der *Liber de Sensu et Sensato* von al-Farabi bei Albertus Magnus," *Oriens Christianus* 48 (1964), 107–16; B. Geyer, "Albertus Magnus und die Entwicklung der scholastischen Metaphysik," in P. Wilpert (ed.), *Die Metaphysik im Mittelalter* "Miscellaenea Mediaevalia," Band II (Berlin: W. de Gruyter, 1963), pp. 3–13; M. Grignaschi, "Les traductions latines des ouvrages de la logique arabe et l'Alfarabi dans l'oeuvre d'Albert le Grand," *Archives d'Histoire Doctrinale et Littéraire du Moyen Age* 39 (1972), 41–107; M. Mignucci, "Albert the Great's Approach to Aristotelian Modal Syllogistic," *Arts Libéraux et Philosophie au Moyen Age* [Acts of Fourth International Congress of Medieval Philosophy] (Paris: J. Vrin, 1969), pp. 901–11; F. Ruggiero, "Intorno all'influsso di Averroè su S. Alberto Magno," *Laurentianum* 4 (1963), 27–58; J. B. Schneyer, "Alberts des Grossen Augsburger Prediktzyklus über den Hl. Augustinus," *Recherches de Théologie Ancienne et Médiévale* 36 (1969), 100–147; F. Van Steenberghen, "Albert le Grand avait-il une philosophie personelle?" *Bulletin de l'Académie Royale de Belgique (Lettres)* 52 (1966), 15–30.

16

Are Plotinus and Albertus Magnus Neoplatonists?

Plotinus (204/5–270) has been receiving considerable attention in recent decades. Paul Henry and Hans-Rudolf Schwyzer published three volumes of their critical edition of his Greek text in 1951, 1959 and 1973.[1] In 1955 Richard Harder initiated the publication of the Greek text of the *Enneads* in chronological order, as well as of a German translation and commentary, in a series of volumes which Rudolf Beutler and Willy Theiler completed by 1971.[2] Harvard University Press published the entire *Enneads* in the "Loeb Classical Library" between 1966 and 1988.[3] Finally, the

---

[1] *Plotini Opera* (Paris: Desclée de Brouwer, 1951–1973), Tomes 1–3. Tome 2 contains *Plotiniana Arabica*, which is the English translation by G. Lewis of Plotinus' text found in Arabic. Henry and Schwyzer's edition also is appearing in the Oxford Classical Texts (Oxford: Clarendon Press, 1964 sqq.), which furnishes textual revisions as suggested by scholars in reviews and critical studies.

[2] *Plotins Schriften* (Hamburg: Felix Meiner, 1956–1971), Bands 1–6, "Philosophische Bibliothek."

[3] In these Loeb volumes A. Hilary Armstrong furnishes a revised Henry-Schwyzer Greek text, as well as a serviceable English translation and introduction to individual treatises. Help in translating Plotinus' difficult Greek can be obtained also from V. Cilento, *Plotino Enneadi* (Bari: Laterza, 1947–1949), 3 vols.; E. Bréhier, *Plotin Ennéades* (Paris: Les Belles Lettres, 1924–1938; frequently reprinted); Marsilius Ficinus' literal Latin translation in F. Creuzer and G. H. Moser, *Plotini Opera Omnia* (Oxford: Typographicum Academicum, 1835). Stephen MacKenna's nineteenth-century translation is, even in its fourth and revised edition (1969), often misleading.

Lexicon Plotinianum of J. N. Sleeman and Gilbert Pollet appeared in 1980.[4]

Besides those publications abundant secondary literature has dealt with Plotinus during the same years, as one can judge by consulting any volume of the *L'Année Philologique* (Paris: Société d'Édition "Les Belles Lettres") from 1951 onwards. For example, volume 22, which covers the year 1951, lists nineteen books and articles; volume 25 lists twenty-three publications for 1954; volume 30 seventeen for 1959; volume 34 seventeen for 1963; volume 39 sixteen for 1968; volume 45 thirty-eight for 1974;[5] volume 50 twenty-seven for 1979; volume 52 thirty-nine for 1981; volume 54 twenty-six for 1983; volume 56 thirty-three for 1985; volume 58 thirty-nine for 1987; volume 60 thirty-five for 1989.[6]

What is noteworthy in that literature is not only its abundance but also the frequency with which scholars point out the differences between Plotinus and subsequent Greek Neoplatonists and express doubts as to whether his is the primary influence upon them. For instance, in *Porphyry's Place in the Neoplatonic Tradition: A*

---

[4] Leiden: E. J. Brill; Leuven: University Press, 1980. This first dictionary of the *Enneads* was worked on by Sleeman (University of London) from 1946 to 1957 and by Pollet (University of Louvain) from 1959 onwards. The latter revised the first draft of the dictionary in the light of Henry-Schwyzer's critical edition (see n. 1 above) and utilized the almost complete but unpublished "Index Verborum" compiled by Ludwig Früchtel (d. 1963).

[5] The increase in the number of studies in volume 45 arises from the publication in 1974 of the acts of the Convegno Internazionale held at Rome, October 1970, and published under the title *Plotino e il Neoplatonismo in Oriente e in Occidente* (Roma: Accademia Nazionale dei Lincei, 1974); it contains twenty-nine studies on Plotinus, on which those by P. Hadot, W. Theiler, H. J. Blumenthal, H.-R. Schwyzer, J. Daniélou, J. Rist and J. Pépin are most relevant for the purpose of this chapter. A similar increase in volume 42 issued from the publication in 1971 of the acts of the Colloques Internationaux du Centre National de la Recherche Scientifique: Sciences Humaines, held at Royaumont, June 1969, and published as *Le Néoplatonisme* (Paris: Éditions du Centre National de la Recherche Scientifique, 1971), in which at least ten papers are devoted to Plotinus.

[6] A source of significant articles on Plotinus (and, more generally, on Neoplatonism) is the volumes published by the International Society for Neoplatonic Studies: R. Baine Harris, ed., *The Significance of Neoplatonism* (1976); *idem, Neoplatonism and Indian Thought* (1981); Dominic J. O'Meara, ed., *Neoplatonism and Christian Thought* (1981); R. Baine Harris, *The Structure of Being: A Neoplatonic Approach* (1981); R. J. Wallis and Jay Bregman, eds., *Neoplatonism and Gnosticism* (1992).

Study of Post-Plotinian Neoplatonism (The Hague: Martinus Nijhoff, 1974), Andrew Smith finds Plotinus and Porphyry differing on points in their conceptions of soul—e.g., its relationship to Intellect and to body, its descent from and ascent to higher levels, its fate after death, its transmigration.[7] As A. Hilary Armstrong observes, Porphyry virtually abandoned "the real distinction between Intellect and Soul, on which Plotinus sometimes insists very strongly." The latter always seems "to have considered it important, from some points of view at least, to assert a certain transcendence of Intellect over Soul. . . . It seems unlikely that he would have approved of Porphyry's tendency to monism here."[8] According to A. C. Lloyd, Porphyry emphasized monism here "because he was prepared to pay the price, a certain belief in the reality of the individual person, which Plotinus . . . was not. . . . [Together with Plotinus Porphyry denied] that the soul 'in itself,' or essentially, was divided into parts. But Porphyry went quite beyond Plotinus as well as Plato in preventing any real distinction between the two [Intellect and Soul] by claiming that the soul could not be affected by anything. Quite consistently, he recognized only one kind of soul, the rational, which was possessed by men and brutes alike" (*ibid.*, p. 288). In general, Porphyry seems "often to present a simpler doctrine than Plotinus; partly it is . . . a matter of going back to second-century writers" (*ibid.*, p. 292).[9]

In fact, Porphyry separates himself from his master also in epistemology and logic to the extent that R. Baine Harris believes Porphyry "set the stage for the formation of another kind of Neoplatonism, namely, a type that focuses upon the logic and categories of Aristotle. A case could be made . . . that there really

---

[7] See Smith, chs. 1–5, the last of which ("An Evaluation of Eschatology in Porphyry and Plotinus," pp. 69–80) is especially informative. For a general summary see pp. 143–47.

[8] *Cambridge History of Later Greek and Medieval Philosophy* (Cambridge University Press, 1967), pp. 266–67. Also see *ibid.*, pp. 267–68: "The doctrine of Intellect was both the weak point and the growing point of Plotinian Neoplatonism; and this seems to be confirmed by what happened in the next few centuries." His account of Intellect "was not acceptable as it stood to any of his successors," although they "still show the influence of this majestic centre-piece of his speculation."

[9] See *ibid.*, p. 276: "For the theory of the active and passive intellect in Aristotle's psychology and the theory of logic they [the Neoplatonists after Plotinus] went, as it were, behind Plotinus and were drawing much more on second-century material."

have been two forms of Neoplatonism operative in the history of Western philosophy, namely, the Neoplatonism . . . of Plotinus and the Neoplatonism of Porphyry and, by and large, the latter has been far more influential than the former" (*Structure of Being*, pp. vii–viii). How, then, are we to characterize the two Neoplatonisms? Plotinus' brand entails a mysticism plus "a way of philosophizing [and of dialectics] that points to a form of knowing that is beyond dialectics" (*ibid.*, p. vii) and that rejects "Aristotle's categories and a portion of his logic" (*ibid.*, p. viii). Porphyry's sort sets aside "Plotinus' categories and logic as inadequate" and relies "heavily on both Aristotle's categories and logic in his own thought, especially in dealing with the physical or sensible world. If the case can be made that there is sufficient difference in the logic of Plato and Plotinus to justify the term 'Neoplatonism,' it can also be said . . . that there is sufficient difference in the logic of Plotinus and Porphyry to serve as the basis for defining and delineating the various historical types of Neoplatonism" (*ibid.*, p. viii).[10]

But what of Plotinus and (say) Iamblichus? Recently John Whittaker inquired whether "the influences upon Iamblicus which do not derive from Plotinus—the influence of the Aristotelian tradition, of Middle Platonism, of the milieu of the *Chaldean Oracles* and the Hermetic writings—" might not be so strong that the career of Iamblichus is "explicable simply as a phenomenon of the third and fourth centuries without Plotinus as a necessary presupposition?" Hence, Plotinus' "historical importance may have been exaggerated. . . . If the role of Plotinus was not as great as has been supposed, then perhaps we should be satisfied to regard Neoplatonism simply as a mode of philosophizing characteristic of the third and following centuries of our era."[11]

---

[10] According to Mary Clark, "Marius Victorinus Afer, Porphyry, and the History of Philosophy," in *Significance of Neoplatonism*, pp. 265–73, Porphyry had great influence upon Victorinus, as well as upon Chalcidius, Boethius and Macrobius, and "it was Porphyry rather than Plotinus who was the point of contact between Latin philosophers and Neoplatonism" (p. 268). His metaphysics of being rather than of unity (as was Plotinus') issued into a triad of Being, Life and Thought, which Victorinus interpreted as the Christian trinity of consubstantial persons. Had Victorinus used the Plotinian triad of the One, Intellect and Soul, his trinitarian doctrine would have been a subordinationism (*ibid.*, pp. 265–66 and 270–71).

[11] *De Jamblique à Proclus*, Entretiens sur l'Antiquité Classique 21 (Genève: Fondation Hardt, 1975), pp. 65–66. On Iamblichus see n. 75 below.

In a paper occasioned (at least in part) by Whittaker's challenging the traditional view of Plotinus as the founder of Neoplatonism, H. J. Blumenthal states that Whittaker's interpretation is perhaps helpful ("it stresses that later Neoplatonists were more liable than Plotinus to accept non-philosophical explanations and procedures") but it is also misleading ("it can easily tend to exaggerate the importance of such elements [the irrational material absorbed from the *Hermetica* and the *Chaldean Oracles*] in later Neoplatonism," which was not so thoroughly corrupted by irrationalism as once was commonly thought).[12] Yet Blumental himself isolates four areas of disagreement between Plotinus and other Neoplatonists: the relationship of soul and intellect (part of our mind remains permanently active in the Intellect *versus* our soul descends as a whole into the physical world; *ibid.*, pp. 214–16), the interpretation of Aristotle's categories (they pertain only to the sensible world *versus* they apply also to intelligible being; pp. 216–19), the nature of time (time is attached to Soul and eternity to Intellect *versus* Time and Eternity are hypostases in the intelligible hierarchy; p. 219), and the nature of evil (evil is matter or the negativity of matter incidentally causes evil in conjunction with soul *versus* evil is not matter, which is directly related to the One, but is a kind of teleological inadequacy; p. 220). Blumenthal's final conclusion: in some areas later Neoplatonists introduced Plotinus' views to corroborate their own but in others they differ substantially with him (p. 220).

The preceding sampling of secondary literature makes clear that subsequent Neoplatonists do diverge from Plotinus in their conceptions of soul and intellect, in their eschatologies and in their epistemology and logic; and, second, that such divergence is a legitimate basis for wondering how influential Plotinus actually was in those areas. But what the literature does not document is disagreement between Plotinus and them in basic metaphysics. This perhaps will prove to be the common ground that makes them all be authentic "Neoplatonists" and compensates for their differences in other and less crucial areas.

In what follows, then, I shall try to isolate what appear to be the main features of Plotinian metaphysics so as to eventually evaluate

---

[12] "Plotinus in Later Platonism," in *Neoplatonism and Early Christian Thought: Essays in Honour of A. H. Armstrong* (London: Variorum Publications, 1981), p. 214. Blumenthal's main aim is to discuss what Plotinus' Neoplatonic successors thought of him (p. 212).

better the fundamental metaphysics of Porphyry, Iamblicus, Proclus and others, who may thereby reveal themselves to be at one with Plotinus in this area and thus to be Plotinian Neoplatonists. But postponing such evaluation to another time and place, I shall in the second portion of this chapter turn instead to Albert the Great (ca. 1200–1280), who is sometimes considered to be a medieval exponent of Neoplatonism. The question guiding my research will be, Is his metaphysics sufficiently like Plotinus' that he deserves to be called "Neoplatonist"?

Plotinus' Metaphysics

My aim in reading Plotinus' *Enneads* is, then, to understand his metaphysics[13] by searching out his replies to these questions: what does "to be real" mean? what sort of causality does God exercise in producing existents which are, to some degree, other and lower than Himself? upon what fundamental principles does his metaphysical position rest? During that search I shall not only attend to the chronological ordering of the *Enneads*[14] but I shall try to discern *what Plotinus himself had in mind* when he was writing this or that

---

[13] Metaphysics is contrasted with ethics, philosophy of man, cosmology and religion, all of which are to be found in the *Enneads* but will receive little or no direct attention. We shall attend rather to Plotinus' position on the real precisely as real and, thus, on unity wherever found. Plotinian metaphysics is then the knowledge of the real as real and not (as Aristotle expresses it) of beings as being, since reality is not being but unity. Were Aristotle's formula taken literally, metaphysics would be restricted to reflection on νοῦς, Soul and the physical world, since the One transcends being.

[14] Fortunately, Porphyry lists Plotinus' treatises as he received them and, thus, provides us with their chronological order (see Porphyry, "The Life of Plotinus," in A. H. Armstrong, trans., *Plotinus*, Loeb Classical Library [Cambridge, Mass.: Harvard University Press, 1966], pp. 12–25). Unfortunately, he did not respect that chronological order but edited them according to topics: see R. T. Wallis, *Neoplatonism* (New York: Charles Scribner's Sons, 1972), pp. 44–47.

I shall indicate the chronological place of each treatise cited below by a number in parenthesis—for example, "VI, 9 (9), 1, 1–8" means "Sixth *Ennead*, Treatise 9, ninth treatise chronologically, ch. 1, lines 1 to 8." The Greek text used is that of P. Henry and H.-R. Schwyzer, *Plotini Opera*, vols. 1–3 (Paris: Desclée de Brouwer, 1951, 1959 and 1973). Unless otherwise indicated, translations are my own.

treatise—that is, my intent will be to study Plotinus on his own terms, within his own era and *Denkenswelt*.

Reality Is Unity

What, then, does he mean by "to be real"? In VI, 9 (9), 1, his answer is inductive because it issues from reflections upon concrete cases. But it is difficult to understand because of the ambiguity of the Greek word εἶναι and its derivatives. In English we can express different dimensions of Plotinus' thought in three distinct ways.

(a) "The One exists" (= the One actually is = He is not merely a figment of the mind but does actually exist);

(b) "The One is real" (= the One is of value, significance, worth— in fact, He is supremely valuable and solely real);

(c) "The Intellect is but the One is not" (= the Intellect is one-many and, thus, is being [see VI, 2 (43), 21, 45–48]; the One is not because He transcends multiplicity and, thus, transcends being).

All those three distinct meanings Plotinus must express by the single verb εἶναι so that τὸ ἓν ἔστιν can signify (depending upon the context) either (a) that God exists or (b) that God is real or, when the negative οὐκ is added, (c) that God is not being. Such ambiguity is one reason why reading Plotinus is difficult and problematical.

But forewarned and thereby forearmed, let us now consider VI, 9 (9), 1, 1–8, where Plotinus sets down the concrete cases which furnish the evidence that reality is unity. All beings (he begins) are beings

> by the One, both those which are primarily so [= the νοῦς and the Soul] and those which are in some way classed among beings [= sensible things]. For what could *be* if it were not one? If beings are deprived of what we call unity, they *are not*. For instance, an army or a choir or a flock no longer *is* if it is not one. In fact, neither a house nor ship *is* if it has not unity, for a house is one and a ship is one and if it loses its unity, a house is no longer a house or a ship a ship.[15]

---

[15] Lines 1–8: Πάντα τὰ ὄντα τῷ ἑνί ἐστιν ὄντα, ὅσα τε πρώτως ἐστὶν ὄντα, καὶ ὅσα ὁπωσοῦν λέγεται ἐν τοῖς οὖσιν εἶναι. Τί γὰρ ἂν καὶ εἴη, εἰ μὴ ἓν εἴη; Ἐπείπερ ἀφαιρεθέντα τοῦ ἓν ὃ λέγεται οὐκ ἔστιν ἐκεῖνα. Οὔτε γὰρ στρατὸς ἔστιν, εἰ μὴ ἓν ἔσται, οὔτε χορὸς οὔτε ἀγέλη μὴ ἓν ὄντα. Ἀλλ' οὐδὲ οἰκία ἢ ναῦς τὸ ἓν οὐκ ἔχοντα, ἐπείπερ ἡ οἰκία ἓν καὶ ἡ ναῦς, ὃ εἰ ἀποβάλοι ἂν ἡ οἰκία ἔτι οἰκία οὔτε ἡ ναῦς.

Comment. What is meant by saying that if something no longer is one it no longer *is*? Possibly and probably, "is" has all three levels of meaning: "exists," "is a being" and "is real," the last of which nonetheless seemingly predominates. After a tornado hits an area (to restrict ourselves to one of Plotinus' examples), what exists is not a house but a pile of rubble; the house no longer is the being that it was; it no longer is real because it is valueless and worthless by losing its unity through the violent storm. This third meaning is especially relevant for our purposes because it stresses that to be real is to be one and a fall from unity is a fall also from reality. In fact, the unity which constitutes the reality of houses, ships, armies and the like, as well as of Intellect and of Soul, points to the One, which makes all of them be one (each in its own way) and thereby be real: "all beings are beings [= are real] by the One" (line 1).

A similar alignment of the One with the onenesses of other existents is also found in a later text. In III, 8 (30), 10, 14 sqq., Plotinus expresses amazement that the many should come from the One. Yet such is the fact: the multiplicity of life does come from what is not multiplicity, since the origin [= the One] is not divided up into the All [= the νοῦς and, eventually, the Soul] lest the All too be destroyed and, since the origin must remain by itself and be different from all else, lest the All not even come into being (lines 14–19). Accordingly, we must (Plotinus advises)

go back everywhere to the one [in each existent]: in each there is some one to which you reduce it and this in every case to the one before it, which [however] is not simply one, until we come to the simply one, which cannot be reduced back to something else. [For example,] if we take the one of the plant—this is its source remaining within it[16]—and the one of the animal and the one of the soul and the one of the physical All, we are taking in each case that which is most powerful and valuable in it. But if we take the one of the beings which truly are—that one which is their origin and spring and power—shall we lose faith and think of it as nothing? [By no means;

[16] This source would be the individual plant's share of what Plotinus had earlier in the same chapter spoken of as "the life of a huge plant, which goes through the whole of it while its origin remains and is not dispersed over the whole, since it is, as it were, firmly settled in the root. So this origin gives to the plant its whole life in its multiplicity, but remains itself not multiple but the origin of the multiple life" (lines 10–14; Armstrong's translation).

the One is truly real even though] it is certainly none of the things of which it is the origin: it is such, though nothing can be predicated of it—neither being nor entity nor life—as to be above all such existents.[17]

Comments. As was the case in VI, 9, 1, 1 sqq. (see above), here Plotinus also proceeds inductively: he moves from the oneness we perceive in plants, animals, our souls and the physical universe to truly real beings (Soul and Intellect) and then to the One, Who is fully real because of His sheer unity and transcendence of being. Second, the One gives them oneness and, thereby, also reality because their unity is what makes each of them worthy of esteem. And the oneness which the One furnishes also is that which is most powerful in them (see lines 25–26: τὸ δυνατώτατον καὶ τὸ τίμιον) and which constitutes their power to contemplate and thereby to make themselves and subsequent existents.[18] In fact, the power in them *is* the One—He is power[19]—just as the oneness in them *is* the One (see lines 26–27): each of them *is* the One-on-a-lower-level, each is a λόγος of the One.[20] This basic identity of each lower existent with

---

[17] Lines 20–31: Καὶ ἐφ' ἑκάστου μὲν τι ἕν, εἰς ὃ ἀνάξεις, καὶ τόδε τὸ πᾶν εἰς ἕν τὸ πρὸ αὐτοῦ, οὐκ ἁπλῶς ἕν, ἕως τις ἐπὶ τὸ ἁπλῶς ἓν ἔλθῃ· τοῦτο δὲ οὐκέτι ἐπ' ἄλλο. Ἀλλ' εἰ μὲν τὸ τοῦ φυτοῦ ἕν - τοῦτο δὲ καὶ ἡ ἀρχὴ ἡ μένουσα - καὶ τὸ ζῴου ἓν καὶ τὸ ψυχῆς ἓν καὶ τὸ τοῦ παντὸς ἓν λαμβάνοι, λαμβάνει ἑκασταχοῦ τὸ δυνατώτατον καὶ τὸ τίμιον· εἰ δὲ τὸ τῶν κατ' ἀλήθειαν ὄντων ἕν, τὴν ἀρχὴν καὶ πηγὴν καὶ δύναμιν, λαμβάνοι, ἀπιστήσομεν καὶ τὸ μηδὲν ὑπονοήσομεν; Ἤ ἐστι μὲν τὸ μηδὲν τούτων ὧν ἐστιν ἀρχή, τοιοῦτο μέντοι, οἶον, μηδενὸς αὐτοῦ κατηγορεῖσθαι δυναμένου, μὴ ὄντος, μὴ οὐσίας, μὴ ζωῆς, τὸ ὑπὲρ πάντα αὐτῶν εἶναι.

[18] See chs. 3 sqq., where Plotinus sets forth his position on contemplation. Θεωρία is found on all levels of reality except the highest (the One transcends contemplation) and the single word expresses both (say) the Intellect's operative state of contemplating and its content (i.e., what is contemplated, what is caused by the contemplating). This content itself is in turn an operative state producing its own content, until one comes to the λόγος of plants, which are the content of Nature's operative state of contemplation but do not themselves contemplate. One may with profit consult John N. Deck, *Nature, Contemplation and the One: A Study in the Philosophy of Plotinus* (Toronto University Press, 1967).

[19] After concluding the previous chapter by observing that the One is other than all things and is before all of them, Plotinus initiates chapter 10 with the statement that the One is "the power of all" (δύναμις τῶν πάντων): not only *can* the One produce all of them but He is in all as their δύναμις.

[20] On λόγος meaning "a higher existent as on a lower level," see Donald L. Gelpi, "*Logos* as a Cosmological Principle in Plotinus" (Master's thesis, St.

the One balances Plotinus' other paradoxical statements that the
One is other than all else (see ch. 9, lines 39–54; ch. 10, line 10): yes,
God is other than all His products inasmuch as God Himself is not
totally identical with God-on-a-lower-level, but this otherness does
not eliminate the fact that whatever reality (oneness, δύναμις) is
found on any subsequent level *is* God and, consistently, Plotinus'
position is a monism. After all, to be real is to be one.[21]

The One as Cause

Now we can take up the question of what kind of causality the
One exercises in producing lower existents. We already find an
answer in III, 8, 10, 3 sqq.: His products flow out from Him as do
rivers from a spring which is itself without origin, which gives
itself wholly to them and yet is not depleted by them but remains
itself at rest and unchanged.[22] A similar but more detailed reply is

---

Louis University, 1958); *idem*, "The Plotinian *Logos* Doctrine," *The Modern
Schoolman* 37 (1960), 301–15.

[21] Do Plotinus' texts themselves underwrite this conclusion? Yes, provided
one realizes that although they disclose existents to be both distinct from and
yet one with one another, the unity there disclosed overshadows their distinctness. (For a listing and discussion of texts see L. Sweeney, *Divine Infinity
in Greek and Medieval Thought* [hereafter: *Divine Infinity*] [New York/Bern:
Peter Lang Publishing, Inc., 1992], ch. 11, pp. 245–47.) The most apt comparison of this relationship between the One, Intellect, Soul and all other existents
is that of a man and his integral parts. "Every man is both other than his
hands or feet and the like and yet is physically joined to them all, each of
which is really different from any other part and is less than the man in his
entirety. In such a living being one finds a sort of real distinction but immersed in genuine unity, which overshadows it. The parts are really but, let
us say, inadequately and only virtually distinct from one another and from
the whole, but they are vitalized by a single soul and thus coalesce into an
essential unity or *unum per se*. The distinction is, so to speak, accidental, the
unity is essential. . . . Something like that sort of inadequate real distinction
seems to exist" between the One and all other existents without eliminating
their radical unity and the basic monism which marks his metaphysics (*ibid.*,
p. 246). Also see A. H. Armstrong, "The Apprehension of Divinity in the Self
and Cosmos in Plotinus," in *The Significance of Neoplatonism*, ed. Harris, pp. 187–
98; Plato Mamo, "Is Plotinian Mysticism Monistic?" in *ibid.*, pp. 199–215 (*vs.*
Zaehner, Arnou, Rist); for references to studies by Trouillard, Carbonara,
Bréhier and de Gandillac, see L. Sweeney, *Divine Infinity*, p. 247, n. 13.

[22] A fuller translation/paraphrase of the initial lines of the Greek is as
follows: "That which is above life is the cause of life for the act which is the
life of the Intellect is not first but itself flows out, so to speak, as if from a
spring. . . ." The Greek for lines 2–10: Τὸ δὲ ὑπὲρ τὴν ζωὴν αἴτιον ζωῆς· οὐ γὰρ

offered by an earlier treatise. In V, 2 (11), 1, 3, Plotinus discusses how all existents come from the One, which is simple and has no diversity or doubleness. It is precisely

> because there is nothing in It that all things come from It: in order that being may exist, the One is not being but That Which generates being, which is (so to speak) its first-born. Perfect because It seeks nothing, has nothing and needs nothing, the One (as it were) overflows and Its superabundance makes something other than Itself. What has thus come about turns back to the One and is filled and thus becomes Its contemplator and so is Intellect.[23]

> The Intellect, because it thus resembles the One, produces in the same way—that is, by pouring forth a multiple power which is a product resembling its maker: just as That Which was before it did, Intellect poured forth a likeness of itself. This act of originating from entity [or Intellect] is Soul, which comes about while Intellect remains at rest, for Intellect too came about while That Which is prior to it remains unchanged.[24]

> But Soul does not remain unchanged when it produces: it is moved and thereby brings forth an image. It looks There whence it came and is filled and thereupon goes forth to

---

ἡ τῆς ζωῆς ἐνέργεια τὰ πάντα οὖσα πρώτη, ἀλλ᾽ ὥσπερ προχυθεῖσα αὐτὴ οἷον ἐκ πηγῆς. Νόησον γὰρ πηγὴν ἀρχὴν ἄλλην οὐκ ἔχουσαν, δοῦσαν δὲ ποταμοῖς πᾶσιν αὐτήν, οὐκ ἀναλωθεῖσαν τοῖς ποταμοῖς, ἀλλὰ μένουσαν αὐτὴν ἡσύχως, τοὺς δὲ ἐξ αὐτῆς προεληλυθότας πρὶν ἄλλον ἄλλη ῥεῖν ὁμοῦ συνόντας ἔτι, ἤδη δὲ οἷον ἑκάστους εἰδότας οἷ ἀφήσουσιν αὐτῶν τὰ ῥεύματα. In lines 10–14 Plotinus compares the source of reality to the life of a huge plant—see note 16 above. In III, 8, 9, 26 he likens the One to a voice filling empty space.

[23] Lines 5–11: Ἢ ὅτι οὐδὲν ἐν αὐτῷ, διὰ τοῦτο ἐξ αὐτοῦ πάντα, καὶ ἵνα τὸ ὂν ᾖ διὰ τοῦτο αὐτὸς οὐκ ὄν, γεννητὴς δὲ αὐτοῦ· καὶ πρώτη οἷον γέννησις αὕτη· ὂν γὰρ τέλειον τῷ μηδὲν ζητεῖν μηδὲ ἔχειν μηδὲ δεῖσθαι οἷον ὑπερερρύη καὶ τὸ ὑπερπλῆρες αὐτοῦ πεποίηκεν ἄλλο· τὸ δὲ γενόμενον εἰς αὐτὸ ἐπεστράφη καὶ ἐπληρώθη καὶ ἐγένετο πρὸς αὐτὸ βλέπον καὶ νοῦς οὗτος. Lines 11–13 are not reproduced here since they relate why νοῦς is also τὸ ὂν and hence, are not crucial for my present purposes.

[24] Lines 13–18: Οὗτος οὖν ὢν οἷον ἐκεῖνος τὰ ὅμοια ποιεῖ δύναμιν προχέας πολλήν - εἶδος δὲ καὶ τοῦτο αὐτοῦ - ὥσπερ αὖ τὸ αὐτοῦ πρότερον προέχεε· καὶ αὕτη ἐκ τῆς οὐσίας ἐνέργεια ψυχῆς τοῦτο μένοντος ἐκείνου γενομένη· καὶ γὰρ ὁ νοῦς μένοντος τοῦ πρὸ αὐτοῦ ἐγένετο.

another opposed movement and thus generates its own image
[= the sentient and vegetal levels of the physical universe].[25]

Comments. The similarity this earlier passage has with III, 8, 10,
3–10, consists in the fact that each portrays the causality exercised
by the One as literally "emanative." In the later text life "flows out"
from the One as if from a spring (III, 8, 10, 4: προχυθεῖσα ... οἷον ἐκ
πηγῆς)—a spring which gives itself wholly to the rivers going forth
from it (line 7: ἐξ αὐτῆς προεληλυθότας), which in turn tarry for a
while all together before flowing forth (line 8: ῥεῖν), although each
knows even then the direction its streams will flow (line 9: τὰ
ῥεύματα).[26] Also in V, 2, 1, 8, the One, as it were, overflows (οἷον
ὑπερερρύη) and thereby It has made (line 9: πεποίηκεν) something
that is, to a degree, other than itself[27]—that δύναμις which Plotinus
will elsewhere call "intelligible matter" (see II, 4 [12], chs. 1, 3–5)
and which becomes the Intellect/Being by turning and contemplating the One and thereby filling and actuating itself. In turn Intellect
produces by similarly pouring forth (lines 14 and 16: προχέας ...
προέχεε) intelligible matter and δύναμις, which, however, is now
prone to plurality and motion and which becomes Soul by contemplating whence it came and thereby filling and actuating itself.[28]

---

[25] Lines 18–21: Ἡ δὲ οὐ μένουσα ποιεῖ, ἀλλὰ κινηθεῖσα ἐγέννα εἴδωλον. Ἐκεῖ
μὲν οὖν βλέπουσα, ὅθεν ἐγένετο, πληροῦται, προελθοῦσα δὲ εἰς κίνησιν ἄλλην
καὶ ἐναντίαν γεννᾷ εἴδωλον αὐτῆς αἴσθησιν καὶ φύσιν τὴν ἐν τοῖς φυτοῖς. The
reference to φύσις in line 21 may foreshadow its appearance in III, 8, chs. 3
and 4, as the Soul in its lowest descent toward matter and as the source of all
λόγοι in plants.
[26] For the Greek text of III, 8, 10, 3–10 see note 22 above.
[27] Other only "to a degree" because it is God-on-a-lower-level: see above,
paragraph corresponding to notes 19–21.
[28] The second moment of causality on the levels of both Intellect and Soul is
exercised by intelligible matter, which fills and actuates itself by contemplating its source (the One and νοῦς, respectively). The difference between V, 2, 1
and III, 8, 10 is that the latter develops and elucidates the twofold notion of
contemplation as operative state and content (see n. 18 above).
On "emanation," see A. H. Armstrong, " 'Emanation' " in Plotinus," *Mind*
46 (1937), 61–66: Plotinus almost invariably uses the metaphors of development and growth from a seed or of the radiation of light from a luminous
source—the latter he derives from the Stoic author Posidonius; John H. Fielder,
"*Chorismos* and Emanation in the Philosophy of Plotinus," in *Significance of
Neoplatonism*, ed. Harris, pp. 101–20; *idem*, "Concepts of Matter and Emanation in the Philosophy of Plotinus" (Ph.D. diss., The University of Texas at
Austin, 1970, pp. 138–207.

Accordingly, both III, 8, 10 and VI, 2, 1 depict the One as causing through emanation, which has in Plotinus' eyes several advantages over efficient causality. The One in causing remains perfect: His effects do not deplete or change Him. Emanative causality occurs spontaneously, automatically, necessarily: products arise thereby because God is totally perfect and not because He freely chooses to produce them. Such causality safeguards Plotinus' monism: what overflows from the One—the intelligible otherness, matter, operative power[29]—is the One-on-a-lower-level. That is, the effects of emanation are not adequately distinct from their cause[30] and thereby differ from what results from efficient causality. For example, Plato's Craftsman in the *Timaeus*[31] is really other than both the Forms serving as exemplary and final causes of the visible world and their participants.[32] The father of whom Aristotle speaks in *Physics* II, 3, 194b29–32, is really distinct from the child begotten or the sculptor from the statue carved.[33] Such adequately real oth-

---

[29] Δύναμις here does not resemble Aristotle's prime matter but operative power (see *Metaphysics*, Delta, ch. 12, 1019a15–21). But Plotinus' δύναμις is not merely a faculty of an individual soul (as with Aristotle) but is the massive overflow from the higher source which helps constitute all lower existents by its actuating and filling itself through contemplation (see above, notes 18 and 28 [first prgr.]) and by "receiving" such actuations.

[30] See n. 21 above.

[31] That the *Timaeus* is to be taken literally, see Gregory Vlastos, "Disorderly Motion in the *Timaeus*," in *Studies in Plato's Metaphysics*, ed. R. E. Allen (New York: Humanities Press, 1965), pp. 379–99; *idem*, "Creation in the *Timaeus*: Is It a Fiction?" in *ibid.*, pp. 401–19 (each article gives many references to scholars holding the dialogue to be mythical).

[32] On the Forms as models and goals, see *Timaeus*, 29D–31A. For a commentary see L. Sweeney, S.J., *Infinity in Plato's "Philebus": A Bibliographical and Philosophical Study* (forthcoming), pp. 89–140 plus notes 175–280.

The fact that the Craftsman makes things be images of the Forms indicates that things participate in Forms. Accordingly, participation in Plato requires that both exemplary causes (Forms) and efficient causes (Craftsman) be operative and that participants be really distinct from both causes—see L. Sweeney, S.J., *Divine Infinity in Greek and Medieval Thought*, ch. 4: "Participation in Plato's Dialogues: *Phaedo, Parmenides, Sophist* and *Timaeus*," especially pp. 60–64. These requirements contrast participation in Plato with participation in Plotinus, for whom the One is emanative and not efficient cause and lower existents are not really distinct in an adequate fashion from Him (see n. 21 above). Accordingly, "participation" is to be taken much more literally in the *Enneads* than in Plato (or, for that matter, Aquinas): each lower existent is a "part" of the One since it *is* the One-on-a-lower-level because of Plotinus' monism.

[33] Also see *Meta.*, Delta, ch. 2, 1013a29 sqq.

erness between effect and agent does not result from the causality Plotinus ascribes to his God: Intellect, as well as Soul, *is* the One deploying on a lower level. The One is not an agent or craftsman. He transcends reasoning, judging, desiring, executing a task.[34] Because perfect, He overflows spontaneously and necessarily and this overflow, which is not really distinct from Him, becomes through contemplation the existents of the noetic, psychic and physical universe.[35]

Fundamental Principles

Let us now take up the third and final question concerning Plotinus: what basic principles are operative in his metaphysics? The first issues from reflection upon the primacy which he gives to unity (as we have already noted) and which can be expressed as follows: "Whatever is real is one" because to be real is to be one.[36] Any item is real because of its unity, with the result that the more unified something is, the more real it is. Consequently, that which is totally simple is also the Primal Reality—namely, the One, which is the absolutely first and highest hypostasis.[37] On the other hand, an existent's lapse into multiplicity is equated with a lapse into unreality—an equation which is equivalent to saying that the emanation of Intellect, Soul and Nature from the One is a movement of what is increasingly less perfect from what is more perfect. To go

---

[34] Such functions Plato attributes to the Craftsman in the *Timaeus*, as is clear even from his initial explanation (29D–30A) of why the Craftsman ordered this world as he did. But Plotinus, when describing the causality of the One, replaces such verbs with "flowing," "overflowing," "pouring forth," as seen above.

One should note, though, that on occasion he ascribes to God a mysterious sort of self-awareness. For listing and exegesis of texts, see J. M. Rist, *Plotinus: The Road to Reality* (Cambridge University Press, 1967), pp. 38–52; W. T. Wallis, *Neoplatonism*, pp. 58–59.

[35] That Plotinus sets a low value on πρᾶξις and, hence, on efficient causality can be gathered from these texts in III, 8: ch. 1, 14 sq.; ch. 4, 30 sqq.; ch. 6, 1 sqq.; ch. 7, 1 sqq. For a good commentary see John N. Deck, *Nature, Contemplation and the One*, ch. 9: "Making and 'Efficient Causality,'" pp. 93–109.

[36] On this and subsequent principles see my *Divine Infinity in Greek and Medieval Thought*, ch. 11, pp. 249–52 (where texts are provided).

[37] See John P. Anton, "Some Logical Aspects of the Concept of *Hypostasis* in Plotinus," *Review of Metaphysics* 31 (1978), 258–71 (with references to studies by Armstrong, Rist, Deck, Wallis); Heinrich Dörrie, "Hypostasis: Wort- und Bedeutungsgeschichte," *Nachrichten der Akademie der Wissenschaften in Göttingen* (1955), pp. 35–92 (on Plotinus: pp. 68–74).

forth from a cause is to proceed from the perfect to the imperfect.[38]
Once this is realized we can formulate a second fundamental principle: "The 'movement' from the One to subsequent existents is a
'movement' from a more perfect to a less perfect state."

This causal situation is, paradoxically enough, linked with a
third metaphysical principle. Even though an effect is always less
perfect than its cause, still whatever is genuinely real must by that
very fact cause subsequent realities, which turn back to their source
because of dependency upon it and desire for it. This principle,
which issues into Plotinus' doctrines of procession and of reversion
(πρόοδος and ἐπιστροφή), can be formulated thus: "Whatever is one,
also is good." Obviously, it is an immediate sequel of his principle
concerning unity, for that which is one is not only real but also is
perfect and powerful. Now whatever is perfect and powerful automatically overflows and thereby produces another (but lesser) reality, which depends upon and tends back to its cause in love. Such
is the twofold status which "good" signifies when predicated of
an item—a reality and unity insofar as it is both the source of
subsequents and the term of their love and tendency.[39] And the more

---

[38] By this process lower existents become increasingly determined and,
thereby, less real. For example, VI, 9 (9), 11, 36 sqq.: "When [the human soul]
goes down, it comes to evil and so to nonbeing." VI, 5 (23), 12, 16 sqq.: [In
ascending back to God] you have come to the All and not stayed in a part of it,
and have not said even about yourself, 'I am so much.' By rejecting the 'so
much' you have become all—yet you were all before. But because something
else other than the All added itself to you, you became less by the addition,
for the addition did not come from real being (you cannot add anything to
that) but from that which is not. When you have become a particular person
by the addition of non-being, you are not all till you reject the non-being. You
will increase yourself then by rejecting the rest, and by that rejection the All is
with you." Determination so conceived helps preserve Plotinus' monism because what alone is real in any existent is the oneness it has from and with the
One and not the apparent additions and individuation it has put on.

If the movement from the One downward is one of decreasing perfection
and is an essential mark of Neoplatonism, Spinoza's position (where the
divine substance progressively manifests itself first through attributes and
then through modes, both general and particular, and thus moves from the
more to the less perfect) is closer to Plotinus' than is Hegel's, whose Absolute
Spirit moves from the less to the more perfect: from Categories (Being, Essence, Notion) through Nature to Spirit (Art, Religion, Philosophy).

[39] Plotinus frequently makes the following two points both in one and the
same text and yet also separately—what is perfect gives rise to products
inevitably, spontaneously, automatically by reason of its very perfection and

unified something is, the more perfect and powerful it is, and the more aptly it can be designated as good. The result is that what is totally simple is also the Supreme Good—as the ultimate source of absolutely all else and the universal goal of all appetition, the One is also the Good. Whatever is one, then, is also good—good *to* others by producing them automatically and necessarily, good *for* others as the object of their seeking.

What Is Neoplatonism?

To conclude the first part of this chapter and before considering Albert the Great, let us try to discern what the essence of Neoplatonism is when viewed in its fundamental metaphysics. From the data Plotinus has furnished, one may say that Neoplatonism is a monism (this mark seems absolutely crucial) and is the sort of monism which has at least these three essential traits.

(1) It posits as the primal reality an Existent
  (a) Who is the One-Good because to be real is to be one—this equation means that reality is neither becoming (no matter how that word is taken—e.g., any sort of motion or change or activity or operation, whether temporal or eternal)[40] nor being (no matter how that word is taken—e.g., one-many, immutability, eternity, intelligibility, meaningfulness, actuation, etc.);
  (b) Who consequently transcends all becoming, being, knowledge, description;
  (c) Who nonetheless actually exists.
(2) It grants that there are existents (e.g., Intellect and intellects, Soul and souls, the physical world) other than that primal reality but in such a way that whatever reality they have *is* the One

---

power and, second, each product turns back to its source because of desire and love. The following list includes examples of both kinds of texts: V, 4, 1, 20 sqq.; V, 1, 6, 15 sqq.; V, 1, 7, 5 sqq.; V, 2, 1, 1 sqq.; II, 9, 8, 10 sqq.; V, 3, 11, 1 sqq. Also see V, 5, 12, 1 sqq.: Desire for beauty is always conscious, but everything desires and aspires to the Good by a natural tendency and innate desire. Hence, the Good is prior to beauty. Also, VI, 7, 20, 16 sqq. and *ibid.*, 21, 1 sqq.: the Good is prior to Intelligence because everything seeks the former and the latter is desirable only because of the former.

[40] Consequently, the One transcends the operations also of intellection and contemplation; see n. 18 above. But see n. 34 on the "self-awareness" occasionally ascribed to the One. On the One's totally transcending all attributes applicable to His effects, see VI, 9, 3, 39 sqq. and 49 sqq.

and, thus, they are at bottom identical with the One and are not adequately distinct from Him.[41]

(3) It finds two sorts of causality operative, the first of which is the spontaneous and inevitable going forth (πρόοδος) of effects from the One and is a movement from the perfect to the imperfect;[42] the second is the return (ἐπιστροφή) of effects to the One and, hence, is a movement of the imperfect to the perfect, which begins with contemplation but terminates with a soul's transcending contemplation and then becoming fully identified with the One.[43]

Albert the Great

Ten centuries after Plotinus there lived a Dominican friar who taught theology and philosophy at Cologne and Paris, who was a capable administrator and a prolific author, who described himself as a "Peripatetic" but who currently is rather often reckoned as a Neoplatonist: Albert the Great (ca. 1200–1280).[44] In order to test that

---

[41] Because of this radical identity in reality of the One with all else, "real" cannot, it seems, be analogously predicated of Him and His effects because analogy rests on similarity (not identity) and genuine diversity. In fact, in any monism would not predication be univocal, not analogous?

[42] Accordingly, the flow of effects from the One is not creation, which requires causality to be free and efficient and an adequately real distinction to hold between effects and cause. See John N. Deck, *Nature, Contemplation and the One*, pp. 96–97. On the three factors which creation, strictly interpreted, entails, see L. Sweeney, S.J., *Divine Infinity in Greek and Medieval Thought*, ch. 13: "Doctrine of Creation in the *Liber de Causis*," pp. 305–6.

[43] On this ultimate identification see Plato Mamo, "Is Plotinian Mysticism Monistic?" pp. 199–215; A. H. Armstrong, "The Apprehension of Divinity," especially pp. 192 sqq.; *idem*, "Form, Individual and Person in Plotinus," *Dionysius* 1 (1977), 58–59; John Rist, *Plotinus: The Road to Reality*, ch. 16: "Mysticism," pp. 213–30.

[44] On Albert as Peripatetic see R. Kaiser, "Zur Frage der eigenen Anschauung Alberts d. Gr. in seinen philosophischen Kommentaren," *Freiburger Zeitschrift für Philosophie und Theologie* 9 (1962), 53 sqq.; L. A. Kennedy, "The Nature of the Human Intellect According to St. Albert the Great," *The Modern Schoolman* 37 (1960), 121–23; James A. Weisheipl, "Albertus Magnus and the Oxford Platonists," *Proceedings of the American Catholic Philosophical Association* 32 (1958), 124–39 (includes data on Albert's life and writings); *idem*, "Life and Works of St. Albert the Great," in *Albertus Magnus and the Sciences: Commemorative Essays* (Toronto: Pontifical Institute of Mediaeval Studies, 1980), pp. 13–51. On Albert

current interpretation let us turn to his treatise *Liber de Causis et Processu Universitatis,* the first fourth of which is an investigation of the perfections attributable to the First Cause (knowledge, will, freedom, omnipotence, causality) and the last three-fourths is a commentary on the *Liber de Causis.*[45] The latter he thinks should be read as the final book of Aristotle's *Metaphysics* and was composed by a certain David the Jew, who culled statements from Aristotle, Avicenna, Algazel and Alfarabi and then added his own comments (*PU,* II, 1, 1, 433D).[46] Albert's own treatise, probably written no earlier than 1265 and no later than 1272,[47] discloses (in my judgment) his own mature posi-

as Neoplatonist see Vernon J. Bourke, *Aquinas' Search for Wisdom* (Milwaukee: Bruce, 1965), pp. 50–51; *idem, Augustine's Quest of Wisdom* (Milwaukee: Bruce, 1944), p. 300; Étienne Gilson, *History of Christian Philosophy in the Middle Ages* (New York: Random House, 1955), p. 431 (*re* the human soul Albert retained elements of "philosophical Augustianism"); F. Copleston, *History of Philosophy* (London: Burns Oates and Washbourne, 1950), II: 297; Francis J. Catania, "'Knowable' and 'Namable' in Albert the Great's Commentary on the *Divine Names,*" in *Albert the Great: Commemorative Essays,* ed. F. J. Kovach and R. W. Shahan (Norman: University of Oklahoma Press, 1980), p. 115.

On Albert's life and writings see F. J. Kovach, "Introduction," *Albert the Great:* pp. vii–xix; T. F. O'Meara, "Albert the Great: A Bibliographical Guide," *Thomist* 44 (1980), 596–97 (esp. references to M. Schooyans and J. Schöphfer). *Re* Aristotle see ch. 14, nn. 14 and 23, above.

[45] This influential but anonymous treatise, which was also called *Liber de expositione bonitatis purae,* was translated into Latin from Arabic by Gerard of Cremona (d. 1187). On its authorship see Richard C. Taylor, "St. Thomas and the *Liber de Causis* on the Hylomorphic Composition of Separate Substances," *Mediaeval Studies* 41 (1979), 506, n. 3 (with references to other secondary literature); *idem,* "The *Liber de Causis:* A Study of Medieval Neoplatonism" (Ph.D. diss., University of Toronto, 1981), pp. 54–70 (the anonymous author was probably a Muslim or Christian philosophical thinker living in the Middle East between A.D. 833 and 922); Denis J. Brand, *The Book of Causes* (Niagara, N.Y.: Niagara University Press, 1981), pp. 1–7.

However uncertain the identity of the author may be, this is clear: he joins data from Proclus' *Elements of Theology* and Plotinus' *Enneads* with a doctrine of creation. See also Leo Sweeney, S.J., *Divine Infinity in Greek and Medieval Thought,* ch. 13, pp. 289–307, and ch. 14, pp. 309–18; A. Badawi, *La transmission de la philosophie grecque au monde arabe* (Paris: J. Vrin, 1968), pp. 60–72.

[46] For my use of the Cologne edition of Albert's *Liber de Causis et Processu Universitatis* [hereafter: *PU*] and for my method of referring to it, see my ch. 15 above, "*Esse Primum Creatum* in Albert the Great's *Liber de Causis et Processu Universitatis,*" n. 14.

[47] On the dating of Albert's *PU* see R. Kaiser, "Versuch einer Datierung der Schrift Alberts des Grossen *De Causis et Processu Universitatis,*" *Archiv für Geschichte der Philosophie* 45 (1965), 129. For other information drawn from

tion on God and reality and this not only in its first seventy pages but also in its last 187 pages, where one finds rather frequent cross-references to the earlier portion.[48]

How shall we approach Albert's book? We shall isolate his metaphysical position by observing how he answers three questions, the first of which is not (as with Plotinus) what "real" means (Albert does not explicitly address that question in *PU*) but concerns what knowledge someone can have of God. The second is what attribute best describes God (here his answer will imply that reality is light and thus unity—see note 54 below). The third is in what sense effects "flow from" Him. In each case we shall be intent first on discerning (as with Plotinus) what Albert himself had in mind when replying to such an inquiry and, thereafter, on evaluating the possible Neoplatonic aspects of his reply.

Our Knowledge of God

What, then, can one know of God? Can we say He is "substance" or "being" or "wise" or "good" or "one"? No, if such terms are taken precisely as they arise within our human way of knowing, for thereby they express substance, being, wisdom and so on [precisely *as caused, as limited*]. But if one concentrates solely on the perfection itself and neglects the way in which it has arisen in our mind, one is aware of substance only as substance, being as being, wisdom as wisdom. Accordingly, such perfections are found in and affirmed of God in a prior and more perfect fashion than in and of His effects ("Et cum talia praedicantur de primo principio, quamvis secundum nomen quo cadunt in nostrum intellectum, non dicantur de ipso; tamen secundum naturam ipsius rei prius

---

Kaiser's publications, see my ch. 15 above: "*Esse Primum Creatum* in Albert the Great's *Liber de Causis et Processu Universitatis*," n. 13.

[48] For indications that Albert is taking a personal stand and is expressing his own thought in *PU*, see I, 4, 3, 45b–c (the opinion of Hermes Trismegistus and others "pessimus error est et destruit omnes gradus entium"); *ibid.*, p. 46a (Avicebron's statement "valde debiliter est probatum . . . [et] valde imperfectum . . . valde inconveniens . . . valde perverse dictum est"); I, 4, 5, 49a (the theory proposed by *quidam* that "omnia esse unum et quod diffusio primi in omnibus est esse eorum" is "pessimus error"); I, 4, 8, 58c: the view of Isaac, Moyses Maimonides and other Jewish philosophers that the celestial intelligences are angels we do not believe to be true: "sed nos hoc verum esse non credimus"; also see I, 4, 7, 54d–55a.

For cross-references to earlier sections of the *PU*, see II, 1, 17, 81a; II, 1, 20, 85a–b; II, 1, 24, 90a–c; II, 4, 11, 164b–c.

sunt in ipso quam in causatis et perfectius incomparabiliter maiori perfectione"). Why so? Because they are present in Him as exemplary cause and, thus, the cause of substance, wisdom and goodness can only be Substance, Wisdom and Goodness ("Oportet tamen quod ista dicantur de seipso et praedicentur per affirmationem eo quod ista per causam et exemplum primo sunt in ipso; et causa substantiae non potest esse nisi substantia; nec causa exemplaris sapientiae potest esse nisi sapientia; nec causa exemplaris bonitatis nisi bonitas"). Because creatures are images of divine substance, wisdom and goodness, such perfections also are predicable of them too but in a less perfect way. They are, then, attributed to God and creatures not univocally but analogously (ibid.: "Et hoc ideo quia causatum imitatur causam sed non consequitur perfectionem ejus; propter quod non est univoca praedicatio quando haec de primo et de secundis praedicantur" [I, 3, 6, 41c–d]).[49]

To this account let us join a later explanation. When establishing in II, 4, 7 that God transcends every name assigned Him because our nomenclature follows upon our human way of knowing Him, which arises from His effects (p. 161a), Albert infers that our naming Him entails negation (e.g., He is not substance as we are) and eminence (His substance exceeds ours infinitely: He is an infinite sea of substance whose limits completely escape us; p. 161a–b). Yet he immediately adds that one can attend to the perfection itself expressed by a "complete" name rather than to the name as such.[50]

---

[49] For an intelligent but controversial interpretation of how Albert intends perfections to be analogously predicated of God and creatures, see Francis J. Catania, " 'Knowable' and 'Namable' in Albert," pp. 97–128. Since he considers Albert to be comparatively "agnostic" re knowledge of God (vs. F. Ruello) because of his interpretation of res significata/modus significandi, Catania's exegesis of PU on this point would differ from mine. The basis of his interpretation apparently is that the res significata is intrinsically permeated by and inseparably linked with the modus significandi and cannot be considered without it—a situation which obtains even with reference to creatures.

In my exegesis of PU I find Albert coming close to echoing Aquinas' acceptance of the theory of absolute natures. See S.T., I, 14, articles 1–12, especially a. 3; In I Sent., II, 1, 3 solution; for my exegesis see ch. 18 below: "Metaphysics and God: Plotinus and Aquinas."

[50] A "complete" name is one which indicates a perfection all existents are better off having than not having (PU, II, 4, 7, 161d–162a: "quod omnibus rebus melius esse quam non esse") and is contrasted with "diminutive" names—namely, those whose meaning entails also imperfection, as is the case with "motion" ("actus existentis in potentia"), "time" ("fluxus ab eo quod abiit in non esse incipit et terminatur in id quod nondum est"; ibid., 161c–d) and "matter."

Thus, "substance" is "that which is self-subsistent and makes all else subsist," "intelligence" is "subsistent light which is the source of all intelligible light." In that case such perfections belong to the First Cause in a prior manner and to His effects only through Him (p. 161b).

Comments. Both I, 3, 6 and II, 4, 7 make two points clearly. Our knowing and naming the First Cause do entail negation: His reality exceeds all our attempts. But, second, we can and do affirm all "complete" perfections of Him: He *is* Being, Substance, Goodness, Unity, Wisdom, Intelligence and so on. Such affirmations are not merely through extrinsic denomination, as Plotinus would have it: the One is said to be being only inasmuch as He is the cause of being in others.[51] Not so for Albert: God causes being or substance or wisdom only because He *is* Being or Substance or Wisdom, as he explicitly says: "Causa substantiae non potest esse nisi substantia, nec causa exemplaris sapientiae potest esse nisi sapientia" (I, 3, 6, 41C). If such positive statements are alien to Plotinian Neoplatonism, as they seem to be, Albert is not Neoplatonic in this area.

"Intellectus Universaliter Agens"

But what of his position on the attribute that best describes the First Cause? What is the heart of God's reality from which all His other perfections flow? Albert replies clearly when discussing how we know God if He cannot be defined. His answer: we know Him from His effects, the first of which discloses Him better than the second or the third. That first effect is Intelligence and, thus, God is best described as "The Universally Agent Intellect" (II, 1, 24, 90d).[52]

---

[51] In "extrinsic denomination" a predicate is applied to a subject not because what is signified by the predicate is intrinsically in the subject but because the subject is related to something which does have that *significatum*.

[52] The passage terminates with Albert's granting that the description of God as "Universally Agent Intellect," even though the best we have, does not reveal *quid Deus sit*. (On why the question *an Deus sit* should not be raised, see I, 1, 8, 16d).

"Intelligentia" has a twofold signification in Albert, the first of which refers (as in the Latin quoted) to the initial created hypostasis ("intelligentia, cuius substantia intellectus est"). The second refers to *esse primum creatum*, which is the initial "flow" from God and which is also called "intelligentia," "simplex conceptus mentis," "lumen," etc.—see II, 1, 19, 83c; II, 1, 21, 85d; ch. 15 above, notes 27 and 56; also n. 64 below. In order to distinguish the two meanings I capitalize the English word to express the intellectual substance (thus: Intelligence) and use lower case to express the initial flow from the First Cause (thus: intelligence).

But what is "intellectus universaliter agens"? Albert had explained the phrase almost one hundred pages earlier. The First Existent, since He efficiently produces all other existents as the divine artist,[53] must be Intellect (I, 2, 1, 25c–d)—namely, the Universally Agent Intellect: He who makes things solely of and through Himself, He in whom *esse* and *id quod est* are identical, He who receives or undergoes nothing from anything, He who has no contrary or equal. Such an Intellect is like the sun, provided the latter is taken as the very essence of light making all things be visible, the very visibility of which consists in that light ("Omne visibile consistit in lumine sol") and is reduced to and grounded in it. Again, such an Intellect is like an art which would be identical with the light producing the artifacts, which would consist in nothing but that very illumination ("Omne artificiatum consistit in lumine artis sicut in effectivo producente") and are reduced to and based on it (p. 25d–26a).[54] Accordingly, the Universally Agent Intellect is in essence subsistent Light,[55] which produces all other existents, either immediately (other intelligences) or mediately on several levels (e.g., souls; natural forms which illumine matter and, thus, constitute our physical universe).[56] They all consist in that light and are resolved back into it and are grounded in it. They all emanate from

---

[53] See I, 1, 11, 24d–25a: the First Principle is efficient cause primarily and, thereafter, is formal or exemplary cause.

[54] The radical unity of all creatures with God as Universally Agent Intellect can be inferred from the Latin text. Just as light is the very essence of the sun and of things visible and just as light is identical with art and with the artifact, so too light (as will be clear in the immediately subsequent lines of the text) is the very essence of the divine intellect and of all created things, which differ among themselves to the degree they entail darkness (see n. 56 below).

[55] See II, 4, 7,161c: "Erit enim intelligentia omnis intellectualis luminis fons per seipsam."

[56] The various grades of existents result from their progressively falling away from light and encountering darkness. See I, 4, 5, 48b–d: "Sicut dicit Isaac, semper posterius oritur in umbra praecedentis. Umbram autem vocamus differentiam per quam coarctatur et obumbratur amplitudo luminis a priori procedentis. . . . Primum autem lumen occumbit in ipso per hoc quod aliud est in ipso esse et quod est; et hoc quidem intelligentia est. . . . Et sic de omnibus, quod semper aliquem occasum et obumbrationem prioris constituitur sequens differentia entis, sicut sensibile in umbra intellectualis et vegetabile in umbra sensibilis; corpus autem contrarietate determinatum in umbra coeli, quod sola corporeitate determinatum est; conmixta vero corpora consequenter constituuntur in obumbratione et remissione qualitatum elementalium. . . .

it and thereby each receives its *id quod est* and *esse:* that Intellect illumines them all, without itself being illumined by anything prior (p. 26a). It thereby differs from all other agent intellects, each of which illumines what is subsequent to them only in dependence upon the divine illumination and not in virtue of its own *id quod est.* Hence, "agent intellect" is not applied to the First Principle univocally [but analogously] (p.26b–d).

Comment. Albert's statement that "God is Agent Intellect" has, in the light of I, 3, 6 and II, 4, 7 (analyzed above) and the currently studied text, several characteristics. It entails negation insofar as the divine intellect is not identical with a human or, for that matter, any created intellect. It also entails eminence, since the divine intellect infinitely exceeds all other intellects: it *is* His very substance and *id quod est,* by and through which He acts. But it is also an affirmation that analogously God is Intellect through intrinsic denomination. He produces all other intellects because He Himself *is* Intellect. This affirmation separates Albert from Plotinian Neoplatonism.

That separation is also suggested by the fact that all creatures not only consist in the divine illumination which constitutes them, to which they are reducible and which grounds them, but they also are present in the subsistent Light Which is God Himself. The First Principle is (Albert writes in II, 1, 20, 84d–85a) absolutely perfect: all perfections and excellences are in Him, although they are completely one and cause no multiplicity in Him at all ("Primum enim principium in omnibus nobilibus bonitatibus est perfectum, quamvis sint unitae, nullam penitus multiplicitatem inducentes"), for privations, motions and compositions are in Him immaterially, nondeficiently, immutably and simply—the manner in which lower existents are always present through their *rationes* in what is higher. These *rationes* or ideal forms, as Plato would express them, are not only found in the light proceeding from the Universally Agent Intellect, where they are incorruptible and more perfect in every way than they are in things. But they are also in the First Principle itself and, thus considered, are all one with one another

---

Per quod patet quod ordinem in gradibus entium non facit nisi casus et occubitus a lumine primi entis." Also see *ibid.,* c. 8, p. 55c sqq.: I, 4, 2, 44a–b, *re* the four ways in which the "flow" from God is linked with recipients— *distans, cadens, occumbens, oppressum tenebris*—and thus comes to constitute diverse levels of creatures (intelligences, souls, heavenly bodies, terrestial things).

and with that Intellect (85a–b).[57] That presence of all perfections in God again contrasts Albert with Plotinus, for whom the One is without any of the perfections He causes: none of them is present in Him.[58]

The "Flow" of Effects from Cause

The third area in which Albert discloses his metaphysics concerns divine causality and, more precisely, the "flow" of effects from God, a topic to which he devotes an entire tractate of twenty-one pages. What are the salient points made there?

In our everyday world water *flows* from a spring and feeds a brook. The spring causes the brook: one and the same water which flows from the spring constitutes the brook. A philosopher observing that situation would call the spring a "univocal" cause of the stream because one and the same perfection (water) is in both cause (spring) and effect (brook). Such univocal causality is one example of "flow": the same identical form is in both the source and the recipient of the "flow" (I, 4, 1, 42b: "Non enim fluit nisi id quod unius formae est in fluente et in eo in quo fit fluxus, sicut rivus ejusdem formae est cum fonte a quo fluit et aqua in utroque est ejusdem speciei et formae. . . . Similiter enim idem est fluere quod univoce causare").[59]

But God is not a univocal cause because He is not in the same genus as any of His effects. And yet (as seen above) their perfections are all in Him; creatures are like Him, "being" and "intelligence" and "wisdom" and so on can be analogously predicated of Him and of them. He is, then, their analogous cause: one and the same perfection ("being" or "substance" or "light") is intrinsically in Him and in them but differently: e.g., He *is* Being, they have being through participation.[60] Consequently, the perfections they have in common "flow" (literally) from Him to them, in much the same

---

[57] For exegesis of II, 1, 20, see ch. 15 above, prgrs. corresponding to notes 68–76. Also see I, 3, 6, 42a–c.

[58] On Plotinus see the portion of this chapter corresponding to notes 23 and 25 above; also n. 40.

[59] Another example of a univocal "flow" would be a ray of light emitted by the sun—see *ibid.*, p. 43c.

[60] On causes as analogous, univocal and equivocal, see L. Sweeney, S.J., *Authentic Metaphysics in an Age of Unreality,* 2d ed. (New York/Bern: Peter Lang Publishing, Inc., 1993), pp. 244–47.

On why *esse* is not predicated of God and creatures univocally but analogously, see II, 1, 17, 81d–82a.

way as the perfection of art "flows" from the mind of the artist eventually and mediately into the artifact (I, 4, 6, 49d–50a: "[Fluxus iste] erit ergo inter ea quae per analogiam dicuntur, sive per prius et posterius, in quibus secundum quasi instrumentale est ad primum. Et forma qua fluit primum, magis ac magis coarctatur et determinatur secundum quod fluit in secundo vel in terito, et sic deinceps, sicut in exemplo diximus de arte quae a mente artificis fluit in spiritum, de spiritu in organa membrorum, de organis in instrumenta, et de instrumentis in materiam exteriorem. In omnibus enim his idem est quod fluit, licet secundum aliud esse sit in primo et secundum aliud in tertio et sic deinceps").[61]

But how does one account for the fact that such perfections "flow" from God at all? What (so to speak) causes Him to pour them out upon creatures? In answering, Albert says nothing of the divine will and freedom[62] but bases God's pouring out perfections on creatures on the fact that He is all perfect and supremely generous (I, 4, 1, 43b). And the "flowing forth" of perfections from Him to creatures is an incessantly ongoing process. As the Universally Agent Intellect God knows Himself, and, as subsistent Light, He is always sending forth forms, by which He constitutes everything which is (*ibid.*, p. 43c: "Fluxus semper est in fieri. . . . Inter omnia autem quae principiorum habent nomen et rationem, praecipue si fluit, est intellectus agens, qui lumine quod sibi essentia est de se, sic semper formas emanat, quibus constituit ea quae agit").[63] The

---

[61] Albert uses the example of art frequently to illustrate the divine "flow"— for instance, I, 4, 2, 44b; *ibid.*, c. 6, p. 49d sq.; *ibid.*, c. 8, p. 56b–c; for more references see my ch. 15 above, n. 74.

[62] In fact, he rejects the divine will as an explanation of the diversity of creatures originating from God: since "ab uno non est nisi unum, nec potest intelligi quod ab omnimode uno per se diversa sint aequali processione. Si enim dicatur quod hoc est verum in agentibus per essentiam et non in his quae agunt per voluntatem, hoc absurdum est. In primo enim est voluntas quod essentia; et sicut primum invariabile est secundum essentiam, ita invariabile est secundum voluntatem" (II, 4, 14, 167a–b). For Albert's long treatment of divine will and freedom, see I, 3, chs. 1–2 and 4.

Perhaps one source of his rejection of the will to explain the origin of creatures may be his hostility to Avicebron, who gave prominence to the will in the First Cause. For indications of Albert's rejection of Avicebron's philosophy see I, 1, chs. 5 and 6; also I, 4, 3, 46a–b; I, 4, 8, 55d. Also see James Weisheipl, O.P., "Albertus Magnus and Universal Hylomorphism: Avicebron," in *Albert the Great*, ed. Kovach and Shahan, pp. 239–60.

[63] That God's knowing Himself produces creatures see I, 4, 8, 55d and 56d.

first of those forms or light is *esse primum creatum*,[64] which flows from God as act from Act,[65] which contains all other subsequent perfections (e.g., *vivere, sentire, intelligere*) as acts too and active powers.[66] As these flow forth and thus enable *esse* to disclose and develop its contents, God as extrinsic and efficient cause and "esse primum creatum" as primal intrinsic cause produce the substantial entities of Intelligences, Souls, the heavens and terrestrial things.[67]

---

[64] See II, 1, 17, 81c: "Relinquitur ergo quod esse sit primum creatum et quod alia causata non creata sint, et quod nullum causatorum prius esse possit quam esse. Esse . . . [ut] processus enim simplex prius a causa prima procedit ut actus in esse constituens omne quod est. Ex hoc autem quod primum est sequitur quod simplicius sit omnibus aliis: simplicissimum enim est quod in aliud resolvi non potest. Esse autem est in quo stat resolutio entium." Also see II, 1, 15, 79a; II, 1, 19, 83c–d; II, 1, 20, 85b–c; II, 3, 10, 148a. For exegesis of these passages (as well as those cited in notes 65–69 below) see ch. 15, prgrs. corresponding to notes 22–43.

Esse primum creatum is also called "simplex intelligentia" and "simplex conceptus mentis"—see n. 52 above, second prgr. On what *esse* itself means (e.g., entity, essence, act of essence, intelligibility of *ens*), see ch. 14 above: "The Meaning of *Esse* in Albert the Great's Texts on Creation in *Summa de Creaturis* and *Scripta Super Sententias*."

[65] See I, 4, 1, 43a: "Dici potest quod [esse] fluat secundum quod est actus ab actu"; II, 1, 20, 85c: God "producit esse ab esse suo increato. . . ; et ideo dicit Aristoteles in VII *philosophiae primae* quod actus est ab actu: actus ejus quod fit [est] ab actu ejus quod facit." Also see II, 2, 23, 117a; II, 5, 15, 181b. On God as Act see I, 2, 3, 28a–b; I, 4, 1 and 2, 43a–b and 44c–d; II, 2, 4, 97b–c.

[66] See II, 1, 17, 81b: "[Esse] non educitur ex aliquo in quo formalis inchoatio sit ipsius, sicut vivere educitur ex esse et sentire ex vivere et rationale ex sensibili. . . . Et quia esse virtutem suam influit super omnia sequentia, propter hoc sicut esse actus est entium, ita vivere viventibus est esse, et sentire est esse sentientibus et ratiocinari est esse rationalibus. . . ; et hanc virtutem, quod scilicet quodlibet istorum sit esse quorum est, sequentia non possunt habere nisi a primo quod est esse"; II, 1, 19, 83c–d; *ibid.*, p. 84a.

[67] For Albert "esse primum creatum" is act. In fact, its contents (*vivere, intelligere, sentire*) are acts too. These, then, are related to *esse* as acts to act and not as acts to potency. Hence, their coming forth from *esse* is not an eduction of acts from potency but an unfolding of acts from act through the threefold extrinsic causality (efficiency, exemplarity, finality) of the Act Who is *esse increatum* and *intellectus universaliter agens*. Together with *esse primum creatum*, they are simultaneously the *potentiae activae* within the procession or 'outflow' of light by which He causes all creatures to be and to be what they are in the cascade of reality reaching from God down to matter" (ch. 15 above, prgr. corresponding to n. 78).

In all of these entities passive potency or receptivity is not itself an intrinsic component but consists in an extrinsic factor: the distance at which each entity stands from its causes and, eventually, from God.[68]

Comments. In this area of his metaphysics Albert would seem to move closer to Plotinus than in those surveyed previously. His very choice of the word "fluere" to express how created existents arise from God, as well as his comparing their origin from Him to a stream fed by a spring, appears to parallel Plotinus' Greek (see paragraphs of this chapter corresponding to notes 23–28). Second, the fact that the German Dominican is silent, when describing creation,[69] on God's free choice and speaks as though the production of creatures is automatic, spontaneous and, in that sense, necessary (created perfections result and flow out from Him because He is fully perfect and contemplates Himself) also makes him resemble the Greek author.

That resemblance, however, encounters obstacles, since Albert's position appears, at first sight, not to be a monism by his stressing in many texts the distinction between God and His effects. Let us take two samples. How is God (he asks in I, 1, 11) the First Principle? As an efficient cause inasmuch as He is Artist. But an artist is distinct from all the artifacts he makes. Therefore, the divine Artist is distinct from all creatures and is a constitutive part of none of them (p. 24d: "Cum vero omnia secundum esse dependeant ad ipsum et emanent ex ipso, . . . oportet quod primum principium sit efficiens sicut artifex, distinctus ab omnibus et nullo modo commixtus ipsis"). Approximately fifty-eight pages later: the first

---

On the origin and differentiation of Intelligences, Souls, etc., see *ibid.*, n. 29 for multiple references; also n. 56 above.

[68] See I, 4, 5: "[Procedens] secundum id quod est, in potentia est et non in actu antequam sit in potentia, ergo esse differentiam facit a primo esse. Tertium autem ens quod a primo et secundo est, similiter in potentia ad secundum, et hoc magis in potentia est quam secundum, et sic est de quarto et de quinto et deinceps"; II, 1, 14, 78b; I, 4, 8, 55d; II, 2, 5, 98c–d; II, 2, 14, 107b–c; II, 4, 1, 156a–b; for commentary on those texts see ch. 15 above, "Conclusions."

[69] Albert has creation in mind, obviously, in the multiple places in which he speaks of *esse primum creatum* and in some of which he defines creation—see, for instance, II, 1, 17, 80d–81a: "Creare ex nihilo producere est. Quod autem causat non supposito quodam alio quo causet, consequenter sequitur quod causet ex nihilo; primum autem causat non supposito quodam alio quo causet; primum ergo causat ex nihilo. Causatio ergo ipsius creatio est."

creature ("esse primum creatum") presupposes nothing but the Creator, Who nonetheless is other than it, for the First Principle does not become an essential part of anything. Thus, *esse* is not predicated univocally of that Principle and its effect (II, 1, 17, 81d–82a).[70]

But does such textual emphasis on God's distinction from His effects clear him of the charge of monism? Plotinus also affirms the One to be other than the Intellect and the other existents which emanate from Him, and yet he simultaneously maintains they are one with the One to the extent they are real: they are the One-on-a-lower-level (see paragraphs above corresponding to notes 14–21). Might Albert's position be similar? We would be more sure if he unequivocally equated reality with unity (as does Plotinus). Although such an equation seems lacking, he apparently does speak as though to be real is to be light,[71] which perhaps is equivalent to giving primacy to unity in reality.

As to Albert's conception that the passive potency which *esse primum creatum* encounters in substantial entities (see lines above corresponding to notes 64–68) is the extrinsic situation in which such an entity finds itself rather than an intrinsic component (see note 68 above), one may at least infer that such a conception marks a departure from a strictly Aristotelian doctrine of potency and act.[72]

---

[70] Other texts on distinction between God and creatures are: I, 4, 3, 45b–c; I, 4, 5, 49b–c sq.; II, 1, 6, 66b–c; II, 4, 2, 157a–c.

[71] See I, 2, 1, 26b: "Omnis res ab illo est in quod resolvitur sicut in suae constitutionis principium. Ex quo ergo omne quod est, sive sit per se sive per accidens, sive sit per naturam sive per animam, sive corporeum sive sit incorporeum, resolvitur in tale lumen intellectus agentis et illud ad aliud ante se resolvi non potest"; I, 4, 8, 55d. In fact, God *is* pure light (II, 1, 25, 91a). In and through that light He pre-possesses the forms of all things and, then, establishes and distinguishes all of them (I, 3, 6, 42a–c). Because the divine light extends everywhere, God is omnipresent (I, 2, 5, 31a). As already argued (see n. 54 above), one can infer from I, 2, 1, 25b–d the radical unity of all things with God as Universally Agent Intellect: light is the essence of sun and of visible things, light is the essence of art and artifact, light also is the essence of the divine intellect and of all creatures.

[72] See ch. 15 above in its entirety.

Conclusions

The immediately preceding section on Albert's theory of causality has disclosed it to be similar to Plotinus'. According to each author effects "flow from" God as a stream from an inexhaustible spring—a "flowing forth" which is spontaneous and necessary. But in the two previous sections Albert appeared to be unlike Plotinus. God for the former *is* Being, Substance, Wisdom and other "complete" perfections: the core of His reality is, in fact, His being "intellectus universaliter agens." The Plotinian God transcends those perfections: He is above being, substance, wisdom and intellect. Moreover, Albert's God is first and foremost an efficient cause and contains all the perfections of His effects: the *rationes* of all creatures are present in the subsistent Light which is God. Plotinus' God is not an agent but an "emanative" cause, Who is Himself without any of the perfections He causes: none of them is present in Him.

Clearly, determining the extent to which the Latin author is or is not Neoplatonic has been made possible by our tracing the basic lines of Plotinus' metaphysics (see above, "What Is Neoplatonism?"). Because for Plotinus to be real is to be one, his God is sheer unity and, thereby, must be above being, intellect and all the other perfections of His effects. The fact that Albert's God *is* Being, Substance, Wisdom and Intellect and contains all perfections suggests that reality for him is not simply unity but is, in some sense of the word, "being" (under the influence of *Exodus* 3:14?), despite his implying that unity and reality are coterminous,[73] and despite the fact of his conceiving of causality as the "flowing forth" of effects from cause.

Accordingly, taking Albert as a test case in which Plotinus' metaphysics is taken as a criterion of authentic Neoplatonism encourages us when we turn to Iamblichus, Proclus, Pseudo-Dionysius and other Greek philosophers. If reality for them is unity, if their primal God is the One-Good, if He transcends being, intellect and all other such attributes, if His mode of causing lower existents is by necessary overflow or procession, then their positions are au-

---

[73] This implication is based on his apparently identifying reality with light (see n. 71 above). This identification becomes less surprising if "being" is for him equivalent to "oneness." If this equivalence proves true, Albert's metaphysical position fits more readily into a Plotinian Neoplatonism.

L. P. Gerson, *Plotinus* (London: Routledge, 1994), grants his book is "difficult" (p. 225). It would also be less disappointing if he had not used Aquinas'

thentically Plotinian Neoplatonisms. This is true no matter how far they may differ from Plotinus in their conceptions of soul and intellect, in their eschatologies, in their epistemology and logic. This is also true no matter how much they may have added to Plotinus' "pure position"[74] such apparently alien elements as theurgy from the *Chaldean Oracles* (as happens in Iamblicus and Proclus)[75] or the Trinity and Incarnation from Christianity (as in Pseudo-Dionysius)[76] or a doctrine of creation from the Koran or Old and New Testaments (as in the *Liber de Causis*).[77] But deciding in this fashion whether or not such authors are Plotinian in their Neoplatonism must be reserved for another occasion.

---

conception of God (e.g., see pp. 26–29, 32) as the being whose essence is existence and creatures as beings whose essences are really distinct from existence in order to portray Plotinus' One and other existents in a similar fashion (see pp. 5–6, 9–12). This portrayal is misleading; Gerson seems unaware that the key to unlocking someone's metaphysics is what to be real (= to be of value, perfection) consists in for that metaphysician. If reality is actual existence, as it is for Thomas, God *is* existence, which thereby constitutes His essence or nature, and the essence of any creature (angel, human or whatever) is really distinct from existence, which however is the primal actuation of that creature. But if to be real is to be one, as Plotinus holds, then God is subsistent oneness, and all other existents (Intellect and intellects, Soul and souls, and so on) are real to the extent each is the One-on-a-lower-level but it is unreal to the extent it is lower and other than the One. It is a fact that the One and all else do exist, but that fact is not evidence of existence as a perfective factor, as it is for Aquinas. See my chs. 5–6 above, and chs. 19–20, 22 and 26 below.

[74] A "pure position" is in contrast to what Gilson (*History*, p. 238) calls a "complex": "A doctrinal complex is a more or less organic whole, made up of interrelated theses which are frequently found united despite the diversity of their respective origins. . . . It is a syncretic combination of elements united together by their common neoplatonist inspiration."

[75] On Proclus see L. Sweeney, S.J., *Divine Infinity in Greek and Medieval Thought*, ch. 12: "Participation and Structure of Being in Proclus' *Elements of Theology*." On Iamblichus see H. J. Blumenthal and E. G. Clark (eds.) *The Divine Iamblichus: Philosopher and Man of Gods* (London: Bristol Classical Press, 1993); Gregory Shaw, *Theurgy and the Soul: The Neoplatonism of Iamblichus* (University Park, Penn.: Pennsylvania State University Press, 1995).

[76] See William J. Carroll, "Participation in Selected Texts of Pseudo-Dionysius the Areopagite's *The Divine Names*" (Ph.D. diss., The Catholic University of America, 1981).

[77] See notes 42 and 45 above.

17

Idealis in the Terminology of Thomas Aquinas

In his *Thomas Lexicon* Ludwig Schütz lists fifteen texts in which St. Thomas uses the word *idealis*.[1] In those passages that adjective occurs nineteen times, most frequently modifying *ratio*,[2] but occasionally characterizing also *forma*,[3] *similitudo*,[4] *relatio*,[5] *respectus*,[6] *species*,[7] *homo*[8] and *infinitum*.[9]

A few of those texts are directly concerned with interpreting Platonist or Neoplatonist doctrine,[10] but most raise questions vital to Thomas' own doctrine. For instance, are such terms as "wis-

---

[1] *Thomas Lexicon* (Paderborn: Ferdinand Schöningh, 1895), p. 362. R. J. Deferrari, M. I. Barry, Ignatius McGuiness, *Lexicon of St. Thomas Aquinas* (Washington, D.C.: Catholic University of America, 1949), I, 496, make no significant additions to Schütz's list.

[2] *Quodl.*, VII, 1, 3 resp. (Marietti, 137); *De Pot.*, 7, 6 obj. 5 (Marietti, 201); *De Spiritualibus Creaturis*, 5 ad 7 (Keeler, 70); *S.T.*, I, 32, 1 ad 1 (Marietti-Leonine, 169); *ibid.*, I, 115, 2 resp. and ad 1 (Marietti-Leonine, 540); *ibid.*, I II, 93, 1 ad 1 (Marietti-Leonine, 421); *ibid.*, II II, 173, 1 resp. (Marietti-Leonine, 805).

[3] *Quodl.*, VII, 1, 3 resp. (Marietti, 137); *De Anima*, 20 ad 6 (Marietti, 357); *In I Post. Anal.*, lect. 1, no. 8 (Marietti-Leonine, 150).

[4] *De Ver.*, 3, 5 ad 2 (Marietti, 71; Leonine, XXII, 112); *De Pot.*, 7, 6 obj. 5 (Marietti, 201).

[5] *De Pot.*, 9, 9 ad 22 (Marietti, 252).

[6] *S.T.*, I, 28, 4 ad 3 (Marietti-Leonine, 155).

[7] *In VII Meta.*, lect. 16, no. 1642 (Cathala, 474).

[8] *In VIII Meta.*, lect. 3, no. 1707 (Cathala, 496).

[9] *In Librum de Causis*, Prop. 16 (Saffrey, p. 94, l. 26).

[10] See texts cited above, notes 7 to 9, together with *In I Post. Anal.*, lect. 1, no. 8 (Marietti-Leonine, 150).

dom," "justice" and the like synonymous when predicated of God?[11] How many persons[12] and real relations[13] are found in God? Are "lex aeterna" and "summa ratio" interchangeable phrases?[14] Can the Trinity be known through natural reason?[15] Is there a divine idea of prime matter?[16] Is an angel completely incorporeal?[17] Does an angel,[18] as well as a human soul after death,[19] know individual material existents? What is the nature of prophetic knowledge?[20] Does corporeal matter involve "seminal reasons"?[21]

Finally, in line with the preceding double textual series, *idealis* itself has two basic meanings. When appearing within Aquinas' interpretations of Platonism, it refers to the realm of Platonic Ideas.[22] Elsewhere it points to the creative knowledge of Thomas' God—to the "divine ideas," to the exemplars which Aquinas, as well as

---

[11] *De Pot.*, 7, 6: "Utrum ista nomina [bonum, sapiens, iustum, etc.] sint synonyma" (Marietti, 200).

[12] *Ibid.*, 9, 9: "Utrum in divinis sint tres personae tantum an plures an pauciores" (Marietti, 246).

[13] *S.T.*, I, 28, 4: "Utrum in Deo sint tantum quatuor relationes reales, scilicet paternitas, filiatio, spiratio et processio" (Marietti-Leonine, 154).

[14] *Ibid.*, I II, 93, 1: "Utrum lex aeterna sit summa ratio in Deo existens" (Marietti-Leonine, 420).

[15] *Ibid.*, I, 32, 1: "Utrum trinitas divinarum personarum possit per naturalem rationem cognosci" (Marietti-Leonine, 168).

[16] *De Ver.*, 3, 5: "Utrum materia prima habeat ideam in Deo" (Marietti, 71; Leonine, XXII, 111).

[17] *De Spirit. Creat.*, a. 5: "Utrum aliqua substantia spiritualis creata sit non unita corpori" (Keeler, 61).

[18] *Quodl.*, VII, 1, 3: "Utrum intellectus angelicus possit intelligere singularia" (Marietti, 136).

[19] *De Anima*, a. 20: "Utrum anima separata singularia cognoscat" (Marietti, 354).

[20] *S.T.*, II II, 173, 1: "Utrum prophetae ipsam Dei essentiam videant" (Marietti-Leonine, 904).

[21] *Ibid.*, I, 115, 2: "Utrum in materia corporali sint aliquae rationes seminales" (Marietti-Leonine, 540).

[22] *In VII Meta.*, lect. 16, no. 1642 (Cathala, 474): ". . . Platonici ponentes species ideales in hoc recte dicunt quod ponunt eas separatas, ex quo ponunt esse substantias singularium" A couple of paragraphs later Thomas gives "per se homo" and "per se equus" as examples of these *species* (*ibid.*, no. 1644).

In VIII Meta., lect. 3, no. 1707 (Cathala, 496): "Nomen enim speciei non dicetur de composito nisi secundum ordinem ad hoc quod dicitur secundum formam tantum, sicut Platonici posuerunt. Ponebant enim quod homo, qui est compositus ex materia et forma, dicitur per participationem hominis idealis, qui est forma tantum."

In I Post. Anal., lect. 1, no. 8 (Marietti-Leonine, 150): "Posuit autem Plato quod scientia in nobis non causatur ex syllogismo sed ex impressione formarum

other medieval Christian theologians, deposited in the divine intellect and through which God knows and causes all finite existents.[23]

Such, then, is the impressive and helpful catalogue of texts that Schütz, together with his American counterparts (Deferrari, Barry and McGuiness),[24] provides. It is, however, incomplete, since Thomas uses *idealis* at least thirteen times in his commentary on the anonymous *Liber de Causis*,[25] of which the German and American

---

idealium in animas nostras, ex quibus etiam effluere dicebat formas naturales in rebus naturalibus, quas ponebat esse participationes quasdam formarum a materia separatarum."

[23] *Quodl.*, VII, 1, 3 resp. (Marietti, 137): "Artifex autem increatus, scilicet Deus, non solum producit formam sed etiam materiam. Unde rationes ideales in mente ipsius existentes non solum sunt efficaces ad cognitionem universalium sed etiam ad singularia cognoscenda a Deo." Later: "Et quia intellectus divinus est altissimus, per unam simplicem essentiam suam omnia cognoscit, nec est ibi aliqua pluralitas formarum idealium nisi secundum diversos respectus divinae essentiae ad res cognitas."

De Anima, a. 20 ad 6 (Marietti, 357): "Sed species influxae [into a separated soul], cum sint similitudines idealium formarum quae sunt in mente divina, possunt distincte repraesentari singularia. . . ."

S.T., II II, 173, 1 resp. (Marietti-Leonine, 805): "Ipsa divina essentia est ratio omnium quae fiunt; ratio autem idealis non addit super divinam essentiam nisi respectum ad creaturam."

Also see *De Spirit. Creat.*, a. 5 ad 7 (Keeler, 70); *S.T.*, I, 32, 1 ad 1 (Marietti-Leonine, 169); *ibid.*, I II, 93, 1 ad 1 (Marietti-Leonine, 421).

[24] See n. 1 above.

[25] Although its Latin translation is commonly attributed to Gerard of Cremona (d. 1187), the authorship itself of the *Liber de Causis* is still an open question. For a survey of positions on its authorship up to 1938, see H. Bédoret, "L'auteur et le traducteur du *Liber de Causis*," *Revue néoscolastique de philosophie* 41 (1938), 519–33. For more recent surveys, see H.-D. Saffrey, *Sancti Thomae de Aquino Super Librum de Causis Expositio* (Fribourg: Société Philosophique; Louvain: Éditions E. Nauwelaerts, 1954), pp. xv–xxv; G. C. Anawati, "Prolégomènes à une nouvelle édition du *De Causis* arabe," *Mélanges L. Massignon* (Paris: A. Maissonneuve, 1957), pp. 73–85.

By and large, the text of the *Liber de Causis* which Saffrey reproduces with his edition of Thomas' commentary (see *op. cit.*, p. lxxiii) is Gerard of Cremona's Latin translation as originally published by O. Bardenhewer, *Die pseudo-Aristotelische Schrift "Ueber das reine Gute" bekannt unter dem Namen "Liber de Causis"* (Freiburg, Germany: Herder, 1882), pp. 163–91 (for Bardenhewer's German paraphrase of the *Liber*, based upon the one extant Arabian MS, see *ibid.*, pp. 58–118). This is the text of the *Liber de Causis* and of Thomas' commentary that we shall use throughout this chapter.

An edition of William of Moerbeke's translation of Proclus' *Elements of Theology* has been published by C. Vansteenkiste, "Procli Elementatio Theologica Translata a Guilelmo de Moerbeke (Textus Ineditus)," *Tijdschrift*

scholars (L. Schütz, R. Defarrari) have included only one.[26]

The present chapter is concerned with those thirteen passages in Thomas' *Super Librum de Causis Expositio.*

The term first occurs when Thomas comes upon Proposition 3 of the *Liber*—"Omnis anima nobilis habet tres operationes, nam ex operationibus eius est operatio animalis et operatio intelligibilis et operatio divina." Obviously, Aquinas begins, the author here aims at disclosing how soul somehow shares both in deity and in intelligence.[27] But what is meant by "god" and by "intellect"? To answer that question, Thomas continues, let us review the four levels of reality within a Platonic universe.

On the lowest level reside bodies, above which are souls.[28] Next come intellects and, at the top, the Forms. Separate, universal and subsistent, these exercise causality over all items within the lower orders and, hence, are called "gods."

> Plato posuit universales rerum formas separatas per se subsistentes. Et quia huiusmodi formae universales universalem quamdam causalitatem secundum ipsum habent supra particularia entia quae ipsas participant, ideo omnes huiusmodi formas sic subsistentes "deos" vocabat, nam hoc nomen "deus" universalem quamdam providentiam et causalitatem importat.[29]

Within this order each Form *seu* god finds its proper place in accordance with the degree of its universality or, to say the same

---

voor *Philosophie* 13 (1951), 263–302 and 490–531 (hereafter: Vansteenkiste). For an account of that translation, together with a lexicon of William's Latin terms, see C. Vansteenkiste, "Procli Elementatio Theologica Translata a Guilelmo de Moerbeke: Notae de Methodo Translationis," *ibid.*, 14 (1952), 503–46.

For further information on the author, translations and content of the *Liber de Causis*, see L. Sweeney, S.J., *Divine Infinity in Greek and Medieval Thought* (New York/Bern: Peter Lang Publishing, Inc., 1992), chs. 13 and 14.

[26] *In L. de C.*, Prop. 16 (Saffrey, 94, 26). See L. Schütz, *op. cit.*, p. 394, no. 14; R. Deferrari *et al., op. cit.*, II, 550, "n." The inclusion by these scholars of only a single text from Thomas' commentary on the *Liber* is easily understandable in view of the fact that Schütz (*ibid.*, p. v) aims at completeness only with respect to the *Summa Contra Gentiles* and *Summa Theologiae*, while Deferrari *et al.* (*ibid.*, pp. vii–viii) intend to be complete only with reference to the *Summa Theologiae*.

[27] *In L. de C.*, Prop. 3 (Saffrey, 17, 1 sq.).

[28] *Ibid.* (Saffrey, 19, 4 sq.).

[29] *Ibid.* (Saffrey, 18, 8 sq.).

thing, in proportion to the extent of its causality: the further its influence extends, the higher the place it occupies.[30] The highest, accordingly, is the One-Good, in which absolutely everything participates, although it itself depends on nothing else, and which, consequently, is the supreme god and absolutely first cause.[31]

---

[30] *Ibid.* (Saffrey, 18, 14 sq.): "Inter has autem formas hunc ordinem ponebat quod quanto aliqua forma est universalior, tanto est magis simplex et prior causa." Thomas expresses this rule of thumb for determining the order of precedence within the realm of Platonic forms under various formulae. For example, *ibid.*, Prop. 2 (Saffrey, 13, 15 sq.): ". . . secundum Platonicorum suppositiones, qui universalium abstractionem ponentes, quanto aliquid est abstractius et universalius, tanto prius esse ponebant." *Ibid.*, Prop. 4 (Saffrey, 27, 14 sq.): "secundum positiones platonicas . . . quanto aliquid est communius, tanto ponebant illud esse magis separatum et quasi prius a posterioribus participatum, et sic esse posteriorum causam." *Ibid.*, Prop. 12 (Saffrey, 78, 14 sq.): ". . . secundum positiones platonicas quibus ponuntur formae separatae subsistentes, quarum . . . unaquaque tanto est altior, quanto est universalior et ad plura suam participationem extendens." Also see *De Subst. Separ.*, c. 1 (Perrier, p. 126, no. 5): "In ipsis etiam speciebus ordinem quemdam ponebat, quia secundum quod erat aliquid simplicius in intellectu, secundum hoc prius erat in ordine rerum."

[31] *In L. de C.*, Prop. 3 (Saffrey, 18, 18 sq.): ". . . ultimum autem quod ab omnibus participatur et ipsum nihil aliud participat, est ipsum unum et bonum separatum quod dicebat 'summum deum' et 'primam omnium causam.' Unde et in libro Procli inducitur propositio 116ᵃ, talis: *Omnis deus participabilis (est)*, id est participat, *excepto uno.*"

Thomas incorrectly interprets the Proposition quoted from Proclus, whose very point is that the One is not participated by anything. (Hence, "participabilis" in William of Moerbeke's translation is passive and not active, as Thomas' interpolation ["id est participat"] would make it.) "In the first place," the Greek author explains immediately after formulating Proposition 116, "it is clear that the One is not participated in, for if it were, then it would thereby become the unity of a particular and cease to be the cause both of existent things and of the principles prior to existence" (E. R. Dodds, ed., *Elements of Theology* [Oxford: Clarendon Press, 1963], [hereafter: *Elements*] p. 102, l. 13 sq.). In fact, one reason why Proclus introduced "henads" into his system may have been precisely to bridge the gap between the One, who is completely transcendent, and beings. (On the "henads," see E. R. Dodds, *Elements*, section L: "Of Divine Henads or Gods," Prop. 113–65, pp. 101–45 and 257–60; T. Whittaker, *The Neo-Platonists* [Cambridge University Press, 1928], p. 172 sq.; A. E. Taylor, *Philosophical Studies* [London: Macmillan, 1934], p. 178 sq.; L. Rosan, *Philosophy of Proclus* [New York: Cosmos, 1949], p. 103 sq.).

Manifestly, Proclus' and Thomas' theories of "participation" must be miles apart, if the former denies and the latter affirms that it establishes the fundamental *rapport* between absolutely all things and the First Cause.

Among these Forms and gods, too, is the (here the term first appears) *Ideal* Intellect: "inter quas formas est etiam intellectus idealis."[32] In this item all intellects within the second level of reality participate—the higher ones thereby becoming both intellects and divine, the lower ones merely becoming intellects.

> Inter intellectus autem superiores quidem dicebant esse divinos intellectus, inferiores autem intellectus quidem sed non divinos, quia intellectus idealis qui est per se deus secundum eos, participatur quidem a superioribus intellectibus secundum utrumque, scilicet secundum quod est intellectus et secundum quod est deus, ab inferioribus vero intellectibus secundum quod est intellectus tantum, et ideo non sunt intellectus divini. Sortiuntur enim intellectus superiores non solum quod sint intellectus sed etiam quod sint divini.[33]

Thus far the first passage, where *idealis* simply describes the status of the First Intellect as a subsistent Form and a deity. It places that item on the fourth and highest plateau of the Neoplatonic universe.[34]

---

[32] *In L. de C.*, Prop. 3 (Saffrey, 19, 1 sq.).

[33] *Ibid.* (Saffrey, 19, 9 sq.).

[34] Thomas thus channels the Neoplatonic universe into four levels or orders (Forms *seu* gods, intellects, souls, bodies) in at least three treatises. Besides the present one (*In Librum de Causis*, Prop. 3 [Saffrey, 18, 8 sq.]; *ibid.*, Prop. 19 [Saffrey, 106, 4 sq.]: ". . . secundum Platonicos quadruplex ordo invenitur in rebus"), it also occurs in *De Substantiis Separatis* (c. 1 [Perrier, p. 125, no. 5 sq.]) and *In II de Coelo et Mundo* (lect. 4 [Marietti-Leonine, p. 163, no. 334]). See n. 61 below.

This exposé of Neoplatonism will perhaps prove to be characteristic of Thomas' late works, since those three treatises belong to the last period of his life. The *terminus a quo* for the writing of *In Librum de Causis* is certainly 1268 or, even, 1270 (see I. Eschmann, "A Catalogue of St. Thomas's Works," [hereafter: Eschmann] in E. Gilson, *Christian Philosophy of St. Thomas Aquinas* [New York: Random House, 1956], p. 407). *De Substantiis Separatis* seems contemporaneous with *In Librum de Causis* (Eschmann, 412). *In Libros de Coelo et Mundo* was probably written in 1272 or 1273 (Eschmann, 412).

This interpretation of Neoplatonism may have suggested itself to Thomas while reading Proclus' *Elements of Theology* in the Latin translation Moerbeke finished 18 May 1268 (Eschmann, 412). For instance, see Proclus' Prop. 20: "Beyond all bodies is the entity of the soul; beyond all souls is the intellective nature, and beyond every intellective *hypostasis* is the One" (*Elements*, p. 22 and p. 206 sq.). The Latin version: "Omnibus corporibus superior est animae substantia, et omnibus animabus superior intellectualis natura, et omnibus intellectualibus ypostasibus superius ipsum unum" (Vansteenkiste, 273).

The next textual locale is Thomas' commentary on Proposition 6 ("Causa prima superior est narratione"), although the term itself shows up when he has turned to Proclus, upon whom he considers the *Liber* to chiefly depend.

"Omne quod ens ipsum quidem propter supersubstantialem unionem," the medieval Latin translation of Proclus' *Elementatio Theologica*, Prop. 123, reads, "indicibile est et incognoscibile omnibus secundis. . . ."[35] In that sentence, Aquinas explains, the word *ens* stands for any ideal form, understood according to the Platonic conception of the universe. Such, for example, is subsistent Man or Life or anything similar, all of which Platonists hold to be gods and all of which are beyond knowledge and description because of their supersubstantial unity.

> Per hoc autem quod dicit *quod ens,* intelligit omnem formam idealem secundum Platonicorum positiones, puta per se hominem, per se vitam et cetera huiusmodi, quae "deos" dicebant, ut supra dictum est; huiusmodi autem habent unitatem secundum ipsos supersubstantialem, quia excedunt omnia subiecta participantia, et ideo dicit quod neque dici neque cognosci potest unumquodque eorum ab inferioribus. . . .[36]

But, Thomas adds, the author of the *Book of Causes* refuses to go along with the Platonists in their theory of such multiple and separate ideal natures and instead holds that the First Cause alone is subsistent.

> Et quia auctor huius libri non concordat cum Platonicis in positione aliarum naturarum separatarum idealium, sed ponit solum primum. . . ."[37]

Accordingly, only the First Cause is above cognition and description and, hence, our author formulates Proposition 6 with reference solely to Him:

---

[35] *In L. de C.* (Saffrey, 43, 18 sq.); Vansteenkiste, 499.

[36] *Ibid.* (Saffrey, 44, 1 sq.).

[37] *Ibid.* (Saffrey, 44, 17 sq.). See also *ibid.,* Prop. 16 (Saffrey, 95, 1 sq.), where Thomas makes the same point and similarly speaks: "Sed quia auctor huius libri non ponit diversitatem realem inter huiusmodi formas ideales abstractas quae per essentiam suam dicuntur, sed omnia attribuit uni primo quod est Deus . . ." See also *ibid.,* Prop. 19 (Saffrey, 106, 4 sq.), where *idealis* is applied generally to all Forms: "Primus erat ordo deorum, id est formarum idealium. . . ."

Causa Prima superior est narratione et non deficiunt linguae a narratione eius nisi propter narrationem esse ipsius, quoniam ipsa est super omnem causam et non narratur nisi per causas secundas quae illuminantur a lumine causae primae.[38]

Here, manifestly, *idealis* is no longer restricted to "intellect" but is applied to any Platonic Form or separate nature. This broader application reveals its meaning to be simply "the condition of any item belonging within the order of Platonic Ideas or Forms." Consequently, one may validly speak of *Homo idealis, Vita idealis, Ens ideale, Unum-Bonum ideale, Infinitum ideale* (as Thomas explicitly does later on), and so on throughout the length and breadth of the realm of Forms.

As our next area of investigation let us join together two passages which treat kindred problems: Proposition 13 ("Omnis intelligentia intelligit essentiam suam")[39] and Proposition 15 ("Omnis sciens [which Thomas interprets as a *soul*] scit essentiam suam. . . .").[40] Obviously both are concerned with self-knowledge—the first, with that of a separate intelligence; the second, with that of a soul. Here Thomas not only offers five instances of *idealis* but also clarifies the function and nature of the First Intellect.

Any being with genuine intellectual knowledge, whether it be a separate intelligence or a soul, has self-knowledge, but the *whence* and *how* of that knowledge must be determined. Does a separate intelligence know itself by apprehending its own essence or, rather, only by knowing the source from which it has come and in which it participates? The answer to that question, Thomas points out, again lies in our understanding the Neoplatonic hierarchic arrangement of reality.[41]

Its top layer consists of separate Forms or Ideas, among which is found the Ideal Intellect—just as there is, say, an Idea of Man in which all individual humans participate, so too there is an Idea called the First Intellect in which all intellects share.

Sicut autem aliarum rerum ponebant quasdam ideas, ita et

---

[38] *Ibid.,* Prop. 6 (Saffrey, 44, 19 sq.).

[39] *Ibid.,* Prop. 13 (Saffrey, 81).

[40] *Ibid.,* Prop. 15 (Saffrey, 88 sq.). Thomas remarks that "omnis sciens" here stands for "soul": ". . . de anima enim est intelligendum quod hic dicitur" (*ibid.* [Saffrey, 90, 8]).

[41] *Ibid.,* Prop. 13 (Saffrey, 82, 3 sq.).

ipsorum intellectuum [ponebant quamdam ideam], quam vocabant primum intellectum.[42]

As subsistent intellect and intellection, this Ideal Intellect has perfect knowledge. As an ideal form and, in fact, as the very form of
subsistent intelligibility ("Nam primus intellectus idealis non participat aliquam priorem formam intellectualitatis, sed ipsemet est
prima forma intellectualitatis"),[43] it is itself perfectly intelligible. In
it, then, *knowing* and *known* are totally identical and, thereby, it
completely knows itself through itself.

Iste ergo intellectus idealis in quantum est intellectus intelligit,
et in quantum est forma idealis est forma intellecta; sic igitur in
eo unitur omnino intellectus et intellectum, et per hoc perfecte
seipsum intelligit, quia essentia sua totaliter est intelligibile
non solum intelligens.[44]

In that Intellect all intellects whatsoever share, but separate intelligences do so to such a degree that not only do they thereby
have intellective powers, together with actual knowledge, but they
also are *intelligible* to and in themselves. Hence, every separate
intelligence knows itself through itself—by apprehending its own
being, which actually is intrinsically intelligible, although in a derived and dependent manner.[45]

In the second place, does a soul know itself?[46] Yes, Aquinas replies, but differently from either the First Intellect or an intelligence. The former, since it is the very ideal form of subsistent
intelligibility ("scilicet est ipsa forma intelligibilis idealis"), through
itself perfectly knows itself and only itself.[47] The latter, because of

---

[42] *Ibid.* (Saffrey, 82, 7 sq.).

[43] *Ibid.* (Saffrey, 82, 20 sq.).

[44] *Ibid.* (Saffrey, 82, 8 sq.).

[45] *Ibid.* (Saffrey, 82, 13 sq.): "Omnis autem intellectus secundum Platonicos
habet intellectum participatum; sed superiores intellectus participant ipsum
intellectum perfectius, unde participant de ipso non solum quod sint intellectus
sed etiam quod sint intelligibiles et quodammodo formales intellectus; sic igitur
coniungitur in eis secundum eorum substantiam quodammodo intelligens et
intellectum, et ideo etiam ipsi intelligunt suam essentiam, sed diversimode a
primo intellectu."

[46] *Ibid.*, Prop. 15 (Saffrey, 88, 1 sq. and, especially, 90, 6 sq.).

[47] *Ibid.* (Saffrey, 91, 15 sq.): ". . . primus intellectus intelligit seipsum tantum,
ut in 13a propositione dictum est, quia scilicet est ipsa forma intelligibilis
idealis. . . ."

its proximity to the First Intellect, thereby shares both in the form of intelligibility and in intellective power. Consequently, such an intelligence apprehends itself not only by knowing the source in which it participates but also through and in itself.[48] But an intellectual soul, by sharing in the Primal Intellect to a lesser degree, does not itself become intelligible but receives therefrom only the power of knowing. Accordingly, it knows itself but not through its own being. This self-knowledge it achieves, according to the Platonists, by knowing that which precedes it and in which it participates or, according to Aristotle, through intelligible species which become forms rendering it actually intelligible.[49]

Throughout the commentary on Propositions 13 and 15, then, *idealis* is used five times with reference either to "First Intellect" or to "form." Each usage aims at locating the item in question within the top level of the Platonic universe. Consequently, its signification continues to be "the condition of any item belonging within the order of Platonic Ideas." Besides these insights into the use and meaning of *idealis*, the commentary also reveals that the Platonic First Intellect, as interpreted by Thomas, bestows upon its higher participants not only the power to know but also intrinsic knowableness.[50] It is at once both subsistent intellect and subsistent intelligibility.

The final selection consists of two short passages in which Aquinas is immediately interested in determining the order of pre-

---

[48] *Ibid.* (Saffrey, 91, 19 sq.): ". . . alii vero intellectus tamquam ei propinqui participant a primo intellectu et formam intelligibilitatis et virtutem intellectualitatis . . . ; unde unusquisque eorum intelligit et seipsum et superiorem quem participat."

[49] *Ibid.* (Saffrey, 92, 3 sq.): "Sed quia anima intellectiva inferiori modo participat primum intellectum, in substantia sua non habet nisi vim intellectualitatis; unde intelligit substantiam suam non per essentiam suam sed, secundum Platonicos, per superiora quae participat, secundum Aristotelem autem in III° *de Anima*, per intelligibiles species quae efficiuntur quodammodo formae in quantum per eas fit actu."

[50] Besides participating in the Ideal Intellect, all intellects also share in other Forms: "Et quia huiusmodi formae quas 'deos' dicebant sunt secundum se intelligibiles, intellectus autem fit actu intelligens per speciem intelligibilem, sub ordine deorum, id est praedictarum formarum, posuerunt ordinem intellectuum qui participant formas praedictas ad hoc quod sint intelligentes. . . ." (*ibid.*, Prop. 3 [Saffrey, 18, 23 sq.]). Also see *ibid.*, Prop. 13 [Saffrey, 82, 3 sq.]): "Ut enim supra dictum est, secundum opiniones platonicas ordo intellectuum ponitur sub ordine formarum separatarum ex quarum participatione fiunt intelligentes in actu; unde formae separatae comparantur ad eos sicut intel-

cedence within the Platonic hierarchy of Forms. What place should therein be assigned to subsistent Infinity and to First Intellect?

The former is to be distinguished both from the Idea of Being, which is one of its participants and which also involves finitude, and from the One-Good, in which the Idea of Infinity itself participates.[51] Accordingly, the Ideal Infinite occupies a middle position between the One-Good, which is at the peak of the Platonic pyramid, and Being, which holds third place.

> Hoc autem infinitum ideale, a quo omnes virtutes infinitae dependent, est medium inter unum et bonum quod est primum simpliciter, et inter ens.[52]

On the other hand, the Ideal Intellect comes after Being and after Life.

> Secundum Platonicos primum ens, quod est idea entis, est aliquid supra primam vitam, id est supra ideam vitae, et prima vita est aliquid supra primum intellectum ideale.[53]

Idealis, thus, recurs as an adjective aptly applied to any item residing within the upper echelon of Neoplatonic reality. Explicitly Thomas here attaches it to subsistent Infinity and Intellect, but he

---

ligibile ad intellectum." Also see *ibid.*, Prop. 4 (Saffrey, 33, 5 sq.); *ibid.*, Prop. 10 (Saffrey, 67, 19 sq.).

What is the result of this participation? Most likely, it accounts for *what* they are actually cognizing. For example, an intelligence is thinking of "horse" rather than "man" because it is currently participating in the Idea of Horse rather than in that of Man. If this interpretation is correct, then, an intellect is intellect and is actually knowing by sharing in the Ideal Intellect, whereas it is actually knowing "horse" by sharing in the Idea of Horse. See *De Subst. Separ.*, c. 12 (Perrier, p. 174, no. 77): "Inferiores vero intellectus separati . . . intelligunt quidem se ipsos singuli per suam essentiam, alia vero quidem intelligunt secundum Platonicorum positionem per participationem formarum intelligibilium separatarum quas deos vocabant. . . ." Also see *S.T.*, I, 84, 4 resp. (Marietti-Leonine, p. 410): "Plato enim . . . posuit formas rerum sensibilium per se sine materia subsistentes; sicut formam hominis, quam nominabat *per se hominem*, et formam vel ideam equi, quam nominabat *per se equum*, et sic de aliis. Has ergo formas separatas ponebat participari et ab anima nostra, et a materia corporali; ab anima quidem nostra ad cognoscendum . . . ; intellectus noster per hoc quod participat ideam lapidis, fit intelligens lapidem."

[51] *In L. de C.*, Prop. 16 (Saffrey, 94, 23 sq.).

[52] *Ibid.* (Saffrey, 94, 26 sq.).

[53] *Ibid.*, Prop. 18 (Saffrey, 103, 16 sq.).

might as easily have extended it to the One or Life or any Form whatsoever.

Before formulating a summary and conclusions on *idealis* itself, let us momentarily reflect on Thomas' conception of the Platonic First Intellect, which commenting upon the *Liber de Causis* necessarily has repeatedly brought to his attention.

At least two other descriptions of this Intellect are found in Thomas,[54] each based upon its own documentary sources. According to the earlier,[55] the Platonic universe is headed by three principal substances, the first of which is God, Who is the Creator and Father of all, and the third of which is the World Soul. Coming between the supreme God and the Soul is "Paternal Mind or Intellect," who has been made by God and is filled with the Ideas, Forms, *rationes* of all things. Augustine and Macrobius are Thomas' authorities here.[56]

A second account occurs in his commentary on Pseudo-Dionysius' *Divine Names.* According to the Platonists, Thomas there explains,

---

[54] There exists a third series of texts, based upon Themistius' commentary on Aristotle's *De Anima*, in which Platonists, as well as Aristotle, are said to have what might be called an "agent intellect." But this, for the former, is a separate intellect which is comparable to the sun, whereas the latter compares it to a light and makes it a faculty of the soul itself. For example, see *S.T.*, I, 79, 4 resp. (Marietti-Leonine, p. 385): "Et ideo Aristoteles comparavit intellectum agentem lumini, quod est aliquid receptum in aere. Plato autem intellectum separatum imprimentem in animas nostras comparavit soli, ut Themistius dicit in Commentario Tertii *de Anima*." Also see *ibid.*, I, 79, 5 ad 8, p. 386; *De Malo*, 16, 12 ad 1 (Marietti, p. 698); *De Spirit. Creat.*, 10 resp. and ad 8 (Keeler, pp. 126 and 131); *De Unitate Intellectus*, c. 4 and c. 5 (Keeler, nos. 86 and 120).

This separate intellect of the Platonists, though, is not the First Intellect and, hence, the texts are not directly relevant.

[55] Although this description of the Neoplatonic *Nous* as "Paternal Intellect" continues to show up in works as late as Thomas' commentary on the Gospel according to St. John and on St. Paul's Epistle to the Romans, chronologically located between 1269 and 1272 (see Eschmann, pp. 378 and 399), its first appearance in his *Expositio super Librum Boethii de Trinitate* (written before 1260–61, according to Eschmann, p. 406) seemingly antedates the first appearance of his other descriptions of that *Nous*. See n. 61 below.

[56] See *Expositio super Librum Boethii de Trin.*, q. 3. a. 4 resp. (Decker ed., p. 126, l. 22 sq.): "Inter has [substantias immortales] autem ponebant Platonici tres primas et principales, ut patet per Augustinum in X De civitate dei et per Macrobium super somnium Scipionis, scilicet deum omnium creatorem, quem dicebant deum patrem propter hoc quod ab ipso omnia derivarentur, et quandam inferiorem substantiam, quam paternam mentem sive paternum

God is above Being, Life and Intellect but *is* subsistent Goodness.[57] Here, manifestly, Being and Life have been inserted between the First Principle and Intellect.

Finally, while writing his commentary on the *Book of Causes* and influenced by Moerbeke's recent translation of Proclus' *Elements of Theology*, Thomas explicitly introduces the First Intellect into the highest of the four levels of Neoplatonic reality—into the order of the Forms themselves. There it takes its place after the One-Good, after the Idea of Infinity, after the Idea of Being and of Life. As subsistent intellection and subsistent intelligibility, it is the "Ideal Intellect"—that Idea which is the First Intellect and in which all separate intelligences on the second level of reality and all intellectual souls on the third participate to some degree.[58]

---

intellectum dicebant, plenam omnium rerum ideis, et hanc factam a deo patre dicebant, et post hoc ponebant animam mundi quasi spiritum vitae totius mundi."

Also see *ibid.*, q. 1, a. 4 obj. 8 (Decker, 75, 11 sq.) and ad 8 (Decker, 78, 13 sq.); *S.C.G.*, IV, 6 (Leonine manual ed., p. 433a); *De Pot.*, 6, 6 resp. (Marietti, p. 174d); *S.T.*, I, 32, 1 ad 1 (Marietti-Leonine, 169); *In Evangelium Joannis Expositio*, c. 1, lect. 1 (Marietti, p. 18a); *In Epistolam Pauli ad Romanos*, c. 1, lect. 6 (Marietti, p. 22d).

For a survey of the use Abelard and other medieval theologians made of this triad (God, Paternal Intellect, World Soul), and for an interpretation of Thomas' use, see R. J. Henle, S.J., *St. Thomas and Platonism* (The Hague: Martinus Nijhoff, 1956), pp. 407–8.

[57] *In Librum Beati Dionysii de Divinis Nominibus Expositio*, XIII, lect. 3 (Marietti, no. 994): "Est autem considerandum quod Platonici posuerunt Deum summum esse quidem super ens et super vitam et super intellectum, non tamen super ipsum bonum quod ponebant primum principium." See also *ibid.*, I, lect. 3 (Marietti, no. 100): "Fuerunt enim quidam Platonici qui processiones perfectionum ad diversa principia reducebant, ponentes unum principium esse vitae, quod appellabant primam vitam, et aliud principium esse intelligendi, quod appellabant primum intellectum et aliud existendi quod appellabant primum ens et bonum."

Also see *In L. de C.*, Prop. 3 (Saffrey, 22, 13 sq.); *ibid.*, Prop. 12 (Saffrey, 78, 14 sq.); *De Subst. Separ.*, c. 9 (Perrier, no. 59); *Super Epistolam Pauli ad Coloss.*, c. 1, lect. 4 (Marietti, p. 120b). For an interpretation, see R. J. Henle, S.J., *op. cit.*, pp. 413–17.

[58] Does this conception of First Intellect as itself an Idea and as occupying a place within the highest level of the Platonic universe occur in other treatises? In both *De Subst. Separ.* and *In de Coelo et Mundo*, Thomas divides that universe in a similar fourfold fashion (see n. 34 above). In the latter (*In II de Coelo et Mundo*, lect. 4 [Marietti-Leonine, no. 334]), however, he does not mention a

Summary and Conclusions

Besides the fifteen texts listed by L. Schütz,[59] in which *idealis* refers to "idea" understood either in a strictly Platonic or in a Christian sense, Thomas also uses the term at least thirteen times in the following excerpts from his *Super Librum de Causis Expositio.*

Prop. 3, p. 19, l. 1 sq.: ". . . inter quas formas est etiam intellectus idealis."

Ibid., l. 11: ". . . quia intellectus idealis qui est per se deus."

Prop. 6, p. 44, l. 1 sq.: ". . . intelligit omnem formam idealem secundum Platonicorum positiones, puta per se hominem, per se vitam et cetera huiusmodi, quae deos dicebant."

Ibid., l. 17, sq.: ". . . auctor huius libri non concordat cum Platonicis in positione aliarum naturarum separatarum idealium. . . ."

Prop. 13, p. 82, l. 8 sq.: "Iste ergo intellectus idealis in quantum est intellectus intelligit, et in quantum est forma idealis est forma intellecta."

Ibid., l. 20 sq.: ". . . Nam primus intellectus idealis non participat aliquam priorem formam intellectualitatis."

Ibid., l. 24 sq.: ". . . illud derivatur a superiori intellectu ideali."

Prop. 15, p. 91, l. 17: ". . . primus intellectus . . . est ipsa forma intelligibilis idealis."

Prop. 16, p. 94, l. 26 sq.: ". . . hoc autem infinitum ideale . . . est medium inter unum et bonum . . . et inter ens."

"First" Intellect and speaks of the higher intellects within the intellectual order as "divine" through proximity to God, Who is subsistent goodness and unity.

In his *De Subst. Separ.* (c. 1 [Perrier, no. 6]), Thomas mentions a "First Intellect," according to their proximity to which separate intellects are ranked as higher or lower. This intellect does not, however, seem to be itself within the order of Forms or gods, because these latter have knowledge without participating *species*, whereas the First Intellect has fullest participation in them. Moreover, Thomas speaks of Intellect as separated from the Forms ("separando intellectum a diis," where the intellect in question seems to be the first one).

If, then, my interpretation of *In II de Coelo et Mundo* and of *De Subst. Separ.* is correct, Thomas elevates the First Intellect into the top level and designates it a Form and Idea only in his commentary on the *Librum de Causis.*

[59] Schütz and Deferrari *et al.* (see n. 26 above) do insert among their texts one passage from *In Librum de Causis*—Prop. 16 (Saffrey, 94, 26 sq.). I include it in my list of excerpts from the commentary for the sake of completeness.

Ibid., p. 95, l. 1 sq.: "Sed quia auctor huius libri non ponit diversitatem realem inter huiusmodi formas ideales abstractas quae per essentiam suam dicuntur. . . ."

Prop. 18, p. 103, l. 18 sq.: ". . . prima vita est aliquid supra primum intellectum idealem. . . ."

Prop. 19, p. 106, l. 5 sq.: "Primus erat ordo deorum, id est formarum idealium. . . ."

In those excerpts *idealis* is derived from "idea" taken solely in its strictly Platonic sense. It expresses the condition of any item belonging within the order of subsistent Forms and, as such, can be predicated of the One-Good, of Being, of Life, of Intellect, of Man and so on.[60] Thus in interpreting Neoplatonists and, more specifically, the author of the *Liber de Causis,* Thomas explicitly applies it to *omnis forma,* to *forma intelligibilis,* to *natura separata,* to *infinitum* and, on at least six occasions, to "First Intellect." This last and most frequent application indicates that the trajectory of his exegesis has moved from his initially conceiving First Intellect as "Paternal Intellect," in which are stored the Ideas of all things, to his introducing it within the upper level of reality as itself an Idea—a feat which few if any Platonists ever accomplished or even attempted.[61]

---

[60] St. Albert also uses the term, and with respect to *ratio* (*Summa Theologiae,* q. 60, membrum 3, sol. [Borgnet, XXXI, 607]; *ibid.,* membrum 4, sol. p. 612); to *forma* (*ibid.,* membrum 3 [ad qu. primam], p. 607); and to *species* (*ibid.,* membrum 4, a. 2 ad 1, p. 617; *ibid.* [ad qu. primam], p. 618).

[61] What of Plato himself? In his *Sophist* (248A sq.) the "Friends of the Forms" most likely include Plato himself in his early works (see F. M. Cornford, *Plato's Theory of Knowledge* [London: Kegan Paul, Trench, Trubner, 1946], p. 242 sq.). This group is there compelled to admit into the realm of true reality not only what is immutable (i.e., the Forms) but also what changes (249B), among which are to be found "intellect and life and soul" (νοῦν μὲν καὶ ζωὴν καὶ ψυχήν). These mobile items, however, are not termed "Forms" (εἴδη) but only "true beings" (ὄντα) (see Cornford, *ibid.,* p. 246 sq.). True enough, "Motion" is later in the same dialogue (*ibid.,* 254B sq.) classified with "Being" and "Rest" as "very important Forms": Μέγιστα τῶν γενῶν . . . τό τε ὄν αὐτὸ καὶ στάσις καὶ κίνησις (254D sq.). But nowhere is "Motion" identified with intellect.

Hence, Plato himself seems to have introduced intellect into the realm of the "really real" but never to have made it a Form.

See J. A. Weisheipl, *Friar d'Aquino: His Life, Thought and Work* (Garden City, N.Y.: Doubleday, 1983) on the chronology of these writings of Thomas: *In Librum de Causis,* Paris, 1271–72 (p. 383); *De Substantiis Separatis:* Paris or Naples, 1271–73 (p. 388); *In Libros de Caelo et Mundo,* Naples, 1272–73 (p. 376); *Expositio super Librum Boethii de Trinitate,* Paris, 1256–59 (p. 382).

18

Metaphysics and God:
Plotinus and Aquinas

At times juxtaposing one author with another results in a better understanding of both by reason of the very contrast between them. In this chapter let us juxtapose the position of Plotinus with that of Thomas Aquinas on the crucial question of whether the human mind can know the sort of existent God is. Perhaps this comparison will enable us not only to understand more fully their doctrines on God but also to appreciate better the metaphysics upon which each rests.

Plotinus

Let us first approach Plotinus with the question, Can a philosopher know what sort of existent God is?[1] As everyone is aware, his answer is negative: we cannot say anything about the divine nature.

---

[1] One should note that the question here asked of Plotinus (and later of Thomas) is not about God's existence but about His nature—if we somehow know God exists, can we know anything of the kind of existent God is?

The Greek text used for *Enneads* is that of P. Henry and H.-R. Schwyzer, *Plotini Opera,* vols. I–III (Paris: Desclée de Brouwer, 1951–1982). The English translation used is frequently that of A. H. Armstrong, *Plotinus* (Harvard University Press, 1966–1988), "Loeb Classical Library."

Since the nature of the One produces all things, He is none of them. He is not a thing or quality or quantity or intellect or soul; He is not in motion or at rest, in place or in time, but exists in Himself, a unique Form; or rather He is formless, existing before all form, before motion, before rest, for these belong to being and make it multiple. . . . Even when we call the One cause, we are not predicating any attribute of Him but of ourselves, because we receive something from Him while He exists in Himself. Strictly speaking, we ought not to apply any terms at all to Him, but we should, so to speak, run round the outside of Him, trying to interpret our own feelings about Him, sometimes drawing near and sometimes falling away in our perplexities about Him.[2]

Clearly, then, the Greek author denies that one can know and describe the kind of existent God is. What is perhaps not so clear is the metaphysical reasons underlying his reply. Let us now try to unearth them.

In many cases a philosopher's stand on whether and to what extent the human mind can know the sort of existent God is will largely be determined by how he answers this question: Does God actually contain the perfections which are to be found in His effects? If He does, then just as I can say, "This man is wise, intelligent, free and the like," so too I can affirm, "God is somehow wise, intelligent, free." But if He does not, then I must be satisfied with saying, "This man is wise, intelligent, free" and stop there. I cannot apply those same terms to God as indicating intrinsic traits of His very nature. If I do say, "God is wise," I mean only, "God is the cause of wisdom in this man."

What stand does Plotinus take on this question? Explicitly and frequently he maintains that God does *not* contain the perfections to be found in what is subsequent to Him. "Since the nature of the One produces all things, He is none of them."[3] Again: "It is because there is nothing in Him that all things come from Him: in order that being may exist, the One is not being."[4] Again: "He is not all things; if He were, He would need them. But since He transcends all

---

[2] *Enneads,* VI, 9 (9), 3, 39 sq. Also see VI, 8, (39), 11, 1 sq.; VI, 8, 13, 1 sq. and 47 sq.; V, 5 (32), 6, 1 sq.

[3] VI, 9, 3, 39 sq.

[4] V, 2, (11), 1, 5.

things, He can make them and let them exist by themselves while He remains above them."[5]

Why is Plotinus so explicit and firm on this point? Because if God did contain those perfections, the absolute simplicity of His nature would be shattered since they would introduce some sort of multiplicity and distinction (however slight) into Him. And the consequences of this introduction? God would no longer be supremely real because He would no longer be absolutely one and simple. And why this? Here the answer furnishes a master key to Plotinus' entire system: *because whatever is real is one.* That is to say, to be real is to be one. Any item is real because of its unity, and a fall into multiplicity is likewise a fall into unreality.[6]

How seriously Plotinus intends this equating of unity with reality to be taken is abundantly clear from his position on a human person. When a human existent achieves a measure of independence from the One by putting on his own unique and distinguishing characteristics, he is to that extent destroying his true reality. Those characteristics are a sign of weakness, evil, unreality. Such an existent only becomes truly real and truly himself when he becomes totally identified with the One, Whom he should never have left in the first place.[7]

---

[5] V, 5, (32), 12, 47 sq.

[6] See VI, 6 (34), 1, 1 sq.; VI, 9, 1, 1 sq.; V, 5, 5, 11 sq. For a discussion of the primacy Plotinus gives to unity, see ch. 16 above: "Are Plotinus and Albertus Magnus Neoplatonists?" prgrs. corresponding to notes 13–43; *idem, Divine Infinity in Greek and Medieval Thought* (New York/Bern: Peter Lang Publishing, Inc., 1992), ch. 11: "Basic Principles in Plotinus' Philosophy," pp. 243–56.

[7] VI, 9, 11, 36 sq.: "When [the human soul] goes down, it comes to evil and so to non-being. . . . And when it travels the opposite way, it comes not to something else but to itself. And so when it is not in anything else, it is in nothing but itself. But when it is in itself alone and not in being, it is in That [= God], for one becomes oneself not in being but beyond being by that intercourse." See also VI, 5 (23), 12, 16 sq., which describes how a soul must divest himself of his unique characteristics as an autonomous human person to achieve union with the Intelligence: "[In ascending back to God] you have come to the All and not stayed in a part of it, and have not said even about yourself, 'I am so much.' By rejecting the 'so much' you have become all—yet you were all before. But because something else other than the All added itself to you, you became less by the addition, for the addition did not come from real being (you cannot add anything to that) but from that which is not. When you have become a particular person by the addition of non-being, you are not all till you reject the non-being. You will increase yourself then by rejecting the rest, and by that rejection the All is with you." May one not

The relevant consequences of this equation between reality and unity are manifold. For example, creatures are not really distinct from God, for otherwise they would become completely unreal (at best, there is an inadequate real distinction between God and creatures, such as exists between an *unum per se* and its integral parts [e.g., lungs, hands, feet]).[8] Again, knowledge by its very nature connotes at least a mental distinction between knower and known (distinction = multiplicity = unreality and imperfection). Accordingly, knowledge is linked with imperfection. Hence, knowledge is not found in God, Who does not know even Himself. Nor is the last end of humans to know God but somehow to become literally identified with Him. Finally, God to be supremely real must be completely one and absolutely simple. Hence, He must transcend all perfections, the presence of which would insert into Him multiplicity and distinction and, thereby, destroy Him.

Plotinus' is a universe, then, in which the question, Can a human know what God is? is not very important, for man's highest achievement is not to know God but rather to become (better: rebecome) Him through some sort of mystic but literal identification. Second, its answer must necessarily be negative. Man cannot know or describe God since precisely because He is supremely real and perfect He is above being, intellection, freedom, beauty, wisdom, and all other perfections which the human mind discovers in His subsequents and is at home with and which would unlock the mystery of God if only He did not transcend them completely. But He does so transcend them and the human knower can know only what God is not—that He is neither form nor being nor beautiful nor wise.

Thomas Aquinas

Let us now turn to Thomas Aquinas and put to him the same question asked the Greek author—Does God actually contain the perfections to be found in His effects?

---

legitimately infer that the divesting process is all the greater to attain union with the One?

[8] For an explanation of what is meant by an "inadequate real distinction" and for its textual justification, see L. Sweeney, *Divine Infinity in Greek and Medieval Thought*, ch. 11, pp. 245–47.

Explicitly and frequently Aquinas maintains that God does contain those perfections.

> To that inquiry I reply that the perfections of all things are in God. Accordingly, He is described as all-perfect (*universaliter perfectus*) because no perfection of any kind whatsoever is absent from Him. . . . [Why so?] First of all, because whatever perfection is in the effect must also be in its efficient cause, and this either in the same manner if that agent is an univocal cause or in a more eminent manner if it is an [analogous or] equivocal cause. . . .[9]

For example, this man is caused by God, Who therefore contains perfections to be found in him. This containment means that just as one can say, "This man is wise, intelligent, free," so too he can affirm, "In His own way God also is wise, intelligent, free," and such an affirmation reveals that the human mind can at least to some extent know something about God.[10]

"But," we can imagine Plotinus interrupting Aquinas, "the presence of such perfections would introduce multiplicity into God and thereby destroy Him, since He would no longer be supremely real."

"Not so," the Latin author answers. "Such perfections actually are present in God but they are all identified with the divine being (otherwise He would not be pure act but a composite of potency/act because any real composition is between potency/act).[11] Nonetheless, they are not mere synonyms: they genuinely are at least mentally distinct from one another and from the divine essence."[12]

"Then you haven't answered my objection at all," the Greek puts in again. "Even a mental distinction is enough to ruin God, for it connotes some sort of multiplicity, which in turn banishes absolute simplicity and unity. And if God isn't totally simple and one, He isn't God because He wouldn't be supremely real."

---

[9] *S.T.*, I, 4, 2 resp. (Leonine manual ed., 22). Also see *S.C.G.*, I, 28: "Amplius. Nihil agit . . ." (Leonine manual ed., 30); *Comp. Theol.*, c. 21; *De Pot.*, 7, 3 resp. (Marietti ed., 193).

[10] See *S.T.*, I, 13, 2 resp. (64) and 5 resp. (67); *De Pot.*, 7, 5 resp. (198 sq.). For a competent study of the divine attributes, see Maurice R. Holloway, *Introduction to Natural Theology* (New York: Appleton-Century-Crofts, Inc., 1959), 194 sq.

[11] *S.T.*, I, 3, 7 resp.: "In omni composito oportet esse potentiam et actum, quod in Deo non est." Also *De Pot.*, 7, 4 resp. ad finem (196).

[12] *In I Sent.*, d. 2, q. 1, a. 3 solutio ad finem (Mandonnet ed., 70); *De Pot.*, 7, 6 resp. (201 sq.); *S.T.*, I, 13, 4 resp. (66).

"Unfortunately, I must disagree again," the Latin rejoins. "God is supremely real not because He is absolute unity but because He is subsistent actuality since, to my way of thinking, to be real is to actually exist or, more simply, to be *actual.* Hence, what makes something be real is what makes it be *actual.* And whatever makes it actual also makes it *perfect,* and the degree of its perfection is proportioned to the degree of its actuality.[13] If an existent is nothing but actuality, he is without any limitation and, thus, is all-perfect. God is such an existent—all-perfect because subsistently actual and thereby supremely real. Far from destroying God, the presence of all perfections in Him guarantees that indeed He *is* God. Supreme reality, subsistent actuality, absolute perfection go hand in glove."[14]

Let us pause for a moment on the important points this dialogue has revealed for our study. Obviously, unity has a very different function in the two philosophies. For Plotinus it is the principle from which all else flows, the pivot on which his entire system revolves. For Aquinas unity is secondary to actuality, a mere consequence, a by-product. For the former, divine unity must be absolute, admitting not even mental distinctions. For the latter, God is one with qualification, since there is real identity and yet mental distinctions between His various attributes. For the former, God is totally one and simple because He is supremely real. For the latter, divine unity is not directly connected with supreme reality. God is genuinely but with qualification simple because otherwise He would be imperfect: He would be a composite of potency/act rather than pure act. For the former, God contains no perfections precisely

---

[13] *S.T.,* I, 3, 4 resp. 2nd prgr. (17); *ibid.,* 4, 1 ad 3 (21); *S.C.G.,* I, 28 (29). Fundamentally, what Thomas is saying in these texts is that perfection is linked with actuality because of the nature of the act of existing (*esse*). This component is the source of all other perfections insofar as, say, this man cannot be wise, virtuous, intelligent, happy unless he actually exists. And this component also actualizes those very perfections of wisdom, virtue, etc., when the man acquires them through his efficient causality. In fact, all such perfections can be looked upon as resulting from the act of existing as the intrinsic, componential cause of those essential perfections thus efficiently caused. In the divine existent, whose very essence is subsistent existence, all those other perfections are there also, each to the fullest possible extent, each identified with that subsistent actuality. See L. Sweeney, S.J., *Authentic Metaphysics in an Age of Unreality,* 2d ed. (New York/Bern: Peter Lang Publishing, Inc., 1993), chs. 4–6.

[14] *S.T.,* I, 4, 2 resp. ad finem (22); *S.C.G.,* I, 28 (29).

because He is supremely real. For the latter, God contains all perfections and this, also, precisely because He is supremely real.

Additional Clarification

In Thomas' doctrine an important point needs to be clarified. He
claims that humans can know something about God but that this
knowledge is indirect and negative.[15]

Our question is why, precisely, this knowledge is indirect and
negative. What is the force of those two adjectives?

Before attempting an answer, let us note that Aquinas commonly
allows four different sorts of predications with reference to God—
the figurative (God is a lion), the relational (God is our Creator), the
negative (God is immaterial), and the affirmative (God is wise,
intelligent). Our current question has little relevance with respect
to the first three, because manifestly such figurative, relational and
negative predications are either indirect or negative or both. Rather,
our inquiry mainly concerns the fourth sort of predication. In what
sense can such an affirmative statement as "God is wise, intelligent,
free, etc." be simultaneously indirect and negative? If we know
God to be wise, intelligent, etc., why and in what sense must we
still say that we do not know God in Himself, that we do not know
what God is but only what He is not?[16]

The answer to that question, as well as the key to Thomas' entire
position on divine attributes, lies in his conviction (based on experience) that the human intellect can know the absolute nature of
things. That is to say, when a human knower knows, for example, a
man, he knows what makes man be man (and, concomitantly,
what makes man be other than dog and the like). If what makes
man be man were simultaneously what makes man be this man,
then there would only be this man, and man would be predicable

---

[15] For example, see *S.T.*, I, 3, Preliminary Remarks: "Sed quia de Deo scire
non possumus quid sit sed quid non sit, non possumus considerare de Deo
quomodo sit sed potius quomodo non sit."

[16] This and subsequent prgrs. are based upon Thomas, *In I Sent.*, d. 2, q. 1,
a. 3 (Mandonnet ed., pp. 63–72). These pages are considered to be Thomas'
insert into his commentary (first composed ca. 1256 in Paris) during the years
1265–68 while in Rome. See I. Eschmann, "A Catalogue of St. Thomas' Works,"
in E. Gilson, *The Christian Philosophy of St. Thomas Aquinas* (New York: Random House, 1956), pp. 384–85; J. A. Weisheipl, *Friar Thomas d'Aquino: His Life,
Thought and Works* (Garden City, N.Y.: Doubleday, 1974), pp. 358–59.

only of this man. But what makes man be man is not what makes man be this or that man and, accordingly, man can be predicated of this man, of that man, of all humans.

Some of the absolute natures known by us involve matter in their intrinsic makeup. Man is such a nature, as are lion, sensation, quantity, and the like. Without delaying on such natures, let us simply note that terms signifying them are applied to God only figuratively (God is a lion) or negatively (God is not sentient nor extended nor in any way material).

But other absolute natures (such as being, true, good, intellection, wisdom, etc.) are not linked with matter in their very makeups. For instance, take wisdom (= presence of such knowledge in an existent as to enable him to bring about order, harmony, well-being, etc.). In knowing wisdom, the human mind is aware of what makes wisdom be wisdom and be other than charity, justice and the like. Moreover, what makes wisdom be wisdom is not what makes wisdom be human wisdom—otherwise, wisdom could be predicated only of humans. Nor is what makes wisdom be wisdom that which makes it be divine wisdom—otherwise, wisdom could be predicable only of God. Rather, neither human nor divine is explicitly included in that absolute nature of wisdom nor in our awareness. Accordingly, wisdom can be affirmed both of humans and of God but, obviously, in a different way: wisdom in humans is an operative habit, distinct from the intellect in which it inheres; wisdom in God is identified with the divine being. Manifestly, such affirmations are analogous inasmuch as they rest upon similarity/diversity—human and divine wisdom are similar insofar as the absolute nature of wisdom is verified in each, and they are also different insofar as human wisdom is an accidental perfection, whereas divine wisdom is the divine actuality itself.[17]

"But such affirmations would seem to indicate," someone may conclude, "that we have a positive and not merely a negative knowledge of God, that we do know God in Himself, that we do know what God is."

That conclusion is partially accurate insofar as wisdom properly is in God (He actually is wise), but it must be supplemented by our simultaneously affirming, "Yet His wisdom is really identified with His being, intellection, freedom and all His other attributes." Moreover, that conclusion must be corrected also by our realizing that

---

[17] On analogy, see my *Authentic Metaphysics in an Age of Unreality*, ch. 6., Sec. 2.

our knowledge of wisdom as an absolute nature (our grasp of wisdom as wisdom) comes from human wisdom, from humans who are wise. Technically, this means that the intelligible species[18] of wisdom as wisdom, which informs the recipient intellect and issues into our awareness of wisdom, has come from the displays of human wisdom we have perceived, from phantasms caused by such displays of human existents.

From this point of view, then, we do not know God in Himself but in His creatures—that is, through formal determinations or actuations arising from them. Thus considered, our knowledge of Him is indeed indirect, imperfect and negative.

But viewed in the light of what we have previously said concerning absolute natures, our knowledge of Him can be proper (= definitions of pure perfections are genuinely but analogously verified in God) and positive. When knowledge is so considered, we can know (however dimly) something of God himself, and to an extent we can describe the sort of existent He is.

Such, then, seems to be Aquinas' position: a human being can know something about God (because of his grasp of absolute natures), but this knowledge is imperfect and indirect (because God is known only in creatures, only through formal determinations or actuations arising from His effects). This second clause highlights the paradox of Thomas' view—humans know absolute natures of perfections which do not intrinsically involve imperfection and matter, even though the formal determinations or actuations upon which that knowledge rests have themselves arisen from imperfect and material existents.

---

[18] "Intelligible species" is the language which Aquinas often uses to express this factor in our knowledge but which can be misleading. By "species" he does not mean "image" or "picture," which might suggest a representationalist epistemology, but "form" or "formal determination" or "formal actuation": it is the entitative and noncognitive means by which the known causes the content of knowledge. This initial actuation is followed by another actuation, which is the cognition itself (sensation or intellection) and which is efficiently caused by the cognitive faculty (the external and internal senses, the recipient intellect) actuated by that initial determination. This faculty now becomes aware of what it had entitatively and formally become in and through its first state of determination caused by the known, and this awareness is the second actuation the cognitive process involves. See my *Authentic Metaphysics*, pp. 326–28; idem, *Divine Infinity in Greek and Medieval Thought*, ch. 23, pp. 560–61; also ch. 21 below, "Preller and Aquinas: Second Thoughts on Epistemology," prgrs. corresponding to notes 16–24.

Conclusion

The basic difference between Plotinus and Aquinas (and, for that matter, between all philosophers) lies in what each means by *real*. For the former, to be real is to be one, and the rest of his position consistently follows from that premise. For the latter, to be real is to be actual, and his position too flows coherently from that insight.

Accordingly, what determines even a philosopher's attitude to God is his basic metaphysics, which in turn grows out of what he means by real. According to Plotinus to be real is to be one. Therefore, God is absolutely simple and thus contains no perfection to be found in His effects. Accordingly we cannot describe Him with terms signifying any such perfections. In a word, we cannot know or describe what He is. According to Thomas to be real is to be actual. God is subsistent actuality and, therefore, contains all perfections. Thus we can describe Him in terms of those perfections. He is, then, knowable and describable at least to some degree.

This contrast between Plotinus and Aquinas has, I hope, somewhat illumined their doctrines on God and revealed the metaphysical foundation upon which each rests.

IV

Existence and Existentialism

19

Existence/Essence in Thomas Aquinas' Early Writings

Etienne Gilson appears to have stated that the real distinction between existence and essence neither has been nor can be philosophically established.[1] He advises his modern readers to acquire an awareness of the act of existing and of its real distinction from essence by following Thomas Aquinas' lead and turning theologian.

> Give up the philosophical way—from creatures to God—and try the theological way—from God to creatures. Thomas Aquinas may well have first conceived the notion of an act of being (*esse*) in connection with God and then, starting from God, made use of it in his analysis of the metaphysical structure of composite substances.[2]

How, precisely, did this new conception occur initially? Possibly by Aquinas' reflecting upon *Exodus* 3:14, "God said to Moses: *I am*

---

[1] *Elements of Christian Philosophy* (New York: Doubleday, 1960), p. 128: In naming God as "He Who is," one has come "to the notion of a God Whose essence is His very act of existing; but [he] does so only if [he] sets out from a world of concrete substances endowed with individual acts of existing. And this does not seem philosophically demonstrable from the notion of substance alone. It can be demonstrated that no essence is the cause of its own existence, from which it follows that whatever has an essence, and exists, must exist in virtue of an external cause; but no one has ever been able to demonstrate the conclusion that, in a caused substance, existence is a distinct element, other than essence, and its act." See also *ibid.*, pp. 130–31.

[2] *Ibid.*, p. 131.

Who am . . . He Who Is has sent me to you." That reflection may have proceeded in some such fashion as this: What is the import of that text? This: God Himself has revealed His proper name to be "He Who Is," which is equivalent to saying He is unlimited existence, total actuality. But creatures are made to the image and likeness of God. Therefore, each creature too involves existence and actuality but, unlike God, as shared, participated, limited by what each is, by its essence. Therefore, each creature has existence as a constitutive part but as limited by and distinct from essence.[3]

In the present chapter we are not directly concerned with the possibility of a philosophical justification of the real distinction but with Aquinas. The primary question, though, is not how and when he did first achieve his awareness of *esse* but, more generally, what his position is on *esse*/essence. Does he explicitly and without equivocation state them to be really distinct? Does he also endeavor somehow to establish that distinction? If so, how?

In answering those questions we first arranged his writings in a chronological order[4] and then isolated passages in which he mentions existence/essence. These turn out to be of three sorts, in the first of which he at least implies *esse* to be somehow other than essence. These are marked below by two asterisks (**). In the second sort he explicitly states that they are other but offers no reason for his statement, while using that otherness in solving some other problem. These are identified below with one asterisk (*). In the final kind he attempts somehow to establish that otherness. These texts have no asterisk at all but are tagged as [Text A], [Text B] and so on whenever there are more than one in a treatise. Obviously, this third sort is most important.[5]

After cataloguing the texts and dividing them according to Early (ca. 1254–ca. 1260), Middle (ca. 1260–ca. 1267) and Late (ca. 1267 sq.), we analyzed them and the results of that analysis for the

---

[3] *Ibid.*, p. 132.

[4] Unless otherwise noted, we follow the chronology worked out by I. Eschmann, "A Catalogue of St. Thomas' Works," in E. Gilson, *The Christian Philosophy of St. Thomas Aquinas* (New York: Random House, 1956), pp. 381–437; also see n. 51 below.

[5] Some care has been taken to make this list complete, but we can hardly hope to have completely succeeded. Accordingly, references to relevant texts other than those here catalogued will be gratefully received.

For a partial list of texts, with analysis, see J. de Finance, S.J., *Être et Agir* (Rome: Librairie Éditrice de l'Univ. Gregor.; 2d ed., 1960), pp. 94–107; L. de Raeymaeker, *Philosophy of Being* (St. Louis: Herder, 1954), pp. 126–39.

"Early Writings"[6] are reported in the second half of the paper, "Comments and Conclusions."

I: *Scriptum Super Libros Sententiarum* (R. P. Mandonnet, O.P. [editor for vols. I and II] and M. F. Moos, O.P. [editor for vols. III and IV] [Paris: P. Lethielleux, 1929, 1933 and 1947]).

In I Sent., d. 2., q. 1, a. 4: "Utrum in divinis sint plures personae," ad 1 (p. 74).

Ibid., d. 4, q. 1, a. 1: "Utrum generatio sit in Deo," ad 2 (p. 132).

**Ibid.*, d. 7, q. 1, a. 1: "Utrum potentia generativa sit in Deo," ad 2 (p. 177).

Ibid., d. 8, q. 1, a. 1: "Utrum esse proprie dicatur de Deo," solutio ad finem (p. 195).

[Text A:] *Ibid.*, d. 8, Expositio Primae Partis Textus (p. 209): "Esse non est accidens Deo."

Ibid., d. 8, q. 4, a. 1: "Utrum Deus sit omnino simplex," sed contra 3 (p. 219).

[Text B:] *Ibid.*, d. 8, q. 4, a. 2: "Utrum Deus sit in praedicamento substantiae," [solutio] (p. 222).

Ibid., ad 1 (p. 222).

Ibid., ad 2 (pp. 222–23).

[Text C:] *In I Sent.*, d. 8, q. 5, a. 1: "Utrum aliqua creatura sit simplex" (pp. 226–27).

[Text D:] *Ibid.*, a. 2: "Utrum anima sit simplex," solutio, pp. 229–30.

Ibid., ad 4 (p. 231).

**Ibid.*, d. 19, q. 2, a. 1: "Utrum aeternitas sit substantia Dei," solutio (pp. 466–67).

[Text E:] *Ibid.*, d. 19, q. 2, a. 2: "Utrum nunc aeternitatis sit ipsa aeternitas," solutio (pp. 470–71).

Ibid., d. 19, q. 4, a. 2: "Utrum in divinis sit totum universale," solutio (p. 483).

**Ibid.*, d. 19, q. 5, a. 1: "Utrum veritas sit essentia rei," solutio (p. 486).

Ibid., d. 24, q. 1, a. 1: "Utrum Deus possit dici unus," solutio (p. 575).

---

[6] The texts from the middle and late treatises are published below but without commentary in Appendices A and B. But some of those texts are used in my *Authentic Metaphysics in an Age of Unreality*, 2d ed. [hereafter: *Authentic Metaphysics*] (New York/Bern: Peter Lang Publishing, Inc., 1993), pp. 78–81.

***Ibid.*, d. 25, q. 1, a. 4: "Utrum tres personae possint dici tres res," solutio (pp. 611–12).

***Ibid.*, d. 33, q. 1, a. 1: "Utrum relationes divinae sint essentia divina," ad 1 (p. 766).

***Ibid.*, d. 34, q. 1, a. 1: "Utrum persona et essentia in divinis sint idem," solutio (p. 788).

**Ibid.*, d. 35, q. 1, a. 4: "Utrum scientia Dei sit univoca scientiae nostrae," solutio (p. 819).

*   *   *   *   *

II: *De Ente et Essentia,* c. 4 (Leonine ed.: Romae, 1976) p. 376, 90–126.[7]

*   *   *   *   *

III: Continuation of texts from *Scriptum Super Libros Sententiarum.*
[Text F:] *In II Sent.*, d. 1, q. 1, a. 1: "Utrum sint plura prima principia," solutio (Mandonnet, pp. 12–13).

[Text G:] *Ibid.*, d. 3, q. 1, a. 1: "Utrum angelus sit compositus ex materia et forma," solutio, pp. 87–88.

[Text H:] *Ibid.*, ad 1 (p. 88).

***Ibid.*, ad 4 (p. 89).

**Ibid.*, ad 6 (p. 89).

***Ibid.*, d. 3, q. 1, a. 3: "Utrum in angelis possit esse numerus," solutio (pp. 93–94).

[Text I:] *Ibid.*, d. 3, q. 1, a. 5: "Utrum angeli sint unius generis," solutio (pp. 99–100).

[Text J:] *Ibid.*, d. 3, q. 1, a. 6: "Utrum angelus et anima differant specie," solutio (pp. 102–3).

[Text K:] *Ibid.*, d. 16, q. 1, a. 1: "Utrum aliqua creatura possit dici esse ad imaginem," ad 3 (p. 398).

[Text L:] *Ibid.*, d. 16, q. 1, a. 2: "Utrum anima humana sit constituta ex aliqua materia," ad 5 (p. 419).

[Text M:] *Ibid.*, d. 37, q. 1, a. 2: "Utrum omne ens sit a Deo," solutio (p. 946).

***In III Sent.*, d. 6, q. 2, a. 2: "Utrum in Christo sit tantum unum esse," responsio (Moos ed., p. 238).

---

[7] Because of a shift in terminology with reference to individuation, M.-D. Roland Gosselin, O.P., has concluded that Thomas wrote *De Ente et Essentia* before *In II Sententiarum* and after *In I Sententiarum*, d. 25. See *Le "De Ente et Essentia" de S. Thomas d'Aquin* (Paris, J. Vrin, 1926), p. xxvi sq. I shall follow his lead and put the *De Ente* excerpt between those from *In I Sent.* and *In II Sent.*

**Ibid.*, ad 1 (p. 239).
Ibid., d. 11, a. 1: "Utrum Filius Dei sit creatura," ad 4 (p. 361).
**Ibid.*, ad 7 (p. 362).

* * * * *

IV: *Quaestio Disputata de Veritate* (Leonine ed.: Romae, 1970–76).
**De Veritate*, q. 1, a. 1: "Quid sit veritas," resp. (p. 5, 131–39).
Ibid., 1, 1: Sed contra 3 (p. 4, 69) and ad 3 [sed contra] (p. 7, 281).
Ibid., 1, 4: "Utrum sit una tantum veritas qua omnia sint vera," ad 4 (p. 14, 233–38).
**Ibid.*, 2, 1: "Utrum in Deo sit scientia," resp. (p. 39–118–39).
**Ibid.*, 2, 2: "Utrum Deus cognoscat vel sciat seipsum," ad 5 (p. 46, 262–69).
**Ibid.*, 8, 6: "Utrum angelus cognoscat seipsum," arg. 4 (p. 237, 27–35) and ad 4 (p. 239, 194–99).
[Text A:] *Ibid.*, 8, 8: "Utrum angelus res materiales cognoscat per formas aliquas, an per essentiam sui cognoscentis," resp. (p. 246, 116–26.).
Ibid., 10, 8: "Utrum mens seipsam per essentiam cognoscat aut per aliquam speciem," arg. 12 (p. 319, 79–86) and ad 12 (p. 323, 400–9).
[Text B:] *Ibid.*, 10, 12: "Utrum Deum esse sit per se notum menti humanae, sicut prima principia demonstrationis quae non possunt cogitari non esse," resp. (p. 341, 174–83).
**Ibid.*, 21, 4: "Utrum omnia sint bona bonitate prima," ad 7 (p. 604, 329–41).
[Text C:] *Ibid.*, 21, 5: "Utrum bonum creatum sit bonum per essentiam," resp. (p. 606, 132–48).
[Text D:] *Ibid.*, 21, 6: "Utrum bonum creaturae sit in modo, specie et ordine," resp. (p. 609, 125–34).
[Text E:] *Ibid.*, 27, 1: "Utrum gratia sit aliquid creatum positive in anima," ad 8 (p. 792, 221–31).
**[Text F:] *Ibid.*, 29, 3: "Utrum gratia Christi sit infinita," resp. (p. 855, 174–95).

* * * * *

V: *Expositio super Librum Boethii de Trinitate* (Bruno Decker, ed. [Leiden: E. J. Brill, 1955]), 5, 4 ad 4 (p. 198, l. 15 sq.).

* * * * *

VI: *In Librum Boethii de Hebdomadibus Expositio* (R. M. Spiazzi,
O.P., ed., *Opuscula Theologica*, vol. II [Romae: Marietti, 1954]).
Lectio 2 (p. 398, nos. 31–35).
***Ibid.*, lect. 4 (p. 405, no. 60, no. 62).
***Ibid.*, lect. 5 (p. 408, no. 71).

*   *   *   *   *

VII: *Quaestiones Quodlibetales* (R. Spiazzi, O.P., ed. [Romae: Marietti,
1949]).
[Text A:] *Quodl.* VII, 1, 1: "Utrum aliquis intellectus creatus
possit divinam essentiam videre immediate," ad 1 (p. 134b).
[Text B:] *Ibid.*, VII, 3, 2: "Utrum angelica simplicitas patiatur
compositionem ex subiecto et accidente," resp. (p. 140b).
**Ibid.*, ad 1 (p. 140b).
***Ibid.*, IX, 2, 2: "Utrum (in Christo) sit unum tantum esse,"
resp. (p. 180d sq.).
**Ibid.*, IX, 4, 1: "Utrum (angeli) sint compositi ex materia et
forma," arg. 4 (p. 184c).
[Text C:] *Ibid.*, resp. (p. 185b).
***Ibid.*, ad 5 (p. 185d).

*   *   *   *   *

Such, then, are the early texts so far discovered in which Thomas
shows his hand on existence/essence. What follows is based upon
an analysis of them.

Initial Comments and Conclusions

(1) A first point to note is that Thomas' position on the otherness
between *esse*/essence is found expressed in many different contexts. It occurs once in an exegesis of a text from Hilary quoted by
Lombard (*In Sent.*, Text A). Occasionally it mingles with topics
concerning the Trinity (**In I Sent.*, d. 2: "Utrum in divinis sint
plures personae"; **Ibid.*, d. 4: "Utrum generatio sit in Deo").[8] Frequently it shows up when he is discussing various divine attributes
(**In I Sent.*, d. 8, q. 1: "Utrum esse proprie dicatur de Deo"; **Ibid.*,
d. 8, q. 4: "Utrum Deus sit omnino simplex"; *Ibid.*, Text B: "Utrum

---

[8] References are to texts as cited and listed above. Thus "'**In I Sent.*, d. 2"
is equivalent to "'**In I Sent.*, d. 2, q. 1, a. 4 ad 1 (p. 74)'"; "'**Ibid.*, d. 4" is
equivalent to "'**Ibid.*, d. 4, q. 1 a. 1 ad 2 (p. 132).'"

Deus sit in praedicamento substantiae"; *Ibid.*, Text E: "Utrum nunc aeternitatis sit ipsa aeternitas"; *Ibid.*, d. 19, q. 4: "Utrum in divinis sit totum universale"; *Ibid.*, Text F: "Utrum sint plura prima principia").

Frequently, also, it enters into his investigation of creatures. At times this is an inquiry into creatures generally. Are they simple (*In Sent.*, Text C: "Utrum aliqua creatura sit simplex")? Are they images of God (*In Sent.*, Text K: "Utrum aliqua creatura possit dici esse ad imaginem")? Is every being a creature (*In Sent.*, Text M: "Utrum omne ens sit a Deo")? How is a creature to be described as good?

> **De Veritate*, 21, 4: "Utrum omnia sint bona bonitate prima"; *Ibid.*, Text C: "Utrum bonum creatum sit bonum per essentiam"; *Ibid.*, Text D: "Utrum bonum creaturae sit in modo, specie et ordine."

Is sanctifying grace a creature (*ibid.*, Text E: "Utrum gratia sit aliquid creatum positive in anima")? Can creatures see God (*Quodl.*, Text A: "Utrum aliquis intellectus creatus possit divinam essentiam videre immediate")?

At other times he concentrates upon angels and human souls. Are such existents absolutely simple or are they somehow composed of act/potency?

> *In Sent.*, Text D: "Utrum anima sit simplex"; *De Ente et Essentia*, c. 4; *In Sent.*, Text G: "Utrum angelus sit compositus ex materia et forma"; *Ibid.*, Text L: "Utrum anima humana sit constituta ex aliqua materia"; *In Boet. de Trinitate*, 5, 4 ad 4; *In Boet. de Hebdomadibus*, Lect. 2, nos. 31–35; *Quodl.*, Text B: "Utrum angelica simplicitas patiatur compositionem ex subjecto et accidente"; *Ibid.*, Text C: "Utrum (angeli) sint compositi ex materia et forma."

Are all angels in the same genus (*In Sent.*, Text I: "Utrum angeli sint unius generis")? Do angels differ specifically from human souls (*Ibid.*, Text J: "Utrum angelus et anima different specie")? How does an angel know himself and material things (**De Ver.*, 8, 6: "Utrum angelus cognoscat seipsum"; *Ibid.*, Text A: "Utrum angelus res materiales cognoscat per formas aliquas an per essentiam sui cognoscentis")? How does a man know himself and God (**Ibid.*, 10, 8: "Utrum mens seipsam per essentiam cognoscat aut per aliquam speciem"; Ibid., Text B: "Utrum Deum esse sit per se notum menti humanae, sicut prima principia demonstrationis quae non possunt cogitari non esse")?

That wide variety of problems within which Thomas expresses himself on esse/essence makes clear that nowhere in his early writings does he directly and ex professo formulate the question Utrum esse differat ab essentia. It is always answered in connection with some other topic. Perhaps he comes closest to that formulation when, under pressure from those holding universal hylomorphism, he asks whether angels and human souls involve compositions of form/matter or, again, whether every creature is simple. Nonetheless, those inquiries are not precisely what we are looking for. The otherness between esse/essence is each time developed only as an answer to them and even this development entails in many cases a strictly theological movement inasmuch as Thomas goes from God to creatures: in God essence is esse, but creatures are not God, therefore in creatures essence is not esse (see especially In Sent., Texts C, D and G).

(2) Aquinas uses several different verbs to express the fact that esse and essence[9] are somehow different. At least once he uses distinguere:

*De Ver., 1, 1, ad 3 (sed contra): Cum dicitur: Diversum est esse et quod est, distinguitur actus essendi ab eo cui actus ille convenit.[10]

Occasionally he uses accidere:

In Sent., Text A: cuilibet quidditati creatae accidit esse. Ibid., Text B: aliter enim (esse) accideret quidditati.[11]

---

[9] Incidentally, the texts quoted in the paragraphs immediately below show that Thomas, when contrasting essence with esse, frequently substitutes quidditas or id quod est for essentia.

[10] This text challenges Cunningham's statement that "St. Thomas never said, 'Essence is distinct from esse,' " since here Thomas seems at least once to have said that very thing. See F. A. Cunningham, S.J., "Distinction According to St. Thomas," New Scholasticism 36 (July 1962), 279; idem, Essence and Existence in Thomism: A Mental vs. "Real Distinction"? (Lanham, Md.: University Press of America, 1988), pp. 227–59; my review of the book in The Modern Schoolman 68 (1991), 337–40.

[11] For a discussion of what Thomas intends by describing esse as accidental, see J. Owens, "The Causal Proposition—Principle or Conclusion?" The Modern Schoolman 32 (May 1955), 323–29.

More frequently he chooses *differre:*

*In I Sent., d. 2: in creatura differt essentia rei et esse suum.

*Ibid., d. 4, q. 1, a. 1, ad 2: Cum enim in omni creatura differat essentia et esse. . . .

*Ibid., d. 8, q. 1, a. 1, sol.: Cum . . . in qualibet re creata essentia sua differat a suo esse. . . .

Ibid., Text B: . . . habet quidditatem differentem ab esse.

Ibid., Text C, 1st prgr.: Boethius: ". . . differt et quod est et quo est."

Ibid., Text E: Actus autem qui mensuratur aevo, scilicet ipsum esse aeviterni, differt ab eo cujus est actus re. . . . Aeternitas et nunc aeternitatis non differunt re sed ratione tantum.

In Boethii de Hebdomadibus, no. 32: Sicut esse et quod est differunt in simplicibus secundum intentiones, ita in compositis differunt realiter.

He also frequently makes use of the phrase *est aliud quam* (or something equivalent):

*In I Sent., d. 8, q. 4, a. 2, ad 1: Substantia quidditatem nominat quae est aliud ab esse ejus.

Ibid., Text E: [Quidditas ipsius Dei] secundum rem non est aliud quam suum esse sed ratione tantum.

De Ente et Essentia, c. 4: Ergo patet quod esse est aliud ab essentia uel quiditate. . . . Unde oportet quod in qualibet alia re preter eam aliud sit esse suum et aliud quiditas uel natura seu forma sua.

In Sent., Text G: In omnibus autem aliis esse est praeter quidditatem cui esse acquiritur.

Ibid., Text I: Omne id quod habet esse aliud a sua quidditate. . . .

Ibid., Text J: Res illa non habet quidditatem aliam nisi suum esse. . . . Anima autem rationalis habet esse absolutum . . . quod est aliud a sua quidditate, sicut etiam de angelis dictum est.

De Ver., Text A: Esse cuiuslibet rei praeter primum ens est aliquid praeter essentiam ipsius.

*Ibid., 10, 8, ad 12: In anima est aliud quo est et quod est.

Ibid., Text B: Cuiuslibet enim creaturae esse est aliud ab eius quidditate.

Ibid., Text E: Oportet quod esse suum sit aliud quam ipsum.

*Quodl., IX, 4, 1, arg. 4: Sed in omni creatura esse est aliud ab essentia eius. . . .

On approximately an equal number of times he simply states that the act of existing *non est* essence:

> **In I Sent.,* d. 8, q. 4, a. 1, sed contra 3: Sed nullum compositum totum est suum esse, quia esse ipsius sequitur componentia, quae non sunt ipsum esse.
>
> *Ibid.,* Text F: . . . ita tamen quod ipsarum rerum naturae non sunt hoc ipsum esse quod habent.
>
> *Ibid.,* Text G: In lib. *De Causis,* propos. 9, dicitur quod intelligentia non est esse tantum, sicut causa prima, sed est in ea esse et forma, quae est quidditas sua.
>
> **In II Sent.,* d. 3, q. 1, a. 1, ad 6: Forma simpliciter subsistens quae non est suum esse. . . .
>
> *Ibid.,* Text M: Alia autem entia . . . aliquod esse participant, quod non est idem quod ipsa sunt.
>
> **In III Sent.,* d. 11, a. 1, ad 4: Unde ipsa [natura quae est ab alio] non est suum esse, ut habeat necessitatem essendi ex se.
>
> **De Ver.,* Text C: Natura autem vel essentia cuiuslibet rei creatae non est suum esse, sed esse participans ab alio.
>
> *In Boethii de Hebdomadibus,* no. 34: Nulla earum [formarum] est ipsum esse, sed habens esse.
>
> *Quodl.,* Text B: Omne quod non est suum esse, oportet quod habeat esse receptum ab alio. . . . Angelus non est suum esse.

He also frequently uses some form of the verb *componere* or the noun *compositio:*

> *In Sent.,* Text C: In qualibet creatura . . . inveniatur quidditas vel natura sua et esse suum . . . et ita componitur ex esse vel quo est, et quod est.
>
> *Ibid.,* Text D: Et hoc modo intelligo in angelis compositionem potentiae et actus, et de "quo est" et "quod est," et similiter in anima. . . . Advenit ibi compositio horum duorum, scilicet quidditatis et esse.
>
> *Ibid.,* Text G: Et sic angelus compositus est ex esse quod est, vel ex quo est et quod est. . . .
>
> *De Ver.,* Text E: Omne quod est in genere substantiae est compositum reali compositione . . . et ideo omne quod est directe in praedicamento substantiae, compositum est saltem ex esse et quod est.
>
> *In Boethii de Trin.,* 5, 4 ad 4: Et hoc est quod dicitur quod sunt compositi ex "quod est" et "quo est," ut ipsum esse intelligatur "quo est," ipsa vero natura angeli intelligatur "quod est."

Quodl., VII, 3, 2, ad 1: Substantialis simplicitas in angelis excludit compositionem materiae et formae, non autem compositionem ex esse et quod est.

Ibid., Text C: Et sic dicimus angelum esse compositum ex quo est et quod est. . . . Ideo est in eo compositio actus et potentiae.

Those texts disclose that Thomas has at least six ways of expressing the otherness between *esse*/essence: *distinguere, accidere, differre, est aliud, non est* and *componere*. The last four are used most frequently, with almost equal frequency and, seemingly, with little or no change in meaning.[12]

(3) The next point is of crucial importance: Aquinas not only states that *esse* differs somehow from essence (see the texts cited above with an asterisk) but he also endeavors to establish, to account for, to give a foundation or proof of that difference. This attempt he makes in at least four ways. Some of these are overlapping and are found in one and the same text, but they can be isolated for purposes of accuracy and convenience.

Intellectus Essentiae Argument

(4) One of those ways is what can be called the *intellectus essentiae* argument and occurs rather often.

In Sent., Text A: Accidens dicitur hic quod non est de intellectu alicujus, sicut rationale dicitur animali accidere; et ita cuilibet quidditati creatae accidit esse, quia non est de intellectu ipsius quidditatis; potest enim intelligi humanitas et tamen dubitari utrum homo habeat esse.

---

[12] With reference to *componere*, see J. Owens, "Diversity and Community of Being in St. Thomas Aquinas," *Mediaeval Studies* 22 (1960), 282–97. His position seems to be that the very being of sensible existents *is* their composition. See pp. 286–87: "The composition of matter and form, substance and accident, takes place in being. So much is this so, that the being of these things . . . *consists* in such compositions. . . . The being which follows upon that composition [of matter and form] and consists in that composition will likewise have to be individual. The real being of sensible things, therefore, will be individual because it is a composition that is individual." However attractive and valid Owens' position may be on other points, if he is saying that *esse* itself is a composition, then one must dissent. According to Aquinas *esse* is not the mere composition of other components but a unique component over and above all other components and with its own function to perform.

Ibid., Text B: Omne quod est in genere habet quidditatem differentem ab esse, sicut homo; humanitati enim ex hoc quod est humanitas non debetur esse in actu; potest enim cogitari humanitas et tamen ignorari an aliquis homo sit.

De Ente, c. 4: Quicquid enim non est de intellectu essentie uel quiditatis hoc est adueniens extra et faciens compositionem cum essentia, quia nulla essentia sine hiis que sunt partes essentie intelligi potest. Omnis autem essentia uel quiditas potest intelligi sine hoc quod aliquid intelligatur de esse suo; possum enim intelligere quid est homo uel fenix et tamen ignorare an esse habeat in rerum natura. Ergo patet quod esse est aliud ab essentia uel quiditate.

In Sent., Text F: Invenitur enim in omnibus rebus natura entitatis, in quibusdam magis nobilis et in quibusdam minus; ita tamen quod ipsarum rerum naturae non sunt hoc ipsum esse quod habent: alias esse esset de intellectu cujuslibet quidditatis, quod falsum est, cum quidditas cujuslibet rei possit intelligi etiam non intelligendo de ea an sit.

Ibid., Text G: Esse autem secundum quod dicitur res esse in actu invenitur ad diversas naturas vel quidditates diversimode se habere. Quaedam enim natura est de cujus intellectu non est suum esse, quod patet ex hoc quod intelligi potest esse cum hoc quod ignoretur an sit, sicut phaenicem vel eclipsim vel aliquid hujusmodi.

De Ver., Text B: Hoc autem quod est esse in nullius creaturae ratione includitur; cuiuslibet enim creaturae esse est aliud ab eius quidditate; unde non potest dici de aliqua creatura quod eam esse sit per se notum etiam secundum se.

(a) Those passages require several comments. The last text manifestly moves in a manner different from the others. Instead of going from the *intellectus essentiae* (here spoken of as *ratio creaturae*) to the otherness between the *esse*/quiddity, it proceeds from the latter to the former. But this procedure is not in conflict with that found in the other five since it aims at emphasizing the ontological foundation of the *intellectus essentiae* argument. The ontological reason *esse* is not included in an awareness of a creature's quiddity is that *esse* is different from the quiddity. The other texts presuppose this foundation and have to do with our way of knowing: the reason *we know* that *esse* is other than essence is that *esse* is not contained within the intelligibility of a creature's whatness.

(b) What, then, is the structure of the argumentation within those first four texts? Basically, this:

> [Because it is the proper object of our intellect, essence is what we immediately and spontaneously know];[13]
> But essence is known only if and because all its intrinsic parts are known (*De Ente*);
> Therefore, what is not known when we know essence
>> is not an intrinsic part of it;
>> is rather extrinsic to it: it comes from without and enters into composition with it (*De Ente*);
>> happens to it (*In Sent.*, Text A);
>> in a word, is other than it.
> But *esse* is not known when we know essence, because we can know what a man is (*De Ente; In Sent.*, Texts A and B) or what a phoenix or an eclipse or any other such thing is (*De Ente; In Sent.*, Text G) without knowing whether they do actually exist;[14]
> Therefore, *esse* is other than essence.

(c) Is that argumentation valid? At least two objections can be lodged against it. The first is that it seems to be merely an intramental, entirely abstract consideration insofar as it has to do with essences as known, with concepts, with intelligibilities of man, phoenix and so on. What can we answer? True, it does deal with intelligibilities and concepts but only as seen against the actual universe as a background, as the texts themselves make clear:

> *In Sent.*, Text B: . . . ignorari an aliquis homo sit.
> *De Ente:* . . . ignorare an esse habeat in rerum natura.
> *In Sent.*, Text F: . . . non intelligendo de ea an sit.

---

[13] The brackets indicate that the point is not made explicitly in the text itself. That Thomas makes the point elsewhere in early writings, see for example *De Ver.*, 15, 2 ad 3 (Leonine ed., p. 487, 326): "Objectum autem intellectus est quid, ut dicitur in III de Anima." Also see *ibid.*, resp. (p. 486, 227); *ibid.*, 14, 2, resp. (p. 441, 203).

[14] Contemporary physics furnishes a good example of what Thomas is driving at: physicists knew *what* the nutrino should be, prior to their discovering *that* there actually is such a subatomic particle.

> *Ibid.*, Text G: Esse autem secundum quod dicitur res esse in
> actu. . . .

Throughout the argument, then, *esse* has to do with actual existence
and not merely with some sort of Boethian *forma totius*.[15] Moreover,
one interpretation of the argument is that a human knower who
knows what (say) "dog" is finds himself confronted with various
actual dogs and realizes that in knowing "dog" he did not know
that *these* dogs existed. This realization underwrites the fact that
the argumentation does entail actuality and, second, suggests that
there is at least some difference between the fact that this dog is
dog and the fact that he actually is; otherwise, why did the human
knower not know this existing dog in knowing dog?

But suppose we say that "to actually exist" for this dog is the
same as "to be this dog." Then the couplet, essence/*esse*, would be
equivalent to the nature-as-specific/nature-as-individual, to dog/
this dog. In such a case one could know the first member of the
couplet without knowing the second. Moreover, a difference exists
between them but it is not a real difference since it is only that
between the indeterminate/determinate. What can be said to this
problem? It threatens the *intellectus essentiae* argument much more
seriously than any previously encountered, but its solution lies in
two facts. The relationship between a nature as specific and as
individual is that of act and potency,[16] whereas the relation be-

---

[15] On the meaning of *esse* in Boethius, see M.-D. Roland-Gosselin, O.P., *op.
cit.*, pp. 142–45; E. Gilson, *History of Christian Philosophy in Middle Ages* (New
York: Random House, 1955), pp. 103–6. That Thomas was himself aware of
the meaning given by Boethius (and Avicenna) to *esse* or *quo est*, see *In Sent.*,
Text D.

[16] That the relationship is one of act/potency can be gathered from the
following line of reasoning. *Receptum/recipiens* are to one another as act/po-
tency (*De Ente et Essentia*, c. 4 [Leonine de., p. 377, 147–9]: "Omne autem quod
recipit aliquid ab aliquo est in potentia respectu illius, et hoc quod receptum
in eo est est actus eius"). But in material things specific essence is *received* in
signate matter, whence it becomes individuated (*ibid.*, c. 5, p. 379, 134: "Et
iterum natura uel quidditas earum est recepta in materia signata. Et ideo sunt
finite et superius et inferius, et in eis iam, propter diuisionem materie signate,
possibilis est multiplicatio indiuiduorum in una specie"). Hence, nature-as-
specific/nature-as-individual are related to one another as act/potency.

Also, an intellectual nature is not received in any matter (*ibid.*, c. 5, p. 378, 1
49: "Sed natura uel quidditas earum est absoluta et non recepta in aliqua
materia") and, hence, is pure act in that order (*ibid.*, 11. 54–58: "Non autem

tween essence/*esse* is that of potency/act.[17] Accordingly, the couplet, essence/*esse*, is not equivalent to species/individual; "actually to exist" for (say) this dog is not the same as "to be this dog," and the problem vanishes.

(d) The second objection against the argument is that *esse* perhaps signifies merely "essence as efficiently caused." If so, one can know essence without knowing *esse* inasmuch as one can be aware of what something is without knowing whether some agent or other has actually produced it yet. There would also be a difference between essence/*esse*—namely, that between something as it is in itself and then in relation to an efficient cause. But once the thing is produced and actually exists, that fact is no intrinsic factor in the thing, and what it is and that it is are not really different. *Esse* is the essence itself as efficiently effected.

That difficulty would seemingly be insurmountable if Thomas in his early treatises did not provide two facts—*esse* is a factor which is most intimate to existents ("esse autem est magis intimum cuilibet rei quam ea per quae esse determinatur")[18] and *esse* is a genuine perfection within them.[19] But an efficient cause is always other than

---

finiuntur inferius quia earum forme non limitantur ad capacitatem alicuius materie recipientis eas. Et ideo in talibus substantiis non inuenitur multitudo indiuiduorum in une specie").

[17] For example, see *ibid.*, c. 4, p. 377, 149 sq.: "Ergo oportet quod ipsa quidditas uel forma que est intelligencia sit in potencia respectu esse quod a Deo recipit, et illud esse receptum est per modum actus. Et ita inuenitur potencia et actus in intelligenciis." Also see below, "Act and Potency" section.

[18] *In II Sent.*, d. 1, a. 4 Sol. (p. 26).

[19] For instance, see *De Ente et Essentia*, c. 5, p. 378, l. 30 sq.: "Similiter eciam quamuis [Deus] sit esse tantum non oportet quod deficiant ei perfectiones relique et nobilitates. Imo habet Deus perfectiones que sunt in omnibus generibus, propter quod perfectum simpliciter dicitur, . . . sed habet eas modo excellentiori ceteris rebus, quia in eo unum sunt sed in aliis diuersitatem habent. Et hoc est quia omnes ille perfectiones conueniunt sibi secundum suum esse simplex . . . et ita Deus in ipso esse suo omnes perfectiones habet." What that text makes clear is this. God is *esse* and, for that very reason, is all-perfect; therefore, *esse* (in God, as well as in creatures) is itself a perfection—in fact, the perfection *par excellence*.

Bernard of Auvergne, Prior at the Dominican convent of Saint-Jacques in Paris in 1303, is a witness to the fact that from the very beginning of the controversy concerning the real distinction some conceived of *esse* as equivalent merely to essence-in-relationship-to-efficient-cause. For example: "Sed quod interim dicit [Henry of Ghent], quod essentia creaturae est essentia in quantum est formalis similitudo Dei et habet esse existentiae in quantum

its effect and thus remains extrinsic to it and is not a perfection of
the effect. Consequently, *esse* as an intrinsic perfective factor of existents is not identical with "essence-as-efficiently-caused," and the
objection collapses.

(e) Such, then, is the first manner in which Thomas undertakes
to establish that *esse* differs somehow from essence. Before the
challenge of various difficulties, it turns out to be a highly complicated process. It discloses that it does have an existential dimension;
that essence/*esse* are not to be identified with species/individual
or with essence-in-itself/essence-in-relation-to-efficient-cause; that
esse is rather an intrinsic and perfective factor within an existent:
that by which the existent actually is. The end result would seem to
be at least this—the implication that *esse* is a constituent of an existent and is genuinely (really?) other than essence.

(f) Finally, is this *intellectus essentiae* argument to be found in any
of Thomas' predecessors? Although he seems never to have claimed
them as *auctoritates* in this connection, both Alfarabi and Avicenna
have somewhat similar procedures.[20]

The *Genus* Argument

(5) Another way Aquinas uses to establish the otherness between *esse*/essence we can call the *genus* argument.

---

refertur ad ipsum ut ad causam efficientem, ita quod esse existentiae nihil
addit super essentiam nisi respectum. . . ." The text is found in Adriaan Pattin,
"La structure de l'être fini selon Bernard d'Auvergne, O.P. (+après 1307),"
Tijdschrift voor Philosophie 24 (1962), 731, l. 42 sq.

Another witness is Giles of Rome: "Secundo opinantes esse non esse rem
ab essentia realiter differentem dicere possent quod nihil est aliud ipsum esse
quam quidam respectus ad agens, ita quod eadem res est essentia et esse, sed
est essentia in se considerata, vel est essentia ut est res praedicamenti et ut
habet ideam in Primo; est autem esse ut est effectus agentis, ita quod esse
creatum nihil aliud addit super essentiam quam quemdam respectum ad
agens. Ergo secundum hunc modum loquendi, si quaeratur quare res creata
nunc habet esse et prius non habeat esse, dicetur quia nunc habet actualem
respectum ad agens et est effectus agentis, prius vero non erat huiusmodi
effectus, nec habebat hunc actualem respectum." See Edgar Hocedez, S.J.,
Aegidii Romani Theoremata de Esse et Essentia (Louvain: Museum Lessianum,
1930), p. 125, lines 10–21.

[20] On Alfarabi, see E. Gilson, *History of Christian Philosophy*, p. 186; on
Avicenna, see D. Saliba, *Étude sur la métaphysique d'Avicenne* (Paris: Les
Presses Universitaires, 1926), pp. 79–80.

In Sent., Text B: Omne quod est in genere habet quidditatem differentem ab esse. . . . Et ratio hujus est quia commune, quod praedicatur de his quae sunt in genere, praedicat quidditatem, cum genus et species praedicentur in eo quod quid est. Illi autem quidditati non debetur esse nisi per hoc quod suscepta est in hoc vel in illo. Et ideo quidditas generis vel speciei non communicatur secundum unum esse omnibus sed solum secundum unam rationem communem. Unde constat quod esse suum non est quidditas sua.

Ibid., d. 19, q. 4, a. 2 sol.: In divinis non potest esse universale et particulare. . . . Primo, quia, secundum Avicennam, II parte *Logicae,* cap. ii, ubicumque est genus et species, oportet esse quidditatem differentem a suo esse, ut prius dictum est. . . .

Ibid., Text H: Non oportet illud quod est in praedicamento substantiae habere quidditatem compositam sed oportet quod habeat compositionem quidditatis et esse; omne enim quod est in genere suae quidditatis non est suum esse, ut Avicenna, *Meta.,* tract. VIII, c. iv, etc., dicit.

Ibid., Text I: Secundum Avicennam, ubi supra [*Meta.,* tract. V, cap. v, vi, vii], omne id quod habet esse aliud a sua quidditate oportet quod sit in genere; et ita oportet quod omnes angeli ponantur in praedicamento substantiae, prout est praedicamentum, cum secundum Avicennam, *loc. cit.,* sit res quidditatem habens, cui debeatur esse per se, non in alio, scilicet quod sit aliud a quidditate ipsa.

Ibid., Text J: Ut Avicenna dicit in sua Metaph., tract. II, c. 1 et tract. VI, c. v, ad hoc quod aliquid sit proprie in genere substantiae requiritur quod sit res quidditatem habens cui debeatur esse absolutum ut per se esse dicatur vel subsistens. . . . Anima autem rationalis habet esse absolutum, non dependens a materia, quod est aliud a sua quidditate, sicut etiam de angelis dictum est; et ideo relinquitur quod sit in genere substantiae sicut species, et etiam sicut principium, inquantum est forma hujus corporis.

De Ver., Text E: Omne quod est in genere substantiae est compositum reali compositione; eo quod id quod est in praedicamento substantiae est in suo esse subsistens, et oportet quod esse suum sit aliud quam ipsum, alias non posset differre secundum esse ab illis cum quibus convenit in ratione suae quidditatis; quod requiritur in omnibus quae sunt directe in praedicamento: et ideo omne quod est directe in praedicamento substantiae, compositum est saltem ex esse et quod est.

(a) What can be said as a commentary on those passages? Unlike his practice with respect to the *intellectus essentiae* process (see #4f above), here he repeatedly acknowledges Avicenna as his authority.[21]

(b) Of the six passages within which the *genus* argument is found, only two explain it somewhat (*In Sent.*, Text B; *De Ver.*, Text E), while the others are content merely to state it. What is the structure of that argumentation?

Genus and species express what things are (*In Sent.*, Text B);
But what things are is that which they have in common (*ibid.;*
    De Ver., Text E);
Therefore, things have in common the fact that they belong to
    such and such a species and genus: this man and that man
    agree in the fact that each is a man; this man and that dog
    agree in the fact that each is an animal;
But the whatness which things entail has *esse* only in indi-
    viduals (*In Sent.*, Text B: Illi autem quidditati non debetur
    esse nisi per hoc quod suscepta est in hoc vel in illo; *In I Sent.*,
    d. 2, q. 1, a. 4 ad 1: [Essentia creata] secundum illud esse
    non est nisi in uno tantum habente);
But individuals are different, unique;
Therefore, the whatness which things entail also involves dif-
    ference and uniqueness, and this through *esse* (*De Ver.*, Text
    E: alias non posset differre secundum esse ab illis . . .);
Therefore, the whatness which things entail
    is that in which they both agree and differ,
    is that which is at once common and unique:

---

[21] Despite Aquinas' frequent references, it is difficult to find Avicenna explicitly stating the *genus* argument as such. The closest he comes to that statement is *Metaphysica*, tr. VIII, c. 4: "Primus etiam non habet genus; primus enim non habet quidditatem sed quod non habet genus non est genus; genus respondetur ad interrogationem per quid est; genus etiam aliquo modo pars est rei; certissimum est autem quod primus non est compositus."

> *common* insofar as it is generic and specific—that is, ultimately it is the basis for intelligibilities predicable of all (*In I Sent.*, d. 2, q. 1, a. 4 ad 1: Essentia creata communicatur . . . tantum secundum rationem suam et non secundum esse; *Ibid.*, Text B: Quidditas generis vel speciei non communicatur secundum unum esse omnibus sed solum secundum unam rationem communem);
> *unique* insofar as it is individual and has *esse* (*ibid.*);
> Therefore, the fact that things are individual and have *esse* and yet also belong to a genus and species
> indicates that in them *esse* is other than whatness (*In Sent.*, B: Unde constat quod esse suum non est quidditas sua);
> points to the composition in them of *esse* and whatness (*De Ver.*, Text E: . . . compositum reali compositione . . . compositum est saltem ex esse et quod est).

(c) Is this complex and awkward line of reasoning conclusive? Obviously, this process would make no sense at all to anyone who refuses to see things as a merger of community/difference. A nominalist is such a one, according to whom actual existents are entirely and absolutely different from one another. The only community between (say) men is the term "human." There is no common human essence. Solely individuals *as individuals* are real. A Platonist is also such a one but for a different reason. Individuals as such are unreal. Their sole function is to reflect the subsistent and separate essences of Man, Dog and so on, which alone are really real and which are self-contained, self-concentrated, self-identical, monolithic, etc.

But even to someone who views actual existents as genuine combinations of community/difference, need the process indicate more than a composition within the quiddity? In the last analysis, this would be that of substantial form (that by which [say] this man is *human*) and of prime matter (that by which he is *this* human). True enough, I would answer, in other authors and with other formulations of the argument. But that is not Thomas' position. For him the process does not point to a composition merely within the quiddity but also within the existent—that between quiddity and *esse*, between *id quod est* and *id quo est*. But even so, why must *esse* mean the act of existing? Why could not it refer simply to essence-as-individual? In this interpretation essence/*esse* would be identical with essence-as-specific/essence-as-individual, with essence-as-common/essence-as-unique. But this cannot stand for the simple fact that for Thomas the relationship of essence/*esse* is that of potency/ act, whereas essence-as-specific is related to essence-as-individual as act to potency (see #4d above).[22]

(d) Here, then, is the picture as I see it. According to Aquinas actual existents involve both community and disparity in what they are—for example, these men are similar as *men* but differ as *these* men. This similarity/difference is not fully explained solely by the composition of substantial form/prime matter within the essence but also rests upon an outside factor: namely, *esse*, that by which each individual actually exists, that by which both form and matter are actualized and are thus enabled to exercise their intrinsic causality of specifying and individuating.

No great surprise should be felt when *esse* is closely linked with the individual essence as individual: a great affinity lies between them. Each is to be found only on the level of the concrete, the actual, the existential. What actually receives and limits *esse* is not quiddity in its generic or specific status (as such it is intramental) but an individuated quiddity. And what *esse* actualizes is this or that individual quiddity and not a specific or generic quiddity.[23]

---

[22] Joseph de Finance also grants that in the texts of the *genus* argument one can interpret essence/*esse* as essence-as-specific/essence-as-individual (*op. cit.*, p. 95): "On pourrait donc se demander si ces textes ne visent pas la distinction de la 'nature' et du 'suppôt' plutôt que celle de l'essence et de l'existence." He eliminates this interpretation by recalling the fact that Thomas applies this argument also to angels, where there is no question of individuals sharing the same specific nature. Accordingly, the essence/*esse* composition of which Thomas speaks is more than that of matter/form: it is a composition of essence/act of existing. See *ibid.*, p. 96.

De Finance's elimination is not entirely adequate. Granted that in the angelic ranks there are no individuals within a species. Still, could not essence/*esse* be simply an angelic-essence-as-indeterminately-viewed/the-same-essence-as-determinately-viewed? Or even as an angelic-essence-in-itself/the-same-essence-as-efficiently-caused-by-God?

On how genus and difference are to be found in angels, see *De Ente et Essentia*, c. 5, p. 379, 1. 85; *In II Sent.*, 3, 1, 5 solutio (pp. 99–100).

[23] It may help to recall that material existents involve two kinds of community/diversity, one of which looks to specific perfections (e.g., "man"), the other to being. With regard to the first, the substantial form is the principle of community (e.g., because of his human soul each of these ten men is human), whereas prime matter is the basic principle of diversity through individuation. But since substantial form and prime matter can perform their intrinsic causal functions of specifying and of individuating only if and as actualized,

An adequate understanding of Thomas' *genus* argument requires, then, that we bring to it a great deal of his metaphysics. This should not be surprising, though, because with a different metaphysics the process itself would have been developed quite differently.

God-to-Creatures Argument

(6) A third way by which Aquinas attempts to establish the difference between *esse*/essence can be designated as the "God to creatures" argument. Each of the several occurrences of this line of reference is so disparate that it seems best to study them separately.

(a) The first (*In Sent.*, Text C) is found in his answer to whether every creature is simple ("Utrum aliqua creatura sit simplex"). Thomas intends to safeguard the simplicity of prime matter and other components, as well as of universals ("materia prima . . . forma quaelibet . . . universale"): they are creatures but are not composite. Hence he distinguishes them from supposits. The relevant sentences occur when he describes the latter.

> Quaedam [creatura] enim est quae habet esse completum in se, sicut homo et hujusmodi, et talis creatura ita deficit a simplicitate divina quod incidit in compositionem. Cum enim in solo Deo esse suum sit sua quidditas, oportet quod in qualibet creatura, vel in corporali vel in spirituali, inveniatur quidditas vel natura sua et esse suum, quod est sibi acquisitum a Deo, cujus essentia est suum esse; et ita componitur ex esse vel quo est, et quod est.

(b) The structure of the inference is clear:

> [A creature differs from God;]
> But in God alone essence is *esse;*

---

esse mediately and ultimately accounts for both community and diversity within a species. See my *Authentic Metaphysics*, pp. 119–29.

With regard to community/diversity in being, *esse* is a common perfection of all beings (for example, see *In Sent.*, Text F; *De Ver.*, Text F; *In de Hebdomad.*, lect. 2, #34): however diverse existents may be in *what* they are, nonetheless they are all similar at least in *that* they all do actually *exist*. Nevertheless, *esse* is also unique in each existent inasmuch as it is determined and limited by the essence of each existent it actualizes and each such essence is unique, diverse, individual.

> Therefore, in every creature essence is not *esse*, which comes
> to him from God;
> Therefore, every creature is composed of *id quod est* and *esse*.

This procedure is to be expected of an author who conceives of a
theologian's proper task as proceeding from God to creatures[24] and
who is here writing a theological treatise. Moreover, the authority
he cites in the *sed contra* of the very text under discussion proceeds
in a similar manner.

> Contra. Boethius, I *De Trinitate*, cap. ii, "In omni eo quod est
> citra primum, differt et quod est et quo est." Sed omnis creatura
> est citra primum. Ergo est composita ex esse et quod est.

(c) But an important question still remains. How does Thomas
establish the minor of his argumentation? How does he know that
in God alone essence is *esse?* Just previously he had faced that
problem and had replied that God *is* His *esse* because the first principle of being must *be* in the best possible manner.

> Illud quod est primum principium essendi nobilissimo modo
> habet esse, cum semper sit aliquid nobilius in causa quam in
> causato. Sed nobilissimus modus habendi esse est quo totum
> aliquid est suum esse. Ergo Deus est suum esse.[25]

He had, moreover, three authorities on his side, all of whom he
cites in texts from *In Sent.*

---

[24] See *In I Sent.*, Prologus, 1, 1: "Utrum praeter physicas disciplinas alia
doctrina sit homini necessaria," solutio (p. 8): ". . . tota cognitio philosophica
quae ex rationibus creaturarum procedit. . . . Homo manuducatur ad illam
contemplationem in statu viae per cognitionem non a creaturis sumptam sed
immediate ex divino lumine inspiratam; et haec est doctrina theologiae." *Ibid.*,
a. 4: "Utrum Deus sit subjectum istius scientiae," solutio (p. 16): "Omnia enim
quae in hac scientia considerantur sunt aut Deus aut ea quae ex Deo et ad
Deum sunt, inquantum hujusmodi." *In II Sent.*, Prologus, p. 1: "Creaturarum
consideratio pertinet ad theologos et ad philosophos sed diversimode.
Philosophi enim creaturas considerant secundum quod in propria natura
consistunt; unde proprias causas et passiones rerum inquirunt; sed theologus
considerat creaturas secundum quod a primo principio exierunt et in finem
ultimum ordinantur qui Deus est."

[25] *In I Sent.*, 8, 4, 1, sed contra 3 (p. 218 sq.).

Boethius, *De Trinitate*, c. 2: "Divina substantia est ipsum esse, et ab ea est esse" (the lines immediately adjacent to this are cited in the *sed contra* of *In Sent.*, Text C);

Hilary, *De Trinitate*, VII, 11: "Esse non est accidens Deo, sed subsistens veritas et manens causa et naturalis generis proprietas" (cited in *In Sent.*, Text A);

Exodus, III, 14: "Ego sum qui sum. Sic dices filiis Israel: Qui est misi me ad vos" (cited in *In I Sent.*, d. 8, q. 1, a. 1 contra [p. 194]).

(d) Thomas asserts, then, that the divine essence *is esse* because of his own theological reflection upon God as primal being and because of the three authorities alluded to.[26] But the fact still remains that both his theological reflection and the exegesis of his authorities must rest upon a prior recognition of what *esse* is and of what being is. Although divine revelation may state (at least, imply) that God is being, still it does not explicate what is meant by "being" or *esse*. Hence, whence came that recognition? Through what sort of process? By what type of reflection? On this point Thomas is silent. In view of his constant position that human knowledge begins with the senses,[27] though, his awareness of *esse* and being could apparently have been triggered only by contact with sensible existents. True, meditation upon *Exodus* 3:14 and other Scripture texts may have been the occasion of that awareness, which accordingly may have come to Thomas the theologian, but its basic source is his

---

[26] These same three authorities Thomas adduces in later works—for example, see *S.C.G.*, I, c. 22 ("Quod in Deo idem est esse et essentia") (Leonine manual ed., p. 24c).

[27] For example, see *In II Sent.*, 3, 3, 1 solutio (p. 113): "In intellectu vero humano similitudo rei intellectae est aliud a substantia intellectus et est sicut forma ejus . . . ; *et huius similitudo est accepta a re.*" *Ibid.*, 3 ad 1 (p. 121): "Unde lumen intellectuale in eo [intellectu humano] receptum non est sufficiens ad determinandum propriam rei cognitionem *nisi per species a rebus receptas.*" *Ibid.*, 4 ad 4 (p. 124): "Intellectus possibilis in nobis est in potentia respectu *specierum acceptarum a rebus* per lumen intellectus agentis actu intelligibiles factas." *Ibid.*, 39, 3, 1 solutio (p. 936): "Et quia rationalis anima corpori conjuncta est, ideo cognitio debita sibi secundum suum proprium ordinem est cognitio *quae a sensibilibus* in intelligibilia procedit." Also see *De Ver.*, 10, 6 resp. (Leonine ed., p. 312, 183); *ibid.*, 11, 1 resp. (p. 350, 264).

direct perception of himself and other actual material existents. To be real is to be actual, *esse* is that by which an actual existent is actual and thereby real, being is any actually existing item—all these realizations are grounded upon the only experience of actuality a human knower has: the actuality embedded in the visible universe.

In the God-to-creatures process under discussion, then, Thomas does move from the identity of essence/*esse* in God to their otherness in creatures. But this movement itself rests, I would say, upon a prior realization of the nature of *esse* and being which has issued from his reflection upon sensible existents.[28] This realization is as

---

[28] What sort of knowledge is this prior realization? Is it philosophical or theological? No easy or simple answer can be given.

Certainly, it involves an induction, because the knower has moved from sensible existents to an intellectual and technical awareness of *esse* and of being. But is that induction purely philosophical? If the methodology of theology is to go from God to creatures and that of philosophy to go in an opposite direction, and if the two movements are absolutely incompatible, then it would have to be described as philosophical. But that absolute incompatibility is very dubious, since some psychological processes actually center upon God as revealed, initiate a general movement from Him to creatures, and still have some moments of induction. For instance, when confronted with points in revelation which revelation does not itself clarify and explicate, the human knower turns to another source of illumination—the sensible universe. To give a parallel: the general direction of a moving boat may be downstream, but this fact does not prevent a passenger within the boat from walking upstream to the rear of the boat, while simultaneously being borne downstream by the boat itself. Similarly, a human knower may, in general, be concentrating upon God as divinely revealed and be understanding creatures in light of Him; nonetheless, he also can simultaneously be knowing God Himself better through insights and information derived inductively from creatures.

To return to our original question, then: what sort of knowledge is the realization which Thomas has of the nature of *esse* and of being and which grounds his theological reflection, as well as his exegesis of *Exodus* 3:14 and of patristic authorities? It is *inductive* because its immediate starting point is himself and other actual material existents. But it is *theological* because it occurs within the more comprehensive psychological process Thomas initiates to understand the data of divine revelation. (Incidentally, this inductive dimension which Thomas imparts to his theology explains why a student of philosophy can read his theological treatises *and learn philosophy* and why Thomas revolutionized philosophy through his authentic existentialism without ever having written a purely philosophical treatise.)

See L. Sweeney, S.J., *Authentic Metaphysics*, pp. 73–81, especially pp. 80–81; also see ch. 2 above: "Can Philosophy Be Christian? Its Relationship to Faith,

latent as the steel girders in a modern apartment building but as necessary and as influential.

(7) The next instance of the God-to-creatures inference (*In Sent.*, Text D) is immediately subsequent to the previous one, but here the inquiry concerns the human soul (a. 2: "Utrum anima sit simplex"). It is while setting up the solution that the soul is not composed of matter/form but of *id quod est/esse* that Thomas writes the relevant lines.

> Cum autem de ratione quidditatis vel essentiae non sit quod sit composita vel compositum, consequens poterit inveniri et intelligi aliqua quidditas simplex, non consequens compositionem formae et materiae. Si autem inveniamus aliquam quidditatem quae non sit composita ex materia et forma, illa quidditas aut est esse suum aut non. Si illa quidditas sit esse suum, sic erit essentia ipsius Dei, quae est suum esse, et erit omnino simplex. Si vero non sit ipsum esse, oportet quod habeat esse acquisitum ab alio, sicut est omnis quidditas creata. Et quia haec quidditas posita est non subsistere in materia, non acquiretur sibi esse in altero, sicut quidditatibus compositis, immo acquiretur sibi esse in se; et ita ipsa quidditas erit hoc "quod est" et ipsum esse suum erit "quo est."

Our author here proceeds almost dialectically.

> A simple quiddity either is or is not *esse*;
> If it is *esse*, then it is the divine essence and is totally simple;
> If it is not *esse*, then it has acquired *esse* from God and is a created essence.

This procedure, like the previous instance (#6d), presupposes a prior position on *esse* and is little more than a contrast between God and a creature.

(8) In contrast to the last instance of the God-to-creatures argument, the current one (*De Ente et Essentia*, c. 4) is complicated. It should more accurately be described as a God-to-angels argument, since the otherness between *esse*/essence with which Aquinas is mainly concerned is not in creatures generally but in angels, as this analysis indicates.

Theology and Religion?" prgrs. subsequent to n. 5 and corresponding to notes 12–30. On induction see *Authentic Metaphysics*, pp. 329–33.

(a) The overall aim of chapter 4 in *De Ente et Essentia* is to investigate the sort of essence to be found in separate substances ("videre per quem modum sit essentia in substantiis separatis").[29] Such an essence does not involve a composition of matter and form but is simple: it is only a form.[30] Nevertheless, such an existent is not entirely simple or a pure act; rather, it is a composite of act/potency.[31]

(b) The key passage follows and consists of three steps.

First Stage

(b1) The *esse* of a material existent is other than what it is because one can know what such a thing is without knowing that it actually exists (*ibid.*, p. 376, 94–99—see #4 above).

(b2) Such otherness is the case of every existent unless there should perhaps be something whose essence is *esse* (*ibid.*, l. 103: "Nisi forte sit aliqua res cuius quidditas sit ipsum suum esse").

(b3) Such an existent must be unique and primal (*ibid.*, l. 104: "Et hec res non potest esse nisi una et prima . . . ").

(b4) Accordingly, if this should be true, in all else *esse* is other than essence and, hence, this state of affairs holds true also in intelligences: in them *esse* is other than form and, thus, an intelligence is a composite of form and *esse*.

Si autem ponatur aliqua res que sit esse tantum ita ut ipsum esse sit subsistens, hoc esse non recipiet additionem differentie quia iam non esset esse tantum sed esse et preter hoc forma aliqua; et multo minus recipiet additionem materie quia iam esset esse non subsistens sed materiale. Unde relinquitur quod talis res que sit suum esse non potest esse nisi una. Unde oportet quod in qualibet alia re preter eam aliud sit esse suum et aliud quidditas uel natura seu forma sua. Unde oportet quod in intelligenciis sit esse preter formam, et ideo dictum est quod intelligencia est forma et esse (*ibid.*, p. 377, 113–26).

---

[29] Leonine ed., p. 375, 1–3. Although Thomas lists human souls, intelligences and God as separate substances ("in substantiis separatis, scilicet in anima et in intelligencia et in prima causa"), still the two crucial paragraphs deal solely with intelligences or angels.

[30] *Ibid.*, p. 376, 33–40.

[31] *Ibid.*, lines 90–93.

Second Stage

(b5) But is the existence of a Being whose essence is *esse* merely hypothetical? No, because material things actually do exist and in them *esse* is other than essence and thus is efficiently caused not by the essence itself but from without: by an Existent who *is esse*.

> Non autem potest esse quod ipsum esse sit causatum ab ipsa forma uel quiditate rei, causatum dico sicut a causa efficiente, quia sic aliqua res esset causa sui ipsius et aliqua res seipsam in esse produceret, quod est impossibile. Ergo oportet quod omnis talis res cuius esse est aliud quam natura sua habeat esse ab alio. Et quia omne quod est per aliud reducitur ad illud quod est per se sicut ad causam primam, oportet quod sit aliqua res que sit causa essendi omnibus rebus ex eo quod ipsa est esse tantum; alias iretur in infinitum in causis, cum omnis res que non est esse tantum habeat causam sui esse, ut dictum est (*ibid.*, p. 377, 127–43).

(b6) Hence, an intelligence is a composite of form and *esse*—this is not a hypothesis but a fact.

> Patet ergo quod intelligencia est forma et esse et quod esse habet a primo ente quod est esse tantum, et hec est causa prima que Deus est (*ibid.*, lines 143–46).

Third Stage

(b7) This composition of form/*esse* in an intelligence is one of potency/act (*ibid.*, 11. 147–53; for a study of potency and act, see #16 below).

(c) Such, then, are the three stages within the relevant lines of *De Ente*, chapter 4:

First: There is at least a hypothetical otherness and composition of form/*esse* in intelligences—if God exists, one has the unique case where essence is *esse*; in intelligences (and, for that matter, in all else except God) essence is other than *esse*.

Second: But the otherness and composition of form/*esse* in intelligence is not merely a hypothesis but a fact since God does exist, as is clear from the existence of material things and the otherness in them of *esse*/essence (known through the *intellectus essentiae* argumentation).

Third: This composition of form/*esse* in intelligences is one of potency/act.

(d) In *De Ente*, chapter 4, then, Aquinas uses two ways to establish the difference between *esse*/essence. The first is the *intellectus essentiae* line of reasoning with respect to material existents (see #4 above). This is also the initial phase of a creatures-to-God process, since he uses the difference between *esse*/essence in sensible existents to prove that God exists and that His essence is *esse*. The second is the God-to-intelligences argument under discussion.

De Ente et Essentia has been acclaimed as containing "if not *the* typical, at least *a* typical instance of Thomistic metaphysical procedure" and to which perhaps "the other expressions of Thomistic metaphysical procedure may in one way or another . . . be reduced."[32] I cannot agree. Although the *intellectus essentiae* argumentation may possibly be conclusive, it is not compelling because of the complications latent within it (see #4c sq.). Thomas himself seems not to have used it widely except in his early treatises. The God-to-intelligences argumentation is obviously restricted to intelligences and is not directly metaphysical but theological.[33]

(9) The next instance of the God-to-creatures inference (*In Sent.*, Text G) perhaps underwrites my interpretation of the preceding one because it also moves from God to angels, and this in a rather closely parallel fashion.

(a) Is an angel composed of matter and form? No, although he does entail a composition. In developing his position, Thomas moves from material existents to God and then back to creatures and, especially, to angels, as this exegesis shows.

(a1) Some natures (a phoenix, eclipse and so on—[in general, any material thing]) are such that *esse* is not contained within their intelligibilities, as is clear from the fact that one can know what they are and yet be unaware of whether they actually are (see #4 above).

(a2) But [on the strength of the fact that material things do exist and are other than their *esse*] one discovers another nature in whose intelligibility *esse* is included—indeed, *esse* is His very nature. Here *esse* is not acquired from someone else but from Himself.

---

[32] J. Owens, "Note on the Approach to Thomistic Metaphysics," *New Scholasticism* 28 (October 1954), 468.

[33] Obviously, this argumentation is valuable in a Thomistic angelology: since we do not sensibly perceive angels, how else could one establish that in an angel *esse* is really other than essence?

Alia autem natura invenitur de cujus ratione est ipsum suum esse, immo ipsum esse est sua natura. Esse autem quod hujusmodi est, non habet esse acquisitum ab alio, quia illud quod res ex sua quidditate habet, ex se habet.

(a3) But everything which is not God has *esse* acquired from another—that is, from God. Therefore, in God alone *esse* is quiddity; in all else *esse* is other than quiddity, which however acquires *esse*.

Sed omne quod est praeter Deum habet esse acquisitum ab alio. Ergo in solo Deo suum esse est sua quidditas vel natura; in omnibus autem aliis esse est praeter quidditatem, cui esse acquiritur.

(a4) But a quiddity which is itself composed is not the *id quod est* or supposit but only that by which the supposit is something or other ("id quo [id quod est] aliquid est, ut humanitate est homo"). Yet a simple quiddity, such as that of an angel, is itself *id quod subsistit*, and *esse*, which is other than the quiddity, is that by which it is (*id quo est*). Therefore, an angel is a composite of *esse* and *id quod est*, or of *id quo est* and *id quod est*, or, in the language of *Liber de Causis*, Prop. 9, of *esse* and form.

Sed quidditas simplex, cum non fundetur ex aliquibus partibus, subsistit in esse quod sibi a Deo acquiritur; et ideo ipsa quidditas angeli est quod subsistit; etiam ipsum suum esse, quod est praeter suam quidditatem, est id quo est; . . . et sic angelus compositus est ex esse et quod est, vel ex quo est et quod est; et propter hoc in lib. *De Causis*, propos. 9, dicitur, quod intelligentia non est esse tantum, sicut causa prima, sed est in ea esse et forma, quae est quidditas sua.

(a5) This composition of *esse*/forma is also a composition of act/potency.

(b) Such, then, is *In Sent.*, Text G, and its similarity to *De Ente*, chapter 4, is rather striking. Its question is basically the same: is an angel composed of matter/form? If not, is he in any way a composite of act/potency? Its structure is similar. It originates with the otherness in material things of *esse*/essence, which is established by the *intellectus essentiae* argument (#a1) and then ascends to God, where alone essence and *esse* are identical (#a2). Thence one returns to creatures (#a3) and, above all, to angels (#4), where *esse* is not

essence and who are now known to be composed of *esse*/essence
(#a4) as act/potency (#a5). Note too that *Liber de Causis,* Prop. 9, is
the authority invoked both here and in *De Ente* (p. 32, l. 3).

True, there are dissimilarities. For example, in *De Ente* the first
movement from material existents to God is hypothetical ("Nisi
forte . . . Si autem. . . ."), with an ensuing initial conditional otherness between *esse*/form in intelligences. Again, the phases of the
argument in *In Sent.* are somewhat less clearly defined and, at times,
are only implied. But the resemblance between the two overcomes
such unlikenesses. Each offers the same two ways of grounding the
difference between *esse*/essence. The first has to do with material
things and is the *intellectus essentiae* inference, from which one rises
to God, where essence is *esse*. The second is the God-to-angels inference, which because of its restricted nature deploys on the strictly
theological level and is not intended to replace properly metaphysical attempts to substantiate the otherness between *esse*/es-
sence in existents we directly perceive.

(10) The last instance of the God-to-creatures argument (*Quodl.,*
Text C) is again a God-to-angels process.

(a) Are angels composed of matter and form? No, because any
sort of materiality is repugnant to the fact that they are intellectual
beings and are incorporeal. Are they, then, simple? The relevant
lines are an answer to that question.

> Sed quia substantia angeli non est suum esse (hoc enim soli
> Deo competit, cui esse debetur ex seipso, et non ab alio);
> invenimus in angelo et substantiam sive quidditatem eius,
> quae subsistit, et esse eius, quo subsistit, quo scilicet actu
> essendi dicitur esse, sicut actu currendi dicimur currere. Et sic
> dicimus angelum esse compositum ex quo est et quod est, vel
> secundum Boethii ex esse et quod est.

(b) As I read that passage, the structure of the argument is clear.

> God is the sole instance of an existent where *esse* comes not from
>   another but from Himself;
> [But what comes from oneself is identical with oneself;]
> Therefore, God alone is *esse;*
> Therefore, the substance of an angel is not *esse;*
> Therefore, an angel involves both substance or quiddity and
>   *esse;*
> Therefore, an angel is composed of *id quod est* and *id quo est* or
>   *esse;*

But the angelic substance is related to *esse* as potency to act;
Therefore, an angel is composed of potency/act.

(c) A couple of questions suggest themselves, the first of which concerns the major premise. Why with reference to God does *esse* come from Himself and not from another? No answer is given in the text itself. Elsewhere (for example, *In Sent.*, Text G) the reason is that the divine essence is *esse*, which scarcely is acceptable here since in the current text the identity of *esse*/essence is a consequence of the self-origin of the divine *esse*.

The second question has to do with the first minor. Why is what comes from oneself identical with oneself?[34] The answer given in *De Ver.*, Text A, is merely a negative restatement: whatever one possesses from another and not from himself is other than his essence ("Omne autem quod aliquid habet non a seipso sed ab altero est ei praeter essentiam").[35] More explicit information has not yet been uncovered.

(d) Although *Quodl.*, Text C, may be ambiguous on those two points, still it clearly differentiates *esse* from essence by stating that although *esse* is an act, it is not an act which is a part of essence, it is not a form ("et ipsum esse sit actus . . . esse non est actus qui sit pars essentiae, sicut forma").

Participation Argument

(11) In *Quodl.*, Text C, we are finished with instances of the God-to-creatures inference. Let us now turn to another and final manner in which he undertakes to validate the difference between *esse*/essence and which we can term the participation argument. This is closely linked with the God-to-creatures texts because most of the

---

[34] The proposition can hardly be classed as self-evident since intellect and will come from the human soul (and, for that matter, all operative powers and other properties from their subjects) and yet are really distinct from the soul. For example, see *In I Sent.*, 7, 1, 1 ad 2 (p. 177): "Egreditur etiam ab essentia alius actus . . . et iste est actus secundus et dicitur operatio. Et inter essentiam et talem operationem cadit virtus media differens ab utroque, in creaturis etiam realiter, in Deo ratione."

A somewhat similar proposition is found in *In Sent.*, Text G: "Illud quod res ex sua quidditate habet, ex se habet."

[35] Thomas continues: "And thus does Avicenna show that in every being except the First Being *esse* is other than essence—*Et per hunc modum probat Avicenna quod esse cuiuslibet rei praeter primum ens est aliquid praeter essentiam ipsius, quia omnia ab alio esse habent.*"

sections in which Thomas develops his doctrine on *esse*/essence according to the rubric of participation also set up parallels between God and creatures.

He does not seem to have applied this rubric to the *esse*/essence problem at the beginning of his early treatises, since the instances so far discovered include only *In II Sent.*, d. 16 (see Text K above), *ibid.*, d. 37 (Text M), *De Veritate*, 21, 5 (Text C) and *In Boethii de Hebdomadibus*, lectio 2.[36] These instances are so disparate that we shall handle each separately.

Let us begin with the last, which could easily be contemporaneous with the other three[37] and which will enable us to understand them better by providing information on participation in general.

(a) If we view *esse* and *id quod est* in their concepts (*loc. cit.*, #22: "Quae diversitas non est hic referenda ad res . . . sed ad ipsas rationes seu intentiones"), Thomas begins, how do they differ? As the *participatum* and *participans*, he replies, and the relevant lines follow.

Est autem participare quasi partem capere; [a] et ideo quando aliquid particulariter recipit id quod ad alterum pertinet universaliter, dicitur participare illud; sicut homo dicitur participare animal quia non habet rationem animalis secundum totam communitatem; et eadem ratione Socrates participat hominem; [b] similiter etiam subjectum participat accidens et materia formam, quia forma substantialis vel accidentalis, quae de sui ratione communis est, determinatur ad hoc vel ad illud subjectum; [c] et similiter effectus dicitur participare suam causam, et praecipue quando non adaequat virtutem suae

---

[36] This is not to say that participation is missing from Thomas' early texts (see L.-B Geiger, O.P., *La participation dans la philosophie de S. Thomas d'Aquin* [Paris: J. Vrin, 1942], pp. 489–90, for a list of texts from *In I Sent.*), but that he seemingly begins to use it with reference to *esse*/essence only in *In II Sent.*, Text K. For background on participation see my *Divine Infinity in Greek and Medieval Thought* (New York/Bern: Peter Lang Publishing, Inc., 1992), chs. 3–4 and 12 (on Plato and Proclus).

[37] Thomas probably began composition of *In de Hebdomadibus* after completing *In I Sententiarum* and certainly before 1260–61. See I. Eschmann, *op. cit.*, p. 406. Let me note: *In de Hedomaoibus*, #24, reproduced in the following prgr., lists three sorts of participation, which I have there distinguished by bracketed and italicized letters—[a], [b], [c]—so as in my subsequent commentary to indicate that such italicized letters refer back to the divisions of the Latin text.

causae; puta, si dicamus quod aër participat lucem solis, quia non recipit eam in ea claritate qua est in sole (*ibid.*, #24).

(b) In the light of those lines, what is participation? Basically, it is possessing an item, but only partially, even though the item of itself is somehow common, general, unrestricted. This possession can be of at least three sorts. The first [*a*] has to do with universal notions. For example, the intelligibility of "man" *participates* "animal" because "man" is "animal," which, however, no longer retains its full generality but has become "rational animal." The second sort [*b*] has to do with substantial and accidental forms (and any other kind of act) and their recipients. In (say) this man prime matter *participates* human soul because, although it has become human through the soul's informing it, still he has become *this* human by the limitation and substantial individuation matter itself effects on the soul. A human person *participates* wisdom by becoming wise because, although he truly is wise, still his is not the wisdom of God or even of a Solomon by the very fact it is *his* wisdom. The last kind [*c*] concerns analogous causes and their effects. Shakespeare's *Hamlet* only *participates* the vision of beauty, emotional depths, imaginative force of the dramatist because for every facet of his poetic inspiration it does convey there are countless facets left unexpressed.

Participation, accordingly, involves these factors. [1] An item which of itself is common, general, ample, unencumbered, indeterminate, free and, in some cases at least, rich, perfect, noble [2] becomes part of another, [3] with the result that this other becomes perfected, enriched, filled out, ennobled [4] but the item itself becomes restricted, confined, limited, determined.[38] The item in question can be [a] an intelligibility, [b] any sort of form or act and [c] the perfection entailed in an analogous cause situation.

(c) But let us return to the text. If we now view *esse* and *id quod est* in what they actually are (#31: "hic autem ostendit quomodo applicetur ad res"), Thomas continues, what do we find? That they differ really and not merely conceptually in things whose essences are themselves composite. Why so? Because the *id quod est* of such a thing is itself composed (that is, of matter and form), whereas *esse*

---

[38] Accordingly, participation is not any sort of reception but only that by which what is received is limited and changed by its being received. For example, when someone catches a baseball, the ball is received but not participated. See n. 45 below.

itself is simple. Hence, in all such things the *id quod est* is really other than the *esse* which it participates.

> #32: Est ergo primo considerandum, quod sicut esse et quod est differunt in simplicibus secundum intentiones, ita in compositis differunt realiter; quod quidem manifestum est ex praemisis. Dictum est enim supra quod ipsum esse neque participat aliquid, ut eius ratio constituatur ex multis; neque habet aliquid extraneum admixtum, ut sit in eo compositio accidentis; et ideo ipsum esse non est compositum. Res ergo composita non est suum esse. Et ideo dicit quod in omni composito aliud est esse, et aliud ipsum compositum, quod est participatum [*read*: participans] ipsum esse.

(d) What of *esse* and *id quod est* in existents which are simple? They are really identical, for otherwise such an existent would no longer be simple but composite.

> #33: Ostendit qualiter se habet in simplicibus, in quibus est necesse quod ipsum esse et id quod est sit unum et idem realiter. Si enim esset aliud realiter id quod est et ipsum esse, iam non esset simplex sed compositum.

(e) Thomas next makes provision under that general rule for immaterial forms by calling them simple only with qualification (#34): "secundum quid simplex, inquantum caret aliqua compositione, quod tamen non est omnino simplex"). Such a form is simple to the extent that it is without matter, but it is other than *esse*, and, thus, such an existent is a composite of essence or form and esse. Why the otherness between form/*esse*? Because they are related to one another as the determinant to the determined and common, the recipient to the received, the participant to the participated. And this otherness holds true whether these immaterial forms are conceived after the manner of Plato or of Aristotle.

> #34: Si ergo inveniantur aliquae formae non in materia, unaquaeque earum est quidem simplex quantum ad hoc quod caret materia, et per consequens quantitate, quae est dispositio materiae; quia tamen quaelibet forma est determinativa ipsius esse, nulla earum est ipsum esse, sed est habens esse. Puta, secundum opinionem Platonis, ponamus formam immaterialem subsistere, quae sit idea et ratio hominum materialum, et

aliam formam quae sit idea et ratio equorum: manifestum erit quod ipsa forma immaterialis subsistens, cum sit quiddam determinatum ad speciem, non est ipsum esse commune, sed participat illud: et nihil differt quantum ad hoc, si ponamus illas formas immateriales altioris gradus quam sint rationes horum sensibilium, ut Aristoteles voluit: unaquaeque illarum, inquantum distinguitur ab alia, quaedam specialis forma est participans ipsum esse; et sic nulla earum erit vere simplex.

(f) The only existent who is truly simple is God, Who does not participate *esse* but is *esse.*

#35: Id autem erit solum vere simplex, quod non participat esse, non quidem inhaerens sed subsistens. Hoc autem non potest esse nisi unum. . . .

(12) Such is the first in the series of participation texts. It has both bad and good points. Among the former is the fact that the first consideration it offers of *esse* and *id quod est* is in terms of their concepts (*loc. cit.,* #22–#29). It investigates them as they actually are only after that consideration (*ibid.,* #31 sq.; see #11c above). Even in the latter investigation when establishing the real difference between *esse* and *id quod est* in material things, it utilizes what was elaborated in the former: because its *ratio* is simple and because it is free of accidents (#32), *esse* is itself simple and thus cannot be the *id quod est,* which is composite. Another troublesome and unusual feature is that with reference to immaterial forms Thomas does not speak of intelligences or angels but only of Platonic forms and of Aristotelian First Movers (see #11e).

Still, the passage is genuinely helpful for our study. It offers clear statements of the fact that *esse*/essence are really different (#32: "differunt realiter"; see above, #11c sq.). Above all, it provides a general doctrine of participation, which Eschmann calls "the starting-point for any study of the Thomistic notion of *participation* and the distinction between 'quod est' and 'esse.'"[39]

(13) The second text in the participation series is *In Sent.,* Text K, where the point of discussion is whether a creature is an image of God. No, according to *argumentum tertium,* because an image always connotes that an image and what is imaged have a unity, agreement, common ground ("convenientia quaedam cum aliquo

---

[39] I. Eschmann, *op. cit.,* p. 406, no. 41.

uno") in something prior and more simple. Such a situation obtains, Thomas replies, when two things are participating some one item. Thus "substance" (*ens in se*) and "accident" (*ens in alio*) both participate *ens*, which is prior to both; or "man" and "horse" both participate "animal," which is prior to each.[40] But the *convenientia* between God and creatures is different: it is that between what *is* an item simply and what is as much as possible like the other through participation of the perfection which the other *is*. Thus God is being because He is His *esse*; a creature is a being only by participating *esse*.

> Convenientia potest esse dupliciter: aut duorum participantium aliquod unum, et talis convenientia non potest esse Creatoris et creaturae, ut objectum est; aut secundum quod unum per se est simpliciter, et alterum participat de similitudine ejus quantum potest. . . . Et talis convenientia esse potest creaturae ad Deum, quia Deus dicitur ens hoc modo quod est ipsum suum esse; creatura vero non est ipsum suum esse, sed dicitur ens quasi ens participans; et hoc sufficit ad rationem imaginis.

(a) In the contrast this text sets up between God and creatures, it is similar to a God-to-creatures process on the question of *esse*/essence. God is *esse* and thus is Being; [but a creature is not God;] therefore, a creature is not *esse* and yet is named a being because it participates *esse*. Why is God *esse*? Thomas here offers no information.[41] Why is not a creature *esse*? Because, as we have said, a creature is other than God. Why does a creature participate *esse*? Not much information is given here, but Thomas' general position on participation sketched in *In de Hebdomadibus* (see #11b above) would suggest that a creature's participation of *esse* is of the second [*b*] sort. It is participation because a created existent does possess *esse* but only partially, in a limited and determined way. It is of the second sort because both the item participated (*esse*) and the participant are components: the former is act, the latter is a potency and recipient.

(b) A creature's participation of *esse* also involves the third [*c*] sort—that of an effect in its analogous cause. God is such a cause

---

[40] "Substance"/"accident" and "man"/"horse" are the examples given in the *argumentum tertium* to which Text K replies. In *In I Sent.*, Prol., 1, 2 ad 2 (p. 10), the examples are "potency"/"act" re "ens" and "substance"/"accident."

[41] On why Thomas holds God is *esse*, see #6c above.

and a creature is His effect. But God is *esse* and, thus, the perfection which God properly causes in each created existent is *esse*, which the existent receives and limits. Hence, a creature through its essence participates [*b*] *esse* because it possesses *esse* but not in the fullness of which *esse* is capable of and in itself. But when *esse* actually *is* of and in itself, it has the fullness, richness, amplitude of a subsistent being—namely, God, Who *is esse*.[42] Hence, by participating [*b*] *esse*, a creature also participates [*c*] God, Who as *Ipsum esse subsistens* is its efficient cause and its exemplar. It is like God, it is an *imago Dei*, it enjoys the *convenientia* of which Text K speaks: "convenientia . . . secundum quod unum per se est simpliciter et alterum participat de similitudine ejus quantum potest."

(c) As I read the text, then, one can find all three sorts of participation. The first [*a*] is exemplified in the situation existing between the intelligibilities of "substance," "accident" and "being"[43] (which also illustrates the first kind of *convenientia*). Both "substance" (*ens in se*) and "accident" (*ens in alio*) participate "being" because each confines, restricts, limits "being," which of itself is common, general, indeterminate. The second [*b*] and third [*c*] are found in the creature's participation of *esse*, as just discussed.

---

[42] *Esse*, as well as any other pure perfection, is a *participatum* which is unlike "animal" and other such mixed perfections, for the latter of and in themselves are only intramental awarenesses, whereas *esse* of and in itself is an extramental subsistent. See *In I Sent.*, Prol., 1, 2 ad 2 (p. 10): "Communitas potest esse . . . ex eo quod unum esse et rationem ab altero recipit; et talis est analogia creaturae ad Creatorem: creatura enim non habet esse nisi secundum quod a primo ente descendit, nec nominatur ens nisi inquantum ens primum imitatur; et similiter est de sapientia et de omnibus aliis quae de creatura dicuntur."

[43] What Aquinas has said in *In I Sent.*, Prol., 1, 2 ad 2 (p. 10) and *In Sent.*, Text K, might lead one to think that *ens*, if predicable of creatures, is not also predicable of God. But such a conclusion would be false since God is being *par excellence* (see, for example, *In Sent.*, Text M: "Illud tamen verissime et primo dicitur ens cujus esse est ipsum quod est, quia esse ejus non est receptum sed per se subsistens").

What, then, is to be said? *Ens* in relationship to substance and accident is other than, over and above, greater in comprehension than, either of them. But that situation does not hold with relationship to God and creatures. God *is* Being and here *ens* is not merely a *ratio* but also an extramental subsistent. This is the very point of *In I Sent.*, Prol., 1, 2 ad 2 ("creatura . . . nec nominatur ens nisi inquantum ens primum imitatur") and of *In Sent.*, Text K ("Deus dicitur ens hoc modo quod est ipsum suum esse; creatura vero non est ipsum suum esse, sed dicitur ens quasi ens participans").

(14) The third participation text (*In Sent.*, Text M) again contrasts God and creatures, while emphasizing God's function as cause.

(a) Is every existent from God? Thomas asks. Yes, and for this reason.

> Being is a perfection found in all existents and yet according to varying degrees;[44]
> But being is said in its primal and truest sense of God, the existent who is His *esse* (because here *esse* is not received but is subsistent);
> But whatever is primal is the cause of all else, where the perfection in question is found only through participation;
> Therefore, God is the cause of all other existents;
> But other existents, even the least, are beings but only in a derived sense (*per posterius*) inasmuch as they all participate *esse* which is other than themselves;
> Therefore, such an existent has whatever being it does have only from God and of itself it has nothing but deficiency in being.

Ens invenitur in pluribus secundum prius et posterius. Illud tamen verissime et primo dicitur ens cujus esse est ipsum quod est, quia esse ejus non est receptum sed per se subsistens. In omnibus autem quae secundum prius et posterius dicuntur, primum eorum quae sunt potest esse causa, et per se dictum est causa ejus quod per participationem dicitur; et ideo oportet quod illud ens quod non per participationem alicujus esse quod sit aliud quam ipsum, dicitur ens, quod primum inter entia est, sit causa omnium aliorum entium. Alia autem entia dicuntur per posterius, inquantum aliquod esse participant quod non est idem quod ipsa sunt, et haec procedunt usque ad ultima entium; ita quod quamcumque rationem essendi aliquid habeat, non sit sibi nisi a Deo sed defectus essendi sit ei a seipso.

---

[44] See *In Sent.*, Text F: "Invenitur enim in omnibus rebus natura entitatis, in quibusdam magis nobilis et in quibusdam minus." But notice that Thomas here proceeds to God not from participation but from the *intellectus essentiae* argument, for immediately thereafter he states: "Ipsarum rerum naturae non sunt hoc ipsum esse quod habent: alias esse esset de intellectu cujuslibet quidditatis, quod falsum est. . . . Ergo oportet quod ab aliquo esse habeant, et oportet devenire ad aliquid cujus natura sit ipsum suum esse; alias in infinitum procederetur."

(b) The underlying structure of the passage seems clear.

I: God is *esse* because his *esse* is unreceived and subsistent;
Therefore, God is primal being;
But what is primal is cause of all the rest;
Therefore, God is cause of all other beings, which *are* only through participation.

II: Other existents participate *esse*, which is other than themselves;
Therefore, other existents are beings in a derivative sense;
But what is derivative is caused;
Therefore, other existents are caused by God;
Therefore, other existents have being from God, nonbeing from themselves.

The thought-process turns on two pivotal truths: (I) God is *esse* because His *esse* is unreceived and subsistent and (II) Other existents participate *esse*, which is other than themselves. The second of these is dependent upon the first and, thus, the process is also a God-to-creatures inference. One knows that a creature participates *esse* because God is His *esse* and a creature is other than God.

Participation here is of the same two kinds as in the previous text (Text L; see #13 sq.). By participating [b] *esse*, the component and act, a creature also participates [c] God, Who is subsistent *esse*, and thus resembles God, its efficient and exemplary cause, to the extent that it is.

(15) The final participation passage to be considered (*De Ver.*, Text C) is brief and again sets up a parallel between God and creatures. The question under discussion is whether a creature is good through what it is (*per essentiam*). No, Thomas answers in the lines relevant to our study, because

Goodness has to do with the *esse* of an existent;
But the essence only of God is *esse*, whereas that of any creature is not *esse* but, rather, participates *esse* from another;
Hence, only God is pure *esse*, because He is subsistent *esse*; the *esse* of a creature is received or participated;
Hence, only God is goodness through His essence; a creature is good only through participation.

Essentialis enim bonitas . . . attenditur . . . secundum esse ipsius. . . . Ipsa autem natura vel essentia divina est eius esse;

natura autem vel essentia cuiuslibet rei creatae non est suum
esse, sed esse participans ab alio. Et sic in Deo est esse purum
quia ipse Deus est suum esse subsistens; in creatura autem est
esse receptum vel participatum. Unde dico quod si bonitas
absoluta diceretur de re creata secundum suum esse sub-
stantiale, nihilominus adhuc remaneret habere bonitatem per
participationem, sicut et habet esse participatum. Deus autem
est bonitas per essentiam inquantum eius essentia est suum
esse.

(a) The identity of *esse*/essence in God and their otherness in
creatures are used to solve another problem: that of how goodness
is found in God and creatures. Because of the contrast between
God and creatures, Thomas again moves apparently from their
identity in God to their otherness in creatures.

(b) What is participation in these lines? The same two sorts as
before (see above, #13a sq.; #14b), to judge by the phrase *esse
participans ab alio*. A creature participates [*c*] God, His cause, by
participating [*b*] *esse*, the component and act.

(c) One should also note that Thomas appears to make participation and reception equivalent ("in creatura autem est esse receptum
vel participatum"). If so, texts in terms of reception only[45] are to be
reduced to the participation series.

(16) Such, then, are at least four ways in which Aquinas endeavors to establish a difference between *esse*/essence in creatures: the
intellectus essentiae argument, the *genus* argument, the God-to-creatures inference, and the participation inference. Before formulating
general conclusions about that endeavor, let us first sketch what
Thomas states on act/potency, since such statements terminate
many of the texts previously studied.

Act and Potency

What, then, does he say concerning act and potency?

---

[45] Accordingly, texts in which Thomas discusses the *esse*/essence relationship in the language of *receptum/recipiens* can be considered as equivalent to
participatum/participans passages. For instance, see *In Sent.*, Text C (sed contra
2); *De Ver.*, Text D; *Quodl.*, Texts A and B. But see n. 38 above.

In Sent., Text D: Et quia omne quod non habet aliquid a se, est possibile respectu illius, hujusmodi quidditas cum habeat esse ab alio erit possibilis respectu illius esse, et respectu ejus a quo esse habet, in quo nulla cadit potentia; et ita in tali quidditate invenietur potentia et actus, secundum quod ipsa quidditas est possibilis et esse suum est actus eius.

De Ente et Essentia, c. 4: Omne autem quod recipit aliquid ab aliquo est in potentia respectu illius, et hoc quod receptum in eo est actus eius. Ergo oportet quod ipsa quiditas uel forma que est intelligencia sit in potentia respectu esse quod a Deo recipit, et illud esse receptum est per modum actus. Et ita inuenitur potencia et actus in intelligenciis.

In Sent., Text G: Et quia omne quod non habet aliquid ex se sed recipit illud ab alio est possibile vel in potentia respectu ejus, ideo ipsa quidditas est sicut potentia et suum esse acquisitum est sicut actus; et ita per consequens est ibi compositio ex actu et potentia.

In Boethii de Trinitate, 5, 4 ad 4: Sed quia non habet esse a se ipso angelus, ideo se habet in potentia ad esse quod accipit a deo, et sic esse a deo acceptum comparatur ad essentiam eius simplicem ut actus ad potentiam.

Quodl., Text B: Ex hoc aliquid est susceptivum formae substantialis vel accidentalis, quod aliquid habet possibilitatis: quia de ratione potentiae est ut actui substernatur, qui forma dicitur. . . . Omne quod non est suum esse, oportet quod habeat esse receptum ab alio, quod est sibi causa essendi. Et ita, in se consideratum, est in potentia respectu illius esse quod recipit ab alio. Et hoc modo ad minus potentialitatem ponere oportet in angelo, quia angelus non est suum esse, hoc enim solius Dei est.

Ibid., Text C: Et quia ipsa substantia angeli in se considerata est in potentia ad esse, cum habeat esse ab alio, et ipsum esse sit actus, ideo est in eo compositio actus et potentiae.

(a) As those excerpts make clear, Thomas uses both *possibile* (*In Sent.*, Text D) and *potentia* (*De Ente; In de Trin; Quodl.*, Text C) to express the counterpart of act, and this sometimes in one and the same text (*In Sent.*, Text G; *Quodl.*, Text B). Again, it is with regard to angels and human souls that he elaborates his doctrine on act/ potency in these texts on *esse*/essence, and this elaboration occurs only at the end of the texts when the difference between *esse*/ essence has somehow been grounded. None of them underwrites the practice of some Thomistic textbooks of beginning with act/ potency to establish the real distinction between *esse*/essence (for example, "Act and potency are really distinct; but *esse*/essence are act/potency; therefore. . . .").

(b) What determines whether one item is act and another is potency? To judge by these texts: if the existent does not have the item from itself but receives it from another, it is act and the recipient is potency. No other reasons are given. This approach to act/ potency is a sort of "extrinsicism": one realizes that *esse*/essence are act/potency not by what they are in themselves but by the relationship the existent has to God. This tends to set them entirely within the framework of efficient causality, of the effect-cause relation between the creature and God, of creaturehood.

(c) In fact, Thomas at least once seems to reduce potency to little more than Avicennian possibility. The question at issue is whether every creature is mutable. Yes, Thomas answers, because motion follows upon potency. Hence, all creatures are mutable since every creature entails some potency inasmuch as only God is pure act ("Cum igitur omnis creatura habeat aliquid de potentia, quid solus Deus est purus actus"). The notable section follows.

> Est autem considerare duplicem possibilitatem: unam secundum id quod creatura habet. . . . Prima consequitur creaturam secundum quod habet esse ab alio: omne quod esse suum ab alio habet non est per se necesse esse, ut probat Avicenna, tract. VIII *Metaphys.*, cap. liv; unde quantum est in se est possibile, et ista possibilitas dicit dependentiam ad id a quo est.[46]

---

[46] *In I Sent.*, 8, 3, 2 solutio (p. 213).

One curious effect of Thomas' conceiving act and potency in an "extrinsic" fashion is that he knows *esse*/essence to be act/potency only after he has established God's existence, although he knows *esse* to be other than essence (through the *intellectus essentiae* or the *genus* arguments) before that establishment. In this prior moment he also knows *esse*/essence to be *perficiens/perfectum* (see n. 19 above), without however realizing that that very fact shows them to be act/potency of a different stripe. This "intrinsic" conception of act/potency

A creature involves possibility, then, insofar as it has *esse* from another. But why the connection between possibility and its having *esse* from another? The very fact that it thus has *esse* indicates that it is not the *Necesse Esse* and, thus, must be possible and be dependent upon Him.

General Summary

(17) In retrospect, what points should one emphasize in Thomas' attitude to *esse*/essence in his early writings?

(a) Nowhere does he formulate the question "Utrum esse differat ab essentia" as the heading of a distinct *articulus* but always discusses the topic in connection with something else (see #1 above).

(b) In those discussions *esse* clearly has to do with actual existence and not with some kind of Boethian or Avicennian *forma totius* (see #4c).

(c) He frequently states that *esse* is other than essence (see #2). Although he generally does not explicitly characterize that otherness as real, still at least occasionally he leaves no doubt but that *esse* does differ from essence really and not merely conceptually. At times he unequivocally says so. For example, *esse* and *quod est* differ only intentionally in existents which are essentially simple but really in existents which are essentially composed ("sicut esse et quod est differunt in simplicibus secundum intentiones, ita in compositis differunt realiter" [*In de Hebdomadibus*, no. 32—see #11c above]). Or, again, whatever is found in the genus of substance involves a real composition, which is at least that of *esse* and *quod est* ("Omne quod est in genere substantiae est compositum reali compositione . . . compositum est saltem ex esse et quod est" [*De Ver.*, Text E ; see #5 above]).[47]

At other times he so contrasts *esse* with essence as at least to insinuate the same conclusion. Is an angel composed of matter and form? He is composed, Thomas replies (*Quodl.*, Text C), of potency and act because of his composition of quiddity and *esse*. If matter/form were synonymous with act/potency, then he would entail a

---

will be achieved only in his later treatises, where *esse*/essence can be known to be act/potency prior to his knowing God.

[47] Apparently, Thomas also explicitly characterizes the difference between *esse* and essence in an angel as real in *In Sent.*, Text E ("Actus autem qui mensuratur aevo, scilicet ipsum esse aeviterni, differt ab eo cujus est actus re quidem"). But the passage is so complex and enigmatic as to be of little use,

composition of matter/form. But an angelic quiddity is not synonymous with matter because of its self-subsistence, and *esse* is not
equivalent to form because although *esse* is an act ("esse eius, quo
subsistit, quo scilicet actu essendi dicitur esse, sicut actu currendi
dicimur currere . . . et ipsum esse sit actus"), still it is not such an
act as to be part of the essence ("esse non est actus qui sit pars
essentiae, sicut forma"). What is Thomas saying? That *esse* is an act
within the existent and, hence, is a constitutive part of it; still it is
an act which is outside of and not part of the essence. What is this
but to affirm that *esse* is really other than the essence?

In another passage *esse* is contrasted not merely with form but
with efficient cause as well. Unless a soul is composed of matter/
form as the recipient of life/the principle of life, the *argumentum*
runs, it would *be* life and thus would usurp God's privileged status.
Not so, Thomas replies (*In Sent.*, Text L), because a soul does involve a composition—namely, of form/*esse*. And *esse* is that by
which the soul *is* and *lives*, and yet it is not itself a form or any part
of the soul's essence. ("Unde sicut anima rationalis est nec est illud
quo est. . . . Sed sicut illud quo est formaliter, non est aliqua forma
quae sit pars essentiae ejus sed ipsum suum esse"). Nor is it God,
Who is the efficient cause by which the soul is and lives ("Sed id
quo est et quo vivit effective est ipse Deus, qui omnibus esse et
vitam influit. . . ."). Through this contrast, then, Thomas appears to
reaffirm that *esse* is really different from the soul and from God.

(d) If in those three passages Thomas clearly affirms the real
difference between *esse*/essence, his attempts at somehow establishing that difference are often complicated and not always conclusive. Those attempts fall into four classes, the first two of which
(the *intellectus essentiae* argument [#4] and the *genus* argument [#5])

---

and at times *esse* seems almost equivalent to an intelligibility ("secundum
esse, scilicet secundum rationem quam accepit prioris et posterioris").

For more general reasons why Thomas seems to indicate that the otherness
between *esse* and essence is real, see J. de Finance, *op. cit.*, p. 108: "Mais la
façon dont il compare et oppose la distinction d'essence et d'existence à celle
de matière et de forme; le rôle qu'il lui fait jouer, à la place de l'universel
hylémorphisme des augustiniens, pour fonder la distinction, éminemment
réelle, des créatures et du Créateur; le parti qu'il en tire, presque jusqu'à la fin
de sa carrière, pour la théologie de l'Incarnation; surtout, le rapport étroit
entre cette thèse et l'ensemble de la doctrine thomiste sur l'origine de l'être
fini et le pourquoi de son activité, rapport que la suite de cet ouvrage s'efforcera
de mettre en lumière, tout cela semble bien imposer une interprétation réaliste."

can be termed "philosophical" as moving from creatures to God. The third and fourth (the God-to-creatures argument [#6–#10] and the participation argument [#11–#15]) are describable as "theological" in the sense that they proceed (with one exception, noted below, #17i) from God to creatures. Let us look at each separately.

(e) The *intellectus essentiae* line of reasoning (#4) is open to two serious charges. Perhaps the couplet essence/*esse* is equivalent merely to essence-as-specific/essence-as-individual (#4c) or, again, to essence-to-itself/essence-in-relationship-to-efficient-cause (#4d). In either equivalence *esse* would be only mentally different from essence. Elsewhere, though, Thomas himself takes the sting out of both objections by furnishing two facts. The relationship between an essence as specific and as individual is that of act and potency,[48] whereas the relationship between essence/*esse* is that of potency/act. Hence, the first equivalence collapses. Second, *esse* is an intrinsic and perfective factor within existents. Accordingly, *esse* is more than essence situated within a framework of efficiency and, thus, the second equivalence vanishes.

The *intellectus essentiae* argumentation, then, needs to be complemented by those two facts if it is to be valid. As so complemented, though, it discloses an existential dimension, and apparently *esse* is the internal component by which the existent actually *is* and is genuinely other than the essence, by which the existent is what he is. One should note, though, that Thomas seems almost to have abandoned this argument in his later writings.

(f) The *genus* argumentation (#5) aims at establishing the difference between quiddity and *esse* by pointing to the fact that things agree in belonging to the same species or genus but differ insofar as they have *esse*. Can any charge be leveled against it? Yes, one similar to that made against the previous argument. Suppose we interpret *esse* as meaning essence-as-individual. Then essence/*esse* would be identical with essence-as-specific/essence-as-individual, with essence-as-common/essence-as-unique, and *esse* would be only conceptually different from essence. True, this interpretation is a natural and intelligent one, but it is hardly consonant with Thomas' position that the relationship of essence/*esse* is that of potency/act, whereas essence-as-specific is related to essence-as-individual as act to potency. Hence, the identity between the two couplets is broken. But even so, the *genus* argument remains so complex and awkward as to be ineffectual.

---

[48] See n. 16 above.

(g) The third sort of attempt Thomas makes at establishing the otherness between *esse*/essence is the God-to-creatures argument (see #6–#10). The first two such endeavors (#6, #7) raise a question which is not resolved within the texts themselves. Granted that the divine essence is *esse*, still for that statement to be meaningful one must have a prior recognition of what *esse* is and of what being is. Whence comes that recognition? On this point Thomas is silent. Presumably it could come only from a metaphysical reflection upon the sole actuality a human knower directly experiences—his own and that of other sensible existents. Here, then, Thomas' exegesis of Scripture and his theology rest upon his metaphysics. The last endeavor (#10) also suggests an unresolved inquiry: why is what comes from oneself identical with oneself?

With the exception of the first, all the endeavors (#7–#10) are primarily concerned with separate intelligences. These are existents which are outside the range of direct human knowledge and, hence, of strict metaphysics. How, then, can one prove that *they* are composed of *esse*/essence? Obviously not by the *intellectus essentiae* or the *genus* arguments. Solely, then, by contrast with God, once He is somehow known to be subsistent *esse*:[49] In God alone essence is *esse*; but an angel is not God; therefore, an angelic essence is not *esse*, which however it receives from God. Within a properly constructed theological context and as applied to separate intelligences, this line of argumentation is valid. But Thomas does not, I would say, intend it to eliminate properly metaphysical attempts to substantiate the otherness between *esse*/essence in existents we directly perceive.

(h) Thomas' final endeavor to account for the difference of *esse*/essence uses the rubric of participation (#11–#15). In three of the instances so far discovered (#13–#15) he proceeds from God to creatures in some such fashion as this: God is subsistent *esse* and thus is Being essentially; but a creature is not God; therefore, a creature is not *esse* and is a being only through participation. Manifestly, such a procedure hangs upon a prior realization of what *esse* and being are and that God is subsistent *esse*.

(i) But participation can initiate a movement from creatures to God, as is clear from the *In de Hebdomadibus* text (#11). What factors does participation involve? At least four: [1] a perfection which of itself is common and unrestricted [2] is found to be part of another,

---

[49] This knowledge is achieved through the *intellectus essentiae* argumentation (see #8 and #9 above).

[3] with the result that this other is perfected and enriched [4] but the perfection itself is limited and restricted. Once one realizes that actual existence is such a perfection, then he can clearly see it is other than the various essences which limit and restrict it; he is next forced to conclude as the only explanation of those existents which truly *are* but are not of themselves that there must be an Existent Who *is* that perfection in its fullness and of Himself. Somewhat later in the same text (#32–#35; see #11c above), Thomas sketches (after a fashion) this journey from creatures to God. In existents which are essentially composite *esse* is really different from essence because *esse* is itself simple, whereas the essence is composed of matter/form (#32). In essentially simple existents it differs from essence because such an essence *is* a form (whether Platonic or Aristotelian) which determines, limits, participates *esse* (#34). Only God is absolutely simple, because He entails no composition of *esse*/essence: He does not participate *esse*, He *is* subsistent *esse* (#35).

But Thomas' is only a sketch and a rather cumbersome one at that (see #12). If we may judge by the other texts (#13–#15), what he does more commonly with reference to *esse*/essence and participation is to move from God to creatures.

(18) Such, then, are notable points in Thomas' attitude to *esse*/essence in his early writings—very frequent affirmations that *esse* is other than essence; an occasional clear statement that the otherness is real and not merely mental; at least four sorts of attempts at establishing why *esse* is different, which are not always satisfactory but which set the stage for an attentive study of his middle and late works.[50]

(19) Finally, why is ch. 19 relevant to our study of Christian philosophy? Because it considers the relationship between philosophy and theology (see p. 462 and n. 24; pp. 484–86). It also focuses upon topics at the heart of philosophical and theological reflection—e.g., God as efficient, exemplary and final cause; creatures as His participants; creatures as each a single but composite entity of actuation/potency, of existence/essence. This last composition has been submitted to a rigouous textual examination, which thus is a good preparation for the subsequent chapters.

---

[50] The texts for that study are provided below in Appendices A and B. Also see n. 6 above.

Appendix A

Middle Writings (ca. 1260–ca. 1267)

Among the texts included in this section are excerpts from *Compendium Theologiae*,[51] *Summa Contra Gentiles*, *De Potentia*, *Quaestio Disputata de Anima*, *De Spiritualibus Creaturis* and *In Librum Dionysii de Divinis Nominibus Expositio*.

I: *Compendium Theologiae* (Raymundi A. Verardo, O.P., ed., *Opuscula Theologica*, vol. I [Taurini: Marietti, 1954], pp. 9–138).

C.T., c. 11: "Quod Dei essentia non est aliud quam suum esse," (p. 16, #20).

Ibid., c. 14: "Quod Deus non est aliqua species praedicata de multis individuis" (p. 17, #27).

Ibid., c. 68: "De effectibus divinitatis, et primo de esse" (pp. 33–34, #117).

Ibid., c. 109: "Quod solus Deus est bonus per essentiam, creaturae vero per participationem" (p. 54, #218).

* * * * *

II: *Summa Contra Gentiles*, Leonine Manual Edition (Romae: Apud Sedem Commissionis Leoninae, 1934).

S.C.G., I, c. 22: "Quod in Deo idem est esse et essentia," pp. 23b–24d.

[Text A] *Ibid.*, I, c. 25: "Quod Deus non est in aliquo genere," prgrs. 3–5, p. 26c.

Ibid., I, c. 26: "Quod Deus non est esse formale omnium," prgrs. 3 and 4, p. 27c.

---

[51] On dating the *Compendium Theologiae* [hereafter: *C.T.*] among the middle rather than the late writings, see J. A. Weisheipl, *Friar Thomas d'Aquino: His Life, Thought, and Work* (Garden City, N.Y.: Doubleday, 1974), pp. 386–87; I. Eschmann, *op. cit.*, pp. 411–12. *C.T.* is now also available in the Leonine edition (1979), Tome 42.

In Appendices A and B Thomas' texts marked by two asterisks (**) are those in which he at least implies *esse* to be somehow other than essence. In those marked by one asterisk (*) he explicitly states that *esse* and essence are other but offers no reason for his statement, while using that otherness in solving some other problem. In texts that have no asterisk at all but are tagged as [Text A], [Text B] and so on whenever there are more than one in a treatise, he attempts somehow to establish that otherness. See prgr. corresponding to notes 4 and 5 above.

**[Text B:] *Ibid.*, I, c. 38: "Quod Deus est ipsa bonitas," prgr. 5, p. 36c.

Ibid., I, c. 43: "Quod Deus est infinitus," prgr. 5, p. 41c.

[Text C:] *Ibid.*, II, c. 15: "Quod Deus sit omnibus causa essendi," prgr. 5, p. 101a.

[Text D:] *Ibid.*, II, c. 52: "Quod in substantiis intellectualibus creatis differt esse et quod est," pp. 145a–46a (entire chapter).

[Text E:] *Ibid.*, II, c. 53: "Quod in substantiis intellectualibus creatis est actus et potentia," pp. 146b–c (entire chapter).

[Text F:] *Ibid.*, II, ch. 54: "Quod non est idem componi ex substantia et esse, et materia et forma," p. 146d sq. (entire chap-ter).

Ibid., III, c. 20: "Quomodo res imitentur divinam bonitatem," p. 243c.

Ibid., III, c. 49: "Quod substantiae separatae non vident Deum per essentiam ex hoc quod cognoscunt eum per suam essentiam," prgr. 8, p. 280b.

Ibid., III, c. 65: "Quod Deus conservat res in esse," prgr. 5, p. 298b.

Ibid., III, c. 66: "Quod nihil dat esse nisi inquantum agit in virtute divina," prgr. 7, p. 299d.

**Ibid.*, IV, c. 40: "Objectiones contra fidem incarnationis," 5th objection, p. 495c.

*   *   *   *   *

III: *Quaestio Disputata de Potentia Dei* (P. M. Pession, O.P., ed. [Romae: Marietti, 1949]).

De Pot., q. 1, a. 2: "Utrum potentia Dei sit infinita," resp. (p. 11c).

Ibid., 2, 1: "Utrum in divinis sit potentia generativa," resp. (p. 24c).

Ibid., 2, 1, ad 7 (p. 26d).

Ibid., 3, 1: "Utrum Deus possit aliquid creare ex nihilo," ad 17 (p. 41b).

Ibid., 3, 4: "Utrum potentia creandi sit alicui creaturae communicabilis vel etiam actus creationis," resp. (p. 46c). (Especially note: "Primus autem effectus est ipsum esse, quod omnibus aliis effectibus praesupponitur et ipsum non praesupponit aliquem alium effectum.")

Ibid., 3, 5: "Utrum possit esse aliquid quod non sit a Deo creatum," resp. ad finem (p. 49c).

Ibid., 5, 3: "Utrum Deus possit creaturam in nihilum redigere," resp. (p. 135c). Also: *resp. ad finem (p. 136b) and ad 8 (p. 137a).

Ibid., 5, 4: "Utrum aliqua creatura in nihilum sit redigenda vel etiam in nihilum redigatur," ad 3 (p. 139b).

Ibid., 6, 3: "Utrum creaturae spirituales sua naturali virtute possint miracula facere," ad 9 (p. 167c).

**Ibid.*, 7, 2 resp. (p. 191c). [On *esse* as *commune omnibus* and the proper effect of God, see *S.C.G.*, II, c. 15, prgrs. 2 and 4 (pp. 100b, 100d).]

**Ibid.*, ad 4–5, ad 7–8; p. 192a sq.

**Ibid.*, ad 9, p. 192b.

**Ibid.*, 7, 3: "Utrum Deus sit in aliquo genere," resp. (p. 193d).

Ibid., 7, 3, ad 4 (p. 194b).

Ibid., 7, 4: "Utrum 'bonum, sapiens, justum' et huiusmodi praedicent de Deo accidens," resp. (p. 195c).

*   *   *   *   *

IV: *Quaestio Disputata de Anima* (P. M. Pession, O.P., *et alii*, eds., vol. II [Romae: Marietti, 1949]).

De Anima, a. 6: "Utrum anima composita sit ex materia et forma," respondeo (p. 302b).

**Ibid.*, a. 9: "Utrum anima uniatur materiae corporali per medium," the first paragraph of the *respondeo* (p. 314a).

*   *   *   *   *

V: *Tractatus de Spiritualibus Creaturis* (Leo Keeler, S.J., ed. [Romae: Apud Aedes Universitatis Gregorianae, 1946]). Article 1: "Utrum substantia spiritualis sit composita ex materia et forma," last two paragraphs of *respondeo* (pp. 11–12).

*   *   *   *   *

VI: *In Librum Beati Dionysii de Divinis Nominibus Expositio* (C. Pera, O.P., ed. [Romae: Marietti, 1950]).

**In De Divinis Nominibus*, c. 4, lect. 5: "De pulchro divino, et qualiter attribuitur Deo" (p. 114, no. 349).

Ibid., c. 5, lect. 2: "Deus est causa particularium entium" (p. 245, no. 661).

**Ibid.*, c. 11, lect. 4: "De divinis perfectionibus secundum quod per se in abstracto considerantur" (p. 347, no. 934).

**Ibid.*, c. 13, lect. 1: "De perfecto et uno" (p. 359, no. 962).

Appendix B

Late Writings (ca. 1267 sq.)

In this section are included passages from *In Libros Physicorum Aristotelis Expositio, Summa Theologiae, Quaestiones Quodlibetales, In Aristotelis Libros Peri Hermeneias, In Metaphysicam Aristotelis Commentaria, Super Librum de Causis Expositio* and *Tractatus de Substantiis Separatis.*

I: *In Octo Libros Physicorum Aristotelis Expositio,* vol. 3 of *S. Thomae Aquinatis Opera Omnia iussu Leonis XIII edita* (Romae: Leonine Commission, 1884).

   In VIII Physicorum, lect. 21, p. 449b, no. 13, and p. 449d, no. 14.

* * * * *

II: *Summa Theologiae* (Leonine text [Romae: Marietti, 1950]).

   [Text A:] *S.T.,* I, 3, 4: "Utrum in Deo sit idem essentia et esse," resp. (p. 17a sq.). [Brings in the notion of *esse* as *actualitas omnium,* and the notion of participation.]

   [Text B:] *Ibid.,* I, 3, 5: "Utrum Deus sit in genere aliquo," resp. 3d and 4th prgrs. (p. 18b–c) and ad 1 (p. 18c).

   [Text C:] *Ibid.,* I, 4, 1: "Utrum Deus sit perfectus," ad 3 (p. 21d) [*esse = actualitas omnium*]

   ***Ibid.,* I, 4, 2: "Utrum in Deo sint perfectiones omnium rerum," resp. (p. 22b) and ad 3 (p. 22c).

   ***Ibid.,* I, 4, 3: "Utrum aliqua creatura possit esse similis Deo," ad 3 (p. 23d).

   **Ibid.,* I, 6, 3: "Utrum esse bonum per essentiam sit proprium Dei," resp. (p. 30d) and ad 2 (p. 31a).

   ***Ibid.,* I, 7, 1: "Utrum Deus sit infinitus," resp. last prgr. (p. 32d) and ad 3 (p. 33a).

   **Ibid.,* 7, 2: "Utrum aliquid aliud quam Deus possit esse infinitum per essentiam," resp. 2d prgr. (p. 33c), and ad 1 (p. 33c).

   **Ibid.,* I, 8, 1: "Utrum Deus sit in omnibus rebus," resp. (p. 36c).

   **Ibid.,* I, 9, 2: "Utrum esse immutabile sit Dei proprium," resp. (p. 41d).

   **Ibid.,* I, 10, 2: "Utrum Deus sit aeternus," resp. (p. 43c).

   ***Ibid.,* I, 11, 4: "Utrum Deus sit maxime unus," resp. (p. 50c).

   **Ibid.,* I, 12, 2: "Utrum essentia Dei ab intellectu creato per aliquam similitudinem videatur," resp. (p. 53a).

Ibid., I, 12, 4: "Utrum aliquis intellectus creatus per sua naturalia divinam essentiam videre possit," resp. (p. 54d sq.).

Ibid., I, 13, 11: "Utrum hoc nomen *qui est* sit maxime nomen Dei proprium," resp. (p. 74b).

**Ibid.*, 14, 4: "Utrum ipsum intelligere Dei sit eius substantia," resp. (p. 79a).

[Text D:] *Ibid.*, I, 44, 1: "Utrum sit necessarium omne ens esse creatum a Deo," resp. (p. 224a).

Ibid., I, 50, 2: "Utrum angelus sit compositus ex materia et forma," ad 3 (p. 254b) and ad 4 (p. 254c).

[Text E:] *Ibid.*, I, 54, 1: "Utrum intelligere angeli sit eius substantia," resp. (p. 266d). [*Actio = actualitas virtutis, esse = actualitas essentiae.*]

**Ibid.*, I, 54, 2: "Utrum intelligere angeli sit eius esse," resp. (p. 267d).

Ibid., I, 54, 3: "Utrum potentia intellectiva angeli sit eius essentia," resp. (p. 268b) and ad 2 (p. 268c).

[Text F:] *Ibid.*, I, 61, 1: "Utrum angeli habeant causam sui esse," resp. (p. 295c).

[Text G:] *Ibid.*, I, 75, 5: "Utrum anima sit composita ex materia et forma," ad 4 (p. 355a).

Ibid., I, 79, 1: "Utrum intellectus sit aliqua potentia animae," resp. (p. 382c).

Ibid., I, 90, 1: "Utrum anima sit facta vel sit de substantia Dei," ad 2 (p. 443d).

Ibid., I, 90, 2: "Utrum anima sit producta in esse per creationem," ad 1 (p. 444c).

Ibid., I, 104, 1: "Utrum creaturae indigeant ut a Deo conserventur," resp. (p. 492b and p. 493a).

**Ibid.*, I, 104, 4: "Utrum aliquid in nihilum redigatur," ad 2 (p. 495c).

Ibid., I II, 3, 7: "Utrum beatitudo consistit in cognitione substantiarum separatarum, scilicet angelorum," resp. (p. 22b).

*   *   *   *   *

III: *Quaestiones Quodlibetales:*[52]

Quodl., X, 2, 4: "Utrum duratio angeli habeat prius et posterius," ad 4 (p. 200b).

---

[52] On the dating of the *Quaestiones Quodlibetales* see I. Eschmann, *op. cit.*, pp. 392–93; J. A. Weisheipl, *op. cit.*, pp. 367–68. For relevant texts in earlier *Quaestiones Quodlibetales*, see those listed at the beginning of this chapter.

[Text D:] *Ibid.*, II, 2, 1: "Utrum angelus substantialiter sit compositus ex essentia et esse," p. 23d sq.

[Text E:] *Ibid.*, II, 2, 2: "Utrum in angelo sit aliud suppositum et natura," resp. ad finem (p. 25c).

*Ibid., ad 1 (p. 25d sq.). [Also includes much information on various kinds of *accidents.*]

*Ibid., ad 2 (p. 26b).

**Ibid., III, 1, 1: "Utrum Deus possit facere quod materia sit sine forma," resp. (p. 40b). [Rather strange text, which actually could be used to show that Thomas does not hold *esse* to be really other than form. For example: "Idem est dictu materiam esse in actu, et materiam habere formam."]

[Text F:] *Ibid.*, III, 8, 1: "Utrum (anima) sit composita ex materia et forma," resp. (p. 60d sq.).

[Text G:] *Ibid.*, XII, 5, 1: "Utrum esse angeli sit accidens eius," sed contra and resp. (p. 227a).

* * * * *

IV: *In Aristotelis Libros Peri Hermeneias* (R. Spiazzi, O.P., ed. [Leonine text; Romae: Marietti, 1955].

**In I Peri., lect. 5 (p. 29, no. 22).

* * * * *

V: *In Duodecim Libros Metaphysicorum Aristotelis Expositio* (R. M. Spiazzi, O.P., ed. [Romae: Marietti, 1950]).

*In IV Meta., lectio II, #558.

**In VI Meta., lect. 1, #1151.

* * * * *

VI: *Super Librum de Causis Expositio* (H. D. Saffrey, O.P., ed. [Fribourg: Société Philosophique, 1954]).

[Text A:] Prop. 4, p. 30, l. 2. sq. and l. 18 sq.; p. 31, l. 14 sq.

**Ibid., Prop. 6, p. 47, l. 11 sq.

*Ibid., Prop. 7, p. 49, l. 23 sq.

[Text B:] *Ibid.*, Prop. 9, p. 64, l. 4.

*Ibid., Prop. 9, p. 65, l. 28 sq.

**Ibid., Prop. 18, p. 104, l. 9 sq.

* * * * *

VII: *Tractatus de Substantiis Separatis* (Francis J. Lescoe, ed. [West
    Hartford, Conn.: St. Joseph College, 1962]).
  [Text A:] *De Subst. Separ.*, c. VIII (p. 79, no. 42).
  [Text B:] *Ibid.* (pp. 80–82, no. 44).
  [Text C:] *Ibid.*, c. IX (p. 86, no. 48, last prgr.).

20

The Mystery of Existence

That things exist was a constant source of wonderment and amazement to G. K. Chesterton. He once bumped his head against a fencepost in the dark and that accidental blow prompted this exclamation against William Butler Yeats and other then current idealists (whom Chesterton called "mystics").

When they [contemporary mystics] said that a wooden post was wonderful . . . they meant that they could make something wonderful out of it by thinking about it. "Dream; there is no truth," said Mr. Yeats, "but in your own heart." The modern mystic looked for the post, not outside in the garden, but inside, in the mirror of his mind. But the mind of the modern mystic, like a dandy's dressing-room, was entirely made of mirrors. Thus glass repeated glass like doors opening inwards for ever; till one could hardly see that inmost chamber of unreality where the post made its last appearance.[1]

His own attitude was quite different.

But I was never interested in mirrors; that is, I was never primarily interested in my own reflection—or reflections. I am interested in wooden posts, which do startle me like miracles. I am interested in the post that stands waiting outside my door, to hit me over the head, like a giant's club in a fairy tale. All my mental doors open outwards into a world I have not

---

[1] *The Coloured Lands* (New York: Sheed & Ward, 1938), pp. 158–60.

made. My last door of liberty opens upon a world of sun and
solid things, of objective adventures. The post in the garden;
the thing I could neither create nor expect: strong plain day-
light on stiff upstanding wood: it is the Lord's doing, and it is
marvellous in our eyes. . . . To me the post is wonderful
because it is *there*; there whether I like it or not. I was struck
silly by a post, but if I were struck blind by a thunderbolt, the
post would still be there; the substance of things not seen. For
the amazing thing about the universe is that it exists; not that
we can discuss its existence.[2]

Consequently,

There is at the back of all our lives an abyss of light, more
blinding and unfathomable than any abyss of darkness, and it
is *the abyss of actuality, of existence, of the fact that things truly are,
and that we ourselves are incredibly and sometimes almost incredulously real.* It is the fundamental fact of being, as against not
being. . . . He who has realized this reality knows that it does
outweigh, literally to infinity, all lesser regrets or arguments
for negation, and that under all our grumblings there is a
subconscious substance of gratitude.[3]

Chesterton's amazement at the actual existence of things should
be weighed against the fact that he lived before contemporary
existentialism came into prominence; and hence he was unaware of
the position which reduces "existence" to merely "the state of being human."[4] As Heidegger explains:

---

[2] *Ibid.*, pp. 160–61.

[3] *Chaucer* (New York: Pellegrini & Cudahy, n.d.), pp. 33. For testimony
from another English literary figure, see Samuel Taylor Coleridge, *Complete
Works*, ed. G. T. Shedd (New York: Harper & Bros., 1864), vol. 2, p. 463: "Hast
thou ever raised thy mind to the consideration of existence, in and by itself, as
the mere act of existing? Hast thou ever said to thyself thoughtfully, It is!
heedless in that moment, whether it were a man before thee, or a flower, or a
grain of sand,—without reference, in short, to this or that particular mode or
form of existence? If thou hast attained to this, thou wilt have felt the presence
of a mystery, which must have fixed thy spirit in awe and wonder. . . . If thou
hast mastered this intuition of absolute existence, thou wilt have learned that
it was this, and no other, which in the earlier ages seized the nobler minds, the
elect among men, with a sort of sacred horror."

[4] "Contemporary existentialism" is what I elsewhere characterize as "radical" (see my *Authentic Metaphysics in an Age of Unreality*, 2d ed. [hereafter:

The being that exists is man. Man alone exists. Rocks are, but they do not exist. Trees are, but they do not exist. Horses are, but they do not exist. Angels are, but they do not exist. God is, but he does not exist. The proposition "man alone exists" does not mean by any means that man alone is a real [read: actual] being while all other beings are unreal and mere appearances or human ideas. The proposition "man exists" means: man is that being whose Being is distinguished by the open-standing standing-in in the unconcealedness of Being, from Being, in Being.[5]

Had Chesterton read Heidegger and had he then continued to predicate existence of any actual thing, human or otherwise, and still felt exhilarated at its very actuality, that would indeed be a startling and gratifying state of affairs.

Such is what some of Chesterton's fellow countrymen have been doing, though. In the final paragraph of a study aimed at demolishing proofs for the existence of God, J. J. C. Smart, the British linguistic analyst, admits he experiences awe when reflecting upon actual existence.

The only rational thing to say if someone asks, "Why does this table exist?" is some such thing as that such-and-such a carpenter made it. We can go back and back in such a series, but we must not entertain the absurd idea of getting back to something logically necessary. However, now let us ask, "Why should anything exist at all?" Logic seems to tell us that the only answer which is not absurd is to say, "Why shouldn't it?" Nevertheless, though I know how any answer on the lines of the cosmological argument can be pulled to pieces by a correct logic, I still feel I want to go on asking the question. Indeed, though logic has taught me to look at such a question with the gravest suspicion, *my mind often seems to reel under the immense*

Authentic Metaphysics] [New York/Bern: Peter Lang Publishing, Inc., 1993], p. 23, n. 15) and as "unauthentic" (see ch. 22 below, "Existentialism: Authentic and Unauthentic," prgrs. corresponding to notes 15–21). It is the philosophical position commonly linked with Martin Heidegger, Jean Paul Sartre, Gabriel Marcel, and so on. Although they differ doctrinally among themselves and some of them dislike being called "existentialists," still they have this in common that they affirm "to exist" is "to be human," "to be a subject."

[5] Martin Heidegger, "The Way Back into the Ground of Metaphysics," in *Existentialism from Dostoevsky to Sartre*, ed. W. Kaufmann (New York: Meridian Books, 1959), p. 214.

significance it seems to have for me. That anything should exist at all
does seem to be a matter for the deepest awe. But whether other
people feel this sort of awe, and whether they or I ought to is
another question. I think we ought to.[6]

Even more surprising, perhaps, is that some radical existentialists themselves make a similar admission. Writes Simone de
Beauvoir:

During the whole journey, leaning out of the window I drank
in the darkness and the wind. I had never seen the country in
the spring; I went walking to the song of the cuckoo, among
primroses and campanulas. . . . The fact of existing here and
now sometimes took on a glorious splendor.[7]

Or Gabriel Marcel:

There is another factor or aspect of the situation [as to how to
build up a concrete philosophy] which seems to be just as
important. Whoever philosophizes *hic et nunc* is, it may be
said, a prey of reality; he will never become completely accustomed to the fact of existing; existence is inseparable from a
certain astonishment. The child, in this sense, is close to existence; we all know children who have asked extremely metaphysical questions at the age of six; but this astonishment
usually disappears, the surprise dies away. . . . Only the ha-
bituated mind, or more accurately, the mind which is estab-

---

[6] "The Existence of God," in *New Essays in Philosophical Theology*, ed. A.
Flew and A. MacIntyre (London: SCM Press, 1955), p. 46. See also S. Hamp-
shire, "Metaphysical Systems," in *The Nature of Metaphysics*, ed. D. F. Pears
(London: Macmillan & Co., 1957), p. 23: "That anything exists at all seems a
problem, in itself puzzling. There might have been nothing. Why should there
be anything? There must always have been moods when people thought like
this and wondered, when they stared at the mere fact of existence, as at a
mystery requiring an explanation."
As reported by Norman Malcolm, *Ludwig Wittgenstein: A Memoir* (London:
Oxford University Press, 1958), p. 70, n. 1, Wittgenstein once said: "When I
have it [a certain feeling of amazement] *I wonder at the existence of the world.*
And I am then inclined to use such phrases as 'How extraordinary that
anything should exist!' or 'How extraordinary that the world should exist!'"
[7] *Memoirs of a Dutiful Daughter* (New York: World Publishing Co., 1965),
p. 281.

lished in its daily routine, cannot feel [the shock of reality] any
more . . . whereas a metaphysical mind never wholly resigns
itself to this routine, viewing it as a state of sleep.[8]

Munitz on Existence

An American philosopher, Milton K. Munitz of New York University, has expressed similar wonderment at actual existence in
his book *The Mystery of Existence: An Essay in Philosophical Cosmology*.[9] Aristotle noted long ago (to paraphrase Dr. Munitz's initial
paragraphs) that philosophy begins in wonder—especially, in wonder at the origin of the universe. The pre-Socratics, as well as
Aristotle himself, understood this to mean: "How did the world
get to be the way it is at the present time? Through what processes
of transformation and growth did it pass before it emerged as the
ordered structure it is found to be now?"[10] But current wonderment arises from a different aspect of the world.

There is another side to human wonderment, not considered
by Aristotle, that finds expression in a different kind of question. . . . It would now be roughly equivalent to what is meant
by speaking of the "mystery of existence." For those who are
provoked by the mystery of existence, and so display another
dimension of human wonderment, the root question is *why
there should be a world at all*. To ask this latter question is not to
ask a scientific question. If we are caught in the toils of this
question, no amount of scientific explanation of how the world
underwent various stages of development, on a cosmological
or on a more restricted level, will serve, in any way, to allay
the difficulty summed up by asking why there should even be
a world in existence, whatever its stages of development or its

---

[8] *Creative Fidelity*, trans. Robert Rosthal (New York: Farrar, Straus & Co.,
1964), pp. 63–64. Also see Paul Tillich, *Philosophical Interrogations*, ed. Sidney
and Beatrice Rome (New York: Holt, Rinehart & Winston, 1964), p. 403:
"There is no doubt that the question, 'Why is there something, why not
nothing?' is not a question in the logical sense of the word. There is no answer
to it. . . . But the question *has* been asked by philosophers (and by children)
and is the most radical expression of the astonishment which makes the
philosopher a philosopher."

[9] New York: Appleton-Century-Crofts, 1965.

[10] *Ibid.*, p. 3.

patterns and qualities. It is with this side, or form, of human wonderment that the present book is concerned.[11]

Manifestly, Munitz has experienced as vivid an amazement at existence as have any of the aforementioned authors. Unfortunately, though, his experience terminates in the conviction that existence is incomprehensible and meaningless. The question of the existence of the universe "has neither been satisfactorily answered by any known rational method, nor can be. . . . [One must realize] that the existence of the world is incomprehensible, and cannot be adequately explained in any way."[12] He does not completely close the door on a possible solution to the mystery of existence some future day.

> If one introduces the idea of a *possible* rational method, uniquely suited to discover whether there is a reason for the existence of the world, then, relative to this possible rational method, the question "Is there a reason for the existence of the world?" is *not* unanswerable.[13]

Nonetheless, such a possibility seems unlikely and is, to us here and now, irrelevant. In our actual state of affairs no solution does or can exist.

> Since, as human beings, we have no way of knowing that there is, in fact, such a rational method, or how we might achieve it through the use of the methods we now have, the possibility that this question might be answered by such a possible method, is, for us, wholly speculative and gratuitous. . . . [Rather] by using the already known rational methods, the question "Is there a reason for the existence of the world?" is [simply] *unanswerable.*[14]

His position is clearly an extreme case of what he himself calls "philosophical agnosticism."[15] The actual existence of the universe

---

11 *Ibid.*, p. 4.

12 *Ibid.*, pp. 12–13.

13 *Ibid.*, p. 262.

14 *Ibid.*

15 See *ibid.*, Part 4: "Mystery and Agnosticism," pp. 177–263, especially pp. 220–54: "Philosophical Agnosticism."

is inexplicable and unintelligible; it offers no guarantee that there is a God.

In arriving at those stark and pessimistic conclusions, Munitz proceeds in an orderly fashion and with intelligent sincerity. But they are not, I would suggest, valid or necessary. If interpreted differently, actual existence reveals itself to be eminently intelligible and provides a firm basis for one's assenting that God does exist.

Before indicating that interpretation, though, let me outline Munitz's procedure. After tracing the meaning of "mystery" from ancient Greece through Christianity up to the present (pp. 14–32)[16] and after discussing the three principal types of questions which are unanswerable (pp. 33–47), he then describes what "world" or "universe" signifies in contemporary scientific cosmologies (pp. 51–63)[17] and what "exists" means to Kant (pp. 73–84) and to Bertrand Russell and P. F. Strawson (pp. 84–90). Immediately thereafter he considers (and rejects) theistic answers to the question "Why does the world exist?" Among these he considers Leibniz's appeal to the Principle of Sufficient Reason (pp. 105–7) and "The Cosmological Argument: The Thomistic Version" (pp. 107–25). The latter turns out to be Aquinas' first three Ways, all of which Munitz judges to be grounded on two claims:

> The first . . . that there is something essentially *incomplete* about ordinary commonsensical or scientific explanatory accounts; the second . . . that not only the various constituents of the world but the world itself is *contingent*. Taken together, the facts of incompleteness and contingency point to what is regarded as the *finite* character of the world and all that it contains; they also point to the need for recognizing an Infinite Being as the ground and source of the world's existence.[18]

---

[16] See *ibid.*, pp. 27–32, where he explains (although not with complete success) the difference between "problem" and "mystery" as Gabriel Marcel uses them.

[17] See Munitz's other books—*Space, Time and Creation: Philosophical Aspects of Scientific Cosmology* (Glencoe, Ill.: Free Press, 1957); *Theories of the Universe from Babylonian Myth to Modern Science* (Glencoe, Ill.: Free Press, 1957).

[18] *Mystery of Existence*, p. 108. According to Munitz (*ibid.*, pp. 103–7, 125), Aquinas' Five Ways are based upon the "Principle of Sufficient Reason." This is a serious misconception of Aquinas, since this "Principle," as originated and interpreted by Leibniz, is known deductively and used in an *a priori* fashion. St. Thomas' Ways proceed inductively and are *a posteriori*. See Etienne Gilson, "Les Principes et les causes," *Revue Thomiste* 52 (1952), 39–64; Joseph

Immediately subsequent to his rejection of theism, our author makes three points. First, scientific cosmology cannot establish that the universe began in time (pp. 126–41). Second, the statement "There might have been *nothing*" is nonsense (he refers here to Tillich and Heidegger, using H. Bergson, R. Carnap and N. L. Wilson to refute them); and the statement "The world might not have been" is a by-product of the Hebraic-Christian theism he has already rejected (pp. 142–59). Finally, although the world is not contingent as dependent on a God or as beginning in time, still it is not necessary either, as Spinoza would have it, "in the sense that its existence is entirely self-sufficient and self-explanatory."[19] Its very existence is unintelligible and, thus, mysterious (pp. 160–73). Accordingly, Munitz has arrived at his destination. There is no reason for the existence of the world since the world is not a statement; it is neither an occurrence nor a regularity; it is not something made (pp. 194–211). Second, if we hyphenate the phrase "reason-for-the-existence-of-the-world" and take it as a single idea, "there is no rational method, known to man, by which it could be established that there is (or is not), in fact, anything to which this idea can be applied, as a referent for it."[20] The existence of the world is mysterious precisely because it is inexplicable.

What "Existence" Means

Under the guidance of Munitz, then, reflection upon existence has terminated in agnosticism. Is such a termination inevitable? The answer is no, provided we interpret "existence" differently.

In the chapter in which Munitz studies what "exists" signifies,[21] he surveys the positions of several other philosophers. For Kant "exists" is not a genuine predicate since a predicate should explicate and enlarge the meaning of the term which serves as subject of a sentence; but "exists" does not at all express what the subject is (as do "white," "barking," "soft" and "angry" when applied to "dog").

Owens, "The Causal Proposition—Principle or Conclusion?" *The Modern Schoolman* 32 (1955), 159–71; John E. Gurr, "Genesis and Function of Principles in Philosophy," *Proceedings of the American Catholic Philosophical Association* 29 (1955), 121–33.

[19] *Mystery of Existence*, p. 160.

[20] *Ibid.*, p. 212.

[21] *Ibid.*, ch. 5, pp. 72–99.

Whenever, then, we are concerned with giving a list of qualities (each of which is derived from some sensed feature of an
object) that tells us *what* that object is, or (what comes to the
same thing), what the meaning is of the concept that designates that type of object, we do not find "exists" among the
qualities listed. Existence, in short, is irrelevant to the specification of the meaning of empirical concepts.[22]

Modern logicians agree with Kant that "exists" is not a bona fide
predicate, although they often add more sophisticated reasons. For
example, Bertrand Russell affirms that "exists" is merely a property of a propositional function. What does he mean?

A form of words containing an undetermined variable—for
instance, "*x* is a man"—is called a "propositional function" if,
when a value is assigned to the variable, the form of words
becomes a proposition. Thus "*x* is a man" is neither true nor
false, but if for "*x*" I put "Mr. Jones" I get a true proposition
and if I put "Mrs. Jones" I get a false one.[23]

What, then, is "existence" in this context?

When you take any propositional function and assert of it that
it is possible, that it is sometimes true, that gives you the
fundamental meaning of "existence." You may express it by
saying that there is at least one value of *x* for which that
propositional function is true.[24]

"Exists," accordingly, is the same as "is sometimes true," and hence
it directly concerns the use of language and the exercise of thought.
It has to do with the truth of propositions and not with actual
things.[25]

---

[22] *Ibid.*, p. 76.

[23] Bertrand Russell, *Human Knowledge: Its Scope and Limits* (London: George
Allen & Unwin Ltd., 1948), p. 468.

[24] *Logic and Knowledge* (London: George Allen & Unwin, 1956), p. 232 (quoted
by Munitz, *Mystery of Existence*, p. 85). Munitz (*ibid.*, pp. 87–90) also gives a
clear and helpful explanation of the view of P. F. Strawson, who clarifies but
does not basically depart from Bertrand Russell's position. According to
Strawson, a sentence in which "exists" occurs is not itself a subject-predicate
statement but only the presupposition for such a statement.

[25] *Mystery of Existence*, pp. 84–90.

When working out his own position, Munitz strongly reacts against this last point by asserting that "existence" is concerned with the actual world. Granted that "within the context of his system of disclosure [a logician] can so choose to define 'exists' that it has, indeed, the meaning he assigns to it." Nonetheless, may one not legitimately ask "whether this restriction does not do violence to other ordinary uses of the same word"? Munitz's answer is a firm yes.

> As I am arguing here, there is at least one other further and normal use of the word "exists" in which it does make sense to say that it *characterizes something*, namely, the world. To say that existence characterizes the world . . . is not to say something about language at all (except indirectly and incidentally insofar as language, and language-users, are themselves part of the world). It is to say something about the world: existence may be predicated of the world. That the world exists, holds of the world whether or not there are any terms in our language by which we could refer to the world, or to its existence.[26]

But what does "exists" signify? What characteristic does it predicate of the world? The answer is to be found in the fact that "exists" is a verb. Like any other verb, it should express some form of activity; it should describe what existents *do*. If applied to individual things within the world, it is

> an elliptical or foreshortened way of saying that the thing or person persists in carrying on some *particular* activity, or group of activities. Thus, when I say "Socrates existed" or "The moon exists" . . . the terms "existed" and "exists" serve as loose and general surrogates for other terms that can be substituted for them. To say that Socrates existed, is to say that Socrates *lived*, or that he persisted in some particular state, and to say that the moon exists, is to say that the moon occupies space and endures in time, that it behaves as a physical object.[27]

The result is that whenever "exists" is used as a "descriptive term for some activity—or group of activities—of something, we can get

[26] *Ibid.*, pp. 89–90.
[27] *Ibid.*, pp. 92–93. Also see Sidney Hook, *The Quest for Being* (New York: St. Martin's Press, 1961), p. 153.

rid of the term 'exists' altogether, and replace it, more informatively and fruitfully, by specifying the particular activity or kinds of activities that the object in question engages in." The terms thus substituted are better able to distinguish one type of entity from another, or one individual from another.[28]

But when Munitz turns to the world itself, he allows no such replacement. Here "exists" does have "a distinctive and unique role to perform: it designates *what the world does.*" Although we can say that a man lives, that a satellite occupies space and time and interacts physically with other bodies, none of these words describes what the world does; it does not live or move or grow or breathe or oscillate or, even, occupy space and endure in time.[29] Hence, "lives," "moves" or any other such verb is inappropriate to express the activity of the world, and "exists" remains the best choice. But what does the world do? Quite bluntly, the world does what a world does. The world "worlds"; it carries on as a world. This function is what "exists" indicates—a unique and distinctive term to express a unique and distinctive activity. The world "exists"; the world is the world; its essence is its existence.

> The term used to describe its mode of "activity" should be irreducible to any other; it should not be replaceable by some other term. It is to serve as such a distinctive and unique term to describe what the world does, and nothing else does, for which we may use the term "exists." The mode of functioning that is appropriate to the world is—to exist. Instead of saying "The world worlds" or "The world carries on as a world," we say "The world exists." To exist is all that the world can do; this is what it is "fit" to do; or—to use traditional terminology—the essence of the world is its existence.[30]

The conviction expressed in the last clause of the quotation enables Munitz to conclude that "The world exists" is, paradoxically, an

---

[28] *Mystery of Existence*, p. 93.

[29] *Ibid.* On the meaning of "the world," see *ibid.*, p. 52: "[The term 'the world' serves] at once, for the astronomical expanse or inclusive spatio-temporal frame for the great variety of natural objects, events, and processes disclosed in human experience, as well as for this variety itself. The latter includes purely physical phenomena, manifested both terrestrially and throughout the astronomical universe, as well as those of life, mind, and human culture." Also see *ibid.*, pp. 69–71.

[30] *Ibid.*, p. 94.

analytic *a posteriori* statement. *A posteriori* because based on one's experience, analytic because "existence" is an essential feature of the very notion of "the world"—"nonexistence" and "the world" are contradictory.[31] It also enables him to apply *Exodus* 3:14 to the world.

> [According to traditional theology] it is appropriate to God, though not to anything else, to be able to say "I am that I am," or, "I exist, for that is my essence." Whatever be the case with traditional conceptions of God, however (and without going so far as identifying God and the world, as Spinoza did), in this respect, we can say of the world exactly what Austin thought was an incomplete predication, namely, "it exists." If the world could speak, it, too, would say "I am," "I exist," and this would be a complete statement coming from the world, though not if made for, or by, anything else *in* the world.[32]

Such, then, is how Munitz understands "exists." It does not exercise a merely logical function within propositions but helps characterize the actual world itself. Because a verb, it expresses the unique and distinctive activity of the world—namely, the world carries on as a world, the world worlds, the world is what it is, the world is the world. His question then becomes: Why is the world the world? Why is there something that has the characteristics of the world? Why does the world have this feature, that it exists?[33] As we have already seen, Munitz finds that question unanswerable. There is no reason for the existence of the world since the world is not a statement; it is neither an occurrence nor a regularity; it is not something made.[34] Such a question "has neither been satisfactorily answered by any known rational method, nor can be. This conviction amounts to the realization that the existence of the world is incomprehensible, and cannot be adequately explained in any way."[35]

---

[31] *Ibid.*, p. 81. Munitz (*ibid.*, pp. 81–84) considers his analytic *a posteriori* statement to correspond to Kant's analytic *a priori* proposition when concerned with an empirical rather than a pure subject.

[32] *Ibid.*, p. 94. The "Austin" referred to in the quotation is John L. Austin, English philosopher, whom Munitz quotes as remarking "that when God called out to Moses from the burning bush 'I am,' Moses . . . should have asked God: 'You are what?' "

[33] *Ibid.*, pp. 95, 96.

[34] *Ibid.*, pp. 194–211.

[35] *Ibid.*, pp. 12–13.

Another Approach

Despite his careful thoroughness and incisive intelligence, Munitz's agnostic conclusion is, I would submit, neither accurate nor satisfactory. Its inaccuracy is grounded in his misconception of existence as an activity. True enough, "exists" is a verb but it is unlike other verbs. "Lives," "runs," "thinks," "occupies space and endures in time," and so on, all point to *what* this or that existent is. They describe some of the constituents which help make a thing be what it is. As Kant correctly understood, "exists" is not such a term. When, say, a man is declared to exist, that statement does not express a constitutive note of him as a man. Existence is other than what he is. What sort of verb is "exists," then? Not one which indicates an activity but rather one which makes a status claim (to use the language of G. E. Moore and of K. E. M. Baier).[36] When predicated of anything, "exists" expresses that the thing in question is not fictitious, imaginary or merely intramental. Rather, it is extramental. It actually *is*. It is actually present outside nothingness. It possesses the status of be-ing rather than of nonbe-ing.[37]

Perhaps an apt way of conveying this signification of "existence" is a concrete case. The following one is somewhat backhanded, since it mainly concerns nonexistence; but it may prove helpful for

---

[36] G. E. Moore, *Some Main Problems of Philosophy* (London: George Allen & Unwin, 1953), pp. 216–33, especially pp. 225–26; K. E. M. Baier, "Existence," in *Proceedings of the Aristotelian Society* 61 (1961), 19–40, especially p. 35: "*To say they* [beasts of fable, etc.] *are non-existent is simply to say they do not exist in the world around us.* Thus, existence and existence in the world around us come to the same thing. . . . To exist is to be in the world around us." See Munitz, *Mystery of Existence*, pp. 90–91.

A word of caution is necessary. One should separate the notion of "existence" from "existence in space/time," "existence in this world," and so on. To be spatial/temporal and the like belong to existents not qua existents but qua material; they all flow directly from what existents are and not from the fact that they are. "Spatial/temporal" is as foreign to existence as such as is "non-spatial/atemporal," "material" as foreign as is "immaterial," "human" as "nonhuman," "American" as "Chinese"—they all are quidditative characteristics.

[37] See *Authentic Metaphysics*, pp. 77–80. Also see William Barrett, "One Hundred Real Dollars (or Doorknobs)," *Journal of Philosophy* 59 (Nov. 8, 1962), 763: "The ordinary everyday understanding of existence: namely, as a characteristic common to all actually existing things that is not possessed by unreal, imaginary, or merely possible entities, and that is lost when the thing ceases to exist, passes away, perishes, becomes extinct, dies, disappears, vanishes, fades, melts away, is no more."

that very reason. It is a report of a conversation between a staff member of the *New Yorker* and a Mr. Joe Gould, who claimed to have been writing "An Oral History of Our Time" for more than twenty years and who lived on money advanced him during those years by many acquaintances (including the staff member) because of that claim. Mr. Gould has just refused to allow a publisher to see his manuscript because he had always "resolved in the back of my head that the Oral History would be published posthumously."

> As soon as Pearce [the publisher] was out of the room, I turned on Gould. "You told me you lugged armfuls of the Oral History into and out of fourteen publishing offices," I said. "Why in hell did you do that and go to all that trouble if you've always been resolved in the back of your mind that it would be published posthumously? I'm beginning to believe," I went on, "that the Oral History doesn't exist." This remark came from my unconscious, and I was barely aware of the meaning of what I was saying . . . but the next moment, glancing at Gould's face, I knew as well as I knew anything that I had blundered upon the truth about the Oral History.
> "My God!" I said. "It doesn't exist." I was appalled. "There isn't any such thing as the Oral History," I said. "It doesn't exist. . . . The woman who owns the duck-and-chicken farm [where Gould claimed to have stored it for safekeeping] doesn't exist," I said. "And her brother who had the stroke doesn't exist. And her niece doesn't exist. And the Polish farmer and his wife who look after the ducks and chickens don't exist. And the ducks and chickens don't exist. And the cellar that the Oral History is stored in doesn't exist. And the Oral History doesn't exist."
> Gould got up and went over to the window and stood there looking out, with his back to me.
> "It exists in your mind, I guess," I said, recovering a little from my surprise, "but you've always been too lazy to write it down. All that really exists is those so-called essay chapters. That's all you've been doing all through the years—writing new versions of those chapters . . . and correcting them and revising them and tearing them up and starting all over again."
> Gould turned and faced me and said, "It's not a question of laziness." Then . . . he turned his back on me again.[38]

---

[38] "Joe Gould's Secret," *New Yorker*, Sept. 26, 1964, pp. 107–8.

My justification for such a long quotation is that it rather vividly illustrates the difference between nonexistence and existence. The owner of the farm, the farm itself, the owner's relatives, the Polish couple, the ducks and chickens, most of the Oral History—all of them are fictitious, imaginary, merely figments of Gould's inventive mind. They are, in a word, nonexistent. But Mr. Gould himself, the member of the *New Yorker* staff, the publisher, the initial chapters of the history are outside any mind and outside nothingness. They actually are and must be reckoned with accordingly. They are all in the state of be-ing, which is not itself an activity but is just that: actually be-ing. In short, they exist.[39]

Besides contrasting it with the merely intramental and depicting it as the state of actually be-ing, what else can we say of existence? We must add that it is a perfection. This is the aspect of themselves which existents convey to attentive minds.[40] As we previously saw, Chesterton called existence "wonderful . . . amazing . . . an abyss of light." Simone de Beauvoir found it a "glorious splendor" and Gabriel Marcel "an astonishment." Ludwig Wittgenstein character-

---

[39] When thus interpreted as a status claim, existence obviously is not restricted to the world solely (as Dr. Munitz would have it) but is applicable to any item which actually is—individual humans, animals, trees, history books, fence posts, and so forth.

[40] How is existence known? Mainly in two ways, the first of which is direct perception and, more precisely, existential judgments. By reason of evidence immediately presented to them in their everyday lives, human knowers affirm, "Yes, there is a fire in the attic; there actually is a fire department in this suburb; and so on" (see *Authentic Metaphysics*, pp. 85, 336–37). To express this in traditional language, we could say that existence is a *sensibile per accidens* (in contrast with a *sensibile per se*, whether *proprium* or *commune*); it is a factor which is closely involved with a *sensibile per se* (a physical object which stimulates and determines our sense powers) and is immediately apprehended in connection with the latter. See Aquinas, *In II De Anima*, lect. 13 (Marietti ed., nos. 393–96); *In IV Sent.*, d. 49, q. 2, a. 2 resp. (Parma ed., VII, 1202a); *Summa Theologiae*, I, q. 17, a. 2 resp.; *ibid.*, I, q. 78, a. 3 ad 2.

Second, existence can be known through intuition: an immediate, unique, sudden, vivid awareness that something exists and that existence is a supremely important factor. See *Authentic Metaphysics*, pp. 91–93 and 391–99.

Although Munitz restricts his remarks on how we know existence to the world, still much of what he says is valid when properly interpreted. See *Mystery of Existence*, p. 79: "[Knowledge of existence of the world] is the most primordial, commonplace, and universally shared experience. We are likely to overlook it, only because it is so trivial and omnipresent. At any rate, the awareness of the existence of the world is primary and not reducible to any other type of experience."

ized it as "extraordinary" and Paul Tillich as "the astonishment which makes the philosopher a philosopher." Actuality is, in brief, a perfection for the existent. That a thing exists is good for it, ameliorates it, helps perfect and constitute it, makes a difference in it.[41]

This last point has an important and relevant sequel. Someone could admit that "exists" has the meaning just elaborated and still overlook its philosophical consequences. "Granted," he might say, "that 'exists' indicates the thing in question to be extramental and to be actual. Nonetheless, its status of actuality points only to efficient causation. The sole difference between a farmhouse as on the drawing board and as actual is that carpenters and bricklayers have efficiently produced it by their labor. The difference between human offspring as possible and as actual is that their parents have begotten them. Their state of actuality is no differentiation within the existents and is not an intrinsic factor—it merely adds the fact that they have been efficiently caused; it only juxtaposes them to the agents responsible for them." This argument is groundless by the very fact that existence is a perfection *of the existent*: its status of being actual ameliorates *it*, helps perfect and constitute *it*, differentiates *it*. Hence, actuality is an intrinsic factor of the existent itself; it helps make up the existent as a constitutive part. Since agents are necessarily other than (and, in that sense, extrinsic to) their effects, actuality itself is not merely efficient causation. This is not to say that efficient causes are not necessary; material things need them (for example, parents, light and heat waves, and so on) in order to exist. But their existence is not the mere presence and activity of efficient causes. It is an intrinsic, constitutive factor.[42]

Accordingly, what one must realize is that an existent (say, this man) consists of two intrinsic factors: what he is and that he is, essence and existence, that by which he is this man and that by which he exists. However closely joined together in fashioning him, these two constituents are really other than each other. To give one reason: that which is the intrinsic cause of difference cannot itself be simultaneously the intrinsic cause of similarity; but

---

[41] For example, consider the difference existence would have made to the purely mental items in Mr. Gould's story, recounted above. The difference would not be that the owner of the farm would be changed from a woman to a man or that the Polish couple would become Italian but rather that the farm owner, the Polish couple, the farm, and so on would all be actually (and, thereupon, also be an owner, Polish couple and farm).

[42] See *Authentic Metaphysics*, pp. 86–89, 100.

this man is similar to all other existents (whether human or other-wise) in that he and they do exist, and he is unlike them in that he and they each exist in their own unique fashion by reason of what each is; but his essence is that by which he is *what* he is, existence is that by which he *is*; therefore, his essence and existence, although they are both intrinsic constituents of him, are not identical. They are really other than each other.[43]

This real otherness between existence and essence brings in its wake an important conclusion: all existents whose existence really differs from essence are contingent. That is to say, they exist in such a way that, as far as they themselves are concerned, they might not have existed and even now they need not be. Why so? Since in such existents essence or nature is really other than existence, no such existent exists in virtue of its very nature. For example, by his very nature this man is intelligent, free, capable of love and anger and self-nourishment, and so on, because human nature is such as itself to be rational, sentient, vegetal, and so forth. But he does not exist by his very nature because this is not itself existence. He exists, in a word, contingently: he exists in such a fashion that he might not have existed and even now he need not be.[44]

---

[43] See *ibid.*, where the following technical points are made. Existence and essence are really other than each other by a real minor distinction (pp. 82–83, 89–93). They are constitutive parts and intrinsic causes, but they are not physical or integral parts (as are lungs, heart, bones, and so on); like sub-stance/accidents and prime matter/substantial form, they are components. They are principles of being rather than beings; they are real without them-selves being realities (pp. 50–56, 56–64, 93–100).

The metaphysics which has elaborated those points is an inductive noumenology. It is inductive since all its conclusions are based upon data gained through perception and experience. It is a noumenology insofar as it enables us through intellection to know existents in their intrinsic causes and, thus, in what they are and not merely in what they appear (pp. 326–38). (It is not a noumenology, though, in the sense of providing determinate, specific knowledges of things. Such information is either impossible of attainment for a human knower or comes to him from various natural sciences.) Because it is constantly turned to actuals for evidence, it is not compatible with any sort of Husserlian phenomenology. The latter brackets actual existence so as to con-centrate on meaning and intentionality, and thus proclaims that existence has nothing to do with reality and, hence, is of no significance.

[44] According to Munitz (*Mystery of Existence*, p. 120), contingency is of no avail in proving the existence of God because it "begs the question or presup-poses what one is trying to prove, namely, that the world is created." Why so? Because "what we need are reasons for believing that the world might not

Yet he does actually exist. He does possess that perfection; he finds himself in that state of "glorious splendor," of wonderful astonishment. Yet that perfection does not come, as we have already seen, from what he is of himself since his nature is not to exist. Hence, he must have it from someone whose very essence is existence and, for that reason, who exists necessarily in that he exists in such a way that he cannot not be. This existent we call God.[45] Since He exists by His very nature, He needs no cause in order to exist; and, second, He can and does efficiently cause all else to exist. This is what we call creation: an efficient causation which is not a change of or in preexisting matter (as is the case of the efficient causality exercised by all material existents) but rather which accounts for the actual existence of what before actually was in no way. It is the efficiency by which God properly (whether immediately or mediately) causes all things to *exist*, each through an act of existing which is a constitutive part and intrinsic cause really other than what each is.[46]

---

have existed. . . . Once grant this manner of describing the world, that it, too, is contingent, then one has not so much prepared the ground for the concluding statements that there is a Necessary Being: one has already used this conclusion in so characterizing the world." I cannot agree. One realizes material existents are contingent not because of efficient causes but because of intrinsic causes (intrinsic in the sense they are constitutive parts of the things in question); such existents are composed of existence/essence. Their existence really differs from their essences, and hence they exist in such a way that they might not have existed and even now they need not be (as far as they themselves are concerned). They are not affirmed to be contingent because God exists. We affirm that God exists because they are contingent.

[45] See *Authentic Metaphysics*, pp. 135–39; James F. McGlynn and Sister Paul Mary Farley, *A Metaphysics of Being and God* (Englewood Cliffs, N.J.: Prentice-Hall, 1966), pp. 116–28.

[46] Munitz claims creation to be impossible because it has never been observed; it is not sensibly verifiable. "What is essential [in order to have a causal making of an object by some agent] is that we have some basis in our experience for saying that such-and-such a feature of the act of making something was observed, even if it was observed only once" (*Mystery of Existence*, p. 208). Munitz's *a priori* claim must yield to inductive evidence and necessary inference, as he himself suggests: "If I have an object which . . . I know to possess a structure that is the outcome of deliberate making, I am prepared to acknowledge that this, too, was made" (*ibid.*, p. 207). Material existents have just the structure required. They are a composition of existence/essence; no one of them exists by its very essence or nature. Yet they do exist. Accordingly, there must be an Existent who is existence and who efficiently causes them actually to exist. Creation is just such efficient causation.

Résumé

In his book, Milton K. Munitz has centered his attention upon an important and difficult topic in metaphysics: existence. He is convinced that existence is a mystery, insoluble and incomprehensible. Is this admission of agnosticism necessary and inevitable? Only if one admits with Munitz that existence is an activity. But if actual existence is seen to be the state of glorious splendor and wonderful astonishment in which existents find themselves when they are no longer merely intramental but actually are, then existence is no meaningless and inexplicable surd of unintelligibility. It can ground a sanely optimistic metaphysics which culminates in affirming the existence of God.[47]

---

[47] See L. Sweeney, S.J., "God Does Exist," *Ensign* (Spring 1967), 5–10.

Appendix

Existence, Being and Analogy

Let us note what psychologically happens as we progressively come to see how "existence" affects what "being" means.

We begin by reflecting upon material existents. Because of various and diverse evidences within them, we realize that *what* they are is accounted for by prime matter, substantial form and accidents; but that they *actually exist* is explained only by a component which is other than those just mentioned. This can be called the "act of existing" (*esse*) and is the source of the existent's perfection, reality and being. Each material existent is real and is being, then, because it actually exists. As the result of that initial stage in our intellectual process, we become aware that "being" means "that which actually exists." Here, then, the term "being" points to a genuine *concept* (or conception or intelligibility—call it what you like, since those three words can be used interchangeably) because within a complex apprehension[48] we have achieved an intellectual realization or awareness of what beings are precisely as being. It is an *analogous* concept, since actual existents themselves are both similar and diverse (similar in that they all exist, diverse in that each exists in its own and, hence, unique way) and the complex awareness which they produce in us joins similarity to diversity. Yet it is *one* concept inasmuch as we have the single awareness that reality for all such existents is rooted not in their materiality or any other essential trait but only in their actuality.

The second stage of our gradual grasp of what being signifies is already implicit in the first, since now we turn to those components discovered within material existents. They too are real because they are actually present within an existent. They too are real

---

[48] A complex apprehension is an awareness which is consequent upon a technical process of thinking (involving judgments, reflection or direct reasoning, and so on). It summarizes those previous operations in a single, dynamic insight into what some item is. Our awarenesses of all the components (substance/accidents, prime matter/substantial form, essence/*esse*), as well as of being, are complex apprehensions.

This sort of apprehension is not restricted to philosophy but is common to all sciences. See *Authentic Metaphysics*, pp. 326–28.

analogously insofar as they are both similar and diverse—similar in that they all exist within one and the same (say) man, diverse in that within that man each has its own intrinsic causal function to perform. Accordingly, our original concept of being is enlarged to cover also those components when we come to realize that "that which actually exists" expresses any actually existing item, whether it be a supposit (for example, this man, this cow) or a component within a supposit. Yet that complex and obviously analogous concept remains genuinely one in meaning, since we therein retain the single realization that reality for components, as well as for supposits, arises from the sole fact that they do actually exist.

The final stage is built upon the previous two, for the existence of God is demanded by the existence of the material universe. Material things do not exist of and by themselves, since in them actuality is other than nature: that by which they exist (*esse*) is really other than that by which they are what they are (essence). Yet they do actually exist. Hence, there must be an Existent whose very nature *is* actuality and existence and who is their cause. God, then, is real because He actually exists. He is real analogously, since all else is both similar to Him and diverse from Him—similar inasmuch as they, as well as He, actually exist and they are images of His infinite perfections; diverse inasmuch as they and He exist in different manners: actuality for them is not their essence, whereas His very nature is to exist and to be actual.[49] Consequently, when we have proved that God actually exists and are thus aware that He too is real and Being, then our conception of being must be extended so as to embrace creatures and Creator. "Being" is "that which actually exists" in such a way that the *that which* can be really distinct from, or totally identified with, actual existence. Yet that complex and manifestly analogous concept continues to be genuinely one because it conveys the single message that reality, no matter where found, is synonymous with actuality. Even though the existents of whom we may be thinking are as disparate as God and creatures, still all are being because they *are*.

When arrived at by the inductive and deliberately elaborated process just outlined, then, our awareness of being is a concept which is richly complex and analogous because it has arisen by our

---

[49] That status of similarity/diversity issues into several sorts of analogy— that of eminence, of proper proportionality, of reference, of denomination— see *Authentic Metaphysics*, pp. 151–60 and 194–96.

reflecting upon actual existents which are complex and analogous. Yet it is one concept because our reflection concentrated upon the single factor which makes them all real—the fact that they do actually exist.[50]

---

[50] On inductive processes see *Authentic Metaphysics*, pp. 329–33. On "being" also see *ibid.*, Appendix B, pp. 401–3.

21

Preller and Aquinas:
Second Thoughts on Epistemology

Victor Preller

In 1967 Victor Preller published a book, *Divine Science and the Science of God: A Reformulation of Thomas Aquinas*.[1] Despite the nearly twenty-five years since its publication its first two chapters are still worth considering: "A Cautionary Note and Assorted Promissory Notes" (pp. 3–34) and "Epistemology Reformed and a Cautionary Note Reissued" (pp. 35–107). In them I shall concentrate upon his interpretation of Aquinas' epistemology and psychology, which seems to be largely a misinterpretation. But it is illuminating for that very reason.

Man for Aquinas, as Preller reads him, is in entity like an angel (pp. 44, 49, 50, 51, 56, 64). This entitative condition has, of course, repercussions upon human cognition. There is innate in each human knower a conceptual system which consists of intentional forms or categories (pp. 43, 53–55, 62–63) and which as such does not directly pertain to actual things (pp. 38, 51, 70). That system has not arisen from things (pp. 51, 52, 54) but from the agent intellect, which "all men possess *by nature* [as] a common power of conceptualization . . . and is the same in all men" (p. 70, italics in original; also see pp. 53, 55, 76).[2] Elements within that conceptual

---

[1] Princeton, N.J.: Princeton University Press, 1967.

[2] Preller makes Aquinas' notion of agent intellect seem much like Avicenna's *dator formarum*, which was a sublunar separate Intelligence "ceaselessly radiating all possible forms and causing them to exist in proportionate matters, or to be known by intellects" (E. Gilson, *History of Christian Philosophy*

system have only a syntactical or logical role—that is, "the 'meaning' of any concept or statement which could be formed within the system would be nothing but the syntactical role played by that concept or statement within the system" (pp. 44–45). Such a system "would be entirely formal—it would have no material content" (p. 45).[3] But can it have no reference to man's empirical experience? Yes, through the imagination, which "is naturally programmed in such a way" as to synchronize "only such regularly repeated patterns of the state of the sensory system as are isomorphic with elements within the conceptual system of the man-angel's intellect" (p. 50).

The "sensory system" just mentioned is fitted into man's angelic nature only after rather radical transformation. Of themselves the senses are not powers of knowing (p. 57): their content is nonintentional and apparently consists merely of the "material alterations of the receiving organs of the sensory systems—alterations caused by the impact on the organs" of external objects (p. 49). Sense knowledge requires that the intellect combine with the senses. Only then is there "an intentional interpretation of the objects of experience, ordered to the intelligible categories of the mind" (p. 39). In fact, "perception (*conscious* experience of external reality) arises *jointly* out of the non-intentional contents of sensation and the forms of conceptual thought" (p. 62). The intelligible categories and the conceptual forms just mentioned are not caused by sense experience, which is "the *occasion* for the actual development of a conceptual system" and nothing more (p. 54).

My previous two paragraphs are an attempt accurately to replay Preller's interpretation of the medieval author. But accuracy is hard to attain, because it is difficult to separate Preller's own position and reformulation of Aquinas from his account of the latter's own position. This difficulty is forecast even in Preller's description of the aim and character of his book. He will use "the writings of

---

in the Middle Ages [New York: Random House, 1955], p. 214; also see pp. 204–5). Aquinas often rejects Avicenna's view—see, for example, *S.T.*, I, qu. 79, art. 4 resp.; I, qu. 84, art. 4 resp.; *De Veritate*, qu. 10, art. 6 resp. (Leonine ed., XXII, 115).

[3] On p. 75 Preller acknowledges his debt to Kant. For another book published in 1967 which is indebted to Kant (among others), see K. R. Hanley and J. D. Monan, *A Prelude to Metaphysics: The Meaning of Being Interrogated Through Reflection and History* (Englewood Cliffs, N.J.: Prentice-Hall, Inc., 1967). For my critique see "Thomas Aquinas and Philosophers of Subjectivity," *Modern Schoolman* 47 (1969), 62–70.

Aquinas . . . as a model of religious language," but he simultaneously feels "free to modify Aquinas' positions on some important points" (p. vii). "Aquinas utilizes the categories of Aristotelian
epistemology to *make* his theological claims concerning the status
of language about God. It is therefore necessary for us to see what
is essentially entailed by his espousal of that epistemology and
how it is related to the theological substance of his own teaching"
(p. 35). Nonetheless, "I shall . . . translate the epistemological doctrine of the *Summa Theologiae* into a fairly contemporary mode of
discourse highly dependent on the insights and terminology of
Wilfred Sellars."[4] In fact, "from time to time I shall modify or
reformulate certain aspects of Aquinas' stated position, eliminating
what I take to be superfluous or contradictory elements" (p. 36). He
believes it possible "to offer an interpretation of Aquinas which—
while it might never have occurred to him—will express what he
intended. At the very least it will not be inconsistent with what he
does say" (p. 44; also see pp. 53–61).

Granted, then, the difficulty of coping with Preller's exegesis of
Aquinas, but if my previous paragraphs are to some degree adequate, anyone acquainted with Thomas' Latin text can rather easily judge that Preller's exposition is incorrect. Aquinas makes abundantly clear that man entitatively is not an angel. The human soul,
he says, specifically differs from an angel (*Summa Theologiae*, I, qu.
75, art. 7 resp.; also see parallel texts given in Leonine-Marietti and
in Ottawa editions). An angel is a subsistent form, which has no
connection whatsoever with matter (*ibid.*, I, qu. 50, art. 1 and 2). A
human being is essentially a composite of form and matter: his soul
(that which is the principle of his intellectual life, as well of course
as of his sensitive and vegetal life) is by its very nature the substantial form of his body (*ibid.*, I, qu. 76, art. 1 resp.). This relation of an
angelic and of a human existent to matter determines the nature of
knowledge in each. Since an angel is entirely immaterial, its intel-

---

[4] On Sellars as a conduit of Kant to Preller see Wilfrid Sellars, *Science,
Perception and Reality* (London: Routledge and Kegan Paul, 1963), pp. 46, 73n,
74n, 90, 100–101, 127, 299. Also see *idem, Science and Metaphysics: Variations on
Kantian Themes* (London: Routledge and Kegan Paul, 1968) in its entirety. For
Sellars' own intellectual autobiography see his "Autobiographical Reflections"
in Hector-Neri Castañeda (ed.), *Action, Knowledge and Reality: Critical Studies
in Honor of Wilfrid Sellars* (Indianapolis: Bobbs-Merrill Co., Inc., 1975), pp. 277–
93 (on Kant, see pp. 283–89 especially). Also see Johanna Seibt, *Properties as
Process: A Synoptic Study of Wilfred Sellars' Nominalism* (Acascaders, Calif.:
Ridgeview Publishing Co., 1990).

lect is a cognitive power which has no corporeal organ and which is in no way joined to matter (*ibid.*, I, qu. 85, art. 1 resp.: "Quaedam autem virtus cognoscitiva est quae neque est actus organi corporalis, neque est aliquo modo corporali materiae conjuncta, sicut intellectus angelicus"). Consequently, its proper object is also whatever is entirely immaterial (*ibid.*, I, qu. 84, art. 7 resp.). But a human being is mind-in-matter, an incarnate intellect, the proper object of which accordingly is intelligibilities existing and concretized in matter (*ibid.*: "Intellectus autem humani, qui est coniunctus corpori, proprium obiectum est quidditas sive natura in materia corporali existens"). These concretized intelligibilities are the content-determining-cause of human knowledge by acting upon the senses so as to help produce sense knowledge and through the senses so as to help produce intellection (the senses and the intellect being efficient causes of their knowledges). The senses, then, are truly powers of knowing: conjoined to corporeal organs, they know material things precisely as individual and particular (*ibid.*, I, qu. 85, art. 1 resp.: "Quaedam enim cognoscitiva virtus est actus organi corporalis, scilicet sensus. Et ideo obiectum cuiuslibet sensitivae potentiae est forma prout in materia corporali existit. Et quia huiusmodi materia est individuationis principium, ideo omnis potentia sensitivae partis est cognoscitiva particularium tantum"). Man's intellect, although itself without an organ, is nonetheless a power of a soul which is the substantial form of matter, and, hence, its proper object (as has already been said) is intelligibilities existing in matter but (this has not yet been said) not precisely as so existing (*ibid.*: "Intellectus . . . humanus . . . non enim est actus alicuius organi, sed tamen est quaedam virtus animae, quae est forma corporis. . . . Et ideo proprium eius est cognoscere formam in materia quidem corporali individualiter existentem, non tamen prout est in tali materia"). Intellection, then, is abstractive, for abstraction is just that: knowing what actually exists as individualized but without considering its individuality. But phantasms disclose to the knower an individual existent precisely as individual. Hence, our intellect efficiently brings about knowledge of material existents only by abstracting from phantasms (*ibid.*: "Cognoscere vero id quod est in materia individuali, non prout est in tali materia, est abstrahere formam a materia individuali, quam repraesentant phantasmata. Et ideo necesse est dicere quod intellectus noster intelligit materialia abstrahendo a phantasmatibus").

As that text suggests, phantasms are crucial to Thomas' theory of cognition. But what are they? What role do they play? As we previously noted, individual material existents (e.g., this running man, this roaring lion, this fragrant red rosebush) are the proper object of human knowledge, whether sensation or intellection (*ibid.*: "Objectum cuiuslibet sensitivae potentiae est forma prout in materia corporali existit. . . . Proprium eius [intellectus humani] est cognoscere formam in materia quidem corporali individualiter existentem . . ."). Such existents are intelligibilities or forms concretized in and individualized by matter. By our external and internal senses we know such existents precisely as concretized and particularized (*ibid.*: "Et quia huiusmodi materia est individuationis principium, ideo omnis potentia sensitivae partis est cognoscitiva particularium tantum"). That is, the content of the initial, entitative and noncognitive actuation (which arises when this running man or this roaring lion or this fragrant red rose physically stimulates our sense organs and which informs and actuates our sense faculties) and of the ensuing sensation is "this running [man]" or "this roaring [lion]" or "this fragrant red [rose]."[5] The content of the phan-

---

[5] In Aquinas' terminology the bracketed word designates a *sensible per accidens* (in contrast with a *sensibile per se*, whether *proprium* or *commune*)—namely, a factor which is closely involved with a *sensibile per se* (a physical object which stimulates and determines our sense powers) and is immediately apprehended in connection with the latter. See Aquinas, *In II De Anima*, lect. 13 (Marietti ed., nos. 393–96); *In IV Sent.*, dist. 49, qu. 2, art. 2 resp. (Parma ed., vol. VII, 1202a); *S.T.*, I, qu. 17, art. 2 resp.; *ibid.*, I, qu. 78, art. 3 ad 2.

See G. P. Klubertanz, "St. Thomas and the Knowledge of the Singular," *The New Scholasticism* 26 (1962), 135–66.

What more can be said of the bracketed word in the phrases "this running [man]," "this roaring [lion]," "this fragrant [rose]"? The bracketed word indicates what is genuinely but only implicitly contained in the initial, entitative and noncognitive actuation and in the sensation, waiting to be explicated in and by the process of intellection. Or one might say that the bracketed noun points to what is virtually present in the initial entitative actuation and in the sense experience itself and which will become formally present through intellection. But no matter whether the couplet used is implicit/explicit or virtual/formal, two important points must be remembered, the first of which is that the content of both sensation and intellection is radically the same (e.g., "this fragrant red rose"), although the former centers on "this fragrant," the latter on "rose." Second, if the intelligibility expressed by "rose" is taken to be identical with form itself (that by which this plant is rosebush), it is actually and not merely potentially present in the rosebush itself and is universal only through extrinsic denomination inasmuch as it causes us intellectually to know "rose" as what several such bushes have in common. But if form is taken precisely as concretized in and individuated by matter, form is an intelligibility only potentially because that concretization and individuation

tasm, which is the cognitive actuation efficiently produced by the internal senses (especially the cogitative power), is no exception. Its content too is "this running [man]" or "this roaring [lion]" or "this fragrant red [rose]." But by intellection we know such individual material existents precisely and explicitly as actually intelligible— that is, as "man" or "lion" or "rose." How does this come about? The agent intellect, serving as principal efficient cause, uses as instrumental cause a phantasm whose content is "this running [man]" or this roaring [lion]" or "this fragrant red [rose]" so as to produce in the possible or recipient intellect the initial entitative actuation whose content is "man" or "lion" or "rose."[6] The recipient intellect, because of the formal actuation thus produced within it and now informing and actuating it, has become what it will know—a becoming which is not physical (men, lions or roses are not actually in it) but intentional.[7] Through that actuation the recipient intellect is genuinely although nonphysically conformed to and assimilated with the actual thing. This conformity and assimilation issues into knowledge when the intellect efficiently causes the concept or *verbum*, the explicit content of which is "man" or "lion" or "rose."[8]

---

so permeates it that it can be intellectually known only if abstracted from those material conditions, as a result of which abstraction form is actually intelligible in actuation #a$_3$ (see diagram below). But even when thus identical with actual intelligibility, form is not in itself intrinsically universal (which is a direct characteristic solely of the content of intellection, of form-as-known) but (as we said earlier) only through extrinsic denomination as that which causes that content, which alone is a direct or reflex universal. See Thomas, *In II Sent.*, d. 3, q. 3, a. 2, ad 1; *S.C.G.*, I, c. 69, prgr. 8: "Praeterea"; *Q. D. de Anima*, a. 20, ad 1; *De Spir. Creaturis*, a. 9 resp.; *In IX Meta.*, lect. 11, n. 1898; *S.T.*, I, 13, 7 ad 6.

[6] See *Quaestio Quodlibetalis*, VIII, qu. 2, art. 3 resp. (Marietti ed., p. 161): "Intellectus agens est principale agens, quod agit rerum similitudines in intellectu possibili. Phantasmata autem quae a rebus exterioribus accipiuntur, sunt quasi agentia instrumentalia: intellectus enim possibilis comparatur ad res quarum notitiam recipit, sicut patiens quod cooperatur agenti."

[7] This stage of the process is precognitive with reference to the intellection which has not yet occurred. "Intentional" should be understood broadly enough to cover all aspects of cognition—thus, actuations #a and #b are both intentional. The word has a restricted meaning in E. Husserl and other phenomenologists—see H. Spiegelberg, *The Phenomenological Movement*, 3d ed. (The Hague: Martinus Nijhoff, 1984), pp. 746–47.

[8] See *Quaestio Disputata De Veritate*, qu. 1, art. 1 resp. (Leonine ed., XXII, vol. 1, pp. 5–6): "Omnis autem cognitio perficitur per assimilationem cognoscentis ad rem cognitam, ita quod assimilatio dicta est causa cognitionis: sicut visus per hoc quod disponitur per speciem coloris, cognoscit colorem. . . . Hoc

In such an epistemology and psychology there manifestly are two causes of human knowledge. The cognitive faculties (external and internal senses; the agent and recipient intellects) are its efficient cause, but actual individual things are its content-determining-cause.[9] A human knower directly and noninferentially knows actual things because they have caused the content of his knowledge. They account for what he knows. Thomas' position on cognition, therefore, is not Kant's. He neither needs nor permits any categories or conceptual forms or first principles which would be in origin independent of actual existents. A second feature of Thomas' theory is that the initial formal actuations are everywhere required as entitative determinants in the intentional order of the cognitive faculties. By them our powers entitatively, intentionally

---

est ergo quod addit verum supra ens, scilicet conformitatem sive adaequationem rei et intellectus, ad quam conformitatem, ut dictum est, sequitur cognitio rei. Sic ergo entitas rei praecedit rationem veritatis, sed cognitio est quidam veritatis effectus."

[9] The distinction between efficient and content-determining-causes is based upon such texts as *De Veritate*, qu. 10, art. 6 resp. (Leonine ed., XXII, vol. 2, pp. 312–13): "[On the question of 'utrum mens humana cognitionem a sensibilibus accipiat'] rationabilior est sententia Philosophi qui ponit scientiam mentis nostrae partim ab intrinseco et partim ab extrinseco esse, non solum a rebus a materia separatis sed etiam ab ipsis sensibilibus. Cum enim mens nostra comparatur ad res sensibiles quae sunt extra animam, invenitur se habere ad eas in duplici habitudine: uno modo ut actus ad potentiam, in quantum scilicet res quae sunt extra animam sunt intelligibiles in potentia, ipsa vero mens est intelligibilis in actu, et secundum hoc ponitur in anima intellectus agens qui faciat intelligibilia in potentia esse intelligibilia in actu; alio modo ut potentia ad actum, prout scilicet in mente nostra formae rerum determinatae sunt in potentia tantum quae in rebus extra animam sunt in actu, et secundum hoc ponitur in anima nostra intellectus possibilis cuius est recipere formas a rebus sensibilibus abstractas, factas intelligibiles in actu per lumen intellectus agentis, quod quidem lumen intellectus agentis in anima procedit sicut a prima origine ... et praecipue a Deo.

"Et secundum hoc verum est quod scientiam mens nostra a sensibilibus accipit; nihilominus tamen ipsa anima in se similitudines rerum format in quantum per lumen intellectus agentis efficiuntur formae a sensibilibus abstractae intelligibiles actu, ut in intellectu possibili recipi possint."

For a discussion on the distinction between efficient cause and content-determining-cause, see L. Sweeney, S.J., *Authentic Metaphysics in an Age of Unreality* [hereafter: *Authentic Metaphysics*], 2d ed. (New York/Bern: Peter Lang Publishing, Inc., 1993), pp. 325–26.

For additional passages in Thomas on potential and actual intelligibility, see *De Ver.*, 19, 1 resp.; *Compendium Theologiae*, c. 83; *S.T.*, I, 84, 6 resp. ad finem; *Quaestio Disputata de Anima*, a. 15, resp. Also see texts listed above in n. 5.

and precognitively become what will be known. Third, the phantasm has several facets. It is the awareness which is efficiently produced by man's internal senses but whose content consists of data from the external senses as well. By it one knows, to use a previous example, this fragrant red rose as "this fragrant red [rose]." Because of its content it also can serve as the instrument which the agent intellect uses to produce within the recipient intellect the entitative actuation whose content is "rose." Because its content is itself determined by the red rose affecting the external and internal sense organs, it is the channel through which the actual rose is the content-determining-cause of that entitative actuation and, thereby, of the concept "rose."

If the previous three paragraphs are correct, one must conclude that Preller has misread Aquinas. Man having an a priori system of conceptual forms and categories within his mind; the senses not causes but only occasions of that system; the senses not themselves powers of knowing; the entitative, noncognitive initial actuation of the faculty (whether sense or intellect) not distinguished from the subsequent cognitional actuation of the same faculty—these points are in conflict with the medieval theologian's texts.

The same conflict shows up in Preller's conception of abstraction and of the phantasm. For example, as he says on p. 53, "To abstract the intelligible species or form which is potentially present in one's experience—to make one's experience actually intelligible—is to express the isomorphism that exists between one's experience and one's conceptual system by *utilizing* that system as a means of consciously perceiving and informing that which one experiences." But he mentions phantasms more frequently. P. 38: They are "remembered images of the objects of sensation." P. 40: "Aquinas maintains, however, that the phantasm contains or represents, not the object itself, but only the sensible accidents of the object." P. 50, n. 51: "The phantasm cannot be an 'intentional image' possessed 'by the mind.' Sensation cannot be a conscious state until the contents of sensation (physical states of the organism) are 'informed' by the intellect"; also see pp. 54–55. P. 56: "Aquinas seems to define the 'phantasm' in such a way that it must be both intelligible and nonintentional—both material and (in some sense) mental. I shall attempt to show that the very notion of a perceptual mental image . . . prior to the operation of the intellect is self-contradictory"; see pp. 58–59. P. 61: "The 'phantasm' is *simply* Aquinas' method of . . . indicating how the physical may affect the 'mental'. . . . I think we must [grant] that it is an impossible entity—a self-contradictory *tertium quid.* . . . The most crucial aspect of the 'logic of phantasms' is that the 'phantasm' is produced by a kind of pre-judgmental and pre-conceptual automatic causality. . . . Nevertheless, the form that the 'image' actually takes is dictated by the presence 'in the mind' of conceptual powers and categories. All that Aquinas can really be saying is that our *conscious experience* of, e.g., 'blue objects' is a result *both* of that which occurs in the physical sensory system when we sense a blue object, *and* of the production by the intellect of the formally significant concept 'blue.' *There are no 'phantasms'"* (italics in original).

His exposition of phantasm, as well as of abstraction,[10] is inaccurate because Aquinas, in my judgment, means something quite different by the two terms.

Second Thoughts

Yet on second thought one can understand why Preller, whose industry and intelligence are beyond question, went wrong in his interpretation: Thomas himself is to blame to some extent because of his occasional careless and misleading language. Take as an instance my paragraphs above corresponding to notes 5–9: where we speak of the twofold stage of sentient and intellectual knowledges as "the initial, entitative, formal actuation" and "the subsequent cognitional actuation," Thomas, even in the passages quoted in notes 6, 8 and 9, speaks of the first stage as "similitudines" and "species," words which can mean likenesses or images and which thus might lead one to think that for Aquinas knowledge terminates directly there rather than at the material existents themselves causing their content. Hence, one could conclude that Thomas' epistemology is a representationalism. That conclusion would be mistaken because even in *De Veritate*, 1, 1 resp., quoted above in note 8, Aquinas makes clear that "similitudines" or "species" are equivalent to what I call the "initial, entitative, precognitive, formal actuations": all knowledge (he says) is brought about when the knower becomes assimilated to, conformed and identified with, the known and then comes to know it:

Omnis autem cognitio perficitur *per assimilationem cognoscentis ad rem cognitam,* ita quod *assimilatio* dicta est *causa cognitionis:* sicut visus *per hoc quod disponitur per speciem coloris, cognoscit*

---

[10] For an exposition of the metaphysics of Thomistic abstraction see L. Sweeney, *Authentic Metaphysics,* pp. 338–50 and Appendix C (pp. 405–7).

colorem. . . . Hoc est ergo quod addit verum supra ens, scilicet *conformitatem* sive *adaequationem rei et intellectus; ad quam conformitatem . . . sequitur cognitio rei.* Sic ergo entitas rei praecedit rationem veritatis, sed cognitio est quidam veritatis effectus [italics added].[11]

But why did Thomas use such possibly misleading language as "similitudines" and "species" in his epistemology? One reason is that traditionally such terms were used when theologians were trying to describe the Trinity: the Word is the image or likeness of the Father. This is a tradition which began with St. Paul and was continued by Hilary of Poitiers.[12] It was further developed by Augustine in his search for analogues between the three persons of the triune God and the human knower. That he thus linked the Trinity and human epistemology can be learned from W. G. T. Shedd's 1887 statement in his "Introductory Essay" to his revision of A. W. Haddan's 1872 translation of Augustine's *De Trinitate:*

Augustin [*sic*] starts with the assumption that man was made in the image of the *triune* God, the God of revelation; not in the image of the God of natural religion, or the untriune deity of the nations. Consequently, it is to be expected that a trinitarian analogue can be found in his [man's] mental constitution. If

---

[11] For additional texts see n. 22 below; also see Jacques Maritain, *The Degrees of Knowledge,* trans. G. B. Phelan (New York: Charles Scribner's Sons, 1959), pp. 95–98.

[12] For Paul see 2 *Cor.* 4:4: "Illuminatio evangelii gloriae Christi, qui est imago Dei"; *idem, Col.* 1:15: "[Filius Dei] qui est imago Dei invisibilis."

For Hilary see his *De Trinitate,* II, 1, 1: "Infinitas in patre, species in imagine, usus in munere"—for Latin text see H. Hurter (ed.), *Sancti Hilarii Pictaviensis Episcopi de Trinitate Libri XII* (Oeniponti: Libraria Academica Wagneriana, 1887). What does "species," here applied to God the Son as image of the Father, mean? In origin it apparently is a translation of "eidos," which comes from the Greek verb "to see," and thus it first means "that which is seen or appears." The connotation is that what one sees in an object is the beauty it conveys to the viewer. Consequently, "species" means beauty. For information on Hilary see my *Divine Infinity in Greek and Medieval Thought* (New York/Bern: Peter Lang Publishing, Inc., 1992), ch. 15: "Divine Infinity: 1150–1250," prgrs. corresponding to notes 30–44; ch. 8 above, "Augustine on Christ as God and Man: Exegesis of *Confessions,* VII, 19," n. 14; Michael O'Carroll, *Trinitas: A Theological Encyclopedia of the Holy Trinity* [hereafter: *Trinitas*] (Wilmington, Del.: Michael Glazier, Inc., 1987), pp. 123–26; E. J. Fortman, *The Triune God: A Historical Study of the Doctrine of the Trinity* [hereafter: *Triune God*] (Philadelphia: The Westminster Press, 1972), pp. 126–33; Aquinas, *S.T.,* I, 39, 8 resp.

man is God's image, he will show traces of it in every respect. All [interpreters] acknowledge that the Divine unity, and all the communicable attributes, have their finite correspondants in the unity and attributes of the human mind. But the Latin father goes further than this. This, in his view, is not the whole of the Divine image. When God says, "Let *us* make man in *our* image, after *our* likeness" (*Gen.*, 1, 26), Augustin understands these words to be spoken *by* the Trinity, and *of* the Trinity—by and of the true God, the God of revelation: the Father, Son, and Holy Spirit, one God [italics in original].[13]

For Augustine, then, the human person images the Trinity, and this in especially the two triads of mind, knowledge and love and, second, memory, understanding and will—see *De Trinitate*, Books IX, X and XV.

Bonaventure continues to set up analogues between the triune God and human epistemology in such a way as to suggest or even welcome a representationalism. For instance, consider his remarks on how sense knowledge comes about. The sensible object causes its "similitudo" in the knower and thus is like a parent producing an offspring. The result is that sensation can serve as a parallel of God the Father's relation to God the Son as parent to offspring or "similitudo" or image.

First of all, let us consider the illumination of sense perception, which is concerned exclusively with the cognition of sense objects. . . . If we consider the medium of perception, we shall see therein the Word begotten from all eternity and made man in time. Indeed, a sense object can stimulate a cognitive faculty only through the medium of a similitude which proceeds from the object as an offspring from its parent, and this . . . for every sense. This similitude, however, does not complete the act of perception unless it is brought into contact with the organ and the sense faculty, and once that contact is established, there results a new perception. Through this perception the mind is led back to the object by means of the similitude ("per illam perceptionem fit reductio ad obiectum mediante similitudine illa"). . . . In like manner, know that from the mind of the Most High. . . , from all eternity there

---

[13] See *Nicene and Post-Nicene Fathers of the Christian Church* (Grand Rapids, Mich.: William B. Eerdmans Publishing Co., 1956; reprint 1976), III, 5. Also see M. O'Carroll, *Trinitas*, pp. 42–45; Fortman, *Triune God*, pp. 139–50.

emanated a Similitude, an Image and an Offspring; and afterwards, when the "fullness of time came," He was united to a mind and a body and assumed the form of man, which had never been before. Through Him the minds of all of us which receive that Similitude of the Father through faith in our hearts are brought back to God.[14]

Bonaventure does, then, set up a parallel of the Father and Son as parent and offspring, but this parallel apparently works only if the "similitudo," which is distinct from the sensible object, is known first and then leads the knower to the object itself. If so, such an epistemology is representational: the similitude or image, which represents the object, is known before the object itself, which thereafter becomes known.

Granted that Aquinas does use such traditional language as "similitudo" or "species" or "imago," but his epistemology is not representational.[15] For him such words do not express what the human knower is aware of before knowing the object. Rather, they express the initial entitative and noncognitive actuation which is the means by which the cognitive powers of the knower nonphysically (intentionally) but noncognitively become the known so as to establish an entitative oneness of knower and known, which results in a second actuation that is the cognition itself, efficiently produced by the actuated faculty. The species or similitude is itself known only subsequently and by inference.

In order to understand Aquinas better let us first turn to Aristotle, whose epistemology is not affected by Trinitarian concerns.

Aristotle's Theory of Knowledge

That Aristotle realized that knowledge is becoming and being the other can be inferred from the twofold actuation of which he

---

[14] *De reductione artium ad theologiam*, #8, *S. Bonaventurae Opera Theologica Selecta* (Ad Claras Aquas: Typographia Collegii S. Bonaventurae, 1964), V, 222—trans. E. T. Healy, *The Works of St. Bonaventure* (St. Bonaventure, N.Y.: The Franciscan Institute, 1955), as quoted by H. Shapiro, *Medieval Philosophy: Selected Readings* (New York: The Modern Library, 1964), p. 375. See O'Carroll, *Trinitas*, pp. 57–58; Fortman, *Triune God*, pp. 212–17; Etienne Gilson, *The Philosophy of St. Bonaventure* (London: Sheed and Ward, 1938), pp. 350–58.

[15] See O'Carroll, *Trinitas*, pp. 132–33 and 210–12; Fortman, *Triune God*, pp. 204–10. Also see n. 22 below.

speaks in *On the Soul*, III, 2, 425b26 and 426a10, quoted and studied below. But it is also a realization based in everyday life on his (and our) experience of sympathy upon learning of misfortunes affecting loved ones, of joy upon learning of their successes, of fear when hearing of threats to their safety.[16]

That realization can also be gained vicariously from what is expressed in drama and other literature. Take as an instance how for Miranda (the heroine of John Fowles' novel *The Collector*), thinking of the world outside the cellar in which she was physically imprisoned made her mentally free because she had intentionally become the boyfriend of whom she was thinking: by her cognitive acts she was with him, and knowledge is thus shown to be becoming and being what is known.

> It's odd (and I feel a little guilty) but I have been feeling happier today than at any time since I came here. . . . I feel happy because *I've not been here for most of the day. I've been* mainly *thinking* about G. P. [her painter friend]. *In his world, not this one here.* I remembered so much. I would have liked to write it all down. I gorged myself on memories. This world makes that [outside] world seem so real, so living, so beautiful. Even the sordid parts of it [italics added].[17]

That dimension of cognition as intentionally becoming and being the known has been well explicated by the playwright Ossie Davis in commenting on the nature of good drama.

> What are we looking forward to in the theater? What will be the source of the pleasure we [dramatists] will provide? Insight.

---

[16] Such experience implies that we feel sympathy, joy and fear for others because their situation has become ours through knowledge. We have cognitively become them and cognition *is* that state of our being one with them.

[17] John Fowles, *The Collector* (New York: Dell Publishing Co., 1963), p. 136. Another example can be gathered from Jimmy Hoffa's interview while in prison. When asked why imprisonment had not beaten him down, he answered: "My body was in the prison, sure. But I never let my mind believe it. That cell is $7\,^1/_2$ feet by 9 feet, and if you want to know what that's like you go home and spend the rest of the day in your biggest closet.

"But my mind was always somewhere else. I read books, and my mind wasn't in the cell. It was away somewhere in the books. . . . And I had people send material for me to study" (Al Stark, "Hoffa on Prisons," *The Washington Post* for April 2, 1972).

The immediate, personal apprehension of truth—of the "feel" of truth—about a thing, or a person, or a situation. For where there is no insight the people perish. And pleasure in art is based upon *the discovery of identity.* I propose as the legitimate business of the theater the eliciting of the simple joy of seeing for the first time, not only what man is, but also what man can be. *By seeing, I mean to experience. For only by experience can we know. And in theater at its best we experience, through our imagination, the* feel *of what is true. And having felt it, we know it; and having known it, we possess it—and are possessed by it—forever.*

Once *I feel the truth, the internal* is-*ness* of, say, a Negro, a Jew, a Gentile, a Catholic, a Communist, a homosexual or a Nazi, I can no longer pretend that he is a stranger, or a foreigner, or an outcast. *What is more, I will be so pleasured in my new knowledge that I would not want to so pretend. I will myself have become, at one and the same time, all of these things* [italics added].[18]

Aristotle would, I am convinced, accept Davis' conception of knowledge as that by which the knower nonphysically and intentionally becomes the known. If so, his next step would be to explain how that nonphysical becoming occurs. His explanation could not consist in any sort of cognitive factor, which would simply initiate an infinite regress.[19] No, it would have to be a noncognitive factor which would entitatively unite the known with the knower prior to the operation of knowledge itself. But this operation would issue from that entitative union of known/knower when the knower through efficient causality comes to be aware of what he/she already had entitatively become.

Such is, in fact, Aristotle's explanation. Knowledge requires two actuations, the first of which is the initial, precognitive, entitative,

---

[18] Ossie Davis, "Plays of Insight Are Needed to Make Stage Vital in Our Lives," *The New York Times* for August 23, 1964. Also see Oscar Wilde, as quoted by Owen Dudley Edwards, *The Fireworks of Oscar Wilde* (Trafalgar Square: Barrie and Jenkins, 1992): "We become lovers when we see Romeo and Juliet, and Hamlet makes us students. The blood of Duncan is upon our hands, with Timon we rage against the world, and when Lear wanders out upon the heath the terror of madness touches us. Ours is the white sinlessness of Desdemona, and ours, also, the sin of Iago."

[19] An initiation he also refused when explaining the actual continua of extension, motion and time, each of which consists of parts which are without extension (points), without movement (places) and without duration (instants or "nows"). See *Physics*, Delta, chs. 10–14.

formal actuation (hereafter: actuation "a") of the faculty; the second is the cognition itself (hereafter: actuation "b"). In *On the Soul*, III, 2, 425b26 and 426a10, he speaks clearly of that first actuation with reference to our sense knowledge.

> The actuation of what is sensed and of the sense is one and the same (although the being of each is not the same), . . . but that actuation is in the sense and [not in what is sensed].

> Ἡ δὲ τοῦ αἰσθητοῦ ἐνέργεια καὶ τῆς αἰσθήσεως ἡ αὐτὴ μέν ἐστι καὶ μία, τὸ δ᾽ εἶναι οὐ τὸ αὐτὸ αὐταῖς· . . . καὶ ἡ τοῦ αἰσθητοῦ ἐνέργεια καὶ ἡ τοῦ αἰσθητικοῦ ἐν τῷ αἰσθητικῷ.

If we transfer that insight from sense perception to any spontaneous or philosophical knowledge (see *ibid.*, III, 4, 429a13 sqq.), we obtain this: the actuation of what is known and of the faculty knowing is one and the same but it is present in the faculty and not in the known. It is an actuation of the known and is caused by the known, while simultaneously it also is an actuation of the knower too and, in fact, is solely *in* the knower. This is truly remarkable. The very same actuation which precognitively conditions, determines, forms the faculty by being present in it is also the actuation of that which is known (precisely as known, though, and not as it is outside the cognitive process, where its actuations are its substantial and accidental forms) and which is causing it in the knower. Through this actuation, which is *in* and *of* the knower and *of* and *by* the known, the object known is the content-determining-cause of my knowledge.[20]

Perhaps the following diagram will help by showing the two actuations of each cognitive faculty.[21]

---

[20] Here *energeia* does not mean activity or operation but the nonoperational and formal actuation which is prior to and content-determining-cause of the operation of knowledge. See Appendix below.

[21] For the diagram I am grateful to Carson R. Yeager, Cherie Rascop and Carol Szablewski. The diagram aims at showing the two causes of non-constructural knowledge (both spontaneous and philosophical)—material existents as its content-determining-cause, the human knower through its cognitive faculties (external and internal senses, recipient and agent intellects) as its efficient cause. Both the five external senses (seeing, hearing, smelling, touching, tasting) and the internal senses (imagination, memory, cogitative and unitive senses) are represented by solid geometrical figures so as to show them to be operative powers within physical organs (the latter are obvious in the case of the external senses; the brain is the physical organ of the internal

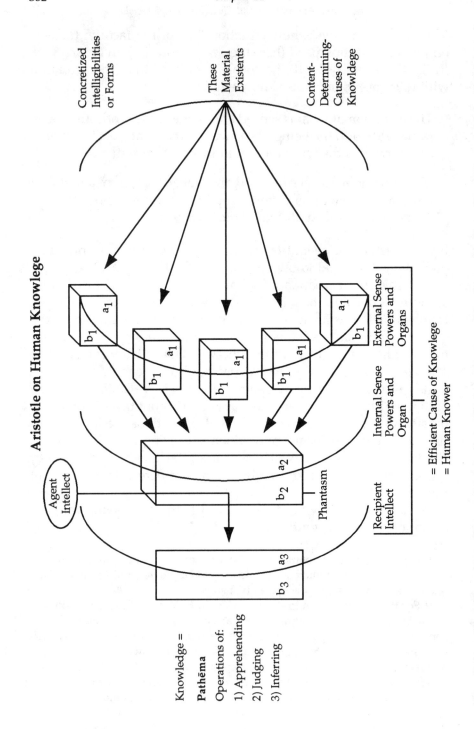

Aristotle on Human Knowlege

In that diagram special attention should be directed to the phantasm, which is crucially important and which is represented as actuation "b_2." The phantasm has these six characteristics.

(a) It is my sentient awareness of an individual sensible object such as this brown, wet, barking dog, which is its content-determining-cause.

(b) It is an awareness efficiently produced by the internal senses and based on data from the external senses, as well as from the imagination and memory of previous such data.

(c) It is an awareness whose content is "this-brown-barking-wet-[dog]."

(d) It is the awareness through which I am one cognitively with that dog as "this-brown-barking-wet-[dog]" because also I am one noncognitively through actuation "a_2" with that dog as "this-brown-barking-wet-[dog]."

(e) The result is that my knowledge terminates directly not at the phantasm (which is a *medium quo*) but at the dog itself.

---

sense powers). The recipient and agent intellects are each represented by a plane geometrical figure because they have no physical organs. In all cognitive powers actuation "a" is noncognitive, entitative and formal; actuation "b" is the cognition efficiently produced by the formally actuated and determined power, which thereby becomes aware of what it had entitatively become by actuation "a." The three intellectual operations of apprehension, judgment and inference, represented as actuation "b_3" on the diagram, are each multiple—for example, apprehension can be simple or complex, judgments can be perceptual or intellectual, inference can be inductive or deductive. See my *Authentic Metaphysics*, pp. 326–33. On the diagram "knowledge" is termed *pathêma* (see Plato, *Phaedo*, 79D; *Republic*, VI, 511D6–E2) because as nonconstructural and *re* its content knowledge is "what is done to us" by material existents as its content-determining-causes.

On the contrast between nonconstructural and constructural knowledge, see *Authentic Metaphysics*, p. 146, n. 10: "What is constructural knowledge? From reflection upon various sorts of constructs found in logic, mathematics, physics, and other empiriological sciences, as well as in our spontaneous knowledge of physical and moral evils, constructural knowledge seems to consist in these two factors: (a) The mental activity involved helps constitute (and thus affects) the very content of the intelligibilities in question, within which it shows up as an integral part. (b) Consequently, the basis of those intelligibilities is not directly any actually existing item, but rather that mental activity.

"By contrast, in nonconstructural knowledge (a) the mental activity involved is merely the means the knower uses to receive the intelligible message which actual existents themselves deliver; (b) accordingly, the basis of the content of such knowledge is directly those actual existents."

(f) The phantasm is that which the agent intellect uses as an instrumental formal cause to produce the spiritual actuation "a_3" in my recipient or possible intellect, which then as an efficient cause produces "b_3" and which is now intellectually aware of "dog" itself as a direct universal.

What is the end result? The human knower knows, and thus is cognitively one with, this brown-barking-wet-dog both as "dog" (through the intellect) and as "this-brown-barking-wet" (through our external and internal senses) so that human knowledge directly terminates not with the content of the phantasm and of the direct universal but with the dog itself (see note 5 above, last paragraph).

Aquinas: Existence and Actuation "A"

What is Thomas' reaction to Aristotle's theory of knowledge as just set forth? Wholehearted acceptance, but with two *caveats*, one of which we have already encountered: he often expresses actuation "a" by "similitudo" or "species" and thus can mislead the unwary reader.[22] Second, actuation "a" if defined as "formal deter-

---

[22] The word "species" has different meanings. Etymologically, it comes from the Greek word "eidos" and, thus, means "that which is seen or appears," which in turn can signify "apparent but misleading" (e.g., "a specious argument") or "beautiful" (because what one sees in an object is its beauty— see n. 12 above). More technically, though, "species" in logic is in contrast to genus and to individual: it is more determinate than genus (e.g., "human" *vs.* "animal") and is less determinate than individual (e.g., "human" *vs.* "Socrates"). In epistemology and psychology "species" has at least two meanings, the first of which is "that which is an image or likeness" and, when so taken, it can lead to a representationalism. On the other hand, it can mean "form" and, when so understood, it is "that by which something is what it is" and, with reference to cognition, "that by which something is known to be what it is."

Thomas uses "species" or form in this last sense: it is "that by which we know," the "modus quo cognoscimus." See, for example, *S.T.*, I, 55, 1 ad 2: "Sicut sensus in actu est sensibile in actu, ut dicitur in III *de Anima* (c. 8, 431b20–28), non ita quod ipsa vis sensitiva sit ipsa similitudo sensibilis quae est in sensu sed quia ex utroque fit unum sicut ex actu et potentia, ita et intellectus in actu dicitur esse intellectum in actu, non quod substantia intellectus sit ipsa similitudo per quam intelligit sed quia illa similitudo est forma eius"; *ibid.*, I, 85, 2 resp.: "Dicendum est quod species intelligibilis se habet ad intellectum ut quo intelligit intellectus. Quod sic patet. Cum enim sit

mination" would not be applicable to our knowledge of existence, since existence is not a form. What can be said on this last point?

Let us first return to Aristotle and investigate actuations "a" and "b" a bit more thoroughly in this schematic fashion.

(1) I spontaneously know what a sensible thing is by my intellect and senses. I technically know what its components are solely by intellection (= by inference). For example, Jim is this human person here and now before me: he is *that which* is human, material and courageous.

That *by which* he is human = substantial form or soul.

That *by which* he is material (i.e., extended) and thus is substantially individuated = prime matter.

That *by which* he is courageous = the accidental form of courage.

(2) When I know him as this human person, *I am him* non-physically, intentionally.

(a) I experience (= actuation "b") him.

(b) I also experience my experience of him.

(c) I do not experience my noncognitive unity with him (which is actuation "a") but I infer actuation "a" as necessary for that noncognitive unity with him.

(d) What, then, is actuation "a"? It is the formal determination of my faculties, just as the accidental forms and substantial forms are the formal determinations of my substance and prime matter, respectively.

(e) Moreover, the content of actuation "a" is whatever the content of actuation "b" is:

(1) If actuation "b" is my spontaneous knowledge of Jim as this human person here and now, then the content

---

duplex actio, sicut dicitur IX *Metaphysicorum* (c. 8, 1050a23 sqq.) una quae manet in agente, ut videre et intelligere, altera quae transit in rem exteriorem, ut calefacere et secare; utraque sit secundum aliquam formam. Et sicut forma secundum quam provenit actio tendens in rem exteriorem est similitudo obiecti actionis, ut calor calefacientis est similitudo calefacti; similiter forma secundum quam provenit actio manens in agente est similitudo obiecti. Unde similitudo rei visibilis est secundum quam visus videt; et similitudo rei intellectae, quae est species intelligibilis, est forma secundum quam intellectus intelligit.

"Sed quia intellectus supra seipsum reflectitur, secundum eandem reflexionem intelligit et suum intelligere et speciem qua intelligit. Et sic species intellectiva secundario est id quod intelligitur. Sed id quod intelligitur primo est res cuius species intelligibilis est similitudo." As complementary passages see *ibid.*, I, 84, 3 resp. and 6 resp. Also see J. Maritain, *The Degrees of Knowledge*, pp. 86–100, 111–28 and 387–418.

of actuation "a" corresponds to the content of that spontaneous knowledge of Jim: by that spontaneous knowledge I am aware that Jim is Jim and is not John, that he is human and not canine.

Hence, actuation "a" is the formal determination or form which makes me *be* Jim nonphysically, intentionally (but not yet cognitively).

(2) But if the content of actuation "b" is Jim as known philosophically as a composite of substantial form, prime matter and accidents, then the content of actuation "a" corresponds to the content of that philosophical knowledge of Jim.

Hence, actuation "a" is the formal determination or form which makes me *be* Jim in this philosophical, technical fashion.

(3) More precisely, then, what does "formal determination" or "form" mean? Form = that *by which,* when received, something is intrinsically caused to be *what it is* [hence, existence is not a form because it makes something *be*].

(a) If that by which, when received, this human person is made to be courageous, it is an accidental form.

(b) If that by which, when received, he or she is made to be human, it is substantial form..

(c) If that by which, when received, a faculty (external or internal senses, recipient intellect) is made to *be* the known precognitively, it is actuation "a."

(d) When that faculty so actuated by "a" efficiently causes cognition itself, that cognition is actuation "b."

(4) Hence, I infer *that* there is actuation "a" from the fact that to know is to be the known. I infer *what* that actuation "a" is from what I experience actuation "b" to be in each case of actual knowing.

The immediately preceding paragraphs have presented the Aristotelian theory of knowledge.

Consistently, what is Aquinas' reaction to it with reference to actuations "a" and "b"? One must ask that question because existence, which is key to Thomas' metaphysics, is not a form.

(5) Therefore, when existence is known, whether spontaneously or philosophically, actuation "a" is not strictly a "formal determination," and accordingly has to be changed and enlarged thus: actuation "a" is *determination through act*

which either is a "form" strictly—namely, *that by which,* when received, something is intrinsically caused to be *what it is;*

or is "existence"—namely, *that by which,* when received, something is intrinsically caused *to be.*

(6) But if the content of actuation "a" corresponds to the content of actuation "b" (see #2*e* above), this situation should hold true *re* existence too.

    (a) If actuation "b" is my spontaneous knowledge of Jim as this human person here and now *existing,* then the content of actuation "a" corresponds to the content of that spontaneous knowledge of Jim.

    (b) But if the content of actuation "b" is Jim metaphysically known as a composite of existence/essence (where existence has primacy, is autodetermining and amaterial),[23] then the content of actuation "a" corresponds to the content of that philosophical knowledge of Jim.

    (c) In the latter case, then, the content of actuation "a" is the determination through the act of existing which makes me *be* Jim in this philosophical and technical fashion.

(7) Thus, when I know Jim spontaneously as this human person here and now *existing* (see #6*a* above), actual existence is an "incidental sense-object" (*sensibile per accidens*)—that which is known intellectually and sensibly when I perceive Jim as this tall, lean, white, perspiring, puffing runner (= "essential sense-object [both proper and common]"—in Latin: *sensibile per se et proprium et commune*).[24]

(8) It is noteworthy that actual existence is such an "incidental sense-object" from the very beginning of our cognitive life, where our first awareness is "this something or other actually here and now existing" and continues to be such a *sensible per accidens* throughout our life.

    (a) The fact that actual existence has been, is and will be a constant accompaniment of our knowledge of actual existents throughout our entire life may help explain why some philosophers take existence for granted as a fact but fail to see that it is evidence of the most important component within such existents.

    (b) That is, it is constantly present to us in knowledge of actual beings, and its content of and in itself is "existence" solely, whereas the content of the other component in a being (namely, essence) varies from situation to situation:

---

[23] See my *Authentic Metaphysics,* ch. 5: "Primacy of Existence in Existents."

[24] See Aristotle, *On the Soul,* II, c. 6, 418a6 sqq.; Thomas, *In II De Anima,* lectio 13 (Marietti ed., pp. 134–38). See n. 5 above.

now I am aware of this existing tall, perspiring runner,
now of this existing growling pit bull chasing him,
now of the shrill siren and flashing red light of the
    existing police car saving him from the attack.
My attention can be so concentrated on *what* I am perceiving that I pay little or no direct attention to the fact that the
runner, dog and squad car do exist.

(c) Thus existence can be passed over and taken for granted
also by philosophers when they look for evidence to understand and explain philosophically such actual situations and thus they miss existence as a component.

(d) They might even be prone to describe the very object of
the human intellect as the "essence" solely of things, as
solely *what* they are. Not so Aquinas—at least in his *Summa
Theologiae* and other late writings. For him the object of the
human intellect is "the essence or nature *existing* in material" and individual things: "intellectus humani . . . proprium objectum est quidditas sive natura in materia
corporali existens" (*S.T.*, I, 84, 7 resp.).

Conclusion

From Preller to Aquinas to Aristotle and back to Aquinas, from
epistemology to metaphysics, from the mystery which is human
knowledge[25] to the mystery of existence (as we described it in
chapter 20 above) and then to the mystery of how we know existence—such has been my journey in this chapter. In terminating it
let me briefly speak again of the role of the phantasm in human
intellection and, second, quote G. K. Chesterton on existence.

Is there any parallel which can illumine how the agent intellect
and phantasm, as Aquinas conceives them, cooperate in effecting
actuation "a_3" (see diagram above)? In making such a suggestion,
one must keep in mind these points. The agent intellect is itself
without content. The phantasm has content, which however is
explicitly particular, concrete and sensible. The actuation "a_3," as
well as the consequent concept, is in content explicitly abstract and
actually intelligible. Consequently, the determinate content of actuation "a_3" and ensuing intellection must come solely from the
phantasm but only when utilized by the agent intellect as its instru-

---

[25] See J. Maritain, *The Degrees of Knowledge*, pp. 110–18.

ment and, thereby, when elevated to a level of activity and to an effect which surpass it if left to itself. Now, do we have anything in everyday life which might illustrate such complicated mutual functions? Possibly this: slides in a projector casting colored pictures on a screen. The light-beam in the projector would correspond to the agent intellect, the slides to the phantasms, the colored pictures on the screen to actuation "a_3," the screen to the possible intellect. But to make the example more exact, one would have to postulate that the slides themselves are in black and white and yet cause colored pictures on the screen under the influence of the light shining through them, which reveals and activates the colors dormant in them from the start.

Such an analogy limps, obviously, and may do more harm than good. At any rate, what one must remember is that Aquinas assents to the actual presence in a human knower of an agent intellect and of actuation "a_3" and to the instrumental function of phantasms in intellection because of an inference based on his views of the human soul as the substantial form of matter, of material existents as concretized intelligibilities and as the content-determining-cause of cognition, and of cognitive powers as its efficient cause.

But behind that intricate attempt to cope with the mystery of human intellection stands existence as astonishing fact, evidence and component. As G. K. Chesterton remarks,

There is at the back of all our lives an abyss of light, more blinding and unfathomable than any abyss of darkness, and it is *the abyss of actuality, of existence, of the fact that things truly are,* and *that we ourselves are incredibly and sometimes almost incredulously real.* It is the fundamental fact of being, as against not being. . . . He who has realized this reality knows that it does outweigh, literally to infinity, all lesser regrets or arguments for negation, and that under all our grumblings there is a subconscious substance of gratitude [italics added].[26]

No one could have said it better.

---

[26] *Chaucer* (London: Faber and Faber, 1932), p. 33. Also see my ch. 21 above.

Appendix

How Translate *Energeia*?

Much depends on what one understands Aristotle to mean in *On the Soul*, III, 2, 425b26 and 426a11: "*Hê energeia* of what is sensed and of the sense is one and the same. . . . But *hê energeia* is in the one sensing and not in what is sensed."[27]

The Greek noun is frequently translated as "activity"—for example, see W. S. Hett, *Aristotle: On the Soul*, in "The Loeb Classical Library" (revised ed., 1957), p. 147: "The activity of the sensible object and of the sensation is one and the same, though their essence is not the same. . . . The activity of the sensible object and that of the sensitive subject lie in the latter." In 1967 George A. Blair compared *energeia* with *entelecheia* and concluded that neither word should be translated by "actuality";[28] that *energeia* is used by Aristotle five times as often as *entelecheia* (537 *vs.* 116); that the former means "activity" (since even "the form of a thing is really a special kind of action of its matter"), the latter means "the internal possessing of an end"; that such possession is equivalent to activity and thus *entelecheia* also signifies "activity" and gradually is replaced by *energeia* in Aristotle's texts.[29] Although Blair does not concentrate on the *De Anima* passage, consistently he would translate *energeia* there as "activity."

In 1981 Hippocrates G. Apostol also chose "activity" for *energeia*: "The activity of the sensible object and the activity of the sensation [of it] are one and the same, but the essence of each of them is not the same. . . . Just as action and [actual] affection are in that which is affected and not in that which is acting, so the activity of the sensible object and of that which can sense is in that which can sense."[30]

Seven years later Terence Irwin uses "actuality": [1] Aristotle "argues that when I perceive an object, the actuality of the object is

---

[27] For the Greek text see above, prgr. corresponding to n. 20.

[28] See my comments below on "actuality" as best used solely for "existence," which is given primacy in Aquinas' position.

[29] George A. Blair, "The Meaning of 'Energeia' and 'Entelecheia' in Aristotle," *International Philosophical Quarterly* 7 (1967), 101–17. This article issued from Blair's Fordham University doctoral dissertation (1964) with a similar title.

[30] Aristotle's *On the Soul* (Grinnell, Iowa: The Peripatetic Press, 1981), p. 44. Also see *ibid.*, p. 138, n. 11, and p. 140, n. 16, where Apostol discloses an uneasiness with "activity" as a translation of *energeia*. He ends the note by remarking, "Perhaps there are other interpretations."

one and the same with the actuality of the perceiver, and that it is in the perceiver, not in the object."[31] [2] In explanation he cites two examples of efficient causality: a builder building a house of bricks, Ann teaching Bert something. In such cases "the actuality of a change is in the patient [the bricks, the pupil] rather than [in] the agent [the builder, the teacher]. . . . The relevant sort of change is essentially doing something *to a patient*, not simply doing *something* (*ibid.*, italics in original). Irwin now turns to perception.

[3] The same argument ought to show why the actuality of the perceiver and of the object are in the perceiver. Though we speak of the object "being perceived," suggesting that it is a patient, the passive verb is misleading, since it is really the object that affects the perceiver. [4] My perceiving the rock is my being affected by the rock; being perceived is not a change in the rock or something that the rock does to exercise one of its proximate potentialities. . . . The event [of perception] counts as its being perceived because of the change in me, not the other way round. The object does not become suitable to have its form absorbed when I perceive it; it was suitable all along, and its being perceived by me is no real change in it. When I perceive it, therefore, I must become aware of it as it has been before I perceived it. Aristotle still implies a realist view of the objects of perception (*ibid.*).

But his realism is challenged, in Irwin's exegesis, because [5] "he assumes further that the relevant actuality of the object is its becoming red, and so he concludes that its becoming red consists in its being perceived as red. . . . Aristotle's conclusion implies that the object is only potentially red before it is perceived . . . and makes . . . the existence [of real perceptible qualities] depend on their being perceived."[32] Or, as Irwin states on page 591, note 29:

---

[31] Terence Irwin, *Aristotle's First Principles*, paperback ed. (Oxford: Clarendon Press, 1990), p. 312. Bracketed numbers are added to make subsequent references easier.

[32] *Ibid.*, p. 313. Irwin's interest in establishing whether or not Aristotle's position is a realism arises because he believes Plato and Aristotle (as Robin Smith points out in a paper on "Foundationalism, Coherentism and Aristotle," presented at a meeting of the Society of Ancient Greek Philosophy, Dec. 28, 1992) to be "engaged in the same project as modern epistemology"—namely, the "Cartesian illusion argument" and "Cartesian-style cases of massive error" (typescript, p. 8; also see *ibid.*, p. 10). Smith concludes his paper by

Aristotle argues as follows, 425b26–426a1: (1) The actuality of the object is the actuality of the perceiver. (2) In perception the perceiver becomes actually red (e.g.). (3) Hence in perception the object becomes actually red. (4) Therefore the object is actually red only when it is perceived.

Comments. Irwin correctly acknowledges that "my perceiving the rock is my being affected by the rock" (#4). But he seems unaware that for Aristotle the rock affects the perceiver in two ways: through physical media it acts upon the sense organs and powers as an efficient cause of the changes in them, whereby and whereupon it also serves as their content-determining-cause. As explained above (see paragraphs corresponding to notes 16–21), it actuates them in an entitative and noncognitive way (= actuation #a) so that the sense powers, thus entitatively actuated and formally determined, can then efficiently produce the perception itself (= actuation #b). Actuation #a it is which both perceiver and perceived have in common, not actuation #b. Actuation #a is *of* and *in* the knower and *of* and *by* the known, which thereby is the content-determining-cause of my knowledge, which I efficiently cause when I am aware of what I entitatively became through actuation #a. Knowledge itself (= actuation #b) is in me solely and not in the object known.

Finally, in light of the primacy Aquinas gives to existence as a fact, perfection and component, it is better to restrict "actuality" to "existence." Moreover, every activity is an *energeia* but not every *energeia* is an activity. Hence, one should use "activity" only when describing such operations of an existent as knowing, loving, freely choosing, feeling, digesting, locomotion and so on, all of which are *energeiai* in it. Perhaps this diagram is helpful.

Energeia:
(1) Common meaning: enrichment, fulfillment, completion of what is potential.
(2) Two sorts:
    (a) operational: all activities
    (b) nonoperational:
        (1) accidents (except activities) *re* substance
        (2) substantial form *re* prime matter
        (3) for Aquinas: existence *re* essence.

---

advising that we "should proceed with much circumspection in applying the taxonomy of modern epistemological theory to Aristotle (and by implication to other ancient philosophers)" (p. 11). I agree wholeheartedly with this advice.

22

Existentialism:
Authentic and Unauthentic

Forty years ago Anthony West wrote words in *The New Yorker* which might have tolled the death knell of existentialism.

> One cannot be sufficiently thankful to Mlle. de Beauvoir [whose novel, *All Men Are Mortal*, he was reviewing] for so explicitly declaring in her novel the vacuities that lie behind the Germanic complexities of existentialist philosophizing. It becomes clearer and clearer that this movement, which originally seemed a sign of France's cultural recovery and vigor, is a disintegration phenomenon and a gauge of the hidden damage done to French intellectual life by the events of the past forty years.[1]

Fortunately or unfortunately, West's diagnosis was not accepted universally, and existentialism in the next ten years became stronger than ever before. In fact, it was characterized in 1965 by another popular magazine as "ubiquitous."[2] If we confine our attention to

---

[1] *The New Yorker*, February 5, 1955, p. 104.

[2] *Time*, May 7, 1965, p. 70: Whitehead's position is "an alternative to that ubiquitous Teutonic import, existentialism."

The "existentialism" of which *Time* (as well as Anthony West—see n. 1) speaks is what we elsewhere refer to as "radical existentialism" (see *Authentic Metaphysics in an Age of Unreality* [hereafter: *Authentic Metaphysics*], 2d ed. [New York/Bern: Peter Lang Publishing, Inc., 1993], p. 23, n. 15) and what we shall call "unauthentic existentialism" once we come to the first section of the

that period in America, its influence could be detected on the practical level in the Free Speech Movement, which dominated the campus of the University of California at Berkeley in the 1964–1965 school year.[3] Those who engineered that movement had counterparts on every campus, Catholic as well as non-Catholic, in what was aptly called the "New Breed"—collegians and seminarians who were less violent and radical, perhaps, but no less dedicated to personal fulfillment and self-determination and who also had existentialism as one of their ancestors.[4]

On the speculative level its popularity could be discerned in the omnipresent paperback editions of Kierkegaard, Jaspers, Heidegger, Sartre, Marcel, Tillich, Buber and others.[5] Moreover, within that decade many Americans published significant, sympathetic books on existentialism—to restrict ourselves to some Catholic authors,

---

present chapter (until that first section, though, we shall designate it simply as "existentialism"). It is the philosophical position developed by Sartre, Jaspers, Heidegger, Marcel, etc.

At times it is also named "philosophy of subjectivity" (in view of the primacy it gives to subjects *vs.* objects), "phenomenology" (because of the methodology it uses), or "personalism" (in view of the prominence it gives the human person). Incidentally, the last two terms can be misleading since not every phenomenology (e.g., that of Husserl himself) is existentialist and there have been personalisms that are not existentialisms (e.g., that of Borden Parker Bowne, William James, R. Le Senne, F. C. S. Scheller, etc.). See F. Copleston, S.J., *Contemporary Philosophy* (Westminster, Ind.: The Newman Press, 1963), pp. 103–24.

[3] Such was the admission of Jack Weinberg, one of its leaders, in an interview: "The word 'existential' is used a lot [to explain the origin and nature of the Movement]. . . . You could call it an affirmation of self." See Calvin Trillin, "Letter from Berkeley," *The New Yorker*, March 13, 1965, p. 88.

[4] A. Greeley, "A New Breed," *America*, May 23, 1964, p. 708: "How has the New Breed come to be? . . . It lives in the midst of a psychological age when even the Sunday magazines talk about existentialism. It has read the philosophy and literature of the day, with its heavy emphasis on significance and personalism."

[5] As an example of the wide dissemination of existentialist literature, consider what M. Friedman said of Martin Buber's writings. In 1944 only two of Buber's books were in English. By 1959 "more than twenty of Buber's books have been published in English, . . . several more translations are underway, five of his books have been reissued in paperback editions, four anthologies of his writings have appeared, and several books in English have been written on his thought" (M. Friedman, *Martin Buber: The Life of Dialogue* [New York: Harper and Brothers, Harper Torchbooks, 1960], p. v).

Robert O. Johann, *The Meaning of Love: An Essay towards a Metaphysics of Intersubjectivity*; Frederick D. Wilhelmsen, *The Metaphysics of Love*; Quentin Lauer, *The Triumph of Subjectivity: An Introduction to Transcendental Phenomenology*; Thomas D. Langan, *The Meaning of Heidegger: A Critical Study of an Existentialist Phenomenology*; Kenneth T. Gallagher, *The Philosophy of Gabriel Marcel*; William J. Richardson, *Heidegger: Through Phenomenology to Thought*; and Vincent P. Miceli, *Ascent to Being* [in Gabriel Marcel].[6]

How has existentialism fared since 1965? In John Furlong's informative survey of "the lush forest of contemporary metaphysics" since that date,[7] "two dominant styles of metaphysical thinking . . . have reigned in this century. Positivism characterizes the spare and wiry Anglo-American style of philosophy, existentialism the aphoristic and dramatic European."[8] The first is exemplified by W. v. O. Quine, the early Ludwig Wittgenstein (*Tractatus Logico-Philosophicus*), Wilfred Sellars and the later Wittgenstein (*Philosophical Investigations* and *The Blue and Brown Books*).[9] In the second "the catalyst in almost all Continental thinking of the last forty years has been Martin Heidegger," who "either made original contributions" to phenomenology (with Edmund Husserl) and to existentialism as such[10] or else "founded" contemporary hermeneutics (practiced

---

[6] To this list should be added W. Luijpen, *Existential Phenomenology* (Pittsburgh: Duquesne University Press, 1963). Although its author is Dutch, the book was published in America, where it was rather widely used as a text. Also see his *Phenomenology and Metaphysics* (Pittsburgh: Duquesne University Press, 1965).

[7] John Furlong, "Recent Developments in Metaphysics," in L. Sweeney, S.J., *Authentic Metaphysics*, pp. 353–89.

[8] *Ibid.*, p. 360.

[9] *Ibid.*, pp. 360–73. For an appreciation of the contrast between the early and later Wittgenstein, see Ray Monk, *Ludwig Wittgenstein: The Duty of Genius* (New York: The Free Press, 1990), who does not conceal or overemphasize his neurotic eccentricities; for an interesting comparison of Descartes and Wittgenstein, see Ian Hocking, "Wittgenstein the Psychologist," *The New York Review of Books* (April 1, 1982), pp. 42–44; for a presentation of religion by someone who is both "a Christian theist and analytical philosopher" indebted to Wittgenstein, see W. Donald Hudson's chapter in R. E. Davies (ed.), *We Believe in God* (Philadelphia: The Westminster Press, n.d.), pp. 97–111.

[10] Furlong, "Recent Developments in Metaphysics," pp. 373–74. This Heidegger does by deepening "the conceptual base of existentialism, working out ideas—care, angst, death, call, *existentialia*, nothingness, thrownness—that became an integral part of existentialist literature" (*ibid.*; also see n. 89). See notes 15–16 below.

currently by Hans-Georg Gadamer), which in turn has issued into deconstructionism (e.g., Jacques Derrida).[11]

What conclusions does Furlong draw from his "brief history of contemporary metaphysics"? First,

> both Continental and Anglo-American philosophy, despite very different starting points, seem to have ended up with strikingly similar insights about the nature of metaphysics. Quine, Wittgenstein, Heidegger, and Derrida, for instance, all declare the project of Western metaphysics, the search for eternal truths, abiding Reality, and certain foundations either dead or moribund. They all seem to share a similar diagnosis: our "form of life," or our "hermeneutic situation" is inarticulable; we can never speak about our own "prejudices," or our primordial contact with the world. Our own situation is "concealed" from us. There is even some consensus regarding the prognosis: Quine, Wittgenstein, Gadamer, Heidegger, and Derrida all point to attention to language, not to Reality or Truth, as our main pursuit. Whether it is scientific language,

---

[11] For an exposition and critique of deconstructionism see Henry Veatch, "Deconstruction as the Vehicle of a New 'Liberation Philosophy,' " in James Reidy (ed.), *Aquin Papers* (St. Paul, Minn.: College of St. Thomas, 1987), pp. 5–12. For a defense see Reiner Schürmann, *Heidegger on Being and Acting: From Principles to Anarchy* (Bloomington, Ind.: Indiana University Press, 1987); Bill Martin, *Matrix and Line: Derrida and the Possibilities of Postmodern Social Theory* (Ithaca, N.Y.: SUNY Press, 1992); Andrew McKenna, *Violence and Difference: Girard, Derrida, and Deconstruction* (Urbana-Champaign, Ill.: University of Illinois Press, 1992). Also see n. 48 below, last prgr.

On Heidegger see F.-J. von Rintelen, *Contemporary German Philosophy and Its Background* (Bonn: H. Bouvier Verlag, 1970), pp. 83–106; H. Spiegelberg with K. Schuhmann, *The Phenomenological Movement: A Historical Introduction*, 3d ed. (The Hague: Martinus Nijhoff, 1984), pp. 336–421; Jacques Taminiaux, *Heidegger and the Project of Fundamental Ontology*, trans. Michael Gendre (Albany, N.Y.: SUNY Press, 1991).

Hermeneutics may have led Heidegger himself not so much to deconstructionism as to poetry. His "later work is allusive and poetical. . . . In fact, what seems to be left after philosophy is another type of thinking, poetry. . . . 'To stand in the presence of the gods and to be involved in the proximity of the essence of things. Existence is "poetical" in its fundamental aspect— which means at the same time: insofar as it is established (founded), it is not a recompense, but a gift' " (Furlong, "Recent Developments in Metaphysics," pp. 385–86).

poetic language, or merely the play of signifiers, we cannot press beyond linguistic forms to a Reality.[12]

If Furlong is accurate in concluding that both Continental and Anglo-American philosophers believe metaphysics as a "search for eternal truths, abiding Reality and certain foundations" is "either dead or moribund" and both wish to substitute "attention to language [whether scientific, poetic or merely the play of signifiers], not to Reality or Truth" as their main pursuit, then those of us who do not share their belief and wish must renew our efforts to set forth "an alternative thinking-through of metaphysical themes . . . one that is sensitive to contemporary human concerns, to the concrete situations in which humans and other existents give evidence directly of themselves, to the objective and eternal truths issuing therefrom."[13]

Such has been our effort in chapters 18 to 21 above, as well as in our *Authentic Metaphysics in an Age of Unreality*,[14] and such will continue to be our goal in this chapter by contrasting an existentialism which is authentic with those which are unauthentic and thereby self-destructive.

Authentic Existentialism?

Let us being by noting that "existentialism," by the force of the term itself, would seem to indicate a philosophical position in which primacy is given to "existence" (whatever that noun may mean), in which "existence" confers reality because it bestows perfection, value, significance upon whatever *is* perfect, valuable, significant. In short, it is a doctrine in which "to be real" is "to exist."

But what is "existence"? How one answers this question is crucial in determining whether the existentialism he espouses is authentic or not. If one replies that "to exist" is "to be actual," then any actual existent, no matter what sort it may be, is real by the very fact that it actually exists. Reality is not restricted to any one kind of being, whether human, subhuman or, for that matter, superhuman, but extends as far as does actuality itself. If, as seems reasonable, "authentic" signifies that the item of which it is predicated is genu-

---

[12] *Ibid.*, pp. 387–88.
[13] *Ibid.*, p. 388.
[14] Publication data are given above, n. 2. Also n. 20 below.

inely what its name indicates it should be and seems to be, then the reply which equates "existence" with "be-ing actually" constitutes an existentialism which is authentic.

But if one answers that "to exist" is "to be this or that sort of thing," then only things of this or that sort are real, and they are so by being this or that sort and not by actually existing. Reality is confined to one or other kind of existent, it resides in *what* things are and not in *that* they are. An answer which is responsible for such confinement is, strictly speaking, an *essentialism* and no existentialism. It is, at best, an existentialism only in an unauthentic sense.

Let us now turn to Heidegger, Jaspers, Sartre, Marcel, and so on, as well as to their European and American followers, in order to discover the sort of existentialism they proposed. Is it authentic or unauthentic? To reply we must inquire what they meant by "existence." However differently they may phrase it, their answer basically comes down to this: "to exist" is not "to be actual" but "to be human."[15] As Heidegger explains:

The being that exists is man. Man alone exists. Rocks are, but they do not exist. Trees are, but they do not exist. Horses are, but they do not exist. Angels are, but they do not exist. God is, but he does not exist. The proposition "man alone exists" does not mean by any means that man alone is a real [that is, actual] being while all other beings are unreal and mere appearances or human ideas. The proposition "man exists" means: man is that being whose Being is distinguished by the open-standing

---

[15] The existentialists do differ doctrinally among themselves. For example, G. Marcel sees his doctrine so divergent from Sartre's as to be unwilling for his own to be classified as an "existentialism"—see his "Existence and Human Freedom," *Philosophy of Existentialism* (New York: Citadel Press, 1964, pp. 47–90, which still remains an excellent indictment of Sartre's views. But despite such stark differences, scholars now rather commonly agree that the positions of Sartre, Marcel, Heidegger, Jaspers, Merleau-Ponty, etc., are all elaborations of the same primitive fact, which is "the intentionality of existence, conceived as man's essential openness, as the encounter of subjectivity with given realities which are not this subjectivity" (W. Luijpen, *Existential Phenomenology*, p. 315). Also see *ibid.*, pp. 34–39; A. Dondeyne, *Contemporary European Thought and Christian Faith*, trans. E. McMullin and J. Burnheim (Pittsburgh: Duquesne University Press, 1958), p. 29; F. Copleston, *op. cit.*, pp. 125–47. On the difference in Marcel between "existence" and "being," see K. Gallagher, *Philosophy of Gabriel Marcel* (New York: Fordham University Press, 1962), pp. 58–62.

standing-in in the unconcealedness of Being, from Being, in Being.[16]

Or A. Dondeyne:

Insofar as it serves to express the fundamental category, or more precisely, the "central reference-point" of existential philosophy, the term "exist" no longer signifies ... the simple fact of being real [that is, actual]; it means rather the manner of being which is proper to *man*. In this sense, only man "exists." Not that there is nothing outside man; man has, however, a mode of being called "existence" by which he is distinguished from all other beings that inhabit the universe."[17]

What, then, does "existence" signify? Not the state of being actual but the condition of being human. This is not to deny that things, as well as humans, actually *are*—a fact which both Heidegger and Dondeyne emphasize.[18] But it is an affirmation that only men and women, only subjects, are real, in the sense of intrinsically and *per se* being perfect, valuable, significant, and that what makes them alone be real is the fact that they are *human*, they are *subjects*. Primacy is not rooted in their actuality but in their humanity, in their subjectivity. A philosophical position which insists upon a primacy so conceived is a humanism, a philosophy of subjectivity, a philosophy of essence (to use Marcel's own phrase),[19] an essen-

[16] "The Way Back into the Ground of Metaphysics," in W. Kaufmann (ed.), *Existentialism from Dostoevsky to Sartre* (New York: Meridian Books, Inc., 1959), p. 214. Also see K. Jaspers, "Existenzphilosophie," *ibid.*, p. 141 and *passim*. On Heidegger's interpretation of existence as "Ek-sistence," see W. Richardson, *Heidegger: Through Phenomenology to Thought* (The Hague: Martinus Nijhoff, 1963), especially pp. 20, 39, 232–38, 536–41, 600–602.

[17] *Op. cit.*, p. 29. Also see W. Luijpen, *op. cit.*, ch. 1, section 2: "To Be Man is To Exist," pp. 14–46.

[18] Also see G. Marcel, "An Essay in Autobiography," in *The Philosophy of Existentialism*, p. 117: "None of the extremist forms of Idealism which deny this reality [of the outward world] ever seemed to me convincing: for to what more certain or more intimate experience could this reality be opposed?" On Sartre's idealism, which he admits "it took me 30 years to shake off," see his *The Words* (New York: George Braziller, 1964), pp. 48–51, 59–60.

[19] "My thought ... is irresistibly drawn towards a philosophy of essence," in "Preface" to Petro Primi, *Gabriel Marcel et la méthodologie de l'invérifiable"* (Paris: Desclée de Brouwer, 1953), p. 7 (quoted by K. Gallagher, *op. cit.*, p. 135;

tialism, since reality is viewed as flowing from *what* human existents are and not the fact that they are. It is not an existentialism except in an unauthentic sense, since "existence" here does not mean genuinely what it seems to mean by force of the term itself.[20] Here "existence" signifies the state of being *human* instead of the state of *be-ing*, period.

But what do Heidegger, Marcel and other philosophers of subjectivity mean by "authenticity"? Of what do they predicate "authentic/unauthentic"? As one might expect, the adjectives point to two disparate ways in which someone can *be human*.[21] If he is unaware of what true selfhood is, if he is sluggishly immersed in the day-in-day-out routine of a depersonalized life within our automated and technological civilization, if his relations with others are conducted on the superficial level of mere talk (*Gerede*) and idle curiosity, if conformity to alien goals and external standards substitute for free and indigenous decisions, if he re-acts to the challenges of the human situation by evasive distractions and passive procrastination, then his is an *unauthentic* existence. His life is not authentically human. But if he is conscious of himself as an original center of free initiative and as a projective power-and-drive-to-the-future; if he courageously carries out that freedom and fashions his unique self by ontologically standing out from the crowd and from his everyday, ontic circumstances; if his communication with others is through loving dialogue, arising from attending to their status as fellow subjects; if he recognizes and then freely acquiesces to finitude as a condition immanent in his being-in-the-

also see p. 117). Marcel uses "philosophy of essence," though, to separate his doctrine from those existentialisms which refuse any place to essences.

[20] See J. de Finance, "Being and Subjectivity," *Cross Currents* 6 (1956), 177: "If the word 'existentialism' did not exist, it would have to be invented to characterize adequately Thomistic thought. We shall not employ it, however, precisely because it does exist and now carries a very special meaning. No, Thomism is not an existentialism. But it is *par excellence* the metaphysics of existence." Whereas de Finance surrenders the word to Sartre, Jaspers, etc., I prefer to wrest it back and to distinguish between authentic and unauthentic existentialisms, thereby underscoring their differences.

[21] See J. Wild, *The Challenge of Existentialism* (Bloomington, Ind.: University of Indiana Press, 1959), pp. 126–50 and 256–57; W. J. Richardson, *op. cit.*, pp. 76–84, 183–93; A. de Waelhens, *La philosophie de Martin Heidegger* (Louvain: Éditions de l'Institut Supérieur de Philosophie, 1948), pp. 109–17, 169–80, 205–9; C. Schrag, *Existence and Freedom* (Chicago: Northwestern University Press, 1961), pp. 42–49, 80–81, 170–74, 200–204; I. Lepp, *La philosophie chrétienne de l'existence* (Paris: Aubier, 1953), pp. 137–63.

world and to death as a constant menace abiding within his being-as-potentiality-to-end, then his is an *authentic* existence. He lives in an authentically human manner.

For Heidegger and company, then, authenticity (*Eigenlichkeit*) and unauthenticity are characteristics of human existence and not of existence, with the result that their philosophical position is again shown to be not authentically an existentialism but a humanism or a philosophy of subjectivity.

Subject/Object and Supposit/Nature

The mention of subjectivity in the preceding paragraphs suggests the next topic: how are subject/object related to supposit/nature, which have prominence in Christian philosophy? Let us discuss the former pair briefly before taking up supposit/nature.[22] "Subject" and "object" have to do with existents precisely as *knowable*. The difference between them is grounded in the fact that existents can be known in two radically different manners, and this difference is in turn rooted ultimately in the fact that there are two radically different sorts of existents. Let us take this as an initial definition: a *subject* is an existent "as experienced from within, i.e., not according to its objective surface, a certain sum of determinations by which it is conceptually definable, but in itself as a unique subsistent, an original center and source of free initiative."[23] In understanding that definition we must stress two important points. The uniqueness, the never-to-be-repeatedness, the originality—in a word, the individuality which characterizes a subject as subject—is directly centered in his freedom. The reason he is unique and uniquely so is that he is *free*. He is a *human* existent, endowed with intellect and will, who thus can freely fashion himself and stand out from all others. This uniqueness is not in the abstract or in the

---

[22] Besides Johann's article referred to in n. 23, see the following on subject/object: G. Marcel, "On the Ontological Mystery," in *The Philosophy of Existentialism*, pp. 9–46; also Marcel, *The Mystery of Being* (Chicago: Henry Regnery Co., 1960), I, pp. 242–70; K. Gallagher, *op. cit.*, pp. 30–36, 137–38; R. Troisfontaines, *De l'existence à l'être: La philosophie de Gabriel Marcel* (Paris: J. Vrin, 1953), I, pp. 77–100, 128–36, 353–55; W. Richardson, *op. cit.*, pp. 154–58, 324–30; J. de Finance, *art. cit.*, pp. 163–78.

[23] R. Johann, "Subjectivity," *The Review of Metaphysics* 12 (1958), 206. The word "subsistent" in the definition can be misleading, for a reason which will be clear at the end of this section.

past or even in the future: it is in the concrete, here-and-now exercise of his freedom in this or that choice, which is *his* and no other's
and which even he himself can never again reduplicate exactly,
because any other decision will be at least numerically distinct and
because he will never again find himself in *these* identical circumstances. Second, subjectivity as subjectivity demands a direct and
experiential awareness of current, concrete, transient choices. A
person must be cognitively caught in his novel, unpredictable exercise of freedom; we must be present to him while and as he freely
chooses. These two points constitute the heart of a subject as subject, and have the following consequences. Only human existents
are capable of such uniqueness and individuality because subhumans are without freedom. Second, human existents are subjects
only in the very act of exercising their freedom and, of equal importance, only as immediately known during that very act.

But what is an *object*? Quite bluntly, it is everything else. It is
everything except a human being actually exercising his freedom
and experientially known in that actual moment. Accordingly, all
subhuman existents are objects, since they are incapable of freedom. Each is a "thing," an "it," "known abstractly or conceptually,
. . . . universally valid-for-all, . . . as circumscribable and determinable in its constitutive notes."[24] Also, human existents are objects
when considered with respect to all the dimensions of their lives
not directly involved in their free decisions. Moreover, such existents are objects even in their free lives when these are known
conceptually, abstractly, impersonally and then described in technical language, as happens in a philosophy of human nature course.
Objectivity also sets in when such existents are looked on concretely but only as serving various functions in the everyday life of
a family, a business, an industry, an army; or as mere data in a
questionnaire, as a statistic in a Gallup poll, etc.[25] Then human
existents are mere "things" to be used and manipulated and numbered. Each is an "it" or, at best, a "he" or "she" instead of an "I"
and "Thou."

Now let us turn to supposit/nature. This pair of terms arose
historically from divine revelation, as developed and defined by
the Church, and initially concerned the Trinity and the Incarnation.
Stated baldly, the triune God is three supposits in one nature,

---

[24] Johann, *ibid.*, p. 204.
[25] See G. Marcel, *The Philosophy of Existentialism*, pp. 10–12; also *The Mystery of Being*, I, pp. 28–42; K. Gallagher, *op. cit.*, p. 56.

Christ is one supposit in two natures.[26] Issuing from that statement are two obvious consequences. What "supposit" expresses in the Trinity or in Christ cannot be identically what "nature" expresses, and this amounts to saying that supposit and nature are not the same. Second, both supposit and nature point to a status of independence, autonomy, uniqueness in the individual of whom they are predicated. The first indicates an independence in the way the individual exists, which is generally expressed by saying that he *subsists*; the second, an independence arising from the fact that he is an individual even in the sort of existent he is—for example, John is *this* man, Rover is *that* dog. If we apply this language to Christ and Judas, we would say that Judas was not only a definite, particular man, thereby different from and independent of all other humans in his very humanity; but he also existed in and through himself, thereby differing from and independent of all other existents in existence itself. He was, then, a subsistent human nature, a human supposit. Likewise, Christ is a man and, thus, possesses intellect, will and all other human operative powers, as well as freedom, vulnerability and various other human characteristics; he is also a determinate, particular man and, thereby, differs from and is independent of all other humans in his very humanity. But he does not exist in and through himself but in and through the Word of God: His human nature, complete, perfect and individualized though it is in its humanness, does not subsist. Christ is not a human supposit. With reference to existence, then, he differs from and is independent of all other existents not as man but as a divine supposit, as the Son of God.

Let us briefly make a last relevant point. Whence is the difference between supposit and nature? What are the intrinsic causes of those divergent sorts of independence and individuality? From what within the nature and within the supposit do they flow? Revelation sheds no light directly on this question, which thus has remained open and controversial. Thomists commonly state the cause of individuality in natures to be the quantified matter within such natures; that of individuality in supposits, the act of existing proper to and actualizing each supposit.[27]

---

[26] For documentation and discussion, see *Authentic Metaphysics*, "Actual Existence and the Individual," pp. 181–93, 196–97. It is important to emphasize that "person" is one sort of supposit—that with an intellectual nature.

[27] Maritain, following Cajetan, is an exception: for him the cause of a supposit's status as supposit is the "substantial mode of subsistence." See *Authentic Metaphysics*, p. 184, n. 81.

Let that suffice as a sketch of what subject/object and supposit/
nature signify so that we can now compare the two sets of terms.
This comparison is necessary in view of what happens when the
former are interpreted in the light of the latter: an injustice is done
to both. If one models "subject" on "supposit," "subject" is not
restricted to human existents but is to be found wherever an existent, no matter of what sort, *subsists*.[28] But then a human's actual
exercise of freedom, as known experientially and nonconceptually,
is no longer the heart of his subjectivity. If, however, one makes
subject/object parallel with supposit/nature by linking subject with
the act of existing and object with essence,[29] then consistently objects should not exist (which, of course, they do) and, second, the
sort of existents subjects are should contribute nothing directly to
their being subjects (which, of course, is not true either: if subjectivity is a human's actual life of freedom, as experienced from within,
then it is rooted in his being a *human*, which is on the side of
essence).

Now, finally, to make the comparison between subject/object
and supposit/nature. First of all, the two pairs of terms have this in
common, that each set refers to actual existents and, in fact, to
human existents.[30] Moreover, "subject," as well as both "supposit"
and "nature," aim commonly at emphasizing the same characteristic in human existents—namely, uniqueness, independence, individuality. Yet the similarity stops there because each set approaches
that emphasis from a different point of view. The contrast between
"subject" and "object" is elaborated so as to highlight the precious
originality and extraordinary value located in human existents by
reason of their free, transcendent lives. Men and women are thereby
reminded to endeavor constantly to rise above the monotony of
their day-in-day-out existence, to fight the depersonalizing influences of mechanized industry, business methods, urban living habits in our contemporary civilizations. The contrast between "na-

---

[28] This apparently is Maritain's position. See *Existence and the Existent* (New
York: Pantheon Books, 1949), pp. 62–68. Also, perhaps, J. de Finance, *art. cit.*,
p. 173.

[29] Perhaps de Finance tends to set up that parallel—see *ibid.*, pp. 173–76.
Possibly also R. Johann, *art. cit.*, pp. 207–8, 217–24, insofar as he approaches
subject from the side of existence and object from the side of essence, even
though subject and object are each affirmed to involve both existence and
essence.

[30] One should remember, though, that supposit/nature do not refer exclusively to human existents, nor does object.

ture" and "supposit," however, is elaborated with a different sort of uniqueness and individuality in mind. It is a proclamation that any existent (not just men and women) can have a twofold independence. One is within the very *sort* of existent they are (expressed, for example, when I say, "I am this man, you are that man; here is one oak, there is another"), and this is the area "nature" is concerned with. The other is with regard to the very *exercise of existence* itself (expressed when I say, "I subsist but my intellect and freedom do not: they exist in and through me; Christ's human nature does not subsist, either: it exists as assumed by the Son of God"), and this "supposit" is concerned with.

Now, since the two sets of terms are developed within different perspectives, they need not conflict, although they do overlap. For instance, a human supposit can be either a subject or an object, depending upon whether or not one has in mind a person's actual life of freedom as known experientially. All subhuman supposits are classified as objects only, for obvious reasons. On the other hand, a subject can be and most frequently is a human supposit, although what directly confers subjectivity upon him is not the fact that he is a supposit but that he is *human*. To give an example: Judas was a subject who was a person—the former status exemplified in his free decision to betray Christ, the latter in his existing independently of any other existent. But Christ is a subject who is not a human supposit—the former condition exhibited in the Garden when He freely acquiesced to the approaching sacrificial death on Calvary ("Not My will but Thine be done!"), the latter because His humanity does not exist independently of His status as the Word of God.

The conclusion to be drawn from the fact that the two sets of descriptions are elaborated from different viewpoints is, manifestly, that no one-to-one correspondence exists between them. Subject is not identical with supposit (which for most Thomists is to deny that subjectivity immediately springs from the act of existing), nor object with nature. In fact, if one is to correlate the two descriptions, "subject" and "object" would both be a subdivision of "nature," since they have to do directly with *what* existents are: some existents are of such a nature as to be free (= subject), others as to be without freedom (= object).

This correlation issues into a conclusion which is most relevant to the present chapter: the study of subject/object does not belong to metaphysics in an authentic existentialism, although it may pertain to metaphysics in the unauthentic existentialism of a philosophy of subjectivity. Why so? In both existentialisms metaphysics is the consideration of existents qua existent. But, as we have seen above, "to exist" for a philosopher of subjectivity is "to be human." Consequently, metaphysics in a philosophy of subjectivity is the study of human beings in their humanness, and this of course involves studying them in their subjectivity. But "to exist" for an authentic existentialist is "to be actual." Hence, in such an existentialism metaphysics studies all actuals precisely as actual, which is equivalent to saying that a metaphysician views human existents as existent and not as human, as actual and not as subjects contrasted with objects.

Does an authentic existentialist, then, fail to consider subjects/ objects? By no means. As he has gratefully learned from contemporary philosophers of subjectivity, subjectivity is an extremely important and valid dimension of a human person and offers a strong bulwark against contemporary dehumanizing forces and tendencies. But an *ex professo* study of subjectivity should be scheduled as the concluding and culminating course in the college curriculum, so that the student can draw upon all previous philosophical and theological disciplines. From metaphysics he realizes the primacy of actual existence, and this even in *what* an existent is (and, thus, *ultimately* in subjectivity also);[31] from the philosophy of man, especially the structure and exercise of human knowledge and freedom;[32] from ethics, the liaison between a human's free acts and

---

[31] This primacy is coupled with analogy: the act of existing of each existent is *similar* to that of all others since in any existent its function is the same: it is that by which each exists and is real; yet it also is *different* because each actuates and thereby is limited by this or that unique essence (see *Authentic Metaphysics*, pp. 151–60).

Also helpful from metaphysics is the doctrine of quantified matter as the principle of individuation, since also the human soul, whence flow the faculties of intellect and will, is thus individuated. Accordingly, quantified matter would have repercussions on one's freedom, in which resides one's subjectivity (see *ibid.*, pp. 188–93). Also helpful is a metaphysician's study of finality, with its consideration of love as telically caused by good-as-known (see *ibid.*, pp. 279–96); also the metaphysics of the true, the good, the beautiful (see *ibid.*, pp. 163–75).

It should also be noted that one's concern with subjectivity helps one in metaphysics and other philosophical disciplines by sharpening his attention, giving some problems precedence over others, etc.

[32] An accurate awareness of the nature of human knowing is of special help for a course on subjectivity, since one then realizes that universal, conceptual, abstract knowledge, given certain safeguards, is not empty, sterile,

law; from natural theology, God's transcendence because of His radical otherness from creatures, coupled with His immanence as the omnipresent efficient cause of our be-ing and acting; from sacred theology, God's presence in our free lives through His grace, the historical development and force of "supposit/nature," Christ as subject *par excellence,* etc. So conceived and so executed, a course in subjectivity has all the relevance and contemporaneity of subjectivity itself, plus a solid underpinning in inductively developed noumenologies of being, of man, of morality, etc. In brief, it would have most of the advantages and few of the disadvantages of the merely phenomenological approaches of unauthentic existentialisms.[33]

Subjectivity, Solipsism, Monism

The final topic chosen for discussion is a problem which subjectivity raises by its tendency to solipsism and ontological isolationism. As we have seen in the preceding section, subjectivity consists

---

feckless (it could amount to what we will see Marcel calls "secondary reflection"); that nonconstructural cognition has contact through the human knower's senses with the concrete, singular existent, and so on.

It is equally important to have an accurate understanding of the *cognitum,* especially when it is subhuman existents (which would be objects for a philosopher of subjectivity). For Johann the existence of each such object "has no depth, is absorbed, as it were, in the pattern it actualizes, in the face it presents to the world. There is no disproportion between an inner reality and its outer manifestations, between a secret center and source of activity and any of its particular concrete realizations" (*art. cit.,* p. 205). Such a description might be accurate for an object in Descartes' universe, where nonhuman substances are nothing but extension, plus local motion. (See Descartes, *Principles of Philosophy,* Part I, Principles 53 and 63 [La Salle, Ill.: Open Court Publishing Co., 1937], pp. 157, 164). But otherwise it would be inaccurate since nonhuman existents actually involve their own kind of uniqueness, autonomy, individuality (and this on the levels both of supposit and of nature); they have their own sort of depths, inner reality, mystery.

[33] On the phenomenology practiced by unauthentic existentialists, see A. Dondeyne, *op. cit.,* pp. 10–35, especially 29–35, and 108–28; W. Luijpen, *Existentialist Phenomenology* in its entirety.

Authentically existentialist metaphysics, as well as philosophy of nature and so on, is a *noumenology* in the sense that one knows existents in their intrinsic causes (substance/accidents, matter/form, act of existing) and, thus, in what they are and not merely in what they appear. Yet is is an *inductive* noumenology since all its conclusions are based upon data gained through perception and experience. See *Authentic Metaphysics,* chs. 3–5, pp. 41–140.

in a human existent's actual exercise of freedom as experienced in itself and from within; but we have such experience only of our own lives of freedom, only of ourselves as original centers of free initiative; therefore, the only subject each of us knows is himself—all other selves are closed to us, all are locked within their own subjectivity.

This is a problem which philosophers of subjectivity are aware of but have left unsolved, if we are to believe John Wild.

> The problem remains where Kierkegaard left it. My existence is subjectively mine. It is due to my own decision. How, then, can it be transmitted to another? Their unqualified attack on theoretical apprehension has made it impossible for existentialists to deal adequately with this question. The absence of any clear account of authentic communication remains a major weakness in the doctrine. . . . According to Heidegger, my ordinary mode of being with others is impersonal, debased, and unauthentic. He briefly refers to the possibility of authentic communication between persons but nowhere explains how this is possible or even reconcilable with his picture of the genuine person who has broken from his fellows to live alone with himself in a world of his own choice. The more authentic we become, the more isolated we seem to be. Jaspers has struggled with this problem, but his rejection of universal concepts and judgments makes an intelligible solution impossible. In Sartre, this weakness emerges with brutal clarity. When two persons meet, each tries to absorb the other as an object into his world. Communication is thus restricted to conflict. Love, friendship, and devoted cooperation for common ends are excluded *a priori*.[34]

Whether or not you agree with Wild, this is noteworthy: the absence of Gabriel Marcel from his list of those who have unsuccessfully encountered that problem. In the curtailed space which remains, let us outline his attitude on the topic, as set forth by Kenneth Gallagher in *The Philosophy of Gabriel Marcel*.[35]

---

[34] J. Wild, *Challenge of Existentialism*, pp. 139 and 165. On Heidegger, see W. Richardson, *op. cit.*, pp. 66–70, 213–15, 577–82; on Jaspers, see E. Allen, *The Self and Its Hazards: A Guide to the Thought of Karl Jaspers* (New York: Philosophical Library, 1951); on Sartre, see W. Luijpen, *op. cit.*, pp. 103–12, 195–206, 313–29.

[35] In subsequent paragraphs page numbers in parentheses will be references to this book. For publishing data see n. 15 above.

Stated bluntly, Marcel's position is that we can and do establish contact with other subjects, and this for at least three reasons. The first is developed within the more general context of mystery/problem (pp. 30–49) and yet seems relevant to the question of interpersonal communication. All human intellection uses concepts, true enough. But one sort, although conceptual, never loses contact with the existent in its singularity (p. 45), nor does it objectify what is known (pp. 42–43). Why this contact? Because it lives off the twofold intuition which our senses and our intellectual faculty provide (pp. 43–44). This knowledge, which Marcel calls "secondary reflection," would apparently allow us to cognize other selves as singular existents, as nonobjectified and, thus, as fellow subjects.

The second reason is what Marcel calls "fidelity," which is a descent into intersubjectivity (p. 68), and which reveals, and in fact creates, the self (p. 69). How does this work? When I respond personally to an appeal from another, I am "faithful" to him. Fidelity thus is a spontaneous, unimposed presence of an I to a Thou, and thereby "I create myself in response to an invocation which can only come from a thou. It is a call to which I answer 'present.' In saying 'here' I create my own self in the presence of a thou" (p. 70). This is an ontological presence but occurring in time because of my open-end unity of direction, will, and response to you in the order of freedom (p. 71). Obviously, if such responses are possible, intersubjective relations are possible also.

The third reason resides in ontological communion, in which "the other is given to me as a thou, as a non-objectifiable presence" (p. 22). In contrast to the human togetherness found in a *community* (e.g., children in a family) or in *communication* (e.g., teenagers' egocentric assertion of themselves), *communion* occurs when I freely and unselfishly open myself to you in a truly personal encounter (pp. 22–23). Communion is founded on love and, in fact, is love (p. 78), which creates the self, for what else is a lover but *one who loves* (p. 79)?[36] It also creates the thou, for to love someone is to say to him, "Thou at least shalt not die!" since love "rises above the entire order of *things* and of the destruction which preys upon things" (p. 80). Manifestly, through love a breakthrough can occur between subjects.

Are Marcel's reasons valid? Instead of evaluating them here, let us use them as an occasion for suggesting another but related topic: the possible connection between intersubjectivity and monism. Theo-

---

[36] Also see *ibid.*, pp. 25–26.

retically, at least, that connection can solve the ontological atomism which conceivably endangers subjectivity. There are interpersonal relations since subjects are, at bottom, identical with one another because of their identity with God, Absolute Spirit, Unique Value, Infinite Being (call Him what you will). We can know, love, respond to one another because we radically are united with one another in God. In brief, subjectivity becomes intersubjectivity by reason of a latent pantheistic basis.

Can that accusation be leveled at Marcel's doctrine? In answering, let us follow this procedure. As a sort of devil's advocate we shall sketch some factors in Marcel which might leave him open to such a charge.[37] This sketch will be followed by a brief rebuttal, which will itself terminate in some words of caution.

(1) "How is one person *with* another?" Marcel asks while speaking of intersubjective communion. Not in an external, spatial, indifferent juxtaposition, as one thing is with another, but in a personal way, as a Thou to an I.

> At that point he is with me in an absolute sense—he is not juxtaposed to me at all. When one debouches upon the spiritual plane, the correlative categories of the "same" and the "other" are at once transcended. Beyond the closed systems in which the logical judgment encloses us, *there is a sort of fecund indistinctness where persons commune.* . . . Between the I and the thou a bond exists which exceeds any means I have to take cognizance of it (p. 27; italics added).

Because a person is constituted by his presence with another, because his is a "reality which only emerges in communion," then

> every relation of person with person must be interiorized in the most extreme manner possible. . . . Personal communion . . . is strictly nonobjectifiable. I cannot dissect it into components one of which confronts the other. It is a "participation without frontiers," and Marcel emphasizes this by the seemingly quaint statement that *we cannot tell how far a personality extends.* We are part of all that creates us (p. 28; italics added).[38]

---

[37] Paragraphs in this sketch are numbered to facilitate references. References in them to page numbers are to Gallagher's book.

[38] Marcel's statement is found in *La Quatuor en fa dièse* (Paris: Librairie Plon, 1925), p. 190.

Just as "in the realm of music everything is bound together in a living communication," so too here: intersubjectivity "is a world of interpenetration, inseparability, where the harmony of the whole is present to every part. 'All is in all'—this is at once a description of musical reality, of communion, and of Marcel's philosophy" (pp. 28–29).

What those statements make clear is that subjects on the personal level, subjects as subjects, are not genuinely distinct from one another. They fuse into, interpenetrate with, one another.

(2) But there is more. We might expect our status of freedom to be an indisputable sign of our independence and distinctness from others. Not so, because freedom of choice is deceptive: it is merely "a surface manifestation. It is a void and uninteresting phenomenon taken in abstraction from the real freedom which underlies it" (p. 91).[39] The latter is a creative action and

> to create oneself is not to belong to oneself, it is to belong to more than oneself. The passage to liberty is effected at the interior of belonging. Liberty is not an anarchic affirmation of self, but an acknowledgement, a welcoming of ontological belonging. . . . There is no denying the paradox involved here. . . . To say "I am free" is equivalent simply to saying "I am I." To be a self is to be free. But it now seems that at that limit where I am most myself, I am no longer autonomous. . . . We are forcibly reminded of the statement of Jaspers: "There where I am myself I am no longer only myself" (pp. 90–91).

True freedom, then, is the discovery of oneself, which is simultaneously coupled with an absence of autonomy and my ontological belonging to something more than myself. And what is this last? The answer comes from the nature of creation.

(3) Any creative experience such as freedom is "the birth of the transcendent in a spiritual subject, and it is the birth of the subject in transcendence. . . . The transcendent is not a mere 'thing' but the eternal and absolute thou at the heart of all communion" (p. 94). And insofar as "I am actually spirit, I am actually part of a communion whose vital principle is a transcendent act which is identi-

---

[39] This refusal to conceive of true freedom as residing in one's free choices is, one must remember, common to all monists (e.g., Spinoza, Hegel, etc.). For them someone is free because nothing external can force him; yet what he does is still automatic, necessitated, determined from within.

cally love and truth. If I could coincide with my own being fully, I could attain to this transcendence. Which again means that the search for the truth of being is a search for the true self" (p. 121).

(4) In brief: to discover one's true self in freedom is to attain to the transcendent, eternal, absolute Thou, to whom each spirit belongs and with whom each is ultimately identified. And in arriving at that absolute and indefectible Presence, I thereby can know, love, respond to other selves, since He is the common ground between them and me. Interpersonal relations are guaranteed, ontological isolationism and solipsism are overcome, but only through a pantheistic monism of spirit.

In our rebuttal of points made in the previous paragraphs, we must first note that Marcel himself has elsewhere explicitly rejected monism. It is a mistake, he affirms, to believe "that the predominance of the mind can only be affirmed on the basis of a universal spiritualism, a monism of the psychical. . . . Real philosophy is beyond monism as it is beyond pluralism."[40] Or again: Once a dualism between thought and the external world is unacceptable,

> thought reaches the point of positing a non-causal unity of the world and of itself, and there lies the real meaning and strongest justification of monism conceived as a doctrine of identity. I appear to myself as bound up with the world by the fact that we derive it and me from an identical act by which the absolute begets itself—I have elsewhere developed at length the motives for which I cannot accept this theory, which fails to make the absolute intelligible.[41]

But even without Marcel's explicit rejection, the previous paragraphs, when accurately interpreted, are themselves no affirmation of monism. The bond between an I and a Thou, spoken of in (1), the indistinctness between persons when communing, does not insinuate that the persons are identified with one another. They transcend the categories of Same/Other, of One/Many. Subjects qua subjects are neither identical nor distinct. Such adjectives are applicable

[40] *Metaphysical Journal*, trans. B. Wall (Chicago: Henry Regnery Co., 1952), p. 94.

[41] *Ibid.*, p. 117; see pp. 115–20. Also see G. Marcel, *Royce's Metaphysics*, trans. V. and G. Ringer (Chicago: Henry Regnery Co., 1956), p. 155.

only to objects, only to existents having definite characteristics, only to the realm of Having (*vs.* Being).[42]

Moreover, the absence of autonomy through true freedom, described in (2), does not necessarily indicate that autonomy is replaced by heteronomy so that subjects entitatively coalesce with one another. In their subjectivity they transcend both autonomy/ heteronomy, which are restricted to the world of Having.

> Autonomy is above all the negation of a heteronomy presupposed and rejected. "I want to run my own life"—that is the radical formula of autonomy. It is here that we can see that tension between the Same and the Other, which is the pulse of the world of having. . . . At a certain depth within me, and in a zone where practical specializations melt away, the terms autonomy and heteronomy become inapplicable.[43]

Finally, although freedom is aligned with belonging to something more than oneself, to transcendent love and truth (3), still "belonging to" is not synonymous with "being one with" (4). Every creature belongs to God and yet is not identified with Him.

When all is said and done, though, a nagging doubt recurs as to whether Marcel actually has cleared himself totally from the charge of monism. That doubt arises not only because he makes occasional ambiguous statements[44] but also because his answers are a bit too facile to be completely satisfactory. "If an I and a Thou somehow are genuinely indistinct," someone objects, "they must be identified with each other and with the transcendent Thou." Not so, Marcel replies. Subjectivity transcends characterizations such as sameness/otherness or identity/distinction. These have nothing to do with subjects as subjects (1). Quite frankly, I wonder. True

---

[42] *Metaphysical Journal*, p. 94; *Being and Having*, trans. K. Farrer (London: Dacre Press, 1949), pp. 153, 167–70.

[43] *Ibid.*, p. 173; also see p. 131.

[44] For example, see *ibid.*, p. 167: "Love treated as the subordination of the self to a superior reality, a reality at my deepest level more truly me than I am myself—love as the breaking of the tension between the self and the other. . . ." Also *Man Against Mass Society*, trans. G. Fraser (Chicago: Henry Regnery Co., 1952), p. 194: "Human beings can be linked to each other by a real bond only because, in another dimension, they are linked to something which transcends them and comprehends them in itself."

enough, subject/object do not pertain directly to the entitative structure of existents, as do supposit/nature. Rather, a subject's subjectivity consists in his actually carrying out his human prerogative
more and more fully through freedom, love, fidelity, etc. These
constitute him as a subject or self. Since they can come and go, so
too his subjectivity can wax and wane or disappear completely. In
this sense, then, the question of whether or not one subject is
entitatively distinct from another is not immediately pertinent. Nonetheless, freedom and love both seem to demand existents which,
although causally related, are still ontologically independent and
distinct. How can someone be authentically free unless it is *he* who
chooses and how can this be unless there *is* a he, entitatively unique
and divergent from all others? How, meaningfully, can there be
love unless there is both someone who loves and someone who is
loved because of the genuine perfections *he* actually and uniquely
possesses?[45] Absence of ontological distinction between loved and
beloved might conceivably generate a sort of narcissism in the
realm of subjectivity.

To mention a final source of doubt: some of those influencing
Marcel were monists—Hegel, Schelling, Fichte, Bradley, Royce.[46]
Has none of their monism rubbed off on him? Actually, Marcel's
position, as outlined by Gallagher, ends by reducing the subject to a
concrete universal. Some may fear, Gallagher writes, that subjectivity turns into a subjectivism. But

> the entire fear is grounded on the misconception that as we
> descend into subjectivity we find a more and more isolated
> particularity, whereas the truth appears to be just the oppo-
> site. The concrete universal is the pearl hidden in the heart of
> authentic subjectivity. The universal is spirit, as Marcel has
> said (p. 141).

---

[45] This Marcel himself appears to admit. See *Metaphysical Journal*, p. 62: "It
is only from the moment at which individuality has an interior that it can
think itself as really distinct from another individuality (and that love becomes possible)."

[46] Marcel's own treatises furnish rather abundant evidence as to which
post-Kantians influenced him. See especially *Metaphysical Journal;* "An Essay
in Autobiography" in *The Philosophy of Existentialism; Royce's Metaphysics;
Creative Fidelity.* Also see H. Spiegelberg, *The Phenomenological Movement,* pp.
448–69, especially 454–59.

Hegel too has said as much. Accordingly, might not Marcel's pearls be lying within a Hegelian oyster of Absolute Spirit?[47]

In Retrospect

These are some of the points made in this chapter. Philosophies of subjectivity are unauthentic existentialisms because in them "to exist" is "to be human." Second, subjectivity can profitably be studied within an authentic existentialism, where "to exist" is "to be actual." Finally, one of the ways in which subjectivity can escape solipsism is to join forces with some sort of monism. This alliance constitutes a constant, albeit hidden temptation which some philosophers of subjectivity conceivably find easier to face than to conquer.

---

[47] For Marcel's own text see *Man Against Mass Society*, pp. 1, 7–8: "This distrust of abstractions explains, for instance, the fascination which the Hegelian system exercised on me for such a long time. For . . . Hegel did make a very splendid effort to preserve the primacy of the concrete; and no philosopher has protested more strongly against the confusion of the concrete with the immediately given. . . . The universal is spirit or mind—and spirit or mind is love. . . . Where love on one side, where intelligence on the other, reach their highest expression, they cannot fail to meet . . . intelligence and love are the most concrete things in the world." See also *ibid.*, p. 200; *Being and Having*, pp. 111, 136.

This reduction of a subject to a concrete universal also occurs in R. Johann. Why, Johann asks, is the self not wholly alien to the realm of reflective formulation? "[Because] the value of selfhood manifests itself *experientially* as in some sense transcending myself. . . . The transcendence of this value, precisely because it is what ultimately makes possible the whole realm of discourse, is presupposed in its being symbolized. This being the case, what is meant by words like the *I*, the *you*, the *self*, is not some structure isolated from experience and situated objectively in the intentional realm, but the concrete, existing ground of that realm. The word *self* does not indicate a generality that is subject to objective analysis, but rather—if I may be permitted the use of a much abused term—a concrete universal, that value to which I am concretely present in myself and you and in terms of which we make up a veritable community of uniques" ("Experience and Philosophy," in I. Lieb [ed.], *Experience, Existence, and the Good* [Carbondale, Ill.: Southern Illinois University Press, 1961], p. 35). Have we here come upon another Hegelian oyster and pearl?

If these points are true, authentic existentialism does have advantages not found elsewhere. May I invite you to try it?[48]

---

[48] For additional information on authentic existentialism, see L. Sweeney, *Authentic Metaphysics in an Age of Unreality*, and chs. 18–21 above. Also see F. J. Kovach, *Scholastic Challenges to Some Mediaeval and Modern Ideas* (Stillwater, Okla.: Western Publications, 1987); Henry B. Veatch, *Human Rights: Fact or Fancy?* (Baton Rouge/London: Lousiana State University Press, 1985), especially ch. 4: "Law and Ethics in Search of a Physics or Metaphysics," pp. 213–49; *idem, Swimming Against the Current in Contemporary Philosophy* (Washington, D.C.: The Catholic University of America, 1990), especially Part III, pp. 201–330.

Additional studies on Jacques Derrida: L. Sweeney, "Three Approaches to Union with God: Plotinus, Aquinas, Derrida" in Daniel Burke (ed.), *Spiritual Life and Intellectual Work* (Catholic Commission on Intellectual and Cultural Affairs; Philadelphia, Pennsylvania; LaSalle University, 1996); *idem*, "Deconstructionism and Neoplatonism: Derrida and Dionysius the Aeropagite" in R. Baine Harris (ed.), *Neoplatonism and Contemporary Thought* (Albany: State University of New York Press, 1997).

23

Gabriel Marcel's Position on God

In one of his very first philosophical writings (winter, 1910–1911) Gabriel Marcel turned his attention to God.

We can say that faith bears on the existence of God. But it is clear that this expression must not be taken literally. God does not exist; He is infinitely above existence since He is beyond all truth and can only be grasped by faith through the act which links Him intimately to thought (*PF*, pp. 80–81; Fr., pp. 64–65).[1]

---

[1] In order to limit the number of footnotes, references to both English and French versions of Marcel's writings will be given wherever possible in the body of the paper itself and according to the following schema of abbreviations:

BH: Being and Having, trans. Katherine Farrer (New York: Harper and Row, Harper Torchbooks, 1965). French ed., *Être et Avoir* (Paris: Aubier, 1935).

CF: Creative Fidelity, trans. Robert Rosthal (New York: Farrar, Straus and Co., 1964). (I have rather frequently had to change this translation to bring it into conformity with the French original.) French ed., *Du refus à l'invocation* (Paris: Gallimard, 1940).

EB: Existential Background of Human Dignity (Cambridge, Mass.: Harvard University Press, 1963).

MB: Mystery of Being, vol. I: *Reflection and Mystery,* trans. G. S. Fraser; vol. II: *Faith and Reality,* trans. René Hague (Chicago: Henry Regnery Co., 1960). French ed., *Le mystère de l'être* (Paris: Aubier, 1951).

MJ: Metaphysical Journal, 1913–1923, trans. Bernard Wall (Chicago: Henry Regnery Co., 1952). French ed., *Journal Métaphysique, 1913–1923* (Paris: Aubier, 1927).

PE: Philosophy of Existentialism, trans. Manya Harari (New York: Citadel Press, 1964). French for initial chapters: *Positions et approches concrètes du*

Approximately twenty years later (July 19, 1929) he was still concerned with God.

> We must try to understand how it is that to pray to God is
> without any question the only way to think of God. . . . When I
> think of a finite being, I restore, in a manner, between him and
> myself, a community, an intimacy, a *with* (to put it crudely)
> which might seem to have been broken. . . . To ask myself how
> I can think of God is to enquire in what sense I can be with
> him (*BH*, pp. 31–32; Fr., pp. 31–32).

Another twenty years later (1949–1950, Gifford Lectures at University of Aberdeen) and God was still at the center of his thoughts.

> From the moment when we open ourselves to these infiltra-
> tions of the invisible [world], we cease to be the unskilled and
> yet pretentious soloists we perhaps were at the start, and
> gradually become members, wide-eyed and brotherly, of an
> orchestra in which those whom we so inaptly call the dead are
> quite certainly much closer to Him of whom we should not
> perhaps say that He conducts the symphony, but that He is
> the symphony in its profound and intelligible unity. . . . [He is
> the] eternal Light of which a reflection has continually shone

---

mystère ontologique (Louvain: Nauwelaerts; Paris: J. Vrin, 1949); French for
final chapter: "Regard en arrière," *Existentialisme chrétien*, ed. E. Gilson (Paris:
Librairie Plon, 1947), pp. 290–319.

PF: *Philosophical Fragments 1909–1914*, trans. and introduction by Lionel A.
Blain (Notre Dame, Ind.: University of Notre Dame, 1965). French ed., *Fragments
philosophiques* (Louvain: Nauwelaerts, n.d.).

PM: *Problematic Man*, trans. Brian Thompson (New York: Herder and
Herder, 1967). French ed., *L'homme problèmatique* (Paris: Aubier, 1955).

On Marcel's position concering God, see Roger Troisfontaines, S.J., *De
l'existence à l'être: La philosophie de Gabriel Marcel* [hereafter: Troisfontaines]
(Paris: J. Vrin, 1954), Tome II, pp. 205–374, especially pp. 277–342; Kenneth T.
Gallagher, *Philosophy of Gabriel Marcel* (New York: Fordham University Press,
1962), especially pp. 125–28; Mary Schaldenbrand, "Gabriel Marcel and Proof
for the Existence of God," *Studies in Philosophy and History of Philosophy*, ed. John
K. Ryan (Washington, D.C.: Catholic University of America Press, 1961), vol.
1, pp. 35–56; Donald McCarthy, "Marcel's Absolute Thou," *Philosophy Today*
10 (1966), 175–81; C. V. Pax, "Approach to God in Thought of Gabriel Marcel,"
Ph.D. diss., University of Notre Dame (Ann Arbor, Mich.: University Microfilms, 1962); Lionel A. Blain, "Marcel's Logic of Freedom in Proving God's
Existence," *International Philosophical Quarterly* 9 (1969), 177–204.

on us all the time we have been in this world—that Light without whose guidance we may be sure that we should never have started our journey (*MB*, II, 210; Fr., p. 188).

If those quotations are representative samplings, Gabriel Marcel has reflected frequently and seriously on God.

Let us now study those reflections, which seem especially relevant today. Interest in various brands of atheism, including the "God is dead" school and current secular humanism, calls attention to the importance of rethinking and restating various theisms. Among these Gabriel Marcel's is certainly of first-rank significance.

Several Intellectual Stages

As the first moment in that investigation let us list several stages in Marcel's intellectual development which may help us understand his views on God better.

The first is the early years of his career as a professional philosopher—from ca. 1909 (his degree at the Sorbonne) up to the mid-twenties, from his *Philosophical Fragments* up to *Metaphysical Journal*. In this period he denies that God exists.

Faith bears on the existence of God. But it is clear that this expression must not be taken literally. God does not exist; He is infinitely above existence (*PF*, pp. 80–81; Fr., p. 65).

This denial of existence was necessitated by what Marcel then meant by "existence." Only that exists which is capable of being given as a datum to consciousness and of being identified by the senses (*PR*, pp. 58–60 [Fr., pp. 40–42]; *MJ*, p. 315). But God is not given to consciousness or verifiable by the senses. Hence, God does not exist.[2]

---

[2] Besides the references just given, also see *MJ*, p. 156: "Only that which can be an object of predication, which can be a datum, exists (to make a judgment of existence one must provide data by predicates). Hence the very clear relation between the fact that there is no meaning in saying that God exists, and the impossibility of attributing characteristics to him, of converting him into a *he* or *it*." Also see *MJ*, p. 35; *ibid.*, "Existence and Objectivity," pp. 319–39, especially 335–39, where Marcel conceives existence as linked with

This refusal to predicate existence of God will cause Marcel uneasiness many years later since on first hearing it sounds like an admission of atheism.[3] In his William James Lectures at Harvard University in 1961–1962 (published as *The Existential Background of Human Dignity* in 1963), he commented:

> The text I have quoted [*PF*, pp. 106–7, as well as pp. 80–81 quoted above] is not to be construed in any way as atheism. On the contrary, my concern was to find a possible way of safeguarding the reality of God, which appeared to me to be inevitably compromised from the moment one speaks of His existence; I thought one might speak of the existence of only that which falls within the purview of experience. In this there was a Kantian echo, to be sure (*EB*, p. 27).

Although God does not exist, He *is*, He is *present* to me. And "presence" is not to be construed as "externally manifesting oneself to the other, but rather as involving a quality . . . of making me feel that he is *with* me," does not fail me, stands up to whatever circumstances may bring, and so on (*CF*, p. 154; Fr., p. 201).

The *second* stage is his baptism as a Roman Catholic on March 23, 1929, when he was forty years old.[4] As one would expect, his conversion exerted a powerful influence on the rest of his intellectual life. Many years after his baptism he wrote:

> A conversion worthy of the name . . . [is] an absolutely sincere and spontaneous conversion at the heart of an individual existence. . . . The convert [says:] "I have not found [a remedy for my ills], *I have been found.*" In other words, he would rightfully point out that everything is explained—or, more precisely,

one's body, with a subject's incarnational state. He will return to this conception frequently in later works. See *CF*, p. 17 (Fr., pp. 27–28); *MB*, I, 111–17 (Fr., pp. 105–10); *MB*, II, 25–32 (Fr., pp. 25–30); *EB*, pp. 46–47; Troisfontaines, II, 210–14.

[3] For Marcel's reaction to atheism, see *CF*, pp. 127–30 (Fr., pp. 167–71); *MB*, II, 81–84 (Fr., pp. 73–76); *MB*, II, 194–98 (Fr., pp. 174–78); Troisfontaines, II, 263–67.

[4] Marcel's father had been brought up a Catholic but ceased practicing his religion at an early age; his mother died when he was three; his mother's sister, who became his stepmother, was Jewish but had been converted to a liberal form of Protestantism. See *PE*, pp. 109–11 (Fr., pp. 299–301); *Searchings* (New York: Newman Press, 1967), pp. 96–97.

illuminated—by the idea of grace, and by the fact that he did not refuse that grace (*EB*, p. 167).

If someone objects, "Aren't you abandoning the role of a philosopher by mentioning and emphasizing 'grace'? " Marcel says no.

The philosopher . . . is the man who comes, not without trembling, to share with those who are willing to hear him out a certain experience which it was given to him to undergo. And of this experience he observes that no understanding can be achieved without taking account of that mysterious and essentially discrete reality which is called grace (*ibid.*, p. 168).

In the light of that 1961 comment let us now read Marcel's remarks at the time of his baptism (*BH*, pp. 15, 24; Fr., pp. 17, 30).

March 5th [1929]. I have no more doubts. This morning's happiness is miraculous. For the first time I have clearly experienced *grace*. A terrible thing to say, but so it is. I am hemmed in at last by Christianity—in, fathoms deep. Happy to be so!

March 23rd. I was baptized this morning. My inward state was more than I had dared to hope for: no transports, but peaceful, balanced, and full of hope and faith.

Marcel will need all the peace and balance he then noted because his becoming a Catholic set squarely in front of him an important, difficult problem (this is the *third* stage in his intellectual career): what was to be his attitude to Thomism, which had become practically identical with Catholic doctrine itself in theology and philosophy?[5] That identity had been initiated by Leo XIII's encyclical *Aeterni Patris* on August 4, 1879. "We exhort you in all earnestness," the pope proclaimed toward the end of that encyclical,

to restore the golden wisdom of St. Thomas, and to spread it far and wide. . . . Let carefully selected teachers endeavor to implant the doctrine of Thomas Aquinas in the minds of students, and set forth clearly his solidity and excellence over

---

[5] This question was not remote or merely speculative for Marcel because of his contacts (see quotations below) with R. Garrigou-Lagrange and J. Maritain, two prominent Thomists of the time.

others. Let the universities already founded or to be founded by you illustrate and defend this doctrine, and use it for the refutation of prevailing errors.[6]

Leo XIII's exhortation was repeated and implemented by succeeding popes (Pius X in 1915, Pius XI in 1923, the Apostolic Constitution *Deus Scientiarum Dominus* in 1931, etc.), and the Code of Canon Law (1918) gave the exhortation the force of law in Canon 1366. The result was that Aquinas' philosophical and theological positions were, in many circles at least, almost synonymous with the Catholic Church.

How did Marcel react to Thomism? Years later he admitted quite bluntly that, despite Jacques Maritain's efforts, he found it unacceptable.

[Maritain and I] saw each other continuously during a winter spent in Versailles, at the home of our mutual friend, Charles Du Bos. What Maritain tried to do was to instruct both of us in certain aspects of Thomist doctrine, but, as a matter of fact, neither Charles Du Bos nor I was converted by any manner of means to this type of thought (*EB*, p. 81).

His first reaction, though, seems to have been one of praise, although in a restrained way and only on some points. On June 26, 1929, he wrote that "I am today rid of whatever traces of idealism remained in my philosophy. I feel exorcised by the influence of Father Garrigou-Lagrange's book on God [presumably *Dieu, son existence et sa nature*, which was first published at Paris in 1915], though it is very far from satisfying me completely" (*BH*, p. 27; Fr., pp. 35–36). On July 17 he again mentioned reading Garrigou-Lagrange and commented on idealism: a thought which is not the thought of something "would be lost in a sort of dream of itself . . . I here join forces with Thomism or at least with what I understand to be Thomism" (*ibid.*, pp. 29, 30; Fr., pp. 38, 39–40).

But three years later one can detect rather open hostility in his remarks.

---

[6] Quotation taken from Jacques Maritain, *St. Thomas Aquinas* (New York: Meridian Books, Inc., 1958), pp. 208–9. See *ibid.*, "Testimonies of the Popes," pp. 167–75, for a list of papal approvals of Aquinas from middle of thirteenth century down to 1956. For text of four important modern papal documents, see *ibid.*, pp. 177–266.

October 7th [1932]. It is a fact that they [the Thomist proofs for the existence of God] are not universally convincing. How can we explain their partial ineffectiveness? The arguments presuppose that we have already grounded ourselves on God, and what they are really doing is to bring to the level of discursive thought an act of a wholly different kind. These, I believe, are not ways, but blind ways, as one can have blind windows [*des faux chemins comme il y a des fausses fenêtres*] (*ibid.*, p. 98; Fr., p. 141).

As the years went on, his hostility became even more explicit and almost harsh. In 1940 he stated that such theological affirmations as Thomists are wont to make (e.g., "God is simple," "God is immutable," and so on) "are a snare; for the 'properties' I have just mentioned, if construed as predicates, seem to be the most impoverished that exist; if they are construed as principles of the understanding [*déterminations du connaître*], it must be conceded that they are in a sense more inadequate than those which are conferred on the humblest and most ephemeral creature in our world" (*CF*, pp. 36–37 [Fr., pp. 53–54]; also see *MB*, II, 147 [Fr., p. 133]). In 1950 he returned to the ineffectual and paradoxical character of the Thomistic proofs for the existence of God.

We stumble on this paradox: the proofs are ineffectual precisely when they would be most necessary, when, that is, it is a question of convincing an unbeliever; conversely, when belief is already present and when, accordingly, there is the minimum of agreement [that is, agreement about ends, about the supreme value], then they seem to serve no useful purpose. If a man has experienced the presence of God, not only has he no need of proofs, he may even go so far as to consider the idea of a demonstration as a slur on what is for him a sacred evidence (*MB*, II, 197–98; Fr., p. 177).

In 1955 he suggested that the phrase "death of God" refers to the Aristotelian-Thomistic deity.

I think we should have done with the idea of a God as Cause, of a god concentrating in himself all causality, or even, in more rigorous terms, with all theological usage of the notion of causality. . . . It could be . . . that the God whose death Nietzsche truthfully announced was the god of the Aristotelian-Thomistic tradition, god the prime mover (*PM*, p. 54; Fr., p. 63).[7]

Finally, in a lecture delivered in 1960 but published in English in 1967 he parallels Thomism with Marxism: "I know of only two instances where such indolence [with respect to truth] gives way to the opposite disposition of fanaticism. I have in mind Marxist dogmatism . . . and theological dogmatism (where it crystallizes into the attitude: Outside Thomism there is no salvation)" (*Searchings*, p. 9).

Such frequent and rather virulent criticisms attest to Marcel's preoccupation with Thomism. They also leave no doubt but that he is completely disenchanted with it and that he has discarded all Thomistic proofs for establishing the existence of God. Does he offer any replacement? Yes (this is the *fourth* stage in his intellectual career), but, as is to be expected, it has a very different character from Thomas' proofs, it comes from a totally different philosophical world. It is a consideration centering around the question, "What am I?"[8] He asked this question first in *Being and Having* on January 19–20, 1933, and returned to it in several subsequent writings. Let us begin with *Being and Having*.

> We must obviously subject it [the notion of proving the existence of God] to a careful revision. In my view, all proof refers to a certain datum, which is here the belief in God, whether in myself or in another. . . . The proof can only confirm for us what has really been given to us in another way (BH, p. 121; Fr., pp. 175–76).

---

[7] No contemporary Thomist would agree with Marcel that Aquinas' God is identical with Aristotle's First Mover. For example, see J. Owens, "The Conclusion of the *Prima Via*," *The Modern Schoolman* 30 (1952–1953), 33–53, 109–21, 203–15; *idem*, "The Starting Point of the *Prima Via*," *Franciscan Studies* 27 (1967), 249–84.

For a reply to Marcel's rejection of causality *re* God, see J. M. Le Blond, "L'usage théologique de la notion de causalité," in *De la connaissance de Dieu*, vols. III–IV of *Recherches de philosophie* (Paris: Desclée de Brouwer, 1958), pp. 15–26; for Marcel's counter reply, see *ibid.*, "Dieu et la causalité," pp. 27–33.

[8] Marcel once said (*EB*, p. 16) that "except for the problem of 'What am I?' there are no other metaphysical problems, since in one way or another they all lead back to it."

January 19th–20th [1933].

[1] Reflection on the question "What am I?" [*que suis-je?*] and upon its implications. When I reflect upon the implications of the question "What am I?" taken as a single issue, I see that it .means: "What is there in me that can answer this question?" Consequently, every answer to this question *coming from me* must be mistrusted.

[2] But could not someone else supply me with the answer? An objection immediately arises: the qualifications which the other may have which enable him to answer me, the eventual validity of what he says, are observed [and evaluated] by me but what qualifications have I for making this observation?

[3] I can, therefore, only refer myself without contradiction to a judgment which is absolute, but which is at the same time more within me than my own judgment. In fact, if I treat this judgment as in the least *exterior* to me, the question of what it is worth and how it is to be appreciated must inevitably be asked afresh.

[4] The question is then eliminated *qua* question and turns into an appeal. But perhaps in proportion as I take cognizance of this *appeal qua appeal*, I am led to recognize that the appeal is possible only because deep down in me there is something other than me, something further within me than I am myself—and at once the appeal changes its index (*ibid.*, pp. 124–25; Fr., pp. 180–81).

Let us complement that version with two excerpts from *Creative Fidelity*.

[5] Into an appeal for whom, however? Can I be sure, have I any justification for thinking, that this appeal is understood and that there is a being—someone—who knows me and evaluates me? We must reject at the outset the postulate on which this question is based. . . . The transcendence of the One to whom I appeal is a transcendence of all possible experience as well as of all rational calculation, which is but experience anticipated and schematized.

[6] "Who am I? You alone really know me and judge me, to doubt You is not to free myself but to annihilate myself. But to view Your reality as problematic would be to doubt You and, what is more, to deny You. . . ."

Marcel terminates this version in *Creative Fidelity* by putting the objection: "Isn't this process a prelude to mysticism?" He agrees but adds that there is ultimately no "precise boundary between metaphysics and mysticism. . . . It is time that the metaphysician understands, if he wants once and for all to get out of the epistemological rut, that adoration can and ought to be a *terra firma* for reflection, a ground where he can find support" (*CF*, pp. 145–46; Fr., pp. 189–90).

Marcel's line of thought (that "proof" only confirms and explicates what is already given by faith, that "proof" culminates in an appeal to and adoration of an Absolute Thou) arises, obviously, within a radically different philosophical world from Aquinas'. In order to understand the French philosopher better, let us now briefly point out how radical that difference is.

Marcel's *Weltanschauung*

Aquinas and others had developed a conception of individuality which issued from divine revelation as interpreted and defined by various ecumenical councils and which was commonly accepted by Christian theologians and philosophers prior to Kierkegaard and other philosophers of subjectivity.[9] According to it an "individual" is that which is unique, irreplaceable, original and, in that sense, independent, autonomous. Uniqueness, irreplaceability, originality—in short, individuality—is a condition of the very entity of an existent, it pertains to his or her entitative structure. And it is twofold—that of nature and that of supposit. Both nature and supposit point to a status of uniqueness, autonomy, etc., in the individual of which they are predicated. They are a proclamation that all existents (not just humans) enjoy two sorts of independence and uniqueness. One is within the very *sort* of existent they are

---

[9] For documentation and explanation, see Leo Sweeney, S.J., *Authentic Metaphysics in an Age of Unreality*, 2d ed. (New York/Bern: Peter Lang Publishing, Inc., 1993), pp. 181–93; *idem*, ch. 22 above: "Existentialism: Authentic and Unauthentic," prgrs. corresponding to notes 22–33.

(expressed, for example, when I say, "I am this man, you are that man; here is one oak, there is another"), and this is the kind of individuality "nature" designates. The other is with regard to the very *exercise of existence* itself (expressed when I say, "I subsist but my intellect and freedom do not: they exist in and through me; Christ's human nature does not subsist, either; it exists as assumed by the Son of God"), and this sort of individuality "supposit" is concerned with. However different they are, though, one must remember that both point to states of individuality which are in the *entitative structure itself* of an existent (whether human or not) and which thus are permanent and cannot slip away.

Philosophers of subjectivity do not attend to such entitative individuality. They choose instead to locate uniqueness, never-to-be-repeatedness, originality, in a psychological state (and thus they restrict individuality to human existents solely). What is that state? That in which someone is actually exercising his freedom. The reason he is unique and uniquely so is that he is *free*. He is a *human* existent, endowed with intellect and will, who thus can freely fashion himself and stand out from all others. This uniqueness is not in the abstract or in the past or even in the future: it is in the concrete, here-and-now exercise of freedom in this or that choice, which is his and no other's and which even he himself can never reduplicate exactly, because any other decision will be at least numerically distinct and because he will never again find himself in these identical circumstances.

Another point needs to be made. The psychological state in which I place myself by my free choice and which constitutes me an individual, a self, a subject (*vs.* object) also makes me genuinely *real*. Whenever I am not in such a state, I am unreal (as is, of course, everything nonhuman because incapable of freedom).[10] Note, though, that my reality lasts only as long as that psychological state and, therefore, is transient; it can wax and wane or disappear entirely if I do not exercise my freedom. In fact, philosophers of subjectivity elaborate the contrast between "subject" and "object" so as to highlight the precious originality and extraordinary value located in human existents by reason of their free, transcendent lives. Men and women are thereby reminded to endeavor con-

---

[10] "Unreal" not in the sense of nonexistent but in the sense of insignificant, valueless, worthless and so on. On the positive side, "real" means not what actually is but what is significant, important, valuable, and these characteristics accrue to someone from and within his or her free decisions.

stantly to rise above the monotony of their day-in-day-out existence, to fight the depersonalizing influences of mechanized industry, business methods, urban living habits in our contemporary
civilizations.

Such a notion of individuality (the psychological state in which I
am exercising my freedom and which constitutes my reality as a
self, a person, a subject) is at the heart of any philosophy of subjectivity, whether that of Kierkegaard, Heidegger, Camus or Sartre. It
is also at the center of Marcel's, although with a difference. His
philosophy of subjectivity is rather a philosophy of *inter*subjectivity.
What does this mean? Marcel grants that what produces the psychological state which genuinely makes me a self or subject and,
thus, individual and real is my exercise of freedom, but (herein lies
the difference) only with regard to a certain kind of choice. I truly
become myself only when I freely choose to break out of the prison
of self-centeredness ("self" understood here in a narrow, pejorative
sense) and to relate to others.[11] This can occur in several ways:
through various sorts of personal communication (e.g., language,
making others welcome, making myself available to others);[12]
through sharing common goals, adventures, prayer, worship;[13]

---

[11] On relations see *MJ*, pp. 155–56; *MB*, I, pp. 222–23 (Fr., p. 196—a very
abbreviated version); *MB*, II, 91 sqq. (Fr., p. 82); *Searchings*, pp. 46–47, 62. Also
see J. B. O'Malley, *The Fellowship of Being: An Essay on the Concept of Person in
the Philosophy of Gabriel Marcel* (The Hague: Martinus Nijhoff, 1966), pp. 19–20.

[12] See *EB*, pp. 31–41, especially p. 40: An example of a subject's relating
with another is "that of the change which can come about during a journey in
the relationship which develops between myself and a stranger. To begin
with, he may be only 'that skinny little man' or 'that short-sighted old man,'
but if the conversation between us, at first entirely commonplace and impersonal, brings us to the discovery of a certain bond between us, the relationship thus transformed becomes one of subject to subject." Also see *CF*, pp.
32–34 (Fr., pp. 48–50); *MB*, I, 91–92 (Fr., p. 87).

Also *CF*, p. 88 (Fr., p. 119): "On what conditions can I communicate with
this other reality? . . . I must somehow make room for the other in myself; if I
am completely absorbed in myself, concentrated on my sensations, feelings,
anxieties, it will obviously be impossible for me to receive, to incorporate in
myself, the message of the other. What I called incohesion a moment ago here
presents itself to me as disposability (*disponibilité*)." On *disponibilité* (which
means "my being available or open to another," "my being on hand for
another"), see *ibid.*, pp. 50–54 (Fr., pp. 71–77), p. 227 (Fr., pp. 291–92); *MB*, I, 201
(Fr., p. 178).

[13] See *CF*, p. 8 (Fr., p. 14); *MB*, I, 138–40 (Fr., pp. 128–30): "We have only to
think of what it means to participate . . . in some ceremony . . . [namely,] that
one is one of a number of people present at it, but such participation can also

through faith (by which he means *fidelity*: I believe in others, I extend myself to others as credit to be drawn upon, I put myself in their hands because of my assurance that they are with me, are present to me, will not fail me);[14] especially, through love, which is "more authentic as I love less for my own sake, that is, for what I can hope to obtain from another, and more for the sake of the other."[15]

The consequence is that such communication, participation, faith and love not only make me authentically myself (I become real through you, remember) but also set up simultaneously a resultant web, skein, network, complex (call it what you will) of real relations between me and several or many others (actually) and, even, between me and all others (potentially, at least).[16] This network of

---

have an ideal character. I can, for instance, though tied to a sick-bed, associate myself with this ceremony through prayer . . . [for example,] a ceremony of thanksgiving to God for the end of some national calamity, an epidemic or a war. . . . I do not really need to know that at a given time and a given place such and such an office of thanksgiving will be celebrated. This thanksgiving ceremony is, after all, only a particular expression of an act of adoration with which I can associate myself, through prayer, at any moment. We thus arrive at the notion of an act of participation which no longer leaves any place for the objectivity of a datum or even of a notification. . . . The more all of us who are praying at the same moment are genuinely melted into a single love, the less significance, obviously, the question of how many of us there may be really has. *Melted*, I say: for nevertheless it is not as if I were alone any more, I do really feel myself strangely strengthened by the fact that it is a multitude who are turning at one moment towards him whom we adore." Also see *MB*, II, 117–20; Fr., pp. 105–7.

Also see John Foley, S.J., "Participation in *Fragments philosophiques* of Gabriel Marcel," Master's thesis, Saint Louis University, 1967.

[14] See *CF*, p. 40 (Fr., p. 57); pp. 134–39 (Fr., pp. 176–79), pp. 147–49 (Fr., pp. 192–94), pp. 166–72 (Fr., pp. 216–24); *MB*, II, 69 (Fr., p. 63), p. 88 (Fr., p. 80), pp. 199–200 (Fr., pp. 178–79).

[15] *MB*, II, 109 (Fr., p. 98). Also see *CF*, pp. 33–34 (Fr., pp. 49–50); also note 17 below.

[16] We can relate even with the dead, and this helps explain Marcel's abiding interest in parapsychology (*PE*, pp. 122–24 [Fr., pp. 312–14]; *CF*, pp. 32 and 149 [Fr., pp. 47 and 195]; *MB*, I, 224 [Fr., pp. 197–98]; *EB*, p. 43) and in the family. On the latter, see *MB*, I, 242 (Fr., p. 213); *EB*, pp. 83–85; *Homo Viator*, trans. E. Crawford (London: Victor Gollancz Ltd., 1951), pp. 68–97, especially p. 71 (Fr., p. 99): "Between my ancestors and myself a far more obscure and intimate relationship exists [than between causes and effect]. I share with them as they do with me—invisibly; they are consubstantial with me and I with them." There is even a continuity between so ancient a personage as Caesar and me: "When I affirm Caesar has existed, . . . I do not mean merely

real relationships (plus, of course, the psychological states which cause them) *is* true reality. It *is* what Marcel calls Being, which transcends any one individual and yet in which I and others find ourselves authentically as beings, as truly real.[17]

Perhaps we might more easily understand what Marcel means by this skein of relationships (grounded, as we have seen, in the psychological states of faith, love, etc., which issue from our free decisions) if we turn to the metaphors and similes he uses to describe it. For example, it is (or, as the case may be, is like)

  a magnetic field and existential orbit (*CF*, p. 18; Fr., p. 28);

  a fecund indistinctness where beings may communicate, where they *are* in and by the very act of communication (*CF*, p. 35; Fr., p. 52);

  not a neutral environment but a kind of vital milieu from which the soul draws its strength and where it is renewed by testing itself (*CF*, p. 35; Fr., p. 52);

  a mystery, which is not to be construed as a lacuna in our knowledge or as a void to be filled but rather as a plenitude, the expression of a profound exigence (*CF*, p. 152; Fr., p. 198);

  a city which is not built of stone and is cemented only with thought (*MB*, I, 90; Fr., p. 85); an ideal or intelligible city which is illuminated by an external truth and which draws its very existence from that light which is truth (*MB*, I, 91; Fr., p. 87);

---

that Caesar would have been perceived by me; I mean that there is between the existence of Caesar and my existence, i.e., my psycho-physical presence to myself, an objectively determinable temporal continuity. . . . Furthermore, the chain of spatial, temporal, and spatio-temporal relations can be compressed by the imagination to the point where the existent that is thought becomes co-present with me" (*CF*, pp. 17–18 [Fr., p. 28], quoting in part *Metaphysical Journal*). Also *Searchings*, pp. 55–72.

[17] Even genuine love needs to be grounded in Being, the complex of real relationships: to answer that love "is the more authentic according as I love less for my own sake . . . and more for the sake of the other . . . is only a cut and dried answer and still implies too dualist a notion of the lover and the loved. Will not the truth be found to lie rather in the more and more indivisible community, in the bosom of which I and the other tend to be continually more perfectly absorbed?" (*MB*, II, 109; Fr., p. 98).

The fact that being consists of a skein of relations, issuing from love and other psychological states, illumines how tenuous and delicate reality is. Little wonder that reality of such gossamer density escapes the grasp of concepts, schemata, abstraction.

the inside of a structure which we cannot imagine having a corresponding outside (*MB*, II, 13; Fr., p. 15);

the world of musical improvisation, in which everything is communication and everything is bound together (*MB*, II, 17; Fr., p. 18); also see *ibid.*, II, 192 (Fr., p. 172);

an orchestra or choir in which we take part and where we find "that joy is fundamentally bound up with a consciousness of being *all together*" (*MB*, II, 134; Fr., p. 120); also see *ibid.*, II, 210 (Fr., p. 188);

a symphony of being—which is a supra-rational unity beyond images, words and concepts (*EB*, p. 83);

the indwelling of Christ in all the faithful—an idea "which corresponds exactly in the religious order to the position which I am trying to define on the philosophical plane (*MB*, II, 156; Fr., p. 140);

the Mystical Body, that on which the philosopher should perhaps concentrate (*MB*, II, 205; Fr., pp. 183–84).

If such comparisons do not help, we can fall back on the words Marcel applies literally to it. The sum total of relations is, he says, a togetherness, a community, fraternity, intersubjectivity.[18] Or, even more revealingly, it is a universal—a living universal (*CF*, p. 9; Fr., p. 15: *cet universal vivant*), a polyphonic universal (*MB*, II, 192; Fr., p. 172) and, most significant of all, a concrete universal (*CF*, p. 100; Fr., p. 135: *la seule universalité concrète*; *MB*, II, 142; Fr., p. 130: *un concret véritable*). Why so? The relatedness, the togetherness which is Being is a universal because it embraces all beings, all realities, all selves (being is, we must recall, restricted to human existents, each of which is real and is a self solely in its freely relating to others through love or some other way of communing-with). But it embraces them not with reference to predication (as is the case of the concept of "man," which is universal as predicable of all humans), not through abstracting from their singularity (as does a concept in order to be universal). Intersubjectivity, togetherness, Being, is not a concept. It is the actual, literal encompassment of all beings (hence, a *universal*) in their uniquenesses, individualities (hence, a *concrete* universal) because beings are relations and, hence, are what they are only within the relational context which helps constitute them and of which they are a part.

---

[18] See *EB*, pp. 40–41; *CF*, p. 8 (Fr., p. 14); *MB*, I, 217–25 (Fr., pp. 193–98); *MB*, II, pp. 16–17 (Fr., pp. 17–19).

Marcel's God

Having sketched Marcel's philosophical universe, let us briefly return to the paragraphs in which he outlined an approach to God and see how they might be paraphrased in the light of that sketch.

[1][19] "What am I?" I am a being, a self, a subject, who becomes so *through you* [that is, another human existent]: I freely relate to you through fidelity, love, etc., and you confer on me reality, being, individuality, selfhood.[20]

[2] But what are you? You are a being, a self, a subject who becomes so *through me*: you freely relate to me by returning my love, fidelity, etc., and thereby I confer on you reality, being, selfhood.

But are we not caught in a vicious circle? *You* give being to me, *I* give being to you. How can *you* make me real who makes you real? Or how can *I* make you real who make me real? Manifestly, we need Someone who transcends both you and me and, for that matter, all other human existents.

[3] We appeal, therefore, to an Absolute Thou, Who needs no other to account for His reality.

[4] He reveals Himself, in fact, through our very appeal: the very fact that you and I experience ourselves as real (that is, as genuine selves and beings through our togetherness or intersubjectivity, which rests on mutual love, fidelity, etc.) and then realize further that we are insufficient ultimately to account for our own reality indicates that there must be Someone Who is realifying us both. "O God, You are that Someone, an Absolute Thou, our Ultimate Recourse."[21]

How may we describe this God who answers our appeal and invocation? The divine attributes favored by a rational theology

---

[19] The numbers in brackets refer to sections of the text as arranged above.

[20] For example, see *CF*, pp. 33–34 (Fr., pp. 49–50): "The being whom I love . . . allows me to discover myself; my outer defenses fall at the same time as the walls separating me from the other person fall. . . . This can be expressed more clearly in terms of the observation that I communicate effectively with myself only insofar as I communicate with the other person, i.e., when he becomes thou for me." Also see Troisfontaines, II, 291.

[21] On our feeling of insufficiency, exigence, metaphysical disquiet, see *MB*, I, 9–10 (Fr., pp. 14–15), p. 26 ("the philosopher's task involves . . . an unusual sense of inner urgent need"; Fr., p. 28), pp. 48–69 (Fr., pp. 47–66); *MB*, II, 3–5, 41 (Fr., pp. 7–8, 38); *EB*, 15–17.

must be replaced by the qualities one can ascribe to a Thou and, in fact, to an Absolute Thou.[22] Accordingly, God is

the unconditional (*CF*, p. 136; Fr., p. 179);

the non-identifiable, which is experienced and apprehended as the Absolute Thou and which is seen in a light that is acknowledged as a presence (*MB*, II, 141; Fr., p. 128);

the Divine Transcendence, in relation to which we can conceive individuality: "the individual realizes himself as such by granting that he is a creature" (*CF*, p. 148; Fr., p. 194); also see *ibid.*, p. 145 (Fr., p. 189); *MB*, I, 187–88 (Fr., p. 167);

He whom I invoke in his reality and not in some idol or degraded image of him and to whom I appeal from the depths of my own insufficiency *ad summam altitudinem* and my absolute resort; to whom I vow absolute fidelity and thus extend an infinite credit (*CF*, p. 167; Fr., pp. 217–18);

He who knows someone as he is, whereas the latter perhaps knows himself only as he is not (*MB*, I, 189; Fr., pp. 168–69); see also *CF*, p. 145 (Fr., p. 189);

He who infinitely transcends me and yet with whom prayer humbly, fervently unites me (*MB*, II, 115; Fr., p. 103); see *MB*, I, 139–40 (Fr., pp. 129–30);

the living God, who is the God of faith, who can only be a spirit, who offers Himself to our love (*MB*, II, 174; Fr., p. 157); who has become incarnate so that "every approach to justice . . . or to charity, in the person of my neighbor is at the same time an approach to this God Himself; and this entails an entirely concrete but quite mysterious relation between this living God and this creature who is my neighbor" (*MB*, II, 147; Fr., p. 133);

He who grants us gifts and yet is not some external power which might be conceived by our imagination but is He whom we shall call the Creator or the Father or, to use a more metaphysical expression, is the unrepresentable and uncharacterizable Being who constitutes us as existents (*MB*, II, 190; Fr., p. 171);

Uncreated Light, without which I am left in the dark, which would mean that I have no being at all (*MB*, II, 199; Fr., p. 178); see *MB*, II, 210 (Fr., p. 188);

[22] See *CF*, pp. 36–37 (Fr., pp. 53–54), pp. 56–57 (Fr., p. 80); *MB*, II, 147 (Fr., p. 133); *PM*, p. 63 (Fr., p. 75); *MJ*, pp. 35, 156, 262–64, 284, 286–87.

He who conducts the symphony of which we gradually become members or, perhaps better, He who *is* the symphony
in its profound intelligible unity (*MB*, II, 210; Fr., p. 188);
Someone who is other than me and yet is further within me
than I am myself (*BH*, p. 125; Fr., p. 181); who alone possesses the secret of what I am and of what I am capable of
becoming (*PM*, p. 63; Fr., p. 75).

Further Questions

In our investigation of Gabriel Marcel, we have discussed his
recommendation that we approach God from the question, "What
am I?"; the *Weltanschauung* within which he intends that approach
to be taken; and, third, the sort of God to which it leads. Let us next
list several questions which call for further reflection.

First of all, is the process Marcel outlines valid? Does it enable us
to assent with certainty to a personal God? Perhaps asking that sort
of question is pointless, since he himself affirms that its starting
point is "belief in God. . . . The proof can only confirm for us what
has really been given to us in another way" (*BH*, p. 121; Fr., p. 175).
One has already assented to God before entering upon the proof.
We must note, though, that the belief in God from which the proof
moves need not be one's own ("belief in God, whether in myself or
in another") and, hence, a proof for God's existence may be helpful
for me in case I start from another's belief. Moreover, although
Marcel excludes any objective verification of one's faith, he does
allow a justification of it.[23] Perhaps a valid proof for God's existence might offer the desired justification.

Hence, the question, Is Marcel's approach to God valid? appears
legitimate. Accordingly, let us ask it again: Does Marcel's process
enable us to assent with certainty to a personal God? Quite frankly,
I am not sure, although it is an attractive and intriguing concept.
But the disquieting question which keeps recurring is why an appeal must have a response. In the view of Sartre and others no such
necessity exists. The emptiness, insatiable desire, tendency, projection toward transcendence are inescapable and ceaseless factors

---

[23] See Troisfontaines, II, 229: "Je sais que j'ai raison de croire et que l'athée
devra reconnaître un jour (ou dans l'éternité) qu'il est dans l'erreur en niant.
Je postule donc une justification de ma foi. Mais cette *justification* n'est pas une
'vérification' à la portée de 'n'importe qui' placé dans les conditions normales
d'expérience 'objective.' "

within every human, but they have no fulfillment, no object, no termination. Such is the human situation and nothing can be done about it.[24] Marcel himself is aware of the difficulty.

> Someone will object, "This appeal may in the first sense be without a real object; it may, as it were, lose itself in the dark" (*BH*, p. 125; Fr., p. 181).

> Into an appeal for whom, however? Can I be sure, have I any justification for thinking, that this appeal is understood and that there is a being—someone—who knows me and evaluates me? (*CF*, p. 145; Fr., p. 189).

He faces the difficulty, too. Such objections, he remarks, are eliminated when one realizes that they are relevant only to problems and not to mysteries and the meta-problematic (*BH*, p. 125; Fr., p. 182), only to what is empirically verifiable and not to what transcends all "possible experience, as well as all rational calculation" (*CF*, p. 145; Fr., p. 189). Marcel's answer seems questionable, I would suggest. If an appeal within the problematic and empirical realm can be without a reply, why and how can I be sure there is a Transcendent answering my appeal on the meta-problematic, meta-empirical, meta-rational level?

But if there should be an Absolute Thou who responds to our appeal, several areas still need examining. Is not an Absolute Thou a contradiction? A "Thou" is another seen in relation to an "I." But God is a Thou. Therefore, He is relational.[25] Yet God is a Thou who is Absolute. Hence, He cannot be relational. Yet, if not relational, how can He be real since reality consists in intersubjectival relations? Or in what sense is God absolute?

---

[24] On Sartre, see William A. Luijpen, *Phenomenology and Atheism* (Pittsburgh: Duquesne University Press, 1964), pp. 264–91; *idem, Existential Phenomenology* (Pittsburgh: Duquesne University Press, 1963), pp. 313–30; James Collins, *The Existentialists* (Chicago: Henry Regnery Co., 1952), pp. 38–79; H. Spiegelberg, *The Phenomenological Movement*, 3d ed. (The Hague: Martinus Nijhoff, 1982), ch. 10, pp. 470–536; W. Desan, *The Tragic Finale: An Essay on the Philosophy of Jean-Paul Sartre* (New York: Harper and Row, 1960), *passim* (bibliography, pp. 213–15); H. Paissac, *Le Dieu de Sartre* (Grenoble: Arthaud, 1950); Jean Wahl, "The Roots of Existentialism," in Wade Baskin, ed., *Jean-Paul Sartre: The Philosophy of Existentialism* (New York: Philosophical Library, 1965), pp. 13–15.

[25] See *MJ*, pp. 137–38, 156–60, 284–87. Also see D. McCarthy, "Marcel's Absolute Thou," p. 178; A. Luther, "Marcel's Metaphysics of the We Are," *Philosophy Today* 10 (1966), 199–202.

Incidentally, however one answers that last question, one must still face the possibility that God's status as the Absolute Thou accounting for our reality results in Marcel's theism involving antihumanistic factors. As analyzed above ("Marcel's God"), his position is that solely God can account for my reality and for yours because we are caught in this impasse: You give being to me, I give being to you. But how can *you* make me real who makes you real? Or how can *I* make you real who make me real?

Manifestly, Marcel argues, we need Someone who transcends you and me and who makes us both real by loving us, and this Someone is God. But God's making me real in that fashion can have one of two results. Either (1) the divinely conferred reality becomes *mine*, it helps constitute *me*. If so, you do not make me real by your love, which instead is itself caused by my reality. (2) Or, that reality does not become truly mine, it is not a constituent of me. Then God alone is real, and I (as well as you) am intrinsically unreal. If so, must we not conclude that Marcel's philosophy, which started out as a humanism, as an affirmation of the primacy of man, becomes almost an antihumanism?

But let us continue with questions concerning God Himself. According to the French philosopher, God is our creator[26] through His freely willing us and things.[27] Yet creation is not an instance of efficient causality, God is not a cause.[28] This denial issues from (among other factors) Marcel's bias against causality, which he restricts entirely to the world of objects[29] and conceives only in a

---

[26] *MJ*, pp. 4–5, 35; G. Marcel, *Royce's Metaphysics*, trans. Virginia and Gordon Ringer (Chicago: Henry Regnery Co., 1956), p. 41; Troisfontaines, II, 290.

[27] *MJ*, pp. 158, 264. For the essential notes in the Judaeo-Christian notion of creation, see L. Sweeney, S.J., *Divine Infinity in Greek and Medieval Thought* (New York/Bern: Peter Lang Publishing, Inc., 1992), ch. 13: "Doctrine of Creation in the *Liber de Causis*," pp. 305–6; for bibliographical data on creation, see *ibid.*, pp. 291–92.

[28] *PM*, p. 54 (Fr., p. 63): "We should have done with the idea of a God as Cause, of a god concentrating in himself all causality, or even, in more rigorous terms, with all theological usage of the notion of causality." Also see *MJ*, p. 35; *Royce's Metaphysics*, pp. 39 (note), 41. On Josiah Royce's refusal to consider God a cause (which most likely influenced Marcel), see *ibid.*, pp. 9, 11, 17, 39, 43, 46, 71–72.

[29] *MB*, II, 172 (Fr., p. 155): "This being whom I love is not only a *Thou* . . . ; he is an object . . . towards whom I can effect all operations whose possibility is included in my condition of physical agent"; *ibid.*, p. 198 (Fr., p. 178): "the domain of intersubjectivity, where all causal interpretations are a mistake."

physical way.[30] But this restriction and this conception form the basis for several questions. Is not my freely choosing to love you an exercise of efficient causality if we interpret an efficient cause analogously as one who produces something by any sort of activity (whether transient or immanent)? If my free choice constitutes me an efficient cause (and there seems to be no good reason for denying this) and if creation results from the free and loving choice of the divine will, why may not one validly (although analogously) view God as our efficient cause? This view would have several advantages, not least of which is that it facilitates one's understanding of the *rapport* between creatures and God. An efficient cause transcends His effects insofar as He is really other than they, yet He is immanent to them inasmuch as He is present to them as agent. As my efficient cause, then, God is transcendent and yet immanent. He is really distinct from me and yet immanent. He is really distinct from me and yet present within me. But if God does not create as an efficient cause, if efficient causality is totally excluded from an intersubjectival universe, how explain divine transcendence and immanence?

Moreover, how are creatures related to God? Would they, in the last analysis, be identical with Him? Marcel has explicitly rejected pantheism.[31] But he has also made statements which somewhat militate against that rejection. Love, he says (*BH*, p. 167), is "the subordination of the self to a superior reality, a reality at my deep-

---

On the exclusion of cause from various areas within intersubjectivity, see the following texts: *MB*, I, 242 (Fr., p. 213; *re* mystery of the family bond); *EB*, p. 85 (*re* family bond); *MB*, I, 257–58 (Fr., pp. 224–25; *re* serious illness as a revelation of how precious yet precarious is life); *MB*, II, 140 (Fr., p. 127; *re* generosity and gifts; *re* grace); *MB*, I, 166 (Fr., p. 150; *re* an artist's environment); *CF*, p. 51 (Fr., p. 73; *re* spiritual life); *ibid.*, p. 87 (Fr., p. 118; *re* influences which being in a situation has upon one).

[30] *PM*, p. 55 (Fr., p. 64): "It is to be feared, indeed, that the idea of causality, whatever effort modern philosophers may have made to spiritualize it, to unfetter it, to detach it from its primitive anchors, is inseparable from the existence of a being provided with instrumental powers; it is, in short, bio-teleological." *MJ*, p. 5: "Causality itself is no more than a purely artificial rationalisation of a totality of becoming." "Dieu et la causalité" (see n. 7 above for full reference), p. 29: "l'interprétation causaliste . . . est inévitablement matérialisante . . . [remaining] au niveau de l'explication physique. . . . C'est dans l'effort—et très spécialement dans l'effort musculaire—que se situe le réduit de la causalité."

[31] *MB*, II, 39 (Fr., p. 37); *MJ*, pp. 94, 115–20; Troisfontaines, II, 288–89.

est level more truly me than I am myself."[32] Or again: there is "a constantly renewed yet creative tension between the I and those depths of our being in and by which we are. . . . There is something which is inexhaustibly concrete at the heart of reality or of human destiny. . . . Each of us gains access to this inexhaustible factor only through the purest and most unblemished part of himself" (CF, pp. 65–66; Fr., pp. 89, 91). Again: "The negation of all autocentrism . . . [is] a property which is only conceivable in terms of a participation in a reality which overflows and envelops me, without my being able to view it in any way as external to what I am" (ibid., p. 144; Fr., p. 188). Granted that such passages can be interpreted so as to avoid monism; but Marcel's rejection of efficient causality and the influence upon him of Bradley,[33] Royce[34] and other post-Hegelians make that interpretation difficult and perhaps suspicious. Hence, the inquiry persists: is Marcel's position open to the charge of a latent monism when one cuts through to its underpinnings?[35]

Such are questions which still need pondering. But they cannot detract from the contribution to religious thought which Marcel has obviously made: a worldview in which human existents have primacy over all subhuman existents, as well as over all dehumanizing forces in our technological cultures, and in which God too plays a primary role as the Absolute Thou and Ultimate Answer to our appeal.

---

[32] Also see *Man Against Mass Society*, trans. G. Fraser (Chicago: Henry Regnery Co., 1952), p. 194; *MB*, II, 19 (Fr., p. 20). Also see ch. 22 above: "Existentialism: Authentic and Unauthentic," prgrs. corresponding to notes 34–47.

[33] For example, see *CF*, p. 22 (Fr., p. 34).

[34] See *Royce's Metaphysics*, pp. 44–46, 58, 64, 71–73.

[35] Another area to be explored is the connection between God, who is "the unrepresentable and uncharacterizable Being" (*MB*, II, 190; Fr., p. 171), and Being *par excellence*, Being-as-such (*MB*, II, 57 [Fr., p. 52]; *CF*, p. 69 [Fr., p. 96], pp. 147–48 [Fr., pp. 192–93], p. 170 [Fr., p. 222], p. 173 [Fr., p. 225]; *MB*, I, 242 [Fr., p. 213]).

24

The Christian Existentialism
of Jacques Maritain

No one can doubt that Jacques Maritain considered himself to be an existentialist, and of a different sort from Sartre, de Beauvoir, etc.: his existentialism is authentic, theirs apocryphal.

Let it be said right off that there are two fundamentally different ways of interpreting the word existentialism. One way is to affirm the primacy of existence, but as implying and preserving essences or natures and as manifesting the supreme victory of the intellect and of intelligibility. This is what I consider to be authentic existentialism. The other way is to affirm the primacy of existence, but as destroying or abolishing essences or natures and as manifesting the supreme defeat of the intellect and of intelligibility. This is what I consider to be apocryphal existentialism, the current kind which "no longer signifies anything at all."[1]

On the strength of that quotation one realizes that Maritain wanted his philosophical position to be taken as an authentic existentialism—i.e., a position in which "existence" (which means, for Maritain, the state of being actual and not, as for apocryphal existentialists such as Sartre, Heidegger, etc., the state of being human)[2] is given

---

[1] *Existence and the Existent* (New York: Pantheon Books, 1948), p. 3; French original, *Court traité de l'existence et de l'existant* (Paris: Hartmann, 1947).

[2] For example, see M. Heidegger, "The Way Back into the Ground of Metaphysics," in W. Kaufmann (ed.), *Existentialism from Dostoevsky to Sartre*

primacy, in which "existence" confers reality because it bestows perfection, worth, significance upon whatever is perfect, valuable, significant. In short, it is a doctrine in which "to be real" is "actually to exist."

Having granted, then, that his metaphysics is an existentialism, we may then ask, is it *theistic*? If the answer is rather obviously yes, an affirmative reply to the next question is not so evident: is it also *Christian*? But first let us reflect on the easier question: why Maritain's metaphysics is theistic.

Theistic Existentialism

The reply to the question, whether Maritain's existentialism is theistic, is that his "primordial way of approach" to the existence of God has the same source as his existential metaphysics—namely, the "natural intuition of being."[3] Accordingly, let us preface our reflections on his existentialist theism by momentarily concentrating on this intuition of being.

Maritain gives his fullest and most detailed account of this intuition in one of his last articles: "Réflexions sur la nature blessée et sur l'intuition de l'être."[4] But for our purposes let us see the simpler and briefer description given in *The Peasant of the Garonne*, the French original of which was published in 1966—just one year before he wrote "Réflexions."

After having dissociated his intuition of being from Bergson's and from "any kind whatsoever of charismatic intuition," Maritain describes it as follows. The intuition of being takes

> place in the heart of the most natural exercise of the intellect, and its only charisma is its *simplicity*—the mysterious simplicity of intellection. There is nothing simpler than to think *I am, I*

(New York: Meridian Books, 1956), p. 214. For the contrast between authentic and apocryphal or unauthentic existentialisms, see my ch. 22 above.

[3] *Approaches to God* (New York: Harper and Brothers, 1954), p. 3. French original: *Approches de Dieu* (Paris: Alsatia, 1953).

[4] *Revue Thomiste* 68 (1968), 17–34. This paper was given first as a seminar on July 21, 1967, and is especially informative on how the intuition occurs psychologically. It is reprinted in the posthumously published book *Approches sans entraves* (Paris: Fayard, 1973), pp. 249–91. For an analysis of the paper see below, Appendix, "The Intuition of Being."

exist, this blade of grass exists; this gesture of the hand, this captivating smile that the next instant will hurry away, *exist*; the world *exists*. The all-important thing is for such a perception to sink deeply enough within me that my awareness of it will strike me some day sharply enough (at times, violently) to stir and move my intellect up to that very world of preconscious activity, beyond any word or formula, and with no assignable boundaries, which nourishes everything within it. Such a descent to the very depths of the soul is doubtless something *given*, not *worked out*—given by the natural grace of the intellectual nature.

And then, if luck should take a hand, and if the eye of consciousness, sufficiently accustomed to the half-light, should penetrate a little, like a thief, this limbo of the preconscious, it can come about that this simple *I am* will seem like a revelation in the night—a secret revelation which will awaken echoes and surprises on all sides and give a hint of the inexhaustible ampleness it permits one to attain. . . .

It is in a judgment (or in a preconscious act equivalent to an unformulated judgment), and in a judgment of existence, that the intellectual intuition of being occurs. The philosophical concept of the *actus essendi*, of the act of existence, will only come later. And the more profound and pure the intuition, the more accurate and comprehensive (barring accidents) will be the conceptualization of the various discoveries philosophy will be able to make by scrutinizing the real in the light of this absolutely fundamental principle.[5]

From that long excerpt, what can be gathered, first, on what the intuition of being is and, second, on how it grounds Maritain's existentialism? This intuition is an intellectual perception or awareness within a judgment of existence ("I exist," "This blade of grass exists") of the value of existence in an existent. It is a striking and deep revelation that the state of be-ing actual is supremely important and significant for someone or something: it is that by which he or it is real, valuable, significant. Reflection upon that state of actuality, thus grasped, leads to the philosophical concept of the act

---

[5] *The Peasant of the Garonne* (New York: Holt, Rinehart and Winston, 1968), p. 138; French original, *Le paysan de la Garonne* (Paris: Desclée de Brouwer, 1966).

of existing as the intrinsic cause or constituent whence flows that reality and value.

Furthermore, that natural although personal and spectacular awareness of actual existence as a fact and as a component in an existent leads to a philosophical position in which primacy is given to existence because it bestows perfection, worth, significance upon whatever *is* perfect, worthy, significant. In short, it results in a doctrine in which "to be real" is "to be actual." This is Maritain's authentic brand of existentialism.

Granted, then, that the intuition of being grounds his existentialism, why and how is it the basis of his theism? He addresses that point best, for our purposes, in *Approaches to God*, chapter 1: "The Primordial Way of Approach: Natural or Prephilosophic Knowledge of God."[6]

In this prephilosophic, natural and "instinctive manner" of knowing, "everything depends on the natural intuition of being—on the intuition of that act of existing . . . in which all the intelligible structures of reality have their definitive actuation and which overflows in activity in every being and the intercommunication of all beings" (p. 3). How does one achieve that intuition? By ceasing to live "in dreams or in the magic of images and formulas, of words, of signs, and practical symbols," one is "awakened to the reality of existence and of his own existence" by really perceiving "that formidable, sometimes elating, sometimes sickening or maddening fact I *exist*" (pp. 3–4). Henceforth one is possessed by the intuition both of his or her own existence and "first and foremost of the existence of things." When this takes place,

> I suddenly realize that a given entity—man, mountain, tree— exists and exercises this sovereign activity *to be* in its own way, in an independence of *me* which is total, totally self-assertive and totally implacable. And at the same time I realize that *I* also exist, but as thrown back into my loneliness and frailty by this other existence by which things assert themselves and in which I have positively no part, to which I am exactly as naught. . . . My own existence . . . I feel to be fragile and menaced, exposed to destruction and death. Thus the primordial intuition of being is the intuition of the solidity and inexorability of existence; and, second, of the death and

---

[6] See n. 3 above for data on French original.

nothingness to which *my* existence is liable. And third, in the same flash of intuition, which is but my becoming aware of the intelligible value of being, I realize that this solid and inexorable existence, perceived in anything whatsoever, implies—I do not yet know in what form, perhaps in the things themselves, perhaps separately from them—some absolute, irrefragable existence, completely free from nothingness and death. These three leaps—by which the intellect moves first to actual existence as asserting itself independently of me; and then from this sheer objective existence to my own threatened existence; and finally from my existence spoiled with nothingness to absolute existence—are achieved within the same unique intuition, which philosophers would explain as the intuitive perception of the essentially analogical content of the first concept, the concept of Being (p. 4).

A second stage follows immediately: a prompt, spontaneous and natural reasoning.

I see first that my being is liable to death; and second, that it is dependent on the totality of nature, on the universal whole of which I am a part. I see that Being-with-nothingness, such as my own being, implies, in order that it should be, Being-without-nothingness—that absolute existence which I confusedly perceived from the beginning as involved in my primordial intuition of existence. But then the universal whole of which I am a part is itself Being-with-nothingness, by the very fact that I am a part of it. And from this it follows finally that since this universal whole does not exist by virtue of itself, it must be that Being-without-nothingness exists apart from it. There is another Whole—a separate one—another Being, transcendent and self-sufficient and unknown in itself and activating all beings, which is Being-without-nothingness, that is, self-subsisting Being, Being existing through itself (p. 6).

This subsistent Being is, of course, God.

But how is this primordial approach to God related to the traditional proofs of His existence? The latter (the five ways of Aquinas) "are a development and an unfolding of this natural knowledge, raised to the level of scientific discussion and scientific certitude . . . and normally presuppose" it. Before attempting the philosophic proofs, then, one must be "alive to the primordial intuition of existence and conscious of the natural knowledge of God involved in this intuition" (p. 11).

Accordingly, if both prephilosophic knowledge and philosophic proofs for God rely on this intuition, it is the foundation of Maritain's theism no less than of his existentialism.

A *Christian* Existentialism?

Finally, is Maritain's existentialism Christian? Nowhere (to my knowledge) has he applied the adjective to his existentialism, which he first elaborated in *Existence and the Existent*, the French original of which appeared in 1947.[7] But he had begun writing on Christian philosophy as early as 1931 for a conference given in December of that year at the University of Louvain, and the essay was published in 1933.[8] This was further developed in *Science and Wisdom*, of which the French appeared in 1935.[9] Hence, his publications on authentic existentialism postdate those on Christian philosophy by more than a decade, and one can understand why he may not have explicitly named his existentialism Christian.

But his interpretation of philosophy in general as Christian discloses why one may validly apply the adjective to his existentialism also. Properly intended, Christian philosophy is "philosophy itself [but] situated in the climate of explicit faith and of baptismal grace" (*SW*, p. 78). To explain: the *nature* of philosophy needs to be distinguished from its *state*. Considered in its pure nature or abstract essence, philosophy "is specified by an object naturally knowable to reason [and] depends only on the evidence and criteria of natural reason." But "taken concretely, in the sense of being a *habitus* . . . existing in the human soul, philosophy is in a certain *state* [and] is either pre-Christian or Christian or a-Christian, which has a decisive influence on the way in which it exists or develops" (*ibid.*, p. 79). In Christian philosophy one receives subjective reinforcement from the "superior wisdoms, theological wisdom and infused wisdom, which rectify and purify in the soul the philosophical *habitus*

---

[7] See n. 1 above for data on French original.

[8] *An Essay on Christian Philosophy* (hereafter: *CP*), trans. E. H. Flannery (New York: Philosophical Library, 1955), p. ix; French original, *De la philosophie chrétienne* (Paris: Desclée de Brouwer, 1933), p. 8.

[9] *Science and Wisdom* (hereafter: *SW*) (London: Geoffrey Bles, 1940); French original, *Science et sagesse* (Paris: Labergerie, 1935).

with which they maintain a continuity not of essence but of movement and illumination, fortifying them in their proper order, and lifting them to higher levels" (*ibid.*, p. 80). Such reinforcement is exemplified in the ability faith gives a "philosopher who knows of the existence of God by purely natural means to adhere rationally to this truth with a sturdier grasp"; in the clarification and spiritualization the contemplative *habitus* contributes to the philosophic *habitus* (*CP*, p. 26); in the self-detachment and relief from ponderousness theology grants to a philosophy accepting its infraposition; in the freedom from futilities and opacities grace bestows on speculative intellects by its healing of nature (*ibid.*, pp. 27–28).[10]

But in addition to such subjective corroborations, philosophy also receives from faith and revelation objective data

> which deal primarily with revealed truths of the natural order. The highest of these have been regularly missed or misstated by the great pagan philosophers. Moreover, these objective data are also concerned with the repercussions of truths of the supernatural order on philosophical reflexion (*SW*, p. 80).

Instances of such data are creation, the human soul as object of salvation, God as subsistent love (*ibid.*, pp. 90–91), substance and accident, nature and person, essence and existence (*ibid.*, p. 102), God as subsistent Being, sin as an offense against God (*CP*, pp. 18–19). Accordingly,

> Christian philosophy is philosophy itself insofar as it is situated in those utterly distinctive conditions of existence and exercise into which Christianity has ushered the thinking subject, and as a result of which philosophy perceives certain objects and validly demonstrates certain propositions, which in any other circumstances would to a greater or lesser extent elude it (*ibid.*, p. 30).

If we now apply his analysis of why philosophy in general is Christian to his conception of existentialism, we can readily see why the term is apt for the latter too.

Philosophy is Christian inasmuch as faith in divine revelation enables the reason more easily and with greater conviction to know (we shall attend only to the areas most relevant) that God exists,

---

[10] Also see *SW*, pp. 86 sqq., *re* subjective reinforcements.

that He is subsistent Being, that His freely creating entails making things which previously in no way existed to now exist actually, that the essence of no creature is existence. The last word is, obviously, at the center of all those areas: God *exists*, He *exists independently* of all else, He causes all creatures *to exist*, every creature *exists* by an act of being other than what he is. But existence is also at the center of authentic existentialism—that philosophical position in which actuality has primacy and "to be real" equals "to exist" and which issues from an intuition of being within judgments of existence. Therefore, Maritain's existentialism is not only theistic (his primordial assent and technical arguments that God exists rest on the same intuition) but also Christian: Christian faith helps the human knower realize that actually to be is supremely important for every existent, whether Creator or creature.

Conclusion

Our aim has not been to praise or blame Maritain but to understand a position that is existential, theistic and Christian and, second, to offer data for reflection and discussion on an often controversial and always difficult notion: Christian philosophy.[11]

All three dimensions of his doctrine are grounded on the intuition of being, which he illustrated always with this testimony from his beloved wife, Raïssa.

> It often happened that I experienced, through a sudden intuition, the reality of my being, of the profound, first principle that places me outside of nothingness. A powerful intuition, whose violence sometimes frightened me, and which has first given me the knowledge of a metaphysical absolute.[12]

Here his existential and Christian metaphysics began, and here my chapter ends.

---

[11] See my "Preface" above on Christian philosophy, esp. prgrs. linked with nn. 17–29.

[12] Raïssa Maritain, *We Have Been Friends Together* (translation, 1942; French original, 1941), as quoted by Jacques Maritain, *The Peasant of the Garonne*, p. 111.

Appendix

The Intuition of Being

In order to understand Maritain on the intuition of being, let us begin by listing some sentences to illustrate what existence ordinarily and spontaneously brings to mind.

"Life does exist in galaxies other than ours"

"Launching pads for intercontinental missiles actually do exist in China"

"Someone actually is downstairs now"

"There actually is a fire in the attic roof"

Although others may consider those propositions existential, Maritain views them as expressing copulative and not truly existential judgments. I say this in light of his last explanation of the intuition of being, "Réflexions sur la nature blessée et sur l'intuition de l'être," *Revue Thomiste* 68 (1968), 17–34 (reprinted in *Approches sans entraves* [Paris: Fayard, 1973] pp. 249–91). For example, in "Someone actually-is-downstairs-now" or "A fire actually-is-in-the-attic," the hyphenated words express a predicate applied to or coupled with the subject. One is on the level not of *Sein* but of *Dasein*, not of be-ing but of being-there. The concept of existence issuing from such judgments is known after the manner of an essence or of a quality. It is univocal. It is abstractive, it pertains to the first level of abstraction (*ibid.*, pp. 24–25 and *passim*).

In order to move from the level of *Dasein* to *Sein*, from univocity to analogy, from abstraction to contemplation, the human knower needs the intuition of being, within which there occurs a genuinely existential judgment ("I am," "This rose exists"), by reflection upon which he achieves a concept of existence which is analogous and not univocal, which is judicative and not abstractive in origin.

What does Maritain mean? We shall realize this if we ask, as he does, How does existence, found in the material things we perceive, become proportioned to the intelligence and spiritualized so that the intelligence can truly *see* it in and by its judgmental act? One must, Maritain answers, distinguish three stages in the process, the *first* of which is (say) my visual perception of this red rose. My eyes have received a sensible species[13] or intentional form from

---

[13] Here and in what follows Maritain means by "species" what I express by "actuation *a*"—see ch. 21 above, "Preller and Aquinas: Second Thoughts on Epistemology."

the surface of the petals reflecting the light which acts on the physical organ of sight so that I can see the color and, simultaneously, the existence of the flower—this last "not by a species but by the intentional action exercised on the sense when receiving the species of the color of the rose" (pp. 20–21), and thus existence would be a *sensibile per accidens* (a point, however, which Maritain does not make).[14]

In the *second* stage I know *that I see,* and this without needing the imagination or phantasms, since the intelligence is aware not only of the color of the rose but also of *seeing* that rose—i.e., of the cognitive activity of the external sense. That activity of seeing is, then, involved in a twofold intentional state: an awareness of its object (the *color* of the rose, intentionally received by the sense faculty through the sensible species) and an awareness of the *rose* (intentionally apprehended by the intelligence through an idea). Accompanying the seeing of the rose is its existence, rendered present in the sense by the intentional activity in receiving the sensible species and made present (implicitly, only) in the intellect by its being implicated in the rose (the object of an *intentio intellecta*)[15] which the intellect knows that I see and which is-there. The intellect is then operating in the first degree of abstraction in saying, "That rose is-there," it is-present-to-me. This is the level of *Dasein* (p. 21), where *Sein* and existence, properly understood, are not present except in a hidden fashion, as implied in something else and without actual recognition yet by the intellect. The existence of the rose is already spiritualized but only potentially within another intelligible.

In the *third* stage the intellect, while the eye is seeing the red rose and while it itself is affirming that the red rose is-there, moves to a higher level, which is not only that of the third degree of abstraction but also that of a natural contemplation in which thought escapes abstraction and where the light of the intuition of being suddenly shines forth. The *existence* of the rose is now grasped explicitly. It is actually spiritualized and actually proportioned to the intellect—not by a species or any *intentio intellecta* but by an *intentio intelligens* in a genuinely existential judgment (p. 22) that

---

[14] But see J. Maritain, *The Degrees of Knowledge,* trans. G. B. Phelan (New York: Charles Scribner's Sons, 1959), pp. 95–98.

[15] See *ibid.,* pp. 111–28 and especially pp. 389–417. There Maritain appears to give no explanation of the "intentio intelligens" which he later contrasts with "intentio intellecta."

the red rose *exists, actually is.* Those verbs now have a fullness of metaphysical meaning, and being in the mystery of its limitless horizon and in its rich analogy discloses itself, even though my awareness of being occurs on the occasion of my seeing an individual thing such as a rose (p. 23).

Such is, in substance, a paraphrase or translation of Maritain's reply to the question he had proposed earlier: how does existence, found in the material things we perceive, become proportioned to the intelligence and spiritualized so that the intelligence can truly see it within itself in and by an existential judgment (p. 20)? It is while the human intellect sees existence within such a judgment that the knower intuits being.

V

Further Contemporaries and Aquinas

25

Whitehead's Cosmology: A Monism of Creativity?

It may seem strange to include a chapter on Alfred North White-head in this book on Christian philosophy in light of Whitehead's rejection of Christianity in favor of Hellenic religion. This rejection he expressed in the last conversation Lucien Price recorded on November 11, 1947, just six weeks before Whitehead died from a stroke on December 30 of that year. In Whitehead's own words:

> It was a mistake, as the Hebrews tried [and Christians contin-ued], to conceive of God as creating the world from the out-side, at one go. An all-foreseeing Creator, who could have made the world as we find it now—what could we think of such a being? Foreseeing everything and yet putting into it all sorts of imperfections to redeem which it was necessary to send his only son into the world to suffer torture and hideous death; outrageous ideas. The Hellenic religion was a better approach; the Greeks conceived of creation as going on every-where all the time *within* the universe. . . . God is *in* the world, or nowhere, creating continually in us and around us. This creative principle is everywhere, in animate and so-called in-animate matter, in the ether, water, earth, human hearts. But this creation is a continuing process, and "the process is itself the actuality," since no sooner do you arrive than you start on a fresh journey.[1]

---

[1] Lucien Price, *Dialogues of Alfred North Whitehead* (Boston: Little, Brown and Co., 1954), p. 370. For Whitehead's other comments (generally hostile) on Christianity, see *ibid.*, pp. 60, 141, 160, 174–77, 262 and 296–97.

The first three sentences in that conversation do indeed make my including Whitehead in this chapter paradoxical. But its subsequent sentences justify that inclusion: "God is *in* the world . . . creating continually in us and around us. This creativity principle is everywhere. . . . This creation is a continuing process."

If the "continuing process" of creation, which here God and elsewhere other creatures are said to engage in, is due to creativity as underlying source and reality, Whitehead's cosmology of process may well be characterized as a monism of creativity. The result? Knowledges need not be really distinct (see my Preface above, section "Monism and Christian Philosophy"). In fact, as Whitehead himself writes, "Cosmology . . . is the basis of all religions" because its theme "is the story of the dynamic effort of the world passing into everlasting unity, and of the static majesty of God's vision, accomplishing its purpose of completion by absorption of the World's multiplicity of effort."[2] This is in line with what he had observed at the start of his book:

> Philosophy frees itself from the taint of ineffectiveness by its close relations with religion and with science, natural and sociological. It attains its chief importance by fusing the two, namely, religion and science, into one rational scheme of thought. Religion should connect the rational generality of philosophy with the emotions and purposes springing out of existence in a particular society, in a particular epoch, and conditioned by particular antecedents. Religion is the translation of general ideas into particular thoughts, particular emo-

---

[2] Alfred North Whitehead, *Process and Reality: An Essay in Cosmology* [hereafter: *PR*], eds. D. R. Griffin and D. W. Sherburne (New York: The Free Press, 1978), p. 349. For other texts on religion, see *ibid.*, pp. 340 and 342–43.

See Stanley L. Jaki, *God and the Cosmologists* (Washington, D.C.: Regnery Gateway, 1989), p. 19: Whitehead "distanced himself from the scientific universe in the measure in which he got entangled in an evolutionary recasting of Kantian epistemology. No wonder that the center of Whitehead's cosmic view was man as co-creator with God of the universe, all three imperfect, all three evolving." Also, p. 20: "The great conclusion of Whitehead's *Process and Reality* that 'cosmology is the basis of all religion,' should be read in that light [namely, of a religion issuing 'from a cosmology that had for its object a cosmos full of quasi-conscious volitions']. The religion in question is radically different from any religion, especially orthodox Christianity, in which the object of worship is an infinitely perfect Creator of a universe which can be perfect only in a strictly limited sense."

tions, and particular purposes; it is directed to the end of stretching individual interest beyond its self-defeating particularity. Philosophy finds religion, and modifies it; and conversely religion is among the data of experience which philosophy must weave into its own scheme. Religion is an ultimate craving to infuse into the insistent particularity of emotion that non-temporal generality which primarily belongs to conceptual thought alone.[3]

The religion of which Whitehead has just spoken would obviously not be Christianity but one aligned and identified with process cosmology.

Bracken on Trinity and Incarnation

But despite Whitehead's own rejection of Christianity, the process theologian, Joseph Bracken, accepts Christianity and, in fact, ingeniously and eloquently inserts its major tenets of God as triune and Christ as incarnate God into Whiteheadian process thought in several publications. Take as an example Bracken's *The Triune Symbol: Persons, Process and Community*,[4] in the initial pages of which he presents its ground plan. In chapter 1 he intends to set forth his "understanding of community as social process, i.e., the dynamic interaction of individual persons with one another so as to create a corporate reality greater than themselves, considered as separate individuals" (*ibid.*, pp. 6–7). He then applies "this generalized notion of community to the traditional notion of Christian doctrine of the Trinity" by proposing

that the nature or essence of God is to be an interpersonal process, i.e., a community of three divine persons who are constantly growing in knowledge and love of one another and who are thus themselves in process even as they constitute the divine community as a specifically social process (*ibid.*, p. 7).

In chapter 2 he jointly considers

---

[3] *PR*, pp. 15–16. See n. 58 below.
[4] *The Triune Symbol: Persons, Process and Community* (Lanham, Md.: University Press of America, 1985).

the doctrines of creation and the incarnation. . . . All of creation, but especially the human community, exists as part of the communitarian life of God. That is, the Father as the source of all life and being expresses himself perfectly in the Son through the power of the Holy Spirit. But he also expresses himself in creation which is thus part of the total reality of the Son. The Son, in turn, responds to the Father in the power of the Spirit; part of this response is the praise and glory given to the Father by creation as a whole, but above all by the human community (*ibid.*).

Bracken now turns to the incarnation.

The Son, moreover, by his incarnation became intimately involved in what was formerly just a part of his own divine being and thus part of his ongoing interaction with the Father and the Spirit. He became part of creation and a member of the human community at precisely that moment in the history of the race when communication between people in different areas of the world was beginning to develop and thus when his person and message could have an ever broader impact on the course of human events.

Accordingly,

everything in creation and indeed the universe as a whole exhibits a basic structure of existence and activity which is ordered to "community" at least in some extended sense of the term. Nowhere do individuals exist simply and solely for themselves. Rather, each individual entity is a dynamic unity in totality of functioning parts or members, and is by the same token ordered to still another totality of which it is itself only a member or part. On the level of human life, this means that human beings are ordered to ever more comprehensive social groupings, until one arrives at the ultimate community, the human race as such. It is this community of which Jesus is the head and through which he gives focus and direction to the creative process as a whole (*ibid.*).

One need only read chapters 1 and 2 of *The Triune Symbol* to realize that Bracken has implemented the "ground plan" presented in its Preface.

Since the publication of that book he continues to insert the Trinity and the Incarnation into process thought in various ways. In his 1990 essay, "The World: Body of God or Field of Cosmic Activity?"[5] he interpreted the three divine persons as "co-constituting from moment to moment a field of activity which is their very reality as one God"[6] and the "eternal 'Son' . . . [as] incarnate in the man Jesus of Nazareth"(*ibid.*, p. 98) according to insights gained "from process-relational metaphysics."[7] What is (he asks) the significance of "field"?

> It both solves the problem of threeness in oneness for Trinitarian theology and renders Whiteheadian process-relational metaphysics internally more consistent. That is, it solves the Trinitarian problem because the divine community or divine field of activity exists only in virtue of the dynamic interrelatedness of the divine persons to one another in the same way because of the structural patterns already resident within the field.

Consequently,

> there is no real distinction between the divine field of activity and its consequent actual occasions, namely, the successive moments in the lives of the divine persons. Furthermore, this field-oriented understanding of the triune God likewise renders Whiteheadian metaphysics internally more consistent because now, even with respect to God, it remains true that only fields survive the becoming and perishing of actual occasions (*ibid.*, p. 99).

Stated more precisely, "God," the "Judaeo-Christian-Islamic name of Ultimate Reality," expresses "the all-comprehensive field of activity in which energy-events in enormous profusion continually take place" (*ibid.*, p. 100).

---

[5] "The World: Body of God or Field of Cosmic Activity?" in Santiago Sia (ed.), *Charles Hartshorne's Concept of God: Philosophical and Theological Responses* (Dordrecht, the Netherlands: Kluwer Academic Publishers, 1990), ch. 6, pp. 89–102.

[6] *Ibid.*, pp. 96–97. Also see n. 62 below.

[7] *Ibid.*, p. 99, where Bracken also finds that "Whiteheadian metaphysics . . . [is] obviously representing a break with the focus on individual substance in Aristotelian metaphysics."

This "revised notion of 'God' as a cosmic field of activity" has (Bracken grants) a major hurdle to cross—namely, "the effort required to set aside accepted ways of thinking about divinity (and indeed about reality as a whole) and to conceive the hitherto inconceivable" (*ibid.*).

His conception of "the hitherto unconceivable" Bracken again sets forth on a large scale in his 1991 book, *Society and Spirit: A Trinitarian Cosmology*[8] by developing further "the Whiteheadian notion of a society as a preconstituted 'environment' or patterned field of activity for the emergence of successive generations of 'actual occasions'" (*ibid.*, pp. 13–14). This development occurs first in chapter 1: "Substance-Society-Natural System,"[9] chapter 2: "Energy-Events and Fields"[10] and chapter 3: "Entropy and Dissipative Structures." After considering Whitehead in the light of Schelling

---

[8] *Society and Spirit: A Trinitarian Cosmology* (London: Associated University Presses, 1991). On p. 14 Bracken admits the heavy influence of Whitehead's *Process and Reality* upon him, even though he is "extending Whitehead's philosophy in a new direction [but] one . . . that is basically compatible with the thrust of his own reflections."

[9] In the first portion of this chapter Bracken takes up (pp. 39–45) Ivor Leclerc's review of such key concepts in the philosophy of nature as "matter and motion, space and time, extension," where Leclerc's heavy indebtedness to Kant, Leibniz and Whitehead is countered by his espousing "a modified Aristotelianism" on these topics. Bracken contests Leclerc's "proposal to repristinate the Aristotelian category of substance as the key concept within a new philosophy of nature" by his own proposal of "Whitehead's notion of society . . . as a more suitable paradigm to describe the functioning unities of common sense experience" (p. 39). See p. 43 also: "Atoms and molecules are structured societies of actual societies, not Aristotelian substances, . . . [societies which] do exercise agency . . . [but] not the agency of an individual existent but rather the collective agency proper to a society," which however "does not make decisions with respect to its on-going self-constitution"—only "actual occasions make such decisions."

[10] See pp. 64–67, where Bracken sets forth in this order Whitehead's own understanding of a subatomic particle as "a society of actual occasions, each of which is a unique subject of experience constituted as such in virtue of its own 'decision'"; the "common element of form," which links together the actual occasions constituting a society; prehension as the internalizing of each actual occasion; analogies of the nexus between various actual occasions; concrescence; ultimate constituents of reality (= subatomic particles) as "momentary subjects of experience that effect an immanent 'decision'" and thereby "indirectly co-constitute . . . the verifiable objective unities of human experience (for example, atoms, molecules, cells, organisms, societies in the macroscopic sense, environments and ecosystems)"—a position which rejects scientific materialism.

(chapter 4) and Hegel (chapter 5), Bracken returns more directly in chapter 6 ("The Triune God")[11] and chapter 7 ("The Cosmic Society") to his own "synthesis of the notions of society and spirit into a new understanding of the God-world relationship" by focusing upon "panentheism . . . the notion that human beings and indeed all finite creatures exist both in themselves and in God at the same time."[12] Accordingly,

> panentheism is vindicated in principle as soon as one accepts a field-oriented approach to reality. For, if the three divine persons of the Christian Trinity co-constitute by their interrelated activity an all-inclusive field within which the activities of all finite entities are located, and if the decisions of the divine persons from moment to moment impact upon their creatures and the self-constituting decisions of creatures are felt by the divine persons, then, one may legitimately say that God and creatures occupy a common world, a joint field of activity that all of them assist in shaping and forming. Because of the primacy of the reality of God, creatures, to be sure, first come into being through the power of God. But they subsequently exist in their own right and make their individual contribution to the field of activity that they share with the divine persons (*ibid.*, p. 140).

Indeed, "a genuinely panentheistic understanding of the God-world relationship . . . [envisions] a community of divine persons within

---

Bracken next (pp. 67–71) discusses societies as "overlapping energy fields" or "environments." Of these the most comprehensive for Whitehead is "the extensive continuum, [which is] the overall scheme of relatedness within which past actual occasions came into being, present occasions are currently concrescing, and future occasions will inevitably take their place" (p. 69); the next most comprehensive field of activity is "the geometrical society"; then come in sequence as we progress toward directly perceptible reality (which Bracken calls "the verifiable objective unities of human experience") the "society of electromagnetic occasions that corresponds to the electromagnetic field in physics"; next energy-waves, then "the individual electrons and protons, atoms, molecules, inorganic bodies, cells, and organic bodies" (*ibid.*).

[11] Bracken grants that what he earlier presented in *The Triune Symbol* (see above) as the "field-oriented approach to the God-world relationship" is here in ch. 6 being spelled out "in greater detail . . . as a cosmic society, which includes God and all finite entities."

[12] A definition taken from his Preface, p. 15, but utilized in chs. 6 and 7, as is evident from the quotation from p. 140 immediately following.

whose all-comprehensive field of activity the field proper to the community of all finite entities has its place" (*ibid.*, p. 148).

Immediately subsequent to *Society and Spirit*, Bracken utilizes panentheism as a compromise position between the classical atheism of scientific materialists and the classical theism of Thomas Aquinas—a utilization which allows a Christian profitably to dialogue with nonbelievers.[13] Bracken's remarks on Aquinas are especially interesting and deserve special attention.

Bracken on Aquinas

[a] Aquinas' "five ways" (see *Summa Theologiae*, I, 2, 3, resp.) appeal to common human experience of movement, causality, contingency, grades of perfection, and order within nature, each of which ultimately requires "a primordial or transcendent agent which stands outside the chain of ordinary causes and effects [and which] Aquinas declares to be God."[14] Although everyone of his generation would regard his "interpretation of the data . . . as self-evident," many intelligent people in the twentieth century would not accept his inference: "for them it would be equally plausible to consider the world itself as the absolute or self-sufficient reality" (*ibid.*). [b] Consequently, no compromise between classical atheism and classical theism is possible unless one is "prepared to accept the doctrine of panentheism, which is the belief that the world is a semi-autonomous finite reality which nevertheless exists in God and through the power of God at every moment." But panentheism has not been well received among classical metaphysicians "because the philosophical categories [of substance-accident] of Aristotle and Thomas Aquinas on which these thinkers rely heavily" do not allow "that one entity can exist in another entity and yet retain its own separate ontological identity" (*ibid.*, p. 209). In light of those categories "panentheism is a logical impossibility." Either "'God' is simply the name for the aggregate of individual entities making up the world at any given moment, or these individual entities are only phenomenal realities with no real existence apart from God as the single, all-comprehensive substantial reality" (*ibid.*, p. 210).

---

[13] See Joseph Bracken, "The Issue of Panentheism in the Dialogue with the Non-believers," *Studies in Religion* 21 (1992), 207–18.

[14] *Ibid.*, p. 208. Letters in brackets have been added for easy reference.

[c] Granted that Aquinas' thought "could be called a form of panentheism" insofar as he argues (*S.T.*, I, 8, 1 resp.) "that God is present to creatures by communicating to them the act of existence, their proportionate share in the divine act of being," and thus "creatures exist in and through the power of God and yet retain their own ontological identity as separate entities." [d] But one must distinguish "between the entitative reality of God and the divine nature." If "God" means "the divine nature or essence, the 'pure act' of existence whereby God is God and whereby creatures are also empowered to exist," then creatures can be said to exist in God and through the power of God. But if "God" means "a personal or, better said, tripersonal being," then creatures cannot exist in God and through the power of God," for they "would be absorbed into the entitative reality of God as the sole infinite being, the entity without limits," and they would be "simply accidental modifications of God" (*ibid.*).

[e] Granted that for Aquinas "God acts upon creatures *per essentiam* [*S.T.*, I, 8, 3 resp.] through the divine nature," yet "God's relation to creatures and their relation to God" are mediated by one and the same nature. Accordingly, creatures "do not exist in God as the Supreme [and tripersonal] Being" (so as to escape their functioning as accidental modifications of the divine being) but "through the divine nature, which . . . thus acts as the common ground of being or source of activity for both God and all creatures" (*ibid.*, pp. 210–11). [f] In summary, then, "Aquinas' approach to the God-world relationship as presented in the *Summa Theologiae* can be regarded as a form of panentheism only if one is willing to adopt a somewhat unconventional, process-oriented understanding of certain key terms such as the divine nature, the act of being, and so on" (*ibid.*, p. 211).

[g] Next Bracken takes up a Whiteheadian notion of panentheism by explaining what Whitehead means by actual entities or occasions, eternal objects, prehension, field of activity, societies, form, decisions, living person or soul (*ibid.*, pp. 211–13). Thereafter he applies Whiteheadian "society" to the three divine persons and to Jesus in order to present a "process-oriented understanding of the God-world relationship" (*ibid.*, pp. 213–15). This presentation culminates in a discussion of creativity, which is "another foundational concept within Whitehead's philosophy" (*ibid.*, pp. 215–16).

[h] Then he returns to Aquinas. Can the Dominican's theory of the God-world relationship be seen as a form of panentheism? Yes,

if one "means the divine nature, understood as the divine act of being which is likewise the underlying principle of being and activity for all creatures." This happens if we equate "the Thomistic act of being . . . with Whiteheadian creativity." Although neither Whitehead nor Aquinas can be directly cited in support of this proposal,

> it is apparent that the two notions fulfill basically the same function within their respective philosophical systems. That is, the notion of creativity empowers God to be God and finite occasions to be themselves within Whitehead's scheme. Similarly, the divine nature or act of being within Aquinas' scheme, when reinterpreted in process-oriented terms, empowers God to be God and creatures to be creatures. In neither case is this principle of activity such that it reduces God and finite beings to accidental modifications of itself, for it does not exist in itself but only in the entities which it empowers to be. It exists primordially in the divine being to make God to be God and secondarily in finite beings to allow them to be themselves as finite entities. Hence, there is no question of its existing apart from God as a rival of God. In the end it is only a principle of activity, the underlying nature of God rather than God in the entitative sense . . . as the Supreme Being" (*ibid.*, p. 216).

[i] This proposal is not claiming that Aquinas was a covert process-oriented thinker but only asserts

> that the logical antecedents of a process-oriented understanding of the God-world relationship are present in the thought of Aquinas. What was only implicit in Aquinas' key concept of the act of being eventually becomes explicit in the Whiteheadian notion of creativity, that activity or process is at the base of reality both finite and infinite. Moreover, if Whitehead's notion of God is given a trinitarian reinterpretation then creativity can be regarded as a principle of intersubjectivity whereby the three divine persons and all their creatures co-constitute from moment to moment an all-embracing cosmic society within the field proper to the intentional activity of the three divine persons (*ibid.*, pp. 216–17).

Thus ends Bracken's "exposition of the doctrine of panentheism from the perspective of a neo-Whiteheadian trinitarian metaphysical scheme," after which he reflects "upon the pertinence of this scheme for the ongoing dialogue between believers and nonbelievers" (*ibid.*, pp. 217–18).[15]

Aquinas Authentically Interpreted

The attention given in my previous two sections to Bracken's neo-Whiteheadian theology may appear to be an obstacle to achieving my main goal—namely, to consider whether Whitehead's process philosophy is a monism. Granted that Whitehead's refusal of Christianity itself excluded any consideration of God as triune or as incarnate—in fact, as seen in the initial quotation of this chapter, he described God's sending "his only son into the world to suffer torture and hideous death" to be "outrageous." But Bracken throughout the publications studied above on the trinity and incarnation stressed his reliance upon Whitehead and he thought them to be developments of Whitehead himself.[16] Let us, then, concentrate upon the areas in which Whitehead is directly and specially influential upon Bracken, a concentration which will however be preceded by my indicating places in which Bracken has misunderstood the thirteenth-century author.

One such misunderstanding occurs when Bracken is determining whether Thomas' position is a panentheism. Yes, Bracken answers when reading *Summa Theologiae*, I, 8, 1 resp., to mean that "God is present to creatures by communicating to them the act of existence, their proportionate share in the divine act of being [and thus] creatures exist in and through the power of God and yet retain their own ontological identity as separate entities" (see #c above). But his answer is no if "God" is taken to mean not "the divine nature or essence" (which is finite and thus allows creatures to be ontologically distinguished from God) but "a personal or, better said, tripersonal being," which is the "sole infinite being, the entity without limits" and which would absorb creatures into His "entitative reality," where creatures would be "simply accidental

---

[15] This reflection was occasioned by a conference at St. Paul University, Ottawa, Canada, on October 11–13, 1991, on "The Situation of Unbelief and Religious Indifference in Canada and the United States." My comments on Bracken's paper there centered on my disagreements with his interpretation especially of Aquinas and may have led to his 1992 article in *Studies in Religion*, just analyzed.

[16] See notes 8–10 and #g above.

modifications" (#d).[17] Bracken's replies apparently rest upon his conception of God as infinite only when taken as "a personal or, better said, tripersonal being" (#d).

But Aquinas' own position on infinity differs greatly from Bracken's exposition. The divine essence or nature *itself is infinite* as entirely without the determination of matter and all other potency. Thus, God's reality or being as subsistent existence is infinitely perfect (and the three divine persons are infinite too inasmuch as they, although distinct as persons, are one and the same infinite God).[18] All this Thomas sets forth clearly when asking in *S.T.*, I, 7, 1, whether God is infinite ("Utrum Deus sit infinitus").

Yes, he answers, because existence as such is the supreme act and perfective factor in any existent whatsoever. Thus, because divine existence is not limited by any recipient but is subsistent, God manifestly is *Himself* infinite and perfect.[19] As a consequence,

----

[17] On how God is infinite for Whitehead see Lewis B. Ford, "The Infinite God of Process Theism," in D. A. Dahlstrom *et al.* (eds.), *Infinity: Proceedings of the American Catholic Philosophical Association* 55 (1981), 84–90, with helpful references to William J. Hill and W. Norris Clarke. The last named seems to be right in finding in God's primordial nature "only an infinity by extrinsic denomination" (see *ibid.*, p. 84).

On "extrinsic denomination" see my *Divine Infinity in Greek and Medieval Thought* [hereafter: *Divine Infinity*] (New York/Bern: Peter Lang Publishing, Inc., 1992), p. xiv, n. 2: "'Extrinsic denomination' is the application of a predicate to a subject not because what the predicate signifies is itself found in the subject but because the subject is related to something in which that signification is intrinsically verified. For example, 'The wind is cold' means not that coldness as such is found in the wind but that the wind causes someone to be cold. Hence, the sentence is equivalent to 'The wind is the cause of coldness in me.' " Applied to Whitehead: the sentence "The primordial nature of God is infinite" means not that infinity as such characterizes the divine nature itself but that, as Clarke says, the "divine mind thinks up in a single act of primordial envisagement from all eternity" the "infinite number of all intelligible possibilities." Thus infinity lies "on the side of the products of the divine mind, and even here only in their number"—see W. Norris Clarke, *The Philosophical Approach to God* (Winston-Salem, N.C.: Wake Forest University, 1979), p. 87. For Whitehead's references to infinity see *PR*, pp. 345, 346, 350; for a commentary see William A. Christian, *An Interpretation of Whitehead's Metaphysics* [hereafter: Christian] (New Haven: Yale University Press, 1959), pp. 277–79.

[18] For Thomas' treatment of the Trinity see *S.T.*, I, questions 27–43. Nowhere does he appear explicitly to speak of infinity with respect to God precisely as triune.

[19] *S.T.*, I, 7, 1 resp.: "Illud autem quod est maxime formale omnium est ipsum esse, ut ex superioribus [*ibid.*, 4, 1 ad 3] patet. Cum igitur esse divinum

divine existence is distinguished from existence in all creatures, each of which has its own actuation of existence, which thereby is distinct from divine existence also.[20] Another consequence: because the divine and subsistent being is itself infinite (and is so through intrinsic denomination), God's knowledge, love, power, wisdom are also infinite.[21]

Aquinas is now prepared to consider in *S.T.*, I, 8, 1 (which, as seen above, Bracken uses to determine whether his metaphysics is a panentheism) whether God exists in all creatures. The Dominican theologian begins his consideration by reflecting on (and thereby understanding and developing) *Isaiah* 26, 12 (see *sed contra*): "O Lord, You do whatever we do" [i.e., You it is who act whenever we engage in activity; You are agent when we are agents].[22] He continues:

---

non sit esse receptum in aliquo sed ipse sit suum esse subsistens . . . , manifestum est quod ipse Deus sit infinitus et perfectus." That "formale" here means "actus," see I, 4, 1 ad 3, a reference which Aquinas himself has just given: "Ad tertium dicendum quod ipsum esse est perfectissimum omnium: comparatur enim ad omnia ut actus. Nihil enim habet actualitatem nisi inquantum est; unde ipsum esse est actualitas omnium rerum et etiam ipsarum formarum. Unde non comparatur ad alia sicut recipiens ad receptum, sed magis sicut receptum ad recipiens."

[20] *Ibid.*, 7, 1 ad 3: "Ex hoc ipso quod esse Dei est per se subsistens non receptum in aliquo, prout dicitur infinitum, distinguitur ab omnibus aliis et alia removentur ab eo—sicut si esset albedo subsistens ex hoc ipso quod non esset in alio, differret ab omni albedine existente in subjecto."

[21] See *In I Sent.*, d. 43, q. 1, a. 1, solutio (Mandonnet ed., p. 1003), where Thomas makes clear that God's power (and by implication such other divine attributes as knowledge, wisdom, love, etc.) is infinite since it is consequent upon an essence which is infinite because the divine *esse* is "absolutum et nullo modo receptum in aliquo" (*ibid.*, solutio, p. 1003). Similarly, in *ibid.*, a. 2, solutio (p. 1005) he indicates that the power of no creature can be infinite because power there follows upon an essence which is not infinite since *esse* in a created existent is not subsistent but is received and limited by that very essence: "Unde impossibile est ut essentiae finitae sit virtus infinita. Impossibile est autem aliquam essentiam creatam esse infinitam eo quod esse suum non est absolutum et subsistens sed receptum in aliquo." See my *Divine Infinity*, ch. 19, pp. 432–37.

On how and why other medieval authors did or did not predicate infinity of God, see *ibid.*, chs. 15–18 and 20.

[22] Brackets are added to indicate that their contents are my commentary.

Thomas here begins by reflecting on the *Isaiah* text because he is acting as a theologian, whose proper function is to understand, develop, defend divine revelation—see my ch. 2 above, "Can Philosophy Be Christian?" pp. 25–27. Theology so conceived is operative also in Thomas' "Five Ways" (I, 2, 3 resp.),

God is in all creatures not indeed as an intrinsic part of them ("non quidem sicut pars essentiae vel sicut accidens")[23] but as an agent must be present to and in that upon which he is immediately acting (Aristotle, *Physics*, VII, ch. 2, 243a3 sqq.).

Now Aquinas goes beyond our (and all other creatures') status as agents to that of our existing.[24]

> But we are agents only inasmuch as we exist; but we exist only if God efficiently causes us to exist—in fact, since God's essence is existence, existence is what He as agent properly causes in us not only when we start to exist but as long as we exist. Thus God must be present to and in us however long and in whatever manner we exist.[25]
>
> But existence is that which permeates us more thoroughly and deeply than any other component because existence is the actuation of all other perfections in a being. Therefore, God is present in us and all other creatures intimately as the agent or efficient cause of our existing.[26]

---

which are his attempts to understand and develop *Exodus*, 3, 14 (see *ibid., sed contra*). Should those "Ways" not help our contemporaries in that theological endeavor (see Bracken, #a above), let them use other "ways"—such was E. Gilson's advice to us during a seminar on the "Five Ways." On Joseph Owens' endeavor to justify philosophically the "Five Ways" by basing them explicitly upon the primacy which Aquinas gives to existence, see (for example) "Aquinas and the Five Ways," *Monist* 58 (1974), 16–35.

[23] Thus Aquinas clears himself of any charge of monism, that position according to which all existents consist of one basic stuff—whether it be unity (Plotinus) or divine substance (Spinoza) or duration (Bergson) or creativity (Whitehead, possibly).

[24] Hereafter for convenience in my translation/paraphrase when I speak of "us" I also intend "all creatures," since what is true of human persons is true also for all creatures.

[25] *S.T.*, I, 8, 1 resp. ad finem: "Cum autem Deus sit ipsum esse per suam essentiam, oportet quod esse creatum sit proprius effectus eius. . . . Hunc autem effectum causat Deus in rebus non solum quando primo esse incipiunt sed quandiu in esse conservantur. . . . Quandiu igitur res habet esse, tandiu oportet quod Deus adsit ei secundum modum quo esse habet."

[26] *Ibid.*: "Esse autem est illud quod est magis intimum cuilibet, et quod profundius omnibus inest, cum sit formale respectu omnium quae in re sunt. . . . Unde oportet quod Deus sit in omnibus rebus et intime." On "formale" meaning "actus," see n. 19 above.

This emphasis by Thomas on God as agent continues when in the *respondeo* of *ibid.*, article 3, he interprets the first noun in the traditional description of God's presence as occurring "per essentiam, praesentiam et potentiam"[27] as meaning presence "in the manner of an agent cause and hence God is present in all things created by Him. . . . [Thus] God is in all things through essence inasmuch as He is present to all as the efficient cause of their existing, as was said above" in *ibid.*, article 1.

> Deus dicitur esse in re aliqua . . . uno modo per modum causae agentis, et sic est in omnibus rebus creatis ab ipso. . . . Est in omnibus per essentiam inquantum adest omnibus ut causa essendi, sicut dictum est."[28]

In *Summa Theologiae*, I, 7, article 1, then, Thomas has explained how God as subsistent existence is Himself infinite *and thereby* is really distinct from creatures. In *S.T.*, I, 8, article 1, he has explained how God is intimately present within all creatures as their proper efficient cause of existence *and thereby* is really distinct from them. Obviously, then, the metaphysics of his theology totally avoids pantheism (and any other sort of monism).

---

[27] This description Peter Lombard himself attributes to "beatus Gregorius super Cantica Canticorum," an attribution which his modern editors change to *Glossa Ordinaria*—see *Sententiae in IV Libris Distinctae*, 3d ed. (Grottaferrata: Editiones Collegii S. Bonaventurae Ad Claras Aquas, 1971), Tom. I, Pars ii, p. 264, lines 6–7, and n. 2. Aquinas repeats Lombard's attribution—see *S.T.*, I, 8, 3 sed contra, and note; Marietti-Leonine ed., p. 564. Also see Thomas, *In I Sent.*, d. 37, q. 1. a. 2 (Mandonnet ed., pp. 859–62).

[28] In *ibid.*, a. 3, ad primum, Thomas makes the same points: "Deus dicitur esse in omnibus per essentiam, non quidem rerum quasi sit de essentia earum sed per essentiam suam quia substantia sua adest omnibus ut causa." On the primacy Thomas gives to God's efficient causality see *ibid.*, I, 4, 1 resp.: "Deus autem ponitur primum principium, non materiale, sed in genere causae efficientis; et hoc oportet esse perfectissimum. Sicut enim materia, inquantum huiusmodi, est in potentia, ita agens, inquantum huiusmodi, est in actu. Unde primum principium oportet maxime esse in actu, et per consequens maxime esse perfectum." In his discussion of creation (see *S.T.*, I, 44) he thinks the question "Utrum Deus sit causa efficiens omnium entium" is the same as asking "Utrum sit necessarium omne ens esse creatum a Deo"—see *ibid.*, article 1 (Marietti-Leonine ed., pp. 223–24).

For Bracken's misinterpretation of Thomas' "Deus est ubique per essentiam" (*ibid.*, I, 8, 3 resp.) by inserting it into his own distinction between the divine nature and God as supreme or tripersonal being, see #e above.

Yet God is immanent to all creatures as initially creating and thereafter conserving them. But He also transcends them, not physically but entitatively in His otherness from them as their efficient cause, a situation which allows Him simultaneously to be really present in them. Thus Thomas' position on God-creatures may be called an authentic "panentheism" since God exists in creatures and creatures exist in and through the power and causality of God[29] and yet not in such a way as to constitute a monism—as though creatures are God and God is creatures because they consist of one basic stuff. This is the challenge which Whiteheadian panentheism must face if for process philosophers and theologians creativity is that basic stuff which constitutes both God and creatures—God in His primordial and consequent natures, things as actual occasions, all joined into an ever developing and all-comprehensive society or community.

Is Whitehead a Monist?

If my reading of Aquinas' texts in the previous section is accurate, Bracken's explanation of them, however eloquent and ingenious, is misleading and inaccurate. Now let us turn directly to Whitehead himself on this crucial question: is his process cosmology a monism because of the role he gives there to creativity?

Commentators on Whitehead have indeed asked whether his position is monistic. For instance, according to Victor Lowe, Whitehead considered Samuel Alexander (1859–1938) to have "leaned a bit too much toward monism, whereas he himself had in *Process and Reality* [published in 1929] leaned too much toward pluralism." But in *Modes of Thought* (published in 1938) he seems "to conceive of the universe somewhat more monistically." Thus, in this later book there is a tendency "to refer 'importance' to the ultimate unity" of God as set forth in *Process and Reality*. But, Lowe adds, "Whitehead is very far from going over to monism."[30]

---

[29] That one more appropriately says that God is in creatures rather than that creatures are in God, see *ibid.*, 1 ad 2: "Licet corporalia dicantur esse in aliquo sicut in continente, tamen spiritualia continent ea in quibus sunt, sicut anima continet corpus. Unde et Deus est in rebus sicut continens res. Tamen per quamdam similitudinem corporalium dicuntur omnia esse in Deo inquantum continentur ab ipso."

[30] Victor Lowe, "Whitehead's Philosophical Development," in Paul Arthur Schlipp (ed.), *The Philosophy of Alfred North Whitehead* [hereafter: Schlipp] (Evanston, Ill.: Northwestern University Press, 1941), p. 120.

William A. Christian ends his study, *An Interpretation of Whitehead's Metaphysics*, with the question "Is Whitehead a Pantheist?" His reply: "Whitehead does not mean to be a monist" because

> in his cosmology there is no room for a self-sufficient entity. According to the principle of relativity, every entity essentially refers to entities other than itself. More specifically, there is no *actual* entity which does not require other actual entities for its own existence. Therefore it is categoreally impossible to reduce actuality to one entity, whether this be called the universe, the absolute, or God.[31]

Moreover, by reason of Whitehead's differentiating himself from Francis Herbert Bradley (1846–1924) (see *ibid.*), he rejects monism, a rejection from which it would follow

> that neither God nor any other entity is identical with a totality of real things. If pantheism is the assertion that God is identical with the totality of real things, that God is "essentially immanent and in no way transcendent," then Whitehead is certainly not a pantheist.[32]

But neither Lowe nor Christian[33] has sufficiently taken into account the possibility that Whitehead's monism is one of creativity (wherein ultimately everything is creativity and creativity is everything) and not a pantheism (wherein everything is God and God is everything). Let us reflect upon Whitehead's own description of creativity in this series of key texts.

---

[31] Christian, p. 403.

[32] *Ibid.*, p. 404.

[33] As instances of Lowe's interpretation of creativity in Whitehead, see Schlipp, p. 96: "The concept . . . called 'creativity' is introduced as a 'substantial activity' 'underlying' the evolution of the organism in which it is embodied . . . [as] required by the doctrine of evolution"; also see p. 115: "That the general aspect of nature is one of evolutionary expansiveness . . . can only be expressed by adopting some such concept as 'creativity' as a metaphysical ultimate." Also see Christian, p. 113: "The conception of original and originative activity" is extended by Whitehead by attributing "creativity to all real individuals, whether subhuman, human, or superhuman, though these individuals vary widely in their complexity, intensity, and effectiveness. As a consequence, the conception of substance needs to be revised so as to conform to this principle of the universality of creativity." See also p. 312: Does the doctrine of God compromise "the real individuality of actual occasions and in

Key Text A: *Process and Reality*, p. 7

Context.[34] [a] In ch. 1: "Speculative Philosophy," sec. 2, Whitehead advises that "the method of rigid empiricism" advocated by Francis Bacon's "method of induction" (pp. 4–5) must be replaced by induction complemented by "the play of free imagination, controlled by the requirements of coherence and logic." This is the method of "imaginative generalization" or, to say the same, "imaginative rationalization." [b] The success of such "imaginative construction" depends upon two conditions, one of which is that it "must have its origin in the generalization of particular factors discerned in such particular topics of human interest" as physics, physiology, psychology, aesthetics, ethical beliefs, sociology, languages or in other "storehouses of human experiences." The result: the imaginative experience is thus "tested by the applicability of its results beyond the restricted locus from which it originated" so that "philosophical generalization" comes to mean "the utilization of specific notions, applying to a restricted group of facts, for the divination of the generic notions which apply to all facts" (*ibid.*, p. 5).

[c] The second condition upon which successful imaginative construction depends is twofold: logical perfection and coherence. The first of these requires no detailed explanation (see *ibid.*, p. 6), but coherence, "the great preservative of rationalistic sanity," does, as is evident in philosophical controversies.[35] Descartes is guilty of incoherence, as his position on "two kinds of substance, corporeal and mental" illustrates, where there is "no reason why there should

---

particular . . . [does] the derivation of subjective aim from God . . . [have] this effect?" No, because by the principle of creativity "no actual entity is completely determined by other actual entities. Other actual entities condition but do not completely determine what shall become in a new concrescence." Thus (Christian now quotes Whitehead [*PR*, p. 339]), "Creativity is not an external agency with its own ulterior purposes. All actual entities share with God this characteristic of self-causation. For this reason every actual entity also shares with God the characteristic of transcending all other actual entities, including God.'"

[34] In studying each of Whitehead's key texts I shall set forth its context, reproduce the capital text itself, comment upon it briefly and then draw forth conclusions.

[35] See *PR*, p. 9: "Rationalism never shakes off its status of an experimental adventure." Although "mathematics and religion, which have so greatly contributed to the rise of philosophy," have unfortunately yoked "it with static dogmatism," rationalism "is an adventure in the clarification of thought, progressive and never final. But it is an adventure in which even partial success has importance."

not be a one-substance world, only corporeal, or a one-substance world, only mental" *(ibid.)*. [d] Spinoza's modification of Descartes achieves greater coherence. "He starts with one substance, *causa sui*, and considers its essential attributes and its individualized modes, i.e., the *affectiones substantiae*. The gap in the system is the arbitrary introduction of the 'modes.' And yet, a multiplicity of modes is a fixed requisite, if the scheme is to retain any direct relevance to the many occasions in the experienced world."

[e] My philosophy of organism (Whitehead continues) "is closely allied to Spinoza's scheme of thought," but with this difference: it abandons the "subject-predicate forms of thought" and thus avoids the "substance-quality concept," with the result that "morphological description" is replaced by a "description of dynamic process." [f] Another result: "Spinoza's 'modes' now become the sheer actualities" needed, which in turn lead to "the discovery that the process, or concrescence, of any one actual entity involves the other actual entities among its components. In this way the obvious solidarity of the world receives its explanation."

The key text follows immediately.

[g] In all philosophic theory there is an ultimate which is actual in virtue of its accidents. It is only then capable of characterization through its accidental embodiments, and apart from these accidents is devoid of actuality. In the philosophy of organism this ultimate is termed "creativity"; and God is its primordial, nontemporal accident. [h] In monistic philosophies, Spinoza's or absolute idealism, this ultimate is God,[36] who is also equivalently termed "The Absolute." In such monistic schemes, the ultimate is illegitimately allowed a final, "eminent" reality, beyond that ascribed to any of its accidents. [i] In this general position the philosophy of organism seems to approximate more to some strains of Indian, or Chinese, thought, than to western Asiatic, or European, thought. One side makes process ultimate; the other side makes fact ultimate.

Commentary. In the preceding sentences (#a to #i) Whitehead has set down several crucial factors of his philosophy. Its cognitive

---

[36] The ultimate of which Whitehead speaks in #g and which he identifies with creativity corresponds in Spinoza not to God but to *conatus*, the dynamic thrust which develops into and lies within the divine substance. So too creativity corresponds to *der Idee* of Hegel and to *la durée réelle* or *élan vitale* of Bergson. See paragraphs corresponding to notes 39–42 below.

operations are induction (#a) from such "storehouses of experiences" (#a) as the particular sciences of physics, psychology, aesthetics and so on (#b), plus "the play of free imagination" (#a). Combining induction with imagination issues into a method of imaginative-generalization or -rationalization (#a) or -construction (#b), which enables the philosopher to apply a restricted group of facts and specific notions to "generic notions which apply to all facts" (#b).

When someone has made that application coherently, as Descartes did not with his theory of two substances (#c) and Spinoza did with his theory of one divine substance (#d), he/she espouses a philosophy of organism, wherein dynamic process replaces "subject-predicate forms of thought" and "substance-quality concepts" (#e) and furnishes the concrescence of actualities in such a way that any one actual entity involves all other actual entities among its components. The result: such a philosophy explains how the world, although complex and changing, is "solid" (#f)—i.e., is one vibrant whole, underlying which however is an "ultimate" (#g) in such a way that it is not Spinoza's God or idealism's Absolute (#h) and that it is not actual in and of itself[37] but only through its "accidents," among which God is primordial and nontemporal (#g). Thus, unlike Western Asiatic and European thought, this ultimate is process (#i) in the sense that creativity is the single active force or field constantly conveying entities from potentiality to actuality, from multiplicity to unity.

Conclusions. In the light of the preceding, may one not infer that the dynamic factor in which all actual entities consist and which all actual entities—God and other creatures—have in common is creativity? Creativity would thus parallel Heraclitus' flux (which

---

[37] On "potential" and "actual" see *PR*, p. 29: "Actual occasions in their 'formal' constitutions are devoid of all indetermination. Potentiality has passed into realization. They are complete and determinate matter of fact, devoid of all indecision." Also see pp. 39–40: In the philosophy of organism "the actualities constituting the process of the world are conceived as exemplifying the ingression (or 'participation') of other things which constitute the potentialities of definiteness for any actual existence. The things which are temporal arise by their participation in the things which are eternal. The two sets are mediated by a thing which combines the actuality of what is temporal with the timelessness of what is potential. This final entity is the divine element in the world, by which the barren inefficient disjunction of abstract potentialities obtains primordially the efficient conjunction of ideal realization." Also see pp. 148–49, 308–9.

Whitehead himself claims "to be one ultimate generalization around which we must weave our philosophical systems"),[38] Plotinus' oneness (which as *dynamis* overflows to become the Intellect and intellects, the Soul and souls—all of which are real only insofar as each is the One-on-a-lower-level),[39] Spinoza's *conatus* (which develops into the divine *natura naturans* and *natura naturata*),[40] Hegel's *der Idee* (which develops triadically, eventually and fully into Absolute Spirit),[41] Bergson's *duration* (within whose evolution both mind and matter are found).[42] If so, may one not conclude that Whitehead's philosophy of creativity-based process is a monism of creativity and thus is like Heraclitus', Plotinus', Spinoza's, Hegel's and Bergson's monistic philosophies? If so, again, may one not infer that God and creatures are the actual entities in which creativity manifests itself and thus constitutes God and other creatures, just as (say) God, the divine attributes and modes are manifestations and products of Spinoza's *conatus*, or the Idea in itself (the Logical

---

[38] *PR*, p. 208. Also *ibid.*: "The elucidation of meaning in the phrase 'all things flow' is one chief task of metaphysics"; *ibid.*, p. 29: "The ancient doctrine that 'no one crosses the same river twice' is extended. No thinker thinks twice; and, to put the matter more generally, no subject experiences twice."

[39] See ch. 16 above, "Are Plotinus and Albertus Magnus Neoplatonists?" section "Plotinus' Metaphysics"; ch. 18 above, "Metaphysics and God: Plotinus and Aquinas."

[40] See James Collins, *A History of Modern European Philosophy* [hereafter: *HMP*] (Milwaukee: Bruce Publishing Co., 1965), pp. 242, 249–50; Paul Seligman, "Some Aspects of Spinozism," in *Proceedings of the Aristotelian Society*, n.s. 61 (1961), 109–28, especially p. 116.

[41] See George Lichtheim, "Introduction," in G. W. F. Hegel, *The Phenomenology of Mind*, trans. J. B. Baille (New York: Harper Torchbooks, 1967), pp. 30–50, especially pp. 32–34 (where *der Idee* is translated as "the notion"). Also see W. T. Stace, *The Philosophy of Hegel* (London: Dover Publications, 1955), especially sec. II: "Modern Philosophy and Hegel," pp. 32–49, and sec. III: "Hegel," pp. 50–119, as well as the helpful "Diagram of the Hegelian System" found inside the back cover. Also see J. Collins, *HMP*, pp. 619–34; *idem, God and Modern Philosophy* (Chicago: Henry Regnery Co., 1959), pp. 210–16, 232–37. Collins (*ibid.*, p. 202) begins his chapter by characterizing Hegel's "master theme of absolute-spirit-as-totality" as "a unique type of dialectical monism," which Whitehead speaks of as "evolutionary monism" (*PR*, p. 210).

[42] J. Collins, *HMP*, pp. 809–47, especially pp. 811–21 and 830–40, where he gives multiple references to Bergson's *The Creative Mind* and *Creative Evolution*. Also see F. S. C. Northrop, "Whitehead's Philosophy of Science," in Schlipp, pp. 168–69: from Bergson "came the doctrine of the primacy of process, which is as basic to Whitehead's philosophy of science as it is to his metaphysics."

Idea), the Idea outside itself (Nature) and the Idea in and for itself (Spirit) are the revelations and (through thesis, antithesis and synthesis) developments of Hegel's *der Idee*?

Perhaps the next capital text will clarify and support that conclusion.

Key Text B: *Process and Reality*, pp. 20–21

Context. [a] Thirteen pages after Text A Whitehead returns to creativity when setting forth the four primary generic "notions which constitute the philosophy of organism," the first of which is "actual entity" or "actual occasion." Such entities "are the final real things of which the world is made up" and extend from God to "the most trivial puff of existence in far-off space." All these comprise the "final facts . . . [the] drops of experience, complex and interdependent" (*ibid.*, p. 18).

[b] The second primary notion is the "ontological principle," which broadens a general principle of John Locke's *Essay Concerning Human Understanding* that "power" is "a great part of our complex idea of substances," with the result that for Whitehead "substance" becomes "actual entity" and "power" accounts for why "the reasons for things are always to be found in the composite nature of definite actual entities—in the nature of God for reasons of the highest absoluteness, and in the nature of definite temporal actual entities for reasons which refer to a particular environment. The ontological principle can be summarized as: no actual entity, then no reason" (*ibid.*, pp. 18–19).

[c] A third primary notion is "prehensions," arrived at when analyzing an actual entity into the most concrete elements of its nature—namely, the actual entity as referring "to an external world" and thus as having a "vector character," as well as involving "emotion and purpose, and evaluation, and causation." The prehension of an actual entity has a "subjective form," determined by the "subjective aim at further integration, so as to obtain the 'satisfaction' of the completed subject" as actual entity (*ibid.*, p. 19).[43]

---

[43] On Whitehead's admission of reliance in his doctrine of prehensions upon Locke's account of mental operations, Descartes' mental "cogitations" and Leibniz' "monads," see *PR*, p. 19, last paragraph. Also see *ibid.*, pp. 80–82.

But one should heed V. Lowe's warning (Schlipp, p. 117, n. 227) that Whitehead's description of his reliance upon Locke and Descartes "gives a misleading idea of the sources from which the philosophy and the concept of prehension, sprang in Whitehead's intellectual development." Lowe adds

[d] Finally, "nexus" is the togetherness, the relatedness of an actual entity arising from its "real, individual and particular" prehensions of other actual entities (*ibid.*, p. 20).

[e] Thus, "the ultimate facts of immediate actual experience are actual entities, prehensions, and nexus. All else is, for our experience, derivative abstraction." Hence, philosophy's purpose is "to explain the emergence of the more abstract things from the more concrete things": the "true philosophic question" is not how concrete particular fact can be built up out of universals but how concrete fact exhibits "entities abstract from itself and yet participated in by its own nature" (*ibid.*).

[f] That is, "philosophy is explanatory of abstraction, and not of concreteness." Hence, by instinctively grasping this ultimate truth some "types of Platonic philosophy retain their abiding appeal: they seek the forms in the facts. Each fact is more than its forms, and each form 'participates' throughout the world of facts" (*ibid.*).

The key text follows straight away.

[g] The definiteness of fact is due to its forms; but the individual fact is a creature, and creativity is the ultimate behind all forms, inexplicable by forms, and conditioned by its creatures. [Creativity is, in short,] the category of the ultimate [and, together with "many" and "one," is] presupposed in all the more special categories [of existence, explanation and obligations].[44]

(*ibid.*, p. 118): "It is neither of these two [Descartes and Locke] but Berkeley, who seems to me ... to have been the philosopher most relevant to Whitehead's own conceptions in their formative stage."

The primacy Lowe gives to Berkeley in Whitehead's development appears less surprising if we reflect upon Berkeley's statement, "Esse est percipi," and the interpretation Whitehead might give it. For Berkeley, being consists in what is thought—mainly by God and subordinately by human minds, the content of whose perceptions are God's thoughts. For Whitehead "esse est prehendi"—becoming consists in prehension: in what is prehended or felt—the influence upon each actual entity by its immediate past, by other actual entities around it, by the eternal objects and, in its own manner, by creativity itself as advancing it from the past through the present to the future. The result is that all such creatures (including God) *are* creativity manifesting and developing itself so that reality in the sense of value and worth *is* that creative advance or process. See n. 56 below.

[44] What are categories? "They are not dogmatic statements of the obvious; they are tentative formulations of the ultimate generalities" (*PR*, p. 8). On existence, explanation and objections as categories, see *ibid.*, pp. 22–28.

[h] "Creativity" is the universal of universals characterizing ultimate matter of fact. It is that ultimate principle by which the many, which are the universe disjunctively, become the one actual occasion, which is the universe conjunctively. It lies in the nature of things that the many enter into complex unity.

[i] "Creativity" is the principle of *novelty*. An actual occasion is a novel entity diverse from any entity in the "many" which it unifies. Thus "creativity" introduces novelty into the content of the many, which are the universe disjunctively. The "creative advance" is the application of this ultimate principle of creativity to each novel situation which it originates. . . .

[j] The ultimate metaphysical principle is the advance from disjunction to conjunction, creating a novel entity other than the entities given in disjunction. The novel entity is at once the togetherness of the "many" which it finds, and also it is one among the disjunctive "many" which it leaves; it is a novel entity, disjunctively among the many entities which it synthesizes. The many become one, and are increased by one. In their natures, entities are disjunctively "many" in process of passage into conjunctive unity. This Category of the Ultimate replaces Aristotle's category of "primary substance."[45]

Commentary. One may (I hope) validly summarize Text *A* as Whitehead's explanation that, although the world is multiple and diverse in its transient contents, it nonetheless is genuinely one—a unity due to an ultimate which is the dynamic basis for the entire world of God and other creatures and which of itself is without actuality and characterization but becomes actual and characterized only through them. This ultimate is creativity (#h).[46] If that

---

[45] On the "category of the ultimate," see #g above. As Whitehead observes immediately after #j, "concrescence" embodies "production of novelty" and "concrete togetherness," which is explicable "not in terms of higher universals or in terms of the components participating in the concrescence. The analysis of the components abstracts from the concrescence. The sole appeal is to intuition." On Whitehead's use of Aristotelian matter, see n. 54 below.

[46] For Whitehead "creativity" is not a Christian notion: it is not linked with creation as God's causing something to exist *ex nihilo* (see *PR*, p. 95). Rather, creation explains how "things" are what and how they are, ironically much as Aristotle's God accounts not for the fact that things exist but for what they are through motion. Hence, "actual" for Whitehead expresses directly not that

hope is well founded, Text *B* seemingly is Whitehead's exposition of how that world, while remaining one, retains multiplicity, diversity and novelty in content and that this retention is due to creativity also.

Let us follow the movement of thought in this second capital text. The philosophy of organism, Whitehead begins, consists of four primary generic notions, the first, second and fourth of which pertain to concrete facts or realities in the universe, the third is the "ontological principle," gained from Locke's understanding of "power" as part of the complex idea of "substance" and broadened by substituting "actual entity" for "substance." This broadening results in our realizing that the "reasons" (of why actual entities are what they are) are to be found in their concrete natures themselves—whether that actual entity be God or be temporal creatures in "a particular environment" (#b). [47]

The first of those primary notions pertaining to concrete facts[48] is "actual entities or occasions," which make up our world and which are all the existents (divine and otherwise) that are the "final facts" our experience issues from and terminates in (#a). "Prehensions"

---

entities actually exist but that they are what they transiently are by proceeding, under the influence of creativity, from the past through the present to the future. See *PR*, p. 342: "The notion of God as 'eminently real' is a favorite doctrine of Christian theology." When combined with "the notion of God as the 'unmoved mover,' " derived from Aristotle [here resides the irony mentioned above], one arrives at "the doctrine of an aboriginal, eminently real, transcendent creator, at whose fiat the world came into being, and whose imposed will it obeys, [and this] is the fallacy which has infused tragedy into the histories of Christianity and Mahometanism." Also see *ibid.*, p. 346: God's role in the universe "lies in the patient operation of the overpowering rationality of his conceptual harmonization. He does not create the world, he saves it: or, more accurately, he is the poet of the world, with tender patience leading it by his vision of truth, beauty, and goodness." *Ibid.*, p. 348: "It is as true to say that God creates the World, as that the World creates God."

[47] Concerning "reasons," see *PR*, p. 24: "Every condition to which the process of becoming conforms in any particular instance has its reason *either* in the character of some actual entity in the actual world of that concrescence, *or* in the character of the subject which is in the process of concrescence." Although "this category of explanation is termed the 'ontological principle,' " it could also be termed the " 'principle of efficient, and final, causation' " and means "that actual entities are the only *reasons*; so that to search for a *reason* is to search for one or more actual entities."

[48] In #a actual entities and occasions are equated, but in *PR*, p. 88, they are distinguished since God is not an "actual occasion" but is an "actual entity" (although not temporally so).

(the second primary notion) expresses those actual entities in their relationships to other actuals in the external world, in their emotions, in their final and efficient causal situations,[49] and in the "subjective forms" resultant from their subjective aims and issuing in "satisfaction" (#c).[50] The final primary notion is "nexus," which directly expresses the togetherness or relatedness of actual entities arising from their mutual prehensions (#d).

The objects which those three generic notions express are what we experience and from which we realize through abstraction the perfections they each participate in (#e). By abstraction, so understood, we gain philosophical knowledge by seeking, as do some Platonists, "the forms in the facts" (= in actual entities) by realizing that "each fact is more than its forms, and each form 'participates' throughout the world of facts" (#f).[51]

The key text comes straight away. What facts or actual entities or creatures are definitely (e.g., that they be divine, human, equine, etc.) is due to the forms they participate in. Creativity, although it itself is inexplicable by forms and is conditioned by the actual entities or creatures it underlies and produces, belongs to the category of "ultimate" and is presupposed and affects other more special categories (#g). It is, then, the most general of all categories.[52] It is the ultimate principle by which the many become one complex actual entity (#h) and by which the many are each novel in their content and thereby are diverse from any other entity.

Creativity is, in fact, the ultimate principle which advances actual entities into the novel situations it originates (#i). As the ultimate metaphysical principle[53] it is not only the advance from dis-

---

[49] See n. 43 above on prehension. For a helpful discussion of the various sorts of prehensions (positive and negative, physical and conceptual) see Edward Pols, *Whitehead's Metaphysics: A Critical Examination of Process and Reality* [hereafter: Pols] (Carbondale: Southern Illinois University Press, 1967), pp. 31–42, with a good diagram on p. 36.

[50] On "subjective aims" and "subjective forms," see *ibid.*, pp. 42–44 and 75–84. On "satisfaction" see Christian, pp. 20–36.

[51] On participation as ingression, see *PR*, pp. 39–40 (quoted in n. 37 above). On ingression see *ibid.*, p. 23: "The term 'ingression' refers to the particular mode in which the potentiality of an eternal object is realized in a particular actual entity, contributing to the definiteness of that actual entity"; also see *ibid.*, pp. 25, 290–91; Christian, pp. 184–89, 208–11.

[52] On category see n. 44 above.

[53] On metaphysical principle see *PR*, pp. 342 and 343. Whitehead uses "metaphysical" in several other contexts. For example, *ibid.*, p. 35: in denying

junction to conjunction by its "creating a novel entity other than the entities given in disjunction" but it also is the advance from conjunction to disjunction since "in their natures, entities are disjunctively 'many' [and remain so] in process of passage into conjunctive unity." And "this category of the ultimate replaces Aristotle's category of 'primary substance'" (#j). [54]

Conclusions. From charting the movement of Whitehead's thought in Text *B*, what have we learned? That his philosophy of organism again appears to be a monism of creativity. The objects which we experience (the actual entities—God and other

---

that "there is a continuing of becoming" while affirming that there is "a becoming of continuity," he states (*ibid.*, pp. 35–36): "The ultimate metaphysical truth is atomism. The creatures are atomic. In the present cosmic epoch there is a creation of continuity. Perhaps such creation is an ultimate metaphysical truth holding of all cosmic epochs." Again, *ibid.*, p. 189: "There is a togetherness of the component elements in individual experience. This 'togetherness' has that special peculiar meaning of 'togetherness in experience.' . . . The consideration of experiential togetherness raises the final metaphysical question: whether there is any other meaning of 'togetherness.'" For philosophers of organism, togetherness arises from experience: "The objectification of one actual occasion [lies] in the experience of another actual occasion. Each actual entity is a throb of experience including the actual world within its scope. The problems of efficient causation and of knowledge receive a common explanation by reference to the texture of actual occasions."

On the coalescence of metaphysical and physical descriptions and theories, see *PR*, p. 116: "If we substitute the term 'energy' for the conception of a quantitative emotional intensity, and the term 'form of energy' for the conception of 'specific form of feeling,' and remember that in physics 'vector' means definite transmission from elsewhere, we see that this metaphysical description of the simplest elements in the constitution of actual entities agrees absolutely with the general principles according to which the notions of modern physics are framed. The 'datum' in metaphysics is the basis of the vector-theory in physics; the quantitative satisfaction in metaphysics is the basis of the scalar localization of energy in physics; the 'sensa' in metaphysics are the basis of the diversity of specific forms under which energy clothes itself."

[54] Although Whitehead replaces Aristotle's "substance" by creativity as the category of the ultimate, he likens it (*PR*, p. 31) to Aristotelian "matter" when the latter is taken as "divested of the notion of passive receptivity, either of 'form,' or of external relations; it is the pure notion of the activity conditioned by the objective immortality of the actual world—a world which is never the same twice, though always with the stable element of divine ordering. Creativity is without a character of its own in exactly the same sense in which the Aristotelian 'matter' is without a character of its own. It is that ultimate notion of the highest generality at the base of actuality."

creatures—concrete and definite by and in their prehensions and nexus; #a, #c, #d) and from and in which we know through abstraction the perfections of forms participated in (#f, #g) entail power in their concrete natures (#b).[55] They are produced by the creativity underlying them (#h), which is the force by which the many become one, each of which becomes novel and diverse through the forms it participates in. Thus, creativity is that which advances actuals into novel situations by moving them from disjunction to conjunction and back again (#h, #j).

In the light of what has just been said, may one not infer again that all actuals (God and other creatures) *are* creativity diversifying, unifying, actuating, externalizing itself through them? The result would be that they *are* creativity, which as process and power is the sole reality.[56] If so, Whitehead's philosophy of organism is here, as in Text *A*, a monism of creativity.

---

[55] On abstraction see Paul Arthur Schlipp, "Whitehead's Moral Philosophy," in Schlipp, pp. 599–601; Christian, pp. 181–83, 206–8 (where the process of abstraction is contrasted with the process of concrescence), and pp. 263–66.

[56] On reality in the sense of value or worth as residing in process (and thus in creativity), see Creighton Peden, "Whitehead's Philosophy: An Exposition," in *Whitehead's View of Reality* [hereafter: Peden] (New York: Pilgrim Press, 1981), p. 29: "On the basis of the quantum theory and theory of relativity, Whitehead made 'process' the key term for describing the nature of reality. . . . His metaphysical considerations were based on science, but now science was related to the ongoing problems of the modern world. The problems of religion, of symbolism, of the function of reason, of nature and life, were now all interrelated within the metaphysical system"; *ibid.*, pp. 40–41: By assuming "that no static maintenance of perfection is possible," Whitehead asserts (*Adventures in Ideas*, pp. 273–74) three metaphysical principles, "the first of which is 'that the very essence of real actuality—that is, of the complete real—is process. Thus each actual thing is only to be understood in terms of its becoming and perishing.'" See n. 43 above.

On how process (so to speak) works, see *PR*, pp. 150–51: "The 'process' is the addition [to indeterminate datum] of those elements of feelings whereby these indeterminations are dissolved into determinate linkages attaining the actual unity of an individual actual entity. The actual entity, in becoming itself, also solves the question as to what it is to be. Thus process is the stage in which the creative idea [and creativity] works towards the definition and attainment of a determinate individuality. Process is the growth and attainment of a final end. The progressive definition of the final end is the efficacious condition for its attainment. . . . The creative process is rhythmic: it swings from the publicity of many things to the individual privacy; and it swings back from the private individual to the publicity of the objectified individual. The former swing is dominated by the final cause, which is the

Looking Ahead, Looking Back

Later passages from *Process and Reality* might be suggested as key texts on creativity. For example, in pages 31–32 and their complement,[57] pages 342–49, Whitehead links creativity with God's primordial and consequent natures in order to indicate the role that their ordering of the world plays in co-operating with creativity in producing the world. But too few entirely new insights into creativity show up there to require treatment as distinct key texts. For example, p. 31: the divine ordering which the primordial nature of God accomplishes conditions creativity and "has a real relevance to the creative advance." Thus, God "is at once a creature of creativity and a condition for it. It shares this double character with all creatures. By reason of its character as a creature, . . . it receives a reaction from the world. This reaction is its consequent nature." Again: "This function of creatures, that they constitute the shifting character of creativity, is here termed the 'objective immortality' of actual entities. Thus God has objective immortality" (p. 32). From the final chapter of *Process and Reality*, "God and the World": God's "unity of conceptual operations is a free creative act," which merely "presupposes the general metaphysical character of creative advance, of which it is the primordial exemplification. The primordial nature of God is the acquirement by creativity of a primordial character" (and thus God *is* creativity as primordial; p. 344). God's "derivative nature is consequent upon the creative advance of the world," an advance which is ultimately due to creativity (p. 345)

---

ideal; and the latter swing is dominated by the efficient cause, which is actual." On efficient and final causalities, see notes 47 and 53 above.

[57] "Complement" because Whitehead in *PR*, p. 31, explicitly refers to "Part V," the second chapter of which is "God and the World," pp. 342–48. On "free creative act" mentioned on p. 344, see Pols, pp. 118–20, on transcendent decision, which is the decision of all actual entities and thus includes God's decision. On transcendence/immanence see *PR*, pp. 93–94: Together with all actual entities, God "is an actual entity immanent in the actual world, but transcending any finite cosmic epoch—a being at once actual, eternal, immanent, and transcendent. The transcendence of God is not peculiar to him. Every actual entity, in virtue of its novelty, transcends its universe, God included." Creativity itself transcends all actual entities—*ibid.*, p. 88: "Every actual entity, including God, is a creature transcended by the creativity which it qualifies." On God as transcendent/immanent, also see Peden, p. 76; *PR*, pp. 239–40.

For Aquinas God's presence in and otherness from creatures (and thus His immanence and transcendence) reside in His being their efficient cause—see paragraph corresponding to n. 29 above.

and, indeed, which *is* creativity. Page 347: "The creative advance
ever re-establishes itself endowed with initial subjective aim derived from the relevance of God to the evolving world." Page 348:
"God and the World are the contrasted opposites in terms of which
Creativity achieves its supreme task of transforming disjoined multiplicity, with its diversities in opposition, into concrescent unity,
with its diversities in contrast." Finally, p. 349: Both God and the
World "are in the grip of the ultimate metaphysical ground, the
creative advance into novelty. Either of them, God and the World,
is the instrument of novelty for the other."

Interesting and inspiring as these additional passages are, they
provide little new information on creativity and its possibly monistic nature in Whitehead's philosophy of organism. They merely
repeat information already given concerning (for example) "creative advance" (pp. 32, 344, 348, 349), creatures (God and other
actual entities) as "conditioning creativity" (pp. 31, 32, 344), creativity through God and the World transforming disjunction into conjunction, opposition into contrast (p. 348). Hence, merely listing
them suffices to corroborate the conclusions reached in Texts *A* and
B: Whitehead's philosophy of organism is a monism of creativity:
this is the underlying force, power, field which constantly advances
actual entities into novel situations and thus continues the process
of their becoming from what they were to what they are now and to
what they will be. Thus all actuals (God and other creatures) *are*
creativity manifesting itself, actuating and conditioning itself, externalizing itself through them. Creativity as process, force and
power, then, is reality.[58]

Knowledge: Constructural or Not?

After this corroboration of Texts *A* and *B*, let us return to Thomas
Aquinas and Bracken, and now on their reactions to knowledge as
"constructural" and "nonconstructural." This distinction historically arose because of Immanuel Kant's position on knowledge *vs.*
thought. Although we *think* of noumena, we *know* only phenom-

[58] See n. 56 above. Another indication of Whitehead's monism is found in
the absence of real distinction between knowledges. In addition to *PR*, pp. 15–
16 and 349 (quoted in the opening paragraphs of this chapter), see *ibid.*, p. 116
(quoted in n. 53 above, last paragraph) on the interconnections between
metaphysics and physics; *ibid.*, pp. 238–39; Peden, pp. 37–41, 43–45, 70–71.

ena, which the mind constructs by imposing its a priori forms of space and time, as well as its twelve categories, upon sense data.[59] All knowledge, then, is "constructural" because the human mind has thus affected intrinsically the content of what it knows. That Kantian conception of knowledge has thereafter raised the question of whether any human cognition is "nonconstructural." The answer is yes if the content of some cognition is not affected by the mind itself contributing to it but has arisen from the objects known, which then would be its sole content-determining-causes.

Aquinas' reply is affirmative: all our direct knowledge (both spontaneous and metaphysical) of actually existing material beings, although efficiently caused by the knower through his/her efficient cognitive powers, is caused in its content by those existents.[60]

What is Bracken's answer? It is negative: there are no nonconstructural knowledges, all human cognition is constructural. One may judge this to be so from what he writes in *Society and Spirit: A Trinitarian Cosmology*,[61] where he aims at developing further "the Whiteheadian notion of a society as a preconstituted . . . patterned field of activity for the emergence of successive generations of 'actual occasions' " (*ibid.*, p. 14). Chapter 2: "Energy-Events and Fields" of that development provides an opportunity for Bracken to touch upon his own epistemology. There he wishes to show "that the ultimate constituents of material reality are Whiteheadian actual occasions, momentary subjects of experience or, in the language of natural science, localized energy-events that objectify themselves to their successors as wave-patterns of energy within a common field of activity. Whiteheadian 'societies,' accordingly, should be understood as 'fields' for the dynamic interrelation of actual occasions" (p. 58). Thus, his intention is "simply to provide a theoretical framework for dealing with the philosophical issues raised by quantum mechanics." In the final portion of that chapter he will "make clear that the notion of field is quite useful for analyzing different societal configurations, from the microscopic (for example, the atom) to the macroscopic (for example, human communities) and thus 'society' rather than 'substance' . . . is best suited to serve as the foundational concept of a new cosmology" (*ibid.*).

---

[59] See J. Collins, *HMP*, secs. 3–5 on Kant's *Critique of Pure Reason*, pp. 468–90.

[60] See my ch. 21 above, "Preller and Aquinas: Second Thoughts on Epistemology," paragraphs corresponding to notes 16–24.

[61] For publication data on *Society and Spirit*, see n. 8 above.

It is when he comes to the end of chapter 2 that he more explicitly discloses his own epistemology when he states that the

[a] objection to the equation of organic and inorganic entities with fields of activity dominated by a common element of form is that these entities do not look like fields of activity. They look like "things," that is, solid, relatively impermeable material realities with purely external relations to one another.

What is Bracken's reply?

[b] In response, all one can say is that appearances deceive. Natural science has already verified that material bodies, both organic and inorganic, are at any given moment a complex network of subatomic energy-events. What is this network, however, but a field of activity such as I have described in this chapter?

He then mentions the reservations of scientists and expresses a hope for their future conversion.

[c] Most scientists, to be sure, are apparently not yet ready to admit that the subatomic energy-events are the effects of the "decisions" of momentary subjects of experience called actual entities or actual occasions. But this, as I see it, is something which may well be achieved over a period of time as the interdisciplinary value of an overarching metaphysical scheme such as that proposed by Whitehead begins to take hold in the minds of these same natural scientists (*ibid.*, p. 72).

But a far greater achievement has already occurred.

[d] The far bigger step is the one already achieved by the scientific community, namely, to admit that the deliverances of the senses to human consciousness represent the end product of an enormously complex process of abstraction and simplification of profuse elementary data. What we see, hear, feel, smell, and taste does indeed correspond to reality but not in the simplistic manner understood in previous centuries. In that sense, the battle over the "substantiality" of the physical world has already been fought and definitively settled within the scientific community (*ibid.*, pp. 72–73).

In summary:

> [e] To sum up, then, the Whiteheadian notion of society, when understood as an ongoing field of activity for successive generations of actual occasions, appears initially well suited to serve as a foundational concept for a new cosmology. For, on the one hand, it seems to be compatible with the results of scientific research done on the submicroscopic level, namely, in quantum mechanics. On the other hand, a preliminary survey of its adaptability to higher-level forms of social organization suggests that it might well be functional there also (*ibid.*, p. 73).

Those excerpts make Bracken's epistemology clear. Consistently it would be a scepticism (at best allowing only probability) concerning the actual existents in the world of which we are a part (#a), since "appearances deceive" (#b). Certitude is rather to be found in the natural sciences, which have verified that all such "material bodies, both organic and inorganic, are at any given moment a complex network of subatomic energy-events"[62]—a network identical with a Whiteheadian "field of activity" (#b). Even though most scientists do not yet accept that identity, one can hope [and pray?] that in time they will see the light and agree (#c). Meantime, though, the far larger achievement of the scientists—namely, that the physical world is not "substantial" but is a complex of mathematically defined atomic and subatomic particles—has freed us from simplistic dependence upon our sensations and the data they deliver to our intellects (#d). Thus, we are ready for the "new cosmology," based on "the Whiteheadian notion of society, when understood as an ongoing field of activity for successive generations of actual occasions" (#e).

In the light of the preceding, what may we infer Bracken's position to be on constructural and nonconstructural knowledge? That knowledge is only constructural because its objects are solely atoms and subatomic particles,[63] the reality of which consists directly

---

[62] Earlier (*ibid.*, p. 58) Bracken had stated that the "ultimate constituents of material reality . . . [are] in the language of natural science, localized energy-events that objectify themselves to their successors as wave patterns of energy within a common field of activity." These constituents correspond to "Whiteheadian actual occasions" occurring within "Whiteheadian 'societies' . . . understood as 'fields' for the dynamic interrelation of actual occasions."

[63] Its objects would also be the counterparts of such particles, which are Whiteheadian actual occasions—see n. 62 above.

in the mathematical formulae which physicists have elaborated and through which they have thereby affected the cognitive contents. Their minds are in large measure the content-determining-causes of the knowledge, which is thereby constructural.

Before turning to Aquinas, let me briefly ask what Whitehead himself thinks on knowledge. To judge by his remarks in *The Concept of Nature*,[64] he would have anticipated Bracken. While protesting "bifurcating nature," he mentions some who maintain "that the molecules and ether of science are purely conceptual. Thus there is but one nature, namely apparent nature, and atoms and ether are merely names for logical terms in conceptual formulae of calculation" (*ibid.*, p. 229). This solution consists, then, in distinguishing "nature" (e.g., the red coals seen in the fireplace)[65] from "atoms, electrons, protons, etc.," which are mere names for the components in the mathematical formulae of an atomic physicist.

Whitehead rejects that solution because it reduces atoms and subatomic particles to mere concepts and names, to mere "assertions about things which don't exist [i.e., the particles of theoretical physics] in order to convey truths about things which do exist [red coals, trees, birds, etc.]." No, let atoms and subatomic particles be *entities in nature* and let scientific laws be expressions of truths concerning them. An atomic particle is hypothetically present in nature only if physicists are not yet fully certain of it.

Obviously, nature for Whitehead consists solely of the particles which a physicist studies and describes. Thus, red coals, hard chairs, singing birds are not as such "natural" and escape certain and true

---

[64] First published by Cambridge University Press (1920), *The Concept of Nature* [hereafter: *CN*] is included in *Alfred North Whitehead: An Anthology* (New York: The Macmillan Co., 1953), pp. 197–294. Its chapter 2, "Theories of the Bifurcation of Nature," pp. 216–32, is especially relevant. According to F. S. C. Northrop in Schlipp, p. 168, in "Whitehead's rejection of 'the bifurcation of nature,'" bifurcation means "the distinction between nature as sensed and nature as designated by scientific theory."

[65] For the example see *CN*, p. 226. Previous examples (p. 219) are "the greenness of the trees, the song of the birds, the warmth of the sun, the hardness of the chairs, and the feel of velvet." Whitehead also gives many instances of things in nature in *PR*—see pp. 62–65: "the contemporary chair" we see and touch, which Whitehead uses to make the point "that real objects for the subject" are "the extensive continuum" and the content "supplied by the eternal objects termed sense-data"; *ibid.*, pp. 170–72: a grey stone, used in an account of "presentational immediacy"; *ibid.*, p. 213: an intense blue color, a lovely shape in the concrescence of one actual occasion.

knowledge. One would, at best, conjecture as to whether and what they themselves are. Hence, to be genuinely true and certain, knowledge must be constructural—i.e., its objects are atomic and subatomic particles, which are found as such, presumably, in extramental reality—as "factors . . . in nature."[66]

"The World Is Charged with the Grandeur of God"

Finally, what is Aquinas' position on knowledge? Obviously he antedates modern physics and other empiriological sciences by several centuries, but he would have accepted them fully and gratefully as a complement to the constructural knowledges he, as well as other medieval authors, was already aware of.[67] In everyday life, for example, he realized that "blindness" is the lack of vision in someone who should see and, thus, a description of it is one's denial of what should be present but is not and, thus, is constructural because the human mind has affected its content as "sight not-present."[68] On the technical level, logic and mathematics were also for Aquinas constructural knowledges, as illustrated by a reflex universal (e.g., "dog as species") in contrast with a direct universal ("dog")[69] or by the edge of this wooden desk in contrast with

---

[66] *CN*, p. 230.

[67] On empiriological sciences see my *Authentic Metaphysics in an Age of Unreality*, 2d ed. (New York/Bern: Peter Lang Publishing, Inc., 1993), p. 6, n. 11: "Empiriological" refers "to an area of research (1) which studies material things (hence, the force of the initial syllables in the adjective, '*empirio*logical') but (2) only as affected by some sort of human activity (hence, the force of the last syllables, 'empirio*logical*'). Because of this second factor every empiriological science is constructural.

"Contemporary physics is an example of an empiriological science because (1) it is concerned with the structure and activities of material things, (2) but only under laboratory conditions and as mathematically formulated. Although constructural, mathematics or logic is not empiriological science because each lacks the first factor."

[68] On why "blindness" is an example of constructural knowledge, see *ibid.*, p. 179, n. 72. All evils (physical and moral) exemplify constructural knowledge.

[69] One's knowledge of direct and reflex universals is characterized in their content by (respectively) "abstraction of whatness" and "abstraction of addition"—see *ibid.*, pp. 338–41 and 346–48.

"straight line" mathematically defined as "that which has length but no width," where obviously the mathematician affects the content of the definition by his denial of width.[70]

But, manifestly, where Thomas differs most from Whitehead and Bracken is in his ready acceptance of that nonconstructural knowledge which is produced efficiently by the human knower and determinately as to its content by the material existents in the concrete situations which confront him/her—this cherry tree circled by honeybees seeking the nectar in its pink blossoms; this singing robin perched in its branches; this Irish setter barking at the gray squirrel run up its trunk but restrained by its owner; this mother comforting her three-year-old frightened by the commotion; Maria walking by and intuitively realizing for the first time how precious it is to be human but, yes, also actually to be. Those and similar situations provide Thomas with evidences for inferring that each tree, bee, robin, dog, squirrel, human person is a single entity composed not only of essence (prime matter/substantial form/ accidental perfections) but also of existence,

(a) which as an actuation distinct from the essence so actuated causes intrinsically each such entity to actually be;

(b) which thereby perfects each such actual existent as one of its intrinsic causes;[71]

(c) but which also limits itself mediately through the essence it is actuating;[72]

(d) which is the source of contingency in such individual existents, each one of which does exist but need not exist as far as it itself is concerned because its essence or nature is other than the act of existing perfecting it;[73]

(e) which thus points to an Existent whose essence or nature must be subsistent existence and who is properly the efficient cause of all creatures and thus is present in and to them but is also other than them.[74]

If the above interpretation is basically correct, existence in Aquinas' position is that by which each actual existent (whether divine, human, equine and the rest) is real. It is the core of their

---

[70] See *ibid.*

[71] *Ibid.*, ch. 4, pp. 75 sqq.

[72] *Ibid.*, ch. 5, pp. 109–21.

[73] *Ibid.*, ch. 5, pp. 135–39. Also see ch. 18 above, "Metaphysics and God: Plotinus and Aquinas," sections "Thomas Aquinas" and "Additional Clarifications." Also ch. 20, "The Mystery of Existence," section "Another Approach."

[74] See section "Aquinas Authentically Interpreted" of this chapter.

reality. It is the perfection which intuitively puts itself across in concrete cases to attentive and receptive minds and enables (for example) a young woman to realize, "Since I *am*, I have the right to be"; a senior in high school to be struck by "the difference between the force of my being and theirs [his schoolmates], between my knowledge of my own being and theirs"; a college student to feel "a real surge of joy in just being"; a high school sophomore to be struck "by what it meant for me to exist for all eternity, that this unique person would be forever";[75] Raïssa Maritain to experience "in a sudden intuition the reality of my own being, the profound first principle which makes me exist outside nonentity";[76] a two-and-a-half-year-old child, remembering the event years later, to notice "how bright the room was [where she had been sleeping] since it was a sunny day, but not brighter than the sudden illumination I had in my mind of my very own being and the keen awareness of my surroundings: I was part of all this, and I realized that I was"; a seminarian sitting on the moist sand of a beach to have been struck by the awareness that "that mollusk existed [which had shot up water from beneath the sand near his foot] . . . [that the] one solitary grain [of sand on the tip of his thumb] actually existed . . . [and] that I too was: I existed. Life then was not a dream but a reality, and the concept . . . stupefied me."[77]

Other instances could be adduced but enough have been presented (I hope) to prove that Aquinas' metaphysics and theology of existence are unique: they are widely divergent from process thought. They also are eminently worthwhile today as complements to contemporary astrophysics and other empiriological sciences and as antidotes to current brands of linguistic analysis, phenomenology, hermeneutics, deconstructionism, secular humanism and other atheisms.

Although we humans are restricted in the immediate knowledge (both philosophical and theological) of God we can have,[78] still

---

[75] For these examples of intuition see my *Authentic Metaphysics*, pp. 78 and 85–86.

[76] *Ibid.*, p. 384; also ch. 24 above, "The Christian Existentialism of Jacques Maritain."

[77] See ch. 20 above, "The Mystery of Existence," for additional instances and reflections.

[78] Aquinas grants that "because we are unable to know what God is but only what He is not, we cannot consider how God exists but only how He does not exist" (*S.T.*, I, 3 introduction: "Cognito de aliquo an sit, inquirendum restat quomodo sit, ut sciatur de eo quid sit. Sed quia de Deo scire non possumus

existence in us and in all other material existents can (as indicated above) so illumine our minds as also to illumine God's presence in this actual world of ours. As Gerard Manley Hopkins exclaims in his sonnet "God's Grandeur":[79]

The world is charged with the grandeur of God.
It will flame out, like shining from shook foil. . . .
There lives the dearest freshness deep down things.

That dearest freshness deep down things, that flaming out like shook shining foil, that charge within the world, which for the poet reveals God's grandeur, is for Thomas actual existence as fact, evidence, perfection and mystery. Existence equally and remarkably discloses God as He Who Is and as the agent properly causing it. Or as Hopkins says in the final lines of his sonnet:[80]

---

quid sit sed quid non sit, non possumus considerare de Deo quomodo sit sed potius quomodo non sit"). In fact, when we speak of God as "existence," what we *directly* know is solely what the verb expresses in the affirmative proposition "God exists," and this we know from the effects He is causing. (*Ibid.*, I, 3, 4 ad 2: "Esse dupliciter dicitur: uno modo significat actum essendi, alio modo significat compositionem propositionis, quam anima adinvenit coniungens praedicatum subiecto. Primo igitur modo accipiendo esse, non possumus scire esse Dei, sicut nec eius essentiam, sed solum secundo modo. Scimus enim quod haec propositio quam formamus de Deo, cum dicimus *Deus est*, vera est. Et hoc scimus ex eius effectibus.") Hence, only in this indirect way do we know existence as divine, existence as God's essence, God as existence.

[79] Peter Milward, *A Commentary on the Sonnets of G. M. Hopkins* (Chicago: Loyola University Press, 1969), p. 4.

[80] Even though devoted to John Duns Scotus, Hopkins will, I hope, forgive me for interpreting this sonnet in the light of "existence" as understood by Aquinas. In this interpretation I am following Marion Montgomery, "The Inescapability of Metaphysics," *First Things* (January 1993), p. 28: Gerard Manley Hopkins is "the poet who immediately supports academic intellectuals called as they are to witness the truth of things in this present moment of the world. Things—*res* in all their gloriously shadowed multiplicity. Hopkins celebrates them through poems whose mediate end is his catching an *inscape* of things in words. . . . That attempt to catch the truth of a thing in words arises out of his response to his own vision of the *instress* of things. And that instress always speaks beyond material manifestation, speaks to the immaterial reality whereby the thing that is, *is* in its first place. For Hopkins knows that 'There lives the dearest freshness deep down things,' despite our seeing with our sensual natures that these are 'dappled things,' . . . We wrestle for the beauty possible in things . . . in the sheer plod that makes us try to reveal that when we say a verb is a word expressing action, being, or a state of being,

Oh, morning, at the brown brink eastward, springs—
Because the Holy Ghost over the bent
World broods with warm breast and with ah! bright wings.

---

we are dealing with a reality spoken to through our words that the words must respectfully attend. In this instance of the verb, St. Thomas' *being* itself is at issue, or Hopkins' 'dearest freshness deep down things.' "

On Hopkins' knowledge of and influence by Scotus, see Alfred Thomas, *Hopkins the Jesuit: The Years of Training* (Oxford University Press, 1969), p. 99: "At the end of his second year in [studying] philosophy, Hopkins discovered for himself the philosophic soulmate he had hungered for since he joined his new Church. This kindred spirit was Duns Scotus"; *ibid.*, p. 183: "Scotus remained [even after his seminary training] for Hopkins 'the greatest of the divine and doctors of the Church.'" Also Eleanor Ruggles, *Gerard Manley Hopkins: A Life* (Port Washington, N.Y.: Kennikat Press, 1969), pp. 137–40, especially p. 137: "Hopkins . . . like Scotus was all his life possessed by his necessity to capture in a word the sense of self of which he was so vividly aware. . . . [This awareness] of the self element in all phenomena was felt by Hopkins more keenly than by most men and the chief clue to his affinity with Scotus lies in a comparison between the philosopher's term *haeccitas* or 'formal difference with respect to the thing' and Hopkins' own coinages which fleck his prose and poetry: 'inscape,' 'pitch' and 'instress.'" Also see B. W. Ward, "Philosophy and Inscape: Hopkins and the *Formalitas* of Duns Scotus," *Texas Studies in Literature and Language* 32 (1990), 214–39; Hywel Thomas, "Gerard Manley Hopkins and John Duns Scotus," *Religious Studies* 24 (1988), 337–64; Austin Warren, "Instress of Inscape," *Kenyon Review* 11 (1989), 216–24; James Collins, "Philosophical Themes in G. M. Hopkins," *Thought* 22 (1947), 67–106; R. V. Young, "Hopkins, Scotus, and the Predication of Being," *Renascence* 42 (1990), 35–50.

On Hopkins' sonnet honoring Scotus, see P. Milward, pp. 68–71.

Bibliographical Addendum. Walter E. Stokes, "The Function of Creativity in the Metaphysics of Whitehead," M. A. Thesis: St. Louis University, 1960; Donald W. Sherburne, "Some Reflections on Sartre's Nothingness and Whitehead's Perishing," *Review of Metaphysics,* 48 (1994), 3–18; Joseph A. Bracken, *The Divine Matrix: Creativity as Link Between East and West* (Maryknoll, N.Y.: Orbis Books, 1995).

26

Can Aquinas Help
Our Contemporary World?

Two situations in our current world can serve as an introduction
to this chapter.

Images: Rwanda, Jupiter, Washington

The first situation is the attention given by *Time*, August 1, 1994,
to Rwanda and then to the comet hitting Jupiter. The magazine's
cover story, "Cry the Forsaken Country" by Nancy Gibbs, provides
pictures and an account of the more than two million refugees from
Rwanda in camps in Zaire and other neighboring countries where
"hunger and disease take up where a vicious war left off" (p. 29).
Such a great exodus was born of an epic betrayal, first, by Western
governments and relief officials by not intervening earlier (p. 34)[1]
and, especially, by the Tutsi and Hutu soldiers and politicians
themselves.

During the last weeks of fighting the Tutsi rebels chased the
Hutu army west, pushing more than a million refugees ahead

---

[1] See also Milton Leitenberg, "Anatomy of a Massacre," *New York Times*,
July 3, 1994, sec. 4, p. 15; Jerry Gray, "Rwanda's Lottery," *ibid.*, p. 1. On why
other African countries fail to intervene in the Rwandan tragedy, see Bill
Keller, "Africa Allows Its Tragedies to Take Their Own Course," *ibid.*, August
7, 1994, sec. 4, pp. 1 and 6. On the continuing tragedy in Rwanda and Zaire,
see John Balzar, "Cholera Ebbs, But Perils For Rwanda on Rise," *Chicago Sun-
Times*, August 6, 1994, p. 9.

of them. The Hutu leaders hid in the safe haven set up more than a month ago by French forces sent to provide humanitarian relief. Once protected, the defeated despots kept broadcasting messages of hate and revenge . . . warning their countrymen to flee or be killed.

Theirs was a brutal strategy of sacrifice; the idea was to cede the land but take the people with them. "The only power remaining in their hands was the population," said one veteran aid worker. "This was why they created the panic." A mass of refugees would pressure the world community to intervene, and show that while the [Tutsi Rwanda Patriotic Front] may have won, it had no country left to govern. "It is the former [Hutu] government that killed half a million Tutsi," says Nigel Fisher [a United Nations representative for Rwanda] "and then instilled fear in its own people: 'You better escape because the Tutsi will kill you in revenge, and if you don't escape, then you're a traitor and we'll kill you.'"

The deadly message did its work. Up and down the rows of refugees in Goma, they tell the same stories, share the same fears (Gibbs, pp. 34–35).

In the same issue of Time Michael D. Leomick furnishes pictures and an account of the aftermath of the twenty-one fragments (some as big as terrestrial mountains) of Comet Shoemaker-Levy 9 hailing down on Jupiter July 17–22.[2]

[Once] the debris from their catastrophic impacts has started to settle . . . , the information superhighway [here on earth] is coming unclogged as Internet users relax their manic electronic search for comet-crash pictures. . . . But amateur astronomers are still peering intently through their backyard telescopes to get a glimpse of the bruises that Shoemaker-Levy 9 left on Jupiter—the most prominent features ever seen on the giant planet. . . . Scientists . . . are finally turning their attention away from the spectacular pictures and starting the long, difficult process of seeing what they can learn from the great comet crash of 1994 (p. 50).

The spots that were made [on Jupiter] by the collisions will undoubtedly blow away eventually . . . but it's much too soon

---

[2] Also see "Jupiter's Inferno," *Time*, July 25, 1994, p. 57.

to tell whether there will be any permanent changes in Jupiter. There is still every chance that the impacts . . . will destabilize the atmosphere and create a new, permanent cyclone like Jupiter's Great Red Spot (p. 51).

That issue of *Time* terminates with Paul Gray's essay, "Looking at Cataclysms," p. 64.[3] The last week of July was one of

[a] visual superlatives, of images both awesome and horrifying. Astronomers said they had never seen anything like the fireworks produced when comet chunks, one of roughly as big as an alp, crashed into the planet Jupiter. International relief workers said the same thing, only they were referring to the tide of refugees streaming out of Rwanda and into overnight cities of misery, disease and death. Certainly the millions of people who watched these two cataclysms unfold through news photographs and televised images had never seen anything like them either.

Gray continues:

[b] In theory, this rush of instantaneous sightings should be a boon to human understanding; the more we notice, the wiser we become. In practice, such cascades of images can prove deracinating. The mind is cut adrift by what the eyes provide. [c] For witnesses, either firsthand or at the remove of film or TV, must supply their own contexts to make sense of what they are seeing. Faced with something new in their visual experiences, they are likely to jump to questionable conclusions.

To avoid such questionable inferences, [d] one must not "mistake the unfamiliar for the unprecedented" or allow the media images of the Jupiter impacts and of the Rwanda refugees to misapprehend their scale. For example,

[e] In absolute measurements, the Rwandan refugees filled infinitely less space than that taken up by a single explosion of Jupiter. But, paradoxically, images could not begin to convey

---

[3] Bracketed lower-case letters are being added to facilitate subsequent references.

the immensities and enormities of these settlements. The frame
was too small to contain such an expanse of anguish. Photog-
raphers had to resort to visual synecdoche, hoping that a
small part of the scene—a wailing child, an emaciated mother,
a pile of corpses in a freshly dug trench—would suggest the
horrors of the whole.

[f] In an important sense, of course, the photographs did
just that. They alerted the world to the plight of the Rwandans,
just as the snapshots of Jupiter gave earthlings an invaluable
cosmic slide show. The danger of images lies not in the information they carry but rather in our propensity to believe—
once we have seen them—that we have seen the whole picture. . . . [But] we should . . . remember that images do not
come with built-in memories or instructions in how they should
be read. If we are to understand them correctly, we must still
do that work ourselves (ibid.).

In his essay what is Paul Gray telling us? Images, however informative and instructive (#a), do not suffice in and by themselves
(#b, #d): those viewing them will understand their content accurately (#c) only if the viewer complements the information they
give by refusing to believe they represent the whole rather than a
part and by amplifying them by his or her relying upon previous
and other current experiences (#e, #f). In short: we must not be
passive but constantly be intellectually active.

Before outlining the second situation which will serve to introduce this chapter, let us even now ask whether Thomas can help us
with the contemporary problems which images raise. The answer
is *yes*, as can be indicated by turning briefly to a publication dated
one day earlier than the *Time* issue just studied: the *New York Times
Magazine* of July 31, 1994. There Michael Kelly's lead article, "Bill
Clinton's Climb," portrays the role "image" plays in Clinton's character and presidency, for whom [g] a successful politician makes
the images needed to convey to the public the reality which he
wishes to be perceived. Why so? Because a tough Texan political
operative taught Clinton "the idea that *perception was reality* [my
italics] . . . and that became the battle cry of the new Clinton
approach" (p. 27).[4] As Kelly explains,

---

[4] This "new approach" Clinton adopted between his defeat in 1980 for a
second term as governor of Arkansas and seeking successfully the office again
in 1982—see ibid., pp. 26–27.

[h] the right words and the right nonverbal signals—the way in which a politician stood, sat, listened, laughed, smiled, frowned—combined to create a message [and image] that overrode the content of the words alone. If a politician was good at this, he could create not only a political reality out of perception, but also several conflicting realities at the same time, subtly manipulating the nuances of language, voice, expression and body posture so that each member of his audience saw and heard what he wanted to see and hear. It was possible to speak even on a subject that aroused sharp division— abortion or affirmative action or welfare—and have people on opposing sides perceive the speaker to be one of them.

[i] Bill Clinton was beyond good at this new political performance art. When he spoke, perception was not only reality. It was a reality that changed quicksilver-quick, from eye to eye and ear to ear. . . . What became increasingly clear in Arkansas was that Clinton . . . [was] blithely and flatly promising what he couldn't deliver, reversing himself on a position to which he had been, only moments before, firmly committed (pp. 27 and 40).[5]

If such describes Clinton in Arkansas, what now happens in Washington?

[j] The President is a ubiquitous electronic presence, always on the go and on the tube, in some vivid new tableau that is a masterwork of the campaigner's art. . . . [There] the President's face is a screen upon which plays a loop of expressions that have become insistently familiar: the open-mouthed grin of

---

[5] See Kelly's earlier article, "The Game: How Image Became the Sacred Faith of Washington," *New York Times Magazine,* October 31, 1993: "The story of this vast change [in journalists and politicians] is the story of how the idea of image became the faith of Washington. . . . In this new faith, it has come to be held that what sort of person a politician actually is and what he actually does are not really important. What is important is the perceived image of what he is and what he does. Politics is not about objective reality, but virtual reality. What happens in the political world is divorced from the real world. It exists for only the fleeting historical moment, in a magical movie of sorts, a never-ending and infinitely revisable docudrama. Strangely, the faithful understand that the movie is not true—yet also maintain that it is the only truth that really matters."

Chapter 26

joyous wonder; the scowl of righteous but controlled anger; the lip-biting, eyes-lowered glance of pondering humility, the near-tears of a man who is not afraid to show that he feels. [k] In an important sense, these expressions are entirely honest; Clinton's empathy is wholly real. *But it exists only in the moment.* The President's essential character flaw isn't dishonesty so much as a-honesty. It isn't that Clinton means to say things that are not true, or that he cannot make true, but that everything is true for him when he says it, because he says it. Clinton means what he says when he says it, but tomorrow he will mean what he says when he says the opposite. *He is the existential President, living with absolute sincerity in the passing moment* [italics added] (p. 45).[6]

What would Aquinas' reaction be to Clinton, as well as to contemporary politicians of similar mentality? Granted that an artist (e.g., a painter, musician, sculptor) makes images which are artifacts (a portrait, a sonata, a statue) so that those viewing them can share in the artist's vision of beauty. But current politicians must deal with actually existing events such as the Rwandan refugees and the Bosnian conflicts, and these demand objective appraisal and solutions. These events also demand that what a politician says and does (and thus the images which his audiences hear and see) be based upon what such actual situations truly are and not upon what the politician wants and makes them be so as to fit into his or her political ambitions and agenda. Hence, what people

---

[6] See Lance Morrow, "Living in Virtual Reality," *Time*, May 16, 1994, p. 94: "Americans inhabit, so to speak, two parallel realities. There is the virtual reality created by media spinning and cultural circuses and gladiatorial spectacles of exemplary pseudomoral combat (Harding v. Kerrigan, Bobbitt v. Bobbitt). . . . And then there is the reality of . . . reality. Places like, say, Bosnia and Haiti [and Rwanda] belong to the reality of reality. . . . A president who, once elected, confuses the two realities is headed for no good outcome. Virtual reality is a dream. The reality of reality always wins in the end. . . . There is a dangerous accumulation of evidence that Clinton operates by the phony physics of virtual reality (appearances, conjurations, evaporating threats, a governance of attitude and feeling) and has not a cold, hard grasp of plain fact. One has a suspicion that Clinton does not know that the reality of reality always wins. Ultimately, in the courtroom of history, life is fair—and often brutal." Also see John Halford, "Virtual Reality: Creating Your Own Values?" *The Plain Truth*, March 1994, pp. 14–19; Richard Corliss, "Virtual, Man!" *Time*, November 1, 1993, pp. 80–83.

perceive should be images which put across honestly the true state of affairs. Reality, then, should determine perception, and not the other way around.

This last sentence expresses precisely Aquinas' position. For him reality is not constituted by perception, as Clinton and his entourage want (#g–#i), but our perception is caused in its content by reality: the actual existents—good and bad, healthy and ill, rich and poor, learned and ignorant, ethnically diverse and talented— in all the concrete cases confronting us and welcoming or, at least, needing our care.[7]

Second, one applies the adjective "existential" to Clinton only as one does (for instance) to Jean-Paul Sartre and other radical existentialists, for whom individual free choices, without any other basis than that they are free, make any action morally good—if today someone freely chooses to save a life and tomorrow to destroy a life, saving or destroying is each equally good because freely chosen. Such a morality is a relativism and can result in social chaos and political anarchy.[8] Sartre's and Clinton's existentialism differs radically from Thomas' authentic existentialism, which rests on the fact that the "real" is "that which is actual," where "actual" expresses an existent as present here in this moment, but "that which" (its essence) expresses not only what it is now but also what substantially it was yesterday and will be tomorrow. This constitutes an authentically existential/essential continuity, which excludes ontological and epistemological relativism: everything real is and is what it is and simultaneously it cannot be and not be what it is; thereby everything real is knowable to the extent it is and is what it is. This continuity also issues into an objective morality by taking into account the fact that (say) human existents in their very being are spiritual/material and deserve corresponding respect, matched by their duties and responsibilities

---

[7] On actual existents in concrete cases as content-determining-causes of our nonconstructural knowledge, see ch. 21 above: "Preller and Aquinas: Second Thoughts on Epistemology." On reality (= value, worth) as consisting in actual existence see ch. 20 above: "The Mystery of Existence"; ch. 22: Existentialism: Authentic and Unauthentic"; ch. 25, especially prgrs. corresponding to nn. 67-68; L. Sweeney, *Authentic Metaphysics in an Age of Unreality* [hereafter: *Authentic Metaphysics*] (New York/Bern: Peter Lang Publishing, Inc., 1993), chs. 4–6.

[8] On Sartre see *ibid.*, especially pp. 21–29, 110–15, 374–84; also see prgrs. corresponding to notes 32–40 below.

to others. In brief, Thomas with his authentic existentialism can rescue contemporary citizens and their leaders alike from political theories centered on anything other than what actually is and the true knowledge such existents cause.[9]

Past, Present and Future: Surveys

The second situation which can serve to introduce this chapter on Aquinas and the contemporary world is the attention given currently in books and articles to contrasting or comparing past decades with current and future ones. For example, some authors restrict themselves to specific topics, such as poverty[10] or the Cold War[11] or religion[12] or abortion.[13] Others trace the history of a spe-

---

[9] See sections "Natural Law Morality" and "Love" below; also see the papal encyclicals *Veritatis Splendor* and *Evangelium Vitae*, referred to in note 13 below; for perceptive commentaries on those encyclicals see Robert Royal, "Freedom and More Truth Must Go Hand in Hand," *Chicago Tribune*, October 11, 1993, and Richard John Neuhaus, "The Gospel of Life," *Wall Street Journal*, April 3, 1995. Also see Karol Wojtyla, *Person and Community: Selected Essays*, trans. Theresa Sandok, and *idem, Ethics and Morality* (New York/Bern: Peter Lang Publishing, Inc., 1993 and 1994). Also see n. 112 below.

[10] Gertrude Himmelfarb, *The Idea of Poverty: England in the Early Industrial Age* (New York: Knopf Publishers, 1984), 2 vols.; *idem, Poverty and Compassion: The Moral Imagination of the Late Victorians* (New York: Knopf Publishers, 1991). Also see R. D. Christy and L. Williamson (eds.), *Land-Grant Colleges and Universities 1890–1990* (New Brunswick, N.J.: Transaction Publishers, 1991).

For a book by Himmelfarb on conceptions of history see *The New History and the Old* (Cambridge, Mass.: Harvard University Press, 1987). On history and politics, see Eli Sagan, *The Honey and the Hemlock: Democracy and Paranoia in Ancient Athens and Modern America* (New York: Basic Books, 1991).

[11] Martin Walker, *The Cold War: A History* (New York: Henry Holt and Co., 1994; John Lukacs, *The End of the Twentieth Century and the End of the Modern Age* (New York: Ticknor and Fields, 1993); Abbott Gleason, *Totalitarianism: The Inner History of the Cold War* (Oxford University Press, 1995).

[12] Stephen L. Carter, *The Culture of Disbelief: How American Law and Politics Trivialize Religious Devotion* (New York: Basic Books, 1993); George M. Marsden, *The Soul of the American University: Protestantism to Nonbelief* (Oxford University Press, 1994); Barry Alan Shain, *The Myth of American Individualism: The Protestant Origins of American Political Thought* (Princeton University Press, 1994); Roger Finke and Rodney Stark, *The Churching of America 1776–1990: Winners and Losers in Our Religious Economy* (New Brunswick, N.J.: Rutgers University Press, 1992).

[13] Ray Kerrison, "Commentary" [on President Bill Clinton], *Catholic Eye*, August 20, 1992, pp. 1–2. Pope John Paul II, "*Veritatis Splendor*: The Splendor

cific people—for instance, Nathan Rotenstreich's books on Jews[14] and Yeshayahu Leibowitz's *Judaism, Human Values and the Jewish State*.[15] Although Morris Dickstein restricts himself to literary criticism,[16] others attend to modern art as well,[17] or to the academic life even more generally.[18] Another example: in his long essay "The Fraying of America," Time, February 3, 1992, pp. 44–49, Robert Hughes speaks of political correctness and multiculturalism and of their effects on campus life and studies.[19]

Gertrude Himmelfarb's *On Looking into the Abyss: Untimely Thoughts on Culture and Society*[20] is a collection of several essays, which a reviewer has characterized as "a coherent and devastating attack on the forces of post-modernism in academic studies, literary, philosophical and historical." A postmodernist such as Jacques Derrida has emitted "a dense cloud of unintelligible verbiage. . . . [He and other deconstructionists are at best] frivolous game-play-

---

of Truth" (August 6, 1993) and "*Evangelium Vitae*: The Gospel of Life" (March 25, 1995); Stephen G. Post, "Abortion and the Triumph of Eros," *America*, April 28, 1990, p. 427.

[14] Nathan Rotenstreich, *Between Past and Present: An Essay on History* (New Haven: Yale University Press, 1958); idem, *Jewish Philosophy in Modern Times: From Mendelssohn to Rosenzweig* (New York: Holt, Rinehart and Winston, 1968); idem, *Man and His Dignity* (Jerusalem: The Magnes Press, 1983); idem, *Jews and German Philosophy: The Polemics of Emancipation* (New York: Schocken Books, 1984); idem, *Order and Might* (New York: SUNY Press, 1988).

[15] Cambridge, Mass.: Harvard University Press, 1992. Also see Herbert Schnädelbach, *Philosophy in Germany: 1831–1933* (Cambridge University Press, 1984).

[16] Morris Dickstein, *Double Agent: The Critic and Society* (Oxford University Press, 1992). For a review see John Sutherland, *New York Times Book Review*, February 7, 1993. Also see Jurgen Kleist and Bruce Butterfield (eds.), *Breakdowns: The Destiny of the Twentieth Century* (New York/Bern: Peter Lang Publishing, Inc., 1994).

[17] Louis A. Sass, *Madness and Modernism: Insanity in the Light of Modern Art, Literature, and Thought* (New York: Basic Books, 1992).

[18] See Richard H. Pells, *The Liberal Mind in a Conservative Age: American Intellectuals in the 1940s and 1950s* (New York: Harper and Row, 1985); Eric Gans, *The End of Culture: Toward a Generative Anthropology* (Berkeley: University of California Press, 1985); Daniel Bell, "American Intellectual Life, 1965–1992," *The Wilson Quarterly* (Summer 1992), 74–107.

[19] Also see Richard Bernstein, *Dictatorship of Virtue: Multiculturalism and the Battle for America's Future* (New York: Alfred A. Knopf, 1994) and review by Judith Kleinfeld in *Academic Questions* 8 (Spring 1995), 90–93.

[20] New York: Alfred A. Knopf, 1994. Hereafter I shall refer to Himmelfarb's book as *Looking into the Abyss*.

ers who make a virtue of their moral irresponsibility. At worst, they are set on destroying the standards that not only make their own activity possible but also enable society to survive at all. Either way they are bad news."[21] Himmelfarb herself discloses that the title of her book comes from the deconstructionists, who use "the image of the abyss" with reference to language—"a purely linguistic [abyss] constructed entirely out of words—indeed, out of a play on words. And having been so willfully constructed, it can be as willfully reconstructed and deconstructed."[22] But, she adds, "philosophy also has its abysses, and some philosophers are confronting them in the same way—playfully and irreverently, as a linguistic construct, having no 'correspondence' with anything posing as 'reality' or truth,'" for, as Nietzsche says, "'Truths are illusions of which one has forgotten that they *are* illusion.'"[23]

In fact, Nietzsche is, together with Martin Heidegger, the forefather of deconstructionism or, more generally, of postmodernism. "Its fathers [are] Derrida and [Michel] Foucault." From the last named, postmodernism "has adopted the idea of power: the 'power structure' immanent not only in language . . . but in the very nature of knowledge which is itself an instrument and product of power" and thus "traditional rational discourse [is impugned] as 'logocentric,' 'phallocentric,' 'totalizing,' 'authoritarian.'"

In literature, postmodernism amounts to a denial of the fixity of any "text," of the authority of the author over the interpreter, of any "canon" that privileges great books over lesser ones. In philosophy, it is a denial of the fixity of language, of any correspondence between language and reality—indeed, of any "essential" reality and thus of any proximate truth about reality. In law (in America, at any rate), it is a denial of the fixity of the Constitution, and of the legitimacy of law itself, which is regarded as nothing more than an instrument of power. In history, it is a denial of the fixity of the past, of the reality of the past apart from what the historian chooses to make of it, and thus of any objective truth about the past.[24]

---

[21] Michael Havard, *New York Times Book Review*, March 6, 1994, pp. 11–12; also see Sanford Pinsker in *Academic Questions* 7 (Fall 1994), pp. 86–92.

[22] *Looking into the Abyss*, p. 13.

[23] *Ibid.* For an exposé and critique of Richard Rorty's agreement with deconstructionists see *ibid.*, pp. 13–17.

[24] *Ibid.*, pp. 132–33.

In the light of Himmelfarb's statements, deconstructionism or postmodernism is obviously one contemporary phenomenon which provides an opportunity to plot how Thomas would react to it. But before turning to that reaction, let us first trace the intellectual history of earlier decades of the twentieth century so as to understand his reaction to them also.

"The Modern Mind": 1920–1960

In 1942 Gerald B. Phelan began an article, "St. Thomas and the Modern Mind,"[25] by referring to Jacques Maritain's 1925 book *Trois Réformateurs*, which found the "roots and primal forces" of the ideas which dominated our minds to have come from three reformers: Luther, who reformed religion, Descartes philosophy, and Rousseau morality. Their influence culminated in the philosophy of Immanuel Kant, who "stands at the meeting of the intellectual streams springing from these three men." As Phelan explains, from Descartes Kant

> inherited the conception of the independence of reason with respect to things; from Rousseau he inherited the conception of the independence of morality with respect to reason; from Luther he inherited the conception of the independence of religion with respect to authority. These ideas became the nucleus of the Kantian doctrine of transcendentalism in the realm of reason, autonomy in the realm of will and immanence in the realm of religion.[26]

From that moment on (Phelan continues) "Kant became the Pedagogue of Europe, the Maker of the Modern Mind." For with few exceptions (Phelan now turns to Cardinal Mercier's 1919 essay, "Le problème de la conscience moderne"), "the men who originated European thought for the last century and a half are permeated with the spirit of Kant."[27] That spirit of the *Critique of Pure Reason* it is (Phelan continues on his own) "which gave rise, though in different manners and with different results, to modern movements of

---

[25] *The Modern Schoolman* 20 (1942), 37–49.

[26] *Ibid.*, p. 39.

[27] See D. J. Cardinal Mercier, *Christianisme dans le monde moderne* (Paris: Perrin, 1919), p. 104.

thought as divergent as the idealism of Hegel, the materialism of Marx, the positivism of Comte, the intuitionism of Bergson, and the pragmatism of William James."[28]

Phelan's 1942 article, together with the attention it gave to Maritain's earlier study, is interesting and useful not only for the information it gives on the "three reformers" and Kant but also for the outline of the cure Thomas offers to "the confusion [in philosophy, in morality, in religion] of the Modern Mind," which has resulted from Kant's influence, whose philosophy (as we have seen) both Maritain and Phelan considered to have resulted form the influence Luther, Descartes and Rousseau exerted on him. And what is that cure? Aquinas makes "order out of chaos in the world of thought" in these steps (p. 40). He firmly grounded "metaphysics on the solid rock of natural reason, i.e., the native capacity of man to know what is *in rerum natura*" (pp. 40–41), to know actual beings themselves, to know noumena. He then established metaphysics as the science of those noumenal beings precisely as being, as actually existing and, next, he stressed that "intelligibility is rooted in being and that knowledge follows, not conditions, being. Thence onward it was a question of ordering all thought in conformity with the order of being" (pp. 41–42). This Aquinas did by distinguishing the "four orders of being in relation to knowledge— the order of things known by the intellect but not made nor ordered by it, the order made by the intellect in its own concepts, the order made by the intellect in the acts of the will and the order made by the intellect in external works (the speculative, the logical, the moral and the artistic orders, respectively)—and the whole plan of the structure of philosophical wisdom was clear" (p. 42).

But interesting and useful as Phelan's paper is for its outline of Aquinas' cure for the confused modern mind, it holds another value: it helps further illumine the intellectual and political movements subsequent to the "three reformers" and Kant. To paraphrase the New Testament:

> Luther, Descartes and Rousseau begot Kant; Kant begot Hegel, Marx, Comte, Bergson and James; Hegel begot Hitler and Mussolini, Marx begot Lenin, Stalin and Mao; Hitler and

---

[28] The movements of thought Phelan mentions were topics for the other papers in the *Schoolman* Symposium, "Kantianism and the Modern Mind," which culminated in Phelan's paper.

Mussolini begot the Nazis of the Third Reich and the Italian Fascists; Lenin, Stalin and Mao begot the Communists in Russia and Eastern Europe, in China and North Korea.

That family record discloses several additional facets of the "modern mind." A few thinkers in Europe (Luther, Descartes, Rousseau, Kant, Hegel, Marx) and the books they authored influenced billions of people throughout the world. Second, what began in speculation ended in practice. What started with abstract ideas soon descended inevitably to the concrete, daily lives of individual women, men and their children.

These aspects of the "modern mind" reveal the importance and difficulty of our reflection, which is not speculative, academic, esoteric, abstract, impersonal, impractical. No, it has repercussions which are intensely practical, concrete, personal and affecting the everyday lives of billions of people. Paul Dezza, S.J., said on October 14, 1941, in a conference given in Rome, "Scholastic Philosophy Faces Modern Thought" (p. 12): "Ideas direct the world and are at the foundation of all social upheavals." Let me illustrate with Etienne Gilson's remarks on Hegel in *The Unity of Philosophical Experience* (1937).[29]

'The truth is the whole,' and the whole itself is nature, which reaches 'its completeness through the process of its own development.' . . . Nature is but the external manifestation of an absolute and eternal Idea [*Geist*], which expresses itself in space and time according to a dialectical law. . . . The Idea which thus 'alienates' itself in nature is finding its way back through the successive moments of its dialectical realization. Each term of a concrete antinomy thus becomes a necessary step to the final self-reassertion of the Idea. That was a master stroke, but it entailed the open recognition of the fact that contradiction was at the very root of reality. . . . Intelligible as part of the whole, each particular thing is unintelligible by itself; rather, by itself, it is but a self-affirmation grounded on the negation of the rest, and denied by the rest. If the realization of the Idea is the march of God through the world, the path of the Hegelian God is strewn with ruins.

---

[29] E. Gilson, *The Unity of Philosophical Experience* (New York: Charles Scribner's Sons, 1937 and 1965), pp. 244–47. Gilson quotes Hegel from J. Loewenberg (ed.), *Hegel Selections* (New York: Charles Scribner's Sons, 1929).

In a metaphysical system wherein the whole of reality is included, such a doctrine does not limit itself to ideas, it applies to things [and men]. . . . That which is contradiction between ideas is war between men, and in such a world war is by no means an accident. It is law. The progressive actualization of the world-leading Idea entails the submission of individuals to the unity of the State. The ideal State itself is progressively working out its unity through the necessary oppositions between particular states.

Indeed, Hegel teaches that "taken by itself, no particular thing can rightly assert itself except by destroying another, and until it is itself destroyed. 'War,' says Hegel, 'is not an accident,' but an element 'whereby the ideal character of the particular receives its right and reality.' These are really and truly murderous ideas, and all the blood for which they are responsible has not yet been shed."

How prophetic Gilson's words were can be gathered from the fact that he spoke them in lectures delivered at Harvard during the Fall semester of the 1936–1937 academic year, and thus shortly before the rise of Hitler.[30]

Such a long quotation from Gilson, together with the paragraphs above on Maritain and Phelan, aids us in understanding what "the modern mind" meant in the decades between 1920 and (say) 1960. It referred to all human individuals during those years as they lived out their day-by-day existence in socialist and fascist nations; also, all human individuals during those years in countries threatened by and, then, at war with those nations. And if we now bring in Auguste Comte, Henri Bergson and William James, "the modern mind" deals with absolutely every human person affected by atheism and capitalism (to the extent these are influenced by Comte's positivism); by relativism in ethics (to the extent influenced by Bergson's conviction that reality is change); by utilitarian and pragmatic conceptions of truth and conduct (to the extent influenced by William James). "The modern mind" expresses, then, an enormous number of human persons—all those affected in their concrete and practical lives by the "makers" of the modern mind Maritain and Phelan listed.

To summarize, then: the phrase "the modern mind" involves several factors: (1) a thinker whose writings or lectures contain (2)

---

[30] See Gilson, *Unity*, p. ix.

ideas which are pivotal, germinal, dynamic, energizing and (3) which come to be disseminated so widely (4) that they infiltrate and deeply affect the majority of people in an era and a place (5) in what they think and say, in how they act and react. These latter (the majority of individuals) are directly the "modern minds"; the former (the man or woman of ideas) is the "maker" of modern minds; in between are the disseminators, propagandizers and popularizers, who are "makers" too in an important but subordinated and derived sense.

"The Modern Mind": 1960–1980

In the light of that summary, a "maker" of modern minds is someone whose ideas are "pivotal, germinal, dynamic energizing and . . . come to be disseminated so widely that they infiltrate and deeply affect the majority of people in an era and a place in what they think and say, in how they act and react." To those "makers" listed in the previous section, George F. Will in his syndicated column of March 13, 1979, added three additional "makers of the modern mind and of the modern sense of disorder today": Darwin, Freud, Einstein.[31] Why so? His answers, the first of which comes at the beginning of his column and the second at its end, are elliptic but provocative.

The essence of modern consciousness, which Einstein did so much to shape, is that things are not what they seem. Charles Darwin asserted a continuum between man and lesser matter. Sigmund Freud's theme, developed in his work on infant sexuality, is that there are uncharted continents of mysterous depths within us. According to modern physics, a person pounding a table is pounding mostly space and electricity— and the person doing the pounding is mostly space and electricity [too]. . . . Matter, Einstein said, is [simply] a form of energy. To increase the speed of an object is to contract the passage of its time. Light is pulled down by gravity because light is subject, at some point, to laws governing substantial objects. And last month scientists announced evidence of gravity waves—evidence that further confirms Einstein's vision:

---

[31] See *Chicago Sun-Times* for March 13, 1979.

gravitic energy is a form of radiation. Things are not what they seem.

In the final paragraphs the columnist turns again to Darwin, Freud and the physicist.

Copernicus removed mankind from the center of the universe, but at least Newton said the universe is intelligible, even decorous. Newton was a great orderer, whose clockwork theory of the universe gave rise, through the seepage of science into the wider culture, to clockwork art—the dignified classicism of the 18th century. And it gave rise to clockwork political theory, the clearest expression of which is the U.S. Constitution, a serene system of "checks and balances." . . .

Then came the three makers of the modern mind and of the modern sense of disorder—Darwin, Freud, Einstein. Darwin imbedded man in the mud, or, more precisely, he said mankind is continuous with the slime from which mankind has crept. Rather than nature's final word, mankind may be an early bead on an endless string.

Darwin gave an unsentimental view of the childhood of the species [but] Freud gave an unsentimental view of childhood. And he linked the artifices of civilization with the uncaged furies in the jungle within man.

Newtonian physics could be explained visually, at least a bit, for laymen, on a billiard table. But Einsteinian physics wraps in uncertainty the concepts we use, from childhood on, to make sense of everyday experience—the concepts of space, time, matter. Modern physics puts laymen severely in their place, which is outside the conversation of science. Yet Einstein, who expanded our sense of life's mysteriousness, insisted that the essential Einsteinian insight is philosophic . . . and it is this: the difference between what the most and the least learned people know is inexpressibly trivial in relation to all that is unknown.

Why does Will consider that famous biologist, psychologist and physicist to have produced the contemporary mind? For two reasons, the first of which is that each of them has caused us to believe that things are not what they seem. However much a man may appear to have immaterial dimensions and powers, he is material since matter is a continuum of which he is a part (Darwin). However normal and well adjusted someone may seem, he contains deep, dark, mysterious forces conditioning or even threatening his psychological equilibrium constantly (Freud). However solid and matter-of-fact physical objects (including humans) may seem, they are mostly space and electrical charges, the matter of which they are made is itself a form of energy, speed is translated into time, gravity into radiation (Einstein). And these beliefs in a thing's not being what it appears result in the conviction (often subconscious but effective) that our spontaneous knowledge must yield to technical knowledge if we are to escape deception: spontaneous knowledge left uncorrected deceives us as to the true nature of reality. And we can be left feeling uneasy, uncertain, wary, depressed, vaguely guilty.

The second reason why Darwin, Freud and Einstein are "makers" of contemporary mentality is that each makes us realize that a human existent does not amount to much—certainly, his cognitive powers and spiritual dimension (if this latter exists at all) are minimal and not worthy of much praise. Each of us has crept from slime and, figuratively, is merely one "early bead on an endless string" (Darwin). Each carries within himself a jungle of uncaged Furies (Freud). No one can make sense of his own everyday spatial, temporal, material universe without assistance from trained scientists, and the intellectual ability and accomplishments of even the best of these are totally trivial in the face of what still remains unknown (Einstein). And, again, feelings of inadequacy, unworthiness, frustration, fright can befall us, and we thereby experience "the modern sense of disorder" which the columnist traces to those three "makers" of the contemporary mind. An inference to be drawn from his account of them is that a human individual is, in the last analysis, of little value and significance.

In stark and explicit contrast to this view is existentialism, according to which each human person alone is real. Worthwhileness and significance—in a word, reality—resides in the uniqueness, never-to-be-repeatedness, originality of a human individual who is "actually exercising his freedom. The reason why he is unique and uniquely so is that he is free. He is a human existent, endowed with intellect and will, who thus can freely fashion himself and stand out from others. This uniqueness is not in the abstract or in the past or even in the future: it is in the concrete, here-and-now exercise of his freedom in this or that choice, which is his and no other's and which even he himself can never reduplicate exactly, because any other decision will be at least numerically distinct and because he will never again find himself in these identical circumstances."[32]

Such is the basic reaction of all radical existentialists, whether atheist or theist, to the downgrading of individual men and women by biology, psychoanalysis or physics. And Sartre, Camus, Marcel, Buber and the rest all take their initial cue from Kierkegaard. "The evolution of the whole world," he wrote in 1847, "tends to show the absolute importance of the category of the individual apart from the crowd." In 1848: "Each human being has infinite reality." In 1850: "In the eyes of God, the infinite spirit, all the millions that have lived and now live do not make a crowd: He only sees each individual."[33]

Fathered by Kierkegaard, those existentialists begot groups in the antiwar years of the 1960s with such interesting names as the "New Breed," the "Free Speech Movement," "Hippies," the "Woodstock Generation" with its hard rock and hard drugs, the "Flower Children"; the "Me-generation" in protests against nuclear energy; in more peaceful circumstances the nameless aspirants to a simple life-style where love and tolerance should reign; the charismatics. But however diverse in name and style, all of them have in common the conviction that each individual human existent is supremely and solely important and, therefore, real. And this conviction issues into two norms for practical life. Each person is to determine *for himself* what he shall do and what his values are.[34] Second, let us all love one another, since each individual is worthwhile and, therefore, lovable—"Make love, not war," so the slogan went.

---

[32] L. Sweeney, S.J., "Gabriel Marcel's Position on God," *New Scholasticism* 44 (1970), 111; reprinted above as ch. 23. This sort of existentialism I shall call "unauthentic" or "radical" below—see portion of this chapter corresponding to n. 35.

[33] The quotations from Kierkegaard are from G. M. Andersen (trans.) and P. P. Rohde (ed.), *The Diary of Søren Kierkegaard* (New York: Philosophical Library, 1960), pp. 102, 103 and 106.

[34] This is Sartre's explicit position: "My freedom is the unique foundation of values. And since I am the being by virtue of whom values exist, nothing—absolutely nothing—can justify me in adopting this or that value or scale of values. And my freedom is in anguish at finding that it is the baseless basis of values." Sartre's statement is given by G. Marcel, *The Philosophy of Existentialism* (New York: Citadel Press, 1964), p. 87.

Aquinas and Those Previous Decades

Our next step in this historical perspective of our contemporary world could be to consider deconstructionism and other postmodern developments (see paragraph corresponding to notes 20–24 above). But first, let us pause to consider how Thomas might help on the topics raised in the decades just sketched and still operative in some areas today—namely, existentialism itself, morality, astrophysics and love.

(a) Existentialism and Humanism

The fact that Aquinas is an existentialist, rightly and authentically understood, should win him, initially at least, an audience, and the fact that his is an authentic existentialism could alert them to the possibility of a genuine humanism which gives a primacy to man but not at the expense of what is nonhuman (e.g., God). Let me explain briefly.

Existentialism is a philosophical position in which primacy is given to "existence" (whatever that noun may mean), in which "existence" confers reality because it bestows perfection, worthwhileness, significance upon whatever is perfect, worthwhile, significant. In short, it is a doctrine where "to be real" is "to exist." But what is "existence"? For Sartre, Marcel, and so on, "to exist" is "to be human." Only humans, only subjects are real in the sense of intrinsically and *per se* being perfect, valuable, significant, and what makes them alone be real is the fact that they *are subjects* actually exercising their freedom (see paragraph corresponding to note 34 above). Such a philosophical position is an existentialism (although unauthentic because "existence" here does not mean—at least in English—what it seems to mean by force of the term itself) and it is an absolute (or exaggerated) humanism because only humans are real and everything nonhuman (God and subhumans) are not real in themselves but solely if and as men and women project or use them.

But "to exist" can also be taken as "to be actual" and then any actual existent, no matter what sort it may be, is real by the very fact that it actually exists. Reality is not restricted to any one kind of being, whether human, subhuman or, for that matter, superhuman, but extends as far as does actuality itself. If, as seems reasonable, "authentic" signifies that the item of which it is predicated is genuinely what its name indicates it should be and seems to be, then the reply which equates "existence" with "be-ing actually" constitutes an existentialism which is authentic.[35]

But this authentic existentialism is also a humanism since it places individual men and women higher than all other existents save God because each human existent by reason of his spiritual powers of intellect and will is free, thereby fashioning a psychological individuality of subjectivity which complements his entitative individuality of supposit and nature.[36] Yet it is a theistic humanism because it culminates in acknowledging God as the efficient, final and exemplary cause that human subjects (and, for that matter, all other existents) do exist.[37] As their creator He sets forth guidelines for them to follow if they are truly to develop themselves to their full stature and attain the happiness they deserve and He intends. Freedom is, indeed, self-determination but not in the sense that each person determines what objectively is valuable[38] but that each can choose whether or not to accept the values presented to him. Freedom has to do, at bottom, with efficient and not with value-determining causality.[39] If unauthentic or radical existentialists would listen to Thomas, their humanism would be better for it.

---

[35] See ch. 22 above: "Existentialism: Authentic and Unauthentic."

[36] See *Authentic Metaphysics*, pp. 181–93.

[37] This acknowledgment occurs when one becomes aware that existence in any actual thing is a gift, and a gift indicates a Giver, who ultimately proves to be God. More fully expressed: the actuation of existence perfects the existent and yet is other than his essence, with the result that no material existent exists of its very nature; yet things do exist, do have that perfection of actuality but, as we said, not of their very nature; therefore, there must be an Existent whose very nature or essence is to exist, who of His very nature is actuality and thus needs no cause, and yet who can and does properly cause all else to exist: God, subsistent actuality. Also see L. Sweeney, S.J., "God Does Exist," *Ensign* 1 (Spring 1967): 5–10.

As a resolute witness to contemporary atheism, see these books by Paul Kurtz and published (with one exception) by Prometheus Press (Buffalo, N.Y.): *In Defense of Secular Humanism* (1983), *Eupraxophy: Living Without Religion* (1989), *Forbidden Fruit: The Ethics of Humanism* (1988), *The New Scepticism* (1992), *Toward a New Enlightenment* (New Brunswick, N.J.: Transaction Publishers, 1994).

[38] On Sartre's interpretation of self-determination see n. 34 above.

[39] This causality is a counterpart of content-determining-cause re knowledge. On this latter see n. 7 above; *Authentic Metaphysics*, pp. 325–26, 346–47.

(b) Natural Law Morality

The fact that Aquinas' existentialism is authentic can also profit radical existentialists, as well even as nonexistentialists, with reference to natural law. "Natural law" is anathema to radical existentialists who accept Sartre's dictum "Existence precedes essence or nature," where the verb "precedes" is equivalent to "eliminates." On the other hand, "natural law" can be taken in too rigid and narrow a sense by traditionalists and essentialists. What better interpretation does Thomas himself offer? In his existentialism "essence" or "nature" includes absolutely everything in someone except existence; therefore, it comprises not only a man's soul and matter (his substantial being), his faculties and their operations, the operative habits (both moral and intellectual) which perfect them, his skills; but also all his relationships—spatial, temporal, ecological, familial, civic, cultural, environmental: all these are the actual situations in which he lives, all these help constitute his nature (see S.T., I, 84, 7 resp.). But the natural law is founded directly upon nature; therefore, natural law is founded upon and must express all those actual and intrinsic perfections, including, yes, his substantial being (which he has in common with other people and which establishes the objective core of natural law), his operative powers, habits and skills, but also his relationships (which may be uniquely his).

Thus existentially conceived, natural law remains an objective norm, based not only on the accidental but also on the substantial aspects of his being (thus it would be much better than the often arbitrary and entirely subjective set of values a radical existentialist such as Sartre might elaborate for himself). But it is more concrete and flexible than more traditional and abstract conceptions of natural law because it takes into account the entire actual person—not only in his substantial being and properties but also in all his individual circumstances and situations (hence, it may offer a greater opening to individual morally justified choices in population control and natural family-planning).[40]

---

[40] On natural law see the papal encyclicals listed in notes 9 and 13 above; Kenneth L. Woodward, "Life, Death and the Pope," *Newsweek*, April 10, 1995, pp. 56–59; Paul Gray, "Man of the Year: Pope John Paul II—Empire of the Spirit," *Time*, January 2, 1995, p. 57; and John Elson, "Lives of the Pope," *ibid.*, pp. 60–76; Dennis Byrne, "Numbed to Death by Individualism," *Chicago Sun-Times*, Column, April 6, 1995; Deal W. Hudson, "Human Nature, Human Rights, and the Crisis among Western Intellectuals," *Notes et Documents* of

(c) Astrophysics and Creation

Aquinas' existentialism also can perhaps hold the attention even of astrophysicists, who increasingly are asking metaphysical questions concerning existence and creation, to judge by the news media. In *Time* for June 27, 1977, the "Science" article was entitled "Witnesses to a Creation," where "witness" refers to an evolving star—called MWC 349—in the constellation Cygnus which is forming its own planets from the enormous glowing disc surrounding it (p. 71). On November 25, 1977, the *Chicago Tribune* carried an article entitled "Another Clue Found to Secret of Creation"—namely, a dipotron, which is a new sort of quark. The long article, "Those Baffling Black Holes," in the "Science" section of Time for September 4, 1978, often speaks of "existence," as these samplings reveal. "If whole stars can vanish from sight within black holes," which figuratively are "rips in the very fabric of space and time" but more literally are mathematical figments solving the complex equations of Einstein's theory of gravity (p. 53), if those stars are "literally crushed out of existence, where has their matter gone? To another place and another time? Where did it come from? In searching for answers to the fundamental questions raised by black holes, scientists are infringing on the realm of philosophers and theologians.

Institut International Jacques Maritain [hereafter: *Notes et Documents*], n.s. 38 (September-December 1993), 31–54, where Hudson gives an impressive defense of the natural law theory of J. Maritain (with references) but also a justified critique of J. Derrida and other postmoderns; Dan M. Crone, "Is Natural Law Innate? A Textual Study in the Writings of St. Bonaventure and St. Thomas Aquinas" (Ph.D. diss., Loyola University Chicago, 1995)—see especially pp. 2–23 for a survey of secondary literature; "Summary and Conclusion," pp. 354–93; Alan Gewirth, "Natural Law, Human Action and Morality," in Rocco Porreco (ed.), *The Georgetown Symposium on Ethics* (Lanham, Md.: University Press of America, 1984), pp. 67–90; Henry Veatch, "A Possible Mis-Step in the Articulation of the Grifinnboyle Moral Philosophy," in W. J. Carroll and F. J. Furlong (eds.), *Greek and Medieval Studies* (New York/Bern: Peter Lang Publishing, Inc., 1994), pp. 145–60; Servais Pinckaers, *The Sources of Christian Ethics* [hereafter: Pinckaers], trans. M. T. Noble (Washington, D.C.: The Catholic University of America Press, 1995), chs. 7 and 14–17.

For a radically opposed view, see Robert Wright, *The Moral Animal: The New Science of Evolutionary Psychology* (New York: Pantheon, 1994)—see Steven Pinker's review in *New York Times Book Review*, September 9, 1994, pp. 3–4. Also see Robert Wright, "Our Cheating Hearts," *Time*, August 15, 1994, pp. 44–52; idem, "The Evolution of Despair," *ibid.*, August 28, 1995, pp. 50–57. Also see A. J. Dyck, *Rethinking Rights and Responsibilities: The Moral Bonds of Community* (New York: Pilgrim Press, 1995).

They are trying to find the meaning of life, of being, of the universe itself" (p. 50). A bit later in the article: "astrophysics intersects metaphysics" when the scientist studies black holes and realizes that "the gravitational collapse of stars suggests that the universe, too, can begin falling back in on itself. If that happens, its billions of galaxies will eventually crush together and would form a super black hole. And what then? Nothing? Or would a new process of creation somehow begin?" (p. 54).

Again: religion and science, as Lance Morrow observes in Time for February 5, 1979, "find themselves jostled into a strange metaphysical intimacy" when they agree "about certain facts concerning the creation of the universe." According to *Genesis* "the universe began in a single, flashing act of creation: the divine intellect willed all into being, *ex nihilo.*" On the other hand, an increasing number of scientists propose the "Big Bang" theory: "the universe had an instant of creation: it came to be in a vast fireball explosion 15 or 20 billion years ago. The shrapnel created by that explosion is still flying outward" to fashion the universe (p. 149). But in this apparent convergence of science and theology in the Big Bang theory of cosmogony and cosmology, has science really validated the biblical myth of creation? However one fields that question, this remains true: "the new coincidence of scientific and theological versions of creation seems to have opened up a conversation [between theologians, philosophers and scientists] that has been neglected for centuries" and that can lead to the most interesting inquiry of all: what came before the Big Bang? (p. 150).

How easily Aquinas can enter into that dialogue and what helpful insights he may contribute to it are readily gathered from the facts that his position gives primacy to actual existence: to be real is to exist; that for him God as agent properly causes all things actually to be since His very nature is existence; that to create is efficiently and freely to cause something actually to exist which before was actual in no way; that creation is simply an exercise of God's proper causality, through which an existent universe replaces nothingness and by which beings are produced *precisely as beings* since "being" is "that which actually exists"—therefore, creation occurs on the very level of being itself, since God properly causes *being* in all beings.[41]

---

[41] For a discussion of creation as production of beings as being, see my ch. 14 above: "Esse in Albert the Great's Texts on Creation in *Summa de Creaturis* and *Scriptum in Libros Sententiarum*," prgrs. corresponding to notes 45–60.

Before departing from this section on contemporary science, let us note at least three of the many developments within astrophysics which have occurred recently. The first is the successful flight of Voyager 2, the "ungainly one-ton craft with its spindly appendages and 12-foot-wide radio disk," which started its journey through the solar system in 1977, passed by Jupiter, Saturn, Uranus, Neptune (and its moon Triton) and Pluto, and then went beyond that system "at a speed of about 35,000 miles an hour, zoomed on on what will probably be a never-ending journey through interstellar space. Voyager will continue to radio back information about cosmic rays and other things for another 25 years, until its nuclear batteries become too weak. Then its creators . . . will send it one last command to turn off its radio antenna, breaking its umbilical connection to Earth." Voyager is, indeed, "destined to go on forever, if it is not destroyed by a meteorite, swallowed by a black hole, or intercepted by intelligent creatures inhabiting other worlds."[42]

The second recent astrophysical development is the challenge to the Big Bang theory which issues from data from the Hubble Space Telescope on the age of the universe. If "the universe is between 8 billion and 12 billion years old," whereas "our own galaxy has stars believed to be as much as 14 billion to 16 billion years old," a "revolution in cosmology" may lie ahead. Either "astrophysicists don't understand stars as well as they thought—but that's considered unlikely." Or "something may be wrong with the revered theory that the universe began with a Big Bang and has been

---

For an attempt to question the need of God as creator, see Stephen W. Hawking, *A Brief History of Time: From the Big Bang to Black Holes* (New York: Bantam Books, 1988): that question arises because of "the possibility that space-time was finite but had no boundary, which means that it had no beginning, no moment of creation" (p. 116) and hence had no place for a creator (p. 141; also see pp. 171–75). For a refutation see Stanley L. Jaki, "Evicting the Creator," *Reflections* 7 (Spring 1988), pp. 1, 20–21 (with references to books on creation by J. S. Trefil and S. Weinberg); *idem, God and the Cosmologists* (Washington, D.C.: Regnery Gateway, 1989), especially pp. 89–94. Also see Paul Davies, *The Mind of God. The Scientific Basis for a Rational World* (New York: Simon and Schuster, 1992).

[42] Ronald Kotulak, "Goodbye, Columbus: Voyager 2," *Chicago Tribune*, August 4, 1989, p. 2. Magellan is another spectacular spacecraft, launched May 4, 1989, to view Venus, the "Evening Star" and Earth's sister planet, "formed about 4.6 billion years ago from a massive ring of gas and dust spinning around the sun"—see "The Secrets of Venus," *U.S. News and World Report*, May 13, 1991, pp. 60–71.

expanding ever since." The result may be that "the Big Bang [theory] may be shot."[43]

A third development is the publication of Frank J. Tipler's book, *The Physics of Immortality: Modern Cosmology, God and the Resurrection of the Dead* (New York: Doubleday, 1994), which its author describes as a "book proclaiming the unification of science and religion" and asserting "that theology is a branch of physics, that physicists can infer by calculation the existence of God and the likelihood of the resurrection of the dead to eternal life in exactly the same way as physicists calculate the properties of the electron" (p. ix). A former atheist, Tipler confesses himself to be "as surprised as the reader . . . that one day I would be writing a book purporting to show that the central claims of Judeo-Christian theology are in fact true, that these claims are straightforward deductions of the laws of physics as we now understand them. I have been forced into these conclusions by the inexorable logic of my own special branch of physics"—namely, "global general relativity," a branch of physics, "created in the late 1960s and early 1970s . . . by Roger Penrose and Stephen Hawking, which enables us to draw very deep and very general conclusions about the structure of space and time by looking at the universe in its *totality* in both time and space" (*ibid.*).

Such a view is not only of "the *visible universe*: that part of the universe whose past can be seen from Earth" and which "is only a tiny fraction of reality. The universe is almost certain to continue to exist for another 100 billion years, and probably much longer" and hence the spacetime of the earth lies mainly in the future. Therefore, "as a global relativist I realized that I would have to study the future of the universe, since the future comprises almost all of space and time. It is not possible to look at the universe in its totality in both time and space while ignoring almost all of space and time" (p. x).

Thereafter Tipler speaks of "chaotic evolution" in all astronomical scales, "chaos in the society of intelligent living beings" (*ibid.*),

---

[43] Michael D. Lemonick, "Oops . . . Wrong Answer," *Time*, November 7, 1994, p. 69. For more information see *idem* and J. Madeleine Nash, "Unraveling the Universe," *ibid.*, March 6, 1995, pp. 76–84. On the discovery by the Hubble that giant black holes do exist, see Michael D. Lemonick, *ibid.*, June 6, 1994, p. 60; on how a new star is formed, see *Chicago Tribune*, June 7, 1995, sec. 1, p. 7.

"biological concepts translated into physics language" so that even human beings are "subject to the same laws of physics as electrons and atoms" (p. xi). The result? "A human being [is] nothing but a particular type of machine, the human brain is nothing but an information processing device, the human soul is nothing but a program being run on a computer called the brain" (p. xi). This very fact "that humans are machines of a very special sort allows us to prove that we humans probably have free will, that we shall have life after death in an abode that closely resembles the Heaven of the great world religions, and that life, far from being insignificant, can be regarded as the ultimate cause of the very existence of the universe itself" (*ibid.*).

One reviewer of Tipler's book finds it to be "a wonderfully ambitious, painfully sincere tour de force—an attempt, sometimes brilliant, sometimes absurd, to stretch scientific reasoning to its breaking point."[44] What would Aquinas make of the book? Probably he would wait until the dust had cleared from the explosion which Tipler's book may cause and then point out how often Tipler speaks of "existence"—e.g., "infer by calculation the existence of God," "the universe is almost certain to continue to exist," "life . . . can be regarded as the ultimate cause of the very existence of the universe itself." Thomas then would strip away the context of constructural knowledge and language within which Tipler places "existence"[45] and refer him back to the paragraph linked to note 41 above—in this physical universe actual existence has primacy since to be of value and worth is actually to exist, God's very nature is existence and as agent He properly causes all things to exist, and so on.

As to Tipler's conception of human freedom proved because "humans are machines of a very special sort," whose brains are "nothing but an information processing device," and the human soul a computer program, Aquinas would replace it with his conception of human freedom of choice as rooted in human persons

---

[44] George Johnson in *New York Times Book Review*, October 9, 1994, pp. 15–16. That the human mind is not a computer see Roger Penrose, *Shadows of the Mind: A Search for the Missing Science of Consciousness* (New York: Oxford University Press, 1994). Also see *idem, The Emperor's New Mind: Concerning Computers, Minds and the Laws of Physics* (New York: Oxford University Press, 1989); John Eccles and Daniel N. Robinson, *The Wonder of Being Human: Our Brain and Our Mind* (New York: The Free Press, 1984), especially ch. 10; John R. Searle, *The Rediscovery of the Mind* (Cambridge, Mass.: The MIT Press, 1992).

[45] On constructural knowledge, see my ch. 25 above, prgrs. corresponding to nn. 59–63; *Authentic Metaphysics*, p. 146, n. 10.

existing as each a single composite entity of spiritual soul and individual body, in human knowledge as integrated sensation/intellection and thus one knows a material object not only as this good but also as good—a knowledge which thereby allows the human person a choice between it and some other good or even a choice not to choose at all.[46]

What would Thomas' reaction be to the two previously mentioned contemporary developments in astrophysics issuing from Voyager 2 and the Hubble telescope? It would be one of sheer awe—awe at the ingenuity of those who made the two crafts, awe at the intelligence of those interpreting the data sent back, awe at the extent and beauty of the solar system and of the universe itself as it discloses how unimaginably vast, intricate and beautiful the heavens really are.[47] Also Thomas would, I am sure, feel dismay at the inaccuracy and inadequacy of Aristotle's conception (necessarily based on then current astronomers—Eudoxus and Callippus) of a geocentric universe enclosed by an outermost sphere of Fixed Stars, which contains either forty-eight or fifty-four lower spheres, of which that of the moon is lowest.[48] Aquinas would open up his

---

[46] See Aquinas, *Summa Theologiae*, questions 59 and 82–83. Also see *Authentic Metaphysics*, pp. 288–89 and 290–93; Austin Fagothey, *Right and Reason* [hereafter: Fagothey], 6th ed. (St. Louis: C. V. Mosby, 1976), ch. 13; James E. Royce, *Man and His Nature: A Philosophical Psychology* (New York: McGraw-Hill, 1961), ch. 12, pp. 186–224 (with good bibliography); G. P. Klubertanz, *The Philosophy of Human Nature* (New York: Appleton-Century-Crofts, 1976), ch. 10: "The Will," especially pp. 235–54; Pinckaers, ch. 16: "Human Freedom According to St. Thomas Aquinas," pp. 379–99.

[47] To quote R. Kotulak again (see n. 42 above): Once the engineers and scientists at the California Institute of Technology and NASA's Jet Propulsion Laboratory have turned off the radio antenna on Voyager 2, "the spacecraft will see many other wondrous things in the galaxy, but it no longer will share them with us. Traveling at the rate of almost one million miles a day, it will come near Barnard's star in the year 8571; pass close to Ross 248 in the year 40176; whiz by Sirius, the brightest star in the sky, about 300,000 years from now, and gaze down at a star called DM + 27 1311 in about a million years. By then, Voyager will be about 282 trillion miles from Earth." On the Galileo spacecraft launched Oct. 18, 1989, the 746-pound robot probe it released into Jupiter's atmosphere on Dec. 7, 1995, and the valuable data sent back to NASA Jet Propulsion Laboratory (Pasadena, Calif.), see Peter Gorner, *Chicago Tribune*, Dec. 7, 1995, p.1; Jane E. Allen, *Chicago Sun-Times*, Dec. 8, 1995, p. 30; Peter Gorner, *Chicago Tribune*, Jan. 23, 1996, p. 3.

[48] On the astronomy grounding Aristotle's cosmogony and cosmology, see Thomas Heath, *Aristarchus of Samos: A History of Greek Astronomy to Aristarchus* (Oxford: Clarendon Press, 1913); Augustinus Nolte, *Het Godsbegrip bij Aristoteles*

own cosmology and cosmogony to all contemporary astronomical
and astrophysical data on the universe, whenever relevant,[49] while
retaining his conception of material things as each a single composite of this or that essence (= substantial form, prime matter, accidental perfections) and existence, which itself actuates the essence
and thereby essentializes and limits itself.[50] Accordingly, his metaphysics, as well as his philosophy of nature in its basics, would not
be changed but rather enriched by new existential evidence of our
expanded and ever expanding universe: it would be as open-ended
as is the universe itself.

(d) Love

Finally, Aquinas has something constructive to say on a topic
outside astrophysics and at the very center of the almost constant
concern in psychological labs and literature, in classrooms, in ecclesiastical centers, in religious and spiritual formation, in novels,
contemporary theater, movies, TV soap operas. That topic is love.
One need not document in any detail the omnipresent interest in
and attempts to practice love. Let these two quotations suffice.
John Powell, S.J., the author of paperbacks on spiritual and psychological matters, states in *The Secret of Staying in Love* (Niles, Ill.:

(Nijmegen-Utrecht: Dekker u. Van de Vegt, 1940); Joseph Owens, *The Doctrine
of Being in the Aristotelian Metaphysics*, 3rd ed. (Toronto: Pontifical Institute of
Mediaeval Studies, 1978), ch. 18, pp. 435–54.

Thomas' dismay at Aristotle's inaccurate astronomical conceptions, as well
as their influence upon his philosophy, may very well have already arisen as
the result of a mystical revelation during Mass on December 6, 1273, after
which he totally ceased writing. He confided to his companion Reginald: "All
that I have written seems to me like straw compared to what has now been
revealed to me" (see James A. Weisheipl, *Friar Thomas d'Aquino: His Life,
Thought and Work* [Garden City, N.Y.: Doubleday, 1974], pp. 320–23). God
may then have revealed to him how erroneous and misleading was the
astronomy upon which Aristotle had necessarily relied—a revelation to
Aquinas which anticipated the amazing data sent back to us by Voyager 2, the
Hubble telescope and other such devices. For other interpretations of Thomas' sudden silence, see *Notes et Documents* (1993), p. 73.

[49] Thomas' openness in his own lifetime to truth wherever found is clear
from his desire to ascertain the exact meaning of the writings of others (e.g.,
Aristotle, *Liber de Causis*, Proclus' *Elements of Theology*, Avicenna, Averroës,
etc.) by procuring the best available translations of them. See James A.
Weisheipl, *Friar Thomas d'Aquino*, pp. 149–53.

[50] See my *Authentic Metaphysics*, chs. 4–5; on existence as limiting itself
through an essence, see *ibid.*, pp. 119–29.

Argus Communications, 1974) in a section entitled "Salvation in and through love," p. 44: "More important than any psychological theory, teaching, or therapeutic technique, that which heals and promotes human change and growth is a one-to-one relationship of love." Second: "It is an absolute human certainty that no one can know his own beauty or perceive a sense of his own worth until it has been reflected back to him in the mirror of another loving, caring human being" (p. 55).[51]

Granted, then, the necessity of love in one's life and our contemporaries' concern about it, but what theory of Aquinas is especially apropos? His proposal that in our nonconstructural knowledge the known makes the knower, that what is known is the content-determining-cause of my spontaneous cognition. Let me explain.

According to Kant and neo-Kantians the knower makes the known; he applies the *a priori* forms of space and time and the categories of his mind to sense data, which thereby are constructed into phenomena.[52] But one loves what one knows; but one has made what one knows; therefore, one loves what he himself has made; therefore, the object of his love is not the beloved herself but the beloved as a phenomenon constructed by himself; consequently, love of another precisely as other and in her own reality is impossible.

Unselfish love flows from Aquinas' epistemological position much more facilely. For him the known makes the knower, inas-

---

[51] Powell's authorities on love are Viktor Frankl, C. G. Jung, Erich Fromm, and Henry Stack Sullivan. Also see Aquinas, *S.T.*, I, q. 20 and I–II, qq. 26–28; Fagothey, ch. 15: "Love," pp. 159–67, with references to Anders Nygren and Martin D'Arcy; my *Authentic Metaphysics*, pp. 201–4 (with references to E. Gilson, R. Johann, F. Wilhelmsen, J. de Finance), pp. 283–84, 290–93. According to the psychologist Gerald G. May, *Addiction and Grace* (San Francisco: Harper and Row, 1988), p. 1: "All human beings have an inborn desire for God. Whether we are consciously religious or not, this desire is our deepest longing. . . . Some of us have repressed this desire. . . . Or we may experience it . . . as a longing for wholeness, completion, or fulfillment. Regardless of how we describe it, it is a longing for love. It is a hunger to love, to be loved, and to move closer to the source of love. This yearning is the essence of the human spirit."

[52] On Kant's influence even upon radical existentialism, as well as upon British analytic philosophy, see E. L. Mascall, "The Gulf in Philosophy: Is Thomism the Bridge?" *Thomist* 38 (January 1974), 22: each of those theories has in common Kant's position that "the object of human knowledge is manufactured by the experiencing subject." Mascall cleverly characterizes the British philosophers as offering clarity without content, the Continental existentialists as offering content without clarity.

much as the known is the content-determining-cause of spontaneous cognition; but the knower loves when a good presents itself
(i.e., the object of love is the good-as-known); but a good presents
itself through knowledge (which is the direct result of the known
affecting the knower); therefore, the good presenting itself through
knowledge causes love in the knower, who thereby loves the good
as it itself is and not as it is constructed by the knower. Hence, the
beloved causes my love: I love a friend precisely as he is in and for
himself. Love is then unselfish.

Obviously, the key to that argumentation is this: what is known
is the content-determining-cause of spontaneous knowledge. Upon
what does Aquinas base that proposition? Upon the brilliant insight Aristotle expresses in *On the Soul*, Book III, ch. 2, 425b26 and
426a10: "The actuation of what is sensed and of the sense is one
and the same (although the being of each is not the same), but that
actuation is in the sense and not in what is sensed."

If we transfer that insight from sense perception to any spontaneous knowledge, we obtain this: the actuation of what is known
and of the faculty knowing is one and the same but it is present in
the faculty and not in the known. It is an actuation of the known
and is caused by the known, while simultaneously it also is an
actuation of the knower too and, in fact, is solely in the knower.
This is, as we have stressed above,[53] truly remarkable. The very
same actuation which precognitively conditions, determines, forms
the faculty by being present in it is also the actuation of that which
is known (precisely as known, though, and not as it is outside the
cognitive process, where its actuations are its substantial and accidental forms and its act of existing) and which is causing it in the
knower. Through this actuation, which is *in* and *of* the knower and
of and *by* the known, the object known is the content-determining-
cause of my knowledge and, thereby, also of my love. Accordingly,
genuine and unselfish love of the other *as other* issues from Aquinas'
epistemology more easily than from other theories of knowledge
and, especially, from Kant's.[54]

---

[53] See prgr. connected with n. 7 above and the reference it gives to my ch.
21 above, especially to prgrs. corresponding to nn. 16-21.

[54] That the beloved must be the other precisely as other, see Powell, op. cit.,
pp. 64–65: " 'Two solitudes that protect, touch and greet each other' (Rainer
Maria Rilke). Here we find the only reality worthy of the name love. The two
partners drop, however gradually, the projected image which was the first
source of attraction to find the even more beautiful reality of the person. They

Selfish love, on the other hand, has disastrous results even when masquerading as "romantic love." As Stephen Post (referring to Peck—see note 54 immediately preceding) remarks: "The passion of romantic love is actually rooted in egocentric sexual inclinations," which in turn issues into sexual indulgence, which "because without commitment and steadfast love has always led to disease, deception, jealousies and emotional pain" (*ibid.*) and, let me add, to countless abortions in the world today.

But the murders occurring in abortion clinics are not the sole sort, if one accepts the interpretation of Barbara Ehrenreich, "Susan Smith: Corrupted by Love" *Time*, August 7, 1995, p. 78: romantic love [of which Stephen Post speaks above] contributed to Smith's killing her two sons. "There is a theme implicit in the Smith story that ought to be familiar to every woman with a functioning heart, and that theme is love. Not the good kind of love, obviously . . . but the ungovernable, romantic kind of love that the songs tell us about, as in 'addicted to love' and 'I would do anything to hold on to you.' Whether Smith intended to kill herself or just wanted to win back her lover by getting rid of the kids, we will never know for sure. Either way, she was an extremist in the cause of love, and her sons, horribly enough, were human sacrifices to it. . . . Everything in her own sorry history taught her to put the pull of sexual, romantic love above the needs of little children. . . . [Let us not] excuse Susan Smith's crime. But we have to forsake the easy, self-distancing explanations like 'evil' and a knowledge . . . that the 'love' we endlessly celebrate can be a source, sometimes, of endless sorrow."

But at odds with Ehrenreich's essay just quoted is, seemingly, her earlier essay, "The Bright Side of Overpopulation," *Time*, Sep-

---

are willing to acknowledge and respect *otherness* in each other. Each person values and tries to promote the inner vision and mysterious destiny of the other. Each counts it his privilege to assist in the growth and realization of the other's vision and destiny." Also see *idem, A Life-Giving Vision* (New York: Thomas More, 1996).

Also see Stephen G. Post, "Abortion and the Triumph of Eros," *America*, April 28, 1990, p. 427, for the definition of unselfish love by M. Scott Peck, *The Road Less Traveled*: "Genuine love is 'the will to extend one's self for the purpose of nurturing one's own or another's spiritual growth.' This definition emphasizes other-regarding virtues. The good of others should shape one's basic commitments. Such love can be a subsidiary hope for reciprocity, but self-interest can never be the controlling motive."

tember 26, 1994, p. 86, where she recommends "an ecologically responsible sexual ethic. This means, at a minimum, guaranteeing contraception, with abortion as a backup, to all who might need it. But it also means telling our teenagers . . . the best news they could get—that sex, in our overpopulated world, is best seen as a source of fun. . . . Sex . . . belongs squarely in the realm of play."

Love of another as other, romantic love of another for one's self, resultant sexual indulgence issuing into disease, emotional pain, abortion and nonabortive murder, sex conceived as "fun . . . in the realm of play"—how fast one has moved in the previous three paragraphs from a perspective of human persons as each a single spiritual/material existent capable of free, loving, unselfish openness to others to considering sexuality to be not sacred or life-giving but irresponsible animal "fun" and "play."

Now: how would Aquinas prevent the slide from good to bad which those paragraphs picture? His prevention would be at least twofold: clean up the communication media of our current times and, second, reinstate the practice of genuine virtue. To begin with the first: Thomas would insist on radically reforming the current media of communication because of his conviction that the known (i.e., that which bombards our ears, eyes and other senses and, thereby, our minds and emotions) is the content-determining-cause of what we know and desire.[55] But today movies, TV shows, video

---

[55] On the known as content-determining-cause of knowledge and desires see paragraphs corresponding to notes 52–53 above.

Edward W. Oakes, "Why Has American Society Become So Violent?" *America*, September 5, 1992, pp. 102–27, is close to Aquinas' view that *what we know* determines the content of our knowing and desiring when he lists the five roots of violence in America: "(1) the transference of the responsibility for sin and evil from the human heart to social structures; (2) the relativization of ethics; (3) the impact of war on modern culture; (4) the technology of mass communication; and (5) the marginalization of religion in contemporary life." See especially his explanation of the fourth. "The very nature of the format of movies and television . . . are too realistic and too pervasive to expect them not to have an effect on the moral sensibilities of the nation. Our attitude toward life is coarsened because of the media. . . . And the effects this is having upon our young is simply devastating." Oakes then refers to Neil Postman's books, *Amusing Ourselves to Death* and *Conscientious Objections*, where Postman "notes the real loss that television has brought in its wake: 'One might say that the main difference between an adult and a child is that the adult knows about certain facets of life—its mysteries, its contradictions, its violence, its tragedies—that are not considered suitable for children to

games, national computer On Line networks, Internet, rap songs, magazines, newspapers and other media are putting across false views (such as those already listed above) on human persons, their nature and goals. And these false, pagan, destructive views are determining what we take human beings to be, how they ought to act, what makes them happy.[56] Consequently, Thomas would advocate a widespread reformation of our communication industry.

---

know. As children move toward adulthood, we reveal these secrets to them in ways we believe they are prepared to manage. But television makes this impossible. . . . It requires a constant supply of novel and interesting information to hold its audience. This means that all adult secrets—social, sexual, physical, and the like—are revealed. Television forces the entire culture to come out of the closet, taps every existing taboo. As a consequence of this, childhood innocence is impossible.' "

[56] On how rap lyrics are coarsening and desensitizing contemporary society, see George F. Will, "America's Slide Into the Sewer," *Newsweek*, July 30, 1990, p. 64; on Hollywood's similar effect, see John Leo, "At a Cultural Crossroads," *U.S. News and World Report*, December 20, 1993, p. 14.

On how schools are harming, not helping, students achieve education in literacy, let alone in morality, see Robert Brustein, "What Price [Political] Correctness?" *Chicago Tribune Magazine*, January 16, 1994, pp. 11–14; Howard Witt, "Bad Grades for New Age Education," *Chicago Tribune*, May 14, 1995, sec. 1, pp. 5–6; Eugene Kennedy, "Dumbing Down American Students," *ibid.*, February 1, 1993, sec. 1, p. 9; *idem*, " 'Do-gooders' don't when they eradicate competition from life," *ibid.*, July 12, 1993, sec. 1, p. 13; Christina Hoff Sommers, "Teaching the Virtues: A Blueprint for Moral Education," *Chicago Tribune Magazine*, September 12, 1992, pp. 14–18; Charles J. Sykes, "The Attack on Excellence: High academic standards and expectations give way to 'feel-good' learning in America's schools," *ibid.*, August 27, 1995, pp. 17–23. In contrast to "government officials in Caroline County, Md., [who] are weighing a proposal to pay teen mothers $30 a month to avoid pregnancy," Haven Bradford Gow, "Teach teenagers moral values," *Chicago Sun-Times*, September 9, 1990, p. 23, commends "school officials in Chesapeake, Va., [who] have been trying to promote moral values like chastity and self-worth, pointing out that chastity is the best way to avoid sexually transmitted diseases and pregnancies. . . . When young people develop noble minds and characters, they will know how to conduct themselves not only in the sexual realm, but also in all other important areas of life."

On morality (or lack thereof) in our current world, see this series of columns by Eugene Kennedy in the *Chicago Tribune*: "It's a spiritual crisis, stupid, not the economy," December 10, 1992, p. 14; "Pseudo-morality must be swept away by the real thing," May 10, 1993, p. 19; "Our life choices show a dearth of what we used to call morality," July 19, 1993, p. 11; "At a time when we need it most, where is virtue?" July 27, 1993, p. 13; "Don't they know the

True virtue would also be high on his list of preventive measures. Virtue is inner control. It is controlling oneself in demanding situations *from within*.[57] I have the virtue of courage if I face and measure up to physical, academic or moral challenges because I see them to be obstacles to my becoming and remaining a free human being and I overcome them. I possess the virtue of charity if I share with others what I have and am because I realize they are God's creatures who are in need. I am chaste if I turn away from illicit sexual pleasures because I know them to be incompatible with my state of life. Likewise for Aquinas courage, charity and chastity (and a host of other like qualities) are virtues and for the reason given—they are the inner controls which human persons need in demanding situations so as to be humanly responsible, free and happy.[58]

---

moral wheel was invented long ago?" August 9, 1993, p. 13; "Truth stands alone, but where are we to find it today?" August 16, 1993, p. 13; "Without standards, we have children sans consciences," August 30, 1993, p. 15. Also see James M. Wall, "Religious beliefs have become a cultural heresy," *Chicago Tribune*, October 14, 1993, p. 17.

[57] On the occasion of the 1992 riots on the streets of Los Angeles and their aftermath, Jerry Schmalz, "Disaffection With National Leaders Sharpens in the Glare of Los Angeles," *New York Times*, May 10, 1992, p. 1, quoted Harry McPherson, one-time counsel to President Lyndon B. Johnson, as saying: "Crime is out of control. Drugs are out of control. The deficit and health-care costs are out of control. Teen-age pregnancy and the welfare loads are out of control. You see L.A. cops backing away when trouble starts, so the rioting is out of control."

In all such instances "control" is external—e.g., to control crime hire more cops, to control drugs stop their flow into this country, etc. But all such extrinsic controls, necessary as they may be, are insufficient unless complemented by inner controls—e.g., help criminals themselves freely desist from their crimes by their realizing that the injustice they are inflicting upon others is *morally wrong* and, thus, they should control themselves *from within*. That inner control would be the virtue of justice.

[58] For a helpful introduction to Thomas' theory of morality in general, see Pinckaers, pp. 221–39; on virtues, see especially pp. 223–29, where he makes these relevant points. The *habitus* (among which are virtues) are "stable dispositions that develop the power of our faculties and render us capable of performing actions of high quality. . . . [Each] *habitus* . . . is a principle of progress and resourcefulness through full commitment. It is through these *habitus* . . . that we acquire mastery over our actions and become entirely free." For Aquinas "virtue was the noblest of human, moral qualities . . . . The virtues are multiple: intellectual, moral, theological. They are perfected by the gifts of the Holy Spirit, to which are added the Beatitudes and the fruits of the

How different our world would be if virtue would replace vice. How helpful to rescuing our world would the application of Thomas' conception of virtues be.

Deconstructionism Again

The immediately prior and lengthy section considered Thomas Aquinas' reaction to the decades 1960–1980 and to developments especially in astrophysics and in love which those years initiated. Let us now take up deconstructionism, touched upon in the section "Past, Present and Future: Surveys" above, which terminated in Gertrude Himmelfarb's account and rejection of it in her book *On Looking into the Abyss: Untimely Thoughts on Culture and Society*.[59] This time let us look at Jacques Derrida himself and decon-

---

Holy Spirit. St. Thomas thus exploited all the riches of the Christian experience. He also investigated the causes, conditions, interrelationships and duration of the virtues."

For a detailed and generally accurate explanation of Thomas' doctrine (with abundant references to *Summa Theologiae*, I–II and II–II) see Jean Porter, *The Recovery of Virtue: The Relevance of Aquinas for Christian Ethics* (Louisville, Ky.: Westminister/John Knox Press, 1990), ch. 4: "The Affective Virtues," pp. 100–23 (Porter here speaks of both temperance and fortitude); ch. 5: "Justice," pp. 124–54; ch. 6: "Prudence; Cardinal and Theological Virtues," pp. 155–71. Also see Jean Porter, *Moral Action and Christian Ethics* (Cambridge University Press, 1995), ch. 4: "Moral Acts and Acts of Virtue," pp. 125–66; ch. 5: "The Virtues Reformulated," pp. 167–299; George P. Klubertanz, *Habits and Virtues* (New York: Appleton-Century-Crofts, 1965), especially ch. 5: "Virtue and Vice"; ch. 6: "The Cardinal Virtues"; Lee H. Yearley, *Mencius and Aquinas: Theories of Virtue and Conceptions of Courage* (Albany: SUNY Press, 1990), especially ch. 2—Mencius is an early Confucian (fourth century B.C.), who lists (p. 36) these as the four central virtues: benevolence, righteousness, propriety, intelligent awareness.

[59] For publishing data see n. 20 above. For another unsympathetic account see David Lehman, *Signs of the Times: Deconstruction and the Fall of Paul de Man* (New York: Poseidon Press, 1991): as its subtitle indicates, the book was occasioned by the December 1987 revelations that Paul de Man had from November 1940 to November 1942 written 180 articles for pro-Nazi newspapers in his native Belgium. See L. Sweeney, "Deconstructionism and Neoplatonism: Jacques Derrida and Dionysius the Areopagite," in R. Baine Harris (ed.), *Proceedings* of International Conference on "Neoplatonism and Contemporary Philosophers," Vanderbilt University, May 1995, prgrs. corresponding to notes 22–25.

structionism by asking, What does he have in mind in his writings?
What does he intend?[60]

(a) The Authentic Derrida

Understanding him is not easy to achieve, and this might seem
to occur at times because of Derrida himself. For example, consider
his commentary on these verses of the poet Angelus Silesius.[61]

> *Nichts werden ist GOTT werden.*
> Nichts wird was zuvor ist: wirstu nicht vor zu nicht,
> So wirstu nimmermehr gebohrn vom ewgen Licht.

> *To become Nothing is to become God.*
> Nothing becomes what is before: if you do not become
>   nothing,
> Never will you be born of eternal light.

"How," Derrida asks, "is this *becoming* to be thought? . . . This
coming to being

> starting from nothing and *as nothing, as God and as Nothing,* as
> the Nothing itself, this birth that carries itself without premise,
> this becoming-self as becoming-God—or Nothing—that is what
> appears impossible, more than impossible, the most impos-
> sible possible, more impossible than the impossible if the im-
> possible is the simple negative modality of the possible.

In the next paragraph Derrida continues by defining deconstruction.

> This thought seems strangely familiar to the experience of
> what is called deconstruction. Far from being a methodical
> technique, a possible or necessary procedure, unrolling the

---

[60] Jacques Derrida was born in Algiers of Jewish parents in 1933. Currently
he teaches in Paris at the Ecole normale supérieure.

[61] Quoted by Derrida in Harold Coward and Toby Foshay (eds.), *Derrida
and Negative Theology* [hereafter: *Negative Theology*] (Albany: SUNY Press,
1992), p. 289. Silesius' verses are from his *The Cherubinic Wanderer*, trans.
Maria Shrady, preface by E. J. Furcha and introduction by Josef Schmide
(New York: Paulist Press, 1986), "The Classics of Western Spirituality." For
biographical data and style-commentary, see *ibid.*, pp. xvii–xxii and 3–33.
Also see *Negative Theology*, p. 322, n. 3.

law of a program and applying rules, that is, unfolding possibilities, deconstruction has often been defined as the very experience of the (impossible) possibility of the impossible, of the most impossible. . . . The possibility of the impossible, of the "more impossible" that as such is also possible ("more impossible than the impossible"), marks an absolute interruption in the regime of the possible that nonetheless remains, if this can be said, in place.[62]

How are we to understand that definition (deconstruction is the experience of the impossible possibility of the most impossible), which on first hearing sounds contradictory? We must turn to what is the starting-point (as Rodolphe Gasché advises) of all modern philosophers from Descartes through the German idealists and Husserl and, apparently, to Derrida himself because of his acceptance (with them) of the Cartesian methodology. That is, one must turn away "from any straightforward consideration of objects and from the immediacy of such an experience toward a consideration of the very experience in which objects are given." Thus by "bending back upon the modalities of object perception, reflection shows itself to mean primarily self-reflection, self-relation, self-mirroring."[63] When one thus severs "the self from the immediacy of the object world," it is given "freedom as a thinking being."[64] And when one severs the self *even from the very experience itself* in which objects are given, it becomes even more free. It now has the freedom to ignore both objects and cognitive experiential states so as to concentrate upon language or, more accurately, upon texts and upon the speaking and writing producing them or, still more accurately, upon endlessly thinking, speaking, writing otherwise than whatever precedes.

A few pages earlier Gasché has correctly pointed out that Derrida has no place for the "reflection" alluded to in my previous para-

---

[62] *Negative Theology*, pp. 289–90. For bibliographical data on the first appearance of this definition of deconstruction, see *ibid.*, p. 323, n. 5.

[63] Rodolphe Gasché, *The Tain of the Mirror: Derrida and the Philosophy of Reflection* [hereafter: *Tain*] (Cambridge, Mass.: Harvard University Press, 1986), p. 13. For reviews of *Tain* see Henry Staten, *Criticism* 30 (1988), 144–49; Charles Altieri, *Comparative Literature Studies* 26 (1989), 376–84; Christopher Fynsk, *Review of Metaphysics* 41 (1987), 137–39; John D. Caputo, *Research in Phenomenology* 17 (1987), 245–59.

[64] *Tain*, p. 14.

graph[65]—not "because he would wish to refute or reject [it] in favor of a dream of immediacy" but because "his work questions reflection's unthought and thus the limits of its possibility." He is concerned with that "unthought," with that "beyond" of the "orchestrated mirror play of reflection that Derrida's [own] philosophy seeks to conceptualize." Thus he is concerned not with the mirror itself but with its "tain"—"the tinfoil, the silver lining, the lusterless back of the mirror. Derrida's philosophy, rather than being a philosophy of reflection, is engaged in the systematic exploration of that dull surface without which no reflection and no specular and speculative activity would be possible, but which at the same time has no place and no part in reflection's scintillating play."[66]

But what are the "unthought" and "beyond" which are symbolized by the mirror's tain? They consist in the infrastructures or undecidables which "command the mirror's play and determine the angles of reflection." Yet since this foil

_____

[65] That is, when one reflects "upon the modalities of object perception"—when one considers the very experience in which actual objects are given—such "reflection shows itself to mean primarily self-reflection, self-relation, self-mirroring."

[66] *Ibid.*, pp. 6 and 7. When speaking of Hegel, Derrida himself (*Dissemination* [see n. 74 below], pp. 32–33) alludes to *tain*: "It is because we have now arrived at the point where the relation between the 'text'—in the narrow, classical sense of the term—and the 'real' is being played out, and because the very concepts of text and of extratext, the very transformation of the relation between them and of the preface we are engaged in, the practical and theoretical problematic of that transformation, are at stake. The new kind of text that retains and seems to limit us here is in fact the infinite excess facing [*débord*] of its classical representation. This lining fringe, this extra edge, this delimitation, invites a rereading of the form of our relation to Hegel's logic and to all that can be subsumed therein. The breakthrough toward radical otherness (with respect to the philosophical concept—of the concept) always takes, *within philosophy*, the *form* of an a posteriority or an empiricism. But this is an effect of the specular nature of philosophical reflection, philosophy being incapable of inscribing (comprehending) what is outside it otherwise than through the appropriating assimilation of a negative image of it, and dissemination is written on the back—the *tain*—of that mirror. Not on its inverted specter. Nor in the triadic symbolic order of its sublimation. The question is to find out what it is that, written under the mask of empiricism, turning speculation upside down, *also does something else* and renders a Hegelian sublation [*relève*] of the preface impracticable. This question calls for prudent, differentiated, slow, stratified readings."

is made of disseminated structural instances, the mirror's tin-foil necessarily becomes semitransparent and, as a correlate, only semireflective. Reflection, then, appears to be affected by the infrastructures that make it possible; it appears broached and breached as an inevitably imperfect and limited *Scheinen*. Total reflection is a limited play, not because of some defect owing to its finitude—as Hegel has shown, it is a *truly* infinite play—but because of the structurally limitless play of the undecidables that make it possible.[67]

Accordingly,

at first the mirror that Derrida's philosophy holds up seems to show us only its tain; yet this opaque tain is also transparent. Through it one can observe the play of reflection and specula-tion as it takes place in the mirror's mirroring itself. Seen from the inside this play gives an illusion of perfection, but ob-served through the tain, it appears limited by the infrastructural agencies written on its invisible side, without which it could not even begin to occur.[68]

Thus Derrida's criticism does not reject reflection and specula-tion (as found, for example, in traditional onto-theologies and onto-philosophies with their search for transcendental signifiers and transcendental signifieds)

in favor of total immediacy, nor does it presuppose an originary unity by virtue of which the traditional problems of reflexivity can be dialectically overcome in absolute reflection or specu-lation. Derrida's debate with reflection and speculation is not

---

[67] *Tain*, p. 238. On the "structurally limitless play of the undecidables," see R. Gasché, "Nontotalization without Spuriousness: Hegel and Derrida on the Infinite," *Journal of the British Society for Phenomenology* 17 (1986), 289–307, where Gasché lists Derrida's statements on the "infinite substitutability" which characterizes language and texts and which aborts "all possible totalization" of language or texts (p. 289).

"Infinity" as Derrida uses it is similar to Aristotle's use, for whom any actual extension is always definite but is potentially infinite as capable of further bisection. See L. Sweeney, *Divine Infinity in Greek and Medieval Thought* [hereafter: *Divine Infinity*] (New York/Bern: Peter Lang Publishing, Inc., 1992), ch. 8: "Aristotle's Infinity of Quantity," pp. 143–65.

[68] *Tain*, p. 238.

dependent on the essentially philosophical problem of the
aporias, contradictions, or negations of reflection, in terms of
which it refuses to criticize or solve the problems of reflection.
As we have seen, both operations are intrinsically speculative.[69]

Rather, by focusing

on an analysis of those heterogeneous instances that are the
"true" conditions of possibility of reflection and speculation
without being susceptible to accommodation by the intended
totality, Derrida's philosophy reinscribes, in the strict meaning of this word, reflection and speculation into what exceeds
it: the play of the infrastructures.[70]

How can infrastructures be more fully described?

Infrastructures are economically and strategically minimal dis-
tributions or constellations—archesyntheses—of essentially
heterogeneous predicates. The principle articulated by each
singular infrastructure applies to itself as well, and although
each one of the by right infinite number of infrastructures can
be replaced (or supplemented) by another, they are not synonymous with or even identical to one another. Thus one can
see clearly how infrastructures contain the *possibility* of tying
elements together into a totality of foundation, as well as of
self-thematization and of element combination and transformation.[71]

Gasché next sounds a warning.

Since infrastructures combine heterogeneous predicates,
however, and apply to themselves only the better to unground
themselves, they also appear to be strangely ambiguous or
ambivalent. Yet it is not the sort of ambiguity that would be
witness to an absence of clarity in the process of their determination, to the negativity of a lack of precision, to vagueness or

[69] *Ibid.*, pp. 238–39.
[70] *Ibid.*, p. 239.
[71] *Ibid.*, pp. 239–40.

looseness of terms, in short to semantic confusion, nor is it an ambiguity concerning the meaning of the infrastructures, owing to some polysemic richness.

Therefore, "it is advisable to avoid the term *ambiguity* altogether in characterizing the infrastructures" and to qualify them "provisionally as undecidables"[72]—a word which "must be understood to refer

> not only to essential incompleteness and inconsistency, bearing in mind their distinction from ambiguity, but also to indicate a level vaster than that which is encompassed by the opposition between what is decidable and undecidable.[73]

Consequently,

> As "originary" syntheses, or economic arrangements of traits, the undecidables constitute both the medium or the element between the binary philosophical oppositions and between philosophy and its Other, as well as the medium that encompasses these coupled terms. They are undecidable because they suspend the decidable opposition between what is true and false and put all the concepts that belong to the philosophical system of decidability into brackets. By virtue of their constituting a space in between conceptual dyads and, at the same time, comprising them, the infrastructural undecidables are "the medium in which opposites are opposed, the movement and the play that links them among themselves, reverses them or makes one side cross over into the other" (*D*, p. 127). Their undecidability, their "floating indetermination," permits the substitution and the play of the conceptual binary oppositions, which, by turning into one another, become incapable of denominating and defining the medium from which they emerge (*D*, p. 93).[74]

---

[72] *Ibid.*, p. 240.

[73] *Ibid.*, p. 241.

[74] *Ibid.*, pp. 241–42. In the quotation the references to "*D*, p. 127" and "*D*, p. 93" are to Derrida's *Dissemination*, trans. B. Johnson (University of Chicago Press, 1981).

So far runs our attempt accurately to present Derrida himself before we consider Aquinas' reaction to him. But first how can Derrida's authentic position be summarized?[75]

(1) Onto-philosophy and onto-theology are instances of the reflections or (literally) speculations on the surface of the human mirror which is the mind (see note 65 above). (2) But those reflections are made possible and are affected by the tain of the mirror—i.e., by the infrastructures which are located on succeeding levels of that tain and which allow the reflections to occur (see notes 66–69 above). (3) These infrastructures are negative discourse; they are constellations of heterogeneous predicates (see note 69), grounded in such a way as to be endlessly open-ended to further combination and transformation (see note 70). (4) Or one may substitute "undecidables" for "infrastructures" and say that reflections on the mirror's surface are made possible by undecidables (see note 71). These are the medium between philosophy and theology in such a way as to encompass both; they suspend the opposition between what is true and false, between the possible and impossible; they are the space between these latter conceptual dyads and yet comprise them; they are the medium within which opposites are opposed, linked together and reversed; they are floating indeterminates which allow conceptual oppositions to combine (thus neither of them dominates) and to make rational what can only be irrational by trying to reconcile undecidables; they are the philosophical and theological conceptual couples which can be misconstrued as dialectical contradiction susceptible (with Hegel) of eventual dissolution; they suspend decidability in all its forms but especially as a mediation of contradictions; because nonsemantic in character these are rigorously irreducible and irresolvable (see note 73 above).

(b) Aquinas' Reaction

Thomas' first comment on Derrida's position would, I think, concentrate upon the centrality which he gives to the tain (= the tinfoil, the silver lining) of the mirror (= the human mind), which allows reflections (= knowledges such as traditional philosophy and theology) to appear there. What literally corresponds to the

---

[75] In the points to be made now, my parenthetical references to note 65, etc., should be read as referring to "the paragraph corresponding to note 65 above," etc.

mirror's tain itself is the infrastructures which ground the knowledges expressed in texts and in which Derrida is primarily or even solely interested. Since the tain is itself semitransparent, the initial layer of infrastructures (or undecidables), which constitute "the unthought" and "the beyond" of knowledges, rests upon ever deepening infrastructures so that Derrida ends up concentrating (as stated above) upon language or, more accurately, upon texts and upon the speaking and writing producing them or, still more accurately, upon endlessly thinking, speaking, writing otherwise than whatever precedes.

Such concentration makes sense in the light of Derrida's following the lead of Descartes by turning away "from any straightforward consideration of objects . . . [thus liberating oneself] from the immediacy of the object world" and thereby achieving "freedom as a thinking being." It makes sense from Derrida's turning away even "from the very experience in which objects are given," and thereby achieving still further freedom to ignore even our cognitive experiential states. But both freedoms condemn him to achieving nothing more today than a similarly infinite process tomorrow of thinking, speaking, writing otherwise than what has preceded today.

No such condemnation awaits Aquinas by the simple fact that he does not turn away from but rather turns directly to actual existents themselves. That is, unlike the Cartesian methodology to which Derrida, along with other modern and contemporary philosophers, subscribes and which severs knowledge "from the immediacy of the object world," Thomas' epistemology consists precisely of "straightforward consideration of objects." These are the content-determining-causes of all nonconstructural knowledges, by and in which the knower is one with the known.[76]

Such an epistemology also leads the knower to affirm that God exists, because the objects in actual concrete cases, which Thomas straightforwardly considers, put themselves across as real (= of value, worth) and to be what they are precisely because they do actually exist, as these paraphrased texts indicate. When is the perfection of being a human person or of being fire actually achieved? When it exists in dry wood [to restrict ourselves to the latter example], or in the hands of the person holding a piece of

---

[76] See prgrs. corresponding to notes 52–53 and 55–56 above.

flint, or in his mind as he thinks about starting a fire? No, fire is *fire* only when it actually exists. This fact shows that the act of existence is the actuality of all actuations and the perfection of all perfections.[77] Again: you actually do not have goodness or humanity unless they actually exist. Hence, existence is the actuality of every form and nature.[78] Again, absolutely nothing has actuality and reality except inasmuch as it exists. Therefore, the act of existing is the actuality of all things, even of forms. Accordingly, existence for a horse, a man, or anything whatsoever is its actuation and perfection.[79]

But why does the primacy which existence has over what existents are indicate that God exists? Because such existents are composed of essences (= that by which each is what it is— e.g., a man, a horse, a tree)[80] and of existence as the actuation by which each essence actually is. Thus the actuation of existence perfects each actual existent as the intrinsic cause distinct from the essence of that existent. That distinction between essence and the actuation of existence also is the source of contingency in such individual existents: although each does exist, it need not exist as far as it itself is concerned because its essence is other than the act of existing perfecting it. That contingency thus points to an Existent whose essence or nature is subsistent existence and who is the proper efficient cause of all creatures and thus is present in and to them but is also other than them.[81] As subsistent existence God is also subsistent and

---

[77] *De Potentia*, q. 7, a. 2 ad 9 (Marietti Ed., p. 192). The Latin for the last sentence: "Unde patet quod hoc quod dico *esse* est actualitas omnium actuum, et propter hoc est perfectio omnium perfectionum." Also see *Summa Contra Gentiles*, I, c. 28 (Leonine Manual Ed., p. 29d).

[78] *Summa Theologiae*, I, 3, 4 resp. (Leonine Manual Ed., p. 17b). The Latin: "Esse est actualitas omnis formae vel naturae: non enim bonitas vel humanitas significatur in actu nisi prout significamus eam esse." Also see *ibid.*, q. 84, a. 7 resp. (p. 414).

[79] *Ibid.*, I, 4, 1 ad 3 (p. 21d): "Ipsum esse est perfectissimum omnium: comparatur enim ad omnia ut actus. Nihil enim habet actualitatem nisi inquantum est; unde ipsum esse est actualitas omnium rerum et etiam ipsarum formarum." See L. Sweeney, *Authentic Metaphysics*, pp. 79–80.

[80] The essence is itself composed of these components: prime matter, substantial form and accidental perfections—see *Authentic Metaphysics*, pp. 93–94 and 97–99.

[81] *S.T.*, I, 8, 1 resp.

infinite goodness, beauty, knowledge, freedom, wisdom, love[82] and with providence over all creatures.[83] Human beings are specially guided to act in morally good ways by participating in the eternal law through the natural law "written within their hearts" and known by reflection upon themselves as created actual existents.[84]

Obviously, Aquinas stands in contrast to Derrida both on God and on law. "God" for Derrida names

> *that without which* one would not know how to account for any negativity: grammatical or logical negation, illness, evil and finally neurosis which far from permitting psychoanalysis to reduce religion to a symptom, would obligate it to recognize in the symptom the negative manifestation to God.[85]

Or, in the light of Rodolphe Gasché's commentary on Derrida's essay, "Violence and Metaphysics,"[86]

> God as the metaphysical name for Being is primarily an excellent example of the unthought. But more important, since God as an existent yields, as can be seen, to ontic conditionality, or to put it differently, since God in onto-theological theology is always represented in an idolatrous manner, the thinking of God, as well as the relation of man to Him, is analogical and schematic by nature: God is always an example (perhaps, ultimately, of himself). Now since this analogical transfer, by which a continuity between God as the supreme being and all other beings becomes established, is itself of the order of the relations that characterize the ontic realm, the thought of Being is that pre-conceptual, pre-

---

[82] *Ibid.*, qq. 6, 7, 19 and 20; see my *Christian Philosophy*, ch. 18, especially prgrs. corresponding to nn. 15-18. On God's being and other perfections as infinite in themselves, see my *Divine Infinity*, especially chs. 18–19.

[83] *S.T.*, I, q. 22. On providence in relation to law, see *ibid.*, I–II, 91, 1 resp.

[84] See *ibid.*, art. 2 *sed contra* and *resp.*, especially *ad finem*: "Lex naturalis nihil aliud est quam participatio legis aeternae in rationali creatura." Also see *ibid.*, I, 14, 8 ad 3 (p. 82).

[85] Jacques Derrida, *Negative Theology*, pp. 76–77.

[86] See Jacques Derrida, *Writing and Difference*, trans. Alan Bass (University of Chicago Press, 1978), ch. 4: "Violence and Metaphysics: An Essay on the Thought of Emmanuel Levinas," pp. 79–153.

relational, pre-analogical thought that by thinking God, for example, lets God be what He is, an example of the unthought Being and of unthought thought.[87]

If such is Derrida's position on God, what stance does he take on law? In Gertrude Himmelfarb's interpretation, he engages in a litany of denials, the last of which concerns law. In literature he would deny "the fixity of any text" as to what it means; in philosophy he would deny "the fixity . . . of any correspondence between language and reality—indeed of any 'essential' reality and thus of any proximate truth about reality"; in history he would deny the "fixity of the past, of the reality of the past apart from what the historian chooses to make of it and thus of any objective truth about the past." Finally, in law he would deny "the legitimacy of law itself, which is regarded as nothing more than an instrument of power."[88]

But Douglas Litowitz, "Derrida on Law and Justice: Borrowing (Illicitly?) from Plato and Kant,"[89] approaches Derrida differently.

---

[87] Rodolphe Gasché, *Inventions of Difference: On Jacques Derrida* (Harvard University Press, 1994), p. 156. See also ch. 6: "God, For Example," in its entirety (pp. 150–70). On "the unthought," see prgrs. connected with notes 65–69 above.

[88] G. Himmelfarb, *Looking into the Abyss*, p. 133—see prgr. corresponding to n. 24 above. If law is linked with ethics, David Lehman's remarks on Julia Kristeva and J. Hillis Miller are illuminating. Kristeva in 1986 approvingly stated that "in America the so-called deconstructionists think that, because ethics and history belong to metaphysics and because metaphysics is criticized by Heidegger or his French followers, ethics and history no longer exist"—for the quotation see D. Lehman, p. 55. Also see *ibid.*, pp. 63–64, where Lehman quotes the deconstructionist J. Hillis Miller: "Ethicity . . . is a region of human life in which lying is necessarily made into a universal principle, in the sense that ethical judgments are necessary but never verifiably true." Lehman's comment: "By rhetorical fiat Miller reduces ethical judgments to the status of lies! His logic is circular and confused: it is based on the dubious proposition that everything not 'verifiably true' is a lie, and on the implicit assumption that nothing is 'verifiably true.' . . . Miller deconstructs 'ethicity' by identifying it with falsehood—by seeing it as it really is not."

For information on Julia Kristeva's position see Madan Sarup, *An Introductory Guide to Post-Structuralism and Postmodernism*, 2nd ed. (Athens: University of Georgia Press, 1993), pp. 122–26.

[89] *The Canadian Journal of Law and Jurisprudence* 8 (July 1995), 325–46. Litowitz concentrates on Derrida's "Force of Law: The 'Mystical Foundation of Authority,'" in David Gray Carlson, Drucilla Cornell and Michel Rosenfeld

When "law" is taken to mean (as Derrida does) "'positive law,' man-made law," it is distinguished from "justice," which is "outside law; it is a relation or debt from one person to another, an irreducible and incalculable duty to act without consideration of repayment. . . . [Justice] is something that 'exceeds' law, and can perhaps even contradict the law in extreme cases. Justice is deemed an 'experience that we are not able to experience,' and involves an experience of aporiai,"[90] one of which is "the ghost of the undecidable." Here Derrida "is focused on the fact that there must be a rapprochement between *justice* (incalculable, infinite, excessive, and unconditional) and *law* (calculable, determined, contingent, and rule-governed). Justice resists formulas, so we can never say that a particular formulation of law is 'just,' in the sense of rendering complete justice to the other. But at the same time that justice resists encapsulation, there is a demand for a decision to be made. So while there is no justice prior to a decision ('for only a decision is just'), no decision can completely capture justice."[91]

This contrast between "law" and "justice" in Derrida is set forth in what Litowitz calls "a charitable . . . explanation of Derrida's position on law and justice" (see *ibid.*, p. 326) and constitutes Part One of his paper (ibid., pp. 326–34). This is followed by Litowitz's showing in Part Two (pp. 334–40) that "Derrida's approach to justice is heavily indebted to Plato's notion of justice as a transcendent idea (or form) and to Kant's notion of regulative ideas," with the result that Derrida himself holds a "quasi-transcendent view of justice which he appropriates from Plato and Kant" but which his own "rejection of traditional metaphysics and epistemology does not permit him to hold." In Part Three (pp. 340–44) Litowitz elaborates "further on the notion that Derrida's position on law and justice has a hidden metaphysics of presence and is therefore undercut by Derrida's epistemic and metaphysical scepticism." Finally in Part Four (pp. 344–46) he concludes that "Derrida's ultimate goal is laudable: to set forth a concept of justice that demands a tireless, impossible, and incalculable vigilance to ensure that justice is done to the other. But however laudable this position may be, it nevertheless carries metaphysical baggage that must be re-

---

(eds.), *Deconstruction and the Possibility of Justice* (New York: Routledge, 1992), ch. 1, pp. 3–67. He also utilizes Derrida's other writings on justice and law— see Litowitz, p. 325, n. 4.

[90] Litowitz, p. 327.
[91] *Ibid.*, p. 332.

jected on Derrida's own critique of logocentricism. This means that Derrida's recent writings on justice and law are inconsistent with his earlier, more deconstructive writings."[92]

Since Litowitz's careful analysis of Derrida's own texts appears completely accurate, what should one conclude? However laudable Derrida's conception of justice may be, one's praise must be tempered by the inconsistency Litowitz has pointed out. Meantime the harrowing moral and physical evils which afflict our societies (both political and familial) and the individual human persons resident therein[93] require immediate attention and remedies. Aquinas' moral stance issuing from an acceptance of human persons as each a single composite material/spiritual entity, of their participating in God's loving providence and law through natural law,[94] which is to guide each of them in dealing with others, who in turn are to be similarly guided in their conduct—Thomas' stance is infinitely preferable to Derrida's by offering hope and help to our morally bankrupt and violent world.

Images Again

In the summer of 1994 I initiated this chapter with accounts of the wars and refugee camps in Rwanda, as well as of Comet Shoemaker-Levy 9 impacting the planet Jupiter. These were accounts which for Paul Gray in his essay "Looking at Cataclysms" in the same issue of *Time* offered "images both awesome and horrifying."[95] But he cautioned that "if we are to understand them correctly, we must still do the work ourselves" of interpreting them accurately by realizing that they represent only a part of the cataclysms and that we must rely upon previous and other current experience—in short, we must constantly be intellectually alive.[96] Gray's speaking of Rwanda and Jupiter as providing "awesome and horrifying images" led to my recalling Michael Kelly's lead article, "Bill Clinton's Climb," in the *New York Times Magazine*, July

---

[92] *Ibid.*, p. 326, which is an anticipatory summary of Libowitz's article itself.

[93] On the immorality and cruelty of the world in which we live, see prgrs. connected with notes 1–3 and 54–58 above, as well as the section "Images Again" immediately below, especially prgrs. connected with notes 101–7.

[94] See section "Natural Law Morality" and n. 40 above.

[95] *Time*, August 1, 1994, p. 64.

[96] See prgr. connected with n. 3 above.

31, 1994, pp. 27 sqq., where Kelly illustrated the role that "image" plays in Clinton's character and presidency and in other Washington politicians.[97]

Now a year later let me return to Rwanda, Jupiter and Washington so as to update those three accounts and Aquinas' reaction to them.

It is easiest to begin with Jupiter because the two hundred scientists (one of whom was Eugene Shoemaker, codiscoverer of the comet) gathered at Johns Hopkins University May 9–12, 1995, agreed on these key findings, issuing from the vast and varied array of data collected since July 1994: (a) Shoemaker-Levy 9 really was a comet, broken into at least twenty-three fragments by a close encounter with Jupiter's gravitation in July 1992. (b) The most dramatic release of energy detected from earth after major fragments of the comet fell into Jupiter's atmosphere did not come from the hot fireballs that erupted from the impact sites. Instead they came from the "splash-back" when the gas plumes that rose thousands of miles above the cloud tops fell back into them. (c) An atmospheric wave formation observed to move away from major impact sites like a ripple in a pond moved at a speed that suggests there may be ten times more water in Jupiter's atmosphere than anyone had thought. (d) Analyses of the comet's orbital history and chemistry indicate it probably was formed early in the solar system's history from water ice, rock and metals that fell together in a loose heap in a region beyond the orbit of Pluto. At some point its own orbit was disturbed and it began a long series of loops toward the sun that eventually allowed it to be captured in an orbit ranging between Jupiter and the sun. About sixty-five years ago it was drawn into a chaotic orbit that whirled once around the planet every two years. Finally on July 7, 1992, it passed too close to Jupiter and was pulled apart. The breakup continued until there were at least twenty-three visible chunks, which in July 17–22, 1994, impacted Jupiter itself.[98]

What would Thomas' reaction be to the scientists' "key findings"? Conceivably it would repeat the *awe* he experienced when

---

[97] See prgrs. connected with notes 4–7 above.

[98] My account of the scientists' key findings closely reproduces Frank D. Roylance, "Scientists Compile Findings on Comet That Hit Jupiter," *Chicago Sun-Times*, May 14, 1995, p. 26. For reports made soon after the impact see Kathy Sawyer, "Comet Left Sonic Wave In Its Wake," *ibid.*, July 23, 1994, p. 14; Lucy McFadden, "The crash of Shoemaker-Levy 9," *Chicago Tribune*, August

confronted earlier with other astonomical feats[99]—awe at the scientists' ability to evaluate the enormous data furnished by the Hubble Space Telescope on the comet; awe at the comet's own history and chemistry (see #a and #d in immediately preceding paragraph); awe at the aftermath of its impact on Jupiter (see #b and #c). Also, Aquinas would, no doubt, again gratefully incorporate all relevant information into his cosmogony and cosmology.[100]

Next, what of Rwanda? Attention to Rwanda, Burundi and other African countries shifted soon after August 1994 to the strife in Bosnia and Herzegovina, which furnish equally abhorrent images. But granted that shift (to which we shall return in a moment), the violence in Africa did on occasion surface in the media, to judge by some headlines: "Gunmen [= members of Tutsi Rwanda Patriotic Front] Kill 54 Rwandans in Burundi" (*Chicago Sun-Times*, October 26, 1994, p. 40); "Dragnet Misses Rwandan Thugs" (*ibid.*, December 15, 1994, p. 18); "Reports: [Medical] Aid to Rwanda was too late" (*Chicago Tribune*, February 10, 1995, p. 16); "Genocide trials begin in Rwanda" (*ibid.*, April 7, 1995, p. 4); "Rwanda Genocide Remembered" (*Chicago Sun-Times*, April 7, 1995, p. 24); "Fears of 'Another Rwanda' [in Burundi]" (*Newsweek*, April 10, 1995, p. 39); "Refugees Flee Zaire to Avoid Expulsion" (*Chicago Sun-Times*, August 22, 1995, p. 24); "Relief Breakdowns Leave Rwanda Refugees Hungry" (*ibid.*, November 26, 1995, p. 20).[101]

But granted the continued violence in Africa, warfare in Bosnia-Herzegovina now is daily news.[102] Beginning in mid-1991, that

---

27, 1994, p. 18; Heidi Hammel, "Jupiter heals from clash with comet," *ibid.*, September 30, 1994, sec. 1, p. 16.

[99] See prgrs. connected with notes 42–43 and 47–48 above.

[100] See prgrs. connected with notes 49–50 above.

[101] On the conflict between the Hutus and Tutsi in the light of the Church's presence in Rwanda, see Wolfgang Shonecke, "The Role of the Church in Rwanda," *America*, June 17, 1995, pp. 9–11. Also see Agustin Karekezi, "The Language of Rwanda," *Mailbox*, November 11, 1994, lines 1–275.

[102] That warfare becomes somewhat more intelligible in the light of these dates: 1054: start of the schism between the Eastern and Western Churches; 1389–1913: Turkish occupation of Yugoslavia; 1918: first official constitution of Yugoslavia as independent nation but replaced by King Alexander's absolute monarchy in 1929; 1941: Nazi Germany invaded Yugoslavia and divided it between Germany, Italy, Hungary and Bulgaria; 1945: under the leadership of Josip Broz Tito (1892–1980), Yugoslavia became the Socialist Federal Republic of Yugoslavia, which consisted of Bosnia and Herzegovina, Croatia, Macedonia, Montenegro, Slovenia and Serbia and which lasted until 1992.

fighting has continued until the cease-fire of October 11, 1995. That interval falls into three periods, in the first of which the Serbs were victorious. But in August 1995 the Muslims and Croats successfully launched an all-out offensive against the Serbs, who fled east toward Serbia. The cease-fire itself allows, supposedly, the three sides at war (the Muslim government, the Croats, the Serbs) to work out a peace agreement involving a "new constitutional arrangement for Bosnia-Herzegovina. Areas under Bosnian Serb control will formally become the Republika Srpska, and areas under Muslim-Croat control will become another political entity. But Bosnia-Herzegovina will remain a unitary state, in the sense that there will be some overarching government structures with at least nominal responsibility for affairs throughout the republic." Under this peace plan "the Muslim-Croat federation will control 51 percent of the territory of Bosnia-Herzegovina, and the Bosnia Serbs will get 49 percent."[103]

On those dates see G. T. Dennis, "Schism, East-West," *Encyclopedic Dictionary of Religion*, vol. 3 (1979), 3213–14; M. Lacko, "Yugoslavia," *New Catholic Encyclopedia*, vol. 14 (1967), 1083–89; Mihailo Crnobrnja, *The Yugoslav Drama* (Montreal/Kingston: McGill-Queen's University Press, 1994), especially pp. 15–34; Vladimir Bakaric, "Yugloslavia," *Encyclopedia Britannica: Macropedia*, vol. 19 (1977), 1098–1107A.

Two quotations from Vladimir Bakaric, *ibid.*, pp. 1098D and 1103A, are helpful in understanding the fighting of 1991 to 1995: "The traditions of ancient Greece and Rome, of Byzantine, and of western and central Europe diffused, clashed, and sometimes took root in this region [of Yugoslavia], and the contemporary landscape and the multinational society bear Slavic, Eastern and Western imprints of great complexity and diversity." Second: "Religious differences, coupled with varying linguistic and ethnic affiliation, have strongly molded the country's social and political life and have occasioned fierce conflicts. The split between the Serbs and Croats, who, although speaking the same language, adhered respectively to Eastern Orthodox and Roman Catholic persuasions, was particularly deep. . . . The Muslim beliefs of Bosnia are a reflection of the Turkish conquest." Also see Eugene Narrell, "How long can Bosnians keep a grudge going?" *Chicago Tribune*, March 15, 1995, p. 25; Paul Mojzes, *Yugoslavian Inferno: Ethnoreligious Warfare in the Balkans* (New York: Continuum, 1994)—see review by Tim McCarthy, *National Catholic Reporter*, February 3, 1995, pp. 29–30; Lenard J. Cohen, *Broken Bonds: The Disintegration of Yugoslavia* (Boulder, Colo.: Westview Press, 1993); Misha Glenny, *Rebirth of History: Eastern Europe in an Age of Democracy* (New York: Penguin Books, 1993), especially ch. 5.

[103] Ray Moseley, "Bosnia peace deal: Doubts and pitfalls," *Chicago Tribune*, October 11, 1995, p. 1. Also see Kit R. Roane, "Bosnia Cease-fire Goes Into

Whether and to what extent that peace plan is successful remains to be seen.[104] But clearly "all three sides have engaged in 'ethnic cleansing,' " and although that plan gives "refugees the right to return to their homes, some will not take the option, but others will risk their lives by returning to homes in areas controlled by their enemies."[105] The risk is great in view of what happened hours before the latest cease-fire was supposed to go into effect.

> Bewildered and dazed men and women staggered today [October 11, 1995] across the lines into Government-held territory here [Zenica, Bosnia-Herzegovina], stripped of everything they owned by Serbian militiamen and in anguish over family members led away at gunpoint to a fate known only to their captors.
>
> The waves of displaced people now reaching Government territory are the last of some 30,000 Muslims and Croats, from a prewar population of half a million, who remained in the Banja Luka region after the Bosnian Serbs seized control in 1992. Most are elderly, and many tell gruesome stories of drunken rampages by Serbian militiamen, looting, rape and murder.[106]

Aquinas' Counsel

What would Aquinas' reaction be to Bosnia-Herzegovina? He would again agree with Paul Gray's emphasis (see paragraph corresponding to note 3 above) that images issuing from the Balkans (as well as from Africa) tell only part of the harrowing story and must be complemented by further information and then by active evaluation and by resolve to help. His evaluation would, conceivably, be twofold: moral and political. The immorality of the looting, robbing, raping, killing on the part of all three sides is obvious.[107] Accordingly, he would strongly

---

Effect as Packet is Signed," *New York Times*, October 12, 1995; William Pfaff, "War does settle things," *Chicago Tribune*, October 17, 1995, sec. 1, p. 19.

[104] On obstacles to that success, see Moseley, *art. cit.*, and Roane, *art. cit.* But the peace-agreement was signed in Paris, Dec. 15, 1995, pp. 1 and 3; for background see *Time*, Dec. 4. 1995. pp. 31–35.

[105] Moseley, *art. cit.*, p. 20.

[106] Chris Hedges, *New York Times*, October 12, 1995, p. 6. Also see Sara Pearsaui, "An American in Croatia," *Chicago Tribune*, May 12, 1995, p. 27.

[107] On the victorious Croats' own immoral acts *vs.* the Serb refugees, see Shawn Pogatchnik, "Croats Vent Anger on Refugees," *Chicago Sun-Times*,

counsel all sides to replace injustice with justice, hatred with charity, violence with kindness, deceit with honesty.[108] But such necessary inner control cannot be initiated and maintained without outer political control from governments not directly involved in the dispute. Here the United Nations and NATO might function usefully. But this its members can do only if their evaluation is based upon the facts of the Balkan situation, upon its complex historical background,[109] and then upon what is morally right and just. This is a big order—especially given the tendency of Bill Clinton and of other politicians in Washington, in Paris, London, Moscow and elsewhere to foster their own careers and countries, to lack foresight and objective convictions, to be indecisive when confronted with global problems.[110]

August 10, 1995, p. 23; Tom Hundley, "Balkan refugee trail grows," *Chicago Tribune*, August 10, 1995, p. 1: "A long convoy of Serb refugees ran a gantlet of Croatian contempt to the Yugoslav border Wednesday, as the war-ravaged frontier known as the Krajina emptied itself of humanity. Their haunted, frightened faces filled the windows of cars and buses that passed in a column stretching for miles . . . a pathetic spectacle"; *idem*, "Croatians claim victory in western Bosnia," *ibid.*, August 19, 1995, p. 8: "There was new evidence of Croatian atrocities during the capture of Serb-held lands in the Krajina this month. . . . UN workers found mass graves and the mutilated bodies of civilians in former Serb areas captured this month by the Croatian army. . . . Many abandoned Serb homes were looted and set on fire." On Muslim suffering, see Roger Cohen, "A War in the Family: Dead Soldier Son. Grieving Father. Slaughtered Mother. Refugee Brother. Enemy Uncle. The Story of the Zecevics—and of Bosnia," *New York Times Magazine*, August 6, 1995, pp. 32 sqq.

[108] See prgrs. in connection with notes 54–58 above.

[109] See n. 102 above.

[110] See prgrs. connected with notes 4–7 above. The situation in Washington has not changed since August '94, to judge by this sampling of the media: George F. Will, "The Restoration [by Newt Gingrich as House Speaker of a commitment to limited government]," *Newsweek*, November 28, 1994, p. 78, where Will also characterizes Bill Clinton as "the least consequential president since Coolidge, who, unlike Clinton, was peripheral by conviction and choice"; *idem*, "U.S. at Crossroads at Home, Abroad," *Chicago Sun-Times*, June 7, 1995, p. 40; Franz Schurmann, " 'Chaos' view is spreading," *Chicago Tribune*, June 7, 1995, p. 21; Timothy J. McNulty, "As Gingrich has learned, GOP freshmen won't bend," *ibid.*, October 15, 1995, p. 3: Such freshmen as Wisconsin representative Mark Neumann refused to vote on some measures advocated by Gingrich, who then removed Neumann from the national security subcommittee; Jeff Greenfield, "Purity of Ethics is in short supply [in Congress]," *Chicago Sun-Times*, August 9, 1994, p. 24; George Anne Geyer, "Showbiz talents [such as the Clintons exhibit] aren't congruent with foreign policy skills," *Chicago Tribune*, April 7, 1995, p. 23; Carl Ronan, "Flip. Flop. Flip. Flop.

But would Thomas be acquainted with and interested in political situations? Yes, given the fact that his brother Reginaldo was put to death in 1246 by Frederick II, Emperor of the Kingdom of Sicily, because of a conspiracy to assassinate the emperor. Reginaldo had served in the emperor's armed forces from at least 1240 to 1245. But when Frederick II was deposed by Pope Innocent IV in 1245 at the Council of Lyons, Reginaldo changed allegiance and fought with the armies of the pope against Frederick, who put him to death because of the assassination attempt.[111] Was Reginaldo a martyr, then? Aquinas' family certainly thought so, but "the utter confusion at the time between what was of faith and what was of politics" suggests that Reginaldo and the other conspirators intended to gain material advantages rather than to serve the interests of the Roman Church. In fact, "the political situation in which Thomas lived and where he was most directly involved through his family was one of the most confused experiences of the Catholic Church"—a confusion which "is reflected in the life and writings of Thomas," who states that the pope, in virtue of his canonical office, is the head of the Church and nothing else; every other political or worldly accretion to this essentially spiritual authority is a historical accident, which may or may not be there without in any way diminishing the Church's inner spiritual nature."[112]

Flip. Flop. Clinton Masters Double-Talk Over Affirmative Action," *Chicago Sun-Times*, April 12, 1995, p. 23; Maureen Dowd, "Smooth image aside, Clinton must finally try to be a leader," *Chicago Tribune*, August 8, 1995, p. 18; Charles Krauthammer, "Clinton vs. Congress: The Race Is Set," *Time*, June 5, 1995, p. 72: Clinton, who "in his Inaugural Address promised to 'make change our friend,' has turned decidedly unfriendly to change," as is evident "in his '96 budget, a stunning defence of the status quo"; conclusion: Clinton is "a man of myriad political skills and few convictions."

[111] See James Weisheipl, *Friar Thomas d'Aquino*, pp. 7–8.

[112] *Ibid.*, p. 8. Aquinas would rejoice in Pope John Paul II's exercise of papal spiritual authority during his October 5–10, 1995, visit to the United States—his call for nations "to live up to their moral responsibility and confront the crises that cloud this century's last decades" (Celestine Bohlen, *New York Times*, October 6, p. 1); his urging compassion, generosity, concern, charity (Mike Dorning and Paul Galloway, *Chicago Tribune*, October 5, p. 3); in his address to the United Nations his request that the UN "be a 'moral center,' and that we learn from the bitter experience of violent ethnic conflicts in Rwanda and the former Yugoslavia a lesson in the consequences of ignoring the 'fundamental commonality' and 'solidarity' of human dignity" (Mike Dorning, *ibid.*, October 6, pp. 1 and 20); his asking that "America's 'magnifi-

Clearly, Thomas and his family were involved in thirteenth-century politics—an involvement which would indicate that in the Balkans he would be concerned to counsel not only virtue instead of vice but also assistance from political entities other than the Muslims, Croats and Serbs. Should one be surprised at his concern with inner and outer controls? Not at all. This theologian utilizes in his theology a metaphysics based on the evidences from the concrete cases in which actual material existents find themselves. Unlike Derrida, who turns away from "any straightforward consideration of the object," unlike Kant, who constructs within himself what he knows,[113] Thomas turns directly to actual existents themselves and welcomes the intelligible data determining the content of his knowledge. But the Croats, Muslims and Serbs precisely are actual existents caught in the concrete skeins of their history, geographical proximity, ethnic backgrounds and religions. Consequently, Aquinas would be concerned to know them and to assist them to gain peace. It behooves us to follow his counsels and also help them gain peace—individual and political peace, lasting peace, however hard it may be to achieve. As the poet says,[114]

When will you ever, Peace, wild wooddove, shy wings shut,
Your round me roaming end, and under be my boughs?
When, when, Peace, will you, Peace? I'll not play hypocrite
To own my heart: I yield you do come sometimes; but
That piecemeal peace is poor peace. What pure peace allows
Alarms of wars, the daunting wars, the death of it?

---

cent scientific and technological civilization' make 'room for the mystery of God,' along with duties to the needy, the value of traditional families" (Mike Dorning, *ibid.*, October 7, p. 1); his telling the "more than 100,000 people from a gigantic stage in Central Park . . . 'to stand up for purity.' As he was decrying abortion, he added that Catholics ought to 'work and pray against violence of all kinds' " (Andrew Herrmann, *Chicago Sun-Times*, October 8, p. 3). Also see James V. Schall, "The Role of Christian Philosophy in Politics," *American Catholic Philosophical Quarterly* 69 (1995), 1–14.

Moral responsibility, compassion, generosity, concern, charity, God-centered morality, purity, fidelity to traditional two-parent families, refusal of violence—all these Thomas advocates too as the inner control required for human persons truly to live humanly.

[113] On Derrida, see prgr. linked with n. 76 above; on Kant see prgrs. linked with notes 51–54.

[114] Gerard Manley Hopkins, "Peace," in Peter Milward, *A Commentary on the Sonnets of G. M. Hopkins* (Chicago: Loyola University Press, 1969), p. 102.

May the peace that comes to Bosnia-Herzegovina, as well as to the rest of the world, not be piecemeal but fullmeal and permanent. May Aquinas help us all work strenuously to achieve that peace. Amen.

Indices

Greek and Medieval Authors

Modern and Contemporary Authors